JOHN CALVIN IN CONTEXT

John Calvin in Context offers a comprehensive overview of Calvin's world. Including essays from social, cultural, feminist, and intellectual historians, each specially commissioned for this volume, the book considers the various early modern contexts in which Calvin worked and wrote. It captures his concerns for northern humanism, his deep involvement in the politics of Geneva, his relationships with contemporaries, and the polemic necessities of responding to developments in Rome and other Protestant confessions, notably Lutheran and Anabaptist. The volume also explores Calvin's tasks as a pastor and doctor of the church, who was constantly explicating the text of scripture and applying it to the context of sixteenth-century Geneva, as well as the reception of his role in the Reformation and beyond. Demonstrating the complexity of the world in which Calvin lived, *John Calvin in Context* serves as an essential research tool for scholars and students of early modern Europe.

R. Ward Holder is Professor of Theology at Saint Anselm College. He is the author of *John Calvin and the Grounding of Interpretation: Calvin's First Commentaries* and *Crisis and Renewal: The Era of the Reformation*. He has edited *A Companion to Paul in the Reformation*; and coedited *Reformation Readings of Romans*, with Kathy Ehrensperger, and *Emancipating Calvin: Culture and Confessional Identity in Francophone Reformed Communities* with Karen Spierling and Erik de Boer. His current work focuses on Calvin's use of the theological tradition as a source for his own doctrinal formulations.

John Calvin in Context

Edited by

R. WARD HOLDER
Saint Anselm College

CAMBRIDGE
UNIVERSITY PRESS

CAMBRIDGE
UNIVERSITY PRESS

University Printing House, Cambridge CB2 8BS, United Kingdom

One Liberty Plaza, 20th Floor, New York, NY 10006, USA

477 Williamstown Road, Port Melbourne, VIC 3207, Australia

314–321, 3rd Floor, Plot 3, Splendor Forum, Jasola District Centre, New Delhi – 110025, India

79 Anson Road, #06–04/06, Singapore 079906

Cambridge University Press is part of the University of Cambridge.

It furthers the University's mission by disseminating knowledge in the pursuit of
education, learning, and research at the highest international levels of excellence.

www.cambridge.org
Information on this title: www.cambridge.org/9781108482400
DOI: 10.1017/9781108687447

© Cambridge University Press 2020

First published 2020

Printed in the United Kingdom by TJ International, Padstow, Cornwall

A catalogue record for this publication is available from the British Library.

Library of Congress Cataloging-in-Publication Data
NAMES: Holder, R. Ward, editor.
TITLE: John Calvin in context / edited by R. Ward Holder, Saint Anselm College,
New Hampshire.
DESCRIPTION: 1 [edition]. | New York : Cambridge University Press, 2019. |
Includes bibliographical references and index.
IDENTIFIERS: LCCN 2019010788 | ISBN 9781108482400 (hardback : alk. paper) |
ISBN 9781108712231 (pbk. : alk. paper)
SUBJECTS: LCSH: Calvin, Jean, 1509-1564.
CLASSIFICATION: LCC BX9418 .J623 2019 | DDC 284/.2092–dc23
LC record available at https://lccn.loc.gov/2019010788

ISBN 978-1-108-48240-0 Hardback

To the memory of
Edward A. Dowey Jr.
Who first kindled in me a love for Calvin

Contents

Contributors

JON BALSERAK is Senior Lecturer in Early Modern Religion at University of Bristol. He works on the religious and political history of sixteenth-century France and Geneva, biblical interpretation, Renaissance and Reformation Latin, tradition, authority, and morality. He has published *Calvinism: A Very Short Introduction* (Oxford University Press, 2017), *John Calvin as Sixteenth-Century Prophet* (Oxford University Press, 2014), and *Establishing the Remnant Church in France* (Brill, 2011). His current work focuses on medieval and early modern prophecy.

CHRISTOPHER BOYD BROWN is Associate Professor of Church History at Boston University School of Theology, where he has taught since 2003. He studied at Harvard University (AB, AM, PhD) and Concordia Seminary, St. Louis (MDiv). He is author of *Singing the Gospel: Lutheran Hymns and the Success of the Reformation* (Harvard University Press, 2005) and serves as General Editor of the American Edition of *Luther's Works*, volumes 56–75 (Concordia Publishing House, 2009–), including the companion volume *Sixteenth-Century Biographies of Martin Luther* (Concordia Publishing House, 2018). His current research includes a study of sixteenth-century wedding sermons and an edition of Luther's academic disputations.

MICHAEL W. BRUENING is Associate Professor of History at the Missouri University of Science and Technology. He specializes in the history of early Calvinism outside of Geneva and the reformer Pierre Viret. His publications include *Calvinism's First Battleground: Conflict and Reform in the Pays de Vaud, 1528–1559* (Springer, 2005), *Epistolae Petri Vireti: The Previously Unedited Letters and a Register of Pierre Viret's Correspondence* (Droz, 2012), and *A Reformation Sourcebook: Documents from an Age of Debate* (University of Toronto Press, 2017). He is currently researching Calvin's Francophone evangelical opponents.

AMY NELSON BURNETT is Paula and D. B. Varner University Professor of History at the University of Nebraska–Lincoln. She works on the Swiss and

South German Reformation, particularly the education and professionalization of the Protestant clergy. Her books *Karlstadt and the Origins of the Eucharistic Controversy* (Oxford University Press, 2011) and *Debating the Sacraments: Print and Authority in the Early Reformation* (Oxford University Press, 2019) both examine the division of the evangelical movement in the early Reformation.

ESTHER CHUNG-KIM is Associate Professor of Religious Studies at Claremont McKenna College in Claremont, California. Her research focuses on problems of authority, ancient tradition in early modern biblical interpretation, and poor relief reform. She has published *Inventing Authority: Use of the Church Fathers in Reformation Debates over the Eucharist* (Baylor University Press, 2011), *Reformation Commentary on Scripture: Acts* (IVP Academic, 2014), and several articles related to poverty, wealth, and social change, including most recently "Aid for Refugees: Religion, Migration and Poor Relief in Sixteenth-Century Geneva," in *Reformation and Renaissance Review* (2018). She is a 2018–2019 recipient of the Sabbatical Grant for Researchers at The Louisville Institute.

KATHLEEN M. COMERFORD is Professor of History at Georgia Southern University. She specializes in clerical education, early modern Tuscany, and the history of Jesuit books and libraries. She is the author of three monographs, most recently *Jesuit Foundations and Medici Power, 1532–1621* (Brill, 2017), and co-editor of three volumes of collected studies, most recently *From Rome to Zurich, from Ignatius to Vermigli: Essays in Honor of J. Patrick Donnelly, S.J.* (Brill, 2017). She is currently engaged in two research projects: one on the relationship between the Jesuits and the Grand Duchesses of Tuscany, and another on the libraries of Jesuit colleges and houses in Spain, central Italy, and the Low Countries prior to the suppression of the Society of Jesus.

CARLOS M. N. EIRE is T. L. Riggs Professor of History and Religious Studies at Yale University, and author of several books on the Protestant and Catholic Reformations, including his most recent, *Reformations: The Early Modern World* (Yale University Press, 2016), which won the Hawkins Award from the Association of American Publishers. He is currently working on attitudes toward miracles in the early modern age.

KIRK ESSARY is Lecturer in Medieval and Early Modern History at the University of Western Australia. His research focuses on the intellectual and religious history of the late medieval and early modern periods. He is the author of *Erasmus and Calvin on the Foolishness of God: Reason and Emotion in the Christian Philosophy* (University of Toronto Press, 2017). He is currently working on the history of emotions in the long sixteenth century, with a focus on Erasmus.

AMANDA EURICH is Professor of History at Western Washington University. She is the author of *The Economics of Power: The Private Finances of the House of Foix-Navarre-Albret during the Religious Wars* (Truman State University Press, 1994). She is also the author of numerous essays on Huguenot culture and the politics and practice of confessional co-existence in early modern France. She is currently writing a biography of Jean de Coras, the legendary sixteenth-century jurist who presided over the most famous case of identity theft in early modern Europe.

JILL FEHLEISON is Professor of History at Quinnipiac University. Her areas of research include Catholic/Protestant relations around Geneva, late Reformation polemics, and teaching the Reformation. Her publications include "The Place of the Cross: The Pamphlet Battle between François de Sales and Antoine de la Faye," in Sarah Alyn-Stacey, ed., *Political, Religious and Social Conflict in the Duchy of Savoy, 1400–1700* (Peter Lang, 2014), "L'Escalade of 1602: History, Myth and Commemoration," for the *Swiss American Historical Review* (Winter 2013), and her book *Boundaries of Faith: Catholics and Protestants in the Diocese of Geneva* (Truman State University Press, 2010). Her current research explores Catholic/Protestant polemical debates between Jesuits and Reformed ministers, and she is co-authoring a Reacting to the Past game about peace negotiations during the French Wars of Religion.

REBECCA GISELBRECHT is Senior Research Associate and Member of the Teaching Staff at the Institute for Old Catholic Theology at the University of Bern, Switzerland, and Affiliate Assistant Professor of the History of Christianity and Spirituality at Fuller Theological Seminary. Her book publications include *Sacrality and Materiality: Locating Intersections* (V&R Publishing, 2015) and *Hör nicht auf zu singen: Zeuginnen der Schweizer Reformation* (TVZ, 2016). She has published numerous chapters and articles on the Reformation. Rebecca is currently writing her habilitation at the University of Bern – a biography and the first edition and translation of the spiritual writings and correspondence of an Alsatian noblewoman, Anna Alexandria zu Rappoltstein (1504–1581).

BRUCE GORDON is the Titus Street Professor of Ecclesiastical History at Yale Divinity School. His recent works include *Calvin* (Yale University Press, 2009), *John Calvin's Institutes of the Christian Religion* (Princeton University Press, 2016), and an online course (MOOC) "A Journey through Western Christianity: From Persecuted Faith to Global Religion." He is currently completing a biography of Huldrych Zwingli for Yale University Press.

BRAD S. GREGORY is Professor of History and Dorothy G. Griffin Collegiate Chair at the University of Notre Dame, where he is also Director of the Notre Dame Institute for Advanced Study. He studies the Reformation era in cross-confessional and comparative ways, as well as the long-term influences of the Reformation era on the Western world down to the present. Among his best-known works are *Salvation at Stake: Christian Martyrdom in Early Modern Europe* (Harvard University Press, 1999) and *The Unintended Reformation: How a Religious Revolution Secularized Society* (Belknap, 2012), both of which received multiple prizes.

CRAWFORD GRIBBEN is Professor of Early Modern British History at Queen's University Belfast. He works on the histories of puritanism and evangelicalism, and is the author of books including *God's Irishmen: Theological Debates in Cromwellian Ireland* (Oxford University Press, 2007), *Writing the Rapture: Prophecy Fiction in Evangelical America* (Oxford University Press, 2009), and *John Owen and English Puritanism* (Oxford University Press, 2016).

R. WARD HOLDER is Professor of Theology and Director of the Honors Program at Saint Anselm College. He works on the thought of John Calvin in its historical contexts and later receptions. He is author of *Calvin and the Grounding of Interpretation: Calvin's First Commentaries* (Brill, 2006) and *Crisis and Renewal: The Era of the Reformations* (Westminster John Knox, 2009); and coedited *Emancipating Calvin: Culture and Confessional Identity in Francophone Reformed Communities* (Brill, 2018). He is currently working on the concept of the justification of religious thought in the early modern world.

MACK P. HOLT is Professor of History at George Mason University. He works on the Reformation in France and is the author of *The French Wars of Religion, 1562–1629* (Cambridge University Press, 2005), *The Politics of Wine in Early Modern France: Religion and Popular Culture in Burgundy, 1477–1630* (Cambridge University Press, 2018), and a recent article on his current project on French vernacular bibles, "Reading the Bible in Sixteenth-Century France," in Karen E. Spierling, Erik A. de Boer, and R. Ward Holder, eds., *Emancipating Calvin: Culture and Confessional Identity in Francophone Reformed Communities, Essays in Honors of Raymond A. Mentzer, Jr.* (Brill, 2018).

ARNOLD HUIJGEN is Professor of Systematic Theology at the Theological University Apeldoorn, the Netherlands. He works on Calvin's theology, the Trinity, and theological hermeneutics. He has published *Divine Accommodation in John Calvin's Theology: Analysis and Assessment* (Vandenhoeck & Ruprecht, 2011). He has co-edited *Calvinus Pastor Ecclesiae* (Vandenhoeck & Ruprecht, 2016), and *Sola Scriptura: Biblical and Theological Perspectives on Scripture, Authority and Hermeneutics* (Brill, 2017). He is Secretary of the Presidium of the International Calvin Congress.

RONA JOHNSTON is Lecturer in the Department of English at Yale and a historian of early modern Austria. Her recent translation projects include Heinz

Schilling's *Martin Luther: Rebel in an Age of Upheaval* (Oxford University Press, 2017) and various articles in the *Companion to the Swiss Reformation* (Brill, 2016), edited by Amy Nelson Burnett and Emidio Campi.

RALPH KEEN is the Schmitt Chair of Catholic Studies, and Dean of the Honors College, at the University of Illinois at Chicago. His works include *Divine and Human Authority in Reformation Thought: German Theologians on Political Order, 1520–1555* (De Graaf, 1997) and *Exile and Restoration in Jewish Thought: An Essay in Interpretation* (Continuum, 2009). His research focuses on early modern polemical literature and includes critical editions of works by Johannes Cochlaeus and other Catholic controversialists.

CHRISTINE KOOI is Lewis C. and Katheryn J. Price Professor in European History at Louisiana State University. She studies the religious culture of the early modern Netherlands. Her works include *Liberty and Religion: Church and State in Leiden's Reformation* (Brill, 2000) and *Calvinists and Catholics during Holland's Golden Age: Heretics and Idolaters* (Cambridge University Press, 2012). She is currently writing a general history of the Reformation in the Low Countries.

GRETA GRACE KROEKER is Associate Professor of History at the University of Waterloo in Ontario, Canada. She studies the theologies of compromise in the early modern period. She is the author of *Erasmus in the Footsteps of Paul* (University of Toronto Press, 2011) and numerous articles on Christian humanism and Reformation era efforts at religious compromise. She is currently working on a project considering sexual violence in the early modern world.

ELIZABETH A. LEHFELDT is Professor of History and Dean of the Mandel Honors College at Cleveland State University. She is the author of *Religious Women in Golden Age Spain: The Permeable Cloister* (Ashgate, 2005). Her articles about female monasticism have appeared in *Sixteenth Century Journal*, *Journal of Social History*, and the *Journal of Medieval and Early Modern Studies*. She is currently at work on a project analyzing female monastic households in early modern Europe.

UTE LOTZ-HEUMANN is Director of the Division for Late Medieval and Reformation Studies and Heiko A. Oberman Professor of Late Medieval and Reformation History in the Division for Late Medieval and Reformation Studies and the Department of History at the University of Arizona. She is the author of *Die doppelte Konfessionalisierung in Irland: Konflikt und Koexistenz im 16. und in der ersten Hälfte des 17. Jahrhunderts* (Mohr Siebeck, 2000), and she has co-authored or coedited nine volumes in Reformation and early modern history. Currently, she is working on two books about spas, holy wells, and healing waters in early modern Germany between the sixteenth and the eighteenth centuries.

KARIN MAAG is Director of the H. Henry Meeter Center for Calvin Studies and Professor of History at Calvin University in Grand Rapids, Michigan. Her scholarly interests include early modern higher education, the training of clergy, and the Reformation in Geneva and France. Her most recent publications include *Lifting Hearts to the Lord: Worship with John Calvin in Sixteenth-Century Geneva* (Eerdmans, 2016) and *Does the Reformation Still Matter?* (Calvin Press, 2016). Her current work focuses on the comparative study of worship practices across confessional groups in the Reformation era.

DIANE C. MARGOLF is Professor of History at Colorado State University, where she has taught since 1993. She is the author of *Religion and Royal Justice in Early Modern France: The Paris Chambre de l'Edit, 1598–1665* (Truman State University Press, 2003) and the co-author (with Kristin Heineman) of a digital textbook, *Western Civilization: From Antiquity to the Age of Expansion* (Dubuque, IA: Great River Learning, 2016). Her current research interests focus on European travel writing and the history of public apology.

ELSIE ANNE MCKEE is Archibald Alexander Professor of Reformation Studies and the History of Worship at Princeton Theological Seminary. Her areas of research are exegetical and worship history, the Calvinist Reformed tradition, and women in early modern Europe. She has published *John Calvin on the Diaconate and Liturgical Almsgiving* (Droz, 1984), *Katharina Schütz Zell: The Life and Thought of a Sixteenth-Century Reformer* (Brill, 1999), and *The Pastoral Ministry and Worship in Calvin's Geneva* (Droz, 2016). Her current research is making the critical edition of Calvin's First Corinthians sermons (chs. 1–9) for the series *Supplementa Calviniana*.

JENNIFER POWELL MCNUTT is Associate Professor of Theology and History of Christianity at Wheaton College. She works on the history of the Reformed tradition from the Reformation through the Enlightenment. She has published *Calvin Meets Voltaire: The Clergy of Geneva in the Age of Enlightenment, 1685–1798* (Ashgate, 2014) and coedited the volume, *The People's Book: The Reformation and the Bible* (IVP, 2017). Her current work focuses on the history of the French Bible.

RAYMOND A. MENTZER holds the Daniel J. Krumm Family Chair in Reformation Studies, Department of Religious Studies, University of Iowa. His research centers on the Reformed community in early modern France. His most recent publications include *Les registres des consistoires des Églises réformées de France, XVIe–XVIIe siècles. Un inventaire* (Droz, 2014), and edited with Bertrand van Ruymbeke *A Companion to the Huguenots* (Brill, 2016). He is currently preparing a study of material culture and the Reformed liturgy.

OLIVIER MILLET is Professor for French Renaissance literature at the Sorbonne. He works on the relations between religion (Bible) and literature in the Renaissance. He has published *Calvin et la dynamique de la Parole, étude de rhétorique réformée* (Editions Slatkine, 1992) and *Précis de culture biblique* (Presses universitaires de France, 2017), and edited works of Marguerite de Navarre, Calvin, and Du Bellay.

CHRISTINA MOSS earned her PhD in history at the University of Waterloo working under the supervision of Professor Greta Kroeker. She has been published in *Doopsgezinde Bijdragen*, the *Global Anabaptist Mennonite Encyclopedia Online*, and *Protestants and Mysticism in Reformation Europe* (Brill, 2019). Her doctoral research focuses on prophecy and religious radicalism in sixteenth-century Strasbourg.

WILLIAM G. NAPHY is Professor of Early Modern History at the University of Aberdeen. He works on social control in Calvin's Geneva as well as the history of plague, witchcraft, and sexuality. He has published both academic monographs as well as more general works: *Calvin and the Consolidation of the Genevan Reformation* (Manchester University Press, 1996; Westminster John Knox, 2003), *Born to Be Gay: A History of Homosexuality* (Tempus, 2004; also published in Spanish, Portuguese, Serbo-Croat), and *The Protestant Revolution* (BBC, 2008; also published in Italian).

PETER OPITZ is Professor of Church History and History of Dogma from the Reformation to the Present at the University of Zurich; he is Director of the Institute for Swiss Reformation Studies. He is editor of the *Works of Heinrich Bullinger* and coeditor of the *Reformierte Bekenntnisschriften*; his publications include *Heinrich Bullinger als Theologe* (Theologischer Verlag, 2004), *Leben und Werk Johannes Calvins* (Vandenhoeck & Ruprecht, 2009), and *Ulrich Zwingli: Prophet, Ketzer, Pionier des Protestantismus* (Theologischer Verlag, 2015).

TIMOTHY J. ORR is Assistant Professor of History at Simpson University. He works on identity formation through the process of flight in the early modern world. He has published articles in *Church History and Religious Culture* and will be in *Crossing Borders: Transregional Reformations in Early Modern Europe* (Vandenhoeck & Ruprecht, 2019) about trans-regional reformations. His current work concentrates on perceptions of gender in relationship to flight from persecution.

G. SUJIN PAK is Associate Professor of the History of Christianity at Duke Divinity School and is currently serving as Vice Dean of Academic Affairs. She works on the intellectual history of the Protestant reformations, particularly the theologies of the Luther and Calvin and their followers, early modern women, history of Christian-Jewish relations, and the history of biblical interpretation. She has published *The Judaizing Calvin: Sixteenth-Century Debates over the Messianic Psalms* (Oxford University Press, 2010) and *The Reformation of Prophecy: Early Modern Interpretations of the Prophet and Old Testament Prophecy* (Oxford University Press, 2018).

CHARLES H. PARKER is Professor of History at Saint Louis University. His research interests focus on the religious and cultural history of early modern Europe and cross-cultural interactions in world history. His publications include *Global Interactions in the Early Modern Age, 1400–1800* (Cambridge University Press, 2010), *Faith on the Margins: Catholics and Catholicism in the Dutch Golden Age* (Harvard University Press, 2008), and *The Reformation of Community: Social Welfare and Calvinist Charity in Holland, 1572–1620* (Cambridge University Press, 1998). He is currently finishing a book manuscript on Calvinism and empire in the early modern world.

ANDREW PETTEGREE is Professor of Modern History at the University of St. Andrews and Director of the Universal Short Title Catalogue. He is the author of more than a dozen books in the fields of Reformation history and the history of communication including *Reformation and the Culture of Persuasion* (Cambridge University Press, 2005), *The Book in the Renaissance* (Yale University Press, 2010), *The Invention of News* (Yale University Press, 2014), and *Brand Luther: 1517, Print and the Making of the Reformation* (Penguin, 2015). His new projects include "Preserving the World's Rarest Books," a collaboration with the international library community funded by the Andrew W. Mellon Foundation. His most recent book, *The Bookshop of the World: Making and Trading Books in the Dutch Golden Age*, is co-authored with Arthur der Weduwen (Yale University Press, 2019).

DAVID H. PRICE is Professor of Religious Studies, Jewish Studies, and History at Vanderbilt University. He specializes in the history of early modern Europe. Among his recent books are *The Works of Hrotsvit of Gandersheim* (University of Illinois Press, 2015), *Johannes Reuchlin and the Campaign to Destroy Jewish Books* (Oxford University Press, 2012), and *Albrecht Dürer's Renaissance: Humanism, Reformation and the Art of Faith* (University of Michigan Press, 2003). His current projects pertain to Christian-Jewish relations during the period 1500–1789 as well as the Bible in early modern visual art.

CHARLES RAITH II is Vice President of Mission and Ethics at Mercy and former assistant professor of religion and philosophy at John Brown University. His research focuses on theological developments between the high-medieval to early reformation eras, ecumenism, and scriptural interpretation. He has published *Aquinas and Calvin on Romans: God's Justification and Our Participation*

(Oxford University Press, 2014), *After Merit: John Calvin's Theology of Works and Reward* (Vandenhoeck & Ruprecht, 2016), and, with R. David Nelson, *Ecumenism: A Guide for the Perplexed* (Continuum, 2017).

JONATHAN A. REID is Associate Professor of Renaissance and Reformation History at East Carolina University. He is author of *King's Sister – Queen of Dissent: Marguerite of Navarre (1492–1549) and Her Evangelical Network* (Brill, 2009). He coedited the volume of essays *Neo-Latin and the Humanities: Essays in Honour of Charles Fantazzi* and served as assistant editor of the journal *Explorations in Renaissance Culture* (2011–2018). He is currently working on a study of the rise of the Reformed churches in the cities of France from the outbreak of the Luther Affair through the first War of Religion, 1520–1563.

RONALD K. RITTGERS holds the Erich Markel Chair in German Reformation Studies at Valparaiso University, where he also serves as Professor of History and Theology. His published works include *The Reformation of the Keys: Confession, Conscience, and Authority in Sixteenth-Century Germany* (Harvard University Press, 2004), *The Reformation of Suffering: Pastoral Theology and Lay Piety in Late Medieval and Early Modern Germany* (Oxford University Press, 2012), and *Reformation Commentary on Scripture: Hebrews and James* (Intervarsity Press Academic, 2017).

KAREN E. SPIERLING is John and Heath Faraci Endowed Professor and Associate Professor of History at Denison University. Her work explores the relationship between ideals and practices in Reformed societies, focusing on Geneva during the time of John Calvin. Her books include *Infant Baptism in Reformation Geneva: The Shaping of a Community, 1536–1564* (Ashgate, 2005; Westminster John Knox, 2009), *Calvin and the Book: The Evolution of the Printed Word in Reformed Protestantism* (editor; Vandenhoech & Ruprecht, 2015), and *Emancipating Calvin: Reformed Communities and Culture in Early Modern Francophone Europe* (coedited with R. Ward Holder and Erik A. de Boer; Brill, 2018). Her current work explores sixteenth-century concepts of scandal and the roles those ideas played in defining and shaping Reformed communities

JESSE SPOHNHOLZ is Director of the Roots of Contemporary Issues Program and Professor of History at Washington State University. His research focuses on social practices of toleration in Reformation-era Germany and the Netherlands, experiences of religious refugees during Europe's Age of Religious Wars, and historical memory of the Reformation. His books include *The Tactics of Toleration: A Refugee Community in the Age of Religious Wars* (University of Delaware Press, 2011) and *The Convent of Wesel: The Event That Never Was and the Invention of Tradition* (Cambridge University Press, 2017), and coedited *Exile and Religious Identity, 1500–1800* (Pickering & Chatto, 2014) and

Archeologies of Confession: Writing the German Reformation, 1517–2017 (Berghahn Books, 2017). He is currently working on a collaborative research project, funded by the Netherlands Organization for Scientific Research, titled *The Rhineland Refugees and the Religious Landscape of the Dutch Republic.*

KEITH D. STANGLIN is Professor of Historical Theology at Austin Graduate School of Theology in Austin, Texas. He writes mostly in the fields of Reformation and post-Reformation theology, the history of biblical interpretation, and Arminianism. His books include *Jacob Arminius: Theologian of Grace* (Oxford University Press, 2012), *The Reformation to the Modern Church: A Reader in Christian Theology* (Fortress Press, 2014), and *The Letter and Spirit of Biblical Interpretation: From Early Church to Modern Practice* (Baker Academic, 2018).

YUDHA THIANTO is Professor of Theology at Trinity Christian College in Palos Heights, Illinois, where he also chairs the theology department. His research focuses on the early history of the Dutch Reformed church in the East Indies in the seventeenth century. He has published *The Way to Heaven: Catechisms and Sermons in the Establishment of the Dutch Reformed Church in the East Indies* (Wipf & Stock, 2014) and "The Genevan Psalms in Javanese," *Calvin Theological Journal* (2017). His current work explores the history of the singing of metrical psalms in the East Indies during the time of the Dutch East India Company.

STEVEN W. TYRA holds an MA and ThM from Fuller Theological Seminary. He is currently at work on a PhD in the History of Christianity at Baylor University. His primary research interests are John Calvin and early Protestant communities in France. His work has previously been published in the *Westminster Theological Journal, Church History and Religious Culture*, and the *Journal of Theological Interpretation.*

MIRJAM VAN VEEN is Professor at Vrije Universiteit Amsterdam. Her work focuses on the polemic between reformation and radical reformation and on the history of religious migration. Her publications include *De kunst van het twijfelen. Sebastian Castellio (1515–1563): Humanist, Calvinist, Vrijdenker* (Zoetermeer, 2012); "The Disputed Origins of Dutch Calvinism: Religious Refugees in the Historiography of the Dutch Reformation," *Church History* (2017; with Jesse Spohnholz); "Johan Jakob Wettstein's (1693–1754) Use of Sebastian Castellio (1515–1563)," *Sebastian Castellio (1515–1563) – Dissidenz und Toleranz. Beiträge zu einer internationalen Tagung auf dem Monte Verità in Ascona 2015* ed. Barbara Mahlmann-Bauer (Vandenhoeck & Ruprecht, 2018).

JEFFREY R. WATT is the Kelly Gene Cook, Sr. Professor of History at the University of Mississippi. A specialist in the social history of early modern Europe, he is the author of three monographs, including *The Scourge of Demons:*

Possession, Lust, and Witchcraft in a Seventeenth-Century Italian Convent (University of Rochester Press, 2009). He is also editing (with Isabella M. Watt) the volumes of the Consistory of Geneva during the ministry of Calvin (*Registres du Consistoire de Genève au temps de Calvin*, vols. 6–12; Droz, 2012–2018) and is currently writing a monograph about that institution.

DAVID M. WHITFORD is Professor of Reformation Studies at Baylor University. He works on Martin Luther, John Calvin, and the Continental Reformations. He is the author of *Luther: A Guide for the Perplexed* (T&T Clark, 2011), *A Reformation Life* (Praeger, 2015), and *The Curse of Ham in the Early Modern Era* (Ashgate, 2009); and has recently edited *Martin Luther in Context* (Cambridge University Press, 2018). His current work focuses on the history of biblical interpretation and the role of gender in the life and writings of Martin Luther.

KENNETH J. WOO is Assistant Professor of Church History at Pittsburgh Theological Seminary. He is the author of *Nicodemism and the English* Calvin, 1544–1584 (Brill, 2019). His research centers on Calvin and the Reformed tradition, especially the history of biblical interpretation.

RANDALL C. ZACHMAN is Professor of Reformation Studies, Emeritus, at the University of Notre Dame, and is currently Adjunct Professor of Church History at Lancaster Theological Seminary. He is the author of *John Calvin as Teacher, Pastor, and Theologian: The Shape of His Writings and Thought* (Baker Academic, 2006), *Image and Word in the Theology of John Calvin* (University of Notre Dame, 2009), and *Reconsidering John Calvin* (Cambridge University Press, 2012). He served as North American Co-Editor of the *Archive for Reformation History*, and is the former president of the Calvin Studies Society and the Sixteenth Century Society and Conference.

Acknowledgments

All scholars know that they stand on the shoulders of those who have gone before. This was a trope in the Middle Ages, the medieval scholars believed they saw further because they stood on the foundations laid by the early Christian and pagan authors. In an age when inspiration can come in a text, a meme, or a passing comment, the debts to others expand exponentially. It also becomes almost impossible to thank people properly because one doesn't know where one idea began and another ended, and who provided its earliest or most trenchant form.

All those caveats aside, some effort must needs be made. The first debt I have is to the wonderful group of scholars collected here. They are an early modern studies faculty that exceeds the wildest dreams of any university or divinity school. Their constant cheerfulness in the face of my reminders, the extraordinary calibre of their work, and their responsiveness to editorial requests have made this book possible.

Beyond this wider group, there is another debt to a smaller group of early modern historians and theologians to whom I regularly turn, friends more than colleagues, whose counsel and advice I seek regularly. They have been stalwarts through this, whether engaging in the initial discussions of the design of the volume with David Whitford, or consulting with Ray Mentzer about chapters and topics to include, or considering some of the possible contributors with Karen Spierling, or debating the possible chapters with Greta Kroeker, or turning to Bruce Gordon to write a second chapter because another contributor needed to step back from the project, or seeking editorial help on my own writing from Kathryn Edwards who asked good but difficult questions – in all these, I recognize I am a very lucky man because I work with people whom I enjoy and admire.

At Cambridge University Press, Beatrice Rehl has been everything for which an editor could ask. She is there to answer questions, she has kept the project on schedule, and she has accepted the vision of what the volume could be, both for the press and for the academy. Her assistant, Edgar Mendez, has been quick to respond to queries and excellent at tracking down contributor questionnaires and contracts.

Finally, my family has made this possible. Whether in allowing me to fret out loud about deadlines, or listening to me discuss the usefulness of the inclusion of a discussion of various early modern topics in the volume, or putting up with deadlines that they had not known were approaching, they have remained cheerful, loving, and supportive. Their support and love is the foundation on which I work.

Abbreviations

CO *Ioannis Calvini opera quae supersunt omnia.* Ed. Wilhelm Baum, Eduard Cunitz, and Eduard Reuss. 59 vols. *Corpus Reformatorum,* vols. 29–87. Brunswick, Germany: C. A. Schwetschke and Son (M. Bruhn), 1863–1900.

H Herminjard, Aimé Louis. *Correspondance des réformateurs dans les pays de langue française,* 9 vols., Geneva, 1878–1897.

LW *Luther's Works.* American Edition. Ed. Jaroslav Pelikan and Helmut T. Lehmann. 55+ vols. St. Louis, MO: Concordia Publishing House; Philadelphia: Fortress Press, 1955–1986, 2009–.

OS *Joannis Calvini opera selecta.* Ed. Peter Barth, Wilhelm Niesel, and Doris Scheuner. 5 vols. Munich: Chr. Kaiser Verlag, 1926–1952.

WA *D. Martin Luthers Werke: Kritische Gesamtausgabe.* Weimarer Ausgabe, Weimar, 1883–1983.

CITATION CONVENTIONS

Normally, Calvin's *Institutes of the Christian Religion* (or simply *Institutes*) without further specification refers to the 1559 Latin version. This is cited by book, chapter, and paragraph number. For example, *Institutes,* I.v.2.

The *Calvini Opera* is cited according to its own volumes, not those of the *Corpus Reformatorum.* This is cited by work, volume, and column number. For example, *De Scandalis Quibus Hodie Plerique Absterreatur, Nonnulli etiam Alienantur a Pura Evangelii Doctrina,* CO 8.12.

Introduction

John Calvin in Context

R. Ward Holder

In 1995, David C. Steinmetz, one of the two deans of Calvin studies in America along with Robert M. Kingdon, published a slim volume entitled *Calvin in Context*. For Calvin studies, that volume became part of the necessary tools of the trade. Steinmetz brilliantly set forth the argument for the history of exegesis method for which he became famous. In so doing, he argued that attempting to understand Calvin apart from those who went before him, his theological and exegetical context, caused a variety of errors.[1]

The present volume seeks to apply Steinmetz's insight, but on a far broader canvas. Certainly Calvin's theological and exegetical insights only take on their true shapes and colors when seen against the backdrop of the traditions out of which they are drawn, but that is just as true for other facets of his life. It was true for the Christianity in which he was formed, for the political realities that he faced, and for the materiality of Genevan life that made up the fabric of his everyday life.

Calvin's various early modern contexts force modern readers to recognize the thick character of his life and career. It is crucial to note the plurality of those contexts, for they influenced him throughout his life. At a single moment, Calvin would be balancing the concerns of northern humanism with the politics of Geneva as well as its relations with its neighbors in Switzerland, along with the polemic necessities of answering Rome or Lutherans or Anabaptists, and with the personalities of his contemporaries. Of course, that was before he would consider the necessities pressed upon him by the demands of explicating the text of scripture and applying it to the contexts of mid-sixteenth-century Geneva.

---

[1] David C. Steinmetz, *Calvin in Context* (New York: Oxford University Press, 1995).

The most important cluster of issues for the student of Calvin comes from the necessity of placing Calvin firmly in his Genevan and intellectual contexts. Modern readers have a tendency to take the rhetoric of medieval and early modern authors as if they were speaking to the same cultural and mental world in which we live. But this is far from the truth. Calvin lived and worked in a town whose elected leaders believed that it was absolutely vital to the future of their city that they answered the religious questions of the day correctly. They could – and did – compel worship, attendance at catechism classes, and appearances before the church's consistory. Further, the Genevans lived within sight of France, a country that had a sizeable minority of French Protestants, termed Huguenots. The very existence of these Huguenots infuriated some French Catholics, and the Wars of Religion began during Calvin's life. Freedom of religion, a fact of life for modern readers whom many take as an obvious right, was a very different idea in Calvin's time.

Given their importance and at times foreignness, this volume will concentrate upon the contextual issues that made up the world in which Calvin lived. Instead of taking the reader deeply into Calvin's thought or into his particular doctrines as some recently published handbooks do in excellent fashion, *Calvin in Context* sets out to be quite different: to supply the background against which Calvin must be seen. This is admittedly curious. Why not concentrate upon Calvin, and his works? One answer to that comes from the history of exegesis school. This method argued that it was insufficient to know what a particular author had written about a particular passage of scripture. Without delving deeply into the prior exegetical traditions, especially those which an author could have known, or even better did know, it is impossible to answer a series of valuable theological and exegetical questions: Was the author being innovative? Conservative? Boorishly obvious? Truly unique? By considering the context of humanism, French Christianity, and the styles of theology that were significant during Calvin's era, we find ourselves in a better place to appreciate his thought and life.

Having achieved a knowledge of the intellectual context, the scholar who would know Calvin must also turn to the social, political, cultural, and societal contexts. Most scholars know that Calvin married Idelette de Bure in August 1540 while living in Strasbourg. That historical fact remains a dead piece of information without knowing something about the relationship of men and women, the social customs, and the everyday character of life in Strasbourg. Likewise, we know that Calvin wrote to Bullinger asking him to enlist his help in a plan to address some of the political issues that were occurring in the Holy Roman Empire. But without some basic information about the political world of the time, one cannot know whether Calvin was making a serious plan or simply passing on news.

A second answer to the question of why not delve deeply into Calvin's thought at each locus is that *Calvin in Context* is not a one-volume guide to Calvin's thought. Handbooks to Calvin's thought exist, and are useful. Herman Selderhuis's *The Calvin Handbook* is enormously helpful on a variety of topics.[2] *John Calvin in Context*, however, puts a variety of other studies into their proper historical, political, and theological contexts.

Therefore, instead of a chapter on Calvin's doctrine of predestination, there is a chapter on predestination in the medieval and early modern theological world. Instead of a chapter on Calvin's religious influences as he grew up, there is a chapter on French Christianity in the early sixteenth century. Instead of a chapter on Calvin's literary output, there is a chapter on the printed word in the early modern world.

John Calvin in Context begins with a biography of Calvin for those students who are novices in Calvin studies. From there, it offers a series of chapters on France, the University of Paris, French humanism, French religious politics, and the French Wars of Religion. In beginning there, we accept what some Genevans considered a fault – Calvin was French and never really put that behind him. From that point, the volume crosses into Switzerland, and the cities in which Calvin ministered. Geneva and Strasbourg are noted, as are Swiss politics, and the structures of social, cultural, and ecclesiastical life in Geneva. After covering this urban context, the volume takes a moment to rise above the smaller concerns to look at the empire and the ways that the upheavals of the early modern period were transforming Europe. One recent study has looked at the way that the religious, military, and cultural changes in the early modern period caused one of the first great refugee crises – and both Geneva and Calvin cannot be understood without that knowledge.[3] The Jewish question was also an ongoing theme. Were Jews the people of Jesus Christ or a sly bunch who should be banished from the empire? Martin Luther made both arguments in his career – and it was Jews who supplied both the skills to examine the Old Testament in its original language, as well as the religious "other," against which Christianity would be measured by so many theologians. Finally, another set of voices too often unheard by modern analysts were those of the women of the early modern period. Calvin had much to say to

---

[2] Herman J. Selderhuis, ed., *The Calvin Handbook* (Grand Rapids, MI: Eerdmans, 2009).
[3] Nicholas Terpstra, *Religious Refugees in the Early Modern World: An Alternative History of the Reformation* (Cambridge: University of Cambridge Press, 2015).

women, and some things to say about women. But all his work must be seen against the backdrop of the multivalent influences of the reforms and counterreforms occurring in the sixteenth century. The era of the Reformations changed women's lives – sometimes positively, and sometimes not. Understanding that context is crucial to grasping Calvin not only from the impression and vantage point of his close circle of friends (with the exception of his wife, all of whom were male) but from the broader perspectives of those women who also lived through those times.

The volume then turns to piety, theology, and ecclesiastical controversy with a section titled "The Religious Question." It is a mark of how much historical context exists to understand Calvin properly that almost half the volume is set before we turn to religion. It was religion that drove the various movements – whether supporters or foes of Calvin's, people were motivated by their religious beliefs at a depth that is frequently shocking to modern readers. Beginning with the ideal of Western religious reform that had a long history prior to the sixteenth century, the volume plunges into the Luther Affair – the spark that lighted an array of differing fuses to metaphorical bombs that rocked the early modern European religious world. Soon, the religious questions raised efforts not merely to chide one's opponents, but instead as a search for truth, so colloquies were called to attempt to do so. Trent and the Augsburg Interim remind us that Catholicism continued to challenge the evangelical movement.

Three historical developments changed the character of the early modern period in basic ways for the religious world, and are the subject of the next three chapters. First, there is a chapter on biblical scholarship. The era of the Reformations was saturated with the Bible, both with editions and translations of it, and with scholarship seeking to understand and apply it.[4] Likewise, the printed word came into its own with printing houses changing the economic, intellectual, and religious landscapes. Finally, a chapter takes up one of the rhetorical devices most commonly associated with the era of the Reformations – the polemic. Whether cleverly satirical or bluntly scatological, polemics were available to the reading and listening public at all times. Doctrinal loci also became the intellectual and religious battlefields of the early modern period. Baptism, the Lord's Supper, predestination, the

---

[4] The term *Reformations* is intentional – there were a variety of different movements that did not all cohere. See Carter Lindberg, *The European Reformations*, 2nd ed. (Hoboken, NJ: Wiley Blackwell, 2009); R. Ward Holder, *Crisis and Renewal: The Era of the Reformations* (Louisville, KY: Westminster John Knox, 2009); and Carlos Eire, *Reformations: The Early Modern World* (New Haven, CT: Yale University Press, 2016).

Trinity – all these are doctrines to which Calvin turned his considerable intellectual and spiritual powers – but all existed in an ecclesiastical and doctrinal world that preceded Calvin, and engaged thinkers in places as near as Bern, and as far away as Italy and Poland. Many Calvin students know his doctrinal positions on these matters, but are not fully versed in the intellectual and religious environment(s) in which Calvin worked.

"The Religious Question" ends with a series of chapters on issues that Calvin frankly deemed heretical. Chapters on the heresies of Servetus and Stancaro supply critical perspective for grasping some of the most famous polemics and events that revolved around issues of heretical belief. Other chapters consider idolatry, Trinitarian heresies, and Nicodemism and Libertinism. In each case, Calvin was one of the most significant voices in the early modern world, but was not alone in considering these issues or issuing statements about them.

The penultimate section of the book, "Calvin's Influences," recognizes the many ways Calvin was stirred to write, teach, and preach. When Alexandre Ganoczy traced Calvin's sources for the first edition of the *Institutes*, he concentrated most of his efforts on those influences Calvin would have acknowledged as complementing his own, such as Luther, Melanchthon, and Zwingli.[5] But Calvin was influenced by a far broader group of theologians than those with whom he could generally agree. Calvin's first serious work of theology was entitled *Psychopannychia*, and was written because of what Calvin believed Radicals were teaching about the sleep of the soul. In much the same way, Catholic writers, as well as Lutherans, other Reformed, and Anglicans all aroused Calvin. This section provides a way for Calvin to be seen among the other voices of the early modern religious world, whether it was supporting or damning him. Though the section begins with Calvin, it does not end with him but stretches well into the seventeenth century, just as his ideas did not die in 1564 but caused debates for the next centuries.

The final section recognizes what good historians have always known, that our reception of historical figures filters through our own *mentalités*. In "Calvin's Reception," we examine how Calvin became both more and less than the sum of his doctrinal teachings during his own lifetime, and how that process did not stop with his being buried in an unmarked grave in Geneva. International Calvinism coursed out of Geneva and took over large

---

[5] Alexandre Ganoczy, *The Young Calvin*, David Foxgrover and Wade Provo (trans.) (Philadelphia: Westminster Press, 1987), 133–182. The exception is Scholastic Theology, and Ganoczy argues that Calvin reduced scholasticism to two twelfth-century authors and used them for polemical purposes because he only learned them after reading Luther (see p. 177).

swaths of Europe, only to relinquish much of that territory in the coming centuries. Calvin had both his hagiographers and those who would demonize him, and some of their conclusions endure in "common" knowledge. Reformed churches sprang up in the Netherlands, the British Isles, and their colonial possessions, and each exported it to further lands, especially to Asia. Outlining of the spread of Reformed churches is significant, but no less so than the intellectual tradition of Calvinism, received from the seventeenth through the twentieth centuries. The volume concludes with a sense of the various portraits analysts have drawn of Calvin, and how that reflects his contexts, and our own.

Steinmetz's *Calvin in Context* put forth the history of exegesis method, and argued persuasively that the understanding of biblical interpreters' significance depended in part on knowing what they knew. Only then could their originality and synthetic ability be discerned. *John Calvin in Context* seeks that same goal, but with a broader canvas that looks to place Calvin in contexts beyond the intellectual. Through all these efforts, John Calvin's contributions to the intellectual and religious heritage of Christianity becomes ever clearer. Seen in his contexts, Calvin appears as one who is a devotee of his own time, dedicated to his intellectual pursuits, but turned toward the needs of a church that he could not but help mold in a pattern that was both traditional and innovative. In some manners, Calvin was a man of the late medieval age, comfortable with patterns of thought that were passing away even as he lived. In others, his efforts linked him to doctrines that would define the next two centuries. But in all cases, viewing the worlds in which he lived and through which he was received gives modern readers the best possible understanding of John Calvin. Neither hero, saint, nor demon, Calvin lived an early modern evangelical life, one that we have received through the intervening traditions.

PART I

❧

FRANCE AND ITS INFLUENCE

1

Ɒ

John Calvin's Life

G. Sujin Pak

John Calvin was born on July 10, 1509 in Noyon, France to his parents, Gérard Cauvin and Jeanne LeFranc; he was a second-born son, between an older brother Charles and two younger brothers Antoine and François. His mother, whom he remembered for her piety, died when Calvin was only six years old. Gérard Cauvin remarried, and his second wife bore two daughters. Gérard had obtained *bourgeois* status in 1497 and served as a city magistrate in Noyon. Intending Calvin for the priesthood, his father made arrangements to fund his education through his connections with the bishop and diocesan chapter of Noyon. Consequently, in the spring of 1521, Charles de Hangest, bishop of Noyon, provided Calvin his first ecclesiastical benefice of a third share of the Chapel of La Gésine. A second benefice was added in 1527 providing revenues from Saint-Martin de Martheville.

After the death of his mother, Calvin was sent to live in the home of his patron, the de Hangest family, thereby receiving his education alongside the children of the Montmorts, a branch of the de Hangest family. Calvin attended the Collège de Capettes with the Montmort sons, and in 1523, they enrolled together in the Collège de la Marche in Paris where they stayed for only three months before transferring to the Collège de Montaigu. Little is known about these years, but Calvin later dedicated his 1550 commentary on I Thessalonians to his esteemed Latin teacher at the Collège de la Marche – Mathurin Cordier – whom Calvin invited to teach in Geneva in 1536 and eventually secured him a post at the Geneva Academy in 1562.[1] At the Collège de Montaigu – one of the 40 colleges of the University of Paris – Calvin was introduced to medieval scholastic disputation methods. Through

---

[1] John Calvin, *Ioannis Calvini opera omnia quae supersunt*, in G. Baum, E. Cunitz, and E. Reuss, eds. 59 vols. (Brunsvigae: C. A. Schwetschke, 1863–1900) 13:525; henceforth cited as "CO."

the prior reforming work of Jean Standonck, the Collège de Montaigu imbued the values of the Brethren of the Common Life to its students, thereby operating as a kind of educational monastery that aimed to shape both the students' learning and moral character. Each day consisted of an interweaving of academic lessons and the recitation of the daily offices (i.e., morning and evening prayers). Regardless of whether he studied under John Major at this time (which scholars debate), Calvin certainly received a thorough grounding in nominalist practices of disputation, logic, and rhetoric.

Sometime between the years of 1526 and 1528, Calvin's father abruptly changed the course of his son's education, switching his studies from theology to law. Reflecting on this change in the 1557 preface to his Psalms commentary, Calvin indicated his father's rationale concerning the greater profitability of a law career.[2] Most scholars, however, point to the more likely reason of his father's changed circumstances due to a property settlement dispute between Gérard Cauvin and the Noyon cathedral chapter that eventually resulted in Gérard's excommunication in 1531.[3] Thus, sometime between 1526 and 1528 Calvin moved from Paris to the University of Orléans to study law. At Orléans, Calvin studied a legal curriculum under Pierre de l'Estoile centered in the *Corpus Juris Civilis* ("The Code of Civil Law"), a form of Roman law tracing back to the Roman Emperor Justinian I (483–565 CE). By spring of 1529, Calvin transferred to the University of Bourges, where he came under the tutelage of the Italian Andrea Alciati, a scholar known for his pioneering humanistic analysis of the *Corpus Juris*. Calvin, however, publicly expressed his preference for the traditional method of his former French teacher Pierre de l'Etoile in a 1531 preface to the book *Antapologia* of his colleague Nicolas du Chemin.[4] Calvin attended the University of Bourges for about 18 months, where he also studied Greek under Melchior Wolmar, to whom he later dedicated his 1546 commentary on 2 Corinthians.[5]

After the death of his father on May 26, 1531, Calvin turned aside from law back to a humanities curriculum focused on biblical languages and classical authors. Returning to Paris, he attended the Collège Royal, where he became

---

[2] CO 31:21.
[3] See Michael Mullett, *John Calvin* (New York: Routledge, 2011), 13; Willem Van't Spijker, *Calvin: A Brief Guide to His Life and Thought*, trans. Lyle D. Bierma (Louisville, KY: Westminster John Knox, 2009), 9.
[4] See Michael L. Monheit, "Young Calvin: Textual Interpretation and Roman Law," *Bibliothèque d'Humanisme et Renaissance* 59:2 (1997): 263–282.
[5] CO 12:364–365.

immersed in the circles of French Humanism such as those inspired by the teachings of Jacques Lefèvre d'Étaples. In the meantime, he wrote his first book, a commentary on Seneca's *De Clementia*, which he published at his own expense in April 1532. While in Paris from 1531 to 1533, several events contributed to what Calvin would later describe in the 1557 preface to his Psalms commentary as his conversion to Protestantism.[6] Calvin had already fostered a friendship with Nicolas Cop, who had been appointed as rector at the University of Paris in 1533. When in October 1533 a group of students at the university performed a play intensely critical of the evangelical teachings of Marguerite of Navarre, Cop disciplined the students, and Calvin provided his own account in support. A few weeks later, Cop delivered a rectorial address on All Saints Day (November 1, 1533) that expressed clear evangelical content traceable to the teachings of Luther and Erasmus, putting himself further at odds with the Sorbonne (i.e., the Paris faculty of theology) who brought charges against Cop. Cop fled to Basel. Calvin also came under suspicion and fled to Noyon. Records show that Calvin was in Noyon in May 1534, when he resigned his benefice with La Gésine and likely his benefice with Saint-Martin de Martheville, as well. He then accepted the invitation of Louis du Tillet to take refuge in the region of Claix and Angoulême, where he began writing his *Institutes*. Calvin appeared to be traveling back and forth between these various cities and Paris from 1533 to 1534 until the affair of the *Placards* in October 1534, in which virulent attacks on the Mass were posted throughout the chief cities of France that led to the issuance of an edict against the "Lutherans." Consequently, Calvin fled in January 1535 to Basel, where Cop, Oecolampadius, Erasmus, Capito, Münster, Bullinger, and Farel were already in residence.

Calvin formed many important friendships in Basel, including those with Guillame Farel, Pierre Viret, and Heinrich Bullinger, and he deepened his engagement with biblical languages by attending the lectures of Hebrew professor Sebastian Münster and Greek professor Simon Grynaeus, to whom Calvin dedicated his first biblical commentary – his 1539 Romans commentary. While in Basel, Calvin completed the first edition of his *Institutes* (1536), which was addressed to the French king with an introduction defending the Reformation in France. He also wrote the preface and introduction to his cousin Pierre Olivétan's 1535 French translation of the Bible.

Meanwhile, in May 1536 the general assembly of citizens in Geneva voted to embrace the Protestant cause. When Calvin visited Geneva three months

---

[6] CO 31:21ff.

later, Farel, who had been supporting the evangelical movement in Geneva, strongly pressed Calvin to take up leadership of the city. He eventually consented and arrived in Geneva in August 1536 and began giving lectures on Romans as a professor of theology and was soon appointed as a pastor. In his biography of Calvin, Theodore Beza wrote, "When, therefore, he was appointed a teacher of this church by a lawful election and approbation, he drew up a brief confession of faith and church order to provide a definite form for this recently established church."[7] Calvin's church order entailed a confession of faith, catechism, and instructions for church discipline and worship, particularly instructions for congregational singing and more frequent communion. In late 1536 and early 1537 Calvin and Farel presented these documents to the Small Council and Council of Two Hundred, who approved them with the exception of maintaining the quarterly celebration of the Lord's Supper (rather than weekly). Yet the public confession of faith was delayed until July 29, 1537, and many citizens refused to take the oath. Pierre Caroli's charges against Calvin, Viret, and Farel of denying the doctrine of the Trinity signified further resistance, as did the inability of the magistrates to ban the numerous persons who refused to take the confession of faith. The elections in February 1538 placed four pro-Bernese syndics hostile to Calvin in charge, who then ordered Calvin and Farel to attend a synod in Lausanne that decreed that all churches of the region should follow the liturgical practices of Bern. When Calvin, Farel, and other evangelical preachers of Geneva refused to conform, they were expelled from Geneva. Calvin and Farel left Geneva on April 23, 1538 and traveled to Basel, where Calvin stayed in the home of his friend Simon Grynaeus.

In September 1538 Calvin accepted Martin Bucer's invitation to come to Strasbourg to pastor a French refugee church. His time in Strasbourg proved deeply formative on a number of levels. First, Calvin observed Bucer's method of introducing church discipline in Strasbourg, which he would later adapt and apply to Geneva. Second, he cultivated his own practices of preaching and pastoral care, as he regularly preached twice on Sunday and oversaw four services during the week. He also implemented the practice of congregational singing and specifically psalm singing. The first French psalmbook (translated and rhymed by Clémont Marot and Calvin) emerged in 1539 out of Strasbourg, a book that would later serve as a key resource in the French Reformation. Calvin also contributed to the formation of a school in Strasbourg under the leadership of Jacob Sturm by serving as one of the

---

[7] CO 21:30.

lecturers in New Testament exegesis alongside Caspar Hedio, with Bucer and Capito as lecturers in Old Testament exegesis. While in Strasbourg, Calvin expanded and revised his *Institutes* to publish a 1539 edition, published a commentary on Romans (1539), and wrote *Short Treatise on the Holy Supper of Our Lord and Only Savior Jesus Christ*, which expressed a more conciliatory position toward Luther in contrast to his earlier criticisms in 1537. Along these lines, in 1539 he traveled to Frankfurt where he met with Philip Melanchthon to discuss the possibilities of a long-term agreement between the Swiss and Germans. Calvin likely intended to stay in Strasbourg, for he purchased citizenship in the city on July 30, 1539.

During his first years in Strasbourg, Calvin received pressure to marry. Bucer, Farel, and his brother Antoine all failed in their attempts to play matchmaker. But Calvin met Idelette de Bure when she and her husband joined his congregation. After her husband died of the plague early in 1540, Calvin and Idelette married later that year, and Calvin adopted the two children from her prior marriage as his own. On July 28, 1542, Idelette gave birth to a son, but the baby was born premature and died within a month. Indeed, Calvin and Idelette's marriage produced no surviving biological children, due at least in part to Idelette's poor health. She fell ill in 1545 and never fully recovered, eventually dying on March 29, 1549. Upon her death, Calvin grieved to his friend Viret, "I [have been] deprived of the excellent companion of my life."[8]

On March 8, 1539 Cardinal Jacopo Sadoleto wrote a letter to the citizens of Geneva strongly exhorting them to return to the Catholic Church. After first asking Viret to reply, the Genevans appealed to Calvin to offer a defense, resulting in his masterly *Reply to Sadoleto* penned on September 1, 1539. This became another turning point in Calvin's career, as the political changes in Geneva made it possible and even desirable for his return. Calvin returned to resume leadership of the Reformation in Geneva on September 13, 1541 and immediately requested the formation of a committee to draft a church order and guidelines for a consistory. The committee drew up and approved the *Ecclesiastical Ordinances* of 1541, which stipulated four biblical offices of the church (pastor, teacher, elder, and deacon) and their duties, the formation of the Company of Pastors who would meet weekly for Bible study and accountability, and the formation of the Consistory (comprised of the Company of Pastors and the elders) to enforce church discipline. Yet, the lack of clarity concerning the scope of the Consistory's authority was a

---

[8] CO 13:230.

problem that would plague Calvin's Geneva for the next decade and a half. Calvin also drew up a new catechism (1542, 1545), prepared a liturgical handbook (1542), and revised the Genevan Psalter (1543).

Calvin spent his days in Geneva often preaching twice on Sunday (on the New Testament) and three times during the week (on the Old Testament) and presiding over the Friday morning Bible study meetings of the Company of Pastors. An organized transcription of his sermons began in 1549; prior to that few of his sermons are extant. On Sundays, Calvin preached on Acts (1549–1554), the Pauline letters (1554–1558), and the Harmony of the Gospels (1559–1564). During the week, he preached on Jeremiah and Lamentations (1549–1550), the Minor Prophets and Daniel (1550–1552), Ezekiel (1552–1554), Job (1554–1555), Deuteronomy (1555–1556), Isaiah (1556–1559), Genesis (1559–1561), and Judges, 1 and 2 Samuel, and I Kings (1561–1564). Furthermore, he devoted himself to the writing of biblical commentaries, producing New Testament commentaries on 1 and 2 Corinthians (1546); Galatians-Ephesians-Philippians-Colossians (1548); 1 and 2 Timothy (1548); Hebrews (1549); Titus, 1 and 2 Thessalonians, Philemon, and James (1550); 1 and 2 Peter, 1 John, and Jude (1551); Acts (1552); John (1553); and the Synoptic Gospels (1555). He also published Old Testament commentaries on Isaiah (1551), Genesis (1554), Psalms (1557), Exodus-Leviticus-Numbers-Deuteronomy (1563), and Joshua (1563). Signifying his contacts with and efforts toward other countries, Calvin dedicated his commentaries on 1 and 2 Timothy to England's Duke of Somerset Edward Seymour, the epistles of James-Peter-John-Jude to King Edward VI, Hebrews to King Sigismund August of Poland, and Acts to King Christian III of Denmark. Lastly, Calvin provided lectures on the Old Testament in Geneva – lecturing on Isaiah (1549), Genesis and Psalms (early 1550s), Hosea and the Minor Prophets (in mid-1550s), Daniel (late 1550s), Jeremiah and Lamentations (early 1560s), and Ezekiel (1564). Even though the 1541 *Ecclesiastical Ordinances* stipulated the formation of an academy at Geneva, construction for a new educational center did not begin until 1558. The Collège was finally opened on June 5, 1559. Calvin completed the conclusive Latin edition of his *Institutes* in this same year.

Calvin's work in Geneva operated with a keen eye toward his homeland and the goals of fostering true Christian faith, piety, and worship, often in refutation of his opponents. Several treatises in the early and mid-1540s (1543: *Petit traicté* and 1544: *Excuse à Messieurs les Nicodémites*) addressed Calvin's perceived problem of Nicodemism, as the French Protestants struggled to live out their faith publicly in Catholic France. Alongside critiques of Roman Catholicism punctuating his commentaries, significant polemical treatises against the Catholic Church include *An Inventory of Relics* (1543), a refutation of the articles published by the Sorbonne (1544), *The Necessity of Reforming the Church* (1544), and *Acts of the Council of Trent with the Antidote* (1547). The mid-1540s also saw Calvin fighting against the Anabaptists (1544: *Brière instruction*) and the Libertines (1545: *Against the Libertines*), who resisted the enforcement of church discipline in Geneva. Nonetheless, Calvin was active in several efforts toward unity, including his work on the 1549 *Consensus Tigurinus* in an endeavor to unite the Swiss and Lutheran churches over the thorny issue of the Eucharist. Unfortunately, the hoped-for unity did not prevail, as this document evoked the Lutheran attacks penned by Joachim Westphal and Tilemann Heshusius, to which Calvin responded in kind, launching a serial polemical exchange from 1554 to 1561.

The years 1546 to 1555 were full of controversies for Calvin in Geneva. As early as 1543, under Calvin's influence, Geneva denied Sebastian Castellio entrance into Geneva's pastoral office due to doctrinal matters (i.e., denial of the Song of Songs's canonicity and rejection of Christ's descent to hell). Castellio would appear again in 1554 publicly criticizing Calvin's handling of Servetus. Early conflicts (1546–1547) focused around the scope of the Consistory's authority in enforcing church discipline, such as conflicts concerning proper baptismal names, the closing of the taverns, and various acts of resistance led by a coalition of prominent interrelated Genevan families (Perrins, Favres, Septs, Vadels, and Bertheliers), known as "Perrinists," whom Calvin called "Libertines." Some Genevan citizens publicly criticized Calvin's doctrine and character: in 1546 councilmen Pierre Ameaux called Calvin "a bad man and preacher of false doctrine"; in 1551 Jerome Bolsec challenged Calvin's doctrine of predestination in a Friday morning Bible study meeting; in 1552 Jean Trolliet (whose desires to be a preacher were thwarted by Calvin) complained against Calvin's predestinarian preaching; in 1553 Robert Lemoine, appearing before the Consistory, likewise attacked Calvin's doctrine of predestination; and also in 1553 Philibert Berthelier refused to adhere to his excommunication by the Consistory. Indeed, the Perrinists won the majority of the elections in 1552–1553, so that Berthelier got off with just a simple apology to the Consistory. The most famous controversy concerning Calvin also occurred in 1553 when Michael Servetus showed up in Geneva – after previously being sentenced to death for heresy by the Roman Catholic Inquisition in Vienna, burned in effigy, and warned by Calvin not to enter Geneva. Servetus was burned at the stake on October 27, 1553 for his denial of the doctrine of the Trinity, among other heresies.

A significant turnaround occurred in 1555 when the Perrinists and their faction were overthrown in the elections. After a feeble (drunken) attempt at an armed insurrection by Perrin and his followers, they fled Geneva and were sentenced to death in absentia, thus permitting Calvin finally to consolidate his leadership of Geneva. With this consolidation of power, Calvin was able to look outward from Geneva, increasingly lengthening his international influence upon churches in France, England, Scotland, the Netherlands, and Heidelberg, Germany. The establishment of the Geneva Academy in 1559 reinforced these efforts, as persecuted Protestants from surrounding territories sought refuge in Geneva, gained theological training, and eventually returned to their home countries to provide key theological leadership. Yet, the 1550s also entailed mounting health issues for Calvin. He suffered from migraines for most of his life; starting in 1558 he was increasingly confined to his room; and by 1561 he was suffering from consumption, hemorrhoids, and gout, along with painful gallstones and kidney stones. On April 27, 1564, sensing his end was near, Calvin bade farewell to the members of the Small Council and to the Company of Pastors the following day. He died a month later on May 27, 1564 at the age of 54. Throughout his life, Calvin struggled with opponents from within and without, but in close identification with his biblical hero David, he comforted himself with the knowledge that he dedicated his whole life to cultivating true faith, piety, and purity of worship to the glory and honor of God.

SUGGESTED FURTHER READINGS

Gordon, Bruce. *Calvin*. New Haven, CT: Yale University Press, 2009.

Selderhuis, Herman J. *John Calvin: A Pilgrim's Life*, trans. Albert Gootjes. Downers Grove, IL: IVP Academic, 2009.

Wendel, François. *Calvin: Origins and Developments of His Religious Thought*, trans. Philip Mairet. Grand Rapids, MI: Baker Books, 1997 (original 1950).

2

◐◉

French Christianity in the Early 1500s

Raymond A. Mentzer

The French religious universe of John Calvin's youth was complex and powerful. Calvin retained and strengthened many of its central beliefs and practices. Others he modified and realigned to reflect his understanding of an authentic scripturally based Christianity. Finally, Calvin emphatically rejected and sought to suppress a third group of religious views and behaviors that he regarded as unfounded, superstitious, and, in some instances, dangerously idolatrous. Whatever Calvin's assessment, late medieval religious practices and the beliefs that undergirded them were elaborate and pervasive. They held great appeal for a substantial number of people from all social strata, extending from the broad oral culture of the unlettered majority to the elite ranks of the learned and privileged.

The fundamental rituals in which all Christians participated were the sacraments. They were, according to the twelfth-century theologian Peter Lombard, visible forms of an invisible grace. The medieval church maintained seven sacraments: baptism, penance, the Eucharist, confirmation, marriage, ordination, and extreme unction. Still, the number and frequency of sacraments received by an individual varied. Only men could be ordained and even then, only a small percentage would have taken holy orders. Confirmation, performed by a bishop, was essentially a reaffirmation of the baptismal vows. Children seem to have been confirmed at an early age, though it may also be that some simply ignored it. As no formal records of confirmation exist, it is difficult to know with precision at what age and how many individuals received the sacrament.

Baptism, marriage, and perhaps extreme unction were far more familiar to ordinary believers. They corresponded closely to the principal stages in the life cycle. Baptism, which was necessary for salvation, occurred soon after birth. It admitted the infant to the community of belief and at the same time was thought to wash away the stain of original sin from the child's soul.

While liturgical routines varied according to local customs, the general practice was for the godparents to take the newborn to the church within a few days of birth. Often as not the father stayed home to organize the ensuing festivities and the mother would still be recovering from having given birth. Indeed, until the postpartum churching ritual, it was not considered appropriate for a new mother to enter a church. The priest met the party at the church door and blessed the infant. He would put a pinch of salt in her or his mouth, symbolizing the child's preservation in the faith, and he blew upon her or him to exorcise any demons. The priest would also spit into his hand and touch the ears and nose of the infant, thus making her or him receptive to the word of God. The party then entered the church, and proceeded to the baptismal font and a blessing of the water. The godparents renounced, in the newborn's name, Satan and his works. The priest would also test their knowledge of the basic prayers that they or the biological parents were to teach the child. He dipped the child three times into the water, and anointed her or him with chrism (consecrated oil).

However, perhaps as many as one-half of all infants were baptized by the attending midwife immediately upon birth. Any Christian, female or male, could, according to medieval interpretation, administer baptism in an emergency so long as he or she used water and baptized the child in the name of the Trinity. Given the fragility of newborns and the belief that a child who died without benefit of baptism would be forever consigned to limbo and thereby denied the eternal comfort of the beatific vision, parents were naturally anxious to have an infant baptized as soon as possible. Thus, the midwife's task frequently extended beyond providing for the physical well-being of mother and child. She or a helpful neighbor woman could, if deemed necessary, prepare a dying infant for salvation.

Marriage, while considered a sacrament, was very much a family affair in the later Middle Ages. Parents regularly made the necessary preparations and the ceremony often took place at home in the presence of family members. Indeed, the clergy's involvement in the sacrament was minimal. The bride and groom officiated. At most, newlyweds might have gone afterward to the parish church where the priest met them at the west portico and blessed the union. Marriage, whose three traditional legal requirements were consent, publicity, and *copula carnalis*, occurred in two stages. The first was a betrothal ceremony in which the couple exchanged reciprocal promises – the words of the future tense – to wed. They often drank wine from a common cup in the name of marriage and might exchange gifts such as a ring or an article of clothing. Wealthier families generally had the promises formalized in a notarial contract, which detailed the economic arrangements between bride, groom, and their relatives. The ritual was public in the sense that it took place in the presence of at least two witnesses. The solemnization of the marital union with final vows, the so-called words of the present tense, took place several weeks later. The established interval was six weeks, a delay that allowed for the publication of the banns on successive Sundays. The process would presumably turn up any impediments or obstacles. Finally, people enthusiastically celebrated betrothals and marriages, and the accompanying promise of another generation of daughters and sons, with food and drink, music and dancing.

Extreme unction was a rite of departure, the final preparation for death and passage from this world into the next, although it may not have been as widely practiced as baptism or marriage. When observed, extreme unction was typically administered as part of the last rites. The priest visited the dying person, who confessed her or his sins and then received the consecrated Host. The sacrament proper began with the appropriate prayers, followed by an anointing of the organs of the five external senses (eyes, ears, nostrils, lips, and hands) as well as the feet. The priest repeated at each unction the plea that the Lord pardon the dying person for whatever sins he or she had committed by sight, hearing, smell, taste, touch, or walking.

The medieval church required individuals to confess their sins to a priest at least once each year during the Easter season. The penitent knelt before the seated confessor in an open space within the church. He or she began by making the sign of the cross and then offered, in the ideal, an open and frank recitation of each and every of her or his sins since last confessing. The priest would ask questions as appropriate, provide spiritual guidance, and impose a penance. Finally, the confessor would absolve the penitent who, in turn, proceeded to perform the assigned penance. Confession was meant to be entirely private and secret, a matter between confessor and penitent alone. Church authorities also regarded it as part of the necessary preparation for reception of the Eucharist.

The Mass was the central liturgical feature of late medieval Christianity. This regular celebration of the Eucharist made a direct and forceful appeal to the senses, but it was decidedly not a participatory event. Its most elaborate form involved colorful vestments, lighted candles, burning incense, and the ringing of bells. The strong sensory elements embedded in the Mass carried over to the decoration of the edifices in which the clergy celebrated it. In addition to the altar, stained glass windows, polychromatic wall paintings, and ornate statuary adorned many churches. Reformed commentators derisively referred to these buildings as "temples of the idols."

The Mass was recited in Latin, as were people's everyday prayers, notably the Ave Maria, Pater Noster, and Creed. The key moment in the service was the consecration and subsequent Elevation of the Host and the chalice containing the wine. The belief was that the two elements had been miraculously transubstantiated into the flesh and blood of the Savior, even if they still "accidentally" appeared to be bread and wine. The ringing of a bell alerted the faithful to the moment and all knelt in reverence and adoration of their Lord's body and blood. Otherwise, those in attendance stood around (pews had yet to be introduced), perhaps praying the rosary or, equally likely, chatting with friends. The centrality of the Mass in late medieval worship was such that converts from Catholicism to the Reformed faith explicitly abjured the "superstition and idolatry" of the Mass.

While people may have attended Mass regularly, their reception of communion was infrequent, perhaps no more than once a year, usually at Easter when the entire congregation gathered to participate. Even then, the laity received only the Host, a highly stylized form of the bread. Wafer thin and unleavened, it was not to be touched by anyone other than the celebrant. The priest placed it upon the recipient's tongue. He or she swallowed the Host whole and never chewed it. This after all was the flesh of the Lord. For analogous reasons the medieval church barred the faithful from taking the wine lest they spill, dribble, or otherwise desecrate the very blood of the Savior. The cup was reserved exclusively for the priestly celebrant. Ordinary believers, however, were included in ancillary practices such as the kiss of peace through the stylized intermediary of the pax board and the distribution of *pain bénit* at the conclusion of the Mass.[1] These routines centered directly on the laity and served to strengthen spiritual bonds and reinforce communal responsibilities.

The celebration of the Mass typically did not include a sermon. Parish priests, especially in the rural areas, tended to have only elementary training. Many seem not have known how to read and write; they simply memorized the Latin prayers. They primarily fulfilled a sacerdotal role; priests administered the sacraments. Few expected them to offer elaborate explanations of belief. Still, there would have been an opportunity at most Sunday Masses for announcements and vernacular prayers. Known as the *prône*, it was essentially a vehicle for communal catechesis – teaching the laity the rudimentary beliefs and practices of Christianity.[2] When sermon services did take place,

---

[1] Virginia Reinburg, "Liturgy and the Laity in Late Medieval and Reformation France," *Sixteenth Century Journal* 23 (1992): 526–547.
[2] Katharine J. Lualdi, "A Body of Beliefs and Believers: Sacramental Confession and Parish Worship in Reformation France," in Katherine J. Lualdi and Anne T. Thayer (eds.), *Penitence in the Age of Reformations* (Aldershot: Ashgate, 2000), 134–151.

they were generally during Advent and Lent in the weeks leading up to Christmas and Easter. Municipal authorities in urban communities often engaged Dominican or Franciscan friars to offer sermons in the vernacular so that the faithful might prepare properly for the principal Christian feasts. For many urban residents, nurturing the soul through the vehicle of the sermon reinforced the significance of fasting and abasing the body. These sermons tended not to have a strict biblical orientation. Rather, they addressed moral corruption and the seven deadly sins.

Fasting and abstaining from certain foods on certain days was an additional, integral part of medieval Christian devotion. The church developed elaborate communal and private practices that focused on food. The liturgical year involved an extensive cycle of fasting and feasting. Christians readied themselves for the two major feasts, Christmas and Easter, with long stretches of collective fasts and abstinence during the four-week Advent season and the famous 40 days of Lent.[3] These penitential seasons were opportunities for the mortification of the flesh and, for some couples, could mean avoiding sexual intercourse. Beyond fasts aimed at atonement and repentance, medieval fasting also attended rituals of purification and mourning. Men and more especially women engaged in powerful, often astonishing individual acts of discipline and self-denial. These fasts were, in the vocabulary of medieval theology, meritorious works, which could contribute significantly in the quest for salvation.[4]

In all this, the divine was always close at hand. Believers felt assured of God's immanent presence in the consecrated Host. In addition, holy relics, various material articles connected to saints, and sacred pilgrimage sites offered the faithful opportunities to interact in tangible ways with these powerful heavenly figures. Saints protected believers and interceded on their behalf with God. The cult of saints was especially pronounced in the practices surrounding relics. These bits of bone and physical objects associated with the departed saint provided a sense of palpable contact with the spiritual world. Saints could help both in the future and the here and now, in the next world and the present. Their veneration, coupled with prayer and monetary donation, was the occasion for the acquisition of indulgences[5] that helped to lessen, for the suppliant or some designated beneficiary, time in

---

[3] Bridget Ann Henisch, *Fast and Feast: Food in Medieval Society* (University Park: Pennsylvania State University Press, 1976), 28–58.

[4] Carolyn W. Bynum, *Holy Feast and Holy Famine: The Religious Significance of Food to Medieval Women* (Berkeley and Los Angeles: University of California Press, 1987).

[5] An indulgence offered the complete or partial remission of punishment in Purgatory due for sins already confessed and forgiven.

Purgatory (the cleansing atonement for sin that was necessary before entry into heaven). In the immediate, townspeople might parade a local saint's relics in hopes of quelling a fire, stemming a plague, or ending a drought. Saints and their relics offered miraculous cures for individuals afflicted with illnesses and infirmities. Thus, pious persons regularly made vows to go to some pilgrimage site and implore a saint's assistance. The most renowned pilgrimages were to Jerusalem, Rome, and Santiago de Compostela, where one could visit the Holy Sepulcher, the church of Saint Peter, or the tomb of Saint James the Apostle. Relatively few, however, had the time or resources to undertake so lengthy and arduous a journey. Most pilgrims were content to visit one or more of the hundreds of local shrines. Among the more prominent and popular sites were Chartres, Conques, Le Puy, and Vézelay.

Another possibility for the laity's participation in the devotional life of the church was through membership in a confraternity. Almost any group, male or female, that had religious objectives and included laypersons could be styled a confraternity. They were extremely popular and widespread. Indeed, confraternities pervaded the medieval parish landscape. They mobilized participants for saints' festivals and members' funerals, and were intricately involved in charity programs and the decoration of churches and chapels. Surviving records indicate that most parishes, above all in urban settings, had at least one pious confraternity, a voluntary association that honored a specific devotion. Some confraternities venerated the parish name saint. Others were dedicated to the Virgin Mary and yet other groups attended to the myriad of ritual forms surrounding the worship of Jesus. A significant number of confraternities were devoted to healing saints such as the saints Sebastian and Roche who protected against plague, Saint Maur who aided those with gout, or Saint Marcou who helped persons afflicted with scrofula. Confraternity members typically met at a local church, where they arranged for celebrating the feast of the saint to whom they were dedicated. Processions, an important element in the celebration, became elaborate affairs as members, led by a standard-bearer carrying the group's ceremonial staff, marched through the town with lighted candles.

A syncretic approach to the sacred allowed people to blend Christian beliefs and practices with time-honored folkloric elements. Predictably, Calvin's followers in France found these customs more "pagan" than Christian. Yet they were extremely common. Everyone seemingly knew of a sorceress to whom a person could turn for magical favors and remedies. When a spouse or child fell ill, the sorceress provided curative powders along with the requisite ritual incantations. She could also assist in finding lost objects and forecasting future events. Other customs bore less association with witchcraft yet remained on the margins of Christianity. Some households, for example, found enjoyment in the custom of the Yule log at Christmas. More pervasive were the celebrations associated with the feast of Saint John the Baptist on June 24. A long-standing event, its principal feature was a large bonfire around which participants danced on the preceding evening. The flames purified and renewed human as well as agricultural fecundity. To bring good luck, people leapt over the blaze. Some tossed herbs on the fire and later gathered the ashes for magical use. This midsummer ritual appears to have had strong associations with an ancient pre-Christian world and the summer solstice, even if the dates do not exactly coincide. Men and women observed with similar enthusiasm the revelries of Carnival. Youthful demonstrations and merrymaking marked the several days before Ash Wednesday and the beginning of Lent. Mardi Gras was an opportunity to play violins and other musical instruments, don costumes and masks, dance, hold banquets, and generally carouse in ancestral follies before embarking on 40 days of fasting and penitence in preparation for Easter and the observance of the central Christian feast of the Resurrection.

In the end, late medieval Christianity had a strong texture and powerful appeal, despite its severe criticism by Calvin and other reformers. A robust communal orientation permeated the ways in which people gathered for worship and sought mutual spiritual protection amid a decidedly precarious environment. The sacraments defined a person's temporal existence – birth, marriage, and death – even as they promised divine salvation. God and the saints were close at hand and could be readily called upon for relief in times of crisis. Collective fasts and corporate associations cemented unity of presence and purpose. Finally, a clearly identifiable malleability allowed the faithful to blend their Christian faith with long-standing ancestral customs and concepts of the sacred.

SUGGESTED FURTHER READINGS

Barnes, Andrew E. *The Social Dimension of Piety: Associative Life and Devotional Changes in the Penitent Confraternities of Marseilles (1499–1792)*. New York: Paulist Press, 1994.

Galpern, A. Neal. *The Religions of the People in Sixteenth-Century Champagne*. Cambridge, MA: Harvard University Press, 1976.

Groupe de La Buissière. *Pratiques de la confession des pères du désert à Vatican II. Quinze études d'histoire*. Paris: Editions du Cerf, 1983.

Mentzer, Raymond A. "The Persistence of 'Superstition and Idolatry' among Rural French Calvinists," *Church History* 65 (1996): 220–233.

Swanson, Robert. *Religion and Devotion in Europe, c. 1215–c. 1515.* Cambridge: Cambridge University Press, 1995.

Taylor, Larissa. *Soldiers of Christ: Preaching in Late Medieval and Reformation France.* Oxford: Oxford University Press, 1992.

3

∾

The University of Paris during Calvin's Life

Greta Grace Kroeker

THE FOUNDATIONS OF THE UNIVERSITY OF PARIS

The university was a medieval invention and therefore a very medieval institution. Its very name, as Hastings Rashdall explained, grew out of the word
universitas, which denoted both "an aggregate of persons," and a "legal
corporation."[1] The University of Paris, like the other early university, the
University of Bologna, emerged at the end of the twelfth century and reflected
the flowering of culture and learning of the 12th Century Renaissance.[2] While
Bologna came to be known for its Faculty of Law, Paris emerged as the
"archetypal" University in the Faculties of Arts and Theology.

The foundation of the university was closely linked to the other dominant
institution of the Middle Ages, the Catholic Church. In fact, in the case of
the University of Paris, it grew out a guild of teachers at the Notre Dame
cathedral school. But all the universities of the Middle Ages had a strong link
to the Church. "The universities of the late Middle Ages were permeated by
Church influence. Universities were usually founded with the authority from
a papal bull.... Of the three higher faculties, Theology, Law, and Medicine,
in which doctorates were awarded, theological studies were regulated and
overwhelmingly carried out by churchmen, while canon law – the law of the
Roman Church – formed at least half the work of Law faculties."[3] Students at
the university were governed and protected by ecclesiastical law, which
offered special status, protections, and privileges. This special status, in turn,
often caused tensions with townspeople, and the unique sociopolitical conflict emerged, which continues today and we call "town versus gown."

[1] Hastings Rashdall, *The Universities of Europe in the Middle Ages*, Vol. 1 (Oxford: Clarendon
Press, 1895), 5.
[2] Ibid., 19.
[3] Euan Cameron, *The European Reformation* (Oxford: Clarendon Press, 1991), 21.

Students often entered university in early adolescence and studied for the bachelor's degree for five or six years. Although technically classified as clerics through their ecclesiastical status, not all students belonged to religious orders, though religious orders often sponsored their members to go to university, and those students lived in houses of their order while studying. Otherwise, students lived where they could find reasonable rent or banded together in houses under their master or with others from their "nation."[4]

Given the strong connection between the university, in general, and the Church, it is no surprise that the University of Paris, which became the center of theological studies in Christendom, was particularly closely aligned with the Catholic Church. In addition to the pastoral, educational, and doctrinal duties performed by graduates of theological faculties, the Church needed educated, literate functionaries to administer their lands and dealings. So did lay rulers. The universities provided young people educated in Latin and able to conduct the business of the Church, the princes, and the magistrates. In this way, the university was not only essential to the spiritual welfare of Christendom but also fundamental to the proper functioning of its more worldly endeavours. As Rashdall explains, "To the university of Paris, whose four faculties were likened by medieval imagination to the fourfold river of Paradise, could be traced as to their ultimate source and fountainhead all the streams of knowledge by which the whole church was watered and fertilized. In the university of Paris – the 'first school of the church' – France possessed her equivalent to the Italian papacy and the German Caesarship in the politico-ecclesiastical system of Europe."[5]

THE MIDDLE AGES, THE CHURCH, AND THE UNIVERSITY OF PARIS

The University of Paris emerged as the primary theater of the development of the foundation of medieval education, the Seven Liberal Arts, which included the *Trivium* (grammar, rhetoric, and dialectic) and the *Quadrivium* (music, arithmetic, geometry, and astronomy).[6] As the institution developed, however, the great thinkers of the Middle Ages primarily focused on dialectic, a method that relied on debate between two opposing philosophical ideas or positions and the application of reason to arrive at a truth. From this

---

[4] For a detailed account, see Rashdall, *Universities*, ch. 5.

[5] Hastings Rashdall, "The Origins of the University of Paris," *The English Historical Review* 1:4 (October 1886): 639.

[6] Rashdall, *Universities*, 33–34.

focus on dialectic grew the scholastic method and theology that came to dominate the Paris Theology of Faculty, and indeed, most theological practice and study of the era.

Scholasticism relied on the study of ancient philosophy. Eventually, scholastic theologians sought to apply Aristotelian questions of logic, primarily the definition and reality of Universals, to theology and questions of Christian faith and truth. The great Parisian theological stars of the Middle Ages, Anselm, Peter Abelard, and Peter Lombard, applied logic through dialectical method to proving questions of faith, like the divinity of Christ, and to the mysteries of doctrine, like transubstantiation.[7]

This preoccupation with dialectic and logic permeated the curriculum at the University of Paris. Bachelor of arts students and master of theology candidates, however, did not normally study the original texts, what we would refer to as "primary sources." Instead, students studied ancient philosophy and the ideas of the medieval theologians in the form of compilations of opinions, known as *sententiae*, which were gleaned from classical philosophy and theology, but "completely divorced from their original context and hence often also divorced from their original meaning."[8]

From the late fourteenth century on, this educational method became the target of a group of scholars known as humanists, scholars who argued that this pedagogical method was deeply flawed and pedantic. On its own, as Charles Nauert points out, humanism was not a philosophy distinct from Scholasticism. Humanism did not challenge the authorities on which scholastic thought relied. Instead, humanists argued that the ways in which scholastics experienced, taught, digested, and argued about ancient and Christian authorities were flawed. "From Petrarch onward, humanists insisted on reading each opinion in its literary context, abandoning the anthologies and subsequent interpretations and going back to the original source in search of the author's real meaning. To put it another way, classical (and early Christian) authors re-emerged as real human beings living at a particular moment in history and addressing their remarks to specific issues that might have no connection at all with the issues for which medieval anthologists used the author's words."[9] In this way, humanists sought to historicize and contextualize the sources of the past.

---

[7] Ibid. offers a comprehensive guide to these developments. See 33ff.
[8] Charles Nauert, *Humanism and the Culture of Renaissance Europe*, 2nd ed. (Cambridge: Cambridge University Press, 2006), 17–18.
[9] Ibid., 18.

Beginning in Italy, humanist challenges to scholastic methods made inroads on the fringes of university life as early as the fourteenth century, but the scholastic educational system dominated theological education at Paris and elsewhere well into the fifteenth century. But as the Italian Renaissance took shape and migrated over the Alps, many young scholars came to apply the questions and priorities of Renaissance learning to theology, and when they did, they took aim at scholastic methods of teaching and study. These scholars, who came to be known as "humanists" because of their love of the study of humane letters, or the *studia humanitatis*, were fundamentally educational reformers who sought to privilege original texts over excerpts and convincing rhetoric and beautiful grammatical style over memorization and rigid dialectical debate. As Lewis Spitz explained, "They criticized scholasticism as harmful to culture, injurious to Latin style, hostile to poetry and the *bonae litterae*, neglectful of natural and moral philosophy, as being precious rather than practical, logical rather than grammatical and rhetorical."[10] In short, they thought scholastic methods in teaching and studying outdated and boring. Instead, humanists sought out ancient manuscripts, studied classical poetry and history, and applied their enthusiasm for sources to the Bible and the Church fathers.

Humanists often operated as tutors outside of the official teaching circles of universities. They developed followers who appreciated their poetry in the style of the ancients and who studied languages and classical literature under their tutelage in their publications. They were greatly aided by the printing press, and they quickly grasped the power they could wield by publishing their own works on religion and philosophy and their critiques of what they viewed as scholastic errors and abuses.[11]

The core of the humanist conflict with the scholastics was about method, and in the field of theology, the stakes were very high – they touched the very heart of Christian belief, practice, and authority.[12] By the early 1500s, humanists began to demand educational reforms, most especially in the field of theology. Humanists saw the scholastic theological method as a "theological science that concentrated on trivial, abstruse questions of little or no real value to the needs of the Church. Scholastic theology, they charged, neglected full and reflective study of what the Bible said. It forced degree

---

[10] Lewis Spitz, *The Religious Renaissance of the German Humanists* (Cambridge, MA: Harvard University Press, 1963), 275.

[11] There remains great debate among scholars about the intensity of the conflict between humanists and scholastics. See Charles Nauert, "Humanism as Method: Roots of the Conflict with the Scholastics," *Sixteenth Century Journal* 29:2 (Summer 1998): 427–438.

[12] Ibid., 430.

candidates to waste years learning what ignorant, half-educated, and Greek-less medieval commentators had written."[13] The humanists were particularly critical of the scholastic reliance on teaching through the *sententiae*, or fragments, taken out of their original sources and unmoored from their contexts. For their part, scholastics rejected "the application of humanistic textual, historical, and linguistic skills to the study of the Bible."[14] This scholastic defense became increasingly strident as humanists turned their attention to Scripture and its interpretation.

Although scholars have disagreed about the depth of the discord between humanists and scholastics in the fifteenth and sixteenth centuries, the stakes were very high, especially in the field of theology.[15] The scholastics bristled at the humanists' critiques, not just because they attacked their approach to education and theological scholarship but also, and more importantly, because the more astute among them, and those at the University of Paris like Noel Beda (d. 1536), the leader of the Paris Faculty of Theology (Sorbonne), certainly among them, realized that the humanistic attack on dialectic as the primary method of theological study threatened the very idea of theological truth and authority as they understood it. If reading the Bible, and in the vernacular, no less, could reveal God's plan and Christian truth, then anyone with access to the Bible could believe that they had the right to interpret and arrive at that truth. The scholastics rejected the humanists as unqualified to "do" theology and dismissed them as mere grammarians with no proper theological training. They worried that uncoupling the biblical text from the formal and closely guarded training afforded by scholastic methods and masters at the University of Paris and their colleagues could have disastrous consequences for Christianity and the authority and unity of the Catholic Church. As they launched attack after attack against humanist theologians, they feared that whoever controlled the biblical text, controlled the faith.[16]

The theologians at the University of Paris were right to be concerned. As the dons of the oldest and greatest of the theology faculties in Europe, they were the frequent targets of humanist attacks, and they positioned

---

[13] Ibid., 431.
[14] Ibid.
[15] See, e.g., Erika Rummel, *The Humanist-Scholastic Debate in the Renaissance and the Reformation* (Cambridge, MA: Harvard University Press, 1998).
[16] Nauert, "Humanism as Method," 434. Nauert writes in reference to Erasmus, "But his scholastic critics quickly sensed, his modest claim to control the text amounted to claiming control of the whole field."

themselves as defenders of both scholastic method and Catholic doctrine and tradition. They saw themselves as protectors of the faith and guardians of the Christian text and orthodoxy. It worried them that those they viewed as unqualified to even discuss theology had altered what they considered the sacred translation of the Bible in the Latin Vulgate and offered uninformed and dangerous theological opinions, unfettered by the agreed upon sources, methods, and opinions of the academics.[17] And to an extent, they were right. Humanism "challenged the whole enterprise of rational philosophy, the scholastic aspiration toward attainment of absolute truth."[18] Humanism introduced skepticism about doctrine and the ability to discern any absolute truth[19] and called for theology and theologians that addressed the pastoral and spiritual needs of believers. They called for access over prestige and clarity over reason.

THE REFORMATION

The seriousness of this debate over who could "do" theology and what sources were best suited for theological study intensified with the arrival of the Protestant Reformation.[20] While not all reformers were humanists and while not all humanists joined the reformers in their critique of the Catholic Church, the reformers did take up the theological products of the humanists, including biblical translations, questions about pastoral care, and patristic sources and translations and used them to create new theological challenges to the hegemony of Catholic doctrine. After 1517, when Martin Luther, a young professor of biblical studies at the University of Wittenberg, posted his *Ninety-Five Theses* and sparked the Protestant movement, Catholic theologians redoubled their efforts to defend theology departments from the inroads of the dangerous humanists and the new theology that came, sometimes unfairly, to be associated with

---

[17] Ibid., 431. This focused on two issues, defense of orthodox doctrine and rejection of the linguistic/philosophical method for the dialectical method. See also the Theology Faculty's 1531 publication of an attack on Erasmus, *Determinatio facultatis theologiae*, and his response, published the next year, *Declarationes ad censuras Lutetiae vulgatas sub nomine facultatis theologiae Parisiensis*. Erasmus's text and much of the Faculty's argument are available in *Collected Works of Erasmus: Controversies. Declarationes ad Censuras Lutetiae Vulgatas sub Nomine Facultatis Theologiae Parisiensis*. Edited, translated, and annotated by Clarence H. Miller (Toronto: University of Toronto Press, 2012).

[18] Nauert, "Humanism as Method," 432.

[19] Ibid., 431–433.

[20] Ibid., 428.

them.[21] Especially in France, as Protestant ideas spread, the University of Paris theologians stepped into the fray to defend orthodoxy. As Bruce Gordon explains, "The Sorbonne took upon itself a new role in French religious politics; whereas previously it had been the defender of orthodox doctrine, increasingly it became an inquisition, not hesitating to attack prominent figures. In August 1532 Beda led the faculty to condemn all editions of scripture in Greek, Hebrew and French.... In what would prove one of its worst decisions, the Sorbonne proscribed translations of the Bible into French; this would later provide the evangelicals with an open door through which to send a flood of vernacular bibles into the country."[22]

It was in this electric climate that John Calvin entered the University of Paris. Calvin began his studies in 1523 when his parents sent him to Paris with the intent that he study for the priesthood. He came under the careful tutelage of a French humanist, Maturin Cordier at the College de la Marche. He moved to the College de Montaigu, an elite but strict place, and progressed through his studies at the University of Paris.[23] The harshness of the discipline at Montaigu had caused the famed humanist Erasmus of Rotterdam (d. 1536), who had also studied there, to term it "Vinegar College."[24] But in the late 1520s, for reasons historians still find unclear, Calvin changed directions and went to Orleans to study law.[25] Despite the fact that he did not go on to study theology at Paris, he could not have helped but be influenced by the religious changes and conflicting ideas that swarmed around him at the university.

Perhaps the most lasting impact of the rise of humanism, however, and the most important for the context in which John Calvin emerged from the University of Paris, was not the challenge humanistic methodology posed to scholasticism, but the broadening of available theological methodologies and thus interpretations that humanism advanced. The humanist toolbelt equipped scholars to study original sources, encouraged the study of biblical Greek and Hebrew, promoted the importance of historical discontinuity when assessing sources, and elevated the vernacular for both Christian study and preaching. These skills enabled many early modern theologians to use the tools of the Renaissance to address Christianity in

---

[21] See Paul F. Grendler, "The Universities of the Renaissance and Reformation," *Renaissance Quarterly* 57:1 (Spring 2004): 17.
[22] Bruce Gordon, *Calvin* (New Haven, CT: Yale University Press, 2009), 13–14.
[23] Ibid., 5–8.
[24] In Erasmus's colloquy of a butcher and a fishmonger, sometimes called, "A Fish Diet."
[25] Gordon, *Calvin*, 18.

new ways. The very fiber of daily Christian life resounded with the effects of the humanistic embrace of the vernacular in song and text. Protestant Christians who were expected to read the Bible in the language of their homes rather than Latin were able to read the Bible for themselves. Although scholastic method remained in the universities through the eighteenth century and heavily influenced Enlightenment and modern philosophy, it was outside the universities that the theological debates about the usefulness of scholasticism and the fruits of humanistic studies found footing in the religious changes of the sixteenth century and beyond.

The Reformation challenged and changed the University of Paris and its golden Faculty of Theology. Like other universities, it both encouraged and fought the religious changes of the sixteenth century. "Bernd Moeller, the well-known historian of the Protestant Reformation in Germany, made the statement, 'Without humanism, no Reformation.'" He was correct. But Moeller should have added another statement: "'Without universities, no Reformation,' because university professors created and sustained the Protestant Reformation through its first century."[26] This is keenly true for the theology faculty at the University of Paris. Not only did Parisian theologians establish the foundations of medieval theological study but they also helped shape the theological debates and conflicts of the Reformation era and, in many ways, defined both Catholic orthodoxy and how it would be challenged.

In the short term, the conservative Paris theology faculty seemed to win the day. They were able to launch bold defenses of orthodoxy through publishing and censorship and cooperation with the French Parlement.[27] But the changes that had been launched by the humanists and the reformers nevertheless made inroads in France as they did elsewhere. Humanists and "humanism eventually earned wide acceptance in French intellectual life and French Protestants were granted toleration in 1598," but the University of Paris played an important role in keeping France within the Catholic fold and promoting Catholic Reform.[28]

---

[26] Paul F. Grendler, "The Universities of the Renaissance and Reformation," *Renaissance Quarterly* 57:1 (Spring 2004), 1–42, see p. 14.

[27] James K. Farge, "Early Censorship in Paris: A New Look at the Roles of the Parlement of Paris and of King Francis I," *Renaissance and Reformation* 25:2 (1989): 174.

[28] James K. Farge, "Noel Beda and the Defense of the Tradition," in *Biblical Humanism and Scholasticism in the Age of Erasmus*, ed. Erika Rummel (Leiden, The Netherlands: Brill, 2008), 143–164, 164.

SUGGESTED FURTHER READINGS

Paul F. Grendler, "The Universities of the Renaissance and Reformation," *Renaissance Quarterly* 57:1 (Spring 2004), 1–42.

Erika Rummel, *The Humanist-Scholastic Debate in the Renaissance and the Reformation* (Cambridge, MA: Harvard University Press, 1998).

4

∾

French Humanism

Olivier Millet

The reign of Francis I (1515–1547) created a cultural shift in France, caused by the importation and adaptation of the humanist tradition, a tradition of Italian origin. The reasons for this were political.[1] The French monarchy aimed to claim for itself the prestige associated with Italian Renaissance culture (in the artistic realm, but also in the scholarly and literary realms) and to strengthen its ties with Italy, a region in which France had important interests. These priorities complemented the concordat between the monarchy and the papacy (1516), which granted the king the right to name bishops and abbots and thus negated any political or financial gains the Protestant Reformation might have offered France. This milieu also produced the social context in which the young Calvin evolved. We will first examine a few stages of his education before offering an assessment of the years 1530–1534, centered around King Francis I's creation of the first royal chairs.

Calvin began his university studies in Paris (in 1521 or perhaps in 1523) in the Faculty of Arts, first at the College of La Marche and then at the College of Montaigu. His father had plans to prepare him for the Faculty of Theology. He spent only a short time at the former, but there he encountered the regent Mathurin Cordier, to whom the reformer later dedicated his Commentary on II Thessalonians and in 1559 entrusted the role of secondary school teacher at the Academy of Geneva. Pedagogically, Cordier was concerned above all with correct and elegant Latin, which he also tied to the use of the vernacular. He was not, however, a true humanist; according to him, neither Plato, nor Aristotle, nor Cicero had ever instilled piety in anyone, and he mistrusted the high status accorded to the elegant but

---

[1] This chapter was translated by Christina Moss.

misleading nature of rhetoric. The College of Montaigu had undergone reforms at the end of the fifteenth century along the lines of radical nominalism (*via moderna*), which rejected scholastic argumentation and was receptive to an ascetic and mystical orientation. This allowed for intensive study of Latin and its rhetorical expression. Nevertheless, the college had a bad reputation among humanists due to the severity of its discipline. There Calvin followed the encyclopedic course of study of the era (no theology), which subordinated rhetoric to grammar and logic, no doubt according to traditional pedagogical methods (the study of *quaestiones* by means of *disputationes*). He may also have received rhetorical and literary instruction from a master such as François Du Bois, a Latinist of thoroughly humanist inspiration who insisted on the link between elegant and ornate language and the responsibilities of civic life. During his time in the Faculty of Arts, might Calvin have studied the editions of Aristotle produced by the most celebrated French humanist of the early sixteenth century, Jacques Lefèvre d'Etaples (c. 1455–1537)? It is impossible to know. This philosopher, inspired by Italian humanist methods of approaching texts, restored the "true" Aristotle, in opposition to an aging scholasticism. His publications on the (Latin) text of Aristotle made use not of *quaestiones*, but of introductory syntheses, paraphrases, and summaries. Moreover, Lefèvre subordinated logic to morality and religion (biblical conformity). There Calvin might have learned the art of selecting and clearly explaining a doctrine's principal points and the ideal of a return to the text, read plainly and freed from the accretions of centuries of commentaries. After his work on Aristotle, Lefèvre turned to religious and mystical authors (1508–1521) before beginning a third evangelical phase (1522–1534) dedicated to translating the Bible (from the text of the Latin Vulgate!) into French for all. Lefèvre's trajectory presented a possible model that began within the highest ranks of humanist scholarship and moved toward direct communication of the fundamental truths of biblical faith in the vernacular.

Calvin's father then steered him toward law, and he made his way to the University of Orleans (1525–1526?), which was home to the most celebrated Faculty of Law in France. It was there, and at the nearby University of Bourges, that Calvin came into direct contact with the humanism of his day. The University of Orleans had begun to teach ancient languages fairly early (Reuchlin in 1480, Aleander in 1510–1511, etc.). Calvin probably took part in a small society of students and humanist teachers (active in the Faculty of Arts?), which introduced him to the humanist aspects of law. Melchior Wolmar, a Hellenist of German origin and more recently from Paris, where he had been active since 1521, opened a boarding house for students in

Orleans in 1527, and he introduced the young men to the Greek language. He became a professor of Greek at the University of Bourges in 1530 (where he went accompanied by his young lodger Theodore Beza) and there taught the language to Calvin, who thanked him by dedicating his Commentary on II Corinthians to him. Later, in his *Icones*, Beza classified Wolmar as a French humanist.

In his legal studies, Calvin attached himself (explicitly, through his contribution to the 1531 *Antapologia*) to the best-known Orleans professor, Pierre de l'Estoile. Though he was not a humanist, l'Estoile was open to new methods of legal study: direct study of Roman legal texts, aided by Latin philology and history, comparisons with common law, critiques of glosses, and so forth. L'Estoile, both in his teaching and in his publications, sought rigor, tight argumentation, and simplicity (cf. Lefèvre on Aristotle). It was, however, at the Faculty of Law at the University of Bourges, in 1529–1530, that Calvin directly encountered legal humanism; he went there to take courses from the renowned Milanese professor Andrea Alciato, who had been called there from the University of Avignon in the spring of 1529 at the initiative of Marguerite of Navarre, protector of the university and its administrators. Alciato was the best-known representative of the *mos gallicus* (French custom), a new humanist method of commentary on Roman law. The goal was not to allege a *communis opinio* as the old glosses did, reconstructed from medieval commentaries on the *Corpus Juris Civilis* (compiled by Justinian in the sixth century CE), but rather to definitively determine the *veritas juris* – that is the meaning of the words and the passages of the *Corpus* on the basis of all available linguistic and historical knowledge to identify the authentic meaning of the texts under examination. In this manner, while still respecting the medieval tradition and its technical vocabulary, Alciato combined the study of law with history, grammar, and rhetoric. This method was inspired by certain fourteenth-century Italian humanists, who considered the Roman legal corpus as a piece of literary and historical heritage and an exemplar of an ancient form of Latin. Guillaume Budé (1468–1540) particularly exemplified this method in his renowned *Annotations on the Pandects*, which appeared first in 1508 and in an expanded edition in 1526. The method consisted of determining the authoritative text by reconstructing its authentic sources through painstaking critical study (whether through comparison with other manuscripts or conjecture) and of removing the interpolations and modifications introduced by Justinian's commissaries by paying particular attention to matters of language and style. In addition to this, it involved using further ancient sources, history, literature, and philosophy. Ancient Roman law was no longer considered a monument outside of time, but rather a source that bore witness to an ancient language and civilization. There existed, in addition to the *mos gallicus*, a second current of legal humanism. It sought to link the entire subject of law with general principles to clarify it and facilitate its study thanks to a rationalist and systematic organization. The idea came from a lost work of Cicero (*De jure civili in artem redigendo*) and from his *De oratore*; the goal was to legitimize law by making it a science. This science was intended to make it possible to deduce solutions applicable to all cases from legal principles, without needing to allow for historical contingencies or particular circumstances as tradition did. Budé supported this ideal, which was also promoted by the spread of Rudolf Agricola's *Dialectic* in spaces where law was taught and by Claude Chansonette, who had published *Topics of Civil Law* in Latin (1520) in service of the same cause. A systematic account of the law could rely on a part of the *Corpus*, the *Institutes*, structured in a fairly systematic manner and distinguishing between people, things, and actions. Calvin certainly did not personally know the principal representatives of this second method, which found a representative at Bourges only in the 1540s (François Le Douaren). In any case, it would be anachronistic to conclude from the fact of Calvin's legal training that he was the most systematic and rationalist of the reformers, when in fact he was not trained in that school of legal thought, even if he adopted, especially from Budé, the idea of law as a form of philosophy. He primarily encountered the *mos gallicus*, which no doubt reinforced his general interest in the historical status of textual sources.

It was in this context that Calvin developed his commentary on *De Clementia*, which demonstrated a marked eclecticism, drawing from literary, legal, philosophical, rhetorical (the criterion of elegance) and historical sources to illuminate Seneca's text. Calvin's commentary stayed close to the text and illuminated as many facts as possible regarding its ideas, context, and form, even as he made use of commonplaces, which allowed him to not only understand the text but also to perceive its contemporary significance. In short, Calvin's commentary was a good example of a humanist work, but one without specifically French features beyond its tribute to Guillaume Budé and, perhaps, the importance it placed on the virtue of clemency for princes at a time when France's monarchy was becoming increasingly absolutist.

Through this publication Calvin attempted to situate himself in the Parisian intellectual milieu, in which he took part during his last two years in France (1532–1534). This coincided with the early years of the future royal college, which the king had begun to finance in spring 1530. In fact, in view of the conservatism of France's universities, Budé had done all he could to convince Francis I to found the French equivalent of the University of Alcalá or the trilingual College of Louvain (created according to an Erasmian model). Prior to this, humanist studies in Paris took place not in programs of study for which the university conferred degrees but in colleges that prepared students for entry into the Faculty of Arts. This was too limited a context in which to institutionalize new forms of study. Thus Budé had the idea to found a sort of academy for advanced studies, independent of the university, its leadership, and its degrees. His goal was train a new type of elite according to a scholarly program that drew on philological (the study of ancient languages), critical (the study of texts), and rhetorical humanism. In humanist ideology, in effect, the ancient paradigm of eloquence had become the universal criterion for competence among the new elites, with two essential values: the social utility of culture in the political realm and the art of efficiently conducting business ("prudence"). These ideas explain a sort of pragmatism shown by Calvin the reformer; his commitment to the paradigm of eloquence formed him into a brilliant and effective writer of Latin and French literature. This conception of communication, both written and spoken, connected linguistic and stylistic perfection with logical rigor, with the goal of persuading its listeners or readers. The young Calvin contributed to this approach to communication by honoring Budé and Erasmus, its two major representatives active in his intellectual milieu, in his commentary on Seneca's *De Clementia* (1532). Only the first of these was French, but the king had conceived of a plan to invite Erasmus to Paris with the goal of creating royal chairs. Moreover, Calvin adhered to the particular form of the ideal of eloquence found in the works of Philip Melanchthon. The latter's rhetorical and dialectical writings were widely distributed in France in the 1520s and 1530s, and, in 1535, the king even had the idea to invite the German thinker to Paris, a project that never came to fruition. The French humanism from which Calvin benefitted thus participated in broader international currents, even as its patriotic themes (such as Budé's superiority to Erasmus) were reprised by the young Calvin. The royal chairs created in 1530 to teach languages and new disciplines using updated methods did not fully meet Budé's hopes for the project, but Calvin was nevertheless able to benefit from them, if not immediately upon their formation (teaching began in the spring of 1530), then at least especially in 1533, when he often resided in Paris. Two chairs were created for the study of Greek, held by Jacques Toussain who taught grammar (and beginners) and Pierre Danès who taught linguistic commentary on texts (for more advanced students). Among the Greek authors studied before 1532–1533 were Demosthenes and

Aeschines; Calvin, who participated in Danès's courses, must have already been at the right level. The students could make use of the *Commentarii Linguae Graecae* by Budé, a sort of dictionary printed in 1529. There were also three Hebrew professors, among them François Vatable of Picardy, who had close ties to the circle of reformers that coalesced in Meaux around Lefèvre d'Étaples, but it is unlikely that Calvin (who never mentioned Vatable's name) pursued Hebrew studies at that time. Instead, he may have had access to these professors' pedagogical publications, Agathius Guidacceri's Hebrew alphabet, printed in 1533–1534, and Paul Paradis's pronunciation manual, printed in 1534 and dedicated to one of Budé's sons. Finally, it should be noted that Barthélemy Latomus was also part of this intellectual milieu; he had close ties to the evangelical movement and he spread the rhetorical conceptions of Agricola and Melanchthon, which were so important for Calvin, throughout Paris, as well as those of the rhetorician and Hellenist Johannes Sturm, who later became Calvin's friend in Strasbourg. Both men used rhetoric as a universal method for the explanation of ancient texts, a lesson that Calvin retained for the Bible.

In this context, the Faculty of Theology at the University of Paris attempted in 1534 to limit the influence of the royal professors on the subject matter of ancient languages (Hebrew and Greek) as they related to the study of the biblical text. The debate focused on the validity of the Vulgate, the traditional Latin version, which was fundamental to the Faculty of Theology, and of the Greek and Hebrew versions of the text, particularly in the context of the conflicts occasioned by the Erasmian edition of the Greek New Testament and later by the Protestant Reformation. The latter often cited original versions in opposition to the Latin text on points of doctrine and promoted the translation of the Bible into the vernacular from versions in the original languages. These debates could not have escaped the young Calvin, who by this point had identified the cause of philological humanism with religious reform. His first reformatory writing was the Latin preface to the French translation of the Bible printed in 1535 in Neuchâtel, a work of his cousin Pierre Robert, also called Olivétan, the first French translation from the original languages (the preface to the New Testament in the same Bible might also have been written by Calvin). Olivétan's French preface mentions the royal chairs in Paris, which, according to him, ought to have been the most important tool for the translation of the Bible into French. It seems likely that, at the time, Calvin and Olivétan had that model in mind. The Genevan Academy, founded by Calvin in 1559, however, operated on a very different model than the Parisian institution; there philological studies were subordinate to religious doctrine.

During the reign of Francis I, France experienced a "humanist revolution" along sociopolitical lines; the king systematically appointed men formed in this new culture to both political and ecclesiastical posts. A humanist education therefore became an important criterion for career advancement – at least outside the military domain. This context must be taken into account in the case of the young Calvin. His commentary on Seneca's *De Clementia* (on a highly political philosophical theme) was not written solely for the purpose of drawing the attention of educated men to an academic work worthy of the new culture. With this publication, Calvin was also gambling socially with everything he had in hopes of securing a career in the Church or in the royal administration. These hopes were not met with success; from 1534 onward Calvin turned away from these types of studies and devoted himself, self-taught, to theology alone (through the writing of his tract, the *Psychopannychia*), motivated not only by social and academic disappointment but also by a conversion to radical evangelicalism. In his dedication to the king in the 1536 edition of his *Institutes*, Calvin responded indirectly to Budé, who had denounced the Protestant subversion in his March 1535 *De Transitu*; the bridges between institutional French humanism and the radical reformist circles that Calvin by then belonged to had been burned. From 1535 onward, with his participation in the production of Olivétan's Bible, Calvin prioritized the criterion of faithfulness to Reformation doctrine and subordinated humanist studies to religious goals. His 1550 treatise *Des Scandales* was explicit on the subject when it condemned the French humanists who turned away from the message of the Reformation. The reformer retained from his humanist past a particular attention to the philological questions that arise from the biblical text, a sense of communication for the sake of persuasion, notably through the medium of print, which allowed knowledge to move beyond the limits of academic circles (and gave rise to the modern treatise), an effective intellectual and literary method for giving accounts of and debating ideas, a high view of law, and, finally, personal connections with certain French intellectual circles (magistrates, printers like the Estiennes, the family of Guillaume Budé, etc.).

SUGGESTED FURTHER READINGS

Battles, F. L. *Interpreting John Calvin.* Grand Rapids, MI: Baker Books, 1996.

Bohatec, J. *Budé und Calvin. Studien zur Gedankenwelt des französischen Humanismus.* Graz: Böhlaus, 1950.

Boudou, B., and A.-P. Pouey-Mounou, eds. *Calvin et l'humanisme. Actes du symposium d'Amiens et Lille III.* Genève: Droz, 2012.

Breen, Q., and John Calvin. *A Study in French Humanism*. Hamden, CO: Archon Books, 1968.

Millet, O. *Calvin et la dynamique de la parole, étude de rhétorique réformée*. Paris: Champion, 1992.

Tuilier, A., ed. *Histoire du Collège de France. I. La création 1530–1560*. Paris: Fayard, 2006.

5

∽

French Religious Politics

Jonathan A. Reid

John Calvin converted to evangelical doctrines in his homeland, France, where Protestantism was officially proscribed. In 1535, during a spike in heresy persecution, like scores of evangelicals before him and thousands afterward, he fled as a religious refugee. By the time of his death in 1564, though ever an exile in Geneva, he had done more than any other person to transform the religious politics of France, which had plunged into the beginning of a long "war of religion" (1562–1598). That civil war's chief protagonists, French Reformed Protestants, "Huguenots," were his disciples. In attempting to put Calvin in proper context, one must describe both the political environment that shaped his and other French people's response to Protestantism as well as his role, among all the other major actors, in reshaping it.

FRENCH RELIGIOUS POLITICS, FOREIGN AND DOMESTIC TO 1559

During Calvin's lifetime, French religious politics had two distinct phases demarcated by the year 1559. As elsewhere, the sovereign power's will mattered most in determining the response to the Reformation. During their reigns, Francis I (1515–1547) and his son Henry II (1547–1559) pursued similar policies. Domestically, the crown backed the efforts of the Faculty of Theology of Paris, church officials, and the royal courts to repress "Lutheran" heresy, weakly at first under Francis and with increasing determination under Henry. These monarchs' dominant concern, however, was waging the dynastic Italian/Hapsburg Wars (1494–1559), which frequently distracted them from the religious question at home. In their foreign relations, moreover, when opportune, they eagerly allied with the Hapsburgs' enemies, including "enemies" of the Catholic faith.

Until 1559 French religious politics had its greatest impact in this international arena by influencing the confessional fates of many lands. Starting in 1525, the French allied with the Grand Turk against Charles V, thus strengthening the sultan's hand as his armies continued to conquer Christian lands in the Mediterranean, the Balkans, and eastern Europe. Similarly, after supporting Henry VIII in his attempt to have his marriage to the emperor's aunt, Catherine of Aragon, annulled, Francis gave him crucial backing after he broke with Rome (1534) by recognizing his new queen, Anne Boleyn, and by maintaining their military alliance.

Most momentous of all, French aid to German Protestants contributed to their survival. After Bern and other Swiss cantons became Protestant in the 1520s, Francis I continued to pay their annual pensions and to hire their mercenary troops. In 1534, French funds enabled members of the Protestant Schmalkaldic League in the empire to reestablish their ally, Ulrich of Wurttemberg, to his territories, which he then made Lutheran. In 1536, France and Bern collaborated in carving up portions of the duchy of Savoy between themselves, with Bern taking full control of the Pays de Vaud, which it converted to its confession. Due to their action, Geneva secured independence from Savoy just as it was declaring for the Reformation, mere months before Calvin settled there as a pastor. While in the mid-1540s Francis I failed to succor the Duke of Cleves and the Schmalkaldic League sufficiently to save them from capitulating to Charles V, in 1552, following the same policy, Henry II conquered Metz, Toul, and Verdun and marched his army to the Rhine, a flanking attack that enabled his ally, Duke Moritz of Saxony, to defeat Charles V. That crushing victory paved the way for Lutheran Protestants to win permanent legal establishment at the Diet of Augsburg in 1555.

The French crown further contributed to the confessional division of Europe by doing little to help popes fight the Protestants or to strengthen the Catholic Church. Neither Francis nor Henry engaged seriously with the first sessions of the Council of Trent (1545–1547 and 1551–1552) because they feared the council would benefit the emperor and undermine their control over the French church. When relations with the papacy were strained, Francis and Henry threatened variously to call an independent church council or even, like Henry VIII, to break with Rome and set up a French patriarchate.

On the domestic front, Francis's and Henry's religious policies were more consistent but less effective. In accord with French monarchical ideology, they regarded heresy as sedition and a threat to the unity of the "Most Christian Kingdom" under "one king, one faith, and one law." In 1521, following the pope, the Paris Faculty of Theology and the Parlement of Paris condemned Luther's and his followers' doctrines and books. Subsequently, enforcement was uneven and often defective in part due to structural problems in the ecclesiastical and royal judicial systems. More decisively, authorities failed to respond to the threat of heresy strongly enough. The king, his courtiers, many prelates, and other power elites spent much of their energies playing the traditional game of politics for control over clerical and royal appointments and revenues. Until 1540, Francis I only backed the persecution of heresy sporadically in reaction to sensational acts, such as the infamous posting in French cities of "sacramentarian" placards and tracts against Catholic mass during the winter of 1534–1535. In the 1540s, as heresy showed signs of growth, the royal court provided stronger leadership, issuing a coherent series of edicts, which established the Paris Faculty of Theology's 23 articles of faith as the law of the land, banned a list of heretical books, many of them Calvin's, and forbade clerics from preaching evangelical doctrines. Henry II decreed more draconian measures, targeting those who had dealings with Geneva as well as crypto-Protestant authorities who were obstructing justice. As Henry lamented in an edict of 1559, all these measures had miscarried. With the Hapsburg wars over, he vowed to eradicate heretics on the home front.

Although repression did increase – the number of heresy trials in Languedoc doubled each decade from 1530 to 1560 – it had indeed failed to stop the number of French evangelicals from growing. From judicial records and other sources, we know French people from all social milieus adhered to the new doctrines in substantial numbers, though many fewer peasants, proportionally. Collectively, as a persecuted minority they constituted an underground subculture with a distinctive profile. They did not aver their full faith publicly, nor did they have overt political champions. Loyal to the crown, they ever hoped for the king's conversion, while trying to stave off repression. However (un)happily, they remained *in* the Catholic Church, carving out enclaves within it. Across France from 1521 to 1559, an estimated thousand or more evangelical clerics preached "purer" doctrine. Some adjusted liturgical practice to conform to it, offering evangelicals a foretaste of a fuller reformation. Such clerics and laypeople also formed para-church groups, "conventicles," in which they prayed and studied together.

As they developed this religious subculture under the constant threat of persecution, evangelicals had to choose between the contrasting examples and advice of their domestic leaders and Calvin and his colleagues. During Francis's reign, his sister, Marguerite of Navarre and a network of other elite figures provided patronage and protection to French evangelicals, while offering such long-suffering dissenters hope that they might succeed in their contested, but not impossible, quest to induce the king to back a full reform of the French church in doctrine and practice. In the 1530s and 1540s, she and a faction of like-minded courtiers including Francis's mistress, Mme. d'Étampes, and youngest son, Charles, had some success in blunting heresy persecution at home and promoting the anti-Imperial, pro-Protestant foreign policies described previously. Upon his accession, Henry II, who had led a rival faction of conservative Catholics, swept them from court. Evangelicals everywhere were thereafter forced to cultivate their religious communities even more discretely.

After his flight, Calvin, who had been a product of Marguerite's evangelical network, contributed more than any other author to the spread of Protestant doctrines through his persuasive theological and polemical works. He also put evangelicals in an impossible bind that all but ensured they would remain politically clandestine and, ironically, within the church. One the one hand, Calvin insisted from the start, as in his dedication of the 1536 *Institutes* to Francis I, that Christians must obey their monarch, however tyrannical, except when (s)he required them to contravene their religious conscience, in which case he allowed them only the right of passive resistance. On the other hand, in his first anti-Nicodemite treatise of 1537 and thereafter, he admonished evangelicals that they could not be members of the clergy and had to abstain from Catholic rites lest they corrupt themselves and damn the souls of others by their bad example. The only options for the faithful trapped in Catholic lands, he advised, were either to suffer persecution for abstention or, like him, to emigrate. In the 1550s, tens of thousands did emigrate to francophone Geneva, the Suisse Romande, and other Protestant havens abroad. Most, however, stayed in France and because Calvin offered them no alternative church or sacraments, they sought to live and worship as faithfully as they could within the realm and church.

FRENCH RELIGIONS POLITICS UNDER THE SWAY OF CALVIN TO 1564

Henry II's accidental death in 1559 created a power vacuum, precipitating a period of revolutionary ferment. As the crown passed to his teenage son, Francis II (July 1559–December 1560) and then Charles IX (1560–1574), who was a minor at accession, royal authority deteriorated. Seizing the opportunity, Huguenots rapidly agitated, organized, and engaged in a desperate "struggle for recognition." Militant Catholics responded with equal determination to eradicate them. Driven by adamant hatred for each other's religion, Huguenots and Catholics at court and in almost every city and town of France fought an escalating battle for dominance, which erupted in 1562 in the first French war of religion.

The gamut of actors, events, causes, and consequences of this complex descent into that civil war is not easily summarized and important aspects remain little understood. Of chief interest here, as attested by contemporaries and modern scholars alike, Calvin and his fellow ministers animated the advent of the chief protagonists, the French Reformed, and were thus substantially responsible for causing this turning point in French history.

The Huguenot movement had three institutional dimensions, which matured with amazing speed before the outbreak of the first war: the local Reformed churches; the regional and national synods that united them; and the "Huguenot party," the political and military wing comprised of Reformed nobles at court, their adherents, and political-military assemblies representing the reformed communities. These dimensions had begun forming before Henry II's death, but they only fully developed and cohered as a national movement from 1560 to 1562. While Calvin and his fellow pastors inspired and guided their development, French evangelicals took the initiative and did the major shoulder work themselves. Prior to the 1550s, Calvin had never encouraged evangelicals by letter or published tract to form separate Reformed churches, let alone organize nationally. In 1555, having solicited and taken Calvin's advice, the faithful at Poitiers and Paris "separated themselves from abomination" and established the first two underground Reformed churches. They did so because they longed to resolve their "Nicodemite" dilemma and enjoy purified sacraments and preaching. In a steady trickle, other evangelicals emulated them. The 65 churches they founded in the year of Henry's death brought their number to 116. To that point, all were clandestine. From 1560 to 1563, as they emerged from underground, the French Reformed churches grew fivefold in number and membership. Hundreds of them asked Calvin and the Genevan Company of Pastors to provide ministers. By 1562, their appeals had exhausted the supply of suitable candidates from abroad. Geneva, the largest supplier had send out some 250. Many of the estimated 1,250 French Reformed churches with their 1.5–2 million members had to carry on without regular pastoral care under local lay leadership.

Further testifying to Calvin's theological and organizational influence over the movement, when the French churches decided in early 1559 to hold their first national synod – secretly in Paris under Henry II's very nose – Calvin responded by sending a draft confession of faith, which they adopted with minor modifications. Ministers loyal to Calvin dominated the next three national synods at Poitiers (1561), Orleans (1562), and Lyon (1563). Most important of all, as members of the Bourbon and Coligny noble families expressed interest in Reformed religion starting in 1557, Calvin cultivated them as defenders of the faith through correspondence and by sending his top lieutenants to serve as their personal chaplains and advisors. Prior to Henry II's death, these noble Huguenots-in-the-making did not yet constitute a coherent political block at court. In 1560, they began revealing themselves as champions of the Reformed movement. While the highest ranking among them, Antoine de Bourbon, King of Navarre, ultimately defected to the Catholic side (March 1562), when his younger brother Condé rose in revolt in April 1562, an estimated 20–40 percent of the nobility rallied to the cause.

The Huguenots' Catholic opponents were more numerous, but divided. At court, the house of Guise/Lorraine, which championed conservative Catholicism, gained ascendancy at the start of Francis II's reign. Pursuing Henry II's policies, they sought to eradicate heresy including their long-standing (heretical) political rivals, the house of Bourbon/Condé. Royalists, anchored by the queen mother, Catherine de Medici, and her advisors, were moderate Catholics who tried to liberate the king from Guise control and maintain order by resolving the emerging Catholic-Protestant conflict. After the accession of Charles IX, acting as regent Catherine pursued a policy of concord. She convoked the religious Colloquy of Poissy (1561), at which Catholic and Protestant theologians failed to find common ground, and gradually lifted restrictions on Protestants, granting them a limited right to worship openly in the Edict of January 1562. These efforts at conciliation satisfied neither Huguenots nor militant Catholics. Meanwhile, foreseeing war, the noble leaders of all parties solicited help from confrères abroad, thus aligning for once French domestic and foreign religious politics. In March 1562, the Duke of Guise provoked Huguenots by having his troops massacre a Reformed church meeting on his lands and marching into staunchly Catholic Paris to a hero's welcome. He, Bourbon, and the other Catholic leaders forced Charles IX and Catherine to join them in Paris. Condé and the Huguenots then rebelled, not in the name of religion, but in the name of justice and of freeing the king from Guise domination. Both sides called in foreign aid and troops. For tactical reasons, Catherine sided with the Guise during the war and sent a French delegation to the final session of the Council of Trent (1562–1563), but resisted the ultra-Catholics' demands for no compromise with the heretics.

The struggle at court enabled turmoil to build concurrently in most French cities and towns. Reformed Protestants agitated to demonstrate their growing strength, defy the "papist" church, win converts, and worship freely.

Militant Catholics opposed them at every turn. Already well-armed, French people turned their weapons on each other and prepared for war. The ensuing violence in its increasingly ritualized, symbolic, and savage forms, stunned contemporaries and has fascinated students ever since. From 1560 to 1562, Catholics and Protestants traded insults and blows, disrupted each other's services, threatened the other's clergy and leaders, and fought street battles. By the time Condé lifted his banner, some regions were already in a de facto state of civil war. Within weeks, half of France's major cities – including Rouen, Orleans, Lyon, Angers Poitiers, and Montpellier – fell, many without a shot, to Huguenot forces. Others, like Paris, Bordeaux, Toulouse, Marseilles, and Amiens remained in Catholic hands, having kept their Huguenot minorities in check with threats or blows. Victors on both sides attempted to purify their towns by driving out or massacring their enemies. Protestants desecrated Catholic religious objects and abolished the Mass; Catholics mutilated Protestant corpses.

The Huguenots, who were outgunned and out led, were losing the war by late 1562. Condé accepted a treaty in March 1563, which granted them safe havens and restricted rights to practice their faith. This ended hostilities, but did not establish the basis for a lasting peace. The end of the war and Calvin's death the following year marked the end of one period and the beginning of another. The birthing of the Huguenot movement under the influence of Calvin and the mother church at Geneva was over. The French Reformed were fully formed as a community and self-reliant thereafter. So too, intransigent Catholics had rallied to the leadership of the House of Guise and formed the regional leagues that would give them staying power similar to Huguenots during the ensuing 35 years of religious civil war.

In light of those subsequent wars and the religious civil wars that erupted in the Low Countries (1566–1648), the empire (1618–1648), and England (1642–1651/1688) – all precipitated by Reformed Protestants – scholars have credited Calvin and his followers with causing a crisis in European religious politics. Wielding no political power beyond the charismatic force of his ideas and example, Calvin stimulated the rise of the Huguenots and the Reformed elsewhere. By commanding true Christians to separate from papal abomination and to disobey tyrannical monarchs in matters of religion as an absolute condition of faith, Calvin advanced a psychological imperative that inspired many evangelicals "under the cross" to form churches and some eventually to revolt. From 1559 to 1563, however, in the welter of rapidly changing circumstances, neither he nor Huguenots leaders developed a sound strategy for establishing Reformed churches within majority Catholic France as had occurred in the empire. The Huguenots had revolted without a coherent resistance theory to guide them. The insuperable problem was that most Catholics and Protestants held adamantly to the post-Constantinian church-state model of "one sovereign, one faith, and one law," which precluded the coexistence of rival religions. As in the first French war of religion, over the following century, Catholics and Protestants were rarely able to resolve the conflict through victory in battle. In making both war and peace, they were perpetually at a practical and theoretical impasse that Calvin had in part provoked, but for which he had died without providing a solution. That dilemma stimulated a rich evolution in political theory as subsequent Catholic and Protestant thinkers such as Hotman, Beza, Du Plessis Mornay, Bodin, Montaigne, James I, Locke, and Hobbes attempted to resolve the downward spiral of European religious politics, of which the Huguenot revolution of 1559–1563 was a first turn.

SUGGESTED FURTHER READINGS

Daussy, Hugues. *Le parti huguenot: Chronique d'une désillusion*. Geneva: Librairie Droz, 2014.

Holt, Mack P., ed. *Renaissance and Reformation France: 1500–1648*. Oxford: Oxford University Press, 2002.

Jouanna, Arlette. *La France du xvie siècle, 1483–1598*. 3rd ed. Paris: Presses Universitaires de France, 2016.

Kingdon, Robert M. *Geneva and the Coming of the Wars of Religion in France, 1555–1563*. Reprint edition with foreword by Mack P. Holt and postface by Robert M. Kingdon. Geneve: Droz, 2007 (First published 1956).

Knecht, Robert J. *The Rise and Fall of Renaissance France: 1483–1610*. 2nd ed. Oxford: Wiley-Blackwell, 2002.

Reid, Jonathan A. *King's Sister – Queen of Dissent: Marguerite of Navarre (1492–1549) and Her Evangelical Network*. 2 vols. Studies in Medieval and Reformation Traditions, 139. Leiden, The Netherlands: Brill, 2009.

Sutherland, Nicola M. *The Huguenot Struggle for Recognition*. New Haven, CT: Yale University Press, 1980.

6

⁓

The French Wars of Religion

Diane C. Margolf

In November 1559, John Calvin wrote to the beleaguered "brethren of France" as follows:

> I am aware what reflections may here present themselves to our minds; that in the meantime the servants of God do nevertheless suffer, and that the wicked from the impunity with which they commit their acts of cruelty, break out more and more into all sorts of excesses. But since it is our duty to suffer, we ought humbly to submit; as it is the will of God that his church be subjected to such conditions that even as the plough passes over the field, so should the ungodly have leave to pass their sword over all of us from the least to the greatest.... We must even hope, that when he shall have tried his church, he will bridle the fury of the tyrants and cause it to cease in despite of all their efforts. In waiting for such an issue it is our duty to possess our souls in patience.[1]

Calvin thus advised the French Reformed communities to await the consequences of King Henry II's sudden death in a jousting accident several months earlier. French Calvinists (hereafter called Huguenots) could hope and pray that the late king's policy of repression might change under his successor. With the historians' gift of hindsight, however, we know that the opposite occurred: Henry II's death catapulted France into an extended period of political, religious, and social upheaval that encompassed the second half of the sixteenth century. We also know that during the French Wars of Religion (1562–1598), Huguenots did not "possess [their] souls in patience." They suffered greatly, but they also organized and fought against

---

[1] John Calvin, "Letter to the Brethren of France, November 1559," in *Letters of John Calvin*, Vol. 4, ed. Jules Bonnet and trans. Marcus Robert Gilchrist (Philadelphia: Presbyterian Board of Publication, 1858), 84–85, https://calvin.edu/centers-institutes/meeter-center/resources/john-calvins-works-in-english/.

their Catholic opponents, defied the French crown, and ultimately became a protected if vulnerable religious minority in a Catholic kingdom.

Calvin may be described as the absent cause of the French Wars of Religion, given that these events unfolded mainly after his death in 1564. He contributed directly to creating the conditions for the conflict through his efforts to promote Reformed religion in France. The model of Christian life and community he advocated in his writings and helped to implement in Geneva also had a powerful impact on sixteenth-century French society and politics. Yet his teachings about the proper response to religious persecution – especially by a secular ruler – reflected a mixed message about submission and resistance. Despite his advice to the "brethren of France" to accept their suffering, Calvin's greatest impact on the French Wars of Religion was to provide the Huguenots with the means to survive the conflict by a combination of obedience, discipline, and militancy.

Calvin worked tirelessly from Geneva to promote the spread of Reformed religion in the country of his birth. Beginning in 1555, pastors trained in Geneva founded many Reformed churches in France, especially in the southern and southwestern provinces of Guyenne, Languedoc, Provence, and Dauphiné. Calvin corresponded constantly with his supporters in France to address their concerns and sustain their faith, and he took an active interest in winning new converts among the French nobility. Noblewomen contributed significantly to the growing strength of the Reformed presence in France; Jeanne d'Albret, Queen of Navarre, would prove to be a more powerful and consistent advocate for the Huguenots than her husband, Antoine de Bourbon. Outside the circles of royalty and aristocracy, Huguenots could be found among the ranks of magistrates, lawyers, clerics, merchants, and artisans in many of France's towns, including Paris, Rouen, and Lyon. The reception of Reformed religion did not strictly align with social, economic, or professional groups, but instead was found throughout all levels of society and across all of France, allowing for regional variations.[2]

For many French Catholics, however, the growing number of Reformed communities and converts represented an alarming spread of heresy and sedition, rather than the triumph of true Christianity. Protestantism in France had become associated with rebellion against both religious and secular authority during the reign of King Francis I (1515–1547). After the

---

[2] Robert M. Kingdon, *Geneva and the Coming of the Wars of Religion in France, 1555–1563* (Geneva: Droz, 1956; reprint 2007); Nancy L. Roelker, *Queen of Navarre: Jeanne d'Albret, 1528–1572* (Cambridge, MA: Harvard University Press, 1968); Mack P. Holt, *The French Wars of Religion, 1562–1629*, 2nd ed. (Cambridge: Cambridge University Press, 2005), 30–41.

"Affair of the Placards" of October 1534, in which broadsheets attacking the Catholic mass were posted publicly in Paris and other nearby towns, Francis launched a prosecution of heresy through the royal law courts that would continue and intensify under his son and successor, Henry II. The Edict of Chateaubriant (1551) established new levels of censorship, required proof of Catholic orthodoxy, and encouraged French subjects to inform the authorities about anyone suspected of heresy – all in the name of preserving public order and obedience to royal law, as well as quashing religious dissent. Such measures were necessary in part because Huguenots enjoyed the protection of their elite co-religionists, including magistrates in the Parlement of Paris, who had refused to enforce earlier edicts aimed at punishing heresy. For the next eight years, Henry II was preoccupied with foreign affairs, including France's ongoing rivalry with the Habsburgs on the continent, negotiations with the papacy, and the troubled alliance of Spain and England through the marriage of Philip II and Mary I. Yet the direction of his religious policy remained constant: to eliminate the Huguenots and the threat to political and social order that they represented.[3]

Nevertheless, by 1559 Calvin's evangelizing efforts both in Geneva and France had borne fruit. Under his leadership, Geneva's civic and religious authorities worked together to enact the social discipline that would become a hallmark of Reformed religion, and that would ideally instill sound morals, modest behavior, and social order among Geneva's populace.[4] Small wonder that Geneva attracted thousands of French refugees fleeing persecution, or that its model of a godly community impressed visitors such as Antoine de Bourbon's younger brother Louis, Prince of Condé. In the 1559 edition of his most influential work, the *Institutes of the Christian Religion*, Calvin envisioned a relationship between secular and ecclesiastical authorities that could produce peace, justice, and a well-ordered state, while maintaining the proper boundary between civil government and the Law of God. He argued that magistrates (including kings and princes) derived their authority from God and thus deserved obedience; when their rule was unjust or contrary to right religion, it was the responsibility of "lesser magistrates" to resist. In general, Christians should submit humbly to persecution and accept the suffering that came with proclaiming their faith, whether in the form of exile; loss of property, family, and friends; or death. They could pray for a ruler who would uphold their faith, but only those who already possessed a

---

[3] Holt, *The French Wars of Religion*, 17–30; N. M. Sutherland, *The Huguenot Struggle for Recognition* (New Haven, CT: Yale University Press, 1980), 40–61.

[4] Holt, *The French Wars of Religion*, 21–26.

claim to powers of governance were supposed to rebel against kings, and only when such rebellion carried divine approval.[5]

Calvin's views on resistance were shaped by contemporary events, especially the situation in France. He was well aware that unlike the inhabitants of Geneva, Huguenots lived in a society that remained largely hostile to their beliefs and practices. Yet there could be little compromise with the papists who surrounded them; Calvin deplored the practice of outward conformity with Catholicism as "Nicodemism."[6] The fact that the king was dedicated to the Huguenots' destruction was even more problematic. In Geneva, civic and ecclesiastical governance became welded together, as the men who held political office also belonged to the Reformed church.[7] In France, as Mack Holt has noted, "[T]he fusion of church and state was in the person of the monarch, who was bound by his office to protect the Catholic Church."[8] Before the Wars of Religion officially began in 1562, the battle between Huguenots and Catholics was also entangled with the conflict between French monarchs and their subjects – Huguenot and Catholic alike – over religion, resistance, and obedience.

The succession of Henry II's eldest son, Francis II, opened the door to an intense power struggle at court for influence over the new king, his realm's resources, and his religious policy. The contenders included Francis, Duke of Guise and his brother Charles, Cardinal of Lorraine; in addition to being the king's uncles by marriage, they commanded enormous wealth and power through their family's lands and offices, and they were dedicated to defending Catholicism and the anti-Huguenot religious policy. However, the Bourbon and Montmorency families sought to check the Guises' ambition. Their ranks included several important converts to the Reformed faith: Antoine de Bourbon, King of Navarre and his brother Condé, as well as Gaspard de Coligny, Admiral of France and his two brothers. These men,

---

[5] Harro Höpfl, "The Ideal of *Aristocratia Politia Vicina* in the Calvinist Political Tradition," in *Calvin and His Influence, 1509–2009*, ed. Irena Backus and Philip Benedict (Oxford: Oxford University Press, 2011), 51; Willem Nijenhuis, "The Limits of Civil Disobedience in Calvin's Last Known Sermons: Development of His Ideas on the Right of Civil Resistance," in *Ecclesia Reformata: Studies on the Reformation*, Vol. 2, ed. Willem Nijenhuis (Leiden, The Netherlands: Brill, 1994), 74; John Calvin, *Institutes of the Christian Religion*, trans. John Allen (Philadelphia: Presbyterian Board of Christian Education, 1936), 770–806.

[6] Nikki Shepardson, "The Rhetoric of Martyrdom and the Anti-Nicodemite Discourses in France, 1550–1570," *Renaissance and Reformation/Renaissance et Réforme* (n.s.) 27:3 (Summer 2003): 37–61.

[7] William Naphy, "Calvin's Church in Geneva: Constructed or Gathered? Local or Foreign? French or Swiss?," in Backus and Benedict, eds., *Calvin and His Influence, 1509–2009*, 102–118.

[8] Holt, *The French Wars of Religion*, 26.

who were princes of the blood with extensive lands and networks of patronage, had emerged as protectors of the French Reformed churches and
communities. Finally, Henry II's widow, Catherine de Medici, would play
an important role in the complex political maneuvers surrounding the
French monarchy. As the mother of three successive French kings – Francis
II, Charles IX, and Henry III – she would strive to preserve her sons' power
at the expense of both the Catholic and Huguenot factions.

In this context, the tension between patient submission and militant
resistance to persecution in Calvin's teaching became apparent. His ambiguous role in the Conspiracy of Amboise – an unsuccessful attempt in March
1560 by a small group of Huguenot nobles to kidnap Francis II and thus
rescue him from Guise influence – illustrates this. Calvin apparently favored
efforts to have Antoine de Bourbon or Condé use their political status to
protect the Huguenots against the king and his Guise councilors, but he
rejected the use of force or bloodshed to do so.[9] Although the conspiracy
failed, it reinforced fears that the Huguenots (with Calvin's approval) were
using protestations of loyalty and obedience to mask their true intentions of
rebellion and violence. The Colloquy of Poissy (September 1561), in which
Catherine de Medici convened Catholic and Reformed theologians to try
and reconcile their differences, was also unsuccessful and provoked suspicions that the monarchy would compromise with the seditious Huguenots at
the Catholics' expense. The Edict of January (1562) seemed to justify such
suspicions: it granted limited privileges of Reformed worship, which proved
to be unenforceable due to Catholic opposition. The Duke of Guise's massacre of Huguenot worshippers at Vassy two months later, in defiance of
royal law, marked the official beginning of France's eight religious wars.[10]

During the period 1562–1572, which encompassed the first three of those
wars, the pattern of conflict among Catholics, Huguenots, and the crown,
which had already developed during the reigns of Henry II and Francis II,
became entrenched. Royal edicts that were intended to regulate relations
between the two confessional groups in the interest of civil peace could not
be enforced effectively at the local level, nor were they consistently supported
through royal law courts or the Estates General, France's most important
representative institution at the national level. The Guise and Bourbon
leaders of their respective political and religious factions likewise continued
to resist royal authority and fight each other. Military battles and sieges were
accompanied by a war of words: polemical works spewed forth from

---

[9] Sutherland, *The Huguenot Struggle*, 62–100.
[10] Holt, *The French Wars of Religion*, 4–49.

Catholic and Huguenot presses, creating texts and images that portrayed each side as anathema to the other, while preachers emphasized each confession's threat to the purity of the body politic.[11] Calvin's sermons on the Books of Samuel, preached in Geneva shortly before his death in 1564, highlighted "the political consequences of the Gospel" and clearly referred to events in France.[12]

The Saint Bartholomew's Day Massacre of August 24, 1572 became the most famous (or infamous) example of violence to emerge from this turmoil. Huguenot and Catholic leaders had converged on Paris to celebrate the marriage of Marguerite of Valois, sister of King Charles IX, with Antoine de Bourbon's son Henry, now King of Navarre and a Calvinist. The wedding celebration gave way to bloodshed when the assassination of Admiral Coligny exploded into a mass slaughter of Huguenots by Parisian Catholics. It was widely believed that the monarchy had sanctioned both Coligny's murder and the popular attacks that ensued, though this is impossible to prove conclusively; Charles IX, Catherine de Medici, and the Guise were all blamed by contemporaries for the massacre. As reports of events in Paris spread to the provinces, conflicting instructions from the royal court also followed, prompting local authorities to respond differently to the Huguenots in their areas.[13]

For many scholars, this event exemplifies the "rites of violence" generally associated with religious conflict in sixteenth-century France.[14] However, the Saint Bartholomew's Day Massacre also launched a new phase in the French Wars of Religion, reopening and intensifying earlier hostilities. The Huguenots now found themselves engaged in a battle for survival against both the monarchy and their Catholic opposition. They responded by organizing a "state within a state" comprised of political assemblies, ecclesiastical synods, and noble protectors who would collect funds and supplies, lead armies, and negotiate with foreign powers to sustain their cause. Calvin's designated successor in Geneva, Theodore Béza, played a critical

---

[11] Luc Racaut, *Hatred in Print: Catholic Propaganda and Protestant Identity during the French Wars of Religion* (Aldershot: Ashgate, 2002); Barbara B. Diefendorf, *Beneath the Cross: Catholics and Huguenots in Sixteenth-Century Paris* (Oxford: Oxford University Press, 1991); Penny Roberts, "Royal Authority and Justice during the French Religious Wars," *Past and Present* 184 (August 2004).

[12] Nijenhuis, "The Limits of Civil Disobedience," 85–94; quotation at 94.

[13] Philip Benedict, "The Saint Bartholomew's Day Massacres in the Provinces," *Historical Journal* 21:2 (1978): 205–255.

[14] Graeme Murdock, Andrew Spicer, and Penny Roberts, eds., *Ritual and Violence: Natalie Zemon Davis and Early Modern France*. Past and Present Supplement 7 (Oxford: Oxford University Press, 2012).

role in these endeavors. The issues Calvin had raised about obedience and resistance took on new urgency, and treatises illustrated with references to historical, legal, and religious sources were published to justify the Huguenots' actions. These works included François Hotman's *Francogallia* (1573), Béza's *The Rights of Magistrates* (1574), and *Vindiciae Contra Tyrannos* (*A Defense of Liberty against Tyrants*), most likely written in 1574 or 1575 by either Philippe Duplessis Mornay or Hubert Languet and published anonymously in 1579.[15]

Many French Catholics found themselves facing divided loyalties as well. After the death of Charles IX in 1574, those who demanded that the monarchy uphold Catholicism at any cost looked to King Henry III for leadership. As Duke of Anjou, he had defeated the Huguenots at the battles of Jarnac and Moncontour (1569), but when faced with a Huguenot army whose force he could not match in 1576, he made peace by issuing the Edict of Beaulieu. This edict, which granted the Huguenots privileges of public worship, access to offices and professions, and defensible towns (*places de sûreté*), undermined Catholic hopes for the Huguenots' suppression. Moreover, the king's younger brother François, Duke of Alençon (known as "Monsieur"), had joined the Huguenot forces and helped to negotiate the edict, which is often referred to as "the Peace of Monsieur." Alençon's positioning himself as the Huguenots' royal ally was significant because he was also heir to the throne, as Henry III was childless. Years of warfare, factional strife, and popular violence led some Catholics to demand peace, even if it meant compromising on the goal of religious conformity. But those who favored renewing the civil war blocked the Edict of Beaulieu's implementation, and they predominated at the Estates General of 1576. Most of all, Catholics in many French cities began to form an alliance known as the Catholic League, whose members were dedicated to eliminating the Huguenots above all. As their confidence in Henry III's leadership waned, these ultra-Catholics looked increasingly to Henry, Duke of Guise, to win the war against heresy.[16]

These events paved the way for the crisis of the late 1580s, which encompassed the last three religious wars. Henry III's talents as a monarch – intelligence, diligence, dedication to fiscal reform – were not enough to impose peace or retain his subjects' loyalty. The king's public displays of

---

[15] Holt, *The French Wars of Religion*, 99–105; Sutherland, *The Huguenot Struggle*, 211–231; Scott M. Manetsch, *Theodore Béza and the Quest for Peace in France, 1572–1598* (Leiden, The Netherlands: Brill, 2000).

[16] Holt, *The French Wars of Religion*, 104–113.

Catholic piety did not accord well with his concessions to Huguenots, while accusations of favoritism and sexual impropriety further weakened his image and invited vicious criticism. When Alençon (known as Anjou after 1576) died in 1584, the royal succession became even more complicated: Henry III's nearest male relative was Henry de Bourbon, King of Navarre and the Huguenots' chief protector and military leader. The Huguenots might envision the possibility of a monarch who would share their religion rather than suppressing it, but their earlier arguments about resistance to tyrants suddenly took on new meaning for Catholics who were appalled at the prospect of a heretic becoming king of France. Meanwhile, the Catholic League turned to an alliance with Spain and the Guise family to defend their cause. In May 1588, the Sixteen (the Catholic League's leaders in Paris) and the Parisian populace drove Henry III from the capital and welcomed Henry, Duke of Guise to enter; after taking over the city, they forced the king to endorse their demands for renewed war against the Huguenots under the Guises' command. In December 1588, Henry III decided to end this rivalry by having the duke and his brother Charles, a cardinal, assassinated at the royal palace of Blois, but the consequences of this bold move proved fatal for the king. Condemned by Catholic authorities on all sides as a tyrant, Henry III was stabbed to death in August 1589.[17]

Henry de Bourbon would become King Henry IV of France only after a prolonged struggle against three adversaries: the Catholic League, Spain (which supported the League and was openly at war with France after 1595), and the Huguenots. Henry gradually subdued many of his Catholic enemies through a combination of military force and amnesty, promising to overlook past opposition in return for assurances of loyalty in the future. He publicly abjured the Reformed faith in July 1593, an act that helped him to regain control of Paris and other towns previously held by the League, as well as to have an official coronation ceremony at Chartres. Many Catholics doubted the sincerity of Henry's conversion, however, and Huguenot leaders responded with fear and threats of rebellion if he did not guarantee their power, privileges, and safety. The Spanish defeat at Amiens in 1597 and the Duke of Mercoeur's submission in January 1598 effectively ended the Catholic League's resistance; Henry then issued the Edict of Nantes (April 1598)

---

[17] Holt, *The French Wars of Religion*, 112–138; R. J. Knecht, *Hero or Tyrant? Henry III, King of France, 1574–1589* (Aldershot: Ashgate, 2014); Katherine B. Crawford, "Love, Sodomy, and Scandal: Controlling the Sexual Reputation of Henry III," *Journal of the History of Sexuality* 12:4 (October 2003): 513–542.

to address the Huguenots' demands.[18] The Edict of Nantes promised to establish a regime of peaceful coexistence among Huguenots and Catholics, but it also recognized Catholicism as integral to France's governance and society. The Huguenots would have to depend upon continued protection by – and obedience to – the French crown to keep their privileges. Henry IV's apparent achievement of civil and religious peace would not long outlast his reign, and the Huguenots' dilemmas about submission or militant resistance to royal authority would resurface in the seventeenth century.

SUGGESTED FURTHER READINGS

Kingdon, Robert M. *Geneva and the Coming of the Wars of Religion in France, 1555–1563*. Geneva: Droz, 1956; reprint 2007.
Roelker, Nancy L. *Queen of Navarre: Jeanne d'Albret, 1528–1572*. Cambridge, MA: Harvard University Press, 1968.
Holt, Mack P. *The French Wars of Religion, 1562–1629*, 2nd ed. Cambridge: Cambridge University Press, 2005.

---

[18] Holt, *The French Wars of Religion*, 156–171; Sutherland, *The Huguenot Struggle*, 283–332.

PART II

SWITZERLAND, SOUTHERN GERMANY, AND GENEVA

The Swiss Confederation in the Age of John Calvin

Bruce Gordon

The Swiss Confederation remained an enigma for the Frenchman John Calvin, and with good reason.[1] This collection of territories was a unique and rather confusing political and cultural entity that had emerged piecemeal in the late Middle Ages. The very term *Swiss*, which makes sense to modern ears, hardly applied in the sixteenth century in a place where there was little sense of national identity.[2] Humanists had begun to valorize *Helvetia*, and the wars against the Habsburgs and the Burgundians had done much to incite forms of patriotism, but loyalties remained largely local. Huldrych Zwingli had embraced a sense of the Swiss as the elect people of God, and even the young Heinrich Bullinger wrote of his countrymen as the Israelites of the covenant. The reality, however, was much less harmonious. By the beginning of the sixteenth century, the newly expanded Confederation (with the addition of Basel and Schaffhausen) was a collection of 13 members bound by a series of alliances but divided by internal tensions. Not least was the problem posed by Zurich, which during the previous century had made repeated, and unsuccessful, attempts to expand its hegemonic interests.[3]

The Swiss lands into which Calvin fled in 1535 were in turmoil. The Reformation had ripped apart the Confederation. The most powerful urban members, Zurich, Bern, and Basel, had embraced the new faith, setting them against the largely rural and mountainous inner Confederates that had

---

[1] For an overview of Swiss politics in the sixteenth century, see Thomas Maissen, *Geschichte der Schweiz* (Baden: Hier + Jetzt, Verlag für Kultur und Geschichte, 2010).

[2] Regula Schmid, "The Swiss Confederation before the Reformation," in *A Companion to the Swiss Reformation*, ed. Amy Nelson Burnett and Emidio Campi (Leiden, The Netherlands: Brill, 2016), 14–56.

[3] Bruce Gordon, *The Swiss Reformation* (Manchester: Manchester University Press, 2002), 6–42.

remained resolutely Catholic. Zwingli's preaching and Zurich's aggressive promulgation of the Evangelical faith had torn at the fabric of the Confederation and by the mid-1520s the city had been isolated and drummed out of the federal Diet. Zwingli, for his part, had long harbored plans to extend the preaching of the Gospel to recalcitrant Catholic lands through coercion, even military force. The results were the two Kappel Wars of 1529 and 1531 that ended in the reformer's death and Zurich's utter humiliation at the hands of its Catholic opponents.[4] Uri, Schwyz, Zug, Unterwalden, and Lucerne had prevailed in the war and their aspirations to eradicate heresy remained undiminished. Years before the Peace of Augsburg of 1555, the Swiss had therefore been forced by circumstances to devise a means of religious and political coexistence for a Confederation now partly Catholic, partly Reformed.

To comprehend how the Swiss arrived at this confessional arrangement we must turn to the character of the Confederation. It is easier to say what it was not than to characterize what it was. This alliance, which originated in 1291, possessed no federal political structure and no head of state. The largely rural and mountainous members were linked together by a series of agreements highly defensive in nature. The character of the Confederation was reflected in the contemporary name "Eidgenossenschaft," meaning oath fellowship. By the middle of the fourteenth century, Zurich and Bern had joined the original eight members and with the addition of Solothurn, Basel, and Schaffhausen the number had increased to 13 by 1513. In addition to the full Confederates, a collection of lands known as Mandated Territories were jointly ruled through complex local arrangements. Further, as the Swiss expanded their influence during the late Middle Ages they made formed agreements with lands such as Graubünden, the abbey and city of St. Gall and Biel together with the German cities of Rottweil and Muhlhausen as associated members of the Confederation. Finally, through military conquest, Aargau, Thurgau, and the Tessin were added, to be governed by several of the full Confederates.

Formally, the Swiss Confederates belonged to the Holy Roman Empire and were subjects of the emperor, but a series of successful military campaigns against the Habsburgs, culminating in the Swabian War of 1499, had resulted in exemption from the decrees of the Imperial Diets. Such freedom, however, was not independence, and the Confederation was only uncoupled from the empire by the Peace of Westphalia in 1648. With the addition of the

---

[4] George Potter, *Zwingli* (New York: Cambridge, 1976), 390–419.

powerful imperial city of Basel, with its culture of commerce and distinguished university, the Confederation grew into a curious mixture of urban and rural members held together by a web of mutual obligations with little sense of common purpose. The Swiss were at their most united when threatened from outside.

Far from its modern image, most of the Swiss Confederation was extremely poor, particularly those members whose population was concentrated in mountain valleys. Following their spectacular defeat of powerful Burgundy during the war of 1474–1477, the Swiss had become a much admired military force courted with financial rewards by kings and popes.[5] This triumph began the age of the Swiss mercenary and the myth of his invincibility. French, Imperial, and papal recruiters traveled through the lands seeking willing young men for their armies, largely for the wars in the Italian peninsula. Money in the form of pensions paid to leading families and political and ecclesiastical figures poured into the Confederation, lining pockets and winning influence. Huldrych Zwingli, priest in Glarus, accompanied the troops into Italian lands and experienced the battles of Novara (1513) and Marignano (1515). The lucrative mercenary trade brought not only wealth to the Swiss but also deep political divisions, as Confederates were divided in their support of political rivals such as the French king and the pope. Zwingli, recipient of a pension from the pope, had supported the papal cause against the French, a sympathy that forced him to leave his parish in Glarus. The Swiss had become entangled in the labyrinthine politics of the belligerent forces of France, the empire, the papacy, and their various allies.

At Easter 1525 Zurich formally broke with the Catholic Church by abolishing the mass and adopting the Reformation. Zwingli was a deeply controversial and divisive figure whose supporters and detractors acknowledged him as the leader of the reform movement in the Confederation.[6] The alliances between the Swiss had never been religious in nature, but with the Reformation religion became the central issue. Zurich was in apostasy and the Catholic Confederates, with the exception of Bern, Basel, and Schaffhausen, called for its expulsion. Zwingli's city remained isolated and vulnerable until Bern adopted the reformation three years later, in 1528, and Basel the following year, in 1529.

The Second Kappel War of 1531, which was less a campaign than a quick rout, nearly ended both the Swiss Reformation and the Confederation. The

---

[5] Thomas Maissen, *Schweizer Heldengeschichten—und was dahintersteckt* (Baden: Hier + Jetzt, 2015).

[6] Emidio Campi, "The Reformation in Zurich," in Burnett and Campi, eds., *Handbook*, 66–83.

backlash against Zwingli and his supporters was fierce, and even Zurich looked for a moment like it might return to the old faith. Bern and Basel had not supported Zurich in its campaign to force the Catholic Confederates to accept the Reformation. The consequences of the war were not only chaos and retribution, for the Swiss were left to determine how to resolve their religious problems and preserve peace. The Kappel Peace of November 1531 was the first major agreement of the Reformation that formally acknowledged the existence of two forms of Christianity. Although Zurich had been defeated, powerful Bern and Basel were also Reformed, leaving open no possibility other than compromise. The terms, however, were more favorable to the Catholics. Each Confederate was free to choose its confession. Likewise, in the Mandated Territories communities could remain with their faith. However, there was an important proviso: Reformed communities could return to Catholicism, but conversions to the Evangelical faith were precluded. The Kappel Peace left the Swiss Confederation a divided body with no federal means to deal with religious questions. For most of the early modern period the Catholic and Protestant members of the Confederation would meet separately.

The Second Kappel War created a new dynamic among the Protestant Confederates. Zurich had overplayed its hand and Bern and Basel had clearly demonstrated that they were not prepared to act as handmaidens. The Reformed states were surrounded by hostile opponents, including their Catholics neighbors, the Habsburgs and France. To survive, the Reformed Confederates needed to work together, but Zurich could no longer expect to dominate. Zwingli's successor as head of the Zurich church, Heinrich Bullinger, would soon emerge as the leader of the Swiss Reformed churches, but he worked closely with his friends in Basel, Bern, and other cities.

With Zurich badly wounded and Basel naturally oriented toward the German Rhineland, Bern emerged as the aggressive Protestant force in the Confederation, seizing the opportunity to extend its authority. In 1536 Bernese forces moved westward into the French-speaking lands of the Pays de Vaud, making the city the most powerful territorial ruler in the Confederation, with authority that reached as far as the gates of Geneva.[7] In 1526 the episcopal city of Geneva had acquired the status of an associate member of the Swiss Confederation following an alliance with Fribourg and Bern. The purpose of this arrangement was to seek protection from the predatory claims of the Duke of Savoy, who persevered in asserting his authority over

---

[7] Michael W. Bruening, *Calvinism's First Battleground: Conflict and Reform in the Pays de Vaud, 1528–1559* (Dordrecht, The Netherlands: Springer, 2006).

Geneva until he was defeated by the Bernese in 1536. On August 7 of that year, Bern and Geneva concluded an "eternal peace" that allowed the Genevans to retain control of their internal affairs. In other respects, however, the small city became a vassal as the Bernese took control of Geneva's rural territories and assumed responsibility for its foreign affairs.[8]

Geneva, therefore, was never a Swiss city in the sense of belonging to the Confederation as a full member. From Calvin's return to the city in 1541 until his death in 1564 Geneva was squeezed between the dangers posed by Savoy, whose lands were visible from the walls, and Bern, which as the city's protector increasingly sought to control its affairs. Nevertheless, with its location at the crux of crucial trade routes and its proximity to France, Geneva became an important point of contact between the Swiss and the French kingdom and was increasingly drawn into the affairs of the Confederation.

The stumbling block was religion. In 1536 the Genevans had thrown out their bishop and established a new Protestant order. Calvin's disastrous first stay in 1536–1538 revealed the problems surrounding Bern and the newly Reformed church in Geneva. Calvin fell into a conflict over a relatively minor question of liturgical practice but the larger point was that the Bernese sought to control the church in Geneva and to impose their theology, polity, and rituals.[9] During the restoration of the Reformed churches after Kappel, Zurich, Basel, and Bern had developed somewhat different approaches to the relationship between temporal and spiritual authority, or between magistrates and clergy. In Zurich, Bullinger had been a strong voice for the independence of the church in preaching the Gospel while allowing for the city's rulers to preside over the institution. Bern, in contrast, which had never had a powerful reformer comparable to Zwingli or Bullinger, saw the development of much greater political control over the church and its clergy.

During the 1540s and 1550s, Calvin's relationship with Bern went from bad to worse. The Bernese refused to sign the 1549 agreement on the Lord's Supper known as the *Consensus Tigurinus* between the Genevan and Zurich churches. The moment was extremely tense. The Genevans were entirely dependent on the Bernese for protection and the powerful Confederate was determined to keep them subservient. During the late 1540s, Geneva had sought to join the Swiss Confederation as a full member, but, largely due to Bern's opposition, had been rejected. In 1550 the formal alliance between

[8] William G. Naphy, *Calvin and the Consolidation of the Genevan Reformation: With a New Preface* (Louisville, KY: Westminster John Knox Press, 2003).
[9] Bruce Gordon, *Calvin* (New Haven, CT, and London: Yale University Press, 2009), 78–81.

Bern and Geneva expired, and only after difficult negotiations was it
renewed for another five years. Bern believed that it had the right to
intervene in Geneva's affairs and viewed with the great suspicion the growing number of French refugees in the city. Calvin had relentlessly sought to
free the Genevan church from the authority of Bern and its rites and
practices. Along with his close friends Pierre Viret and Theodore Beza in
Lausanne, Calvin became increasingly influential among the French-
speaking ministers of the Pays de Vaud, further poisoning his relationship
with Bern.[10]

Although the confessional situation was largely determined by the Kappel
Peace of 1531, events continued to destabilize the religious and political
situation in the Confederation. The first followed the Schmalkaldic War of
1546–1547 and triumph of Charles V over the badly organized Protestant
forces in the empire. The victory established the emperor's authority in the
southern German lands and his eye fell on the city of Constance, which had
been closely bound to the Swiss and the Reformation. The city was besieged
and Charles declared the imposition of the Interim in 1548. The Reformed
Swiss, led by Bern, called for support for their co-religionists, but their hopes
came to nothing. The chief reformers offered words of comfort, but the
Confederation decided, wisely, against taking on the imperial forces. By
October 1548, Constance was lost to the Reformation and the Swiss, and
the process of recatholicizing was begun. The leading reformers in the city
were exiled, with Ambrosius Blarer fleeing to serve in the Swiss churches in
Winterthur and Biel. The Swiss lost a major ally and point of contact with
the empire.

A second defeat for the Reformed came several years later in the Italian-
Swiss city of Locarno, where from the early 1540s a significant evangelical
community had developed. Such leading figures as Bernardino Ochino and
Peter Martyr Vermigli were among the community members.[11] The Catholic
Confederates objected to the presence of these reformers, and by 1550, after a
series of failed disputations and increasing hostility from Catholic officials,
the community was required to convert to the old faith. The Reformed
Confederates of Zurich and Bern were not able to offer support beyond
words. The Swiss diet upheld the majority principle of the Kappel Peace to
declare in 1555 that the Reformed in Locarno had the option of converting or
leaving the land by March 3. Zurich rejected the decision but was powerless

---

[10] Bruening, *Calvinism's First Battleground*.
[11] Mark Taplin, *The Italian Reformers and the Zurich Church, c. 1540–1620* (Aldershot, and
      Burlington, VT: Ashgate, 2003).

to act. Over two hundred individuals sought refuge, primarily in Zurich but also in Basel and Bern. Their reception was, however, less than warm as they were viewed as an economic threat to the local craftsmen and merchants. While Zurich took a direct interest in the case, Basel remained distant and Bern was far more concerned with its influence in the west. The division of the county of Greyerz, half of which became Reformed, marked the last territorial advance for the Reformation in Swiss lands.

The situation in the Confederation following the Second Kappel War of 1531 was determined by the zeal with which the Catholic states reinforced their victory by creating alliances to defend the old faith.[12] On all sides the Catholics were pressed against opponents: to the north lay Zurich and Bern, while in the east were Reformed Glarus and Graubünden. The greatest unease, however, was caused by the Mandated Territories, lands jointly governed by rulers from both confessions, with the Frei Ämte, Baden and Bremgarten, in the north and Rapperswil, Gaster, and Sargans in the east. Following the war these lands had been largely returned to the Catholic fold. In other Mandated lands the Reformed were dominant, for example in Thurgau, Rheintal, and Zwingli's native Toggenburg. The situation for the Catholics in the Abbey of St. Gallen and Graubünden was extremely tense. In the west, following its conquest of the French-speaking lands, Bern was dominant. Only in the county of Greyerz, divided in the 1550s between Catholic Freiburg and Reformed Bern was there some form of equitable settlement. Basel for the most part did not involve itself in internal Swiss politics, remaining largely consumed with its struggle with its prince bishop. In many respects, the Confederation was effectively divided into two parts along confessional grounds. Although the federal diet, or Tagsatzung, continued to meet and both sides had to engage in their shared rule of the Mandated Territories, Catholic and Reformed Confederates held their own meetings, in Lucerne and Aarau, respectively. The glorious days of the Confederation that dated to its famous victories of the fifteenth and early sixteenth centuries had passed into a period of extended stasis.

By the late 1550s, following the Treaty of Cateau-Cambrésis (1559) France once more emerged as a major player in the Swiss Confederation. French interests had moved away from the long wars in Italy, where the Spanish were now dominant, toward the religious threat posed by the Huguenots.[13]

[12] Peter Stadler, "Das Zeitalter der Gegenreformation," in Hanno Helbling (ed.), *Handbuch der Schweizer Geschichte* (Zurich: Buchverlag Berichthaus, 1980), 1: 575.

[13] Andreas Mühling, *Heinrich Bullingers europäische Kirchenpolitik* (Bern: New York: Peter Lang, 2001).

Following the treaty of 1521, which Zurich under Zwingli's influence had refused to join, Swiss men continued to find employment in the French armies, while pensions continued to flow to leading families and politicians, particularly in the Catholic Confederates, but not exclusively. From 1529 Bern had also refused to honor the terms of the agreement with France, but the proximity of kingdom had real economic benefits for the Swiss, who continued to enjoy favorable trade terms.

Before Calvin's death the Catholic Church in the Swiss Confederation began a long period of revitalization based on close relations with Rome. The first location for conflict was the land of Glarus in the east, where the Catholic Confederates were prepared to go to war to reverse the advances of the Reformation. In 1560 a delegation was sent to Rome to discuss such a plan. The war did not take place, but the Catholics were emboldened, and in the same year concluded a treaty with the newly restored Duke of Savoy.[14] The threat to Geneva was immediate. The Duke undertook to support the seven Catholic Confederates should a religious war break out among the Swiss. A similar attempt by the Catholic Swiss to win support from Philip II of Spain met with less success, but the threat of religious war in the Confederation remained real. A taste for conflict with the Reformed states was not, however, shared by either Rome or Spain, and the situation in Glarus was peacefully resolved.

The papacy was opposed to war in the Swiss Confederation because of its preoccupation with the Council of Trent. The Swiss showed little interest in the council until the sessions beginning in January 1561. All 13 Confederates had been invited, but the Reformed, led by Heinrich Bullinger, had declined to attend. The five Catholic states, however, accepted the papal invitation and sent the talented Melchior Lussy as one of their two delegates. The close connection between the Swiss and Rome was confirmed in 1565 by an alliance with Pope Pius IV, whose nephew had been crowned bishop of Constance four years earlier. The agreement was entirely defensive as the pope promised the Swiss Catholic Confederates support in the case of attack by the Reformed. The arrangement did not last long, ending with Pius IV's death that same year. Nevertheless, the Swiss Catholics had formed strong external bonds that bolstered their position against their adversaries.

By the time of Calvin's death, the situation within the Confederation for the Reformation was precarious. Savoy was hostile and Henry II had been moving against the heretics in his kingdom. Henry's death in 1559 had been

---

[14] Stadler, "Das Zeitalter," 582.

greeted by Calvin as a sign from heaven, but relations between the Swiss and France remained tense. Calvin tried to aid matters by acting as an agent to encourage the Swiss Reformed to ally with France, an intervention that caused considerable consternation in Zurich.[15] Bern was involved in complex negotiations with Savoy that nearly led to military conflict. When an agreement was reached in Lausanne in 1564, Bern had to surrender lands directly to the south of Geneva, which was now largely isolated.

The Swiss Confederation that John Calvin knew had been shaped by the events of the Reformation and the Kappel Peace of 1531. Confessionally divided and largely isolated from the German Empire, the Swiss were politically paralyzed. Despite the peace and arrangements for coexistence, Catholics and Reformed continued to threaten civil war, which would only have been possible with the intervention of foreign forces. The balance between the two sides was such that neither was strong enough to ensure victory. In many respects, it was the changing interests of foreign powers that shaped events in the Confederation. The leading Reformed cities of Zurich, Bern, and Basel largely followed their own agendas, creating little sense of harmony. The Catholics, led by the Jesuits, were beginning a period of revival that would grow in the seventeenth century. In the sixteenth century, however, the situation remained tense and volatile, held together only by a shared sense of the ruinous consequences of civil war. The Swiss were defensive, cautious, and vulnerable, creating a religious and political climate that John Calvin struggled to comprehend.

SUGGESTED FURTHER READINGS

Bruening, Michael W. *Calvinism's first battleground: conflict and reform in the Pays de Vaud, 1528–1559*. Dordrecht: Springer, 2006.

Gordon, Bruce. *Calvin* New Haven/London: Yale University Press, 2009.

The Swiss Reformation. Manchester: Manchester University Press, 2002.

Mühling, Andreas. *Heinrich Bullingers europäische Kirchenpolitik*. Bern: New York: Peter Lang, 2001.

Naphy, William G. *Calvin and the Consolidation of the Genevan Reformation: with a new preface*. Louisville: Westminster John Knox Press, 2003.

---

[15] Gordon, *Calvin*, 178–179.

8

ᴕ

Strasbourg in the Sixteenth Century

Steven W. Tyra

INTRODUCTION

"Strasbourg, that most ancient and magnificent city, is called 'Argentuaria' by the Swiss and is situated along the Rhine."[1] So Hartmann Schedel introduced Strasbourg to readers of his *Liber Chronicarum* (usually dubbed the *Nuremberg Chronicle* in English) in 1493. In keeping with the universalizing aim of his book, he proceeded to weave the *ciuitas vetustissima ac permagnifica* into the events of biblical, Roman, and ecclesiastical history, with the patriarch Abraham, Julius Caesar, and Atilla the Hun all making an appearance. The account was accompanied by a lavish full-page illustration of the city's skyscape centering on its gothic cathedral, whose soaring spire remains iconic to this day. Strasbourg was thus ranked historically and visually alongside the likes of Constantinople, Rome, and even Jerusalem.

While modern historians may have good reason to question the details of Schedel's narrative, there can be no doubt that Strasbourg or *Argentina,* as it was still called it Latin, boasted an impressive civic legacy by the end of the Middle Ages. Its prominence explains in part why the city attracted major Protestant figures such as Martin Bucer and Wolfgang Capito, not to mention a young John Calvin. This chapter will sketch Strasbourg as these early modern people would have encountered it. Perhaps the first thing that citizens would have pointed out to a newcomer like Calvin was the privileged position they enjoyed in that most bewildering of political institutions, the Holy Roman Empire.

---

[1] Hartmann Schedel, "Argentina ciuitas vetustissima ac permagnifica argentuaria dicta Heluitios proter rhenum sita," *Liber Chronicarum figuris et imaginibus* (Nuremberg, 1493), fol. 139v.

FREE IMPERIAL CITY

"Many were very pleased that these loyal folk had come so far on such short notice, that they arrived so well armed and ready for action . . . that the city of Strasbourg could justly regard them with all the more affection and trust," remarked the local luminary, Sebastian Brant.[2] The occasion was the ceremonial entry of the new prince-bishop, William of Honstein, in 1507. The city fathers had quickly assembled a formidable peasant militia to greet his excellency at the gates, lest there be any misunderstanding about who truly exercised power within them. Thomas A. Brady has pointed to this and similar episodes as illustrating the city's fiercely guarded independence at the dawn of the sixteenth century.[3] Despite its titular ecclesiastical prince, Strasbourg was a "Free Imperial City," meaning that it occupied one of three political estates within the empire. The "Golden Bull" of 1356 had designated seven great princes (three ecclesiastical, four secular) as Electors – those who cast votes for a new emperor. Below them were the numerous prelates and potentates of lesser territories, followed by 55 or so Free Cities. These latter received their own chamber and representatives at Imperial Diets and yet often struggled to assert themselves against the territorial rulers in matters of taxation and policy.[4] Strasbourg's own position in the rich Alsatian Rhineland made it an attractive plum that many lords were eager to pluck. The city's identity during the later Middle Ages was therefore forged in a struggle to maintain its privileges, a long campaign that was just entering a new phase as the crises of the Reformation arrived.

Prior to the sixteenth century, the Strasbourgeois had cultivated strong ties to the city-states of the Swiss Confederacy to help ensure their own relative autonomy. The Swabian War of 1499, however, had pitted them against their erstwhile allies to the south, leading to a major realignment in foreign policy. From then on the city fathers looked to the rising power of the Austrian Habsburgs under Maximilian I for protection; close relations with the Holy Roman Emperor were intended to stymie the ambitions of lesser lords. Maximilian rewarded his clients with at least two personal visits during his reign. He did not live to see the Reformation's advent in Strasbourg in the 1520s. That reckoning would be left to his nephew and successor, Charles V, whose Catholic majesty naturally looked askance at the

---

[2] Quoted in Thomas A. Brady Jr., The *Politics of the Reformation in Germany: Jacob Sturm (1489–1553) of Strasbourg* (Atlantic Highlands, NJ: Humanities Press, 1997), 52.

[3] Brady narrates Bishop William's fraught entry and subsequent relations with the city in detail in ibid., 50–55.

[4] See ibid., 16–17.

Strasbourgeois' embrace of "heresy." Matters came to a head when the city joined the Smalkaldic League in 1531, thus casting its lot with the Lutheran princes of Saxony, Hesse, and other territories. The architect of this new Protestant foreign policy was the mayor or *Stettmeister*, Jacob Sturm, the city's most dominant political figure during the first half of the century and a statesman greatly respected by Calvin. While the League's defeat at the hands of Charles in the Smalkaldic War (1546–1547) led to the exile of preachers and theologians such as Martin Bucer, it failed to dislodge Strasbourg's Protestant loyalties. The city's position in the empire remained closely bound up with the Lutheran princes, which included the adoption of a thoroughgoing Lutheran Orthodoxy by the end of the century. Citizens who lived through the Reformation and its aftermath thus witnessed a considerable irony. The Free City that had so long resisted the ambitions of the great territorial princes ended up abetting the consolidation of their power in the confessional age.[5]

LOCAL GOVERNMENT AND ECONOMY

How do we account for the Strasbourgeois' *volte-face* with regard to Habsburg power in the empire, not to mention the late medieval religion of their mothers and fathers? What local factors made Strasbourg amenable to embracing the Reformation at home and abroad? Any answer must begin with the political and economic structures that held sway over the approximately 620 acres encompassed by the city's medieval walls. Strasbourg was in many respects a model for the "Guild Revolution" that swept through southern German city-states in the late Middle Ages.[6] For the majority of citizens, participation in political life entailed membership in a professional guild, of which Strasbourg had 20. (When Calvin purchased citizenship in July 1539, he was enrolled, somewhat incongruously, among the Tailors). Representatives from the guilds in turn formed a body of about three hundred known as the *Schöffen*. They were presided over by the *Ammeister*, who served as the city's chief executive and was required by law to be a guildsman of nonaristocratic lineage. While the *Schöffen* were often consulted on important matters of policy, effective power lay with the Senate,

---

[5] Lorna Jane Abray argues that the Reformation was ultimately "disastrous" for local governance as it led "to the decay of the cities and the strengthening of the princes." See *The People's Reformation: Magistrates, Clergy, and Commons in Strasbourg, 1500–1598* (Ithaca, NY: Cornell University Press, 1985), 211. For a more measured appraisal, see Brady, *Politic of the Reformation*, 249–250.

[6] The details in the section are indebted to Brady, *Politics of the Reformation*, 44–49.

whose 51 members were composed of roughly one-third aristocrats and the remainder common guildsmen. Above even these were the two privy councils – the "XV," which oversaw domestic governance, and the "XIII," which handled foreign affairs. By tradition the higher bodies were referred to collectively as the "Senate and XXI." Finally, the titular head of the government was the noble *Stettmeister,* a role that by the sixteenth century was meant to be largely ceremonial. Nonetheless, in the hands of a brilliant politician like Jacob Sturm, the office served as a rudder to steer policy both foreign and domestic (Sturm also sat on the XIII for most of his career). The *Stettmeister*'s continued dominance points to the reality of oligarchic rule in Strasbourg. Brady has described the system as a "rentier-merchant aristocracy" wherein a small cadre of wealthy families, including "common" leaders within the guilds, monopolized the highest offices.[7]

Of course, such a system depended on the goodwill or at least the nonviolence of the majority to function, and in this respect Strasbourg's elites enjoyed an enviable position vis-à-vis their peers in neighboring territories. Theirs was relatively large commonwealth, boasting around 20,000 inhabitants (by comparison, Geneva had 12,000). So many people within the walls could pose challenges, and Strasbourg like many late medieval cities was forced to develop an elaborate system of poor relief to combat indigence.[8] All the same, the ready supply of labor conspired with the rich resources of the Rhineland to produce a robust artisanal and manufacturing economy. Strasbourgeois journeymen were well organized and assertive about their rights, and the city was the seat of the stonemasons' federation in the empire. Brady also notes active organizations for gardeners, butchers, and bakers within the city, in addition to the revenue generated by its location on major trade routes.[9] To these might be added a more recent industry. Beginning in the late fifteenth century, Strasbourg had become a center of printing and bookmaking. This lively trade in words would attract ambitious journeymen of more than one ilk, including a young Frenchman recently registered as a tailor. It was from Strasbourg's active presses that John Calvin would begin to stitch together an international reputation as a theologian and biblical exegete.[10]

---

[7] See Thomas A. Brady Jr., *Ruling Class, Regime, and Reformation at Strasbourg, 1520–1555* (Leiden, The Netherlands: Brill, 1978), 195.

[8] See the helpful study by Carter A. Lindberg, *Beyond Charity: Reformation Initiatives for the Poor* (Minneapolis, MN: Augsburg Fortress, 1993), esp. 44–45, 138–139.

[9] See Brady, *Politics of the Reformation,* 48.

[10] Among other important works, the second edition of the *Institutes of the Christian Religion* (1539), the *Commentary on Romans* (1540), and the *Psychopannychia* (1542) were printed at Strasbourg.

THE REFORMATION OF THE 1520S

"You of the laity, you hate us clergymen!," fumed Johann Geiler von Kaysersberg, Strasbourg's most popular preacher at the turn of the century.[11] The city's religious life in the decades preceding Geiler's outburst offers a study in contrasts. On the one hand, it is not difficult to find evidence of flourishing piety; well-to-do Strasbourgeois continued to donate substantial sums to ecclesial works, including the casting of a magnificent cathedral bell in 1520. The souls of their fellow citizens were shepherded by clergy in 9 parish churches, 4 collegiate churches, 19 religious houses, and approximately 200 chapels.[12] On the other hand, Lorna Jane Abray has argued that "the rising tide of German anticlericalism is one of the most striking aspects of religious feeling in and around Strasbourg."[13] It has been noted already how the prince-bishop served as the chief political rival to the Senate and XXI, who on at least one occasion felt the need to arm peasants with halberds to drive their point home. At other times, the peasants acted on their own initiative. The 1490s saw a series of anticlerical riots in the countryside protesting priests who had grown rich off investment in rural debt.[14] Such flare-ups only intensified the typical late medieval grievances concerning ecclesial taxation and clerical exemptions from the law. The resulting animus was lamented by Geiler and his colleagues from the pulpit, but to little effect. Whether from "hatred," self-interest, or a genuine desire for reform, the city fathers and a significant portion of the populace were ready to entertain alternative proposals for how to organize the church.

The opportunity arrived in 1521. That year another popular preacher from Kaysersberg, Mathias Zell, embraced teachings associated with Martin Luther and began propounding them from his pulpit in the cathedral, much to the consternation of Bishop William (still reigning after all this time) and the higher clergy. In truth Zell was one of a number of younger clerics and intellectuals who were experimenting with reform. Erasmian humanism already had an influential following in Strasbourg, including the future *Stettmeister*, Jacob Sturm.[15] Zell, however, was the "people's preacher" in both title and effect; he emerged over the next few years as the chief spokesman for a popular movement that saw demonstrations, iconoclasm, and bouts of violence against priests. Meanwhile, the evangelical cause was

---

[11] Quoted in Abray, *People's Reformation*, 25.
[12] Statistics in this section are drawn from ibid., 22–23.
[13] Ibid., 25.
[14] See ibid., 24–25.
[15] See Brady, *Politics of the Reformation*, 69–73.

gaining adherents in high places. Sturm converted in 1523, along with the provost of the St. Thomas collegiate church, Wolfgang Capito, and his student, Caspar Hedio. Before long the freshly excommunicated Martin Bucer arrived in the city and established himself as a leading theologian, engaging in a public debate with the conservative cleric, Thomas Murner. Despite their initial caution, the Senate and XXI took the fateful step of protecting Zell and his colleagues from their ecclesiastical superiors on the grounds that they were merely preaching the "gospel." The magistrates also mandated in 1524 that the clergy become full citizens and so subject to the civil law. The long medieval debate over clerical exemptions had been settled, at least in Strasbourg.

What had moved the city fathers to side with the evangelicals against the old church? Some were doubtless persuaded by the "gospel," among whom Jacob Sturm might be counted. Nonetheless, Brady highlights the chaos of 1524–1525, which saw the outbreak of the Peasants' War across the empire and during which armed mobs and social revolutionaries prowled Strasbourg's streets.[16] In this charged atmosphere, "moderate" reformers like Zell, Bucer, and Capito could present themselves to the rattled magistrates as a sensible *via media* – one that would satisfy the widespread desire for reform while putting its final shape in the hands of the Senate and XXI. The evangelicals, in other words, convinced the city fathers that their reformation would lead to neither an encrusted clericalism nor marauding hordes of peasants. This strategy won the day. However, the price in years to come was a permanent weakening of pastoral authority as reformers like Bucer learned who really were the masters, and who the servants in the new order. The Church Ordinance of 1534 allowed for no pastors' consistory with disciplinary powers, much to Bucer's chagrin. Violations of doctrine and morality were now matters for the secular courts and pastors employees of the state.[17] Thus, when John Calvin fled to Strasbourg in the late 1530s, he encountered a city and church that had been profoundly shaped by the upheavals of the previous decade. The lessons he learned in its service would not soon be forgotten.

WORSHIP AND LEARNING IN THE NEW ORDER

Strasbourg's reformation had been "magisterial" in the truest sense: religious life, including the city's specific doctrinal commitments, were now firmly under the direction of the Senate and XXI. Bucer and Capito might have

---

[16] See for Brady's case, see *Ruling Class*, 199–215; See also Abray, *People's Reformation*, 36–38.
[17] Abray, *People's Reformation*, 45.

authored the "Tetrapolitan Confession" in 1530, but only Jacob Sturm and his peers could authorize it.[18] That is not to say that Strasbourg's religious life in the 1530s and 1540s was a monolith. Pockets of Anabaptism, present since the mid-1520s, persisted among the laboring and artisanal classes even after the expulsion of Pilgram Marpeck and his circle in 1532. It was from one of these communities that a wife was found for John Calvin, who married the Anabaptist widow, Idelette de Bure, in 1540. The magistrates also permitted the establishment of a parish for about four hundred French refugees in 1538, of which Calvin became the pastor. Still, the most fascinating instance of piety in these years was arguably furnished by Katharina Schütz Zell. She had been wed to Mathias in 1523 – a radical act – and ever since had served as his "assistant minister."[19] The title was no mere endearment. Not only did this native woman of artisanal class help to lead the reformation, publicly catechizing Strasbourgeois of both sexes in the new faith, she also managed to vex the likes of Bucer with her assertiveness and depth of biblical learning.[20] The relationship was on poignant (not to mention amusing) display in 1548, when Bucer was tasked with preaching the funeral homily over Mathias's corpse. No sooner had he concluded his somber oration than Mathias's widow sprang to the fore and declared that she too had a word to share:

> [Do] not be irritated with me for what I am doing, as if I wanted to place myself in the office of preachers and apostles: not at all! But it is only as the dear Mary Magdalene without any prior thought became an apostle and was charged by the Lord Himself.... So I also now speak.[21]

Having denied being a preacher, Katharina proceeded to deliver a passionate sermon on the final resurrection that quoted extensively from Scripture, the city's catechism, and Martin Luther.

At the institutional level, no venture was more emblematic of Strasbourg's new status as an evangelical capital than the Gymnasium, founded in 1538 under the rectorship of the humanist scholar, Johannes Sturm (who bore no relation to Jacob the *Stettmeister*). The city had lacked a medieval university, and the Gymnasium was intended to raise its reputation as a

---

[18] Brady describes Bucer and Capito as preparing the Confession "under Sturm's supervision." See *Politics of the Reformation*, 88.

[19] This was Mathias's own title for her. See Elsie McKee, "Volume Editor's Introduction," in Katharina Schütz Zell, *Church Mother: The Writings of a Protestant Reformer in Sixteenth-Century Germany*, trans. Elsie McKee (Chicago: University of Chicago Press, 2006), 19.

[20] Ibid., 19.

[21] Zell, "Lament and Exhortation of Katharina Zell to the People at the Grave of Master Matthew Zell," in *Church Mother*, 104.

center of Protestant and classical learning. The experiment was a success: Sturm's humanistic curriculum and innovative pedagogy soon became a model for schools throughout the empire.[22] The rector also initiated a series of public lectures featuring Strasbourg's leading intellectuals. Among them was the recently arrived Calvin, who expounded John's Gospel and several Pauline epistles. These lectures form the immediate backdrop for the publication of his first biblical commentary, on Romans, which came off Strasbourg's presses in 1540.

CONCLUSION

Strasbourg's experience in the sixteenth century has often been studied; the "suggested reading" that follows is merely the first step into a vast field. It is not hard to see why. The Free City in many ways embodied the tensions, violence, and astonishing creativity of the urban reformations. Its break with the Roman church had deep medieval roots, while also pointing toward a future of "great powers" and confessionalized states, to use Brady's phrase.[23] It is telling that Strasbourg would move steadily toward a more rigid Lutheran Orthodoxy in the 1570s and 1580s, well after the Zells, Bucer, and the first generations of reformers had passed on.[24] In the end, the "ancient and magnificent city" that was the site of so many transitions in John Calvin's career was also a mirror of the changing world around him.

SUGGESTED FURTHER READINGS

Abray, Lorna Jane. *The People's Reformation: Magistrates, Clergy, and Commons in Strasbourg, 1500–1598*. Ithaca, NY: Cornell University Press, 1985.

Brady Jr., Thomas A. *Ruling Class, Regime, and Reformation at Strasbourg, 1520–1555*. Leiden, The Netherlands: Brill, 1978.

The Politics of the Reformation in Germany: Jacob Sturm (1489–1553) of Strasbourg. Atlantic Highlands, NJ: Humanities Press, 1997.

Lienhard, Marc. "Strasbourg in Calvin's Time." In *John Calvin: The Strasbourg Years (1538–1541)*, ed. Matthieu Arnold. Eugene, OR: Wipf and Stock, 2018.

---

[22] See the helpful study by Barbara Sher Tinsley, "Johann Sturm's Method for Humanistic Pedagogy," *Sixteenth Century Journal* 20:1 (1989): 23–40.

[23] See Brady, *Politics of the Reformation*, 249.

[24] One reformer who lived to see the shift was Johannes Sturm, who was finally dismissed from the Gymnasium in 1581 (after 43 years!) for his opposition to the *Book of Concord* and Reformed views.

McKee, Elsie Anne. *Katharina Schütz Zell: The Life and Thought of a Sixteenth-Century Reformer*. Leiden, The Netherlands: Brill, 1999.

Ozment, Steven E. *The Reformation in the Cities: The Appeal of Protestantism to Sixteenth-century Germany and Switzerland*. New Haven, CT: Yale University Press, 1980.

Zell, Katharina Schütz. *Church Mother: The Writings of a Protestant Reformer in Sixteenth-Century Germany*, trans. Elsie McKee. Chicago: University of Chicago Press, 2006.

9

℘

Geneva and Its Protectors

Charles H. Parker

The mottled confessional map of Europe at any of the major junctures of the Reformation, say in 1555 or in 1648, hints at the complex tangle of political alliances, military campaigns, and dynastic aspirations that led to Catholic, Lutheran, and Reformed territorial holdings. Throughout the course of the Reformation, contingent political and military circumstances established the parameters of religious reform. In the early 1520s, for example, Charles V's need for support among German princes against enemies foreign and domestic enabled Lutherans to gain traction in Saxony and Hesse. Decades later in the fall of 1588, storms in the North Atlantic blew ships in Spain's Armada into the coastlines of Scotland and Ireland, helping preserve the Elizabethan settlement in England. And in 1620, the Count of Tilly's imperial forces overran Bohemian troops at White Mountain, a victory that cleared the way for the recatholicization of Czech lands. Strokes of (mis)fortune at courts, on seaways, and on battlefields such as these carried unforeseen and far-reaching implications for the religious map of Europe in the sixteenth and seventeenth centuries. It makes sense, therefore, when considering John Calvin and Calvinism in their fullest contexts to reflect on the conditional political and military incidents that befell the Republic of Geneva in the Reformation period. Calvin's leadership in propagating his brand of Reformed Protestantism with such vigor and success derived in no small part from the independence Geneva achieved among regional powers.

This chapter sets the political context for understanding Calvin and the Reformed movement in Geneva by delineating the triangular regional conflicts between the Confederation of Swiss Cantons (especially Bern), the Duchy of Savoy, and the Kingdom of France. The struggles between these parties created a measure of political autonomy for Geneva that enabled Calvin to turn his conclusions about scripture and the church into a comprehensive theological system and ecclesiastical reform program.

Throughout the sixteenth century, the dukes of Savoy sought to bring Geneva and the surrounding countryside under their political authority. Bern's conquest of the area and alliance with Geneva kept Savoyard dukes at bay for most of the century. Yet tensions that emerged between Bern and Geneva in the 1540s and 1550s aggravated disagreements among ministers in the Swiss cities and regional Francophone parishes. These local political and theological disputes compelled Calvin to look beyond the region to build an international network of Reformed churches in France and across Europe. As Savoy reemerged as a threat at the end of the 1500s, the city increasingly looked to France for support. By the early seventeenth century, however, Geneva stood on its own as the guarantor of its independence.

BERNESE-SAVOYARD RIVALRY AND THE COMING
OF THE REFORMATION

The city of Geneva in the early sixteenth century belonged to a flourishing regional economy located in close proximity to several powers ambitious to expand their political and economic reach. A lively market town since the Middle Ages, Geneva lay to the south and west of the Swiss Confederation and at the southern tip of the Pays de Vaud. Geneva and the Vaud, excepting the bishopric of Lausanne, fell under the jurisdiction of the dukes of Savoy who governed the city through a prince-bishop normally from the ruling dynasty. In principle the Savoyard lands belonged to the Holy Roman Empire, though this feudal relationship meant little in everyday political practice until the Hapsburg-Valois conflict brought open division to the region in the sixteenth century. The prosperity of the Vaud and other local territories had long set the governing oligarchy of Bern and the dukes of Savoy on edge with one another, as each regarded the other as the primary threat to their expansionist intentions in the region.[1]

---

[1] I thank Jill Fehleison and Karin Maag who offered very helpful comments and suggestions. This chapter is based on the following works: Jill Fehleison, *Boundaries of Faith: Catholics and Protestants in the Diocese of Geneva* (Kirksville, MO: Truman State University Press, 2010), 23–28; William G. Naphy, *Calvin and the Consolidation of the Genevan Reformation* (New York: Manchester University Press, 1994), 13; Michael W. Bruening, *Calvinism's First Battleground: Conflict and Reform in the Pays de Vaud, 1528–1559* (Dordrecht, The Netherlands: Springer, 2005), 2–3, 12–13, 19–20, 23–25, 35–60; Bruce Gordon, *The Swiss Reformation* (New York: Manchester University Press, 2002), 46–68, 101–108; Robert M. Kingdon, *Geneva and the Coming of the Wars of Religion in France 1555–1563* (Geneva: Librairie Droz, 1956), 1; Matthew Vester, "Introduction," in *Sabaudian Studies: Political Culture, Dynasty, and Territory 1400–1700*, idem ed. (Kirksville, MO: Truman State University Press, 2013), 6; E. William Monter, *Calvin's Geneva* (London: Wiley, 1967), 84–86, 202–207; Jeffrey R. Watt and Isabella

In the fifteenth century, Geneva came more directly under the authority of Savoy and its prince-bishops, a condition the city resisted increasingly by the early 1500s. In an attempt to offset Savoyard rule and reclaim traditional liberties, leading citizens formed a brief, unsuccessful alliance with the city of Fribourg in 1519. Duke Charles III exacted revenge by having the Genevan instigator of the treaty, Philibert Berthelier, executed and by imposing himself more directly on the city. The heavy-handed actions of Charles pushed Genevan leaders into the arms of the Swiss cantons. In 1526 syndics in Geneva signed alliances (*combourgeoisie*) with Bern and Fribourg to recapture the city's privileges against the duke and his prince-bishop.

During the 1520s, evangelical ideas originating from Germany and from Zurich gained traction in Swiss parishes and cities, eventually finding their way into Geneva. The powerful preaching of Ulrich Zwingli in Zurich found a warm reception among its municipal authorities, which over time adopted the principle features of Zwingli's teachings. By 1525, Zurich stood as the first Protestant city in the Swiss Confederation, and Bern followed suit three years later. Between 1522 and 1528, Zwinglians, Lutherans, and Catholics battled one another for influence among Bernese magistrates and ordinary parishioners. The critical moment came in the Bern Disputation in 1528, in which Zwinglian theologians won debates against Catholic counterparts, and the city council adopted a Reformed Protestant order. As evangelical activity emerged in Geneva, the Bernese magistrates put pressure on its dependent ally to permit public preaching in the city. In the military conflict that ensued between Protestant and Catholic cantons, Zurich's defeat in the second Battle of Kappel in 1531 left Bern standing as the strongest pillar of Reformed Protestantism in the Swiss Confederation. Though both evangelical and Catholic worship continued to take place in Geneva, the city came securely within Bern's orbit by 1530.

The critical event that pushed Geneva solidly into the Reformed Protestant camp was the Bernese military campaign throughout the Vaud against Savoy early in 1536. Bern had long nurtured expansionist intentions in the Vaud; the city government and Duke Charles III had clashed over control of Geneva since the city signed the alliance in 1528. In 1530, the duke sent troops to retake the city only to be rebuffed by Bernese forces. Then again in the fall

of 1535, Charles III again laid siege to Geneva, compelling Bern to invade the
Vaud, along with neighboring territories in Gex, Chablais, and Lausanne.

In addition to these local struggles that engulfed Geneva, the broader
European contest between the Hapsburgs and the French Valois dynasty
over Italy brought Bern and the Swiss Confederation into conflict with
Savoy. The dukes remained loyal to the Hapsburgs, whereas the Swiss
Confederation signed a 30-year treaty with Francis I of France in 1521.
Consequently, at the same time that Bernese forces were pushing into the
Vaud, France was also deploying troops against Savoy. Bern's forces put
Savoyard companies to flight and easily conquered the region. In short
order, Bern sponsored a theological disputation in Lausanne in October
1536, which overwhelmingly supported a Protestant church order. Thus, as
John Calvin was making his way into Geneva in 1536, the city had already
expelled its prince-bishop and declared for the Reformation, a stance driven
and guaranteed by the political and military power of Bern.

TENSIONS IN THE BERNESE-GENEVAN ALLIANCE

Geneva's political alliance with Bern held throughout most of the sixteenth
century, giving the city independence from the duchy of Savoy. Yet at the
same time, the amity between the two cities came under serious strain in the
1540s and 1550s because of foreign policy disagreements and because of
Calvin's vision of the church. It is also worth noting that Bernese military
support came at a high price, as Geneva had to shoulder the heavy expenses
for troops provided by Bern (and Basel) in 1536. These tensions, Michael
Bruening argues, carried important ramifications for the development of
Reformed Protestantism outside of the Swiss lands and the Pays de Vaud.

The Franco-Swiss connection strengthened Geneva's hand against Savoyard encroachments through its alliance with Bern. Out of a concern for
Reformed congregations in his homeland, Calvin held a very strong pro-
France outlook. Genevans believed their security lay not only with Bern but
also with the Confederation's pact with France, thus they grew quite anxious
whenever it appeared to falter. Geneva appealed to join the Swiss
Confederation on several occasions in the sixteenth century, but the cantons
rejected its overtures every time, keeping the city under Bern's long shadow.
In this precarious environment, the truce between the Valois King Francis I
and the Hapsburg emperor Charles V between 1538 and 1542 raised fears
among the Swiss Protestant cantons (namely Bern and Zurich) and Geneva
that the two Catholic powers would now turn their attention to crushing the
enemies of the Roman Church. When Charles and Francis renewed their

hostilities in 1542, Protestants in Swiss lands, Geneva, and the Vaud breathed a collective sigh of relief.

Five years later, the new French king, Henri II, sought to renew the alliance with the Swiss Confederation, even though the agreement was not set to expire until 1551. Henri needed the protection the cantons afforded on France's southeastern frontier, and consequently he was eager to strike a deal. Bern and Zurich, however, did not trust the new king, wary that he might step up his father's campaign against Reformed congregations in France. Calvin stood prominently in support for a renewed alliance, so much so in fact that he and William Farel served as delegates for France in the negotiations with the Swiss. The two ministers believed that a pact would protect French Protestants from persecution. When Bern and Zurich withdrew their backing and the partnership fell through, enmity between Geneva and its protector grew. The failure of the Franco-Swiss alliance left Genevans feeling quite vulnerable to its hostile neighbor to the south.

Theological differences within Reformed Protestantism likewise contributed to a breach between Geneva and Bern. Calvinists and Zwinglians differed on several important doctrinal matters, including the nature of the Lord's Supper and the theological centrality of predestination. Issues involving the relationship between the church and civil authority, however, emerged as the most hotly contested at the time. Calvin championed a church independent from magisterial authority to preach the gospel, administer the sacraments of baptism and the Lord's Supper, and carry out ecclesiastical discipline. This unwavering stance, especially on the matter of discipline, formed a hallmark of Calvinist churches throughout Europe and other parts of the world in the sixteenth and seventeenth centuries. It often met with resistance among theologians and political rulers in Reformed lands, like those in Bern, enemies that Calvinists condemned as Libertines. Ministers and magistrates within the Zwinglian branch of Reformed Protestantism rejected a self-governing church, largely free from civil authority.

The theological differences pitted Genevan Calvinists against Bernese Zwinglians who were both at work reforming religious practice in the Vaud. After the Bernese conquest and Lausanne Disputation of 1536, Bern, Zurich, Geneva, and other Protestant centers sent out missionaries and pastors to cultivate Reformed faith and worship in the region. During the 1540s and 1550s, Bern resisted efforts for reform along Calvinist lines. In the early 1550s, Calvin's toxic dispute with Jerome Bolsec over the doctrine of predestination further soured Bern's attitude toward Calvin. At the height of the controversy, Bern's city government issued prohibitions against preaching on predestination and disciplining around the Lord's Supper in the Calvinist fashion. As a result of bitterness over the lapsed treaty with France and the theological standoff with Calvin, Bern even allowed its alliance with Geneva to lapse in 1556. It was Savoy's renewed sense of purpose in retaking the Vaud that brought Bern and Geneva back into alliance in 1558.

TRANSITIONS TO GENEVAN INDEPENDENCE

The last five years of Calvin's life coincided with two major political events that greatly affected Geneva's incessant need for protection against Savoy. First, the Treaty of Cateau-Cambresis, which concluded the Valois-Hapsburg conflict, put in motion an agreement that France and Bern would restore lands to Savoy, except for the Pays de Vaud, taken in the 1536 conquest. The negotiations to transact this transfer culminated in the Treaty of Lausanne in 1564. Second, the outbreak of the wars of religion in 1562 in France eventually pushed Geneva and Bern onto the sides of both the Huguenot champion, the Prince of Navarre (later Henri IV), and the French crown under Henri III. Savoy remained faithful to a pro-Hapsburg policy, allying itself with the Holy League and the Spanish king, Phillip II. The brutal civil wars that raged in France reinvigorated the old regional dispute between Bern, France, and Savoy regarding control over the Vaud and Geneva. As these conflicts played themselves at the end of the sixteenth century, Geneva would ultimately shed its need of a protector to stand independent from all local powers.

Until 1584, Duke Charles Emmanuel I concentrated most of his energies on consolidating authority over his Italian-speaking lands, though he did threaten Geneva and instigated coup attempts that were foiled. Disagreements over discipline and church organization continued to plague relations between Bern and Geneva under the pastoral leadership of Theodore Beza. Geneva at times reached out to Henri III and cultivated an equally supportive relationship with the Prince of Navarre. Concerns by the French crown and the Swiss Protestant cantons over Savoyard aggression in the Vaud led to the mutual defense Treaty of Solothorn in 1579, which also provided for Geneva's protection. Five years later, Geneva, Bern, and France agreed to a triple alliance directed against Charles Emmanuel I and his designs in the Vaud. Perhaps most importantly for the future security of Geneva, the Prince of Navarre dispatched a military engineer to inspect and fortify the city's walled defenses in 1581.

Finally in 1584, Duke Charles Emmanuel I initiated hostilities that led to a long and difficult struggle for Geneva, but resulted in its definitive chapter in the quest for political autonomy. The duke established a blockade around the city that crippled it economically and devastated villages in the country-side. After five years of miserable deprivation, Harley de Sancy, a French military commander raised 12,000 troops, most of whom were Swiss, and joined with Bern and Geneva in a campaign against Savoyard positions in de Vaud. Sancy's forces easily retook territory and pushed Charles Emmanuel's forces out of the region. But a critical reversal occurred in May 1589, when Henri III recalled Sancy (and his Swiss troops) back to France, leaving de Vaud vulnerable to a counteroffensive. To make matters even worse for Geneva, Bern subsequently signed a truce with Savoy giving up all claims to the Vaud and promising to relinquish defense of Geneva. Thus, Geneva was left on its own to fend off Charles Emmanuel I.

During a four-year war of attrition from 1589 to 1593, the city did just that. Geneva's fortifications held and small bands of troops harassed, ambushed, raided, and thwarted Savoyard positions in de Vaud. When France signed a general truce with Savoy in 1593, the standoff came to an end, though Geneva's status remained disputed. Nevertheless, the war prompted a decisive Genevan pivot away from a Bernese and Swiss alliance for French support, a turn reinforced by Henri IV's accession to the French throne in 1589.

An ill-fated, final attempt by Charles Emmanuel I in December 1602 to retake Geneva, known as the Escalade, sealed the city's independence. The civic militia defeated Savoyard efforts to sneak over the city wall and executed all the conspirators. As a result, Geneva and Savoy signed a treaty recognizing the city's independence.

CONCLUSION

Geneva's security enabled John Calvin and the Company of Pastors to launch a Reformed Protestant movement on an international stage. Yet the political sanctuary for Calvinism relied on the very local triangular tug of war between the powerful city-state of Bern, the fractious kingdom of France, and the overreaching duchy of Savoy. Engulfed in the Valois-Hapsburg conflict in the first half of the sixteenth century and overshadowed by the French religious wars in the second, Geneva gained and maintained independence for Calvinism and its refugees from Savoy by virtue of Bern's military prowess and political will. As intra-confessional disputes sapped the vigor of the Protestant alliance, Geneva increasingly looked to France for support against its pro-Hapsburg rival. By the mid-1580s, however, Geneva found itself isolated and stood on its own against Savoy. The narrative of struggle, persecution, and triumph endemic to Calvinism in the Reformation owed much to political and military circumstances in the Pays de Vaud.

SUGGESTED FURTHER READINGS

Bruening, Michael W. *Calvinism's first battleground: conflict and reform in the Pays de Vaud, 1528–1559*. Dordrecht: 2005.

Fehleison, Jill. *Boundaries of Faith: Catholics and Protestants in the Diocese of Geneva*. Kirksville, MO, 2010.

Gordon, Bruce. *The Swiss Reformation*. New York, 2002.

Manetsch, Scott M. *Theodore Beza and the Quest for Peace in France, 1562-1598*, Leiden, 2000.

Naphy, William G. *Calvin and the Consolidation of the Genevan Reformation*. New York, 1994.

ɞ

Daily Life in Geneva

Jill Fehleison

In the grand narrative of the European past, Geneva's history begins with the arrival of the Reformed faith. Historian Herbert D. Foster noted in 1903 that there was not a good history of Geneva written in English prior to the arrival of John Calvin. Sadly, this hole in the scholarship has not been filled more than a century later. The bulk of the works about Geneva focus on the period of John Calvin's residency there. Louis Binz offers a detailed study in French of the episcopal world of the diocese of Geneva prior to the Reformation, but there is still much to be learned of what life was like in Geneva prior to the changes brought by the introduction of the Reformation. By exploring the civic life of Geneva after the Reformed faith transformed many aspects of the landscape and function of the city within the larger history of the place, a richer picture through multiple lenses emerges.[1]

The geography of the place shaped its physical, cultural, economic, and religious development from the first settlement on the site that we know as Geneva. Julius Caesar mentioned a settlement along a lake and a bridge over the Rhone in 58 BC that is most likely on the spot we know today as Geneva. Its location made Geneva a natural commercial center, but it also had its downside as troops would use the natural paths near the city to make their

---

[1] The Following articles and books were used for this chapter: Louis Binz, *Vie Religieuse et Reforme Ecclesiastique Dans le Diocese De Geneve, Pendant le Grand Schisme et la Crise Conciliaire, 1378–1450* (Geneva: Alex Jullien, Libraire, 1973); E. William Monter, *Calvin's Geneva* (New York: John Wiley and Sons, 1967); Carrie F. Klaus, "Architecture and Sexual Identity: Jeanne de Jussie's Narrative of the Reformation in Geneva," *Feminist Studies* 29:2 (Summer 2003): 278–297; Herbert Darling Foster, "Geneva before Calvin (1387–1526): The Antecedents of a Puritan State," *The American Historical Review* 8:2 (January 1903): 217–240; Nicole Bouvier et al., *Geneva, Zurich, Basel: History, Culture, and National Identity* (Princeton, NJ: Princeton University Press, 2014); Jeffrey R. Watt, "Calvinism, Childhood, and Education: The Evidence from the Genevan Consistory," *The Sixteenth Century Journal* 33:2 (Summer 2002): 439–456.

way to wars in Northern Italy and the Low Countries. In the early modern period, Geneva was unique from other "Swiss" cities as it was not part of the Swiss Confederation. It shared a much larger border with France than with the Swiss states. While Geneva had relationships with other cities, its unique place in Europe gave it a singular culture. It was always a crossroads for other peoples and cultures based on its location. Geneva served as the center of distribution in the region for merchandise and amenities.

The geography of a hill, the Rhone River, and Lake Geneva naturally split the city into two. The hill was probably first a citadel for the Helvetic Tribe and then the bishops built their cathedral there in the sixth century. The main distinction of the layout was the divide between the Upper and Lower City, and this division can probably be traced back to the late Roman period. The lower city grew up along a plain that was near natural trade routes of the river and the lake. This was the commercial area since the Romans and was the place of the great fifteenth-century fairs. Men of letters, lawyers and jurists, and clerks and city officials tended to live in the Upper City while businessmen and merchants lived in the Lower City. The streets of the Lower City were lined with tiny shops known as *hauts-blancs*, which were small wooden structures erected for the fifteenth-century fairs and rented to foreign artisans and merchants. Like many towns and cities of the early modern world, crafts could sometimes be confined to a particular area. For example, tanners were located in a small area near the Rhone River because of the smell produced by their trades and their need for water.

Domestic dwellings were scattered throughout the city and style was based on economic status. With security always in mind, houses of the wealthy built in the fourteenth and fifteenth centuries were known as *maison-forte* because they could withstand a military attack. They were imitations of homes built in northern Italian cities that worried about sieges from the frequent invasions of French and Imperial armies. The wealthy would have a courtyard or garden near their fortified homes. Artisans would typically have narrow rectangular dwellings usually made of tile as wood had been forbidden since the fourteenth century due to fire dangers. The ground floor would hold the shop and storeroom, and there would be a back stairwell to the owner's living quarters on the second floor. Some had a third floor for children and servants. Home furnishings were simple with only a wood table, benches, stools, and maybe a storage cabinet. There might also be a bed with a curtain for the head of the household and his wife. Small lots of 20 × 50 feet divided up in the fifteenth century were large enough for a small garden in the back. It was a compact city designed for safety and commerce.

Geneva was an important town but not a great city even by medieval norms. The city grew over the course of the fourteenth century despite the arrival of the bubonic plague. The population was between 10,000 and 11,000 for much of the fifteenth century, but it was never religiously diverse. There were no Jews in Geneva after 1490 when the leaders decided to expel them from the city. When the Reformation arrived, the population had risen to almost 12,000, and it was the most populated of the Swiss cities. Geneva was a city that periodically needed replenishing from outsiders and was a city of immigrants prior to the Reformation, with people migrating from the countryside, Italian cities, and France. Most of the immigrants that settled in Geneva were from Savoy and France, particularly from Burgundy, but some wealthy Italians also settled in the Alpine city.

The city grew more important and powerful economically during the fifteenth century as a result of successful merchants and craftsmen. The Swabian printer Adam Steinschaber arrived the 1470s after working under Johannes Gutenberg in Mainz, Germany. Several other printers soon followed and the city saw the establishment of a printing industry that would be critical to the Reformation. Printing was not the only economic driver in the city. Geneva was the site of important fairs with each one lasting 10 days. As a result of its successful economy, it became an important banking city with the Medici of Florence opening a branch bank in 1424. The fairs declined during the second half of the fifteenth century largely as a result of Louis XI, the king of France, forbidding French merchants from selling their wares at the fairs in Geneva because he was promoting similar fairs in Lyons, a neighbor downstream on the Rhone River. As a result of this decline, Italian banking houses also began to shift from Geneva to Lyons. The fairs continued with German and Swiss merchants and were important enough to the Swiss cantons of Fribourg and Berne for them to aid Geneva in the late fifteenth century when the House of Savoy tried to assert itself over Geneva. Its economic fortunes remained closely tied to the region.

Like most towns of the early modern world, walls and gates controlled access to the city. Visitors had to present themselves at one of the city's gates and the walls would also prove crucial to Geneva's defenses against military attacks. The city was built for defense but depended on food and other services from outside the walls. It could never completely be closed off to outsiders, and even after the Reformation, it maintained personal economic ties to inhabitants from the surrounding area despite many of them remaining Catholic. Its fortifications proved crucial on numerous occasions in the early modern period in preventing the dukes of Savoy from taking the city, notably in the War of 1589 and during the *Escalade* of December 1602.

While Geneva was a regional center, it would not be called an international city even though it had a regular influx of visitors and settlers from other places. Being a city of merchants and craftsmen, the population of the city was culturally different from those that lived in the countryside and provided much of the food consumed by the city's inhabitants. Agriculture of the mountainous region included herds of sheep and cows, and the cheese of the area was sought after. The land along the shores of Lake Geneva also proved to be fertile for viticulture. After the Reformation, the Catholic/Protestant divide between the city dwellers and the rural populations highlighted their differences further. So, while not an international city before the Reformation, Geneva was an important regional hub to commercial enterprises and to the house of Savoy during the early modern period. Annecy was the only other city in the region that possessed important industry.

Geneva is often described as a sober town not possessing the culture or nightlife of other European cities. It did not grow at the same rate over the course of the sixteenth century as a city like London, which more than tripled in population during the same period and produced unprecedented creative works. Immigration patterns changed as a result of the Reformation and the arrival of John Calvin. No longer were new arrivals just looking for better economic opportunities. Religious and war refugees made up the bulk of new inhabitants of Geneva from the middle of the sixteenth century onward, and the city saw large swings in its population as a result. During the 1550s, when persecution increased against the Huguenots in France, Geneva saw its population double from 12,000 to 13,000 to more than 25,000. Many of these refugees proved to be temporary and returned to France in the 1560s when the conditions improved there for them. There was also a flood of temporary refugees from the surrounding region in 1589 due to war with the Duke of Savoy. Between the peak of population in 1560 (at around 25,000) to 1590, the number of inhabitants returned to its previous levels of about 12,000. The only city near Geneva that was a similar size was Lyons. Population may have risen to around 13,000 by the end of the sixteenth century as a result of more refugees coming from the civil wars in France and religious persecution in other places. While the events of the sixteenth century dramatically changed and disrupted the population of Geneva, the city did not see the same sustained growth over the course of the century that other European cities did, as the geography of the rugged Alpine terrain made it difficult for any city to expand.

Geneva's place as a center of international Calvinism is well established, but prior to the Reformation, Geneva was an episcopal city, home to the bishop and his cathedral. The diocese and much of the influence and power that goes along with being a Catholic See were in the city. Until the 1520s, the bishops had come from the ducal family and the majority were absent from the city for much of their tenure of office. The last bishop left the city for good in July 1533. The rhythm of the city would have followed the traditional Catholic calendar observing important feast days throughout the year, celebrating the period of Advent and the birth of Christ in December, observing Lent in winter, and participating in confession and the Eucharist at Easter. The annual cycle provided structure for those inside and outside the city walls.

There were seven parishes established in Geneva to which families would have belonged. By the middle of the thirteenth century, the Cathedral of St. Pierre was completed in the upper city. In the fifteenth century, the century prior to the Reformation, Geneva had an important building boom, particularly parish churches under the leadership of the bishops. Over the course of the fifteenth century, four parish churches of Geneva were reconstructed: Madeleine, which became the Temple de la Madeleine; Notre-Dame-la-Neuve, a quaint chapel that became a lecture hall, "the Calvin Auditory," for the Reformed Church and was frequented by John Calvin; St. Germain, one of the oldest churches in the town with Gothic architectural style where Guillaume Farel preached; and St. Gervais, which became the Temple of St. Gervais. Much of the religious art created during this fifteenth-century construction was destroyed in the iconoclasm of the Reformation and the churches either became Protestant temples or secular buildings.

Unlike other cities in the fifteenth century such as Florence, religious houses never played a huge role in the life of the city. As of 1450, there was only a Franciscan house and one Dominican house within the city. Several convents were founded near the city. The best known religious house associated with Geneva was the convent of St. Clare founded in 1473 and located near the cathedral, today the location of the Palais de Justice. It was the only female religious house located in the city and a relatively recent addition when Geneva embraced the Reformation. One of the nuns, Jeanne de Jussie, wrote an account of how the women were forced to abandon their house and take up residency in Annecy in 1535 after Geneva's acceptance of the Reformation. All the religious houses were ultimately removed from the landscape of the city.

One of the most important changes brought by the new ideas of the Reformation was the remaking of the sacred space by the civic and religious leaders of the city. The church landscape changed as a result of the Reformation. The official residence of the bishop on the square of the cathedral was converted into a public prison. A chronicle of Michel Roset composed in

1562 mentions that there were four main churches in the city down from the seven Catholic parishes. They included St. Pierre and St. Germain in the Upper City and St. Gervais and La Madeleine in the Lower City. In 1536, after the Grand Council adopted the Reformation, school was made mandatory for all children in Geneva. The increase of the number of children in school would have changed the daily life of families and required new spaces to house the schools. The secondary school was housed in the former Franciscan monastery at Rive. Beyond the reuse and remaking of former Catholic spaces, much of the physical layout of the city remained the same. Town squares included the Place du Bourg-de-Four near St. Pierre, which was a crossroad of the routes leading into the city; the Place de la Fusterie; the Place du Molard near the lake; and the Place de Longemalle. There were three butchers' markets, two grain markets, a few fountains, and enough wells to supply the inhabitants of the city with water. There were two hospitals with one for the poor and another for plague victims, which was located outside the city in the Plainpalais. Despite the changes to people's spiritual lives as a result of the new doctrine, material needs remained the same.

The architecture and physical layout changed little from the days of being an episcopal city to becoming the center of the Reformed faith under Calvin in the sixteenth century. Calvin's Geneva was not particularly prosperous and could not afford to build grand new buildings in her often overcrowded spaces. The narrow facades and Gothic windows were not replaced by styles inspired by the Renaissance until the seventeenth century. The home of the Turrettini family on the rue L'Hotel de Ville built in the second decade of the seventeenth century was the beginning of the new style. No private home that existed during the time of Calvin survives today.

After the Reformation, Geneva's relationship with inhabitants inside and outside the city walls changed. Many of those who lived outside the walls remained Catholic. In addition, religious leadership was in the hands of French immigrants like Calvin. While the majority of those who lived and worked in and around Geneva communicated in a French dialect that differed from that spoken by the pastors, the differences were not so great as to prevent communication between the locals and the new arrivals from France. There were cases of families continuing to socialize and even intermarry with Catholic family and friends who lived outside the city. This continued contact often had to do with the material care and support of children. Parents would sometimes decide to send their children to live with Catholic relatives and friends. These families would be brought before the consistory for failing to raise and educate their children in the Reformed tradition. Civic supervision of the material well-being of its inhabitants led to church deacons overseeing the distribution of charity to needy children and families and heads of household being responsible for the support and education of children and servants. The city became less connected to its neighbors outside the walls, and the French language introduced by the pastors became more widely used.

Geneva is a city with a long and rich history prior to the arrival of the Reformation. The commercial and religious life was deeply tied to the region through trade, immigration, and episcopal activities. While the religious culture and immigration patterns changed after the arrival of John Calvin and other reformers, the physical layout of the city changed very little. Industries like printing that began in the late fifteenth century flourished in the sixteenth century as a publishing center for Protestant works. Catholic space was repurposed for both sacred and secular purposes. There is still much to be uncovered about what life was like in this Alpine city for its less famous inhabitants before and after the Reformation.

SUGGESTED FURTHER READING

Binz, Louis. *A Brief History of Geneva*, trans. Jean Gunn. Geneva: Chancellerie d'Etat, 1985.

Engammare, Max. *On Time, Punctuality, and Discipline in Early Modern Calvinism*, trans. Karin Maag. New York and Cambridge: Cambridge University Press, 2010.

Jussie, Jeanne de. *The Short Chronicle: A Poor Clare's Account of the Reformation of Geneva*, ed. and trans. Carrie F. Klaus. Chicago: University of Chicago Press, 2006.

Monter, E. William. "Historical Demography and Religious History in Sixteenth-Century Geneva," *The Journal of Interdisciplinary History* 9:3 (Winter 1979): 399–427.

Calvin's Geneva New York: John Wiley & Sons, 1967.

Naphy, William G. *Calvin and the Consolidation of the Genevan Reformation*. Louisville, KY: Westminster John Knox Press, 2003 (1994 Reprint).

Scott, Tom. *The Swiss and Their Neighbors, 1460–1560: Between Accommodation and Aggression*. Oxford: Oxford University Press, 2017.

11

Reforming the City-State

Government in Geneva

William G. Naphy

Whenever Geneva is mentioned one thinks of Calvin, Beza and the establish-ment of Reformed structures and theology. The great names that stand out are other ministers (Des Gallars), famous printers (Estienne) and Calvin's great opponents: Castellio, Servetus and Bolsec.[1] Thus, Geneva becomes more the place where Calvin lived and wrote and less a locale with its own history and idiosyncratic historical context.[2] In particular, one forgets that Geneva was a city-state Republic squeezed by an expansionist Berne, a revanchist Savoy and a turbulent France. By focusing on Calvin and the Reformation one forgets that Geneva's adoption of Protestantism was the direct result of the city's Revolution from Savoy. By discussing the city's government, the spotlight returns to this political upheaval that created the city-state in which Calvin found refuge. Geneva's political structures were critical in facilitating (and complicating) Calvin's work and must be understood in their own right.

In 1519, Geneva's merchant elite took part in a failed attempt to free Geneva from the suzerainty of Savoy and attach the city to the Swiss Confederation. The revolt's failure led to a period of direct, personal rule by the duke who took up residence in what was the largest and most profitable city in the duchy. However, his residence simply reminded everyone of the problematic nature of Geneva's 'constitutional' situation in the early decades of the sixteenth century and led to a second, and successful, revolt in the early 1530s.

The first problem for the now independent (and Protestant) republic was to apportion the powers previously held by Savoyard and ecclesiastical authorities.

---

[1] See William Naphy, *Consolidation of the Genevan Reformation* (Manchester: University Press, 1994), 88–89 (Castellio), 172–174 (Bolsec), 182–185 (Servetus).
[2] John B. Roney and Martin I. Klauber, eds., *The Identity of Geneva* (London: Greenwood, 1998).

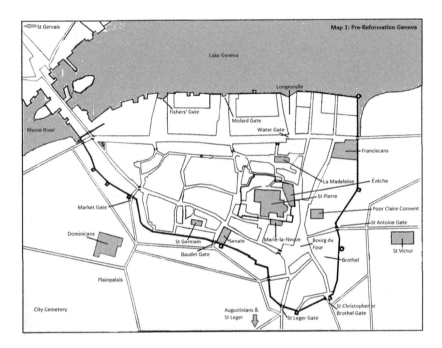

Map 1: Pre-Reformation Geneva

Ducal power had been exercised by the resident *vidomme*. In addition, the prince-bishop held both secular and ecclesiastical power around Geneva. Finally, the cathedral canons and the various monastic communities held secular powers. As landowners, the bishop, the canons and the abbots all exercised judicial roles, especially 'low justice'. 'Higher justice' (e.g., appeals as well as significant capital) crimes were referred to superior secular authorities (e.g., the *vidomme*). Church officials also had powers of presentment to various benefices in the area. Finally, they controlled major buildings within the city and significant property in the countryside (see Map 1 and Map 2). In other words, key judicial powers were held by the duke's representative and church officials. These were balanced by the traditional 'rights and privileges' (*libertes et franchises*) wrung from the duke in the medieval period. These were exercised and protected by the Senate (Small Council, *Petit Conseil*). One of the key problems for the new republic was the 'nationalisation' and integration of these judicial and landowning powers into a constitutional framework built around the city's existing structures.

This meant the nationalisation of the (geographical and judicial) 'possessions' of the Church. Map 2 shows the fractured nature of the Genevan 'nation'. Because it had appropriated the church's lands upon converting to Protestantism, it had a physicality that was not contiguous. Map 2 also highlights the complexity of seizing church possessions. Not only were the

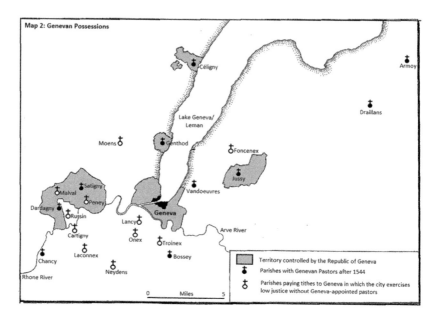

Map 2: Genevan Possessions

physical holdings of the city-state disparate, power was not exercised everywhere in the same way.[3] The city had the significant power to appoint
ministers. But, appointing ministers did not mean full control of the parishes – superior justice often was in Bernese hands. Thus, Geneva's government did not rule over a unified geography nor were its powers complete in
all the areas over which it held sway. Trying to deal with a situation that was
so fractured caused considerable institutional and, more importantly, political problems for the nascent republic.

The wider political reality in which the city found itself meant these administrative, judicial and governmental problelms were all but insoluble. The government wanted complete control over its rural parishes but could not risk a
confrontation with Berne who provided the military support necessary to
secure the city's independence. The city was also relatively poor until the influx
of French religious refugees brought significant sums of money (i.e., 'hard
currency') into Geneva in the 1550s.[4] This made Geneva's government militarily
dependent on Berne and financially dependent on Zurich and Basel who
funded, in particular, Geneva's 'national defence' spending for decades.[5]

---

[3] William Naphy, 'From Prince-Bishopric to City-State', in E. Nelson and J. Wright (eds.),
   Layered Landscapes (Oxford: Routledge, 2017), 134–149.
[4] Antoine Babel, *Histoire économique de Genève* (Geneva: Jullien, 1963).
[5] William Naphy, 'Genevan National Security and Defence Spending', *War in History* 5:4
   (1998): 379–399.

This situation presented the new government with a quandary. How was it to maintain its independence and its Swiss, Protestant (financial and military) support? This issue split the city's governing elite in the late 1530s resulting not only in a political crisis but also a clash with its ministers (Guillaume Farel and Jean Calvin). The Senate agreed to a treaty ('articles') with Berne effectively ceding control over its rural holdings. The resulting political clash between the articles' supporters (*Articulants*) and their opponents (Farel's supporters, hence *Guillermins*) nearly destroyed the government and the revolution.[6] In the end, the Guillermins prevailed, Calvin returned and the city set about creating a 'constitution' to regularise the post-revolutionary situation. The government also committed itself to a policy aimed at joining the Swiss Confederation.[7] While a discussion of politics is not necessary to understanding the city's governmental structures it is essential to understanding why those structures came into existence in post-*Articulants* 1542 and why that settlement was unable to last beyond the mid-1550s. They were born in a political crisis and papered over significant political issues.

The structure of the city's body politic also had an impact on its governmental institutions and how they operated in practice.[8] The city recognised four types of 'residents'. First were Geneva's *citoyens* (citizens). They were the children of (at least one) Genevan citizen and had been born in the city. By right they held the vote (if male and older than 25) and could hold all civic offices. The city also had naturalised citizens (*bourgeois*). These were men (and their families) who received civic status for a fee and, occasionally, free for 'services rendered'. The fee was modest though increased dramatically in the 1550s to take advantage of the coin-rich refugees who wanted status – and security.

Naturalised citizens passed full citizenship to their Genevan-born children. In addition, they voted, but could not be senators. This contrasts with the contemporary European norm in which naturalised citizens only occasionally could vote and were normally prohibited from a wide range of offices. Geneva's relatively lax attitude to naturalised citizens was the result of its traditional use of naturalisation – to turn Genevans from its rural hinterland into *citoyens*. In effect, the system never anticipated mass migration.

The last two categories had few civic rights though some civic security. Registered aliens (*habitants*) were given residency papers allowing them to live, work, and rent in the city. *Natifs* were poor locals who came from

---

[6] Naphy, *Consolidation*, 34–43.
[7] See William Naphy, 'Genevan Diplomacy and Foreign Policy, c. 1535–1560', in W. Kaiser, C. Sieber-Lehmann and C. Windler (eds.), *En Marge de la Confédération* (Basel: Schwabe, 2001), 189–219.
[8] Alfred Perrenoud, *La population de Genève XVIe–XIXe siècles* (Geneva: Jullien, 1979).

families that had never gained civic status in the past – or they were poor migrants from Geneva's rural possessions unable to afford naturalisation. However, throughout the sixteenth century the vast majority of the residents of the city were either *citoyens* or *bourgeois* – that is, able to vote and hold (most) offices. This meant a very active and engaged body politic.

This voting population met, as the General Assembly, twice a year. In November, secondary elections were held for the *Lieutenant* (investigating magistrate) and his assistants (*auditeurs*), and to set the annual price for grain (hence, bread) and wine. In late January, the city held its main elections, which elected all the councils (see following text) and other civic officers. This was not a 'democracy' though. The slate of candidates (normally twice those needed for the available posts) was provided by the outgoing Senate. The General Assembly was also expected to ratify the decisions of the Senate for the previous year. On occasion, especially during a period of crisis or political chaos, the General Assembly could be convoked to advise (and consent) to possible solutions. These two elections were held to ensure 'continuity'. In November, the full panoply of magistrates was in place for the election of the *Lieutenant* and, in January, the *Lieutenant* provided magisterial authority for the election of the rest of the government. So, while Geneva had an annual turnover of magistrates at no point was it 'without a government'.

What did the magistrates do? The *Lieutenant* and his assistants were responsible for investigating and prosecuting crime (akin to the Scottish procurator-fiscal). Legislative and executive power (along with supreme judicial authority) resided with the Senate. This was comprised of four ruling syndics two each from the 'Upper' and 'Lower' City, which ensured representation for the part of Geneva (St Gervais) on the other (right) bank of the Rhone. The syndics could not be closely related and individuals could only serve as syndic once every four years. In addition there were 20 senators and a *saultier* (or factor/steward) who, with the syndics were the full Senate (*Petit Conseil*). The Senate also had a secretary who kept minutes and a treasurer for accounts. The Senate met almost every day and their minutes were copious annually comprising about 400 folios.

There were a further 35 counsellors who were elected to serve, with the Senate, as the Council of Sixty (*Conseil des LX*). The Sixty met exceptionally and most often to discuss foreign affairs. In effect, they were the Senate's senior advisors. In addition, this body of magistrates (syndics, senators and senior advisors) could be augmented by a further 140 elected counsellors to form the Council of the Two Hundred (*Conseil des CC*). This body passed legislation and was the main way of involving the wider body politic short of invoking the full General Assembly.

There were also a whole host of other magisterial positions though these were often held by counsellors.[9] For example, rural justice and governmental oversight was exercised by *chastellains*. The city also had a *hospitalier* and assistants (*procureurs*) to oversee the city's poor relief system (the General Hospital), which replaced the plethora of small monastic foundations.[10] The General Hospital was based in the former Franciscan monastery (see Map 1) and funded through rents from secularised church lands.[11] The city also supported the pre-Reformation school system, which had been greatly enhanced by moving into the Poor Claires convent. However, the school-teachers were employees of the state not magistrates.[12] Nevertheless, elected officials were actively involved in the management of the school system.

As one might expect in an early modern republican system, there was an attempt to include 'checks and balances'. However, this was less about balancing institutions (e.g., legislative, executive, judicial) than ensuring 'voices' for leading families and political viewpoints. This was most apparent in the limitations on election to the syndicate. Likewise, the frequency of elections and the large number of elected magistrates further ensured a large percentage (c. 10%) of the eligible voting male population held some office. Moreover, by creating the post of *Lieutenant* the city apportioned much of the judicial power of the ducal and ecclesiastical away from the Senate while ensuring it remained the 'supreme court'. This maintained the most important element of the traditional 'rights and privileges': citizens, in the final analysis, judged their peers – other Genevan citizens.

Unsurprisingly, in a new constitutional order, these traditional rights were under pressure from the new structures. This was most apparent in the other 'novel' creation of the post-Revolution/Reformation – the Consistory.[13] Although the government had discussed the creation of a church court during Calvin's exile (1538–1541), the institution that came into existence in 1542 was very much the creation of the post-*Articulants* constitutional committee on which Calvin sat.

Magisterial concern about the Consistory's potential to upset the traditional rights and privileges was apparent from the outset. Two

---

[9] For full details, see Naphy, *Consolidation*, 38–40.

[10] Refugees had the privately funded *Bourse française*, Jeannine Olson, *Calvin and Social Welfare* (Selinsgrove, PA: Susquehanna University, 1989).

[11] On the hospital, see Bernard Lescaze, *Sauver l'âme, nourrir le corps* (Geneva: Hospice Général, 1985).

[12] William Naphy, 'The Reformation and Evolution of Geneva's Schools', in B. Kümin (ed.), *Reformations Old and New* (Aldershot: Scolar, 1997), 185–202.

[13] On the Consistory's 'constitutional position', see William Naphy, 'Calvin's Consistory: Secular Court?', in M. Engammare, A. Vauautgaerden and F. Bierlaire (eds.), *L'Intime du Droit à la Renaissance* (Geneva: Libraire Droz, 2014), 397–408.

characteristics of the Consistory, as a constitutional body, were unique. First, every Genevan pastor (c. 12 ministers) sat on the court. This is important. Unlike consistories in other Reformed polities (most especially Scotland, which came closest to the Genevan model), the Genevan consistory included as many ministers as lay members and, in effect, was a body constituted by the nation-states' entire ministerial cadre.

The state strongly supported the Consistory's efforts to coerce adherence to religious practice and belief. Attendance at weekly sermons was a legal obligation. Failure to attend resulted in an appearance before the Consistory and, potentially, a fine and brief jail sentence imposed by a secular court. It also had the power to excommunicate or, rather, recommend for excommunication.[14] Clearly, there was magisterial concern that a body with so many ministers might be judging citizens. This arose from two issues. The first, obviously, was the tradition that citizens would, on final appeal, be judged by the Senate and, second, all but one of the city's ministers during Calvin's ministry were foreign.

To serve as a check and balance in this potentially problematic situation, the constitutional arrangement introduced a novelty: all elders had to be elected counsellors.[15] The chairman of the Consistory was a ruling syndic and two further senators served as elders. The final (normally) eight elders were elected from the Sixty and the Two Hundred (in theory 3 and 5, respectively). This meant that the Consistory was comprised of the nation's entire ministerial corps *as well as* a subcommittee of the city-state's three elected councils.

There were two further bodies that were integral to the Genevan political structure albeit they had no official governmental role. It would be wrong to assume they were not part of the system governing Geneva, however. The Company of Pastors was the collection of all the city's ministers (i.e., the ministerial 'half' of the Consistory – hence, the reason for seeing it as part of the city's 'government'). It met weekly (as did the Consistory) with a key 'constitutional' role of vetting potential ministers. In addition, the ministers held a form of peer-reviewed Bible exposition (*congrégations*) that was open to the public on a weekly basis.[16] This meant that the ministers developed a strong sense of internal cohesion, which has to be borne in mind when thinking about their role on the Consistory.[17]

---

[14] Christian Grosse, *Les rituels de la Cène* (Geneva, Droz, 2008).
[15] On the elders see William Naphy, 'Consistories', in C. Parker and G. Starr-Lebeau (eds.), *Judging Faith, Punishing Sin* (Cambridge: Cambridge University Press, 2017), 104–116.
[16] Erik De Boer, *The Genevan School of the Prophets* (Geneva: Droz, 2012).
[17] On the ministers' weekly work, see Elsie McKee, *The Pastoral Ministry and Worship in Calvin's Geneva* (Geneva: Droz, 2016).

The Company's ability to affect politics and government albeit with no official governmental role is also evident in the Baptismal Name Controversy.[18] Without going into details, the key point is that the ministers, acting on their own initiative, 'outlawed' certain names. The Senate validated this after the fact and fined and jailed Genevans who protested as well as giving ministers the power to add names to the list of proscribed names. Thus, with no formal role, the Company exercised considerable quasi-judicial and quasi-legislative power.

Finally, from 1559, the city founded the Academy (using proceeds from the confiscated estates of Calvin's political opponents of the mid-1550s, the so-called Libertines or *Enfants de Genève*).[19] The Academy became (as with the Consistory, though to a lesser extent) a possible flashpoint between ministers and magistrates. For the Senate, the Academy was meant to be an educational 'jewel' to attract prominent fee-paying students while the ministers saw it as a seminary to train French pastors.[20] As such, it highlighted a continuing debate in Geneva (not wholly settled in the mid-1550s) whether the republic should face east (toward closer integration with the Swiss) or west (to the conversion of France). This final civic institution founded at the end of a decade that saw constitutional clashes that almost tore the nation apart, it is hardly surprising that the city established a second constitutional committee in 1562 that included Calvin. Its most important result was codifying the independence of the Consistory – it had the absolute right to excommunicate without appeal.

In sum, was the Genevan republic democratic? No. Was it representative? Again, not really. Did it have important and effective checks and balances? Somewhat. Most importantly, because of the large number of magistrates and the restrictions on the syndicate, the city was politically responsive. It was also, through its *bourgeois*, very 'open'. In the aftermath of two waves of French immigration (1550s and after the 1572 St Bartholomew's Day Massacre), the body politic was changed substantially becoming more 'French'. Likewise, unsurprising post-revolutionary problems with new structures and institutions were apparent and wracked the republic for more than two decades. Indeed, laying aside those theological disputes (Bolsec, Castellio, Servetus) that troubled the city little, but that are the focus much historical research, the main crises (*Articulants*, slashed breeches, baptismal names, libertines),[21] which nearly broke the city and certainly endangered Calvin's ministry, were the result of problems arising in the governing of the city-state with its new structures and officers.

[18] Karen E. Spierling, *Infant Baptism in Reformation Geneva* (Aldershot: Ashgate, 2005).
[19] Naphy, *Consolidation*, 188–199.
[20] Karin Maag, *Seminary or University?* (Aldershot: Scolar, 1995).
[21] On slashed breeches see Naphy, *Consolidation*, 145.

SUGGESTED FURTHER READINGS

Maag, Karin. *Seminary or University?* Aldershot: Scolar, 1995.

McKee , Elsie. *The Pastoral Ministry and Worship in Calvin's Geneva*. Geneva: Droz, 2016.

Naphy, William. "From prince-bishopric to city-state," in E. Nelson & J. Wright, eds., *Layered Landscapes*. Oxford: Routledge, 2017, 134–49.

  "Consistories," C. Parker & G. Starr-Lebeau, eds., *Judging Faith, Punishing Sin*. Cambridge: Cambridge University Press, 2017, 104–116.

  Consolidation of the Genevan Reformation. Manchester: University Press, 1994.

Roney, John B. and Klauber, Martin I., eds., *The Identity of Geneva*. (London: Greenwood, 1998.

12

ᐸᗌ

Consistories and Discipline

Jeffrey R. Watt

John Calvin and other Reformed Protestants placed a great deal of emphasis on discipline, and one noted historian has even argued that Calvinist discipline contributed to "the making of the modern mind."[1] Some Reformed leaders, such as Martin Bucer, claimed that discipline was the third mark of the true church, the other two being the pure preaching of the Gospels and the proper administration of the sacraments. There were differences of opinion among Reformed thinkers, however, about how discipline was to be carried out. In Zurich, Ulrich Zwingli asserted that the Christian magistrates had the exclusive authority to discipline the faithful, including the right to excommunicate. By contrast, Bucer maintained that discipline should be under the purview of the pastors who were to be assisted by elders.[2] John Calvin, who had gotten to know Bucer during his stay in Strasbourg (1538–1541), reflected the older reformer's ideas on discipline. Although he never specifically recognized it as the third mark of the church, he placed enormous emphasis on discipline, describing it as the "sinews" of the church, and made the establishment of a new disciplinary institution, the consistory, a condition for his return to Geneva in 1541. Calvin composed the Geneva's ecclesiastical ordinances that prescribed that the consistory be comprised of the city's pastors and elders. Consistories became the prime instrument of discipline among the Reformed in sixteenth-century Europe.

Geneva's consistory was not the first Reformed disciplinary institution; that distinction went to Zurich's *Ehegericht*, which was founded in 1525 and had jurisdiction over issues concerning marriage and sexuality. Three years

---

[1] Heinz Schilling, *Civic Calvinism in Northwestern Germany and the Netherlands, Sixteenth to the Nineteenth Centuries* (Kirksville, MO: Sixteenth Century Publishers, 1991), 40.

[2] Amy Nelson Burnett, *The Yoke of Christ: Martin Bucer and Christian Discipline* (Kirksville, MO: Sixteenth Century Publishers, 1994), esp. 180–207.

later, inspired by the Zwinglian Reformation, Bern, Switzerland's most powerful state, embraced Protestantism, and it played an enormous role in spreading the Reformed movement in what would become French-speaking Switzerland. In 1528 Bern established in the city a morals court known as the *Chorgericht* (also known as the *consistoire suprême*). Starting in 1529, a consistory was established in each parish in Bernese territory, consisting of the pastor and at least two elders. These local consistories had the power to impose fines, brief jail terms, and certain forms of public humiliation; serious cases, such as suits for divorce, could be appealed to the *Chorgericht* in Bern.[3] Bern also supported William Farel, who, starting in 1530, led the conversion of Neuchâtel, today a Swiss canton, and through pressure from Bern, four consistories were eventually established there too. Reformed Protestants established similar disciplinary institutions in France, the Netherlands, and Scotland. These institutions all had much in common as far as structure is concerned. The consistories were all comprised of pastors and elders, and French consistories and Scottish kirk sessions often also included deacons. In most consistories, laymen easily outnumbered pastors. Geneva's consistory stood out from others by the prominence of its clergymen; a typical meeting was attended by roughly equal numbers of pastors and elders, and Calvin dominated this institution during his ministry.

Consistories were characterized by their localism. Apart from the territory of Bern, where local consistories were subordinate to the *Chorgericht*, consistorial discipline was generally highly decentralized; most consistories had jurisdiction only over the community in which each was found. Wherever they were established, consistories attacked a wide range of sins, such as fornication and adultery, blasphemy, drunkenness, attending Mass, marital discord, playing cards, dancing, and truancy from church. In France, their responsibilities extended beyond morals control to poor relief and financial administration.

Some of these Reformed disciplinary institutions, such as Bern's *Chorgericht* and other Swiss consistories were actual tribunals, which had the power to impose a range of secular punishments. The same was true of Scotland's kirk sessions, which actively collaborated with magistrates – some of whom were elders who served on the sessions – and even meted out corporal punishments. Most consistories, however, could not impose any secular penalties. In France, the royal government and, more often than not, even the local government were hostile to Protestantism. With the exception of a

---

[3] Heinrich Richard Schmidt, "Morals Courts in Rural Berne during the Early Modern Period," in Karin Maag (ed.), *The Reformation in Eastern and Central Europe* (Aldershot, and Brookfield, VT: Scolar Press/Ashgate, 1997), 155–181.

few that were located in towns dominated by Protestants, French consistories enjoyed no support from local magistrates and accordingly had no direct or indirect means of seeing miscreants punished for their misdeeds. In the Netherlands as well, membership in a congregation was voluntary, and so Reformed discipline did not have the coercive support of government. Geneva's consistory was, strictly speaking, not a tribunal and could not impose secular penalties. It did, however, work closely with the city council – all lay members of the consistory were in fact members of one of the three city councils – which could impose mundane punishments. From its inception, Geneva's consistory passed three types of sentences against sinners: it could admonish them (the most common sentence), excommunicate them, and refer them to the city council for criminal sentencing. By the later 1540s, Calvin's consistory could also oblige people to do *réparation*, a public confession of their sin in church, a penalty that was commonly used later for people who had committed apostasy in France during the Wars of Religion. The Scots also relied on public shaming, aptly seen in their use of the "seat of repentance" upon which sinners were obliged to sit facing the congregation for a prescribed number of Sundays.

There was considerable variation by region in the power consistories had over the sacrament of communion or, as the Reformed preferred to call it, the Holy Supper. In France and the Netherlands, consistories enjoyed a great deal of independence in admitting and excluding people from the Supper. In Scotland, the kirk sessions had the power to excommunicate, though they used it sparingly. In Switzerland, by contrast, Zwingli and Heinrich Bullinger insisted that all disciplinary powers resided with the magistrates alone, and both demonstrated a strong distaste for excommunication; as Bullinger noted, if Jesus allowed Judas to participate in the Last Supper, why should people who were guilty of much lesser sins be excluded from the sacrament? Starting in 1542, Pierre Viret for years pushed Bern to allow the church in Lausanne to excommunicate unrepentant sinners, but Bern never accorded this right.[4]

While all consistories sought to promote morality and attacked a wide range of sins, some disciplinary institutions also took aim at simple disputes between neighbors. Both Calvin's consistory and Bern's *Chorgericht* viewed hatred as incompatible with Christian piety and strove to eliminate conflicts and reconcile feuding parties; the *Chorgericht* even heard cases of violence whereas in Geneva, apart from domestic violence, violent acts usually were

---

[4] Michael W. Bruening, "Francophone Territories Allied to the Swiss Confederation," in Amy Nelson Burnett and Emidio Campi (eds.), *A Companion to the Swiss Reformation*, (Leiden, The Netherlands: Brill, 2016), 378.

under the purview of the city council, not the consistory. Actions against quarrels were in fact among the most common found in the registers of the consistory in Calvin's Geneva. In May 1550, for example, Calvin and his associates summoned two couples, Jean and Louise Bernard and François and Jeanne Bossey for quarreling. Jean Bernard insisted that he did not wish anyone ill, but the Bosseys accused Bernard of often insulting his own wife, calling her a "whore" and other shameful terms. Bernard denied this accusation, and the consistory urged them all to reconcile. They agreed to do so and "touched each other" to show this resolution.[5] This common expression of touching each other refers to a ritual of reconciliation made before the members of the consistory. It involved either a simple handshake or perhaps an embrace, and it was understood as a sign that both parties were pledging to put an end to all rancor and forget the original cause of the dispute. The effort in Geneva to settle quarrels through official channels predated the Reformation. In 1527, nine years before the conversion, the city council established the "peace council" (*Conseil de paix*) for the express purpose of settling disputes. This continuity may explain why Genevans did not resist the consistory's efforts to quell quarrels, unlike its claims to power over the Supper.[6]

As the Bernard/Bossey case shows, when two parties were quarrelling, the consistory was less interested in determining who the guilty party was than in settling the conflict. We of course cannot know how sincere these reconciliations were, but we do know that it was rather unusual for people, other than married couples, once reconciled to return before the consistory for the same disputes. The principal goal of the consistory was to maintain social order and assure that people bore no hard feelings toward others. Calvin and the consistory were convinced that animosity toward one's neighbor was incompatible with authentic piety. As Robert Kingdon aptly put it, in handling such disputes, the consistory resembled more a type of mandatory counseling service than a tribunal.[7]

When it first started functioning in the early 1540s, though it convoked people for a wide range of sins, the consistory of Geneva was most

---

[5] *Registres du Consistoire de Genève au temps de Calvin* (hereafter *R. Consist.*) 12 vols., ed. Isabella M. Watt et al. (Geneva: Droz, 1996–2018), 5: 76.

[6] Christian Grosse, "Aux origines des pratiques consistoriales de pacification des conflits: Le 'Conseil de paix,' (1527–1529)," in Sandra Coram-Mekkey (ed.), *Les registres du Conseil de la République de Genève sous l'Ancien Régime: Nouvelles approches, nouvelles perspectives* (Geneva: Archives d'Etat de Genève and Fondation de l'Encyclopédie de Genève, 2009), 29–63.

[7] Robert M. Kingdon (with Thomas A. Lambert), *Reforming Geneva: Discipline, Faith, and Anger* (Geneva: Droz, 2012), 101–129.

concerned with the religious practices of Genevans. They aggressively tried to root out Catholic practices such as attending Mass, saying prayers to the Virgin Mary, or abstaining from meat during Lent. One continues to find references in the registers to similar cases, particularly attending Mass in neighboring Savoy or France, but by 1550 it was rather unusual to find natives of Geneva who persisted in respecting practices that were specifically Catholic, such as saying prayers to the saints or for the dead. People truly committed to Catholicism had left Geneva by the mid-sixteenth century.

It is safe to say that most consistories encountered at least some resistance. Some members of prominent local families resented the power of Geneva's consistory and the strong influence of the pastors, who were all recent arrivals from France. The baptism of children occasioned many bitter quarrels in Geneva between parents and clergy over the selection of names. Throughout Christian Europe, the choice of names for children had always been the prerogative of parents and godparents. Calvin and other pastors demanded that Genevans give only biblical names to their children and aggressively tried to eliminate the names of certain saints. The competing aims of clergy and parents in the selection of names exploded in a number of acrimonious disputes starting in the 1540s. "Claude," for example, was a popular name for both boys and girls, but it was also the name of a local saint whom Genevans had long venerated. The pastors decried the existence of an "idolatrous" chapel in honor of Claude just seven leagues from Geneva. Though some magistrates were wary of the zeal with which Calvin and other ministers proscribed names as idolatrous or superstitious, they nonetheless came down in favor of the pastors on this issue. At Calvin's request, the city council banned the use of the name "Claude" and mandated that parents choose only among those names found in the Bible. The disputes over the naming of children pitted the native Genevan laity against the French clergy. Calvin and other pastors viewed the names of saints, among others, as utterly inappropriate for Christians. Genevans were understandably upset, however, at being told that their own names were linked to paganism and superstition and could not be passed on to their children and godchildren. Many natives, including members of influential families, expressed their anger and frustration at what they perceived as pastoral arrogance, but Calvin eventually succeeded in eradicating names such as Claude. Their actions were heavy-handed, but pastors succeeded in effecting conformity in the baptizing and naming of children.[8]

---

[8] Jeffrey R. Watt, "Childhood and Youth in the Genevan Consistory Minutes," in Herman Selderhuis (ed.), *Calvinus Praeceptor Ecclesiae: Papers of the International Congress on Calvin Research* (Geneva: Droz, 2004), 41–62.

From the early to the mid-1550s, there was disagreement in Geneva over
the question of the power to excommunicate, as a significant number of
Genevans were becoming increasingly upset by the growing authority of
Calvin and the consistory. Many locals, including some prominent lay
officials, proclaimed that only the city council had the right to excommunicate. Philibert Berthelier was a member of an influential Genevan family and
a bitter critic of Calvin who denied the powers of the consistory. Calvin
became most upset in 1553 when Berthelier, whom the consistory had
excluded from the Supper, petitioned and received permission from the city
council, not the consistory, to be readmitted to communion. Refusing to
admit defeat, Calvin and the other pastors protested that they would rather
die than allow Berthelier to take communion without first coming to the
consistory and apologizing for his errors.[9] This and similar conflicts were
not resolved definitively until 1555, when a drunken riot gave Calvin's
supporters the pretext to purge Geneva of opponents of the disciplinary
regime. The consistory's authority was never again questioned for the
remainder of Calvin's lifetime.

Notwithstanding the preceding examples of resistance, consistories
tended to enforce values that were shared by the community at large. To
investigate and reproach or prosecute sins, consistories everywhere
depended on the rank and file to denounce others for sins. The Scottish
laity, especially community leaders, widely supported the invasive moral
discipline of the kirk sessions, clearly seen in the significant number of
people who voluntarily confessed to sins that could not have otherwise been
discovered. In the Netherlands, Calvinist women viewed consistories as a
more effective venue than secular courts for redress of grievances and
defense of their honor. Genevans obviously embraced the notion that it
was everyone's duty to reproach anyone who blasphemed. To give just one
example, in July 1557 one man accused Humbert Troillet of a nearby village
of blasphemy, asserting that one day while working in a vineyard, Trolliet
cried out, "the body of God" (corps Dieu). The other man rebuked Trolliet,
who immediately prostrated himself and kissed the earth and begged God
for mercy. Two other men asserted that on another occasion, Trolliet yelled
at another, "Goddamn you," and kissed the earth right after they reproved
his words.[10] Clearly these other rural laborers considered it their duty to

[9] Christian Grosse, *L'excommunication de Philibert Berthelier: Histoire d'un conflit d'identité
     aux premiers temps de la Réforme genevoise (1547–1555)* (Geneva: Société d'Histoire et
     d'Archéologie de Genève, 1995).
[10] *R. Consist.* 12: 224, 231–232, 233–234.

scold anyone who blasphemed, and Trolliet's dropping to his knees to kiss the earth and ask forgiveness from God indicates that he, too, recognized this as a serious sin.

Some consistories had not only disciplinary but also pedagogical functions. Most striking is the fact that in the first years of its existence, the consistory of Geneva regularly questioned people who may have been summoned for something altogether different – such as fornication, swearing, or quarrels – about their church attendance and their knowledge of prayers and the Apostles' Creed. From 1542 to 1544, such questions were asked of about two-thirds of defendants, roughly half of whom demonstrated a satisfactory knowledge of the creed, for example. Those whose knowledge fell short were instructed to attend the sermons and the catechism and had to reappear to show their progress.[11] When summoned for their ignorance, one woman excused herself by saying that she had a "bad head" while a man complained that he had "such a thick head that he cannot retain anything of the preaching."[12] Such questions about people's knowledge of the faith, however, were rare starting in the mid-1540s. Although this could conceivably mean that the new scribe just did not bother recording such questions, a more plausible interpretation is that church leaders believed that Genevans had become better versed in the basics of the Reformed faith through the catechism and regular church attendance. By contrast, various Swiss consistories summoned people who were truant from church or did not participate in the Supper but never questioned them about their knowledge of prayers or creeds. Bern's authorities never gave pastors the authority to question those appearing before the consistories about their knowledge of the faith, and it has accordingly been argued that the consistory of Lausanne had only a repressive function, not an educational one, a conclusion that by and large could also be applied to Neuchâtel's consistories.[13]

Not surprisingly, consistories tended to enjoy the greatest success in changing behavior when they were backed by the coercive authority of magistrates. Through the kirk sessions, the Scots were no doubt the most effective in trying to implement Reformed discipline throughout an entire country. Among small city-states, Geneva almost certainly enjoyed

[11] Jeffrey R. Watt, "Women and the Consistory in Calvin's Geneva," *Sixteenth Century Journal* 24 (1993): 430–433.

[12] *R. Consist.* 1: 138, 104.

[13] Sylvie Moret Petrini, "'Ces Lausonnois qui 'pappistent': Ce que nous apprennent les registres consistoriaux lausannois (1538–1540)," *Revue historique vaudoise* 119 (2011): 139–151; Jeffrey R. Watt, "The Reception of the Reformation in Valangin, Switzerland, 1547–1588," *Sixteenth Century Journal* 20 (1989): 89–104.

unparalleled success in influencing the behavior of its residents. Though not adverse to employing punitive measures to enforce Reformed morality, throughout Europe consistories generally preferred persuasion over persecution in effecting social change. While religious and secular leaders were likely never entirely satisfied with the behavior and religious knowledge of common folk, we can say unequivocally that people in these various polities eventually truly became Reformed. Though it almost certainly took longer to take hold in rural areas, in the long run the Reformation was a success, thanks in part to the discipline of the consistories.[14]

SUGGESTED FURTHER READINGS

Benedict, Philip. *Christ's Churches Purely Reformed: A Social History of Calvinism*. New Haven, CT: Yale University Press, 2002.

Kingdon, Robert M. (with Thomas A. Lambert). *Reforming Geneva: Discipline, Faith, and Anger*. Geneva: Droz, 2012.

Mentzer, Raymond A., ed. *Sin and the Calvinists: Morals Control and the Consistory in the Reformed Tradition*. Kirksville, MO: Sixteenth Century Publishers, 1994.

Parker, Charles H., and Gretchen Starr-LeBeau, eds. *Judging Faith, Punishing Sin: Inquisitions and Consistories in the Early Modern World*. Cambridge: Cambridge University Press, 2017.

Spierling, Karen E.; Erik A. de Boer; and R. Ward Holder, eds. *Emancipating Calvin: Culture and Confessional Identity in Francophone Reformed Communities. Essays in Honor of Raymond A. Mentzer, Jr*. Leiden: Brill, 2018.

Watt, Jeffrey R. *The Making of Modern Marriage: Matrimonial Control and the Rise of Sentiment in Neuchâtel, 1550–1800*. Ithaca, NY: Cornell University Press, 1992.

---

[14] For more on consistories, see pertinent articles in *Emancipating Calvin: Culture and Confessional Identity in Francophone Reformed Communities. Essays in Honor of Raymond A. Mentzer, Jr.*, ed. Karen E. Spierling, Erik A. de Boer, and R. Ward Holder (Leiden, The Netherlands: Brill, 2018); and Charles H. Parker and Gretchen Starr-LeBeau, eds., *Judging Faith, Punishing Sin: Inquisitions and Consistories in the Early Modern World* (Cambridge: Cambridge University Press, 2017).

13

Reformed Education and the Genevan Academy

Karin Maag

On June 5, 1559, the Genevan Academy held its opening ceremonies. Gathered together in Saint Pierre Cathedral, the Genevan community came together to hear the academy's statutes read out loud and to listen to a speech by the new rector, Theodore Beza. In his address, Beza brought together what he saw as the two central strands of education: to gain knowledge and to grow in virtue and faith. He noted,

> The saying of Plato is well known: Knowledge that is devoid of righteousness must be called shrewdness rather than knowledge.. ... Yes indeed, you have not gathered in this place as many of the Greeks used to do, heading to their gymnasiums to engage in vain endeavors, but rather, imbued with the knowledge of true religion and liberal arts, to be able to magnify the glory of God and to be a support to your families and an honor to your homeland.[1]

Beza's opening speech set the tone for the Genevan Academy's approach to education: students were to gain knowledge in the humanities, ancient biblical languages, Scripture, and theology, but were also to develop their moral character and lives of faith. This double purpose shaped the Genevan Academy but was rooted in the wider understanding of education at the time.

Set up as a two-tier Reformed educational institution, offering training at both high school and university level, this academy was the culmination of many years of planning and fundraising. As envisioned by John Calvin and his colleagues in the Genevan Company of Pastors, the Genevan Academy's

---

[1] See the text of Beza's address in English translation (amended by this author in the light of the original) in Lewis Spitz, "Humanism and the Reformation," in Robert Kingdon (ed.), *Transition and Revolution: Problems and Issues in European Renaissance and Reformation History* (Minneapolis, MN: Burgess, 1974), 176–179.

purpose was to train boys and young men to become the next generation of leaders of Reformed communities, especially as pastors. Over the next decades, the Genevan Academy served as a highly effective educational center, preparing students for future careers in ministry, government, law, and other fields.

To understand the Genevan Academy's impact in the early modern era, we have to gain a better sense of the context from which it emerged. What schooling options existed in Geneva prior to 1559? What models did the Genevans look to when setting up their academy? A closer scrutiny of this educational context will help us assess how far Geneva borrowed its structure and aims for its academy from other institutions versus offering unique features. Increased knowledge about these preexisting or contemporary educational offerings can help explain the origins of the academy's key features and shed light on the reasons for the academy's longer-term success.

SCHOOLING IN GENEVA BEFORE 1559

The Medieval Legacy

To understand the context of schooling in Geneva before its official Reformation in 1536, it is worth recalling Geneva's political and religious situation in the late medieval era. At the time, Geneva was neither French nor Swiss: instead, it was one of the main cities in the territory of Savoy, ruled by a count (later a duke). Geneva was governed by a bishop, who held both spiritual and temporal power in the city. At various points, the ruler of Savoy and the bishop of Geneva worked hand in hand, but at other times, they were rivals vying for political dominance in the affairs of the city. Meanwhile, the bishop's temporal authority in Geneva also faced challenges from the growing confidence of the Genevan magistrates. These magistrates made known Genevans' increasing desire to run their own affairs, including in education.

Prior to the Reformation, education in Geneva was only available in two forms: either in vernacular schools (usually privately run, accessible to both boys and girls) or in a Latin school (either private or city-run, in practice only open to boys). Due to their ephemeral character, Geneva's medieval vernacular schools have left few traces in the records. However, Geneva's municipal Latin school, the Collège de Versonnex, is relatively well-attested in archival and secondary sources. In 1428, the Genevan magistrates called for the creation of a school and even designated a location near the Franciscan friary. The following year, a wealthy Genevan merchant, François de

Versonnex, made the project a reality by donating funds to set up the school. The words of the donation document are worth noting, as Versonnex's desire to link education and virtue formation proved to be a lasting feature of Genevan education.

> In the name of God, Amen.... The honorable and prudent François de Versonnex, Genevan citizen and merchant, ... wants ... to make use of some of the goods God entrusted to him for pious and salutary purposes, adding that in his opinion, educational discipline is a good work because it dispels ignorance, cultivates wisdom, shapes morals, confers virtues, and facilitates and encourages ethical public service.... He has therefore set up and built a house or building for instruction, to be used now and henceforth by rectors of schools dedicated to grammar, logic, and the liberal arts.[2]

Versonnex's aim to establish a school that would produce educated but also virtuous students dedicated to the public good was shared by many merchants, civic leaders, and humanist scholars in the fifteenth century. Indeed, the creation of a network of municipally run public Latin schools in the fifteenth and sixteenth century owed much to this collective vision.[3] Versonnex's donation document also made religious observances part of the regular school day, a practice that continued in Geneva's schools (albeit in a Reformed version) after the Reformation. Students at the Collège de Versonnex had to recite an Ave Maria and a Pater Noster on a daily basis in front of the altar in the school to honor the memory of François de Versonnex.[4]

Schooling in Geneva after 1536

The aim to provide quality Latin school education that emphasized not only academic preparation but also moral formation and religious instruction persisted after Geneva officially accepted the Reformation in 1536. The government's interest in having high-caliber schools had not abated in spite of the turmoil caused by the process of confessional change. Indeed, the urgent need to revitalize Geneva's Latin school was the second item on the

---

[2] English translation mine. See the short history of the Collège de Versonnex, an image of the donation manuscript, and a Latin and French transcription of the document at http://ge.ch/archives/1-moyen-age-college-de-versonnex (accessed March 12, 2018).

[3] For more on these schools see George Huppert, *Public Schools in Renaissance France* (Urbana: University of Illinois Press, 1984).

[4] For more on the Collège de Versonnex, see the opening chapter in Louis-J. Thévenaz, *Histoire du Collège de Genève* (Geneva: Département de l'instruction publique, 1896; Geneva: Slatkine reprints, 2009), 2–11.

agenda at the same meeting that accepted the Reformation in May 1536. The Genevan general council decided "One should find a learned man for this purpose [i.e. to teach] and that one should pay him a large enough salary so that he can teach and feed the poor [pupils], without asking them for fees, and that all must send their children to school and have them learn."[5] The new institution, known as the Collège de Rive, was up and running already by June 1536. This Latin school built on the legacy of the Collège de Versonnex but also expanded its offerings, adding the study of Greek and elementary Hebrew. The curriculum also now deepened religious instruction, including daily recitations of the Lord's Prayer, the Ten Commandments, and the Apostle's Creed and daily instruction in the Christian faith provided by the school's rector.[6] Much of what is known about the curriculum and pedagogical outlook of the Collège de Rive stems from an anonymous pamphlet detailing the school's aims, published in 1538 and likely penned by the school's first rector, Antoine Saulnier. The pamphlet detailed the school's healthy location, offerings, and mission, rejecting critics' assertions that Reformed schools were narrow-minded institutions focused solely on the Bible. The author noted,

> Even though we give priority to the Word of the Lord, this is not to say that we reject the knowledge of good letters, which certainly can follow and appropriately can take second place. And indeed, when these two things are united in this fashion, there is great uniformity and agreement that the Word of God should be the basis of all doctrine and that the liberal arts act as ways and means (not to be disdained) serving for the true and complete knowledge of that Word.[7]

This intent to balance a faithful focus on Scripture as the ultimate source of knowledge along with the desire to make use of the best of secular learning surfaced again in the Genevan Academy, as evidenced in Theodore Beza's inaugural address. Hence the Genevan Academy did not wrestle with these issues in a vacuum. Indeed, the Genevan Academy's leadership could look back to the Collège de Rive's 1538 pamphlet as an early exemplar of how these diverse streams of knowledge could be brought together in one curriculum.

---

[5] Ibid., 12.
[6] See William Naphy, "The Reformation and the Evolution of Geneva's Schools," in Beat Kümin (ed.), *Reformations Old and New: Essays on the Socio-Economic Impact of Religious Change c. 1470–1630* (Aldershot: Scolar Press, 1996), 185–202.
[7] *L'ordre et la manière d'enseigner en la ville de Genève au college*, in E.-A. Bétant, *Notice sur le Collège de Rive* (Geneva: Fick, 1866). Translation mine.

Although the Collège de Rive benefitted from the support of the Genevan government and from able instructors in the first years, the later years of the institution were troubled. The school faced a perennial shortage of qualified teachers willing to stay for the longer term, largely due to the poor level of pay. Underinvestment in the facilities also led to a challenging work environment, with some rectors complaining that the poor state of the buildings was causing the students to fall ill.[8] The other main challenge was the absence of any university-level instruction apart from the public lectures on Scripture given by Calvin and some of his fellow pastors. If Geneva wanted to offer educational opportunities that went beyond a Latin school, it had to look elsewhere for models.

MODELS FOR UNIVERSITY-LEVEL EDUCATION

The Genevan Situation

There was no university-level training available in Geneva prior to the Reformation, in spite of a plan in 1365, and again between 1418 and 1422, to establish a university in the city. In 1365, Amédée IV, Count of Savoy, obtained a charter from Emperor Charles IV for a Genevan university. The count hoped that a university would heighten his prestige and that of the territory, and would train clergy who would then support his cause against the bishop of the time. However, when the count went on crusade, the bishop of Geneva promptly seized the opportunity to petition the pope to quash the project. From 1418 to 1422, Bishop Jean de Rochetaillée prepared a plan for a Genevan university and obtained a papal charter. However, he was transferred before the plans could take shape, and his next two successors died soon after they were appointed, leading to a quiet shelving of the project.[9] With no university in the city, the nearest option for young Genevans seeking higher education was the University of Basel, set up in 1460.

Models outside Geneva

Thus the upper tier of the Genevan Academy as set up in 1559 was not modeled on any pre-Reformation instance of higher education within the

---

[8] Karin Maag, *Seminary or University? The Genevan Academy and Reformed Higher Education, 1560–1620* (Aldershot: Scolar Press, 1995), 8.

[9] Charles Borgeaud, *Histoire de l'université de Genève: l'académie de Calvin* (Geneva: Georg & Co., 1900), 2–13.

city, meaning that Calvin and his colleagues had to look elsewhere to find institutions of higher learning to emulate. In that regard, it is worth remembering that Geneva's academy was founded quite late, 20 or 30 years after its peer institutions got underway. That late start could be an advantage, as there were more examples of other educational models to emulate or adapt to Geneva's particular circumstances. Some of these options were relatively close at hand and operated within the same Reformed confessional framework, namely within the Swiss lands. The Swiss cities of Zurich and Bern, for instance, each created their own institutions of higher learning already in the 1520s, offering both Latin school and university-level training.[10] However, most scholars agree that the impact of these schools on Geneva was indirect rather than direct, flowing instead through other centers of learning that were both linguistically and chronologically closer to Geneva in terms of their foundation date.

Historians analyzing the roots of the Genevan Academy usually point to one or more of the following as possible models: the Academy of Lausanne (1537), the Strasbourg gymnasium (1538), and the université des arts et collège (1539) in Nîmes in southern France.[11] Like the later Genevan Academy, these three institutions shared a common feature of bringing together in one institution both a lower-tier Latin school and an upper-tier university level, albeit without offering degrees. Lausanne and Strasbourg were also durably shaped by their confessional allegiance to Protestantism, giving their educational institutions a strong religious emphasis. The Genevan Academy also had direct links with all three of these institutions. For Nîmes, the link was Claude Baduel, who had served as rector of the Nîmes school beginning in 1540. Baduel first met Calvin in Strasbourg in 1538, and eventually settled in Geneva by 1555 where he became a pastor and (briefly) a professor in the Genevan Academy from 1560 to his death in September 1561. Calvin learned about Strasbourg's educational system directly, through his time in the city during his exile from Geneva from 1538 to 1541. Finally, the Genevan Academy benefitted from several direct contacts with the teaching faculty at Lausanne, many of whom moved to Geneva in the mid- to late 1550s. The most significant transfer was Theodore Beza, who had taught in the Lausanne Academy from 1549 to 1558. Given its proximity, its shared

---

[10] Karin Maag, "Schools and Education," in Amy Burnett and Emidio Campi (eds.), *A Companion to the Swiss Reformation* (Leiden, The Netherlands: Brill, 2016), 520–541, esp. 534–536.

[11] The best recent study of the Academy of Lausanne is in French: Karine Crousaz, *L'Académie de Lausanne entre Humanisme et Réforme* (Leiden, The Netherlands: Brill, 2012).

linguistic and religious context, and the transfer of knowledgeable teaching personnel, the most likely educational institution serving as a model for the Genevan Academy was indeed the neighboring Academy of Lausanne.[12]

The Genevan Academy's Distinctives

Thus the Genevan Academy took note of other peer institutions in setting up its curriculum and governance. Many of its features, such as its humanist curriculum, the progression of students through the various levels of the Latin school, and focus on biblical languages and exegesis in its university-level instruction were modeled on these other schools. Yet the Genevan Academy also offered several distinctive characteristics.

The most salient aspect of the Genevan academy's curriculum in the lower-level Latin school was the pervasive role of religious instruction. As in the earlier Collège de Rive, students daily recited the Lord's Prayer, the Ten Commandments, and the Apostles' Creed in turn, but they also had to attend worship in the city's churches on Wednesdays and twice on Sunday with their class, accompanied by their teachers. In the week prior to the quarterly celebration of the Lord's Supper, one of the city's pastors was to visit the school and teach about the upcoming celebration of the sacrament, and "exhort all to concord and piety."[13]

In the upper level of the Genevan Academy, the emphasis on faith continued. Although church attendance was not explicitly mandated for the older students, these young men all had to sign their agreement to a lengthy confession of faith before they could begin attending lectures. This confession of faith spelled out in detail the parameters of orthodox belief, explicitly rejected Roman Catholic and Anabaptist teachings, and left no room for a Lutheran interpretation of the Lord's Supper. This elaborate confession of faith was distinctive to the Genevan Academy, though it only remained in force for about 25 years. By the mid-1580s, when Geneva sought to recruit a wider range of students, particularly in law, the confession of faith was replaced with a much shorter and generic statement pledging obedience to Geneva's political authorities and rejecting Catholic superstition and manifest heresies.[14]

The other distinctive that shaped the course of the Genevan Academy was its ability to recruit teaching faculty who drew students to Geneva, beginning with Calvin and Beza, but including later major figures such as the Hellenist

---

[12] See Crousaz's careful analysis in ibid., 61–68.

[13] Maag, *Seminary or University?*, 16. See also Borgeaud, *Histoire*, 628.

[14] Maag, *Seminary or University?*, 16–17, 52.

Isaac Casaubon, the Hebraist Corneille Bertram, and the law professor François Hotman.[15] These professors and others made Geneva a prime academic destination especially during the latter part of the sixteenth century.

CONCLUSION

The Genevan Academy thus built on a tradition of local Latin schools and learned from models of higher education in Reformed contexts within the Swiss lands and further afield. In Theodore Beza's preface to the Genevan Academy's statutes, he noted the challenge that had faced Geneva prior to 1559:

> In the past, even though God had provided her with his most precious gifts, Geneva had to ask for her children to be trained in the humanities in the cities and nations which Geneva, from her own resources, had been teaching about that which is much more important, namely the knowledge of the true religion. Such a situation had its disadvantages and difficulties. However, God in his goodness has granted to this republic a privilege which very few have had before her, namely to have the same city as mother of its learning and of its faith.[16]

Geneva did not invent this model of academic instruction. Indeed, other cities and states established effective hybrid centers of instruction within a strongly confessional context well before the Genevan Academy opened its doors. Yet Geneva's combination of faith formation and high-caliber instruction provided by outstanding faculty made the Genevan Academy a magnet for students from across Europe throughout the early modern era.

SUGGESTED FURTHER READINGS

Huppert, George. *Public Schools in Renaissance France*. Urbana: University of Illinois Press, 1984.

Maag, Karin. "Schools and Education" in Amy Burnett and Emidio Campi, eds, *A Companion to the Swiss Reformation*. Leiden: Brill, 2016, 520–41.

    Seminary or University? The Genevan Academy and Reformed Higher Education, 1560–1620. Aldershot: Scolar Press, 1995.

Naphy, William. "The Reformation and the evolution of Geneva's schools" in Beat Kümin, ed., *Reformations Old and New: Essays on the Socio-Economic Impact of Religious Change c. 1470–1630*. Aldershot: Scolar Press, 1996, 185–202.

---

[15] See the list of the Genevan Academy faculty in ibid., 196–198.
[16] Ibid., 18–19.

Worship, Pastorate, and Diaconate in Early Modern Europe

Elsie Anne McKee

Religious life in late medieval Latin Christendom was intense. A turn toward pastoral theology and increasing lay literacy and activism led to criticism of and rising expectations for clergy (more preaching, better morals), multiplication of devotions (e.g., prayer books promising indulgences, elaborate church decoration, new saints' shrines, and pilgrimages), and anxieties about means of salvation and good works (e.g., chantries and Mass foundations, practices of charity in face of the "undeserving poor"). Among the responses were reformulations of the understanding and practice of worship and the roles and characters of ministries.

WORSHIP

Worship has many facets; each heading gives the medieval starting point, common reforming stances, the range of choices, and Calvin's position.

Space

In Roman tradition specific places and times are intrinsically more holy than others. All who broke with Rome rejected this as a principle, although almost all practiced some kind of nonessential distinctions (recognizing particular places or times as proper for corporate worship). God can be worshiped wherever the church-as-people gathers, so pilgrimage sites were discontinued. Anabaptists did not usually worship in buildings dedicated to that purpose; their common practice at first was house churches, although some (e.g., Hutterites) constructed their own all-purpose community buildings.

Protestants continued to use parish buildings that they inherited. Where they were minorities they might build churches until these were destroyed (e.g., le Paradis, Lyons, France). However, interiors were modified. Additions were common to all: if the place did not have benches and pulpit (with sounding board), these must be installed because worship required preachers who could be heard and places for listeners to sit. Subtractions had to do with altars, décor, and musical instruments. Lutherans retained organs and altar furniture. They removed statues but allowed paintings; many places retained choirs and rood screens. Reformed churches removed virtually all visual material, although some added written biblical verses (e.g., the Decalogue). They consistently replaced altars with tables; there was no choir and the sacraments took place in the nave. They generally removed organs unless these were civic property (in the Netherlands). Furnishings in Church of England (CofE) parishes had a mixed record: removed under Edward VI, (partially) restored under Mary I and later under Archbishop Laud, with some "ornaments" under Elizabeth. Practice was probably not entirely uniform; some had more decoration, others less; some had organs, others none.

Calvin's Geneva was fairly typical of Reformed practice. Parish buildings were furnished with benches and pulpits if they lacked them, tables replaced altars, simple bowls replaced baptismal fonts, and all worship took place in the nave. When parishes were combined for practical reasons, unneeded buildings were turned to other uses until population changes required them to be recommissioned for refugee communities. Artwork and organs were removed.

Time

Approaches to revising worship time illustrate a similar range of changes. All who broke with Rome gave Sunday central prominence; saints' days were essentially eliminated, though Lutherans and the CofE kept some biblical or historical ones. The temporal calendar was revised slightly by Lutherans but most of the rhythm of holy time was maintained. The CofE followed a similar pattern. Reformed communities trimmed Christological observances considerably but in different measures. At issue here is what constituted observance. Was it commemoration or holiday or both? Commonly "observance" has not been explicitly defined, which has led to confusion about what marked one day as different from another. Zwinglians kept six specific Christological days: Christmas, Circumcision, Annunciation, Easter, Ascension, and Pentecost, observing them as holidays on the traditional dates. (They also kept some other local observances.) Scottish Presbyterians and puritans eliminated any markers except Sundays and the day of prayer, plus special celebrations of the Lord's Supper (though not at the traditional times of Christmas and Easter). Anabaptists removed all markers except Sundays.

Calvin's Geneva was instrumental in establishing the typical Reformed rhythm of worship time, focusing on Sundays and the weekly day of prayer, with regular celebrations of the Lord's Supper four times per year. Calvin maintained the special observance of Easter and Pentecost on the traditional days, and the Nativity on the Sunday closest to December 25; all were honored with the celebration of the Lord's Supper. He also added observance of the passion by special sermons the week before Easter, but only Sundays were holidays, with a partial holiday (delayed start of business) on the day of prayer.

Liturgies

All who broke with Rome rejected the tradition that (sacramental) liturgies as such are sacrosanct, but most affirmed the use of planned forms for guiding corporate worship. Protestants regularly published liturgies for the edification of the people and expected these to be used consistently in the community (they could be altered but not at the whim of any one person, even the preacher). Anabaptists usually did not consider liturgical edification necessary for a gathered church, so few wrote liturgies. Balthasar Hubmaier's texts, which gave shape to biblical actions such as baptism or fraternal admonition, were probably used fairly widely but mostly as a convenience. By the seventeenth century, Anabaptists had more fully developed forms.

Although they agreed on the real importance of Sunday liturgies, Protestant forms spanned a wide range, from ones closely modeled on the Mass to those patterned on prone, a medieval vernacular preaching service. Lutherans generally eliminated what was theologically objectionable from the Latin Mass, translated it, and added biblical preaching and congregational singing. The CofE Book of Common Prayer (BCP) also maintained the traditional shape but made a number of modifications in a Reformed direction. Zwinglian Reformed based their very spare Sunday outline on prone. The Bucer-Calvin Reformed developed a balanced Sunday word-and-sacrament pattern, even though the balance was often not apparent because the Supper was celebrated more rarely than they wanted. The goal was to follow scripture and the early church; the result had much in common with the mass, but in Bucer's hands developed a thoughtfully shaped character of its own. Calvin borrowed this for Sunday and his distinctive liturgical creation, the weekly day of prayer, which became one of the marks of the Reformed tradition.

All who broke with Rome modified funeral liturgies (no masses for the
dead). Most practiced varied forms of funerals with sermons. Calvinist
Reformed stood out (uncomfortably) by their decision not to have special
funeral liturgies.

Preaching

A revival of preaching in the Latin West began in the thirteenth century;
more sermons were available than old polemical legends acknowledged.
However, preaching was not necessary for salvation; the sacramental system
was the means of grace. Parish clergy were not required to preach, although
a considerable range of aids were available if they were sufficiently educated
to use them. The main agents of sermons were friars, so most preaching
happened in urban areas and/or on an occasional basis (especially in Lent).
Sermons to laity were normally in the vernacular but the aids were in Latin;
virtually only "heretics" like the Lollards produced written vernacular
sermons. Sermon topics could be chosen from any church-approved source:
e.g., saints' lives, teaching on virtues and vices (e.g., seven deadly sins),
theological miracles (e.g., St. Gregory's Mass), instructions about the sacraments (e.g., how to do penance), moral admonitions (e.g., how to be an
obedient wife), as well as the lectionary. Although stories of Old Testament
heroes were told and retold in visual form, and mystery play cycles of
salvation history were popular, the actual biblical passages in the lectionary
were almost all from the New Testament.

For those who broke with Rome, there were common reactions. Preaching
became an essential part of right worship and its source should be only the
Bible or catechetical points drawn from scripture. Anabaptists continued to
cite the apocrypha, but for Protestants this was generally excluded from the
authoritative biblical canon. Protestants published vernacular sermons to
help uneducated preachers stick to scripture. There was considerable diversity about choice of text and pattern of exposition. Lutherans, who maintained the liturgical year, continued to use the traditional selected lectionary
with some minor modifications. Their exposition was a kind of *loci communes* form that gave particular attention to theologically significant verses
but did not treat every word.

Reformed commonly rejected the constraints of the selected lectionary
along with the full liturgical year, and actively reintroduced regular preaching on the Old Testament for the first time in centuries. (Usually Old
Testament sermons were on weekdays, but Scottish Presbyterians and puritans also selected these books for Sunday worship.) Zwinglian Reformed

adopted a modified *lectio continua* approach but also retained some of the traditional lectionary. Zwingli expounded his texts in straight *lectio continua* fashion, but his successors for the next century used a partial *loci communes* style. Calvinist Reformed rejected the lectionary virtually completely. Calvin consistently expounded all scripture, Old Testament well as New Testament, in straight *lectio continua* fashion, with interruptions to expound traditional texts on the major Christological feasts (Nativity, Passion, Easter, Pentecost). This style reigned in Geneva for a century, before a *loci communes* approach was introduced. Calvinist preaching stood out for its consistent exposition of each biblical book straight through, attending to virtually every verse, and to historical context as well as doctrine.

Sacraments

The place of sacraments in worship was changed in many ways by those who broke with Rome. Partly this was a redefinition of sacrament, partly a change in relationship to the worshiping community. Traditionally, sacraments were the means of grace performed by ordained clergy with a specific form; laity could perform baptism and marriage. Most sacraments did not require the presence of the community to be effective; the individuals who received baptism, penance, and extreme unction might be the only laity involved. Even the mass was not dependent on the congregation's presence or communion; it was effective by the priest's action for them in their absence. Those who broke with Rome agreed that sacraments were not automatically effective; faith and understanding of the biblical teaching were required. For Anabaptists, the emphasis on personal faith and the community was crucial; the ordinances were biblically defined and necessarily communal actions by adult believers (including ordinances such as fraternal admonition, or foot washing, which others did not identify as sacraments).

For Protestants there were two sacraments, baptism and the Lord's Supper/Eucharist. (Marriage, ordination, etc. were still important actions but not defined as sacraments.) There were a considerable range of views regarding the Supper. Theological distinctions will be covered elsewhere; the focus here is the place of sacraments in worship. Everyone who broke with Rome insisted that preaching and the active presence of the community were necessary for the celebration of the Supper/Eucharist; ministers could not commune alone. Lutherans, Calvinist Reformed, and CofE agreed that the sacrament was a means of grace (though they explained this differently) and defined the ideal Sunday service as a combination of preaching and Supper, but they differed on requirements for participating in communion. For

Lutherans and CofE, individuals who felt spiritually prepared could commune while the rest remained in their pews. Zwinglian Reformed saw preaching as the means of grace; the Supper was a memorial on specific occasions when the whole body pledged their faith together. Calvinist Reformed linked purpose, participants, and frequency in distinctive ways. The Supper was a means of grace, first, and second confession; celebration required proper preparation (knowledge and reconciliation with God and neighbors); and the whole community should participate whenever it is offered. Frequent communion was desired but had to be correlated with preparation of the whole church.

Reformed baptisms must be celebrated in the context of the gathered community of faith by a pastor. Lutherans and the BCP allowed private baptisms. Most Protestants continued the practice of godparents but modified the roles and gave primary responsibility to the parents. For Calvin, the godfather was to second the parents to insure the child was taught the faith until she/he could make a personal profession to be admitted to communion.

Prayer Music

For all who broke with Rome, prayers must be biblically based and intelligible. For theological reasons many popular prayers (e.g., for the dead, to the saints) were eliminated, so the ones retained (e.g., Lord's Prayer) stood out more clearly. For practical reasons, corporate participation meant praying and singing in the vernacular. Some (Zurich based) confined congregational voices to spoken words, but the great majority of Protestants and Anabaptists chose song. Everyone sang versions of Psalms. Lutherans added hymns, Anabaptists contributed their own teaching-martyr songs, and Calvinist Reformed made metrical forms of all 150 Psalms. Protestants reintroduced prayers for civil rulers (1 Tim. 2:1–2) found in prone but dropped from the Roman Mass; Calvin and Reformed refugees added a distinctive prayer for those persecuted by civil rulers.

Ethical Concerns

Medieval almsgiving was generous but not formally related to worship (beggars might address people attending Mass). The offertory was not an alms offering but expression of the Mass as a sacrifice. Protestants eliminated the offertory (the BCP alone kept a "sacrifice of praise and thanksgiving"), but most introduced an alms offering, often associated with the

Supper/Eucharist. The Calvinist Reformed saw this as "koinonia" in Acts 2:42, their paradigm of right worship.

Household Piety

Fasting, reciting Latin prayers to saints or for the dead, and pilgrimages were common traditional forms of piety. Protestants replaced these with vernacular songs and prayers from corporate worship. Lutherans added many individual prayers; for the CofE, the BCP supplied others. For Calvinist Reformed, the Psalter became the identifying staple of piety.

PASTORATE

Function and Status

The primary function of medieval parish clergy was to assure the availability of the sacraments; celibacy was considered a necessary condition for that function. Some parish clergy developed the ability to preach, but it was not obligatory. For Protestants, usually the primary role of ministers was to preach and teach, though administering sacraments was also important. The definition and location of holiness changed; given the priesthood of believers, ministers are not essentially different from other Christians. Scripture replaced canon law as the norm, so marriage was appropriate for pastors. Often new clergy were reformed members of the old priesthood, now married and required to preach in the approved (biblical) way. Because knowledge of apostolic teaching was the primary necessity for salvation, pastoral care might focus more on preaching than sacraments, although this varied among the different groups, but all emphasized ministering to sick and dying.

Education and Gender

Medieval university theological education was shaped by scholasticism, although a strong pastoral orientation developed in the fifteenth century and humanism brought new sources and pedagogy. Those who broke with Rome reoriented pastoral education to concentrate on the Bible. Protestants gave an important role to patristic exegesis. They thought every Christian should know the basics but that preachers and teachers needed advanced education: ideally, university training and knowledge of the biblical languages. Anabaptist educational criteria were different; vernacular Bibles sufficed and usually these were read literally. For all groups, formal religious leadership remained firmly in the hands of men.

Pastoral ministry in Calvin's Geneva was typical of Protestants in status, function, and gender, but distinctive in its radicalness: personal break with the past, regulation of educational criteria, and collegial organization. Only one native Genevan friar became a preacher and he soon moved to a rural parish. The rest were university-educated foreigners, fervent religious exiles; few had been priests. They were led and taught by a humanist lawyer, a gifted autodidact in theology, himself an exile. None had longstanding ties with either Geneva or traditional clerical training. This may have contributed to how Calvin distinctively reorganized their collegial ministry, in ways more like early church urban contexts than the parish structures of other Protestants.

Function and Context

Catholic deacons were a rank of sacramental ministry in transition to priesthood. Acts 6:1–6 was cited but reinterpreted because it describes seven men chosen to serve tables, a secular business that did not qualify for ordination. Those who broke with Rome saw no problem in setting apart men to handle money and care for the poor, but most Protestants assigned this task to Christian rulers. Anabaptist groups developed their own religious office of men who cared for physical needs.

The Poor and Social Reform

Traditionally both poverty and almsgiving were virtues. Eventually the "deserving poor" were distinguished from "undeserving" and the salvific value of alms became correlated with giving to monks or other holy people whose prayers would most benefit the donor. By 1500, Western Europe was struggling with a vast (vastly disturbing) problem of vagrants. Civic authorities were concerned for social control, religious authorities for preservation of the mendicant virtue of voluntary poverty; people generally wanted deserving poor cared for and undeserving excluded. In response, new structures developed: centralized resources, rationalized lists of recipients, and two-part civic administration to handle finances and physical care. Protestants found this social welfare entirely compatible with biblical injunctions to care for the poor and needy. Lutherans, Zwinglians, and CofE alike continued the idea of Christendom that did not distinguish between ecclesi-astical and civil bodies, so they identified poor relief as a function of Christian rulers.

Calvin's Diaconate

Geneva established the welfare reform just before Calvin arrived. Like other Protestants, Calvin affirmed civil involvement in poor relief and the religious value of this activity, and shared the interpretation of Acts 6 and 1 Timothy 3 as deacons caring for the poor. He understood the combination of texts as evidence that this ministry was established as second to presbyters but also permanently necessary in every rightly ordered church, thus making a distinctive church office of "lay ecclesiastical ministers." Calvin did not follow the Protestant view that ecclesiastical and civil are one entity; he based his church polity on the New Testament, a time when there had been no Christian rulers. Therefore, ecclesiastical and civil are necessarily distinct and separable, even if their cooperation is preferred. The social welfare reform was an appropriate though not necessary expression of the diaconate; refugees in Geneva created "voluntary" diaconates for their members.

Calvin's teaching on the diaconate also included women. His determin-ation to model polity on the New Testament, and his consistent *lectio continua* practice, meant that he had to deal with texts which other Protest-ants skipped (e.g., Rom. 16:1–2, Phoebe the deacon[ess]). He also needed to counter the Roman interpretation of 1 Timothy 5:9–10 (the widows) as a prooftext for religious vows. The result was his affirmation of two kinds of deacons (Rom. 12:8): men who administer money (Acts 6, 1 Tim. 3) and women who do the nursing (Rom. 16, 1 Tim. 5). Significantly, the Calvinist Reformed diaconate was the only Protestant or Anabaptist church order that included the teaching (if not often the practice) of a (subordinate) place for women in the regular offices of ministry.

SUGGESTED FURTHER READING

Elsie McKee. *The Pastoral Ministry and Worship in Calvin's Geneva.* Geneva: Droz, 2016.
John Calvin on the Diaconate and Liturgical Almsgiving. Geneva: Droz, 1984.

PART III

EMPIRE AND SOCIETY

15

ॐ

The Politics of the Emperors

Ute Lotz-Heumann

The early modern Holy Roman Empire of the German Nation, usually just called "the Empire," was a huge and complex political organization in central Europe. The emperorship was an elected office, and the emperor had the difficult task of ruling over a loose political union of mostly German and largely self-governing principalities and towns, collectively called "the imperial estates." As a result, imperial politics cannot be neatly defined as either domestic or foreign; rather, dynastic, internal, and European considerations were closely intertwined in the politics of the emperors.

Beginning with the second emperor from the House of Habsburg, Frederick III, who ruled from 1440 to 1493, the Habsburgs held the emperorship almost continuously until the end of the early modern period – and the empire – in 1806. During John Calvin's lifetime, three emperors occupied the imperial throne: Frederick's son Maximilian I (1493–1519), Maximilian's grandson Charles V (1519–1556), and Charles's brother Ferdinand I (1558–1564). Maximilian was the emperor who laid the groundwork for the vast composite monarchy ruled over by Charles V.

Many of the territories of the Habsburgs were not acquired through wars, but through marriage: "Bella gerant alii, tu felix Austria nube" – "Let others wage war, you, happy Austria, marry." Maximilian, through his own marriage and those of his son Philip and his grandson Ferdinand, set the stage for Charles V's empire and the Habsburg's European multiple kingdom. In 1477, Maximilian married Mary of Burgundy, heir to the Burgundian lands. This brought the rich Burgundian heritage, including the Low Countries, into the dominions of the Habsburgs, but it also resulted in war with France. Maximilian's son Philip the Handsome married Joanna of Spain (also called the Mad) in 1496 as part of a strategic alliance between Habsburg and Spain against France. And in 1515, Maximilian arranged the marriage of Archduke Ferdinand of Austria (later Emperor Ferdinand I, brother of Charles V) to

Anna, the sister of King Louis of Bohemia and Hungary. In 1526, after Louis's death, Ferdinand was elected king of Bohemia and Hungary, thus making the Austrian Habsburg lands and the powerful Ottoman Empire neighbors in east-central Europe. Conflicts with France and the Ottoman Empire came to determine the imperial policies of Charles V to a large extent.

Under Maximilian, other important developments for the House of Habsburg and the empire were also set in motion. When Charles VIII of France invaded Italy in 1494, thus violating the imperial right to rule over the Northern Italian territories, Maximilian turned to the imperial estates for help. The estates demanded reform measures in return for taxes, which led to the so-called imperial reform of 1495. This reform resulted in the establishment of an imperial court, the administrative division of the empire into districts, a new form of taxation, and the stabilization of the assembly of the imperial estates, the imperial diet. When the members of the Swiss Confederacy refused to accept these changes, the "Swiss" or "Swabian" War broke out in 1498–1499. As a result, Maximilian was defeated, lost the ancestral lands of the Habsburgs for good, and the Swiss Confederacy became de facto independent of the empire.[1]

Maximilian's grandson Charles V ruled over "an empire on which the sun never set." He inherited Spain, including its southern Italian and overseas territories, the Burgundian lands, and the hereditary Austrian Habsburg lands (until 1521–1522, when he made his brother Ferdinand ruler of Austria). And in 1519, he was elected emperor of the Holy Roman Empire of the German Nation, defeating the French king Francis I with the help of bribes from the merchant house of Fugger. Charles's attempt to establish a universal monarchy that would guarantee his dynasty's hegemony over Europe ultimately failed, and the emperor abdicated in 1556.

Charles's imperial politics were torn in many directions, and his ability to rule effectively over his vast empire was constantly strained by wars with France, the Ottoman Empire, and the German Protestants. Charles came to the empire in 1521–1522 to take his crown. In 1521, he presided over the Diet of Worms at which Luther defended his teachings. The Protestant reformer was subsequently put under an imperial ban, the Edict of Worms.[2] However, Charles then became an "absentee ruler"[3] until 1530, a crucial time for the

---

[1] For more details see Chapter 7 by Bruce Gordon.
[2] For more details see Chapter 20 by David Whitford.
[3] Volker Press, "The Habsburg Lands: The Holy Roman Empire," in Thomas A. Brady Jr., Heiko A. Oberman, and James D. Tracy (eds.), *Handbook of European History 1400–1600: Late Middle Ages, Renaissance, and Reformation, Vol. 1: Structures and Assertions* (Grand Rapids, MI: Eerdmans, 1996), 450.

spread of the Protestant Reformation and the expansion of the Ottoman Empire. Charles's focus at that time was his southern European lands, and his goal was to establish his power over Italy as an important part of gaining dominion over Europe. With Francis I of France controlling Milan and laying claim to territories in southern Italy, and Charles controlling Naples and Sicily and laying claim not only to Milan but also to Burgundian territories occupied by France and to territories in southern France, a war was soon inevitable.

The first war between Charles and Francis (1521–1526) ended with a victory by Charles in the battle of Pavia in 1525; Francis was taken prisoner. The emperor regarded the Peace of Madrid of 1526 as a compromise that spared Francis's life and was supposed to be a first step toward building a coalition to fight heretics (Protestants) and the Turks. Francis, who, under the terms of the peace treaty, had given up his claim to the Burgundian territories, Milan, and Naples, among others, declared the peace invalid as soon as he was released and back in France.

A second war between Charles and Francis ensued. Francis was able to form a coalition that included Pope Clement VII and Milan. The alliance had some military success, but then came an unexpected turn of events. The German and Spanish mercenaries of the imperial army, unpaid and practically leaderless, made their way to Rome and plundered the city in 1527. Pope Clement had to seek refuge in the Castel Sant'Angelo. Although Charles V distanced himself from this "Sacco di Roma," the pope effectively became the prisoner of the emperor. This was also the time when the English king Henry VIII tried to have his marriage to Catherine of Aragon, Charles's aunt, annulled by the pope, a request that was – unsurprisingly, considering the pope's circumstances – denied.

The anti-Habsburg coalition continued to fight, and peace was only negotiated in 1529, with the help of the mother of Francis, Louise of Savoy, and Margaret of Austria, Charles's aunt and regent of the Netherlands. The Treaty of Cambrai, also known as "Paix des Dames" (Peace of the Ladies), brought another compromise: Francis gave up his territorial claims in Italy, but he retained his Burgundian lands. In the Peace of Barcelona of the same year, Pope Clement accepted Habsburg hegemony in Europe and agreed to crowning the emperor (which he did in Bologna in 1530). However, contrary to Charles V's wishes, the pope did not agree to convene a general council.

During this decade, which saw the first two wars between the emperor and France, the situation in Germany and in east-central Europe became more difficult for the Habsburgs. In 1524–1525, the Peasants' War broke out and threatened the Habsburg territories. In 1526, the first Diet at Speyer effectively put the Edict of Worms on hold by allowing each imperial estate to act "in such a way as he will be responsible for to God and the emperor."[4] This effectively led to the further expansion of Lutheranism in the empire.

During the preceding years, the Ottoman Empire under Sultan Suleiman II, the Magnificent, had begun to expand in the Mediterranean and in southeastern Europe. In 1526, the king of Bohemia and Hungary, Louis II, fell in the battle of Mohács against the Ottoman Empire. Ferdinand of Austria secured the crowns of Bohemia and Hungary, but he was unable to prevent the partition of Hungary and the advance of the Ottoman army. During the Ottoman advance westward, the second Diet of Speyer took place in 1529. When Ferdinand asked for taxes to help stop the Turks, but also demanded to reinstate the Edict of Worms, the Lutheran estates balked; their official minority "protest" against the majority decision earned them the name "Protestants." Later that year, Suleiman laid siege to Vienna, but ultimately retreated.

After having been crowned emperor by the pope in 1530, Charles V returned to Germany that year for the first time since 1522. He called an imperial diet to Augsburg and intended to solve the religious schism in the empire. However, at the diet, the Protestant estates presented him with a statement of their faith, the "Confession of Augsburg," which Catholic theologians countered with the "Confutatio." Rather than submit to the emperor, several Protestant estates, led by the Elector of Saxony and the Landgrave of Hesse, formed a defensive alliance, the Schmalkaldic League, in 1531. The League subsequently grew to include more evangelical princes and cities.

During the following years, Charles continued to fight the Ottoman Empire, and war with France resumed, which led to concessions to the German Protestants and repeated attempts to find a peaceful solution to the religious schism in the empire. Already in 1532, in the Peace of Nuremberg, the emperor had to accommodate the Protestants' demands in view of their military alliance and his need for new taxes to defend against the Turks. He granted them freedom of worship until a general council would meet.

In 1535, Charles V conquered Tunis, thus pushing back against the Ottoman presence in the western Mediterranean. However, Francis I now saw his own position in jeopardy. In response, he renewed his claim to Milan and formed a league with the Ottoman Sultan. Thus, a third war between

---

[4] Quoted in Thomas A. Brady Jr., *German Histories in the Age of Reformations, 1400–1650* (Cambridge: Cambridge University Press, 2009), 215.

Charles V and Francis I began in 1536. It ended with a 10-year truce brokered by Pope III. During those years, Charles granted another temporary religious peace to the Protestants in the empire, the Frankfurt "truce" of 1539. Facing more pressure from the Ottomans who conquered Buda in 1541, Charles supported various religious colloquies in the empire in the early 1540s.[5] When Francis I, still allied with Suleiman, began another, the fourth, war with Charles in 1541, the imperial diets, including the Protestants, granted the emperor's requests for aid.

However, as the years progressed and no religious compromise was found, the situation in the empire eventually deteriorated. Several different developments converged and led to religious war between Charles V and the Schmalkaldic League. First, the emperor was able to turn his attention to Germany because he achieved an end to hostilities with France and the Ottoman Empire. In 1544, the Peace of Crépy ended the fourth war between Charles and Francis. The treaty basically confirmed the compromise of the Peace of Cambrai. Francis and Charles abandoned their conflicting territorial claims; the emperor gave up his claim to the Duchy of Burgundy, and the King of France relinquished his claim to the Kingdom of Naples. In secret additions to the treaty, Francis gave up his alliance with the Ottoman Empire, promised troops to fight it and the German Protestants, and also promised to support efforts to reform the church and convene a General Council. In addition, he undertook to help the Duke of Savoy in his fight against Geneva, the city that was rapidly turning into a center of Protestantism under Calvin's leadership. In 1545, the Habsburgs were also able to enter into an armistice with the Ottoman Empire, which led to a peace agreement in 1547, so that the eastern border of the empire no longer needed to be constantly defended.

Second, Charles decided to solve the problem of the "pacification d'Allemaigne"[6] by military force rather than negotiation. Two developments led to this decision. Pope Paul III convened a General Council that began to meet in Trent in 1545 (after previous unsuccessful attempts in Mantua in 1529 and Trent in 1542).[7] In addition, the pope promised Charles troops for a war against the German Protestants. The Regensburg colloquy of 1546 ended without results, and the diet of Regensburg in the same year turned out to be a prelude to war. The members of the Schmalkaldic League refused to attend

---

[5] For more details see Chapter 21 by Ronald Rittgers.
[6] Quoted in Heinrich Lutz, *Reformation und Gegenreformation: Oldenbourg Grundriss der Geschichte* (Munich: Oldenbourg, 1997), 48.
[7] For more details see Chapter 22 by Kathleen Comerford.

the Council of Trent, and Charles prepared for a war by looking for allies among the German princes. Eventually, the Catholic Duke of Bavaria and Maurice of Saxony, a Protestant, sided with the emperor. Both princes hoped to gain the electorships that were in the possession of rival lines of their respective noble houses.

When Charles V attacked the Schmalkaldic League, he did not legitimize his war as a religious war. Rather, he invoked imperial law and proceed against the members of the Schmalkaldic League as disturbers of the peace who threatened the integrity of the empire. The two leaders of the League, Elector John Frederick of Saxony and Landgrave Philip of Hesse, had provided him with this convenient reason by illegally conquering the lands of their Catholic neighbor, the Duke of Brunswick, and deposing him in 1542.

At the Battle of Mühlberg in 1547, Charles defeated the Schmalkaldic League. At the height of his power, he was able to dictate the terms for peace, and these came in the form of the Augsburg Interim of 1548.[8] The Interim, as it is known for short, required Protestants in the empire to return to Catholic beliefs and practices. There were only two concessions: married Protestant clergymen were allowed to stay married, and Protestants were granted communion in both kinds until a general council of the Church would resolve the question. Protestant resistance against the Interim was widespread, aided by a massive propaganda campaign, which had already accompanied the Schmalkaldic War.

Protestant princes in northern Germany sought to renew the war, and they forged an alliance with the French King Henri II, the successor of Francis I. Maurice of Saxony, now elector, joined his fellow-religionists in this Princes' War against the emperor in 1552. The result was a complete victory for the German Protestants; their troops chased the emperor into the Austrian Habsburg territories, and he barely escaped capture. Charles, having failed to achieve his ambition to root out Protestantism in the empire, left the task of making peace to his brother Ferdinand. A preliminary peace agreement was found in the treaty of Passau of 1552.

Charles tried one last time to win the upper hand against France. First, he laid siege to the town of Metz, which was held by the French. When the town had successfully withstood the imperial siege, the burghers put up a banner that inverted Charles V's motto "Plus ultra" ("Further beyond"). It read "Non ultra Metas" ("Not further than Metz").[9] Second, Charles hoped that

---

[8] Ibid.

[9] Quoted in Alfred Kohler, *Karl V. 1500–1558: Eine Biographie* (Munich: Beck, 1999), 340.

France could be encircled by another dynastic marriage: the Catholic Queen Mary Tudor ascended the English throne in 1553, and Charles, her cousin, convinced her to marry his son, Philip of Spain. However, Charles's hopes of establishing another Habsburg dynasty and stronghold across the channel from France did not become reality because Mary remained childless.

In 1555, Ferdinand, as designated successor of his brother, also led negotiations at the diet of Augsburg. At this diet, a more stable and lasting religious agreement was made. The Peace of Augsburg granted legal status to Lutherans in the empire, but not to other Protestant movements and churches. Through the so-called *ius reformandi*, the "right to reform," each ruler was allowed to choose between Catholicism and Lutheranism. This was later enshrined in the phrase "cuius regio, eius religio" ("whose territory, his religion"). Subjects had to either conform to their ruler's religion or emigrate. Religious reunification was still the goal, but it was postponed indefinitely.

In 1556, Charles V, suffering from gout and in pain, abdicated. This marked the end of his idea of a universal monarchy, his attempt to establish a Habsburg-dominated peace in Europe, and his unsuccessful fight against, as he put it, "the heresies of Luther."[10] In his abdication speech, he expressed his deep resignation about these failures. The Spanish and Austrian lines of the House of Habsburg were to be divided. Charles gave Spain, the Habsburg lands in Southern Italy, the Spanish colonies, and the Low Countries to his son Philip. His brother Ferdinand became head of the Austrian House of Habsburg and, in addition to holding the crowns of Bohemia and Hungary (since 1526), be became emperor in 1558.

The Peace of Augsburg brought a period of peaceful coexistence to the empire, but at the end of Calvin's lifetime, new clouds were already forming that eventually led to confessional and political rivalry and the Thirty Years' War. In 1563, the Council of Trent concluded its work. At the diet of Augsburg in 1566, the Catholic princes accepted the decrees of the council. As a result, a slow process of Catholic reform and Counter-Reformation began in the empire, which contributed to rising tensions in the long term. In addition, questions about the interpretation of the Peace of Augsburg arose. The peace had granted legal status to the adherents of the Augsburg Confession, but it soon became clear that this was open to interpretation. There were two versions of the Confessio Augustana, one called *invariata*, of 1530, and another one called *variata*, of 1540, both written by Philip

---

[10] Quoted in Brady, *German Histories in the Age of Reformations, 1400–1650*, 229.

Melanchthon. When the Elector Palatine, Frederick III, converted to Calvinism and began to transform the Palatinate into a Calvinist territory, it became questionable whether he still adhered to the Lutheran Augsburg Confession.[11] At the diet of Augsburg in 1566, Catholics moved to have Frederick excluded from the Peace of Augsburg, but the Elector insisted that the religion of his territory conformed to the Augsburg Confession (he meant the *variata* rather than the *invariata* version), and the Lutheran princes did not move to exclude Frederick. As a result, Calvinism spread in the empire.

SUGGESTED FURTHER READING

Brady Jr., Thomas A. *German Histories in the Age of Reformations, 1400–1650.* Cambridge: Cambridge University Press, 2009.

Soly, Hugo, and Willem Pieter Blockmans, *Charles V, 1500–1558, and His Time.* Antwerp: Mercatorfonds, 1999.

Volker Press. "The Habsburg Lands: The Holy Roman Empire." In *Handbook of European History 1400–1600: Late Middle Ages, Renaissance, and Reformation, Vol. 1: Structures and Assertions,* ed. Thomas A. Brady Jr., Heiko A. Oberman, and James D. Tracy. Grand Rapids, MI: Eerdmans, 1996, 437–466.

---

[11] In 1563, Frederick promulgated the Heidelberg Catechism, which became one of the most influential Reformed catechisms.

Judaism in Europe during the Late Middle Ages and Renaissance

David H. Price

In the Middle Ages and the sixteenth century, Jews and Jewish communities faced severe existential threats nearly everywhere in Western and Central Europe. The many types of persecution included banishment, forced conversion, confiscation of property, cancellation of debts, as well as assault and murder. Sometimes anti-Jewish violence erupted spontaneously, and sometimes it resulted from legally conducted prosecution of Jewish victims. During this long period, the number of territories that permitted Jewish residency contracted steadily until the second half of the sixteenth century, when more favorable conditions slowly began to develop in some areas of Europe. The wave of expulsions began with England in 1290, followed by France in 1394, and crested, but did not entirely dissipate, with the banishment of Sephardic Jews from Spain in 1492 and from Portugal in 1497. Significant Jewish communities in Sicily (1493) and the Kingdom of Naples (1511–1541) were also banished in the aftermath of the Spanish decree. The Sephardic expulsions as well as the preceding century of anti-Jewish agitation in Spain (beginning with widespread pogroms in 1391) resulted in tens of thousands of coercive baptisms and, subsequently, the development of a large *Converso* population. As many *Conversos* continued to practice Judaism surreptitiously, they became the targets of the Spanish and, later, Portuguese inquisitions (established in 1478 and 1536, respectively). Moreover, the Iberian expulsions dispersed the thriving Sephardic communities to the Ottoman Empire, parts of Italy, and, as of circa 1600, to the northern port cities of Amsterdam and Hamburg, as well as, beginning in the 1650s, to London. These port cities became important venues for the foundation of new, highly influential Jewish communities.

The situation in the Holy Roman Empire was similarly bleak, even though some imperial communities would ultimately survive. For the period

1399–1520, some 705 communities were lost within the empire,[1] leaving only
three major Ashkenazi communities – Worms, Frankfurt, and Prague –
intact at the end of the sixteenth century. In the territories that comprise
present-day Switzerland, the fifteenth century also unfolded in a series of
banishments (e.g., Basel 1397, Bern 1427, Fribourg 1428, and Geneva 1491),
with the result that no Jewish communities are known to have survived as of
1500. The severe pressure on Jewish communities in Central Europe resulted
in a major migration eastward, especially to Poland and Lithuania. Nonetheless, some conditions for Jewish life in the empire began to improve with
the rule of Charles V (1519–1556) and his successors.

Medieval and early modern Jewish communities typically lived in accord
with special charters or regulations that varied significantly from place to
place. The ecclesiastical and imperial law codes included general provisions
that allowed Jews to be tolerated legally and to practice their faith without
molestation, provided they gave no offense to Christian culture. The papal
bull *Sicut Judaeis*, which functioned as a legal foundation for toleration of
Jewish communities in many areas, permitted construction of synagogues
and cemeteries, worship services (with prayer books), observance of Sabbath
and high holy days, as well as protection against unwarranted seizure of
property. Although derived from the policies of Pope Gregory the Great
(ruled 590–604), *Sicut Judaeis* was first formulated by Calixtus II in 1120 as a
response to the atrocities of the First Crusade and was reissued by many
subsequent medieval popes. During the Middle Ages, the emperor claimed
direct sovereignty (most importantly, direct taxing authority) over Jewish
communities, which were recognized formally as his "cameral servants."
This imperial status eroded in many places by the end of the medieval
period. With the constitutional reform in the Golden Bull (1356), the seven
electoral princes gained direct control over Jews in their territories. Moreover, emperors often mortgaged their taxing authority over Jewish communities to urban or territorial governments. Individual charters and patents of
protection defined specific limitations on residency, economic activity, and
taxation, but also made allowances for limited communal self-government.
In many instances, Christian governments viewed Jewish communities as
important sources of tax revenue and economic stimulus, although Jewish

---

[1] See Dean Phillip Bell, "Jewish Settlement, Politics, and the Reformation," in Dean Phillip Bell
and Stephen G. Burnett (eds.), *Jews, Judaism, and the Reformation in Sixteenth-Century
Germany* (Leiden, The Netherlands: Brill, 2006), 426, summarizing the analysis of Michael
Toch, "Siedlungsstruktur der Juden Mitteleuropas im Wandel vom Mittelalter zur Neuzeit,"
in Alfred Haverkamp and Franz-Josef Ziwes (eds.), *Juden in der christlichen Umwelt während
des späten Mittelalters* (Berlin: Duncker and Humblot, 1992), 37.

banking (money lending and pawn broking) and many commercial ventures often contributed to high levels of social tension.

These economic tensions were compounded by religious animosities that developed over centuries of sustained anti-Jewish agitation. Beginning in the thirteenth century, the Franciscan and Dominican Orders undertook aggressive missionary campaigns with the ultimate goal of eradicating Judaism from Europe. The Franciscan Order even established banks, called *monti di pietà*, that offered low-interest loans to less affluent people in part to push Jewish moneylenders out of some credit markets. The Dominicans also controlled most of the inquisitions that targeted *Converso* populations.

Although anti-Jewish agitators depicted Jews in broad brushstrokes as perilous threats to Christian societies, they also fabricated accusations of specific crimes, such as ritual murder of Christian children, desecration of the Eucharist, and well poisoning. One of the earliest major atrocities against Jews occurred during the First Crusade (1096), when some crusading armies en route to Jerusalem slaughtered several leading Rhineland communities, including those of Speyer, Worms, and Mainz. Among the subsequent persecutions was the widespread murdering of Jews accused of well poisoning during the outbreak of the Great Plague in 1348–1349. The Great Plague pogroms, which were especially devastating in Switzerland and parts of Germany, usually entailed legal cases formally prosecuted by local governments that resulted in the conviction and execution of alleged perpetrators as well as the banishment of entire communities. Some authorities, most importantly Emperor Charles IV and Pope Clement VI, opposed these persecutions, and, in most instances, surviving Jews were allowed to return to their previous residences after the plague subsided. But persecution in general did not abate in the least. Since the twelfth century, Jews were sometimes charged with ritual murder (also known as blood libel), the allegation that they murdered Christian children and used their blood in religious rituals. Beginning in thirteenth century, Christians also alleged that Jews desecrated stolen Eucharistic wafers, an innuendo that is connected to the portrayal of Jews as Christ's executioners in passion devotions. All the host desecration cases have fabricated accounts of Jews torturing the "body of Christ" in the consecrated host, which usually bleeds miraculously. Such legal hoaxes not only typically resulted in the execution of individual Jews and the banishment of entire communities but also became the basis of new religious devotions, as Christians often made shrines for venerating the child as a martyred saint or, in a few cases, the recovered Eucharistic host. The most famous case, that of Simon of Trent (1475), became a major pilgrimage site. Nonetheless, popes and nearly all emperors opposed blood libel prosecutions, with the important exception of Emperor Maximilian I (ruled 1493–1519), who cited ritual murder and host desecration as justifications for his policy of approving banishments from the Habsburg Austrian territories in the 1490s. Jews were also subjected to abusive missionizing campaigns, frequently being compelled to attend anti-Jewish sermons. An important trope in the growing body of anti-Jewish discourse was the accusation that in their prayers and rituals Jews blasphemed the Trinity, Jesus, Mary, and other aspects of Christianity. As the Talmud became a special focus of anti-Jewish agitation, some anti-Jewish campaigners contended that Jews should even be subjected to heresy prosecutions on the grounds that their adherence to the Talmud was a heretical aberration from biblical Judaism. All these efforts and, above all, the growing list of precedents for expulsion destabilized the economic and fiscal rationales for continuing the policy of tolerating Jewish communities.

An important innovation of the sixteenth century was the emergence of Christian Hebrew studies. In 1506, drawing on the expertise of contemporary Jewish scholars as well as medieval Jewish research, Johannes Reuchlin published the first grammar and lexicon of biblical Hebrew designed for Christian students. Some Jewish scholars, preeminently Elijah Levita, and some Jewish converts to Christianity advanced Christian learning significantly. In the aftermath of Reuchlin's research, Christian scholars such as Sebastian Münster made major advances in Hebrew philology, with the result that during the 1520s the study of Hebrew started to become standard curriculum at European universities. With their new command of Hebrew, Christians were able not only to enrich their biblical research but also to undertake extensive study of Jewish theology and culture. In a few instances, this expert knowledge informed more benevolent portrayals of Judaism, but most Christian Hebraists were willing to use their new knowledge to support anti-Jewish efforts. Drawing on his knowledge of Hebrew literature, Reuchlin composed a defense of Jewish writings (1510) against an imperial campaign to confiscate and destroy all Jewish books except the Hebrew Bible. The Protestant humanist Andreas Osiander, a leading minister in Nuremberg and a Reuchlin student, composed a defense of Jews against blood libel based on his expert knowledge of Jewish practices and thought; he demonstrated that Jews simply do not use blood in their rituals. This tract was first published in circa 1530 and then republished in 1540 as part of an effort to undermine another blood libel prosecution. However, many Christian Hebraists wrote critical and even inflammatory portrayals of Judaism, based on their biased use of authentic Hebrew sources. Sebastian Münster and Johannes Buxtorf, both with long academic careers in Basel, were among the most learned of the sixteenth-century polemicists. The most extensive Christian-Hebraic attack on Judaism was the later *Judaism Revealed* (1700/1711) by Johann Andreas Eisenmenger, a Calvinist professor in Heidelberg. It was so vitriolic that its initial publication was blocked by Catholic Emperor Leopold I.

Overall, the emergence of Protestantism did not improve Christian-Jewish relations. Nonetheless, in the 1520s, some Protestants advocated undertaking somewhat less coercive missions to convert the Jews. Martin Luther published his *That Jesus Christ Was Born a Jew* (1523) partly as an anti-Catholic tract, arguing that the historical obstinacy of the Jews was due in large measure to the theological corruption and oppressive measures of the Catholic Church. With an extensive presentation of Christian views of Messianic prophecy in the Hebrew Scriptures (especially focused on Genesis 49:10), Luther expressed the hope that with proper understanding of the Gospel, as provided by his movement, Jews would become more willing to convert.

By the 1530s and 1540s, Luther and several other Protestant theologians and governments adopted harshly anti-Jewish positions. Luther published several brutal condemnations of Jews and of any Christian policy of tolerating Judaism, including his notorious *On the Jews and Their Lies* (1543), which called for the violent eradication of Jewish life from Germany. He also urged Protestant ministers to preach against toleration of Judaism. In specific political interventions, Luther opposed Elector Joachim II's readmission of Jews to Brandenburg and, at the end of his life, insisted that the counts of Mansfeld should expel all Jews from their lands. Most historians now acknowledge that Luther's anti-Judaism had a significant impact. Jews were expelled from Electoral Saxony in 1543 (and forbidden to transit through the territory); the Protestant leader Philipp of Hesse enacted a draconian new Jewish charter in 1543; and Jews were banished from Protestant Braunschweig in 1546. The Lutheran professor (and colleague of Luther) Johann Forster claimed that banishments from Silesia and Neumark were also motivated by Luther's writings. Yet Luther was hardly the only Protestant to oppose toleration of Judaism. Martin Bucer, the leading reformer of Strasbourg, wrote a major tract against toleration of Judaism, *A Recommendation Concerning the Jews: Whether and How They Should Be Kept among Christians* (1539; *Von den juden Ob/ vnd wie die vnder den Christen zů halten sind*), and also urged Philipp of Hesse to ban Jews from his territories. Although he objected to the violence of Luther's *Against the Jews and Their Lies*, the Swiss reformer Heinrich Bullinger composed a strong condemnation of Christian toleration of Judaism in 1572. Catholic

writers were often equally caustic. Johannes Eck, a strident opponent of
Luther and professor at the Catholic University of Ingolstadt, published
Refutation of a Jew Pamphlet (1541; *Ains Judenbüechlins verlegung*) against
Osiander's defense of Judaism.

Very few records of Jewish reactions to the Reformation survive. There are
indications that at least a few Jews initially welcomed the Reformation
because of the perception that it was combating Christian idolatry, especially
the use of religious images. The most important evidence of Jewish reactions
to Protestantism comes from Rabbi Joseph of Rosheim (ca. 1478–1554), a
powerful and effective leader of Jewish communities in the Holy Roman
Empire. At the 1530 Diet of Augsburg, Joseph defended Judaism in a public
debate with the anti-Jewish polemicist Antonius Margaritha (a Jewish convert to Christianity who published a widely influential tract, *The Entire
Jewish Faith*, 1530). Joseph also wrote a book against Martin Bucer's attacks
on Jews and vigorously opposed Luther's efforts. Citing dangerous agitation
in Alsace, Joseph convinced the Strasbourg magistracy to ban publication
and distribution of Luther's *On the Jews and Their Lies*. Joseph was also the
major actor in the negotiations for Charles V's *Letter of Protection*, issued in
Speyer on April 3, 1544, a milestone marking a turn to more favorable
policies toward Jews in the empire. It promised protection of synagogues
and cemeteries, and outlawed banishments without imperial permission. It
also forbade prosecution of blood libel charges and even freed Jews traveling
outside their communal jurisdictions from the obligation of wearing the
Jewish badge. The 1544 imperial patent of protection was confirmed by
subsequent early modern emperors: Rudolf I (1562), Maximilian II (1566),
Rudolf II (1577), Matthias (1612), Ferdinand II (1630), Leopold I (1663), and
Charles VI (1714).

In the sixteenth century, a number of Jewish communities thrived in
northern Italy, the most important ones being Venice and Mantua. Excluded
since 1397, Jews were finally readmitted to Venice in 1516 but immediately
subjected to strict ghetto enclosure. Although that was unprecedented for
Italian Jewry, ghettoization soon became a norm. The Venetian ghetto grew
prodigiously, in both numbers and wealth, reaching a population of approximately two thousand by the end of the century. Venice also became a major
center of Jewish printing, with Daniel Bomberg, a Christian who collaborated with Jewish scholars, operating a prolific Hebrew press there during the
years 1517–1549. In general, the innovation of the ghetto had a mixed impact
on Jewish life. Even if the walls were unquestionably permeable, the ghetto
contributed to severe social segregation and humiliation. Nonetheless, it also
facilitated Jewish self-government, and Jewish culture and learning certainly

flourished in Venice during the sixteenth and seventeenth centuries. In the Papal States, however, toleration of Judaism plummeted to a low point in the sixteenth century. In 1555, Paul IV issued the papal bull *Cum nimis absur-dum*, which effectively abrogated the medieval *Sicut Judaeis*. As of the 1550s, Jews in the Papal States were subject to the inquisition; some were burned at the stake; a strict system of ghettos was imposed in 1555; and in 1569 Jews were expelled from all parts of the Papal States except the recently formed ghettos of Rome and Ancona.

Although John Calvin spent most of his life in France and Geneva, places from which well before his time Jews had been banished, he probably had some direct contact with Jews during his stay in Ferrara, 1536, and his exile in Strasbourg, 1538–1541, especially during extended visits to Frankfurt, Hagenau, and Worms. In his 1561 commentary on Daniel, he wrote: "I have often spoken with many Jews, but I never saw a drop of piety, never a grain of truth or natural intelligence, indeed, I never perceived any common sense in any Jew" (*CR* 58:605). Moreover, like many other Christian theologians, Calvin caricatured Jewish messianic hopes, claiming that Jews expected the Messiah would "come into the world to bring an abundance of goods so that each may have his fill to eat, that there will be no wars, that each should rest and indulge in various delights; this is how the Jews have imagined their savior" (*CR* 70:113). He also complained about Jewish money lending, in 1556 saying that, although Jews are permitted to be moneylenders, that does not mean that "today they may aggrieve and burden God's children" (*CR* 56:117). He occasionally mentioned host desecration, in one instance lambasting the ongoing idolatrous veneration of a prominent host desecration relic in Paris (from 1250), but without questioning the validity of the anti-Jewish innuendo.[2] Calvin also accused theological adversaries of "Judaizing," a common trope in Christian polemics on images, ceremonies, and doctrines of justification: "Thus we see that such a multitude of ceremonies in the Mass is a type of Judaizing, patently contrary to Christianity"(*CR* 33:456).

Calvin's most sustained focus on contemporary Judaism occurs in *Response to the Questions and Objections of a Certain Jew* (*Ad quaestiones et obiecta Judaei cuiusdam responsio*; *CR* 37:657–674), a work that was published posthumously in 1575. The *Response* consists of Calvin's answers to 23 Jewish objections that were printed in a 1555 Paris edition of Shem Tov ibn Shaprut's *Eben Bohan* (*Touchstone*), a work that included a Hebrew translation of the Gospel of Matthew. The Jewish objections, which Calvin

---

[2] Achim Detmers, *Reformation und Judentum: Israel-Lehren und Einstellungen zum Judentum von Luther bis zum frühen Calvin* (Stuttgart: Kohlhammer, 2001), 317.

included in Latin translation, pertain mainly to Christological aspects of the Gospel text. Although most of the responses are concise theological explications (which suggests the work may have been intended for missionizing Jews), in a few instances Calvin lapses into strident anti-Jewish polemic, as, for example, in question 6, where he labels Jews "profane people, indeed, filthy dogs" (*CR* 37:662). Thus, while Calvin never advocated persecution (or banishment) of Jewish communities, his theological perspectives informed a profound rejection of Judaism.

SUGGESTED FURTHER READINGS

Baron, Salo W. "John Calvin and the Jews." In *Harry Austryn Wolfson Jubilee Volume*, ed. Saul Lieberman. Jerusalem: American Academy for Jewish Research, 1965, 1:141–163.

Bell, Dean Phillip, and Stephen G. Burnett, eds. *Jews, Judaism, and the Reformation in Sixteenth-Century Germany*. Leiden: Brill, 2006.

Breuer, Mordechai. "The Jewish Middle Ages." In *German-Jewish History in Modern Times*, ed. Michael A. Meyer. New York: Columbia University Press, 1990, 1:7–77.

Detmers, Achim. *Reformation und Judentum: Israel-Lehren und Einstellungen zum Judentum von Luther bis zum frühen Calvin*. Stuttgart: Kohlhammer, 2001.

Israel, Jonathan I. *European Jewry in the Age of Mercantilism 1550–1750*. 3rd. ed. London: Littman, 1998.

Kaufmann, Thomas. *Luther's Jews*. Oxford: Oxford University Press, 2017.

Price, David H. "Maximilian I and Toleration of Judaism." *Archiv für Reformationsgeschichte* 105 (2014): 7–29.

Ruderman, David B. *Early Modern Jewry*. Princeton, NJ: Princeton University Press, 2010.

Schreiner, Stefan. "Jüdische Reaktionen auf die Reformation." *Judaica* 39 (1983): 150–168.

Weldler-Steinberg, Augusta. *Geschichte der Juden in der Schweiz vom 16. Jahrhundert bis nach der Emancipation*. 2 vols. Zürich: Schweizerischer Israelitischer Gemeindebund, 1966–1970.

17

Refugees

Jesse Spohnholz

John Calvin may be the most famous Reformation-era refugee.[1] Born in northern France, Calvin fled probable persecution in 1534, finally settling in his new home of Geneva in 1541, where he became a towering religious reformer. Historians have treated Calvin not just as a reformer *of* Geneva but also as a reformer *in* Geneva, who understood the Reformation as part of a broader international (or perhaps better put, universal) struggle for truth in a battle that went beyond the confines of any civic jurisdiction. During Calvin's time, Geneva – a city of about 10,000 inhabitants – doubled in size as a result of Reformed Protestant refugees coming from France. As Geneva became known as a welcome asylum for Reformed Protestants fleeing persecution, refugees came from elsewhere as well. As the English exile John Bale living in Geneva wrote of that city, "[I]s it not wonderful that Spaniards, Italians, Scots, Englishmen, Frenchmen, Germans, disagreeing in manners, speech, and apparel . . . being coupled only with the yoke of Christ, should live so lovingly and friendly . . . like a spiritual and Christian congregation."[2] Reformed Refugees fled France not just for Geneva, but for Strasbourg, Basel, Metz, Montbéliard, and elsewhere. Meanwhile, English Protestants made temporary homes in Basel, Zurich, Wesel, and other continental cities. Estimates suggest that as many as 100,000 Flemish and Walloon Protestants fled the Low Countries for cities in England and the Holy Roman Empire, including London, Cologne, Hamburg, and Frankfurt. Like Geneva, exile centers like Emden and Wesel doubled in size by the 1560s and 1570s. There

---

[1] This chapter uses *refugee*, *exile*, and *forced migrant* as synonyms not because it is inattentive to possible differences in meaning, but because clearly categorizing types of sixteenth-century migrants confuses more than it clarifies, for reasons touched on in the conclusion.

[2] Quoted in Graeme Murdock, *Beyond Calvin: The Intellectual, Political and Cultural World of Europe's Reformed Churches, c. 1540–1620* (London: Palgrave Macmillan, 2004), 34.

is no doubt that these experiences profoundly shaped Calvin and his co-religionists. But how distinctive were those changes? To answer that question, this chapter will summarize the experience of religious expulsion as a mass phenomenon across the long sixteenth century (1490s–1610s).

The most dramatic mass expulsion of this era began a few years before Calvin was even born. In 1492, King Ferdinand and Queen Isabella of Spain issued an edict ordering the removal of all practicing Jews from their lands. That act can be seen as either the start of more than a century of mass expulsions or the culmination of a process that had been developing for more than a century. Looking backward, the English government had expelled all Jews from its lands in 1290; the French crown did the same in 1394. In the fifteenth century, we see an intensification of expulsion orders in the politically decentralized lands of Italy and Germany. Jurisdictions that banned Jews included Vienna (1421), Linz (1421), Cologne (1424), Zurich (1436), Augsburg (1438), Bavaria (1442 and 1450), Florence (1494 and 1527), Perugia (1484), Vicenza (1486), Parma (1488), Milan (1489), Lucca (1489), Nuremberg (1499), Ulm (1499), Treviso (1509), Conegliano (1511 and 1522), and Regensburg (1519). What was distinct about the expulsion of 1492 was its scope. Estimates range widely about the number of exiles – was it 35,000 or 200,000? – but scholars acknowledge that the scale was unprecedented. Many Jews first fled to Portugal, but when the king there issued his own expulsion order in 1497, many thousands left. Large numbers went to North Africa and the Ottoman Empire. In 1492, there were few Jews living in the Ottoman city of Salonika (present-day Thessaloniki, in Greece). By 1519, Iberian Jews made up more than half of the population and worshiped in 24 separate synagogues. By the late sixteenth century, many former Iberian Jews had also made their way to the Netherlands, where they formed a significant community in Antwerp and later in Amsterdam.

These expulsions targeted Muslims too. After 1492, hundreds of thousands of Muslims still lived under Spanish rule. From 1499, the government coerced Muslims to accept baptisms, converted their mosques into churches, and suppressed Muslim religious texts, halal foods, and the practice of circumcision. These efforts sparked rebellions, which only further stoked fears among Christians. In Castile in 1502 and Aragon in 1525, the government gave Muslims the choice to covert or leave. By 1526, any Muslim who remained in Spain was considered to have converted – and called a *morisco*. Further tensions exploded in a massive revolt in 1568. By 1609, fears of rebellion and the failure to suppress Islam encouraged the Spanish king to order the expulsion of all people of Muslim dissent. An estimated 300,000 moriscos fled, mostly to North Africa and the Ottoman Empire.

After the Reformation broke out, Christians started expelling Christians in large numbers as well. Facing persecution as heretics, early evangelicals were expelled from or fled Catholic lands frequently. In 1521, Martin Luther famously had to escape certain persecution in disguise, fleeing the imperial city of Worms for the safety of the Electorate of Saxony. The experience of fleeing into exile became even more common as theological controversy spilled out into war, and as princes equated political obedience with conformity to their church. After the Schmalkaldic War in the Holy Roman Empire, the Peace of Augsburg (1555) guaranteed all imperial subjects the right to emigrate (*ius emigrandi*) if they disagreed with the religious order in a territory. Thus after 1555, many thousands of Lutherans fled their homes; serving as an "Exile of Christ" became critical to Lutheran identity. Lutheran theologians who experienced peregrinations embraced this moniker (in Latin, *Exul Christi*), wrote comfort letters for fellows exiles, and encouraged co-religionists to join them as a sign of their devotion to God. Perhaps the first Lutheran to call himself an "exile" was Nicolaus von Amsdorf, who fled Saxe-Anhalt to Magdeburg in 1547. Other Lutherans who spent considerable time reflecting on the spiritual implications of widespread exile of their day included Urbanus Rhegius, Matthias Flacius Illyricus, Nikolas Gallus, Cyriacus Spangenberg, and Tilemann Heshusius.

Given their pariah status across Europe, it is not surprising that Anabaptists and other radical reformers faced expulsions in large numbers as well. Anabaptists were banned from nearly every community where they developed a substantial following. In the 1520s, many Swiss Anabaptists fled to Poland and Transylvania. Radical reformers from across the German-speaking lands also escaped to the Margraviate of Moravia, a Habsburg state nestled between Austria, Bohemia, Hungary, and Silesia. While many of these dissenters moved to villages where they could escape notice, a larger group settled in the town of Nikolsburg (in Czech: Mikulov). The Austerlitz Brethren, the Swiss Brethren, and the Hutterites also had extensive experiences with forced migration and exile. Anabaptist and radical thinkers were so vulnerable to persecution that they often never formed stable communities at all. One recent author describes "moving communities" of Christian brothers and sisters to capture this transient lifestyle.[3] Most leaders among radical Christians – including David Joris, Menno Simons, Kasper Schwenkfelt, Sebastian Franck, Hans Denck, Johannes Bunderlin, Ulrich Stadler, and Jakob Hutte – experienced life as a refugee, most multiple times.

---

[3] Mathilde Monge, *Des communautés mouvants. Les 'sociétes des frère chrétiens' en Rhénanie du Nord Juliers, Berg, Cologne vers 1530–1694* (Geneva: Droz, 2015).

Michael Servetus, the Spanish anti-Trinitarian, was chased out of Catholic Spain and France, only to seek safety in Calvin's Geneva, where he was burned at the stake for heresy. The eclectic spiritualist doctor from The Hague, Justus Velsius, was decried by people as diverse as the Jesuit Martin Delrio and John Calvin. Velsius was forced out of Catholic Leuven, Protestant Strasbourg, Catholic Cologne, Protestant Frankfurt, Catholic Cleves, Protestant Heidelberg, Protestant Zurich, Protestant London, Catholic Groningen, and Protestant Leiden.

Wherever Protestant regimes were able to establish themselves, Catholics also became refugees. When Protestant rebels captured the Northern Netherlands, Dutch Catholics fled to Germany and the Southern Netherlands. In the Holy Roman Empire, Kevelaer, Kalkar, and Cologne became hubs for followers of the Roman Church who had fled the Protestant Dutch Republic. During the reign of the Queen Elizabeth, English Catholic refugee communities popped up in the Southern Netherlands, France, Italy, and Spain. Wealthy English Catholics also established convents and schools in Catholic territories on the continent, so that their children could be educated in their faith rather than in the Protestant schools back home. Protestant and Catholic refugees alike printed books for smuggling into their home territories and conspired against their home government, in hopes that their vision of divine order might rule.

Thus, no religious group in sixteenth-century Europe was untouched by the experiences of persecution and expulsion. In a world defined by the norms of sacral communalism, life as an exile or refugee could be profoundly unsettling. Often exiles drew on preexisting intellectual tools to cope with loss. Living abroad could sometimes promote a kind of exile mentality, which reinforced a sense of righteousness on account of suffering for divine truth. John Calvin reflected on the devotion to God and the pious marginalization from the material trappings of this earth that life in exile inspired. Jewish exiles often saw expulsion as a reenactment of stories of the Tanakh; writings like Samuel Usque's *Consolation for the Tribulation of Israel* (1553) described expulsion as part of an ancient tradition of the suffering of the Israelites. Among Muslim exiles, the experience of expulsion intensified the sense of martyrdom in the face of oppression. Muslim refugees from Spain living in Morocco, Algiers, and Tunis circulated anti-Christian polemics, including Ahmad bin Qasam al-Hagari's influential *The Supporter of Religion against the Infidels* (1637). The *Gospel of Barnabas*, an account of Jesus's life that matched Islamic teachings rather than Christian ones, also circulated among Muslim refugees living in North Africa. Among Lutheran exiles after 1555, exile emboldened authors – Wolfgang Walder, Nicolaus von

Amsdorf, and others – to celebrate divine truth and warn against making concessions to ungodly governments. For Anabaptists and radical reformers like Leonard Schiemer and Jakob Hutter, exile offered an opportunity to emphasize the immateriality of the true church and reflect on the religious command to abandon worldly attachments. As the Hutterite leader Peter Walpot wrote, "[T]he church should [just as the Israelites] also be in the wilderness of this world."[4] Dutch Catholics living in German exile celebrated their suffering in the Catholic tradition of martyrdom for the true church. The Catholic exile Jan Gerritz Stempelse was regarded as "a living saint" in Cologne. When Reformed Protestant authors like Calvin consoled their readers by praising the pious suffering of exiles and assuring them that suffering was a mark of righteousness, they may have had different emphases from authors of other religions, but they were participating in a pastoral tradition that had parallels in all Abrahamic faiths.

While the experience of living in exile could intensify devotion, it sometimes also forced people to learn new traditions in ways that could undermine dogmatism, facilitate cultural exchange, and promote intellectual creativity. Jacob Montino ben Samuel, the Jewish exile from Spain who moved to Bologna, spent much of his career translating Hebrew editions of medieval Arabic texts into Latin for Christian readers. The Spanish Protestant exile, Antonio del Corro, produced the first Spanish grammar book in English, but also promoted reconciliation between Reformed Protestants and Lutherans as well as antipredestinarian ideas that ran him afoul of orthodox Calvinists. The French Protestant in Basel, Sebastian Castellio, promoted similar antipredestinarian ideas, but also developed perhaps the most comprehensive argument for religious toleration of the century. The Italian Protestant refugee in England, Jacobus Acontius, used his engineering skills to help Parliament drain swamps and improve military fortifications. In 1565, he also published his *Stratagematum Satanae*, which promoted a wide-ranging tolerance of religious difference. The bickering promoted by dogmatism, Acontius argued, was the product of Satan's work that threatened the unity of Christianity.

The experience of exile by sixteenth-century Europeans could lead to all sorts of diverse social, cultural, and institutional impacts on the exiles. Among Sephardic Jews in the post-1492 diaspora, the *kahalim* took on a more coherent and central role than they ever had before, such that Jewish communities were often remarkably self-regulated. The development of a

---

[4] Quoted in Hans Leaman, "The Consolation of Exile: Confessional Migration and Identity in the German Reformation" (PhD dissertation, Yale University, 2014), 482.

distinct Sephardic identity seems to have been largely the result of Iberian Jews' exilic experience. For Dutch Reformed Protestants lacking government support, consistories and classes took on central roles of community organizing apart from secular authorities. Later, many retrospectively saw this independence from governmental supervision as a matter of principle rather than necessity. Spanish moriscos came to see themselves as apart from and superior to their Arab Muslim neighbors in North Africa. English Catholics living on the continent developed an intense devotion to their Englishness. Meanwhile, in Germany, having family who had fled to foreign lands for their faith became a mark of pride among people who operated in multiple worlds at once.

Exile impacted hosts in profound ways too. In the short term, populations often regarded newcomers as threats to their well-being and social order. In Calvin's Geneva, locals feared that French refugees would take their jobs and passed laws restricting foreigners' economic activities. We find similar xenophobia elsewhere, including anti-Jewish attitudes in Italy and the Ottoman Empire, anti-Dutch attitudes in England and Germany, anti-*morisco* attitudes in North Africa, and anti-English attitudes in Spain. In some cases, refugees did put a short-term drain on charity coffers and upward pressure on the cost of food, clothing, and housing. But if local populations were often quick to see the downsides of welcoming refugees, many were usually not good at noticing the positive economic impacts. When Jewish exiles arrived in the Ottoman lands, Italy, or the Netherlands from Spain and Portugal, they brought with them skills and capital as merchants, bankers, interpreters, diplomats, and doctors. In eastern and southeastern Europe, governments actively courted Jewish exiles to move to their underpopulated lands. In the Dutch Republic and Germany, Jewish residents sometimes secured increased freedoms from city officials by threatening to take their business to competing jurisdictions nearby. Muslims fleeing Spain for Tunisia, Morocco, Algeria, and the Ottoman Empire brought valuable skills as farmers, weavers, ceramic workers, masons, and carpenters. In their new homes, they built irrigation canals, which allowed for more efficient farming and demographic expansion, and introduced new weaving industries that boosted exports across the Mediterranean. Similarly, Protestant refugees fleeing the Low Countries for England and the Holy Roman Empire brought weaving skills with them. Foreign weavers taught locals to make fancy silks and laces that were sought after by wealthy elites. Production of these "new draperies" required the construction of factories and the hiring of apprentices, spurring on international trade.

Foreign merchants escaping persecution brought trade connections with them, but also accessed new markets. However, we should be careful not to imagine that the experience of exile benefited merchants. There were too many challenges to trading in foreign lands to think that merchants in exile were *more successful* than those who were left unhindered to operate their businesses back home. Merchants in exile often lacked contacts and reputations so critical for traders, and transportation and communication links during times of war and persecution could be risky. Yet, when wealthy merchants fled persecution for other lands, they transformed economies. Most notably, refugees played a critical role in the economic expansion of sixteenth-century London, Amsterdam, and Istanbul. Of course, there are plenty of examples where exiles did not transform economies. In 1562, the Elector Palatine gave a tract of land to Dutch Protestant exiles to found a new city, hoping to promote economic development in his territory. Unfortunately for him, few migrants found the settlement attractive and those who did move often left soon after in disappointment. There were all sorts of other social and cultural impacts of exiles on host communities as well, most of which have never been studied in detail. But refugees introduced new ways of speaking and thinking to their communities, new artistic and literary traditions, as well as new fashions and foods.

It's important to conclude by recognizing that religious persecution was not the only factor encouraging increased migration in the sixteenth century. The expansion of international commerce, improving sailing technology, changing military practices, expanding educational institutions, and other social changes were leading men and women to uproot for new lands in unprecedented numbers. Sometimes it is difficult to tell whether "push factors" or "pull factors" were the most important motivators for migrants. In addition, it is often impossible to discern whether migration was forced or voluntary, or to distinguish between religious, economic, and political motivations for uprooting one's home. In conclusion, historians need to be careful about confusing lofty celebratory rhetoric with the more complicated reality, or making hasty conclusions about the nature and impact of sixteenth-century migrations on any group of believers or a specific refugee, including Calvin.

SUGGESTED FURTHER READINGS

Burke, Peter. *Exile and Expatriates in the History of Knowledge, 1500–2000.* Waltham, MA: Brandais University Press, 2017.

Carr, Matthew. *Blood and Faith: The Purging of Muslim Spain.* New York: The New Press, 2009.

Janssen, Geert H. *The Dutch Revolt and Catholic Exile in Reformation Europe.* Cambridge: Cambridge University Press, 2014.

Luu, Lien Bich. *Immigrants and the Industries of London, 1500–1700*. Aldershot: Ashgate, 2005.

Oberman, Heiko. *John Calvin and the Reformation of the Refugees*. Geneva: Librarie Droz, 2009.

Ray, Jonathan. *After Expulsion: 1492 and the Making of Sephardic Jewry*. New York: New York University Press, 2013.

Rodriquez, Mercedes Garcia-Arenal, and Gerard A. Wiegers, eds. *The Expulsion of the Moriscos from Spain: A Mediterranean Diaspora*. Leiden, The Netherlands: Brill, 2014.

Spohnholz, Jesse, and Gary Waite, eds. *Exile and Religious Identity, 1500–1800*. London: Pickering & Chatto, 2014.

Terpstra, Nicholas. *Religious Refugees in the Early Modern World: An Alternative History of the Reformation*. Cambridge: Cambridge University Press, 2015.

18

ℭ

Calvin and Women

Elizabeth A. Lehfeldt

The question of how the transformations of the early modern era changed – or did not change – the lives of women has become a familiar question for historians. Joan Kelly's pathbreaking "Did Women Have a Renaissance?" challenged scholars to interrogate the impact of watershed moments, like the Renaissance, and to resist assuming that women necessarily benefited from them.[1]

When we apply this approach to the religious changes of the era, the scholarship on the impact of Luther's reforms is robust and instructive.[2] We do not know as much, however, about the impact of Calvin and Calvinism on women.[3] This chapter proposes a preliminary examination of this issue that focuses on three areas: Calvin's theology, his interactions with his female adherents, and the reception of Calvinism among women.

---

[1] Joan Kelly, "Did Women Have a Renaissance?," *Women, History, and Theory: The Essays of Joan Kelly* (Chicago: University of Chicago Press, 1984), 19–50.

[2] Lyndal Roper, *The Holy Household: Women and Morals in Reformation Augsburg* (Oxford: Oxford University Press, 1989); Merry Wiesner, "Beyond Women and the Family: Toward a Gender Analysis of the Reformation," *Sixteenth Century Journal* 18:3 (1987): 311–321; Susan Karant-Nunn, "Continuity and Change: Some of the Effects of the Reformation on the Women of Zwickau," *Sixteenth Century Journal* 13:2 (1984): 17–42. Although as Merry Wiesner-Hanks aptly notes, much of this scholarship has moved beyond querying whether a particular religious movement was good or bad for women "because of the stress on difference and diversity" in the experiences of women; see her "Protestant Movements," in Allyson M. Poska, Jane Couchman, and Katherine A. McIver (eds.), *The Ashgate Research Companion to Women and Gender in Early Modern Europe* (Burlington, VT: Ashgate, 2013), 130.

[3] Amanda Eurich's essay is an important corrective in this regard, but it is focused on Huguenot women and not Calvin more generally; see her "Women in the Huguenot Community," in Raymond A. Mentzer and Bertrand Van Ruymbeke (eds.), *A Companion to the Huguenots* (Leiden, The Netherlands: Brill, 2016), 118–149.

From his pulpit and those of his Calvinist followers, women would have heard Calvin's ideas and specifically his theology of gender. As with Luther before him, Calvin's theological ideas about women were a decidedly mixed bag and simultaneously asserted the worth of women while also highlighting their inferiority to men. Calvin recognized "women, just as men, as the elect creatures of God," created in his image.[4] Women shared in both human-kind's sinfulness and propensity for redemption. Thus, Calvin held both Adam and Eve responsible for the transgressions in the Garden of Eden. At the same time, he also extended the promise of salvation to both men and women equally.

When Calvin attempted to reconcile this position of what we might call the spiritual equality of women with the prevailing social and cultural assumptions about women's inferiority, however, his ideas became more complicated. Like other Protestant reformers before him, Calvin's ideas about the earthly kingdom – as opposed to the heavenly one – upheld sixteenth-century notions about women's inferiority. So while both sexes were created in God's image, women were so "to a lesser degree."[5] Even before the fall, Calvin believed that Adam had dominion over Eve and that she existed to be his submissive helpmate. And Calvin expected that this hierarchy would be duplicated in all human relationships between men and women. When others (see the example of Marie Dentière in the following text) challenged this position and wondered about the biblical example of female prophets and leaders, Calvin was not swayed. For Calvin, these women were extraordinary and did "not annul the ordinary rules"[6] that governed everyday society.

If this was Calvin's assessment of the status of women, what did this mean for their vocation and roles in society? Assessing this requires a consider-ation of the ways in which women encountered Calvin and his message and their subsequent response. Rather than seeing Calvin's message as some-thing they passively received, we should look to the evidence of how they grappled with the reformer's new ideas and institutions. Some became enthusiastic converts, some conducted daily lives governed by Calvinist structures and strictures, and some resisted Calvinism.

Not surprisingly, Calvin had many female adherents who found his message compelling and acted upon it. A particularly noteworthy group of

---

[4] Mary Potter, "Gender Equality and Gender Hierarchy in Calvin's Theology," *Signs* 11:4 (Summer 1986), 726.
[5] Quoted in ibid., 727.
[6] Quoted in ibid., 729.

these proponents were French royal and noblewomen of the mid-sixteenth century.[7] During this period a distinctive Calvinist party, which became known as the Huguenots, emerged in France and Huguenot women played a variety of roles in support of the movement, ranging from offering safe haven to their fellow partisans to helping to create policy to overseeing specific Protestant reforms. The seriousness with which Calvin regarded the role of these women and their devotion to his reforms is demonstrated in his extensive correspondence with them.[8]

One of the more celebrated examples of such involvement comes from the case of Jeanne d'Albret, queen regnant of Navarre and mother of the future Henry IV of France. She waded into the fraught waters of religious turmoil in France in 1560, declaring herself a Calvinist after a mid-century conversion experience. Jeanne's mother, Marguerite of Navarre, had been an early supporter of religious reform (though she studiously avoided being labeled either Catholic or Protestant). Marguerite had gone so far as to offer safe haven to Calvin and to allow various Protestant texts to circulate at her court. Jeanne undoubtedly received some of the preparation for her eventual conversion to Protestantism as a result of Marguerite's enthusiasm for religious reformers and their new ideas.

Jeanne's high-profile endorsement was a definite boost for the Huguenot cause. And she did not hesitate to wield her authority in support of the movement. She sponsored public preaching and created a Protestant academy in imitation of the one in Geneva.[9] She held openly Calvinist services at court.[10] Calvin admired her devotion, writing to her that "when I see how the spirit of God rules you I have more occasion to give thanks than to exhort you."[11]

Calvin also clearly regarded Jeanne as an important source of leverage at the French court and sought to capitalize on her influence. He leaned heavily on her to try to convert her husband, Antoine. This proved to be a daunting task. He ultimately had to acknowledge that Jeanne faced significant challenges from Antoine, who was threatening her with repudiation and banishment from the court. But Calvin, convinced of her pivotal role, urged her to

---

[7] Nancy L. Roelker, "The Role of Noblewomen in the French Reformation," *Archiv für Reformationsgeschichte/Archive for Reformation History* 63 (1972): 168–195.

[8] Charmarie Blaisdell, "Calvin's Letters to Women: The Courting of Ladies in High Places," *Sixteenth Century Journal* 13:3 (Autumn 1982): 67–84.

[9] Roelker, "Role of Noblewomen," 183.

[10] Ibid., 179.

[11] Nancy Lyman Roelker, *Queen of Navarre: Jeanne d'Albret, 1528–1572* (Cambridge, MA: Harvard University Press, 1968), 153.

stay the course and wrote to her saying, "do not fail to stand firm."[12] Yet Jeanne would not succeed in converting her husband. After her husband's death, she did, however, exercise sovereign power in her territories of Béarn and Navarre, seeking to consolidate them as Calvinist strongholds.[13] In 1563, for example, she issued an edict in Béarn that outlawed the Catholic Mass and rejected papal authority.[14]

Calvin's attitude toward the role of women in the movement, however, was not consistent. He welcomed the advocacy of some, like Jeanne, but not others. His reaction to the efforts of another woman, Marie Denitère, reveals much greater skepticism and even disdain. Like Jeanne d'Albret, Marie was a strong and outspoken proponent of Calvinism, but ultimately, Calvin characterized her as "unruly."[15]

Marie was a former Augustinian nun from Tournai who had left her convent in the 1520s and married a former priest. The two had eventually moved to Strasbourg, a hotbed of reformation ferment that attracted such thinkers as Martin Bucer and Guillaume Farel. Upon the death of her first husband she married one of Farel's followers, Antoine Froment. The couple would soon move to Geneva and become embedded in the evangelical reform efforts there. In 1535, for example, Marie joined her husband and another reform partisan, Pierre Viret, to lead an attack on the local convent of Poor Clares, urging the nuns to abandon their monastic lifestyle and reject their vow of celibacy.[16] In the wake of Calvin being driven out of Geneva in 1538 Marie wrote an account of those events and the religious turmoil that had rocked the city. This account, her *Very Useful Epistle* (1539), was addressed to the French queen, Marguerite of Navarre. Marie took full advantage of this letter to express her support for religious reform, her condemnation of the city officials who had driven Calvin and Farel from the city, and her critique of the Catholic Church.

Yet Marie also used the letter to promote the right for women to be active in the church and religious matters. Her support for Calvin's reforms in Geneva became a platform from which she argued for the spiritual authority of women. Meeting the reformers on their own terms and drawing examples from Scripture, she praised female biblical figures like Sarah, Deborah, and

[12] Ibid., 182.
[13] Roelker, "Role of Noblewomen," 180.
[14] Kirsi Stjerna, *Women and the Reformation* (Malden, MA: Blackwell Publishing, 2009), 167
[15] Marie Dentière, *Epistle to Marguerite de Navarre: And, Preface to a Sermon by John Calvin*, ed. and trans. Mary B. McKinley (Chicago: University of Chicago Press, 2004), 19.
[16] Ibid., 2–9.

the Queen of Sheba for their wisdom and faith.[17] She posited that the message of the Bible was available to all, and famously contended that there was not one scripture for men and another for women: "Therefore, if God has given grace to some good women, revealing to them by his holy scriptures, something holy and good, should they hesitate to write, speak, and declare it to one another.... Ah, it would be too bold to try to stop them, and it would be foolish for us to hide the talent that God has given us."[18] Dentière was clearly empowered by the message of Calvinism. She was excited by a world in which she "could be engaged in the pure and serious enterprise of reading and talking about Scripture."[19]

But Calvin's reactions to her efforts revealed the limits of women's participation in the movement. It is unclear what fueled his discontent with her activities, but there are a few possibilities. To begin with, unlike her royal and noble counterparts, she did not have an overtly political role to play. Her *Epistle* was addressed to the queen – a savvy move – but she did not move in noble or royal circles. She was not in a position to sway national politics like Jeanne d'Albret. Perhaps her lack of direct access to the highest levels of political power dampened Calvin's enthusiasm for her efforts. He was also probably troubled by her bold assertions about women's rights to offer theological commentary and instruction.

Jeanne and Marie were highly visible advocates of Calvinism. Though it is more difficult to track and document, it is also clear that Calvinism appealed to women in more everyday ways. This appeal probably derived from various features of the movement. For women who already enjoyed a degree of freedom, such as widows or women who held independent occupations like midwives or dressmakers, Calvinism "complemented in a new sphere the scope and independence that the women's lives already had."[20] Access to the Bible also clearly compelled their enthusiasm for the new religion. Inspired by opportunities like special catechism classes and other incentives to become literate, women sought the opportunity to read and interpret Scripture on their own. As the case of Marie Dentière has demonstrated, however, there were limits to women exercising this access. Overall, like their Lutheran and Catholic brethren the male Calvinist hierarchy deplored anything that hinted at women teaching, preaching, or prophesying and

[17] Ibid., 54.
[18] Ibid., 55–56.
[19] Natalie Zemon Davis, "City Women and Religious Change," *Society and Culture in Early Modern France* (Stanford, CA: Stanford University Press, 1975), 79.
[20] Ibid., 81.

invoked Paul's all-too-familiar dictum that women "keep silence in the churches."[21] Instead Calvin upheld motherhood as a woman's most natural vocation and believed that the home was the most appropriate venue for their participation in religious instruction.[22]

Calvin's efforts to limit the role of women, however, did not, stop them from assuming other kinds of dramatic roles in support of the Calvinist movement. In France the ascendant popularity of Calvinism had created deep rifts within the royal family and nobility that eventually escalated into the armed conflict of the Wars of Religion. Because the war disrupted "traditional patterns of patriarchal authority and privilege,"[23] women had the opportunity to play a significant part in how events unfolded. Women "participated actively in the defence of their communities."[24] They ferried letters and information and offered various kinds of material assistance and lodging.[25] In all these ways, they asserted, through actions that were not overtly religious, their support of Calvinism.

Women also encountered Calvinism when they were held to account for its precepts and teachings. In Geneva, the Consistory, a council composed of pastors and lay elders, enforced Calvinist teachings and church discipline. This gave the Consistory a wide-ranging remit and meant that they often heard cases involving women. Historians have mined these cases as a rich source for how particular groups fared under Calvinism. Interestingly, any comprehensive analysis of how women were treated by the Consistory yields a mixed picture.

In the early years of the Consistory its leaders frequently investigated the piety of women. In fact, despite more men than women appearing before the Consistory between 1542 and 1544, women constituted 55 percent of those questioned about church attendance and 60 percent of those asked to demonstrate their ability to recite prayers and creeds.[26] It would appear that the Consistory expected women to be more tied than their male counterparts to the remnants of Catholic piety.

---

[21] Ibid., 82–83.
[22] Eurich, "Women in the Huguenot Community," 140.
[23] Ibid., 124.
[24] Brian Sandberg, "'Generous Amazons Came to the Breach': Besieged Women, Agency and Subjectivity during the French Wars of Religion," *Gender and History* 16:3 (November 2004): 667.
[25] Susan Broomhall, *Women and Religion in Sixteenth-Century France* (New York: Palgrave Macmillan, 2006), 126–131.
[26] Jeffrey R. Watt, "Women and the Consistory in Calvin's Geneva," *Sixteenth Century Journal* 24:2 (1993), 430.

The Consistory also had a decisive role to play in the regulation of marriage. In many ways it perpetuated a double standard when it adjudicated cases involving husbands and wives. Although in principle it upheld the same punishments for men and women in cases of simple fornication, adultery between a married and an unmarried person, or adultery between two married people, it did not uphold this equity in practice, and tended to punish female offenders more severely than male.[27]

Even though Calvinism supported the right of married couples to divorce under certain circumstances, this did not seem to create any particular benefit for women. In its first two years, the Consistory adjudicated three requests for divorces, all of which had been brought by men, and granted only one.[28] A reluctance to grant divorces would continue to characterize the work of the Consistory well into the eighteenth century.[29] If anything, the Consistory sought to keep marriages intact whenever possible.[30] This could work to the disadvantage of women. Cruelty did not constitute grounds for separation or divorce, and Calvin and his fellow reformers only cautioned husbands not to use excessive violence against their wives.[31]

Women did, however, clearly regard the Genevan Consistory and its counterparts in France and the Netherlands as a mechanism that might provide support and redress. In this, they "used" the consistories in ways that have been documented for other courts in early modern Europe.[32] So the consistories might be a place where they could seek restitution in cases of things like sexual assault. This did not mean, however, that the consistories were always sympathetic. Well-entrenched assumptions about the "natural" weaknesses of women often made it difficult for them to get support from these tribunals.[33]

So far this discussion of Calvin and women assumes an at least perfunctory acceptance of Calvinist reform. The impact of Calvin and his ideas, however, was also felt by women within the Catholic tradition. Though Geneva eventually adopted his reforms in a wholesale fashion with no toleration for Catholicism, that process was not immediate. So some women

---

[27] E. William Monter, "Women in Calvinist Geneva," *Signs* 6:2 (Winter 1980), 192–193.
[28] Watt, "Women and the Consistory in Calvin's Geneva," 436.
[29] Monter, "Women in Calvinist Geneva," 195.
[30] Ibid., 194.
[31] Watt, "Women and the Consistory in Calvin's Geneva," 436.
[32] For example, Laura Gowing, *Domestic Dangers: Women, Words, and Sex in Early Modern London* (Oxford: Oxford University Press, 1998).
[33] Eurich, "Women in the Huguenot Community," 133–140.

were implicated in Calvinism due to their resistance to it. A primary example of this was women who lived in convents and had a monastic vocation.

Jeanne de Jussie, a professed nun in the convent of Poor Clares that Marie Dentière stormed with her evangelical compatriots in 1535, provides a vivid account of what this disruption to Catholic tradition could look like. Monastic institutions were often one of the first things that the Protestant reformers attacked, and Calvinists were no different. Reformers did not believe that monasticism was a calling higher than marriage and thought that its insistence upon celibacy was misguided. Thus, a powerful way of making a statement about the ascendancy of reformed ideas was to shutter any local monasteries and convents, which is precisely what the Genevan reformers sought to do in the mid-1530s.

We get firsthand knowledge of what this looked like from within a convent from the chronicle written by Jeanne de Jussie. From her we learn that zealous evangelicals stormed the convent in 1535 and destroyed images and paintings. They soon departed, leaving the previously enclosed convent wide open. The continued enforcement of the evangelical platform in Geneva would eventually result in the nuns leaving the convent on August 30, 1535. They would reestablish their community in Annecy. The reconstituted community endured for two hundred years before being dissolved following the French Revolution.[34] The nuns, however, always referred to themselves as the "Sisters of Saint Clare of Geneva in refuge in Annecy,"[35] providing powerful testimony to the endurance of their sense of identity and the disruption wrought by Calvinism.

Laywomen also felt the impact of the loss of Catholicism and the expectation that they replace it with Calvinism. As the evidence from Consistory records cited previously reveals, women continued to cling to various Catholic practices. Chief among these was an attachment to the cult of the saints and the veneration of the Virgin Mary. In the first two years of the Consistory, for example, it "convoked more than twice as many women as men for adoration of the Virgin."[36] Ascendant Calvinism did not guarantee the obliteration of female Catholic devotion.

If we return to where this chapter began with an assessment of the transformations of the early modern period and their impact on women we find that Calvinism was like many other watershed religious movements

---

[34] Jeanne de Jussie, *A Short Chronicle: A Poor Clare's Account of the Reformation in Geneva*, ed. and trans. Carrie F. Klaus (Chicago: University of Chicago Press, 2006), 12.
[35] Quoted in ibid., 12.
[36] Watt, "Women and the Consistory in Calvin's Geneva," 434.

of the period. In the early stages, the message of Calvinism – like that of Lutheranism and even some of the Catholic reform movements – created opportunities for women, providing them with a voice and a platform. Women taught and preached and put their own distinctive stamp on these religious changes. As these movements solidified and became more institutionalized, though, such opportunities were closed off and the prevailing gender hierarchy limited what religious change could offer women.

In the specific case of Calvin, all the aforementioned evidence demonstrates that he and his ideas wrought broad changes – theological, political, and social. As a consequence, these changes in turn inspired a range of reactions among women. They became staunch partisans, even when their actions incurred disapproval. They supported war efforts. They sought redress in the Consistory. And some even resisted Calvinism. Calvin's theology and teachings extended a glimmer of hope to women like Jeanne d'Albret and Marie Dentière, who asserted their voices in the name of Calvinism. More ordinary women even were empowered by his message that encouraged literacy and theological engagement. At the same time, however, Calvinism created structures of social discipline like the Genevan Consistory that scrutinized women's lives and decisions. And where Calvinism prevailed, Catholic women lost trusted forms of devotion. Experiences of these women demonstrate that Calvin and the movement that he initiated ushered in significant changes. Through their voices and their actions women demonstrated what these changes meant to them.

SUGGESTED FURTHER READINGS

Blaisdell, Charmarie. "Calvin's Letters to Women: The Courting of Ladies in High Places." *Sixteenth Century Journal* 13, no. 3 (Autumn 1982): 67–84.

Davis, Natalie Zemon. "City Women and Religious Change," in *Society and Culture in Early Modern France*. Stanford: Stanford University Press, 1975. 13.

Eurich, Amanda. "Women in the Huguenot Community." In *A Companion to the Huguenots*, edited by Raymond A. Mentzer and Bertrand Van Ruymbeke, 118–149. Leiden: Brill, 2016).

Monter, E. William. "Women in Calvinist Geneva," *Signs* 6, no. 2 (Winter 1980): 189–209.

Potter, Mary. "Gender Equality and Gender Hierarchy in Calvin's Theology." *Signs* 11, no. 4 (Summer 1986): 725–739.

Roelker, Nancy L. "The Role of Noblewomen in the French Reformation." *Archiv für Reformationsgeschichte/Archive for Reformation History*, 63 (1972): 168–95.

PART IV

THE RELIGIOUS QUESTION

19

ℭ

Western Ideals of Religious Reform

Brad S. Gregory

The high ideals of the faith to which medieval Latin Christians were repeatedly exhorted had rendered ideas and initiatives of reform virtually coextensive with Christendom for centuries before the Protestant Reformation. The imitation of Christ through the practice of the virtues was not so much hard to understand as it was difficult to enact, whether among lay Christians, members of the secular clergy, or those men and women whose solemn vows in religious orders obliged them, at least in theory, self-consciously to pursue this virtuous imitation. "You must be perfect as your heavenly father is perfect"; "Love your enemies and pray for your persecutors"; "None of you can become my disciple if you do not give up all your possessions." Such admonitions were all but guaranteed to produce a gap between prescription and practice. No sooner were Jesus's commands proclaimed than Christians more often than not failed to realize them, whether they were members of the unlettered rural laity, skilled artisans and merchants in Western Europe's burgeoning cities, parish priests scraping by on meager benefices, or powerful prelates whose positions offered constant opportunities to indulge sinful desires. No medieval Christian with the scantest grasp of the faith could have doubted that sins abounded in Christendom.

When people care about something that is troubled, they typically seek to fix it. Hence reforming ideas, aspirations, and practices also abounded in medieval Christendom, both regarding Christians' exercise of the virtues at large and with respect to the Church's institutions. The question was just how to pursue this obviously pressing need – what forms the reforms should take. And the answer to that question depended on what, most fundamentally, one thought the character of the problem was.

Most commonly the problem was seen as a failure to enact Christ's commands as conveyed by the Church. "Why do you call me 'Lord, Lord,' and not do what I tell you?" Christians needed to walk the walk much better.

Between the start of the Gregorian revolution in the later eleventh century and Erasmian humanism in the early years of the sixteenth, the vast majority of efforts to reform either the tenor of Christians' lives in general or ecclesiastical institutions in particular took the Church's fundamental teachings and structures as given. The main problem plaguing Christendom, on this view, was that Christians in all stations of life, clerical and religious as well as lay, neglected to live as they should. The Church's basic doctrines and institutions were the framework within which reforming efforts were pursued, whatever forms they assumed. Such was simply a corollary of the acceptance of the Roman Church's authority, even when, at the height of its "constitutional crisis" in the early fifteenth century, conflicts raged between the respective defenders of councils and popes about where, within the Church, final authority reposed.

The Church's doctrines could be and were augmented, never more during these centuries than at the Fourth Lateran Council in 1215, which produced a body of reforming legislation more extensive than anything previously seen in the history of Latin Christianity. Reforming efforts were expressed in devotional practices and spiritualities that varied widely: the friars of the thirteenth century, for example, differed dramatically from the new monastic orders of the twelfth in their deliberate mobility and urban ministry to the laity, whose own appropriative imitation of monastic and mendicant piety increased substantially as the Middle Ages wore on, and was hugely aided in the 1450s by the invention of print, that great boon to late medieval piety. When self-critical members of these same religious orders belittled their own diminished commitment and fervor, they enacted reforms from within: the Observantine movement, from the later fourteenth century on, affected hundreds of monasteries and friaries whose members sought to observe their orders' respective founding rules with rigorous fidelity.[1] Different idioms of learned engagement with the faith, too, served ambitions of reform in the medieval Roman Church: the Carthusian commitment to monastic *lectio divina* differed from the careful distinctions through which Dominican, Franciscan, or Augustinian scholastics endeavored better to understand and thus to teach and preach the faith, which diverged yet again from the sacred philology and rhetoric of reform-minded Erasmian humanists who sought the renewal of Christendom through erudition in the service of education. And the aesthetic sensibilities that accompanied reform movements varied enormously: Cistercians liked their churches bare and spare,

---

[1] *Reformbemühungen und Observanzbestrebungen im spätmittelalterlichen Ordenswesen*, ed. Kaspar Elm (Berlin: Duncket & Humblot, 1989).

lest exterior distractions sabotage disciplines of contemplative interiority, in stark contrast to the fulsome decorative schemes pursued in some Franciscan or Dominican churches, where beauty sought to inspire holiness. The medieval Church was loaded with sins and alive with reforms. The basic idea behind them was to narrow the gap between prescriptions and practices, ideals and realities, between what the Church taught and how too many Christians lived.

By contrast, small minorities alert to the problems in medieval Latin Christendom had a different view about its sins and shortcomings. Their ideas of reform differed accordingly. In their respective ways, the Waldensians and Albigensians, and later the Lollards and Hussites, did not think Christians needed to heed the Church's teachings more closely because they thought its teachings were mistaken in crucial respects.[2] The discrepancy between doctrines and deeds was a symptom of deeper difficulties. A genuine imitation of Christ involved not following, but in key ways repudiating, what the Church prescribed, not least because its most exalted leaders "preached renunciation and gave a lesson in greed."[3] The Church's hierarchical structure created a stage for the avaricious sins of clergy and religious; the higher their rank, the more visible were their roles, and the ranker did their hypocritical greed appear. The attention was greatest and the criticisms sharpest of the "servant of the servants of God," the popes, who as the "vicars of Christ" oversaw a burgeoning bureaucracy at the curia in Rome before 1309, at Avignon for nearly 70 years thereafter, in both cities between divided rival papal claimants during the decades of the Western schism (1378–1415), and then again in Rome, where the papal court was again ensconced from the 1450s in what turned out to be the beginning of the Renaissance papacy. Where was Christian renunciation, poverty, and humility, in the conspicuous papal striving for acquisition, wealth, and power? Where was it in the agglutination of episcopal sees, the acquisition of property by religious orders, the accumulation of benefices by secular clergy, or the familially aggrandizing pursuit of profit by lay merchants?

All these problems were also obvious to reformers who worked within the Church and sought to get Christians to behave better. Where the dissenters departed from them was in their conviction that the gap was not being closed – and could not be closed – because the Roman Church was not what

---

[2] Malcolm Lambert, *Medieval Heresy: Popular Movements from the Gregorian Reform to the Reformation*, 3rd ed. (Oxford: Wiley-Blackwell, 2002).

[3] R. H. Tawney, *Religion and the Rise of Capitalism*, intro. Adam B. Seligman ([1926] New Brunswick, NJ: Transaction, 1998), 62.

it claimed to be. Its avaricious leaders had fatally twisted the faith entrusted
to their care to serve themselves, shielding themselves from any reforms that
might threaten their standing through institutions and canon law of their
own making. The Church was not, as it had originally been, the congregation
of Christ's faithful followers on the path to salvation; prelatical tyrants had
made it an irreparable anti-church-of-oppression, occluding the way while
they lined their own pockets. Reform demanded not repair but rejection,
whether in favor of the Waldensian following of a genuinely apostolic life,
the Albigensian acknowledgment of authority among their antimaterial
perfecti, the Lollard repudiation of the Mass and clerical privilege, or the
Hussite denial of the papacy's supposedly divine origin and insistence on lay
reception of the consecrated wine and host in Eucharistic communion.

Even the most successful of reform-minded medieval popes, Innocent III (r.
1198–1216), was unable to achieve anything close to a uniform reform of the
Church's manifest problems in the early thirteenth century, less severe as they
were compared to those of the two centuries between the early Avignon
papacy and the Fifth Lateran Council (1512–1517). It is unlikely whether any
popes could have done so, regardless of their efforts. Historians have long
corrected older confessional-historical conceptions of the medieval Church as
a homogeneous monolith, and therefore ostensibly either, as the Protestant
view would have it, an oppressive ecclesiastical fascism or, in the Catholic
assessment, a hierarchically well-ordered harmony. Its basic institutions, practices, and teachings had been unsystematically built up and layered on one
another over centuries, stretching back through the early Middle Ages to the
late Roman Empire, not implemented according to a top-down blueprint,
whether by Benedict of Nursia, Gregory VII, Innocent III, or anyone else.
Those teachings, practices, and institutions were at the same time variegated
and particularized in countless ways at the local level, where all life was lived.
The realities of medieval communication, travel, and technology, even after
the advent of printing in the mid-fifteenth century, precluded either a proto-
Soviet papal totalitarianism, or a pope, however saintly and willful, who could
have legislated by fiat a reform of all Christendom. By the early years of the
sixteenth century, Latin Christianity was marked both by the inherited results
of past reforms and the ongoing efforts of reforms in the present – including
the proceedings of the Fifth Lateran Council, Erasmian humanism, the Observant religious orders, and booming, voluntary lay piety – as well as by
conspicuous sins and shortcomings. And so it seemed things would continue.

They didn't. By no later than the summer of 1519, the Observant Augustinian friar Martin Luther showed that he was not one of those Christian
reformers that aimed to bring Christians' behavior more closely in line with

the Church's teachings. Nor, it turned out, would he work within the institutions, teachings, and practices of the Roman Church. Instead, like other medieval dissenters, Luther came to reject that the Roman Church was what it claimed to be. He did so because his fellow theologians who defended the papacy discounted his own experience of what he called "the Gospel" – a new understanding, which Luther claimed to be the original and divinely intended understanding, of how God works in and saves sinful human beings. It produced the experience of serene certainty that came through God's gift of faith alone, bestowed by God's grace alone, on human beings who could do literally nothing to help themselves save to admit their sinful impotence.[4] The emergent answer to Luther's years of spiritual struggle with his own scrupulous sense of sinfulness as an Augustinian, this was his foundational key to Christian life that reset the criteria for what reform in the Church should be. It was for him the distilled essence and salvific meaning of God's Word in scripture – the Law crushed and the Gospel saved. If the Roman Church refused to adjust its doctrines, practices, and institutions to conform to the true, long-obscured, but now rediscovered meaning of God's Word, then those who understood scripture aright were bound to reject that Church and to reform themselves and their lives by conforming to scripture alone, the sole and final authority for all Christian faith and life.

Some earlier dissenting reformers had also emphasized the authority of scripture over against the Roman Church as its putative arbiter, but none with anything close to the success of the movement that Luther inadvertently initiated. All the medieval movements were contained and controlled through the dutiful efforts of ecclesiastical and secular authorities to suppress them; even the Hussites, the most successful among them despite their movement's internal divisions, remained rooted in Czech lands. By contrast, the Protestant Reformation garnered sustained political support in two among its many expressions: in Lutheranism and Reformed Protestantism, it ended up exercising a demographically widespread, enduring influence on the formation and persistence of new Western Christian traditions, separated socially, doctrinally, liturgically, and theologically from Roman Catholicism. Aided by the new technology of print, it quickly spread beyond Germany and Switzerland to the Low Countries, England, France, Denmark, Sweden, and beyond. Besides the many doctrinal divergences between the anti-Roman medieval reformers and the anti-Roman Protestant reformers of the sixteenth century, one major difference between them was the sustained

---

[4] On the striving for and experience of certainty as the key to Luther's theology, see Richard Rex, *The Making of Martin Luther* (Princeton, NJ: Princeton University Press, 2017).

political support afforded Lutherans and Reformed Protestants. Another was
the shared insistence on the Word of God among sixteenth-century Protestants, which, no sooner than it had appeared as an adamant rallying cry
against clerical corruption and papal tyranny in the heady days of the early
1520s, also revealed itself as a new, and in practice insuperable, problem
among those who embraced it.

It was one thing to champion scripture alone as the sole final authority for
Christian doctrine and life, the touchstone and tool with which to criticize a
Church riddled with sinfulness. It was quite another thing to say what
scripture means, and how it should be applied. Socially and politically
divisive disagreements among Christians who agreed with Luther's
reforming principle of *sola scriptura* were manifest in Wittenberg even
before he returned from the Wartburg Castle in March 1522; they emerged
in Zürich between Huldrych Zwingli and his colleagues who disagreed with
him about infant baptism and became the earliest Anabaptists; they divided
Luther and Zwingli and their respective allies over the proper understanding
of Christ's presence in the Eucharist, a critical source for the split between
Lutheran and Reformed Protestants; they pitted leaders in the German
Peasants War, the most extensive expression of the early German Reformation, against Luther and his insistence that the Gospel had nothing to do
with changing socioeconomic or political structures; they rent Anabaptists,
who rejected Luther as well as Zwingli, among themselves over the (il)
legitimacy of Christians' use of coercive political power and a host of other
issues; they set all Anabaptists against Christians who thought that not only
baptism, but all external expressions of faith, were unimportant. And so on.
All this had transpired before 1530 and just in the Germanic lands of central
Europe where the Reformation began. The vast majority of claims about the
meaning and application of God's Word were not politically supported;
these "radical Protestants" demonstrated that not all anti-Roman Christians
thought justification by faith through grace was Christianity's key doctrine.
The divisiveness that issued directly but unintentionally from the Reformation's central reforming principle never went away during the remainder of
the sixteenth century, or indeed down to the present. In contrast to the
character of recurrent medieval reforming efforts within the sprawling
Roman Church, in the sixteenth century the Church became the churches
in what had been Latin Christendom. Unlike medieval reforms, this reform
would transform Christendom into Europe.[5]

---

[5] Mark Greengrass, *Christendom Destroyed: Europe 1517–1648* (New York: Viking, 2014).

Wherever the Reformation spread in the sixteenth century – and virtually no regions from Scandinavia to Spain remained entirely untouched by it – rulers had to decide how to respond. Those who opted for it had to decide whose version of Protestant Christianity they would adopt and try to implement. The Roman Catholic Church was no less dependent on rulers who elected to oppose the Reformation in all its expressions, continuing instead, like their medieval predecessors, to protect and exercise influence over an institution now newly vulnerable to powerful alternatives and more dependent than ever on political support. Sixteenth-century rulers who supported Catholicism extended a medieval tradition of reform that accepted existing Christian teachings, practices, and institutions. As in centuries past, they patronized religious orders, including new ones such as the Society of Jesus and the Capuchins, the latter yet another Franciscan reform from within. The evangelizing zeal of missionaries from these and other religious orders inspired both their reforming efforts to create Catholics in Europe more moral and devout than their medieval predecessors had been, and to make new converts of non-Christians abroad as Roman Catholicism started to become geographically a global religion as it accompanied Spanish and Portuguese colonization and trade.

Despite delays pursuant to political infighting that echoed spats between medieval popes and rulers, the Council of Trent finally convened in late 1545, nearly a decade after it was first planned for Mantua and many years after some Christians started calling for a new council even before the "Luther affair" had become the early Reformation. The reforming vision of the bishops and theologians at Trent was no more conciliatory toward Protestants than the vision of their thirteenth-century predecessors at Lateran IV had been toward Albigensians; they wanted "the extirpation of heresies and the reform of morals," once again seeking prescriptive means and practical measures to narrow the distance between Christ's commands and his followers' shortcomings.[6] Interrupted by threats of epidemics, war, and Pope Paul IV's resistance to its continuation, the council did not conclude its on-and-off work until 1563. Its doctrinal condemnations and clarifications, disciplinary and institutional prescriptions, dwarfed those of Lateran IV and would not be surpassed again until Vatican II in the 1960s. As it turned out, the Tridentine decrees not only extended the medieval tradition of Catholic reform, but established the parameters for early modern and modern Catholicism, including the efforts of its many subsequent reformers.

---

[6] *Canons and Decrees of the Council of Trent: Original Text with English Translation*, ed. and trans. H. J. Schroeder (St. Louis, MO, and London: B. Herder, 1941), 15 (Latin p. 294).

Over the long run, in a manner parallel to their Lutheran, Reformed Protestant, and Anglican contemporaries, those who acted on the decrees would succeed in shaping religious identities on a scale that would have astounded their forebears in the Middle Ages.

Those identities were informed by rival reforming visions rooted in incompatible claims about Christian truth. Because Christianity was intended to influence politics and society no less than worship and piety, an ambition inherited from the Middle Ages and shared by Catholic and magisterial Protestant reformers in their respective ways, the disagreements affected every major domain of human life. The long-term repercussions have been massive and multivalent. Rival reforming ideas, their adoption and implementation, the unresolved disputes they entailed, and the recurrent wars of more-than-religion in which they were implicated, made the Christianity at the heart of Christendom into an unprecedented problem. Its eventual solution – or at least, the course of action eventually adopted and adapted in every European and North American nation-state – was to redefine religion narrowly as individually chosen interior beliefs, personally preferred expressions of collective worship, and voluntary devotional practices. Thus redefined, religion could be tolerated because it could be managed; it could be politically protected and controlled, regardless of its content. We continue to live with the consequences.

SUGGESTED FURTHER READINGS

Eire, Carlos N. M. *Reformations: The Early Modern World, 1450–1650.* New Haven, CT, and London: Yale University Press, 2016.

Gregory, Brad S. *The Unintended Reformation: How a Religious Revolution Secularized Society.* Cambridge, MA, and London: Belknap Press of Harvard University Press, 2012.

Lambert, Malcom. *Medieval Heresy: Popular Movements from the Gregorian Reform to the Reformation.* 3rd ed. Oxford: Wiley-Blackwell, 2002.

Swanson, R. N. *Religion and Devotion in Europe, c. 1215–c. 1515.* Cambridge: Cambridge University Press, 1995.

The Luther Affair

David M. Whitford

The Luther Affair, or the *causa lutheri*, refers to a collection of theological controversies and events following Martin Luther's posting of the *Ninety-Five Theses* in 1517. The theological disputes were wide ranging, but they focused mainly on the power and efficacy of indulgences, Luther's developing understanding of justification by faith alone, and the extent of papal authority. There were three phases in the debates that culminated in Luther's excommunication by the pope in 1521 and his trial before the Holy Roman Emperor later that spring at the Diet of Worms. The first phase ran from 1513 to 1517 and centered on Luther as he explored the question of justification and its implications for the medieval practice of indulgences. The *Ninety-Five Theses*, which focused on indulgences, were posted in late October 1517. From 1518 to 1519, Luther defended his new theological positions in lectures, monastic colloquies, public debates, and, most importantly, in short pamphlets, published sermons, and longer theological treatises. Defenders of the church's authority and tradition met him in those debates and responded with their own theological tracts. The final phase ran from 1520 to 1521, during which time his theological views were further clarified, he was excommunicated, and then was tried in Germany. While theological debates continued for many years, the parameters of those debates and Luther's legal situation were largely set by the end of 1521. In what follows, we will look at each episode briefly and end by looking at the reactions among University of Paris theologians to the Luther Affair. John Calvin arrived at the University of Paris at the tail end of the Luther Affair, but its reverberations would be felt throughout his education there.

1513–1517: LUTHER'S DEVELOPING THEOLOGY

The University of Wittenberg was a small, rural university when Martin Luther was appointed as Professor of Bible in 1512. Though it was small, it had an important benefactor. The Elector Frederick the Wise established the university in 1502. The elector had two great passions in life: the establishment of the University of Wittenberg and his relic collection – which he worked hard to ensure had no rival beyond Rome. Until Luther's fame in the late 1510s, he was far more successful in the second pursuit than the first. He had thousands of relics, and praying at each relic could reduce one's penalties in purgatory 1,900,000 days. Both the university and the relic collection were housed in Wittenberg Castle.

Luther's first lectures were on the Psalms and extended from 1513 to 1515. He lectured in a traditional format, highlighting significant vocabulary, the history of exegesis on text, and his own theological views on each psalm. He largely used two resources for his lectures, a medieval compendium of biblical scholarship called the *Glossa Ordinaria* and a new commentary by the Paris Bible scholar Jacques Lefèvre d'Etaples. Calvin may have met Lefèvre years later, but he was certainly a teacher of many of Calvin's friends, including Guillaume Farel. Lefèvre was significant to Luther's theological development because Luther first learned the phrase "sola fide" – by faith alone – from Lefèvre. The idea that grace is given by God to the lamenting sinner, by faith alone, is a theme that runs throughout Lefèvre's commentary, and though Luther would not arrive at a mature understanding of "justification by faith alone" for a few more years, it was during his lectures on the Psalms that he first encountered the phrase and first began to ruminate on the implications of salvation by faith without works.

In 1514, while still lecturing on the Psalms, Luther was assigned to preach at St. Mary's Church in the center of Wittenberg. It was during his time as preacher and pastor to the laypeople of Wittenberg that Luther truly began to call into question the efficacy and then the very essence of indulgences. Indeed, as his roles as pastor and professor influenced one another, his critiques of indulgences grew sharper. In 1515, he completed his lectures on the Psalms and turned to Romans. In late 1515, his lecture on Romans 1.17 demonstrates the first real evidence of a more mature understanding of justification by faith. If the sinner is justified by faith alone – not works – then this had direct ramifications for the doctrine of penance and the trade of indulgences that was built on penance. If justification is by faith alone, then penance ought to be a change in heart, not a work one does. If true penance is not a thing one does, then indulgences were a waste of time and money, both of which would be better used to help others.

By the middle of 1516, Luther had nearly arrived at the theological presuppositions that would make the *Ninety-Five Theses* possible. He no longer had confidence in works of penance. He no longer had confidence in the use of indulgences. And while lecturing on Romans, he purchased or was given a copy of Desiderius Erasmus's Greek New Testament (*Novum Instrumentum Omnia*), which he immediately began to use for lecture preparations. Erasmus did not offer exegesis of the text in the same way as Lefèvre had. Instead, Erasmus offered a new translation of the original Greek into Latin and provided extensive translation notes for any changes he had made to the traditional Vulgate Latin translation. For Luther, the most important change was Erasmus's retranslation of the verb *metanoeo*. This word appears twice in the beginning of Matthew (Mt 3:3 and 4:17). In Matthew 3, it is the first word of John the Baptist's sermon at the River Jordan. In Matthew 4, it is the opening word in Jesus's first sermon in the Gospel that was preached immediately after returning from his temptation in the desert. The Vulgate translates the word *poenitentiam agite* (do penance*)*. It was this translation, from the mouths of John the Baptist and Christ, that provided the main scriptural basis for the medieval doctrine of penance. But Erasmus translated it *"poeniteat vos"* (repent ye). In the translation notes, Erasmus explained why *metanoia* could not mean "do penance" and instead meant something closer to "repent of your former ways," or perhaps "to come to one's senses" – given with an allusion to the Prodigal Son. Erasmus confirmed Luther's suspicions concerning penance and indulgences. Penance was not a thing to be done, but a change in heart. And if that was so, then indulgences were a useless waste of time and money. When the indulgence seller Johannes Tetzel arrived near Wittenberg in 1517, he sold indulgences with a vigor that embarrassed even the practice's defenders. Luther erupted into an almost visceral righteous anger, which resulted in his *Disputation on the Power and Efficacy of Indulgences* – better known as the *Ninety-Five Theses*. The opening line of the theses quotes Matthew 4:17 and reads, "When Our Lord and Master Jesus Christ said, *poenitentiam agite*, he willed that the whole life of believers should be repentance." In the theses that follow, Luther derides the sale of indulgences, states that the pope would never countenance their sale if he knew how they were being hawked, and declared that it would be better for people to give pennies to the poor than to purchase worthless pieces of paper.

1518–1519: ELEUTHERIUS

Up until 1517, Luther wrote his name either as Luder or Luter. In 1517, he began to use Luther. This was a play on the Greek word *eleutherius*. *Eleutherius* comes from the Greek word for freedom and liberation. The Greek god Dionysus was called *eleutherius* – "the liberator." The word could also mean "the one who has been freed." Luther would have appreciated both connotations. In late 1517, he began to see himself as one who had been freed by the Gospel and also called to preach this free gift of grace to others.

At the same time, the *Theses* continued to sell broadly throughout Germany. Luther became an almost overnight celebrity. In early 1518, he was invited to expound on his theological insights that gave rise to the *Ninety-Five Theses* at a general convention of his monastic order to be held in April in Heidelberg. The so-called Heidelberg Disputation expounds on Luther's theology more generally, and while there is an implicit critique of indulgences, it is nowhere near as pointed as the *Ninety-Five Theses*. It did, however, continue to develop the idea of justification in significant ways.

Johannes Staupitz, the head of the monastic order and Luther's mentor, invited Luther to the Heidelberg meeting in the hope that by explaining himself more clearly and less passionately, he might defuse a situation that was growing more controversial with each passing day. The opposite seems to have been the effect. The Heidelberg Disputation seems to have placed Luther ever more clearly into the view of Johannes Eck, who as a result of it challenged him to a debate to be held in Leipzig. In Rome, authorities grew ever more alarmed. The official papal theologian, Sylvester Prierias, responded to Luther with a treatise entitled *A Dialogue against the Theses of Martin Luther Concerning the Power of the Pope,* in which he denounced Luther's *Theses.* Prierias argued that, at its heart, the *Ninety-Five Theses* were not just an attack on the sale of indulgences but of papal authority. Luther would reply that he meant no such thing, but this seems a bit forced. A number of the *Theses* do directly criticize the pope and deny that he had the authority to issue some of the types of indulgences that were, in fact, being sold. Prierias cuts straight to the heart of this point when he writes, "He who says regarding indulgences that the Roman Church cannot do what she in fact does is a heretic." This was the first time that someone within the official hierarchy of the church accused Luther of heresy. In August 1518, Luther received a copy of Prierias's treatise against him, together with a summons to appear in Rome to answer for the charges of heresy. Over the summer, Rome also sent a letter to the papal legate in Germany, telling him to have Luther arrested for heresy. Heresy was a crime often punished by burning at the stake. Luther's passionate attack on indulgences had now become a matter of life and death for the young professor.

That Luther was not arrested was due to the intervention of Frederick the Wise. As noted earlier, Frederick had two great passions, his relics collection and the university he founded. Luther criticized indulgences most directly, but it cannot have been lost on Frederick that he also called into question the relics amassed in Wittenberg. Nevertheless, if he had to choose one or the other, and the accusation of heresy made such a choice necessary, Frederick chose the university and the man who had – almost single-handedly – made it famous. It did not hurt Luther's cause that it was Rome who sought him. Frederick was like most other Germans and, though a deeply pious man, he did harbor some suspicions of Italians in general and the papal curia in particular. Frederick the Wise worked together with Staupitz to find a solution wherein the church would be satisfied and the University of Wittenberg would keep its most famous professor. To that end, an appearance was arranged before Cardinal Thomas di Vio Cajetan (d. 1534). Cajetan was a reforming prelate, who was well educated and had distinct humanist leanings. A more perfect person could not have been hoped for. Luther appeared before Cajetan in October 1518. Cajetan told Luther he had read what Luther had written and found him to be in error. However, should Luther publicly recant his heresy and revoke what he had written, Cajetan would ensure leniency. Luther – who had arrived at his convictions over a fairly long period – was not convinced by Cajetan's appeal to his own authority as a cardinal. Instead, he asked Cajetan to show him where he was wrong by pointing out his errors from scripture. Cajetan had no intention of debating Luther, but the conversation quickly degenerated into an argument. The attempt at healing the rupture between Rome and Luther failed. Staupitz released Luther from his vow of obedience following the meeting. When Luther returned to Wittenberg, there did not seem to be any solution possible for the Luther Affair.

The situation only got worse when Luther finally participated in the debate with Johannes Eck in July 1519. Initially, Luther was not going to take part, to avoid further exacerbating his precarious position. Instead, his colleague at Wittenberg, Andreas Bodenstein von Karlstadt, was going to debate Eck. However, as the debate continued, Luther could not resist joining the fray. Eck was a brilliant theologian and an eloquent debater. He challenged Luther again and again on papal authority, the role of the church in salvation, and the authority of church councils. At one point, Eck got Luther to concede that the Council of Constance had erred in its decision to condemn Jan Hus. Luther argued that the Council had erred because it misinterpreted scripture. What would later emerge as the theological concept of *sola scriptura* now began to emerge prominently in his theology – all church actions and decisions, whether made by bishop, pope, or council, were to be judged by the weight of scripture. In a very real sense, then, Luther had placed himself beyond the authority of either pope or council, which made a church resolution to the Luther Affair all but impossible.

Frederick, for his part, now sought a political solution and began to advocate for a trial to be held in Germany instead of Rome – believing that a German trial would be less likely to convict the popular Luther. When the

Holy Roman Emperor Maximilian died in January 1519, Frederick became the ruler of the empire during the interregnum. He exacted a promise from Charles V, Maximilian's grandson and successor, that Luther would be tried in Germany before being handed over to Rome.

1520–1521: TRIAL AND TREATISES

In 1520, Luther produced three of his most significant theological treatises: *Address to the Christian Nobility of the German Nation, On the Babylonian Captivity of the Church*, and *On Christian Freedom*. Between the publication of the *Babylonian Captivity* and *On Christian Freedom*, he received his formal charge of heresy through the papal bull *Exsurge Domini* (promulgated June 15, 1520). He was given 60 days to recant his heresies and revoke his writings. Not only did Luther refuse to recant but he also burned the bull in December 1520 together with colleagues and some of his students. In January 1521, Pope Leo X issued *Decet Romanum Pontificem*, a formal bull of excommunication that denounced Luther as a confirmed and unrepentant heretic. This triggered the need for a German trial, and Charles V summoned Luther to appear before him at the upcoming imperial parliament that was meeting in Worms and assured him of his safe conduct to and from the diet (or parliament). Luther appeared before the emperor at the Diet of Worms in April 1521. Again, he was told to recant, this time by the emperor. Again, Luther refused. It is likely Luther thought he would be arrested and perhaps executed. It is not entirely clear whether he said at the end of the meeting, "Here I stand, I can do no other." A century earlier, Jan Hus had received a similar safe conduct pledge but was still arrested and executed. Luther had every reason to presume he was already a condemned man and that might well have steadied him in such a pronouncement. Luther was not arrested, however. Charles V was a newly crowned emperor and Frederick was a seasoned and senior noble in the empire. The safe conduct was as much an assurance to Frederick as it was to Luther, and so Luther was allowed to leave Worms. A few weeks later, Charles V issued the Edict of Worms, which formally labeled Luther an outlaw and a heretic. People were told to burn his writings and hand him over to imperial authorities if found.

Luther had gone into hiding in a remote castle in Saxony. While there, he collaborated with colleagues back in Wittenberg on a German translation of the New Testament, which was published in 1522. He returned to Wittenberg permanently in 1522 and, because of an imperial ban seeking his arrest, he never left Saxony and the protection of the Saxon nobility, again.

THE UNIVERSITY OF PARIS AND LUTHER

John Calvin arrived in Paris to study as an undergraduate in August 1521. Just five months earlier, the theology faculty of the University of Paris – the Sorbonne – had publicly condemned Luther's theology. The primary mover in this condemnation was Noël Beda. Beda was the leader of the conservative wing of the theology faculty. Even before Luther posted the *Ninety-Five Theses*, Beda had attacked both Lefèvre and Erasmus for their biblical humanism, finding them dangerous. For Beda, Luther was confirmation of his greatest fears. Beda held Lefèvre and Erasmus responsible for Luther.

It is certain that Luther came to the attention of the theology faculty sometime in 1518. He was becoming famous, and word of the controversy in Germany would have reached France quickly. Some written works of Luther's would also have made their way to Paris. In 1519, however, two things happened that brought the Luther Affair to the Sorbonne directly. In April, Christoph Froben sent a large order of Luther's works printed in his shop in Basel to Paris to be sold. He reported to Luther that they were selling well. He also noted that the Sorbonne had copies and were examining them. In July, Paris was chosen as one of the two faculties that were to be sent transcripts of the Leipzig Disputation between Luther and Eck to make a determination of who won and whether Luther had slipped into heresy. Beda led the charge against Luther on both counts. He was ultimately condemned by the faculty in April 1521.

The lasting effect of the Luther Affair in Paris was the fact that anyone of either a reforming bent or a disposition to biblical humanism was labeled a "Lutheran." Beda accused many of being Lutherans, he even succeeded in forcing Lefèvre to flee Paris not once but twice. Others followed, including Guillaume Farel and, ultimately, John Calvin.

SUGGESTED FURTHER READINGS

Fabisch, P. *Dokumente zur Causa Lutheri: 1517–1521*. Münster, Westfalen: Aschendorff, 1988.

Farge, James. *Orthodoxy and Reform in Early Reformation France: The Faculty of Theology of Paris, 1500–1543*. Leiden: Brill, 1985.

Hendrix, Scott H. *Martin Luther: Visionary Reformer*. New Haven: Yale University Press, 2015.

Jensen, De Lamar. *Confrontation at Worms: Martin Luther and the Diet of Worms*. Provo, UT: Brigham Young University Press, 1973.

Leppin, Volker. *Martin Luther: A Medieval Life*. Grand Rapids: Baker, 2017.

Luther, Martin, and Kurt Aland. *Martin Luther's 95 Theses: With the Pertinent Documents from the History of the Reformation*. Saint Louis: Concordia Pub. House, 2004.

Pettegree, Andrew. *Brand Luther: 1517, Printing, and the Making of the Reformation*. New York: Penguin Press, 2015.

Roper, Lyndal. *Martin Luther: Renegade and Prophet*. New York: Random House, 2017.

Religious Colloquies

Ronald K. Rittgers

One of the most important legacies of the Protestant Reformation was the splintering of the western Catholic Church into competing confessions. Protestants introduced permanent schisms into Latin Christendom, both between Protestants and Catholics and amongst Protestants. But even as these divides began to form in the sixteenth century, earnest theologians and rulers, both Protestant and Catholic, sought to reverse and heal them, hoping to recover the unity among Christians for which Christ had prayed (John 17:21). John Calvin participated in a number of these religious colloquies, or formal conversations about contested theological issues. He was present at colloquies in Hagenau (summer 1540), Worms (autumn 1540), and Regensburg (January 1541), although he was more interested in unity among Protestants than between Protestants and Catholics.[1] Such colloquies, which were supposed to be cordial in nature, should be distinguished from disputations, where the goal was to prove the truth of one's position against all claims to the contrary. The English word *colloquy* comes from the Latin *colloquor*: to talk together or hold conversation. The goal of Reformation-era religious colloquies was not to arrive at complete uniformity of belief and practice, rather, it was to determine where reconciliation on matters of belief and practice might be possible.

Beginning in the late 1530s, Martin Bucer introduced Calvin to the world of religious colloquies, affording him the opportunity to meet Philipp Melanchthon, after which Calvin began to hope for reconciliation between Lutheran and Swiss Protestants. (Calvin approved of the 1536 Wittenberg Concord, an effort by Martin Bucer to achieve unity among Protestants on the Lord's Supper by arguing for a modified Lutheran view of the sacrament; in

---

[1] Bruce Gordon, *Calvin* (New Haven, CT, and London: Yale University Press, 2009), 101.

1540, Calvin signed Melanchthon's *Confessio Augustana variata*, which was a reworking of the Augsburg Confession and its Apology that incorporated the Wittenberg Concord and other efforts by Wittenberg theologians to prepare for colloquies with Catholics.) But important colloquies took place before Calvin's entrance into this world. In 1529, Landgrave Philipp of Hesse convened a colloquy at his castle in Marburg to settle differences between Protestants about the Lord's Supper. At the 1529 Diet of Speyer, the evangelical estates had protested the repeal of the 1526 Diet of Speyer's Recess and its temporary suspension of the enforcement of the 1521 Edict of Worms. After the majority of Catholic estates rebuffed this protest, Philipp of Hesse was eager to form a Protestant alliance in the face of a growing imperial threat. He knew such an alliance was impossible until the theological rift between Wittenberg reformers and those in southern Germany and Switzerland on the Lord's Supper could be mended. Luther was hesitant to participate in the proposed colloquy but finally agreed to do so, while Zwingli was eager for the conversation from the start. The two reformers were the main figures at the gathering, but others played an important role, including, in Zwingli's camp, Oecolampadius, and, in Luther's, Melanchthon. The colloquy began on October 1, with Johann Feige, Philipp's chancellor, addressing the assembled theologians, who numbered well more than a dozen, and urging them to achieve unity.

The next day, October 2, the reformers addressed their differences on the Lord's Supper, with Luther famously writing *Hoc est corpus meum* (This is my body) in chalk on the table, insisting on the literal meaning of the words. Luther persisted in this view, holding that Christ's body and blood are truly present in, with, and under the bread and wine, because, according to Luther, at the Last Supper Christ promised that this would be so. Zwingli held that Christ's body and blood are spiritually present, not mingled with the physical elements of the Lord's Supper, which Zwingli feared would lead to superstition. Behind this disagreement lay larger Christological differences, especially regarding the meaning of Christ's session at the right hand of the Father. Neither party was able to win the other to its side, although they did affirm concord on 14 of 15 points of doctrine concerning the Trinity, the virgin birth, the authority of Scripture, infant baptism, salvation by grace through faith, and so on. On the disputed matter of the Lord's Supper, they agreed that it should be given in both kinds to the laity and that the mass is not a work that merits grace. They acknowledged their differences on the nature of Christ's presence in the Lord's Supper and pledged to display Christian love in the meantime and to pray that God would lead them to the right understanding. Thus, this early Protestant colloquy failed in its effort to effect theological unity among Protestants.

The 1530 Diet of Augsburg was not convened as a colloquy; rather, it was, among other things, an opportunity for Lutherans to present a statement of their faith to the emperor, the Augsburg Confession. The Catholic theologian Johann Eck sought to refute the Augsburg Confession in his *Confutatio*, which prompted Emperor Charles V to convene a colloquy among leading Protestant and Catholic politicians and theologians to assess if reconciliation might be possible. The two sides achieved important agreement on such matters as original sin, justification, and confession, but still disagreed on the meritorious nature of good works, the invocation of the saints, communion in one kind, clerical marriage, and the sacrifice of the mass. The colloquy concluded that agreement on all articles of the Augsburg Confession was not possible at the present time, and it therefore called for a general council to be convened by the pope within six months to address the remaining disagreements. Pope Paul III attempted to convene such a council in the late 1530s but without success. Religious division continued to grow within the empire.

In his efforts to deal with this division and thus to strengthen his hand against threats to his empire from both within and without Christendom, namely, from France and the Turks, Charles V convened another colloquy in April 1540, frustrated that a general council had still not taken place. He had also recently brokered a tentative peace with the Protestant Schmalkald League. The colloquy was supposed to meet in Speyer, but plague forced a relocation to the Alsatian city of Hagenau in June. The emperor's brother, Ferdinand I, oversaw it. Catholics wanted renewed negotiations based on the Augsburg Confession. (There was some dispute among Catholics whether Zwinglians who had signed the Wittenberg Concord could be recognized as adherents of the Augsburg Confession.) Catholics also wanted Protestants to renounce claims to Catholic ecclesiastical property, recognize the authority of the Imperial Chamber Court, and reduce the number of territories admitted into the Schmalkald League. The assembled Protestants, which included Bucer and Calvin, rejected these terms, and the colloquy ended because of disagreements over procedure. Undeterred, the emperor announced another colloquy to be held at Worms: the Augsburg Confession and its Apology were to be the basis of this discussion.

The colloquy in Worms was convened in November 1540. It was here that Calvin and others signed the *Confessio Augustana variata*. Initially there were to have been 11 representatives from both sides but eventually just two spokesmen emerged: Melanchthon and Eck. In January 1541 the two theologians reached agreement on original sin, drawing on the earlier work of the colloquy at Augsburg in 1530. Melanchthon and Eck did not pretend that Protestants and Catholics held identical views on the subject, but they contended that there was enough common ground to preclude serious division on this front. The colloquy in Worms thus achieved important success but was soon moved to Regensburg as part of an imperial diet that was to take place there.

The Regensburg Colloquy of 1541 was arguably the most important of the religious colloquies in the Reformation period. It was, in the words of one scholar, the "only truly ecumenical discussion of the sixteenth century."[2] Discussions at Regensburg centered on "The Book of Regensburg," a mediating document that was drafted by Martin Bucer and the humanist Catholic theologian Johannes Gropper, rather than on the Augsburg Confession. The emperor, still eager for unity in the empire, appointed the participants in the colloquy: Catholic theologians Julius Pflug, Eck, and Gropper; Protestant theologians Melanchthon, Bucer, and Johannes Pistorious. Presiding over the colloquy were the Palatinate Count Friedrich and Antoine Perrenot de Granvelle. The papal legate Gasparo Contarini, who was also present, called for a number of changes to the Book of Regensburg, and after these were made, the revised version became the basis for the colloquy, which began on April 27, 1541. Calvin was in attendance but did not play a significant role in the colloquy's proceedings. From the beginning, he was skeptical about its potential for success.

The Regensburg Colloquy ranged widely over a whole host of theological issues. The Protestant and Catholic theologians reaffirmed agreements that had been reached in the past and also identified a number of doctrines where common ground might be found, including repentance after the fall, baptism, confirmation, sacramental confession, marriage, unction, and the sign of the Word. Old disagreements persisted, such as on transubstantiation and the veneration of the consecrated Host, the sacrifice of the mass, papal and conciliar authority, the enumeration of sins in confession and subsequent works of satisfaction, the veneration of the saints, clerical celibacy, vernacular liturgy, and communion in one kind. Protestants created a number of separate draft articles on such issues that were appended to the Book of Regensburg.

The discussion of justification at Regensburg reached important common ground. Eck and Melanchthon found the Book of Regensburg's treatment of the subject unsatisfying and therefore called for an open discussion of justification. These conversations yielded a final draft that was accepted on May 2, 1541. According to this draft, which appeared as article 5 in the

---

[2] Suzanne Schulz Hequet, *The 1541 Colloquy at Regensburg: In Pursuit of Church Unity* (Saarbrücken, Germany: VDM Verlag Dr. Müller, 2009), 4.

revised Book of Regensburg, sinners are justified by "living and efficacious faith" that makes them "pleasing and acceptable to God on account of Christ." Such faith is produced by the Holy Spirit, who is received by this same faith. Love is also "infused" at the same time, and this love heals the will and enables the Christian to begin to fulfill the law.[3] The assembled theologians, drawing on both Scholastic and evangelical principles, thus sought to secure the gratuitous nature of grace that was based solely on divine mercy and the merit and righteousness of Christ while also stressing the necessity of growth in grace. An earlier draft had referred to "double righteousness," that is, the gift of Christ's imputed righteousness that justifies sinners and actual or inherent righteousness produced in the Christian by the Holy Spirit that God rewards. While this term does not appear in the final draft, the basic idea is still present. Calvin approved of article 5 and was amazed that Catholics had conceded so much ground, although he observed that the article was not as clear as he wished. Luther and the pope were more dubious. The colloquy's treatment of justification had a direct influence on the 1999 Joint Declaration on Justification.

On May 31, 1541, the participants presented the revised Book of Regensburg along with the Protestant counter articles to the emperor, who shared the materials with the assembled imperial estates. Eck rejected the revised Book of Regensburg – though not its treatment of justification – and the majority of the Catholic estates equivocated, preferring to have the relevant materials submitted to the papal legate for review rather than take a position themselves. For his part, Contarini argued that everything should be forwarded to the pope, who could convene a council to settle matters. The Protestant estates called for a number of clarifications, elaborations, and changes before they could approve of the materials in good conscience. Thus, the colloquy did not achieve the intended unity. The recess to the diet called for a general council to address the colloquy's findings and for peace to be observed in the meantime. Another colloquy took place in Regensburg in 1546, but the Catholic participants insisted on making the Augsburg Confession, not the revised Book of Regensburg and its treatment of justification, the basis for conversation. The colloquy soon became mired in procedural difficulties and achieved little of note.

---

[3] See A. N. S. Lane, "A Tale of Two Imperial Cities: Justification at Regensburg (1541) and Trent (1546–1547)," in Bruce McCormack (ed.), *Justification in Perspective: Historical Developments and Contemporary Challenges* (Grand Rapids, MI, and Edinburgh: Baker Academic/Rutherford House, 2006), 144. Lane provides a full translation of article 5.

Religious colloquies gave way to war in the empire and, after much bloodshed, Lutherans and Catholics finally agreed to a policy of toleration in the 1555 Peace of Augsburg. In some ways, the preceding colloquies prepared the way for this settlement by granting imperial recognition of those who held to the Augsburg Confession. Efforts to mend the rift between Lutherans and Catholics continued; the two sides met again in Worms (1557), although without much success. A similar effort to reconcile Calvinists and Catholics took place in Poissy, a village west of Paris, in 1561. Convened by Queen Catherine de Medici, it featured Calvin's successor in Geneva, Théodore Bèze, along with Peter Martyr Vermigli, as spokesmen for the Reformed Protestants, and Charles de Guise, the cardinal of Lorraine, for Catholics. The French crown not only feared anarchy and war at home but also the alternative and potentially anti-Gallican ecumenical designs of Rome and the Council of Trent. Debates about the Eucharist scuttled the colloquy, with Bèze championing the Calvinist position and Lorraine supporting the Catholic one. (At one point in the conversation, Lorraine also required Bèze to ascribe to the Lutheran theology of the Lord's Supper in the Augsburg Confession, whether to promote or frustrate the discussion is not clear.)

Inter-Protestant colloquies also took place. In 1564, after the Palatinate was converted to Calvinism, Lutherans and Reformed Protestants met in Maulbronn (in nearby Lutheran Württemberg) to seek common ground on the Lord's Supper and Christology, but to no avail. A similar meeting took place in Montebéliard in 1586 and expanded to consider issues of baptism, church art and music, and predestination. Théodore Bèze represented the Reformed Protestants, Jakob Andreae, the Lutherans. Although located in Lutheran Württemberg, the Francophone Montebéliard had early on adopted the Swiss Reformation and in the 1580s was home to many French refugees who had fled Catholic persecution. This colloquy also figured in the larger desire of Henry of Navarre to seek German Lutheran support for French Huguenots in the French Wars of Religion. The Lutherans refused this support unless the Huguenots rejected the Calvinist view of the Lord's Supper in favor of the Lutheran one. Queen Elizabeth I was also interested in the colloquy, as she saw in it hopes for mending inter-Protestants rifts and establishing a pan-Protestant alliance against the papacy. All these hopes disappointed, for the colloquy only produced partial agreement on music and art.

Despite the best intentions and efforts of Christian theologians and rulers to recover Christian unity, as a general rule and for a variety of reasons – political, personal, and pious – claims of religious truth won out over the demand for Christian charity. Christian unity in the West would remain elusive for centuries to come.

SUGGESTED FURTHER READINGS

Armstrong, Clinton, trans. and Jeffrey Mallinson, ed. *Lutheranism vs. Calvinism: The Classic Debate at the Colloquy of Montbéliard 1586, Jakob Andreae and Theodore Beza*. St. Louis, MO: Concordia Publishing House, 2017.

Hillerbrand, Hans, ed., *The Oxford Encyclopedia of the Reformation*. 4 vols. New York: Oxford University Press, 1996. For dated but still helpful overviews, which have informed this article, see the following entries: Vinzenz Pfnür, "Colloquies," 3: 375–383; Alois Schmid, "Hagenau, Colloquy of," 2: 208; Alois Schmid, "Marburg, Colloquy of," 3: 2–4; Robert Kolb, "Maulbronn, Colloquy of," 3: 34–35; Jill Raitt, "Montebéliard, Colloquy of," 3: 84–85; Donald Nugent, "Poissy, Colloquy of," 3: 281–282.

Lane, A. N. S., "Calvin and Article 5 of the Regensburg Colloquy." In *Calvinus Praeceptor Ecclesiae: Papers of the International Congress on Calvin Research, Princeton, August 20–24, 2002*, ed. Herman J. Selderuis. Geneva: Librairie Droz, 2004, 233–263.

"A Tale of Two Imperial Cities: Justification at Regensburg (1541) and Trent (1546–1547)." In *Justification in Perspective: Historical Developments and Contemporary Challenges*, edited by Bruce McCormack, 119–145, Grand Rapids/ Edinburgh: Baker Academic/ Rutherford House, 2006.

Neusner, Wilhelm, "Calvin's Beitrag zu den Religionsgesprächen von Hagenau, Worms und Regensburg (1540/41)." In *Studien zur Geschichte and Theologie der Reformation. Festschrift für Ernst Bizer*, ed. Luise Abramowski and J. F. Gerhard Goeters. Neukirchen-Vluyn: Neukirchener Verlag, 1969, 213–237.

Schulz Hequet, Suzanne. *The 1541 Colloquy at Regensburg: In Pursuit of Church Unity*. Saarbrücken, Germany: VDM Verlag Dr. Müller, 2009.

The Council of Trent and the Augsburg *Interim*

Kathleen M. Comerford

The Augsburg *Interim* ("Declaration of His Roman Imperial Majesty on the Observance of Religion within the Holy Empire Until the Decision of the General Council") was adopted at the 1548 Diet of Augsburg, marking the victory of Emperor Charles V (r. 1516–1556) in the Schmalkaldic War (1546–1547) by attempting to impose a religious reconciliation between followers of Martin Luther and the Catholic Church. Charles, also king of Spain, was beset by problems throughout his European possessions, stemming largely from the Reformation. The *Interim* was one effort to control these problems. The purpose of the document was to create a temporary compromise, to promote religious and political stability while waiting for a more definitive statement from the Council of Trent (which was in session at the time). The provisional nature did nothing to lessen Protestant fears of attempting to suppress dissent or to dampen concerns on the part of some Catholics that heresy was going unpunished; instead, it hardened divisions. Its failures contributed to a breakdown in Habsburg authority in central Europe.

In the 1520s, Imperial Diets alternately outlawed and allowed the practice of Luther's interpretation of Christianity. This impasse culminated in the 1529 Protestation of Speyer, in which 6 princes and 14 free cities stated that they could not accept the prohibition of Lutheranism, and requested a council. Later in 1529, Lutherans and Zwinglians met at Marburg to discuss the mass, in particular the question of the Eucharist. Philipp of Hesse hoped to unify the non-Catholic groups under a single statement. They managed consensus on multiple points, but not on the Lord's Supper; indeed, the different Protestants never reconciled on that issue. In 1531, Philip and John Frederick I of Saxony established the Schmalkaldic League, initially as a defensive maneuver against a possible attack by Charles V, but later developing into a territorial alliance, complete with economic activity.

Attempts at religious unification among non-Catholics continued, unsuccessfully, through the mid-1530s. These included the Tetrapolitan and Augsburg Confessions (both 1530) and the Wittenberg Concord (1536). Meanwhile, Catholics continued to insist on conformity from those they labeled schismatics or heretics, and many would not support a council, despite a proposal from Pope Paul III (r. 1534–1549). King Francis I of France (r. 1515–1547) refused to send representatives.[1] Some Catholic theologians, including Girolamo Aleander and Johann Eck, advocated crushing dissent, violently if necessary. Mistrust and bitterness thus grew. Examples of increased rancor include the Schmalkald Articles of 1537, in which Luther accused the papacy of lying, cheating, and other shameful behavior. Paul did establish a reform commission, led by Gasparo Contarini, in 1536. The resulting report, *Consilium ... de Emendenda ecclesia* (1537), frankly acknowledged abuses in clerical behavior, church finances, and education. It was leaked and seized upon by proponents of a wide reform, but first ignored and then condemned within the Catholic Church.[2]

In 1541, at the Regensburg Colloquy, Catholics and Protestants met by invitation of the emperor and failed to reach agreement on Eucharistic theology. They issued a statement on justification general enough to satisfy both sides, and Charles V conceded several points in secret, including a promise not to prevent citizens from leaving the Catholic faith in favor of Protestant interpretations. Nevertheless, the Regensburg *Interim* was widely rejected – first by the Lutheran party and later by the Catholics. Within a year, Paul III established the Congregation of the Holy Office of the Inquisition, demonstrating little desire for negotiation. In 1543, John Calvin wrote an open letter, *Supplex exhortatio ad Caesarem*, appealing to Charles V to reform the church and heal the divisions that attempted reform had already produced. Granting that reformers ought to act with respect toward authorities, Calvin argued that the governance of the church was so flawed as to be in opposition to God's word, and therefore must itself be opposed. Charles, responding to various pressures, promised a council. Paul reminded him that emperors did not have that authority, but then announced that a council would meet in Trent in March 1545.

---

[1] Hubert Jedin, *A History of the Council of Trent*, trans. Ernest Graf (St. Louis, MO: Herder, 1957–1961), 1: 326–327. The original German (*Geschichte des Konzils von Trient* [Frieburg: Herder, 1950–1975]) is five volumes; only two have been translated into English.

[2] Printed in Rome, 1538. English translation in John Olin, ed., *The Catholic Reformation: From Cardinal Ximines to the Council of Trent* (New York: Fordham University Press, 1990), 65–79.

The initial sessions of the Council of Trent were poorly attended, and were marred by conflicts and challenges to its authority, including late and lukewarm support from France.[3] The first meetings of the Council (1545–1549) focused on the canon of scripture, original sin, justification, sacraments in general, and baptism and confirmation in particular. Thus, some of the most controversial issues, including the nature and meaning of the Eucharist, were not addressed before the Augsburg *Interim* was written. Both Luther's and Calvin's writings at this point show little hope or desire for compromise. In March 1545, Luther penned *Against the Roman Papacy, an Institution of the Devil*, and in 1547 Calvin authored the *Antidote to the Council of Trent*, the preface of which admonishes readers "never to imagine that, either by the individuals here present, or by the whole Council, were all the Pastors throughout the world here met, could a cure be provided for the great evils by which the flock of Christ is now oppressed" – only Christ could resolve the problems.[4]

Meanwhile, Charles faced multiple challenges to his authority during the mid-1540s, as he sought greater centralization of bureaucracy and governance in Spain and the empire and an alliance with France to defeat the Ottoman Turks. In July 1546, the Schmalkaldic League rose against the empire to protect the right to adhere to Lutheran beliefs. In less than a year, Charles defeated the Protestant princes in the Battle of Mühlberg, and imprisoned Johann Friedrich I of Saxony and Philip of Hesse. The League was thus crushed, and as a result Lutherans were (temporarily) left with little political power. The overconfident monarch then sought to consolidate his power by introducing standardized finances, coinage, administrative procedures, and religious practice within the empire. The year progressed with struggles between pope and emperor over control of the proceedings at Trent, an epidemic, and an attempted transfer of the Council of Trent to Bologna (which failed because some members refused to leave). These crises culminated in a prorogation of the Council (1549–1551). It was still in session

---

[3] An extended excerpt from the *Supplex* is in Philip Schaff, *History of the Christian Church*, Vol. 8: *Modern Christianity: The Swiss Reformation*, 3rd ed. rev. (New York: Charles Scribner's Sons, 1892). On the deal struck with France to support the Council at the 1544 Treaty of Crépy, see Dermon Fenlon, *Heresy and Obedience in Tridentine Italy: Cardinal Pole and the Counter Reformation* (London: Cambridge University Press, 1973), 100.

[4] German version: Martin Luther, *D. Martin Luthers Werke: Kritische Gesamtausgabe*, Vol. 54 (Weimar: Hermann Böhlaus Nachfolger, 1928), 206–299. English version: Jaroslav Pelikan and Helmut T. Lehman, eds., *Luther's Works*, Vol. 41 (Philadelphia: Fortress Press, 1966), 263–376); John Calvin, trans. Henry Beveridge, "Acts of the Council of Trent: With the Antidote," in Henry Beveridge (ed.), *Calvin's Tracts: Tracts Relating to the Reformation*, Vol. 3 (Edinburg: Calvin Translation Society, 1851), 3–188.

(though not meeting) in 1548 when, without consulting either it or the pope, Charles appointed Catholic and Lutheran theologians to draft a temporary agreement.

The *Interim* consisted of 26 articles, outlining both doctrinal and ceremonial precepts. It was presented to the Imperial and Swiss leadership with no opportunity for debate or emendation. The terms were intended to address both Catholic and Protestant concerns according to a centralized, standardized set of liturgical and religious practices. The *Interim* insisted on seven sacraments, but granted the right to communion in both kinds for the laity where already allowed (at least until the Council of Trent ruled otherwise). It required acceptance of transubstantiation, purgatory, memorial masses, and devotion to the saints, yet it opened with Lutheran interpretations of justification by faith. Later clauses point to the necessity of works, thereby apparently embracing Martin Bucer's "double justification" argument from the Regensburg Colloquy. It reimposed Catholic worship practices, but allowed Protestant clergy to retain their wives while waiting for a ruling from the Council. Two months later, Charles issued a "Formula of the Reformation for His Imperial Majesty of the Ecclesiastical State," meant for the Catholic princes, acknowledging scandals and abuses – financial as well as religious – within the clergy.

Both the *Interim* and the "Formula" were efforts to create a peaceful solution to religious unrest in the empire. They confronted an issue that had unsettled Charles V: because the pope wanted to address dogma first, the Council had not yet discussed disciplinary matters, particularly the conduct of the clergy with regard to celibacy or other controversial considerations. In early 1546, Paul softened his position and allowed the discussion of beliefs and behavior simultaneously. Subsequently, the Council dealt with scripture, printing, vernacular languages, original sin, the teaching and preaching of scripture, justification, episcopal residence, the sacraments in general, baptism, the Eucharist, penance, extreme unction, ecclesiastical benefices, and justification.[5] The last was not a matter that had occupied Catholic theologians in any depth before the sixteenth century. The theologians at the Council thus warned against dismissing Luther's position on the basis that it had been Luther's, and counseled colleagues instead to study the question thoroughly, advice those present took. While anathematizing those who argued for justification by works, they also criticized those who posited that works without faith were dead, that works done before justification are

[5] Guy Bedouelle, *The Reform of Catholicism, 1480–1620*, trans. James K. Farge (Toronto: Pontifical Institute of Medieval Studies, 2008), 65–73.

sins, or that faith without good behavior was the basis for justification. The decrees and anathemas from this session, written beginning in July 1546, were put on hold during the Schmalkaldic War and not issued until January 1547. The final version also addressed residence for bishops, so that an item focused on discipline was added to one focused on theology. The conclusion to the matter of residence, explained by Hubert Jedin as "the principle that office and benefice are inseparable," paralleled the justification decision: while the two aspects of the question (faith/works and office/benefice) may be considered separately, they are in fact interdependent.[6] Many issues had been discussed, but few resolved, before the 1547 suspension, so Charles took matters into his own hands. The difficulty was that both the *Interim* and the "Formula" were issued by the emperor, and thus stood on ecclesiastically shaky ground.

That dubious status, combined with widespread resistance, meant that the *Interim* was difficult to enforce. Most Lutheran pastors and theologians rejected it (Philip Melanchthon was a notable exception), some bitterly; they faced exile, imprisonment, or death. Charles V demanded submission by the princes and electors. While Maurice, Elector of Saxony, and several others remained opposed, Philip of Hesse accepted it (and compelled the clergy in his territory to comply).[7] The emperor punished resisting cities with loss of privileges or of independence. Thus the *Interim*, while promising a cooling of tensions, produced greater unrest. In the time following its imposition, hostility to the plans for a Catholic-centered solution grew. The city of Magdeburg expressed its discontent with the *Interim* and its supporters using a flood of broadsheets and pamphlets in 1550–1551, criticizing not merely the theological statements regarding justification and the mass but also the notion of compromise. In response, Maurice besieged the city. Critics, noting ambiguities and contradictions within the document, leveled charges of hypocrisy, contrasting the *Interim* with what they considered more sincere statements of Protestant faith. The Imperial statement could not be trusted on matters of doctrine or practice, they argued, and so its supporters could not be trusted on any point. They were in league with the devil.[8] As John Calvin wrote in the treatise *Interim adultero-germanum, cui*

---

[6] Hubert Jedin, *A History of the Council of Trent*, trans. Ernest Graf. Vol. 2, *The First Sessions at Trent: 1545–47* (London: Thomas Nelson and Sons, 1957), 172–173 and 352.

[7] William Bradford Smith, "Lutheran Resistance to the Imperial Interim in Hesse and Kulmbach," *Lutheran Quarterly* 19 (2005): 249–275, at 256–259.

[8] Nathan Baruch Rein, "Faith and Empire: Conflicting Visions of Religion in a Late Reformation Controversy – The Augsburg Interim and Its Opponents, 1548–50," *Journal of the American Academy of Religion* 71 (2003): 45–74, at 62 and 67.

adiecta est Vera Christianae pacificatinois et ecclesiae reformandae ratio (1549): "Peace is indeed to be longed for and sought with the utmost zeal; but rather than it should be purchased by any loss of piety, let heaven and earth, if need be, go into confusion!"[9]

Seven months after the Augsburg *Interim* was introduced, Melanchthon and others wrote a proposal that Matthias Flacius Illyricus and others dismissively called the Leipzig *Interim*. It offered more concessions to Protestants, but treated justification with ambiguity; restored the Latin liturgy; and revived many ceremonial actions associated with Catholic worship. The Leipzig document, which created a rift within German Protestants over adiapohora (Philippists vs. Gnesio-Lutherans), labeled the theological virtues (faith, hope, and love) as good works necessary for salvation. It did not use the word *sacrament* but gave implicit support to the Augsburg *Interim*'s upholding of seven sacraments.[10] It too was a religious failure. Unlike the earlier document, though, the Leipzig *Interim* was not accepted by the Imperial Diet. A later summary proposal, referred to as "the Excerpt" or "the Small Leipzig *Interim*," which allowed vestments and images of saints, was published as an accompaniment to the 1549 *Kirchenordnung* by Georg von Anhalt.

Catholics moved on, with Pope Julius III (r. 1550–1555) reconvening the Council of Trent (1551–1552). This was the only period attended by Protestant representatives, whose desire for reopening discussion on questions decided in the earlier session was rebuffed. The decrees and anathemas from this period promised to deepen divisions between Catholics and Protestants, with, for example, a reaffirmation of transubstantiation and statements about the necessity of employing properly ordained priests to administer the sacraments. Such categorical statements of difference, along with Charles's attempts at suppressing Lutheranism in Spain, exacerbated tensions in the empire and led to a surprise 1552 attack by Maurice of Saxony, and to the alliance of the Protestant princes of the Empire with Henri II of France against Charles. Unwilling to grant real concessions to Lutherans, yet unable to defend himself because he was unprepared, the emperor was forced to retreat and to grant the Treaty of Passau, allowing religious

---

[9] *Calvin's Tracts*, Vol. 3, "The True Method of Giving Peace to Christendom and Reforming the Church," 234.

[10] Irene Dingel, "The Culture of Conflict in the Controversies Leading to the Formula of Concord (1548–1580)," in Robert Kolb, *Brill's Companion to the Christian Tradition: Lutheran Ecclesiastical Culture, 1550–1675* (Leiden, The Netherlands: Brill: 2008), 15–64, at 22–24; and Charles Arand et al., *The Lutheran Confessions: History and Theology of the Book of Concord* (Minneapolis, MN: Fortress Press, 2012), 177–183.

freedom to Lutherans within the confines of the Holy Roman Empire. This spelled doom for any remaining hope regarding either the Augsburg or Leipzig documents. Worse still for the Catholic cause, the Saxon troops were at that point within a few hours of marching on Trent, causing Julius III to adjourn the council.

Over the next three years, Charles faced multiple international crises. His Italian territories were under nearly constant threat, and several Catholic and Lutheran princes created the League of Heidelberg (1553) to prevent his son Philip from becoming Holy Roman Emperor. The final straw was the election of Gian Pietro Carafa as Pope Paul IV (r. 1555–1559). This patriotic Neapolitan, who hated the Habsburgs in general and Charles in particular, attempted (unsuccessfully) to destroy both the sitting emperor's and his son's power in the Italian peninsula. The burdens of rule and the crises of the early 1550s took a toll. By January 1556, Charles abdicated as ruler over all his territories, and retired to a monastery in 1556.

Paul IV was opposed to councils, and refused to recall the Council of Trent during his pontificate. Pope Pius IV (r. 1559–1565) reconvened the Council in 1562, in part in response to increasing religious crises in France. The French participated in these final sessions, where the topics considered included marriage, the cult of the saints and associated issues, indulgences, purgatory, and the education and behavior of clergy. As with earlier meetings, the participants worked to define doctrine clearly, meaning that they worked against compromise and anathematized the widening range of Protestant interpretations. At the same time, they sought a greater centralization of church administration, blaming lax discipline within religious orders for the Reformation (as so many of the Reformers had been regular clergy).[11]

Both the Augsburg *Interim* and the Council of Trent attempted to clarify doctrine and heal wounds, while favoring the Catholic position. Each focused on belief as well as practice. The *Interim* was intended to be a compromise, but the Council proceeded from the position that it must uphold correct doctrine regardless of expediency. Even though Catholic Church leadership invited Protestants to participate at the Council of Trent, they did not intend the kind of open dialogue that German and Swiss reformers wanted. The result for both initiatives, therefore, was a deepening of divisions. Charles V, a central figure for both, failed to achieve either political peace or religious stability. In the long run, the Council of Trent was

---

[11] Bedouelle, *The Reform of Catholicism, 1480–1620*, 118.

far more influential, providing the basis for doctrinal and disciplinary definitions for centuries; the *Interim*'s legacy lies more in what might have been than in what was achieved.

SUGGESTED FURTHER READINGS

Gordon, Bruce. *The Swiss Reformation.* Manchester: Manchester University Press, 2002.

McNally, Robert E. "The Council of Trent and the German Protestants." *Theological Studies* 25 (1964): 1–22.

O'Malley, John. *Trent and All That.* Cambridge, MA: Harvard University Press, 2002.

Rabe, Horst. "Zur Entstehung des Augsburger Interims 1547/48." *Archiv für Reformationsgeschichte* 2003: 6–104.

Schroeder, H. J., ed. *The Canons and Decrees of the Council of Trent.* St. Louis, MO: Herder, 1941.

Whitford, David M. *Tyranny and Resistance: The Magdeburg Confession and the Lutheran Tradition.* St. Louis, MO: Concordia Publishing House, 2001.

23

Biblical Scholarship

Jon Balserak

"The die is cast."[1] Calvin's words in his 1532 letter from Paris to François Daniel indicated his enthusiasm at publishing his commentary on Seneca's *De Clementia*, which Calvin hoped would launch his career as a brilliant humanist. His audience, in this case, was the Republic of Letters; that pan-European collection of scholars, notaries, court officials, poets, lawyers, and academics to whom he sought to ingratiate himself. Eight years later, he published his *Commentarii in epistolam Pauli ad Romanos*, from Strasbourg. The juxtaposition of similar and dissimilar elements in these two works opens up a fascinating window into the character of biblical commentaries and, more broadly, scholarship in the sixteenth century.

In large measure, the audiences for the two commentaries would have been the same. Both works were written in Latin, saturated with classical references, constructed and formatted in the same way, addressed philological issues and ransacked history for guidance, and conveyed the same ethical tone. These qualities would not, in fact, distinguish Calvin's commenting endeavors from many of his contemporaries, Protestant, Catholic, or otherwise. The *Commentarii in epistolam Pauli ad Romanos* of Benedictus Aretius is similar in numerous ways to Calvin's work as is Philip Melanchthon's exposition of Romans, which bears the same title, and Gerardus Matthisius's *In epistolam B. Pauli ad Romanos commentaria*. But to say more about the character of early modern biblical scholarship, let us glance back briefly at its history.

---

[1] May 23, 1532 letter from Calvin to François Daniel, in *Ioannis Calvini Opera quae supersunt omnia*, G. Baum, E. Cunitz, and E. Reuss (eds.), 59 vols. (Brunswick and Berlin, Germany: C. A. Schwetschke et Filium, 1863–1900), 10: 19–20.

ANTIQUITY AND THE DEVELOPMENT OF COMMENTARIES

The origins of the commentary genre are disputed. It would appear that it arose around the second century B.C. as witnessed in the Dead Sea Scrolls. Known as *pesharim*, these seem to have influenced early Christians who, then, bequeathed the approach to the Christian church of both East and West.

The form of this loosely defined genre could vary markedly from one commentator to the next and from one era to the next. Glosses, scholion, intertextual notes, paraphrase, and suchlike were all incorporated into the commentary. Developing alongside it and blurring lines further were things like catenas and florilegia. It will be recalled, too, that commentaries developed within a culture that prized memory as a mark of superior moral and intellectual character (the legacy of the Myth of Theuth in Plato's *Phaedrus*). This being so, the genre included within it a wide variety of ideas associated with written notes organized toward the end of aiding memory. This would include the development of the idea of *topoi*, that is, the *loci* method. Also of note is the fact that commentaries developed initially in the ancient world as expositions on classical writings, such as Homer and Orphic religious texts, and were subsequently transferred to biblical studies.

MEDIEVAL COMMENTARIES

The rise of monasticism provided a fertile breeding ground for the growth of commentaries. For the West, this meant the *lingua franca* remained Latin, with vernacular commentaries not becoming common until after Calvin's death (though exceptions existed; e.g., Richard Rolle [†1349]). It also meant that many of the commentaries contained the monk or canon's process of meditation in written form. Augustine's *Enarrationes in Psalmos* provides an excellent example of this. This coupled with the commonly used fourfold method of interpretation meant that biblical expositions moved into sometimes-bewildering reflections as they moved away from the literal sense (*sensus literalis*) of the scriptural text in pursuit of the spiritual senses (*sensus spiritualis*: the analogical, tropological, and anagogical). Sermonic literature, which also employed the quadriga, exhibited the same quality.

Several standard commentaries were produced during this period. In the eighth and ninth centuries, Remigius of Auxerre, Rhabanus Maurus, and other Carolingian authors produced biblical commentaries consisting simply of citations from the church fathers, specifically a single sentence or short paragraph on each verse, or portion of a verse, of a given biblical book.

Around 1100 A.D., Anselm of Laon, the French theologian and chancellor of the cathedral school of Laon, together with several students such as Gilbert de la Porrée, produced the important standardized commentaries, the Ordinary Gloss (*Glossa Ordinaria*) and the Interlinear Gloss (*Glossa interlinearia*), which has recently been republished.[2] Scholars in the Abbey of St. Victor at Paris, founded in 1110 A.D., also wrote enormously important exegetical works – specifically, Hugh, Richard, and Andrew of St. Victor, who were known as the Victorines. Their writings passed down groundbreaking work on the literal sense and Jewish exegesis to subsequent generations.

Other influential medieval commentaries include those of Hugh of St. Cher, Thomas Aquinas, and Nicholas of Lyra. The last of these, Lyra's *Postilla super totam Bibliam*, is a repository of Jewish thought, which is – along with several other developments – important for the present discussion of the context from within which Calvin produced his biblical scholarship.

SCHOLASTICISM, JUDAISM, AND RENAISSANCE HUMANISM

The twelfth century saw the rise of two movements extremely significant for shaping that context. One was the appearance of Jewish exegetes like Rashi and Abraham ibn Ezra and, in the thirteenth century, Joseph, David, and Moses Qimhi, who pursued cutting-edge work on the Hebrew Bible and specifically its literal sense (*peshat*). Their work, which Lyra compiled, summarized, and engaged within his *Postilla*, would come to be hugely respected by Reformation commentators.

The other movement was the rise of scholasticism, which brought both a further focus on the literal sense (through the influence of Aquinas's assertion in *Summa Theologicae* I, Q10 of the literal sense's priority) and also a new style of biblical commentary that was replete with theological questions. One finds this superbly illustrated in something like Peter Lombard's *Commentarius in psalmos Davidicos* or Albertus Magnus's *In XII prophetas minores luculentissimae quaedam Enarrationes*. While not moving away from the pursuit of the spiritual senses, these *quaestio*-oriented expositions devoted considerable attention to the theological and philosophical curiosities radiating from the text.

---

[2] See *Biblia Latina cum Glossa Ordinaria, Facsimile Reprint of the Editio Princeps Adolph Rusch of Strassburg 1480/81*, introduction by Karlfried Froehlich and Margaret T. Gibson (Brepols: Turnhout, 1992).

A third movement worth mentioning here is the Renaissance, which arose in quattrocento Italy and was characterized by a love of all things ancient. It furthered *inter alia* the idea of the *Veritas Hebraica* (the doctrine that the original Hebrew was superior to the Septuagint and Old Latin translations of the Old Testament), and made it the aspiration of every humanist to be trilingual. Though the Renaissance predated the printing press by more than 100 years, the latter profoundly influenced the spread of the former, allowing humanists to edit, publish, and circulate new editions of patristic and classical sources – not merely medieval *florilegia* but full editions of Origen, Justin Martyr, Athanasius, Augustine, Cicero, Livy, Quintilian, Virgil, Horace, Ovid, Juvenal, and a myriad of others. The results for biblical scholarship were noteworthy.

RENAISSANCE, REFORMATION, AND THE BIBLICAL TEXT

Moving into the fifteenth and sixteenth centuries, many commentators began adopting a text-oriented exposition of the scriptures which sought to imitate the church fathers and move away from (what they regarded as) the dry, philosophically oriented, and lifeless scholastic approach to biblical exposition. These early modern commentators did not, it should be said, jettison theological inquiry. Rather, with the developments introduced by Rudolph Agricola and others, whose work on dialectic prompted renewed appreciation of the *loci* method, they collected their treatments of theological subjects under different headings. Sometimes, as was the case with, for instance, Peter Martyr Vermigli or Martin Bucer, these were found in the biblical commentaries while at other times they were extracted from the commentaries and collected together into books that were published separately; hence, Andreas Karlstadt's *Loci communes sacrae scripturae* or Konrad Klinge, O.F.M.'s *Loci Communes Theologici Pro Ecclesia Catholica*.

These commentaries often focused on the Hebrew or Greek text, which exegetes analyzed with extraordinary care and philological acumen. Carrying on and intensifying the habits of the Victorines in their careful work on the Hebrew text, humanists like Giovanni Pico della Mirandola, Wolfgang Capito, Johannes Oecolampadius, Sanctes Pagninus, O.P., Benito Arias Montano, and Isaac Casaubon exhibited not only an interest in the Hebrew Bible but also, at times, an almost-obsessive fascination with and reverence for Jewish exegesis and (in some cases) the Kabbalah. They interacted patiently with the school of literal Jewish exegesis, and also published Hebrew grammars and dictionaries as well as versions and translations of the Bible that were extremely impressive for their scholarship. This was true of Roman Catholic as well as Protestant exegetes. Thus, we see in Tommaso de Vio Cajetan's *Commentarii illustres planeque insignes in quinque mosaicos libros* the regular appearance of "Iuxta hebraeum habetur [according to the Hebrew]"[3] followed by critical discussion of the Hebrew text. The Catholic cardinal's respect for the Latin Vulgate did not alter his intention to work with the original. Conrad Pellican's *Commentaria Bibliorum* offers a superb Protestant example of the same.

The Hebrew text had become more widely available during this period. Daniel Bomberg, together with editors Felix Praetensis and Jacob ben Hayyim, created the Rabbinic Bible of 1517, which was to be followed by others as well as works such as Sebastian Münster's *Hebraica Biblia*. The same was done for the New Testament when in 1516 Erasmus published his enormously influential *Novum Instrumentum*, which being a bilingual edition with the Greek text in the left column and the Latin in the right, was a landmark of contemporary scholarship – the first Greek New Testament to be published (i.e., put on the market). This enabled New Testament Greek manuscript evidence to be examined to a degree previously unimaginable. Also produced at this time were Erasmus's *Annotationes* and *Paraphrases* of the New Testament, which were timely, provocative Latin paraphrases of scripture that spread swiftly throughout Europe.

The availability of the original texts brought about a sea change in biblical studies. Lorenzo Valla had pioneered text-critical work on the New Testament almost a century before Erasmus. His work, further developed by Erasmus and Theodore Beza, represented the beginning of modern textual criticism. To be sure, similar labors had (to some extent) been engaged in by Jerome and by the Carolingians who revised their copies of biblical texts in the eighth and ninth centuries, but not to the scale of these sixteenth-century scholars. Indeed Erasmus and Beza both grappled with fundamental questions related to the authenticity of specific biblical material – such as *pericope adulterae* and the Johannine Comma – and to vexing problems concerning whether, and how, one could emend the text of sacred scripture. Treatment of text-critical issues would gradually become more common within biblical studies as the early modern era gave way to the Enlightenment.

The significance of biblical scholarship to the period also made it an obvious center for polemical engagement. While some authors reserved polemics for separate tracts and treatises devoted to that purpose, numerous

---

[3] Tommaso de Vio Cajetan, *Commentarii illustres planeque insignes in quinque mosaicos libros* (Paris: Guilielmus de Boffozel, 1539), clxxx *et passim*.

theologians allowed themselves liberty to argue vehemently with opponents in their commentaries, lectures, and especially sermons.

KABBALISM, ESOTERICISM, AND PROPHECY

Pico's *Heptaplus* (a Kabbalistic commentary on the creation account in Genesis), Jacques Lefèvre d'Étaples's *Quincuplex Psalterium*, and Johannes Reuchlin's *De arte cabalistica* and *De verbo mirifico* are all excellent examples of the link between scripture and esotericism. More careful consideration of this link would need to mention Marsilio Ficino, the Italian humanist and founder of the Platonic Academy in Florence, as well as Franciscus Patricius and others.

Melanchthon's *Initia doctrinae physicae* offers a lovely example. In it, he mixed intensive study of patristic and classical writings with a careful reading of biblical texts, inserting himself into a tradition that went back to the Babylonians and was crowded with representatives from the Latin as well as the Arabic worlds. He repeatedly described astrology as one of the liberal arts, insisting that it is just like medicine or politics. When confronted with scriptural prohibitions against astrology, magic, and the like (Deut. 18:10–14; Isa. 47:13), he distinguished between two kinds of astrology: one in which a person watches the movement of the stars and planets and another that is the illicit practice of divination or soothsaying. On the former, he made clear that it draws from arithmetic and geometry, both gifts of God. Astrology is also affirmed, he insisted, in Genesis 1:14. Given this, astrology should not be spurned or condemn but gratefully accepted. Calvin would, of course, argue vehemently against astrology in 1549 (possibly with his friend, Melanchthon, in mind), as had Pico earlier and, before him, Augustine.

The Bible's prophetic literature was also the focus of an enormous amount of exegetical work during this period. Here Anabaptists, not always known for their biblical expositions, made important contributions with Melchior Hoffman's *Das XII. Capitel des propheten Danielis ausgelegt, ... christen nutzlich zu wissen* and Thomas Müntzer's *Ausslegung des andern Unterschyds Danielis dess Propheten* being worthy of mention. Not all prophecy was focused on apocalyptic themes. The *Prophezei* began in Zurich in 1525 by Ulrich Zwingli as a weekly forum for Bible interpretation that focused on exhaustive scrutiny of the biblical text in their original languages. With colleagues like Heinrich Bullinger, Conrad Pellican, Theodore Biblian-der, and Rudoph Gwalther, Zwingli sought to return to what they saw as the practice of the early church, namely, the habit of working their way *lectio continua* through entire books of the Bible. Similar were the *lectiones publicae* of Bern and *christliche Übung* of Strasbourg. The ultimate goal of these, perhaps especially the *Prophezei*, was preaching.

BIBLICAL SCHOLARSHIP AND PREACHING

Preaching handbooks (*artes praedicandi*), such as the *Manuale Curatorum*, and circulated sermon collections, such as the *sermones ad status*, have been common throughout the church's existence and were during the early modern period as well. The era saw alterations made by humanists and reformers to the character and content of sermons, enlivening their homiletical efforts through the fresh study of works on rhetoric and oratory such as *Rhetorica ad Herennium* and Cicero's *De oratore* and the homilies of Chrysostom, Augustine, and other church fathers. The importance ascribed to sermons in the Middle Ages continued into this era, with numerous works on homiletics being produced including Erasmus's *Ecclesiastes*, Melanchthon's *De officiis concionatoris*, *Elementa rhetorices* and *De arte concionandi formulae* (which included pieces by Melanchthon, Johannes Reuchlin, Johannes Aepinus, and an anonymous contribution), the Council of Trent's *De lectoribus et praedicatoribus Sacrae Scripturae*, and Cyprian Soarez's *Ratio studiorum*, a synthesis of the rhetorical theory of ancient authors like Aristotle, Cicero and Quintilian that was extremely important to Jesuit homiletics. François Lambert's *Commentarii de Prophetia*, for instance, was published in 1526 and explored a range of topics from rhetorical devices that a preacher might employ in his sermons to appropriate topics, study of the biblical text, how to preach on the Decalogue, the promise of the land (and other aspects of the Old Testament), organization, and other material. Likewise, in Melanchthon's writings on preaching, he divided sermons along the lines of classical oratory into seven parts: exordium, narration, proposition, division into parts, confirmation, refutation, and conclusion. He also added a fourth *genus*, dialectic, to the three standard classical *genera* of oration. He and many others saw the sermon's purpose as circumscribed by the aims of classical rhetoric, namely, to move, instruct, and delight. With the vernacular becoming more common for sermons in Europe and the British Isles during this era, sermons were still often translated into Latin for publication as can be seen, for instance, in Heinrich Bullinger's *Decades*. Before him, Martin Luther published collections of sermons, called *postilla*. The aim throughout was to circulate material for the aid of preachers. Of overarching significance for all this was book four of Augustine's *De doctrina Christiana*, which – like Augustine's theology generally – held enormous sway particularly in the Latin West.

CALVIN AND HIS WORLD

Calvin's relationship to the context mapped in the preceding text contributed to his departure from Catholicism and embracing of evangelicalism, though precisely how is difficult to say. That relationship was complex. For instance, he gives the impression of having only a piecemeal acquaintance with medieval writings. But he was, in fact, influenced deeply by things like scholastic thought, though he seldom explicitly interacted with it in print. The influence of medieval exegesis is harder to discern, though still present. By contrast, his knowledge of ancient Christian and "pagan" *corpora* appears easily to anyone perusing his oeuvre. Renaissance humanists and contemporary evangelicals' publications were likewise well known to him, though infrequently mentioned, except in his letters.

Calvin tended to mention individual thinkers in his theological writings when wishing to use them as polemical appeals to authority. He did this most often, unsurprisingly, with patristic authors. Rarely do Calvin's citations point to sources of his thought, which are extraordinarily hard to discern. As he grew older and became drawn into more and more disputes, his engagement with contemporary thinkers, movements, and ideas tended to become more captious and characterized by obstinacy regarding the truthfulness of his own judgments.

Becoming more specific, Calvin's predilection for Augustine's theology, particularly soteriology, was not accompanied by a love for the African's hermeneutics or the tradition's embracing of the quadriga – which Calvin dismissed, on more than one occasion, as an invention of Satan. He also reserved such vituperative language for Anabaptist ideas and Jewish exegesis. By contrast, he praised Oecolampadius's Psalms commentary, and was enamored of the literal exegesis of contemporaries like Bucer, Bullinger, and Vermigli. He employed the *loci* method when organizing his *Institutio Christianae Religionis*, the organization of which was likely influenced by Melanchthon's early writings on Romans. His New Testament commentaries exhibit his use of text-critical methods similar to those found in Valla, Erasmus, and Beza. When expounding both testaments, he worked with the original languages. And under Calvin's leadership, Geneva developed its own version of the *Prophezei* called the *congrégations*.

SUGGESTED FURTHER READINGS

Carruthers, Mary. *The Book of Memory: A Study of Memory in Medieval Culture.* Cambridge: Cambridge University Press, 1990.

Froehlich, Karlfried. "Always to Keep the Literal Sense in Holy Scripture Means to Kill One's Soul: The State of Biblical Hermeneutics at the Beginning of the Fifteenth Century." In *Literary Uses of Typology from the Late Middle Ages to the Present*, ed. Earl Miner. Princeton, NJ: Princeton University Press, 1977, 20–48.

Fumaroli, Marc. *La République des Lettres*. Paris: Gallimard, 2015.

Gordon, Bruce, and Matthew McLean, eds. *Shaping the Bible in the Reformation: Books, Scholars and Their Readers in the Sixteenth Century*. Leiden, The Netherlands: Brill, 2012.

Krans, Jan. *Beyond What Is Written: Erasmus and Beza as Conjectural Critics of the New Testament*. Leiden, The Netherlands: Brill, 2006.

Lane, Anthony N. S. *John Calvin: Student of the Church Fathers*. Edinburgh: T&T Clark, 1999.

Lehner, Ulrich L., Richard A. Muller, and A. G. Roeber, eds. *The Oxford Handbook of Early Modern Theology, 1600–1800*. New York: Oxford University Press, 2016.

Minnis, A. J., and A. B. Scott. *Medieval Literary Theory and Criticism, c. 1100– c. 1375: The Commentary-Tradition*. Oxford: Oxford University Press, 1988.

Muller, Richard. *The Unaccommodated Calvin: Studies in the Foundation of a Theological Tradition*. Oxford: Oxford University Press, 2000.

Rummel, Erika. *The Humanist-Scholastic Debate in the Renaissance and Reformation*. Cambridge, MA: Harvard University Press, 1995.

Sæbø, Magne, ed. *Hebrew Bible/Old Testament*. Vol 2: *From the Renaissance to the Enlightenment*. Göttingen: Vandenhoeck & Ruprecht, 2008.

Smalley, Beryl. *The Study of the Bible in the Middle Ages*. Notre Dame, IN: University of Notre Dame Press, 1964.

24

~

The Printed Word

Andrew Pettegree

Jean Calvin and Martin Luther never met, a circumstance neither of them had much cause to regret. While Martin Luther fought his existential struggle with the papacy in the 1520s, Calvin was still in receipt of a clerical prebend; the German church was well established before Calvin was forced, with some hesitation, to throw in his lot with the reformers. What both men shared was a clear understanding of the power of print. For Luther, this was an instinctive grasp of pamphleteering, how a direct appeal to a lay audience could neutralise the traditional sources of church power. Calvin's journey was more studied. His first quest for authorial fame was a painful humiliation, a callow and premature attempt to walk in the footsteps of Erasmus. From the failure of this project the young scholar learned an important lesson, that if the print industry had ever hastened to follow the humanist agenda, those days were long gone. This was now a pragmatic alliance. Printers loved Luther because he made them money; his Catholic opponents struggled with the medium because they did not. Calvin, too, in his studied, thoughtful way, would conquer print, and in the process make of Geneva a second powerhouse of Reformation publishing. But like so much else in his life, this was a pragmatic triumph, an application of his extraordinary intelligence to a necessary task.

The success of Calvin's *Institutes* in 1536 was as unexpected as the failure of his commentary on Seneca had been painful; the spreading reputation of this masterly encapsulation of the Protestant creed paved the way for his invitation to help fashion a new church at Geneva. His expulsion from Geneva in 1538 allowed him three years to learn the art of leadership, but also to observe the workings of the printing press in one of the citadels of Protestant publishing, Strasbourg. Calvin established a close relationship with Strasbourg's printers. For some years after his return to Geneva, Calvin continued to send his Latin works to Strasbourg for publication; only his brief, more ephemeral texts were consigned to Geneva's, at this point, more rudimentary presses.[1] This arrangement came to an abrupt halt when a manuscript was lost in transit. Calvin took this hard, and in the anxious months before it miraculously reappeared he could undertake little new writing. From this point, local printers would receive the Latin texts too, and with this Calvin was content, for several experienced French publishers had now transferred their presses to Geneva, attracted by the growing reputation of Calvin's city. Several would go on to play a major role in the promotion of Calvin as a major force in the publishing world. Jean Girard had held a virtual monopoly of Calvin's works to 1550, including the first major Latin text, Calvin's commentary on Hebrews in 1549; from this date Jean Crespin, a publisher and author most famous for the French martyrology, played an increasingly important role. Later, exiled members of the great Parisian publishing dynasty Estienne would lend their skills and business expertise to the expanding industry of printing Calvin.

In the course of his career, Calvin brought to the press some 80 original works. This extraordinary productivity in a writing career of just 30 years was not exceptional among the reformers, but it was still remarkable: especially as it excludes the sermons, published from the transcripts made in church by a secretary appointed by the *Bourse Française*, the body charged with poor relief for French refugees. Calvin was not altogether happy that the sermons should be published because he thought of these extemporary performances very differently from the Latin biblical commentaries to which he devoted careful study. What is perhaps more extraordinary, given the austere face he turned to the world, and the rather disdainful attitude to the publication of the vernacular sermons, was his versatility as a writer. We know that Calvin was one of the most powerful interpreters of scripture, not only in his commentaries, but also in the regular gathering of the Genevan ministerial cadre in the *congregations*. Here ministers had the chance to test their own exegetical abilities in the presence of Calvin and Beza, and in turn have their abilities and orthodoxy proved. The commentaries were the most substantial of his published works, even set alongside the *Institutes*, which, in the definitive edition of 1563 (the last of Calvin's lifetime), was already double the size of the work that made his name in 1536. It is in these longer works that Genevan printers showed what the local industry was now capable of; a steady progression of elegant folios

---

[1] Rodolphe Peter and Jean-François Gilmont, *Bibliotheca Calviniana. Les oeuvres de Jean Calvin publiées au XVIe siècle*, 3 vols. (Geneva: Droz, 1991–2000). Jean-François Gilmont, *John Calvin and the Printed Book* (Kirksville, MO: Truman State University Press, 2005).

culminating in the commentary on the Psalms, and the revised commentary on Genesis, each more than 400,000 words long.

These are the works we would have expected of Calvin, and most correspond to his carefully cultivated scholarly self-image: although we might still wonder that in later life, so seriously sick that he had to be carried the few yards from his home to the church to preach, he still turned out an average of 100,000 words of writing a year. Just as remarkable was Calvin's unexpected proficiency as a vernacular and polemical writer. Calvin's career did not begin, like that of Luther, in a torrent of passionate pamphlets, defending his teaching and pouring scorn on his critics. But from the years in Strasbourg onwards, Calvin too addressed contemporary issues facing his church and the wider Protestant community in works of forensic fluency, and he too had sharp words for those who took a contrary view. Calvin's exhortations to fellow believers in France during the 1540s are written in a French so beautifully constructed that they are often studied as a model of the developing language.[2] His interventions in international controversy were written in Latin. During his career, Calvin would pen 24 separate works under 10,000 words in length. These were not quite *Flugschriften*, but nevertheless a precious gift to the printers of Geneva, who found here works from which they could make a quick cash return.

Like most of the sixteenth century's most successful authors, Calvin was very familiar with the mechanics, rhythms and disciplines of the printer's workshop. The international Latin market revolved around the Frankfurt Fair, the Easter and September sales where the publishers and booksellers of Europe congregated to buy, sell, browse and examine the latest typographical innovations. In the weeks leading up to Frankfurt, print shops would work long hours to have texts necessary, for to miss a fair was to have a bulky expensive text taking up space in a warehouse, and no return on the capital invested for a further six months. Authors were expected to play their part in smoothing the path, if necessary putting aside other tasks to complete promised works, or correct proofs. Calvin's correspondence is full of fretful references to the strain of rushing works to press in time for the fair, and the frustration when a text had to be shelved for lack of time.[3]

Once they had made the long trip to Frankfurt, publishers would hope to dispose of at least half of a new edition at the first fair, even if this meant

---

[2] Francis M. Higman, *The Style of John Calvin in His French Polemical Treatises* (Oxford: Oxford University Press, 1967). Id., *Jean Calvin: Three French Treatises* (London: Athlone Press, 1970).

[3] Gilmont, *Calvin and the Printed Book*, 220–222.

accepting other texts in exchange, rather than payment in cash. So Geneva became, almost by default, a major centre of bookselling. All the more important then, that with the growth of the Geneva Academy, there was a growing class of students requiring texts, and serious scholars settled in Geneva keen to build a library. Many of the personal libraries that featured neat rows of Calvin's works would have begun in early student days on the banks of the Léman.

Calvin's death in 1564 came at a testing time for the Genevan print industry. It was quite normal for the sales of authors' works to fall off very sharply after their death. With no new texts from the master's pen, printers had to rely on sales of the back catalogue, and new editions inevitably faced competition from the circulation of old stock through the second-hand market. In this respect, the success of Luther and Erasmus in bucking this trend, with a steady flow of new and collective editions through to the end of the century, was another proof of their exceptional position in the early development of the printed book. Calvin's death also came at a time when his movement was undergoing a period of turbulent growth, with new churches springing up in France, the Netherlands, Germany, Scotland, and England. These movements brought new opportunities for the printed word, not least in the provision of books for worship in the new congregations, and of translations of Calvin's own pastoral writings into other languages. This gave new opportunities for printers in other parts of Europe to share in the profits of publishing Calvin, but posed new challenges for the Genevan industry. To this point, Geneva had enjoyed something close to a monopoly on the publication of Calvin's works. But the growth of Calvinist churches in France in the years after 1559, and the subsequent collapse of persecution, made it for the first time possible to contemplate the establishment of a Protestant press within France, far closer to this rapidly growing market. These new presses, in Lyon, Normandy, and Orléans, played a major role in the printing, in 1562, of the enormous collective edition of the newly completed French psalter, a massive feat of organisational virtuosity given the need for each participating printer to have the necessary musical type. This project, generating more than 35,000 copies in under a year, demonstrated not only the enormous growth in the French Protestant church but also the enormous potency of the publishing industry that had been built around Calvin.[4]

---

[4] Eugenie Droz, 'Antoine Vincent: La propaganda protestante par le psaultier', in Gabriel Berthoud (ed.), *Aspects de la propagande religieuse* (Geneva: Droz, 1957), 276–293.

The Genevan church continued to play a major role in printing works for the new churches, but it would never again enjoy the same exclusivity. Theodore de Bèze, though a capable organiser and a thoughtful exegete, did not have Calvin's totemic role in the church, and his published works never enjoyed the same success. Calvin's legacy to his movement would be a print industry in a constant state of evolution. His works were taken up in a new wave of translations, first in England, then in the new Dutch state. For 40 years, indeed, England became the major centre of publication of Calvin's works, providing a welcome source of income for an otherwise rather under-developed local industry.

A persistent tradition of English exceptionalism has allowed scholars of the British Reformation to present the new English Church settlement as a third way, somewhat removed from the Calvinist mainstream. The history of Protestant printing during the reign of Queen Elizabeth would suggest otherwise. Calvin was far and away the most popular of the continental Protestant authorities who, in the absence of a major local patriarch, dominated English theological publishing.[5] This is true both in terms of ownership of his works and of an extraordinary wave of translations of Calvin's works into English.

In a way the first of these is more important because Calvin made his way into the consciousness (and onto the bookshelves) of ministers and laymen all over Europe through the dissemination of copies of his major Latin works, largely in the original Genevan editions. In England, evidence from postmortem inventories shows that Cambridge scholars collectively owned a full range of all the major commentaries and multiple copies of the *Institutes*.[6] The *Institutes* was by far the most popular of Calvin's work for English collectors, both in Latin and in English translation. An English edition formed part of the great wave of Protestant publishing after the Elizabethan settlement, and was reprinted thereafter at regular intervals to the end of the century.[7]

The *Institutes* was indeed unusual in that this was one of the few of Calvin's works where the market was so robust that it justified foreign reprints in Latin as well as the vernacular, in England, Germany, and later in the Dutch Republic. But local reprints were not necessary for Calvin's

---

[5] Andrew Pettegree, 'The Reception of Calvinism in Britain', in Wilhelm Neuser and Brian Armstrong (eds.), *Calvinus Sincerioris Religionis Vindex. Calvin as Protector of the Purer Religion* (Kirksville, MO: Sixteenth Century Journal Publishers, 1997), 267–289.

[6] E. S. Leedham-Green, *Books in Cambridge Inventories*, 2 vols. (Cambridge: Cambridge University Press, 1986), 2: 172–180.

[7] With seven editions between 1561 and 1600.

scholarly works to be generally available in the growing family of European Calvinist churches. This can be attested not only by the evidence of inventories and personal libraries but also indirectly through the significant numbers of these serious scholarly tomes that survive today. Many books published in the sixteenth and seventeenth centuries can today be traced only in a single copy, and many more have vanished altogether. The sixteenth-century Genevan editions of Calvin's lectures and commentaries can in contrast regularly be found in 30, 40 or 50 copies, dispersed in libraries around Europe and North America.[8]

The *Institutes* has a special status in the history of Calvin's works in print, not only as the definitive statement of Calvin's theology but also because it crossed the boundaries between professional theologians and lay readers. In this respect it took its place among an extraordinary range of Calvin's smaller writings that made their way into English during the reign of Elizabeth.[9] In translation, English readers found a Calvin for all occasions, the biblical exegete, the polemicist, the father of the church. The wave of translations engaged many of the leading figures of the emergent Anglican Church, either as translators or patrons and dedicatees. Ultimately, English versions would outstrip even the loadstar: between 1560 and 1600, more editions of Calvin's works would be published in London than in Geneva. Calvin was good business for all parts of the English print industry, booksellers, who handled the imported books, published and printers, not to mention the burgeoning community of translators.

The seventeenth century brought a sea change in the market for Calvin in print. The centre of gravity shifted again, from England to the Dutch Republic, even as the number of new editions fell precipitately. This did not necessarily mean that Calvin's influence was receding, after all, the central defining issue that shaped the religious and political culture of the new Dutch state revolved around different interpretations of Calvin's central teachings. The *Institutes* was republished throughout the century, in Latin and in Dutch translation. A magnificent set of Calvin's Latin works, in nine volumes, was published in Amsterdam in 1671. But in the developing churches of the seventeenth century, Calvin would be known as much through interpreters as through reprints of his own works: men like William

---

[8] Peter and Gilmont, *Bibliotheca Calviniana*, 60/2, 61/20, 63/19, etc.
[9] Francis Higman, 'Calvin's Works in Translation', in Andrew Pettegree, Alastair Duke and Gillian Lewis (eds.), *Calvinism in Europe, 1540–1620* (Cambridge: Cambridge University Press, 1994), 82–99.

Perkins, immensely popular both in the original Latin and English editions, and in Dutch translation.[10]

In the seventeenth century, the full extent of Calvin's continuing role in theological pedagogy cannot be gauged through the continuing output of the publishing industry, either of his own works or those of his disciples. The canonical Genevan imprints of his own lifetime continued to be cherished. To establish the full extent of this trade, we have a new and extraordinarily valuable body of evidence, auction catalogues and surviving publishers' stock catalogues. The Dutch were pioneers in the sale of books by auction, and between the first auction sale in 1599 and the end of the seventeenth century, we have now identified something in the region of 4,000 printed book catalogues.[11] An analysis of their holdings demonstrates how much Calvin's works remained an integral part of any serious theological library.

Judging from this evidence, in the seventeenth-century Dutch Republic Calvin remained one of the most frequently purchased authors, easily outstripping other patriarchs of the sixteenth century, such as Luther and Bullinger, and popular contemporary theologians, such as André Rivet and Gisbertus Voetius.[12] Only two other authors challenge this ascendency: Hugo Grotius, because of his enormous versatility as a writer, with significant contributions to theology and classical studies as well as politics and jurisprudence, and Erasmus. Erasmus, so frustrated to be overshadowed by the print sensation that was Martin Luther in his lifetime, gained a posthumous revenge as the most popular author of the seventeenth century in his homeland: one suspects not just for his wit and erudition but also as a totemic antithesis to the partisan severity of orthodox Calvinism.

The *Institutes* was overwhelmingly the most popular of Calvin's works on the shelves of Dutch collectors, though a surprising number also invested in the *Opera Omnia* of 1671, at the cost of around 50 guilders. This was more than a month's salary for a minister of the Reformed Church. This was a serious investment, but many others spent similar sums amassing a study collection of Calvin's commentaries. Significantly, a very high proportion of the Calvin editions that crop up in these catalogues were expensive folios, very different from the general market in theological books, which in the

[10] Cornelis W. Schoneveld, *Intertraffic of the Mind: Studies in Seventeenth-Century Anglo-Dutch Translation* (Leiden, The Netherlands: Brill, 1983).
[11] Andrew Pettegree and Arthur der Weduwen, *The Bookshop of the World: Making and Trading Books in the Dutch Golden Age* (London: Yale University Press, 2019).
[12] A study based on consultation of more than two hundred catalogues, completed with the help of Forrest Strickland, author of a forthcoming study of ministerial collecting in the Dutch Republic.

Dutch Republic consisted predominantly of texts in octavo and duodecimo, smaller, far less expensive formats. In assembling these collections, the age of the edition seems to have been largely immaterial. Dutch libraries contain a considerable number of sixteenth-century Genevan imprints, both in French and Latin. This was a tribute both to the quality of the original editorial work and the workmanship of Genevan publishing houses, turning out clean, elegant editions, on good quality paper, still serviceable 150 years later. Indeed the same could be said today, as anyone who has turned the unyellowed pages of these magnificent books could attest. They form a dignified monument to a man who was a church leader by vocation rather than choice, and whose service as an author took him in quite different directions from the fame he had first sought. Few exploited the mature printing industry of the first century of print more effectively, and few left behind such a substantial and enduring print legacy.

SUGGESTED FURTHER READING

Gilmont, Jean-François. *John Calvin and the Printed Book*. Kirksville, MO: Truman State University Press, 2005.

Higman, Francis. 'Calvin's Works in Translation'. In *Calvinism in Europe, 1540–1620*, ed. Andrew Pettegree, Alastair Duke and Gillian Lewis. Cambridge: Cambridge University Press, 1994, 82–99.

Pettegree, Andrew, and Arthur der Weduwen. *The Bookshop of the World: Making and Trading Books in the Dutch Golden Age*. London: Yale University Press, 2019.

Universal Short-Title Catalogue. www.ustc.ac.uk/.

25

Polemic's Purpose

Amanda Eurich

Sixteenth-century Reformers would not have understood Michel Foucault's postmodern assault on polemic as the antithesis of truth because the defense of truth – divine truth, that is – was the guiding purpose of their endeavors. They would, however, have recognized Foucault's description of their tactics as a no-holds-barred contest against an "enemy who is wrong, who is hurtful, and whose very existence constitutes a threat."[1] Across the confessional divide, early modern polemicists believed they were engaged in a war of words as deadly serious as the bloody confrontations taking place in the streets and on the battlefields of Europe. The new medium of print became a critical instrument in their efforts to win princely support; mobilize public opinion across broad geographical, linguistic, and confessional boundaries; and vanquish the heretic in their midst.

In an era when religious polemic was an integral feature of the fierce battle for the hearts and minds of European Christians, Calvin's contemporaries recognized the Genevan reformer as one of most gifted and prolific controversialists among them. Over the course of his career, Calvin penned at least 45 polemical texts in Latin and in French, taking aim at fellow Protestants, Libertines, Anti-Trinitarians as well as the champions of Catholicism. Like his contemporaries, Calvin viewed his more explicitly polemical work as an extension of his pastoral responsibility to equip Christians to discern truth from error. As Calvin explained in his *Commentaries on Matthew*, Christ had admonished his followers "to prepare themselves for battle since it is

---

[1] Michel Foucault, *Essential Works of Foucault 1954–1984*, Vol. 1: *Ethics: Subjectivity and Truth*, ed. Paul Rabinow and trans. Robert Hurley (London: Penguin, 2000), 112. As cited in Almut Suerbaum, George Southcombe, and Benjamin Thompson, eds., *Polemic: Language as Violence in Medieval and Early Modern Discourse* (New York and London: Routledge, 2016), 4.

necessary to fight to give the witness to the truth."[2] For Calvin and his contemporaries, the heuristic purposes of polemic were inextricably linked to its more militant, defensive objectives.

Protestant polemicists faced the particular challenge of dismantling the established authority of medieval Catholicism whose rituals and beliefs were deeply embedded in daily life. Luther notoriously took aim at practices, such as the sale of indulgences, that he deemed corrupt as well as the personalities who legitimized them, often using coarse language, scatological imagery, and profane references to denigrate his Catholic opponents. He and others defended the necessity of deploying extreme measures and graphic language as the only way to liberate the laity from dangerous delusions and thus reform the Church and society at large. By the mid-1520s, the nascent reform movement was increasingly assailed on several fronts. The emergence of even more radical voices, inspired less by theological training than prophetic vision, threatened any unified program of reform and broadened the field of attack. Second-generation reformers, such as Calvin, thus found themselves engaged in an unwieldy offensive directed toward a rapidly expanding arena of challengers.

Not surprising perhaps, Calvin's overtly anti-Catholic tracts comprised less than a quarter of his polemical production, the majority written in the 1540s as the reformer was consolidating his own ministry in Geneva. Although Calvin was no less determined than his predecessors to repudiate medieval error, he was keenly aware of the precarious situation of Genevan republic, positioned between the Swiss confederation and Catholic France, and often more inclined in his early polemical works to engage in what Francis Higman has called "gentle polemics."[3] Calvin's *Letter to Sadoleto*, written in the wake of his expulsion from Geneva, illustrates his ability to moderate his tone to suit his audience and his purpose. A well-known figure in humanist and curial circles, Cardinal Jacopo Sadoleto, had addressed an open letter to the Council of Geneva, imploring the body to reject the dangerous innovations introduced by Calvin and Farel and return to the Catholic fold. Calvin refuted the Sadoleto's claims, penning his clever Latin riposte in less than a week. In his opening salvo, he issued a masterful denunciation of Catholic tradition and papal authority, accusing the cardinal of willingly misrepresenting the reformist agenda. "All we have attempted,"

---

[2] Higman, "I Came Not to Send Peace but a Sword," in Wilhelm Neuser and Brian Armstrong (eds.), *Calvinus Sincerioris Religionis Vindex* (Kirksville, MO: Truman University Press, 1997), 123.

[3] Ibid., 124.

he argued, "has been to renew the ancient form of the Church, which at first sullied and distorted by illiterate men of indifferent character, was afterward flagitiously mangled and almost destroyed by the Roman pontiff and his faction."[4] In the passages that followed, however, Calvin attempted to disarm his adversary by adopting a more conciliatory attitude. As he observed, "God had never so blessed his servants that they possessed full and perfect knowledge of every part of their subject. It is clear that his purpose in so limiting our knowledge was first that we should be kept humble and also that we should continue to have dealings with our fellows."[5] Impressed by the persuasive force of Calvin's rhetoric against Sadoleto, the Genevan Council authorized a French translation of the text that helped inspire the campaign to recall the reformer from exile.

On both sides of the confessional breach, early modern polemicists recognized that they were engaged in a high-stakes game with immediate political as well as eternal consequences. Polemical texts were openly addressed to potential princely and aristocratic patrons, soliciting their moral as well as political and military support. The power of polemic to effect political change inspired a series of pamphlets Calvin directed toward Charles V and imperial authorities in the 1540s as he sought to reinforce diplomatic efforts toward confessional reconciliation enshrined in the Augburg Interim. In a series of bruising battles with so-called Nicodemites, Calvin took his fellow French Protestants to task for their willingness to compromise their public profession of faith and the progress of reform in his native country. Calvin's stinging rebuttals of the Spiritualist movement in France have also been described as driven by political fears that its wide reach within courtly circles threatened efforts to secure aristocratic support for the fledging Reformed movement.[6]

Renaissance traditions of satire heavily influenced Reformation polemical practice, reflecting the humanist training of many Protestant theologians. Reformers embraced parody and ridicule as useful tools to lay bare the pretentions and expose the dangerous fallacies of the opposition, recognizing the seductive, persuasive power of humor. In works in both Latin and in the vernacular, controversialists often consciously eschewed tendentious

---

[4] John Calvin, *Selections from His Writings*, ed. John Dillenberger (Missoula, MT: Scholars Press, 1975), 92.
[5] As cited in Charles Partee, "Calvin's Polemic: Foundational Convictions in Service of God's Truth," in Wilhelm Neuser and Brian Armstrong (eds.), *Calvinus Sincerioris Religionis Vindex* (Kirksville, MO: Truman University Press, 1997), 100.
[6] Wulfert De Greef, *The Writings of John Calvin*, trans. Lyle D. Bierma. (Grand Rapids, MI: Baker Books, 1993), 169–171.

theological arguments, appealing instead to fundamental principles of common sense. John Calvin was not the first reformer, Catholic or Protestant, to pillory the spurious trade in saints' bones, but his *Treatise on Relics* (1543) revealed how effectively he enlisted readers' sympathies by invoking reason and common sense.[7] In this first foray into the world of vernacular polemic, Calvin sounded familiar themes, ridiculing the fraudulent proliferation of relics and the materiality and sensuality of popular devotion. As he writes of that most peculiar of Marian relics, the Virgin's milk: "How they obtained all this milk they do not say.... Indeed had the Virgin been a wet nurse her whole life, or a dairy, she could not have produced more than is shown as hers in all these ports."[8] Calvin's *Treatise on Relics* was the first of a number of tractates that he wrote in the vernacular. Like his contemporaries, Calvin recognized that the use of the vernacular facilitated the pedagogical intentions of polemic, rendering God's design accessible to a broader audience.

In Calvin's preface to Viret's *Disputations chrestiennes*, the Genevan reformer delineated the importance of satire as well as its limitations. "Christianity can be discussed in two ways," he asserted, "firstly, in denouncing the mad superstitions which have grown up among Christians under the disguise of religion ... secondly, in showing the pure and simple truth." When engaging in the defense of doctrine, "[N]o jokes should come into our discourse ... [or the] reverence we feel toward His Majesty."[9] It would be wrong, however, to assume that satire was not used to establish profound theological principles. In works, such as the *Treatise on Relics* and *Against Astrology*, Calvin subtly reinforced his own positions on the Eucharist, predestination, and the sovereignty of God. Calvin's ability to shift registers and modulate syntax to elevate abstract truths or to ridicule the logic of the opposition is readily apparent in his reply to the theologians of the Sorbonne, who had repudiated key Reformation teachings in 23 articles in 1543. Calvin took great delight in parodying the tortured Latin cadences of his adversaries and, by extension, their faulty scholastic logic. Three years later, he took on some of the greatest prelates and theologians of the Catholic Church, annotating the *Acts of the Synods of Trent* in Latin and French in 1547.[10]

---

[7]   John Calvin, *Treatise on Relics*, ed. Anthony Uyl (Edinburgh: Johnson and Hunter, 1854).
[8]   Ibid., 249.
[9]   Higman, "I Came Not to Send Peace," 131–132. See also Francis Higman, *The Style of John Calvin in His French Polemical Treatises* (Oxford: Oxford University Press, 1967), 7–8, 83–102.
[10] Higman, "I Came Not to Send Peace," 127–128.

As Bernard Cottret has argued, the practice of polemic was an integral part of the "process of confessional construction."[11] Protestant reformers sought to define, clarify, and consolidate doctrinal boundaries in their polemical works, a project that bought them into conversation and debate with each other as well as their Catholic opponents. Driven by a desire to restore unity to the Church as prescribed by scripture, the divisive power of polemic also troubled Protestant reformers, especially as they found themselves drawn into internecine doctrinal battles that complicated efforts to present a common front to the Catholic opposition. Throughout his career, Calvin was particularly attuned to these dangers. He circulated his first polemical tractate *Psychopannychia,* a prolonged Latin diatribe denouncing the Anabaptist belief in the sleep of the soul embraced by a number of other Protestant groups, for eight years before finally publishing it in 1542. Calvin's willingness to consult fellow theologians, rethink his positions, and revise his arguments suggests the collaborative nature of his polemical process.

Over the course of the sixteenth century, the failure of public colloquies and print debates, even within the Reform movement, to achieve consensus hardened confessional fault lines and increasingly polarized discourse. Intra-Protestant polemic followed the same rhetorical conventions used to discredit Catholic adversaries, weaponizing what Antònia Szabari has called "the politics of caricature."[12] Early modern theologians proceeded from the conviction that the lines between truth and falsehood could be clearly delineated. The desire for clarity reinforced the pedagogical purposes of polemic, but it also encouraged reductive arguments that identified opponents not merely as misguided but as active agents of evil. Polemicists cleverly manipulated the graphic elements of print to underscore visually the stark contrasts between rival systems of belief and practice, presenting opposing tenets in a dialogical or binary format on the page. Calvin too deployed this technique effectively in his tractates against Spiritualists and Anabaptists in the 1540s.

Both Protestant and Catholic controversialists utilized the inversion of gender roles to excoriate their rivals, playing upon contradictory cultural anxieties concerning the female power and weakness. Mainstream Protestant reformers were singularly unified in their attack on radical reform movements, such as Anabaptism, and often marshaled gender and sexual innuendo to denigrate them. By 1545, Calvin's earlier efforts to parse out the

[11] Bernard Cottret, *Jean Calvin: A Biography* (Grand Rapids, MI: Eerdmans, 2009), 364.
[12] Antònia Szabari, *Less Rightly Said: Scandals and Readers in Sixteenth-Century France* (Redwood, CA: Stanford University Press, 2009), 89.

distinctions between Anabaptists' belief in soul sleep and other more conventional practices gave way to a robust and thoroughgoing condemnation of Anabaptism. Penning a point-by-point deconstruction of Matthew Sattler's *Schleitheim Confession,* Calvin gave free rein to his capacity for vitriolic attack.[13] Writing in simple, clear phrases, Calvin eschewed theological and linguistic subtlety and employed derogatory images to diminish Anabaptist radicals. In the service of doctrinal purity, he was willing to paint with a fairly broad brush, eliding Anabaptist communalism with the polygamist practices of the Munsterites and deftly mobilizing gender tropes common to early modern religious polemics.

Gender was only one of a number of strategies used by early modern polemicists to discredit rival theologies by association. Crude comparisons to earlier heretical sects served the same function by allowing authors to ascribe similar doctrinal affiliations and diabolical motives to their contemporary opponents. Luther repeatedly accused his critics of Pelagianism. Luc Racaut has shown how French Catholic authors effectively linked Calvinists to Catharism, the arch-heresy of the Middle Ages.[14] Calvin too employed this technique in his works, famously inferring the close connections between so-called Libertines and early Christian movements that had been denounced as heretical for centuries.[15]

Renowned figures, such as Luther and Calvin, frequently found themselves the subject of religious invective. Racaut has described Calvin as a reluctant polemicist, forcibly drawn into conflicts not necessarily of his own making.[16] Nevertheless, Calvin turned his polemical energies from the 1550s onward almost fully toward doctrinal controversies, penning 19 Latin treatises on a variety of thorny subjects. His prodigious output in the last decade of his life was most certainly a reflection of his increasing international stature within the Protestant world. A number of these works addressed ongoing Eucharistic disputes among Lutherans, Zwinglians, and Calvinists. The failure to achieve any lasting agreement over the meaning and purpose of the Lord's Supper had divided Protestants for more than three decades, compromising efforts to combat the combined forces of the Holy Roman emperor and the Roman Catholic Church and threatening the autonomy of

---

[13] John Calvin, *Treatises against the Anabaptists and against the Libertines,* trans. Benjamin W. Farley (Grand Rapids, MI: Baker, 1982); see also Wilhelm Balke, *Calvin and the Anabaptist Radicals* (Grand Rapids, MI: Eerdmans, 1981), 28.

[14] Luc Racaut, *Hatred in Print: Catholic Propaganda and Protestant Identity during the French Wars of Religion* (Aldershot: Ashgate, 2002), 99–129.

[15] Higman, *Style in French Polemical Treatises,* 16–17.

[16] Racaut, *Hatred in Print,* 12.

the Swiss confederation. Nearly every reformer of note had penned a treatise on the subject. In 1549, Swiss reformers finally reached an agreement articulated in the *Consensus Tigurinus* published two years later. Calvin's French translation of the Latin text bolstered support for those who rejected both Lutheran and Catholic positions on the bodily presence of Christ in Lord's Supper. From 1555 to 1557, Calvin thus found himself embroiled in a series of bitter exchanges with Joachim Westphal, a German-Lutheran theologian, who denounced the Genevan reformer as a heretic. Pressed by Bullinger to respond on behalf of the Swiss party, Calvin penned the *Defensio sanae et orthodoxae doctrinae de sacramentis,* publishing it only after rigorous vetting by various colleagues. A year later in 1556, he authored a second, even more thorough reflection, running to 172 pages, hoping to silence his Lutheran critics to no avail. A final, even more heated response to Westphal – *Ultima defensio ad Westphalum* – followed in 1557, in which Calvin abandoned any pretense of compromise and accused the German theologian in turn of heresy and slander.[17]

Calvin's efforts to discredit Westphal, and Westphal's vicious retorts, underscore the highly personalized nature of early modern polemics. As many scholars have noted, the rules of engagement often closely mimicked noble conventions of dueling. An aggrieved party registered a challenge in print, a gesture that demanded a response or the subsequent loss of honor. Respondents often found themselves caught up in a flurry of accusations and counteraccusations that escalated religious tensions, radicalized discourse, and rarely led to definitive victories for either side. In the last decade of his life, Calvin engaged in a number of one-on-one battles with his adversaries and detractors, defending his personal reputation as well as his theological legacy. His debates with Jerome Bolsec over predestination triggered a cascade of counterattacks that continued after Calvin's death, posthumously tarnishing his reputation as Bolsec raged against him, penning a savage biography of the Genevan reformer in 1577. Perhaps the most infamous of Calvin's late-career controversies involved Michael Servetus, a Spanish physician and theologian who had gained notoriety with the publication of *On the Trinity* (1531) and *The Restoration of Christianity* (1550). Catholics and Protestants alike condemned both anti-Trinitarian works as heretical. Nonetheless, Calvin felt pressed to acquit himself before his contemporaries after Sebastian Castellio, a former colleague and ardent advocate for religious

---

[17] Richard Gamble, "Calvin's Controversies," in Donald McKim (ed.), *The Cambridge Companion to Jean Calvin* (Cambridge: Cambridge University Press, 2004), 190–199; De Greef, *Writings of John Calvin,* 184–193.

liberty and toleration, published his own critical account of the Servetus's trial and execution for heresy in Geneva in 1553 and Calvin's role in the process. Calvin's *Defense of the Doctrine of the Trinity against Servetus* published in 1554 sealed his reputation not only as chief apologist for the Reformed movement but also as a habile defender of classical Christian orthodoxy.[18] Over the following decade, Calvin was thus drawn into other Trinitarian and Christological disputes with prominent members of the Italian refugee community in Geneva, Menno Simmons, and further afield, with Unitarian thinkers in Poland.

Throughout the sixteenth century, theologians remained convinced of the power of polemic to convict even their most obstinate opponents of God's truth. The humanist belief in the transformative power of language heralded exhilarating possibilities but competing visions of reform and renewal splintered even those ostensibly on the same side into warring factions. "The gradual declension of Reformation rhetoric into propaganda," as Peter Matheson has written, locked polemicists in a zero-sum game in which defamation and demonization of the opposition were the accepted tools of the trade.[19] Early modern writers, nevertheless, championed the value of polemic and its unique potential to expose falsehoods, provide instruction in true doctrine, and fortify the resolve of the faithful. Calvin's lifetime engagement in debate informed and enriched his theological work, especially later editions of the *Institutes,* and reflected his unwavering belief in the power of language to illuminate the Word of God.

SUGGESTED FURTHER READING

Balke, Wilhelm. *Calvin and the Anabaptist Radicals.* Grand Rapids, MI: Eerdmans, 1981.

Cottret, Bernard. *Jean Calvin: A Biography.* Grand Rapids, MI: Eerdmans, 2009.

De Greef, Wulfert. *The Writings of John Calvin: An Introductory Guide.* Trans. Lyle D. Bierma. Grand Rapids, MI: Baker Books, 1993.

Gamble, Richard. "Calvin's Controversies." In *The Cambridge Companion to Jean Calvin,* ed. Donald McKim. Cambridge: Cambridge University Press, 2004, 188–203.

Higman, Francis. *The Style and Polemics of John Calvin in His French Polemical Treatises.* Oxford: Oxford University Press, 1967.

---

[18] See Christopher Elwood, *Calvin for Armchair Theologians* (Louisville, KY: Westminster John Knox Press, 2002), 128.

[19] Peter Matheson, *The Rhetoric of the Reformation* (Edinburgh: T&T Clark, 1998), 249.

Matheson, Peter. *The Rhetoric of the Reformation*. Edinburgh: T&T Clark, 1998.

Neuser, Wilhelm, and Armstrong, Brian, eds. *Calvinus Sincerioris Religionis Vindix: Calvin as Protector of the Purer Religion*. Vol. 36. Kirksville, MO: Sixteenth Century Essays and Studies, 1997.

Racaut, Luc. *Hatred in Print: Catholic Propaganda and Protestant Identity during the French Wars of Religion*. Aldershot, UK: Ashgate, 2002.

Szabari, Antònia. *Less Rightly Said: Scandals and Readers in Sixteenth-Century France*. Redwood, CA: Stanford University Press, 2009.

26

The Style of Theology

Editions of the *Institutes*

Randall C. Zachman

The style of the various editions of the *Institutes* is directly related to the audience for which the book was written, for Calvin was convinced that any book had to be accommodated to the capacities of its intended audience. John Calvin originally wrote the *Institutes* to be a catechism for the pious evangelicals in France, who had come to faith in the Gospel but who needed to have their faith built up and strengthened. "My purpose was solely to transmit certain rudiments by which those who are touched with any zeal for religion might be shaped to true godliness." Because the audience was ordinary believers who needed to be edified, Calvin adopted a style that was accommodated to their capacities. "The book itself witnesses that this was my intention, adapted as it is to a simple and, you might say, elementary form of teaching."[1] As many scholars have noted, the format of Luther's *Small Catechism* is clearly evident in the form of the first edition of the *Institutes*, as it is structured along the lines of the Ten Commandments, the Creed, and the Lord's Prayer, followed by an extended discussion of the sacraments.

Calvin's experience as a teacher and pastor in Geneva from 1536 to 1538 convinced him that the *Institutes* was not in fact accommodated to the capacities of ordinary evangelical believers, and in light of this experience he produced an entirely new, and much shorter, catechism in 1538.[2] After he and Farel were expelled from Geneva in 1538, Calvin wound up reconceiving both the purpose and the audience for the *Institutes*, and he appears to have concluded that the 1538 *Catechism* still failed to meet its objective, as he

---

[1] John Calvin, *Institutes of the Christian Religion*, 1536 edition, trans. and annotated by Ford Lewis Battles, rev. ed. (1975, repr. Grand Rapids, MI: Eerdmans, 1986), 1.
[2] I. John Hesselink, *Calvin's First Catechism: A Commentary*, trans. Ford Lewis Battles (Louisville, KY: Westminster John Knox, 1997).

wrote a new French catechism in Strasburg, and then yet another catechism upon his return to Geneva in 1541.[3] While he was in Strasburg, Calvin changed the audience of the *Institutes* from ordinary pious evangelicals in need of edification to future pastors and teachers of the church in need of a summary of all the parts of the doctrine of piety, which would teach them what they are to seek in their reading of scripture. "For I believe that I have so embraced the sum of religion in all its parts, and have arranged it in such an order, that if anyone rightly grasps it, it will not be difficult for him to determine what he ought especially to seek in Scripture, and to what end he ought to relate its contents."[4] Moreover, Calvin envisioned the *Institutes* as being the necessary preparatory work for the reading of his commentaries on scripture, which were also written for the sake of future pastors and teachers. They should come to the commentaries with a knowledge of the *Institutes* as a "necessary tool," for the *Institutes* were intended to "pave the way" to the right comprehension of scripture.[5]

The idea of preparing a handbook as a guide for the reading of scripture has a long history in the Christian tradition, going back to Origen's work *On First Principles*. In Calvin's day, the book that served this purpose in European universities was *The Sentences* of Peter the Lombard (1150), which organized different theological topics in four different books, starting with the Trinity and ending with the Four Last Things. The scholastic theologians in the universities did much of their training by commenting on the *Sentences* in preparation for their own interpretation of scripture, and they also developed their own summaries of doctrine, most famously in the *Summa Theologica* of the Dominican Thomas Aquinas. Calvin clearly thought that these handbooks were unreliable guides to scripture in terms of their content, but he adopted the form of the *summa* in preparing his own handbook to prepare future teachers and ministers in their interpretation of scripture, guided by his own commentaries.

The change of purpose and audience also brought about a change in the structure of the book. Calvin abandoned the catechetical style of the first edition, and adopted the "common place" style of Melanchthon's *Loci communes* of 1535. From this point on, the *Institutes* were decisively

---

[3] See Randall C. Zachman, "Building Up the Faith of Children: Calvin's Catechisms, 1536–1545," *John Calvin as Teacher, Pastor, and Theologian: The Shape of His Writings and Thought* (Grand Rapids, MI: Baker Academic, 2006), 131–146.

[4] John Calvin, "Preface to the Reader," *Institutes of the Christian Religion*, ed. John T. McNeill and trans. Ford Lewis Battles, 2 vols., Library of Christian Classics (Philadelphia: Westminster, 1960), 1:4; henceforth LCC 1:4.

[5] Ibid., 5.

influenced by Melanchthon's work, for Calvin had great respect for Melanchthon's effectiveness as a teacher, especially the way he could present a topic of theology with such great clarity that it was placed before the eyes of the reader. This kind of clarity is what Melanchthon understood to be eloquence, which is comprised of both dialectics and rhetoric. Dialectics informs the right method of teaching, including the selection of the common places, or *loci communes*, of teaching, whereas rhetoric has to do with the right method of speaking, which teaches us to set the topic being taught before the eyes of the reader. Calvin may have come to know of Melanchthon's work on dialectics and rhetoric as early as his student days in Paris, but he clearly drew on Melanchthon's dialectic and rhetoric in the various editions of the *Institutes* from 1539 to the final Latin edition of 1559.[6]

Both Melanchthon and Calvin defended the necessity of dialectics and rhetoric, which undergird the practice of eloquence, against the apparent rejection of such classical tools by the apostle Paul. Even though Paul appears to reject classical eloquence when he warns believers to beware of being deceived by vain philosophy (Col. 2:8), Melanchthon also pointed out that Paul advises bishops to be apt teachers. Melanchthon rhetorically asked, "Now, how could anybody teach, who had no prior dialectical or rhetorical knowledge? These are especially useful for teaching inexperienced people a method or way of reasoning. This needs to be done in a way that is clear and to the point." Indeed, Melanchthon went on to insist that without the knowledge of dialectics and rhetoric, that is, without the practice of eloquence, "the sacred text can in no way be understood."[7] Calvin made the same defense of eloquence in light of Paul's apparent rejection of eloquence in his preaching of the Gospel. When Paul rejected the "wisdom of the world" (1 Cor. 1:17), Calvin took him to be setting aside "true eloquence, which consists in the skillful choice of subjects, in clever arrangement, and fineness of style [thereby echoing Melanchthon's description of eloquence as involving dialectics and rhetoric]."[8] However, like Melanchthon, Calvin thought that Paul would approve of eloquence when it is brought into the service of the Gospel, for "eloquence is not in conflict with the simplicity of the Gospel at all, when, free from contempt of the Gospel, it not only gives it first place, and is subject to it, but also serves it as a handmaid serves her

---

[6] Zachman, *John Calvin as Teacher*, 37–38.
[7] Philip Melanchthon, *Paul's Letter to the Colossians*, trans. D. C. Parker (Sheffield: The Almond Press, 1989), 51–52.
[8] John Calvin, *The First Letter of the Apostle Paul to the Corinthians*, trans. John W. Fraser (Grand Rapids, MI: Eerdmans, 1960), 32.

mistress." Indeed, Calvin claimed that the proper use of eloquence can "obtain a hearing for those fishermen and uneducated common people [i.e., the authors of scripture], who have nothing attractive about them except the power of the Spirit."[9] The changes Calvin made to the *Institutes* from 1539 to 1559 were all guided by the quest for eloquence, having to do both with the choice and arrangement of topics and the fineness of style, and he thought that he had obtained these objectives in the final Latin edition of 1559.

Calvin was convinced that the eloquence of teaching must be accommodated to the capacities of the reader to be effective. What assumptions did Calvin make about those who would read the various editions of the *Institutes* from 1539 onward? To begin with, he assumed that they were all pious, which means that they trusted in, prayed to, thanked, and obeyed God as the author and fountain of every good thing set forth both in creation and in Christ. They should also be teachable, meaning that they would not seek to cling to their own opinions, but would rather humbly submit to be taught by the Holy Spirit in scripture. They would also be sober and moderate, in that they would not seek to know any more, or any less, than the Spirit teaches them in scripture. They would be sane and of sound mind, meaning that they would not hallucinate like some of the ungodly, and would know how to make sound judgments and recognize indisputable statements. Calvin did not expect them to be brilliant, but rather to be of average intelligence and insight, moderately discerning, and of average judgment.[10]

In terms of the kinds of knowledge Calvin assumed his readers to have, he expected them to have a grasp of the central figures of classical and ecclesial writing. From the references he made in the *Institutes*, he clearly expected his readers to know classical authors such as Plato and Cicero, and he encouraged them to read further in these authors to confirm the points he made. He also expected them to be moderately versed in the writings of the early church, especially in those of Chrysostom and Augustine, but also in later figures such as Peter the Lombard and Gratian, as well as the scholastics who comment on Lombard and Gratian. He expected his readers to be familiar with other evangelical teachers such as Luther, Melanchthon, Bucer, Zwingli, and Bullinger, as well as the authors with whom Calvin strongly disagreed, such as the Anabaptists, Osiander, and Servetus. Above all, he expected his readers to be moderately versed in scripture, so that they could confirm for themselves what Calvin is saying by their own reading of

---

[9] Ibid., 34–35.
[10] Zachman, *John Calvin as Teacher*, 79–81.

the Bible. In sum, it seems that Calvin wrote the *Institutes* to reeducate those who had likely already been educated in the schools and universities of the Church of Rome, and who needed to come to a clearer grasp of scripture so that they could teach and preach it to others.[11]

The style of the *Institutes* was not only adapted to the capacities of its intended readers, but it was also oriented to serve the goal or *scopus* of the book, which was to offer a summary of evangelical doctrine so that its readers might know what they are to seek in their reading of scripture, beginning with their reading of Calvin's commentaries. Calvin was aware that his readers do not have an abundance of time because they were likely being reeducated by his book even as they were already working as evangelical preachers and pastors. Hence he sought to give a comprehensive summary of evangelical doctrine with as much brevity as possible. This means that he could not pause to give each locus of doctrine as much development as possible, but must rather touch on each doctrinal locus with an eye toward moving on to the next topic. Calvin repeatedly reminded his readers that he loved brevity and was incapable of prolixity.[12] Calvin's love of brevity kept him from giving as many testimonies as possible in support of his teaching. Instead, he gave one or two examples and then depended on his assumption that the reader was moderately versed in scripture and other ecclesiastical writers.[13] Calvin was convinced that brevity was essential to true eloquence, for it sets forth the teaching of doctrine with clarity and simplicity, and not with elaborate ostentation and show.

A summary of evangelical doctrine should also be comprehensive, and thus Calvin did not allow his love of brevity to keep him from touching on every doctrine of importance to the meaning of scripture.[14] Calvin also did not hesitate to include in his comprehensive summary doctrines that had previously not been included, such as his understanding of the descent of Christ into hell, which Calvin thought he endured from Gethsemane to his cry of abandonment on the cross.[15] However, this concern for comprehensiveness was always qualified by his desire for brevity, for he was aware that his reader was going to be fatigued by a more fulsome treatment of the doctrinal locus.

---

[11] Ibid., 81–83.
[12] Inst. 3.6.1, LCC 1:685.
[13] Inst. 1.18.1, LCC 1:231.
[14] Inst. 3.19.1, LCC 1:833.
[15] Inst. II.16.8, LCC 1:513.

Finally, a summary of doctrine should follow the right order and method of teaching, and here the influence of Melanchthon's understanding of dialectics is especially apparent through all the editions of the *Institutes*. For the summary of doctrine to be as clear and compelling as possible, it must follow the proper order of doctrinal topics, which Calvin called the *series docendi*, the series or order of teaching. Calvin attended to this order throughout his career from 1539 to 1559, and was only convinced that he had found the right order of topics in the final Latin edition of 1559. The clarity of teaching depends on the way one doctrinal locus rightly opens up to the next topic, all the way through the whole series of teaching. Calvin was convinced that the order of teaching must begin with that which is known by all people, even if they had never read scripture or heard preaching, namely, their awareness that there is some god whom all ought to worship and obey, and that this deity is revealed in the works done in the universe. By 1559, Calvin made a distinction between the knowledge of God the Creator, which reveals who the true God is whom all know they must worship and obey, before moving on to the knowledge of God the Redeemer, which reveals how God redeems us from sin in Jesus Christ. However, throughout every edition of the *Institutes*, Calvin insisted that the knowledge of God leads to the knowledge of ourselves, even as the knowledge of ourselves leads to the knowledge of God.

At the heart of the series and order of teaching were the definitions developed by Calvin in each doctrinal locus. Calvin seemed to follow Cicero in seeing the definition as "a statement giving the subject of discussion in the briefest possible form."[16] The definition was therefore central to Calvin's desire to be as brief and as clear as possible, for such is the nature of true eloquence. The definition should be accommodated to the capacities of the reader, and it should also reflect the genuine meaning of scripture; it should not simply be a sentence from scripture, but should rather be an interpretation of the meaning of scripture regarding that particular locus of doctrine. Calvin was aware that the brevity of the definition could also be a liability, as it may not be able on its own to remove all possible misunderstandings. To clarify the definition and refute false interpretations of the definition, Calvin resorted to the art of rhetoric, which is the art of speaking clearly and forcefully. When writing for the godly, Calvin sought to explain what might be obscure in the definition by means of edifying and uplifting rhetoric, seeing the possible confusion as understandable, and trying in the

---

[16] Cicero, *Orator* 33.116–17, trans. G. L. Hendrickson and H. M. Hubbell, Loeb Classical Library (Cambridge, MA: Harvard University Press, 1988), 393.

explanation to give the pious a firm standing ground. This may involve breaking the definition down into its component parts, so that the explanation can remove all doubts the reader may have, as Calvin did in his discussion of the definition of faith.[17] However, when writing against the calumnies and objections of the ungodly, Calvin adopted agonistic rhetoric, which seeks to destroy both the opponent and his argument. In these passages, Calvin described his opponents as beasts and monsters, and their opinions as mad hallucinations, rather than seeing them as rational human beings who have legitimate opinions. There are times when such rhetoric seems to have gotten the better of Calvin, so that it interfered with the clarity of the series of teaching, as in his long polemical digression against Osiander regarding the doctrine of justification in the final edition of the *Institutes*.[18] However, even in these polemical and agonistic digressions, the goal was to give readers a firm standing place in their reading of scripture.[19]

Each definition should especially set forth the *nature* and *force* of the reality being discussed in a given doctrinal locus. The nature of a reality distinguishes it from all other natures – hence God's infinite and spiritual essence distinguishes the nature of God from all images of human devising. However, it is possible to have the right understanding of the nature of something and still miss the force of that reality, as Calvin thought happened in the scholastic definition of original sin, which came from Anselm. "Although they have comprehended in this definition the whole meaning of the term, [they] have still not expressed its power and energy."[20] The definition therefore not only identified the reality to be sought in the reading of scripture but also brought the reader into an experience of the force and power of that reality. The definition therefore points to a reality that must be experienced and, when this happens, the reality is seen to transcend our ability to define it in language: "to speak more plainly, I rather experience than understand it."[21] Such experience confirmed the truth of the doctrine Calvin was teaching, and also confirmed the legitimacy of the ordinary experience of the pious, no matter how learned they may be. "I speak of nothing other than what each believer experiences within himself – though my words fall far beneath a just explanation of the matter."[22] The truly eloquent teacher of the Gospel not only knows the capability of language to

[17] Inst. 3.2.14, LCC 1:559.
[18] Inst. 3.xi.5–12, LCC 1:729–743.
[19] Inst. 1.13.21, LCC 1:146.
[20] Inst. 2.1.8, LCC 1:252.
[21] Inst. 4.17.32, LCC 2:1403.
[22] Inst. 1.7.5, LCC 1:80–81.

set forth the nature and force of the realities taught in scripture with brevity, clarity, and power but he also knows the limitation of language, and the need to transcend language by means of a vivid experience of the realities being taught.

SUGGESTED FURTHER READINGS

Gamble, Richard. *The Organizational Structure of Calvin's Theology.* New York: Garland, 1992.

Millet, Olivier. *Calvin et la dynamique de la parole.* Geneva: Slatkine, 1992.

Zachman, Randall. *John Calvin as Teacher, Pastor, and Theologian: The Shape of His Writings and Thought.* Grand Rapids, MI: Baker Academic, 2006.

27

Baptism

Karen E. Spierling

John Calvin, like all Protestant reformers of the 1520s and 1530s, was born into a Roman Catholic society and baptized as an infant, according to Catholic practice. When Calvin began to work with Guillaume Farel to lead the Reformation in Geneva, they were interacting with a community of individuals who had all received Catholic baptisms, whether at a baptismal font by an ordained priest, or in the birthing room by a midwife. Those late medieval rites of baptism reflected a number of theological concerns and assumptions, including the teachings that the sacrament of baptism was essential to salvation and that infants who died without baptism would be consigned to limbo. At the same time, traditional baptismal practices also embodied a series of social and familial priorities, including the importance of godparents in building and solidifying social networks and the desire to honor those godparents in the name of a child. As a result, Calvin's understanding of baptism challenged core beliefs and social traditions with which both he and his Genevan followers (both enthusiastic and reluctant) had been raised, complicating the implementation of his ideas and shaping the development of his teachings across the mid-sixteenth century and well beyond Geneva.

In modern theological and ecclesiastical discussions and debates, perhaps the most controversial aspect of Calvin's baptismal theology is his preservation of baptism as a ritual applied to newborn infants, rather than a ceremony undertaken by young adults old enough to declare their faith. Although all sixteenth-century mainline reformers shared this stance, modern scholars have spilled vast amounts of ink (and printer toner) trying to demonstrate that baptizing infants is or is not consistent with Calvin's overall theology. But in sixteenth-century Geneva, as well as in France, Scotland, the Netherlands, and other places where Reformed congregations appeared, baptizing infants was perhaps the *least* controversial aspect of Calvin's baptismal theology and liturgy. More important to contemporaries was that Calvin rejected the teaching that baptism was essential for salvation, instead emphasizing the sacrament as a seal of God's promise to faithful Christians and as a rite of initiation into the visible Christian community. He also rejected what he considered to be "superstitious" Catholic practices in the baptismal ceremony – including exorcisms and anointing the infant with holy oil – and designed a pared-down baptismal ceremony that retained the water and triune formula ("in the name of the Father, Son, and the Holy Spirit") of Catholic practice. Calvin also insisted that this ceremony should not only be public but also must occur in connection with a sermon. And he taught that ideally parents, rather than godparents – and especially fathers, rather than godfathers – should present their own infants to be baptized. By the mid-1540s, he had also persuaded the Genevan city council to draw up a list of forbidden names – predominantly traditional saints' names – that ministers were required to reject.

We cannot fully understand Calvin's articulation of his baptismal theology or his decisions as a Genevan reformer and pastor without recognizing that both late medieval baptismal theology and practices *and* early Reformation-era debates on the subject shaped his thinking. Late medieval Roman Catholic baptismal practices varied to some degree across Europe, depending on local traditions. But based on what we know from medieval liturgies, Catholic baptismal ceremonies generally included the presentation of the infant by godparents; multiple exorcisms of evil spirits from the infant's body; the application of holy chrism (oil) to the child's head; dipping the child into the water in the baptismal font three times; and the godparents' role of answering the priest's questions on behalf of the child. The ceremony began at the door of the church and ended inside the church, at the baptismal font. The exorcisms reflected the belief that baptism purified the infant of original sin, so any evil spirits needed to be removed from the child's body before the infant was washed in the holy water of the font. Aside from the godparents' speaking for the child, the ritual seems to have been based on early Christian practices for baptizing adults, including the participation of a sponsor (the godparent). In late medieval practice, the godparents were often accompanied to the church by a group of people celebrating the baptism. Already in 813, the Council of Mainz had forbidden parents to present their own children for baptism, in part out of concern that the presence of the people who had physically created the child might pollute the spiritual relationship between godparent and godchild.[1] During the

---

[1] Joseph H. Lynch, *Godparents and Kinship in Early Medieval Europe* (Princeton, NJ: Princeton University Press, 1986), 298.

baptismal ceremony, mothers were meant to be recovering from childbirth, and were not supposed to enter a church building until they had undergone the rite of churching (purification). Fathers were expected to be at home organizing the community meal and party that would follow the baptism. After the ceremony, the godparents would return home with the child, accompanied by celebrating neighbors, and the festivities would begin.

While this church ceremony was the expectation, infant mortality rates were high, and it was not uncommon for a child to die within hours or days of birth, or even to be stillborn. The Roman Catholic Church taught that infants who died without being baptized could not gain entrance into heaven, yet there were not enough local priests to ensure that one could be present for the birth of every child. Instead, the Catholic Church permitted laypeople, especially midwives, to perform emergency baptisms in situations in which the death of an infant seemed imminent. Such emergency baptisms did not require exorcism, chrism, or the presence of godparents. The main standard was that the midwife should baptize the child with water and in the name of the triune God. In the case of a stillborn child, there are even sources describing techniques used by both midwives and priests to show that the child was still breathing long enough to receive baptism. If the child survived, no rebaptism was required; the midwife's baptism counted as a legitimate sacrament based on extenuating circumstances.

When Calvin was still a child, Martin Luther and others were already facing the challenge of persuading their communities to set aside some if not all of these traditional practices. By 1536, when Calvin first published his *Institutes*, he was joining a well-established debate among reformers regarding the role of baptism as a sacrament and the appropriate practices to constitute the ceremony.[2] Luther asserted that baptism was a divinely ordained sacrament, that it should be applied to infants, and that it cleansed the infant's soul of sin. Luther reduced the number of exorcisms in his baptismal ritual, but he did not omit them altogether. Because he still saw baptism as a crucial step on a Christian's journey toward salvation, and also because he was concerned not to change too many practices too quickly, Luther was willing to tolerate emergency baptism by midwives.

---

[2] For a useful comparison of changes in the rituals of baptism across the German-speaking lands, see Susan C. Karant-Nunn, "'Suffer the Little Children to Come unto Me, and Forbid Them Not': The Social Location of Baptism in Early Modern Germany," in Robert J. Bast and Andrew C. Gow (eds.), *Continuity and Change: The Harvest of Late Medieval and Reformation History* (Leiden, The Netherlands: Brill, 2000), 359–378.

In Zurich, Ulrich Zwingli taught that baptism was a symbolic communal act that did not effect any particular change in the baptized infant. Instead, the sacrament marked the child's entrance into the earthly Christian community and served as a reminder of God's commitment to faithful Christians. Zwingli developed a covenantal defense of infant baptism – an idea that Luther addressed but did not elaborate on – arguing that with the coming of Christ, baptism replaced circumcision as the sign and seal of God's promise to God's faithful people. In Strasbourg, Martin Bucer also emphasized the importance of infant baptism as a community event that welcomed the new child and provided assurance that the infant would be raised and educated in the Christian community.

Calvin developed his thinking on baptism in the context of such Reformation debates. Like Zwingli, Calvin developed a covenantal understanding of baptism, emphasizing its supersession of circumcision as the primary symbol of the covenant established between God and Abraham, which now applied to sixteenth-century Christians. Calvin also interpreted baptism both as a seal of God's promise and grace and as a mark of initiation into the Christian community. With some echoes of Bucer, Calvin asserted that God intended the sacrament of infant baptism to provide comfort to parents as a visible sign of God's grace and promise to their child.

Despite this general agreement that baptism applied to infants, a smaller group of "radical" reformers – often grouped together as Anabaptists – rejected any biblical basis for infant baptism and taught, instead, that the only legitimate form of baptism was believer's, or adult, baptism.[3] For Anabaptists such as Michael Sattler, Conrad Grebel, or Menno Simons, the sacrament of baptism required a declaration of faith, meaning that an individual's faith had to be fully developed before he or she could be baptized into the community of faithful Christians. Zwingli was the first to confront these teachings in Zurich, starting with a public disputation in 1525, when some of his followers insisted that he was not adhering closely enough to strict biblical teachings. By the time Calvin arrived in Geneva in 1536, believer's baptism had become inextricably associated with social revolutionaries. This view developed first during the German Peasants' War of 1524–1526, in which many of the leaders of the uprisings espoused the more radical ideas of the Reformation, and then further during the Anabaptist takeover of the city of Münster in 1534–1535, which provoked an alliance

---

[3] For a clear and concise comparison of mainstream and Anabaptist views, see Egil Grislis, "Martin Luther and Menno Simons on Infant Baptism," *Journal of Mennonite Studies* 12 (1994): 7–25.

among Catholic and Protestant rulers to lay siege to the city and wrest it back under Catholic control. In response to these violent events, secular rulers and social elites came to see anyone who espoused believer's baptism as a threat to society. As a result, reformers such as Calvin, who were convinced that secular governments had a role to play in enforcing religious reform, did not have the practical option of even considering the theological merits of believer's baptism.

In addition, all the mainline reformers accepted *Catholic* infant baptism as legitimate; in other words, infants who had received a Catholic baptism were not required to be rebaptized to become part of a Protestant congregation. Neither, of course, were the many adult converts to Protestant confessions who had received Catholic baptisms as babies. Perhaps even more surprisingly, the Catholic Church also grudgingly accepted Protestant infant baptisms as valid. This was reasonable, based on its tradition of emergency lay baptism and emphasis on the key elements of water and the triune formula. For Calvin, accepting Catholic baptism as legitimate was necessary to discourage superstitious beliefs about the powers of the actual rite of baptism; he did not want to do anything to encourage the belief that a particular set of words, motion of the hands, or elements applied to a child could provide physical protection to an infant's body or soul. For Catholics, the opposite held true: it was the combination of water and the triune formula that mattered and was efficacious regardless of who performed the ceremony.

Such traditional beliefs died hard, especially among the general population who were not immersed in the details of theological debates. As Calvin, the Genevan pastors and consistory, and the Genevan city council began to put his baptismal teachings into practice, they confronted challenges from Genevans who still believed Catholic teachings on baptism and those who wanted to maintain familial and social traditions. Sometimes these challenges even came from within the city council, which did not always prioritize correct theology to precisely the same degree that Calvin did.

Among the most persistent of traditional beliefs was the Catholic teaching that baptism was necessary for salvation, as well as the connected belief that the various elements of the Catholic ceremony, such as exorcism and chrism, made the Catholic sacrament more fully efficacious than the simple Reformed ritual. Calvin attempted to address this concern by insisting that baptism was meant to comfort parents as a sign of God's promise to accept their children as Christians. But the Genevan consistory records show us that some parents remained skeptical, choosing to take their children to neighboring villages for Catholic baptisms. In some cases, they would also have a public Reformed baptism, perhaps because the baptismal registry also served as a record of

birth and citizenship in Geneva. In other cases, when parents were not
persuaded by Calvin's teaching that God did not require baptism for salvation,
they would have a midwife perform an emergency baptism on a sickly
newborn. Over time, as the Reformation set in and more Genevans had grown
up with Reformed practices, emergency baptisms seem to have declined. But
they were a persistent enough concern throughout Calvin's life that he added a
substantial section to his 1559 *Institutes* explicitly dismissing both the necessity
of emergency baptisms and the validity of baptism by women.

While Calvin remained firm – and even became increasingly staunch – in his
teaching against emergency baptism and rebaptism of any kind, more local and
social concerns seem to have shaped Calvin's thinking and teaching on other
issues. The clearest example of this is the matter of godparents' participation in
the baptismal ceremony. Calvin's baptismal liturgy does not acknowledge the
presence or participation of godparents, but it also does not state explicitly that
parents must present their own children. At the same time, the text of the liturgy
seems to assume that that parents would have been present at the ceremony.
Taking Calvin's liturgy alone as the basis for understand baptismal practice in
Geneva would lead one to believe that parents participated in the sacrament of
baptism, that godparents played no special role, and that baptism always
occurred at a public service, after a sermon. But evidence from the baptismal
registries and consistory records demonstrates otherwise.

Despite Calvin's ideal vision for baptism, in Reformed Genevan practice,
mothers rarely attended the ceremony. Fathers attended somewhat more
often, but it was not always the father who presented the child to be
baptized. Most strikingly, not only did godparents almost always participate
in the ritual, but their names were recorded in the official baptismal registries as the person presenting the infant and, when necessary, they could be
called on by the consistory or city council as a responsible party for a child's
education or welfare. Calvin stood as godfather to at least 47 Genevan
children, perhaps the clearest sign that he was willing to set aside his
theological hesitations about the necessity of godparents in recognition of
their traditional religious and social roles.

A related issue that looms large in Genevan sources is the controversy
over acceptable names. As noted previously, one of Calvin's primary concerns was to strip the baptismal ceremony of any possible encouragement to
"superstitious" thinking. In the case of naming babies, Calvin's definition of
superstition came into direct confrontation with local beliefs about the
power of saints and about the importance of family honor. In Genevan
practice, as in most of Western Europe, the selection of a child's name was
often connected to the particular saint's day on which the child was born, or

to the name of a godparent. Naming a child after a saint was thought to bring that saint's protection to bear on the child as he or she grew up. Naming a child after a godparent solidified a social and emotional connection and, it was hoped, would help to ensure social and economic support for the child. In 1546, Calvin and the Company of Pastors persuaded the Genevan city council to promulgate a list of banned names, including the names of Catholic saints, as well as "absurd" or "ill-sounding" names. The list included "Claude," the name of a local saint popular for both boys and girl. Efforts to enforce this legislation led to angry confrontations between pastors and parishioners during church services and at consistory meetings. Ultimately Calvin prevailed, at least temporarily, as the name "Claude" disappeared from Geneva baptismal registries for the remainder of his life.

Nevertheless, the naming controversy is an excellent example of the challenge of dismantling traditional practices that Calvin (and other reformers) labeled as superstitious and of the importance of understanding historical context. In the case of baptism, if the idea of a name offering protection truly was superstitious, then why should reformers have cared what name people chose? In the historical moment of the 1540s and 1550s, it was most important for Calvin and his colleagues to work to break the hold that Catholic traditions and beliefs still had on Genevan inhabitants. But decades later, in 1638, the Genevan Company of Pastors seems to have acknowledged the paradox of the name ban when it did away with the legislation altogether, asserting that maintaining the prohibition would in fact be an act of superstition.

Context does not determine everything, of course, but to read Calvin's teaching on baptism, in its various forms and venues, without understanding the context in which he was living, thinking, and working is to leave ourselves open to significantly misunderstanding the development of his thought, as well as his role in history. As it had developed throughout the Middle Ages, the practice of infant baptism lay at the heart of parents' social *and* religious concerns and hopes for the future of their children. In implementing his baptismal theology in practice, Calvin the pastor had to navigate not only doctrinal debates but also the daily concerns of congregants focused on caring for their children, protecting their honor, and cultivating social networks to provide for their families.

SUGGESTED FURTHER READINGS

Fisher, J. D. C. *Christian Initiation in the Medieval West: A Study in the Disintegration of the Primitive Rite of Initiation*. Chicago: Hillenbrand Books, 2004.

Hill, Kat. *Baptism, Brotherhood, and Belief in Reformation Germany: Anabaptism and Lutheranism, 1525-1585*. Oxford: Oxford University Press, 2015.

Karant-Nunn, Susan C. *The Reformation of Ritual: An Interpretation of Early Modern Germany*. London: Routledge, 1997.

Old, Hughes Oliphant. *The Shaping of the Reformed Baptismal Rite in the Sixteenth Century*. Grand Rapids, MI: William B. Eerdmans, 1992.

Spierling, Karen. *Infant Baptism in Reformation Geneva: The Shaping of a Community, 1536-1564*. Aldershot: Ashgate, 2005 (repr. Louisville, KY: Westminster John Knox, 2009).

Trigg, Jonathan D. *Baptism in the Theology of Martin Luther*. Leiden, The Netherlands: Brill, 2001.

28

∾

The Eucharist

Amy Nelson Burnett

There was no more divisive theological issue in the sixteenth century than the Eucharist, the ritual understood by Christians as establishing their unity with Christ and with each other. The rite separated Catholics from Protestants, Lutherans from Reformed, and state-supported reformers from a variety of dissenting groups. Modern preoccupation with the question of Christ's "real presence," a term that only became common in the nineteenth century, has led to both a misconception of the sixteenth-century debate and an artificial narrowing of its scope. Disagreements were much broader than Christ's presence and included not only the definition, purpose, and content of the sacrament but also when, where, how, how often, and with whom it should be celebrated. John Calvin's discussions of the Eucharist reflected these many disagreements, and they must be read with an understanding of the audience he addressed and the particular issues that audience considered central.

TERMINOLOGY AND CONTESTED ISSUES

Rival parties could not even agree on what to call the ritual. The early church used the Greek *Eucharistia*, or thanksgiving, for the rite commemorating Christ's Last Supper with his disciples, but by the early Middle Ages that term was replaced by *missa* or *Mass*, and the term *Eucharist* was restricted to the elements of bread and wine. Andreas Karlstadt rejected the word *missa* because Johannes Reuchlin's Hebrew grammar derived the word from the Hebrew term for an offering. Karlstadt therefore argued that the very name taught that the Mass was a sacrifice, and he said it should instead be called the Supper (*Abendmahl* or *Nachtmahl*). Martin Luther also used "the Lord's Supper" for the sacrament, but he did not insist on the name, and he called his revised liturgy a German Mass. He more often referred to "the sacrament of the altar," or simply "the sacrament," and he could use "sacrament" to refer either to the entire rite or specifically to the elements of bread and wine. Influenced by the Augustinian idea of a sacrament as "a sign of a holy thing," Huldrych Zwingli spoke of "the sacrament of Christ's body," but in his Latin writings he preferred to call the rite *the Eucharist*, which was translated into German as thanksgiving (*Danksagung*) or remembrance (*Widergedächtnis*). Echoing the wording of 1 Corinthians 11, the Swiss reformers also referred to "the Lord's Table" and "the Lord's bread and cup," names that were criticized because they were perceived as desacralizing the elements and reducing the ritual to a common meal.

This disagreement about terminology was important, for it reflected the underlying theological priorities of each party. For Catholics, the sacrifice of the Mass was as important an issue as transubstantiation. The two chief components of the rite, sacrifice and communion, could not be separated, and they both highlighted the special position of the priest, who turned the elements into Christ's body and blood when he consecrated them and who consumed both elements every time he celebrated the Mass. This distinguished him from the laity, who generally received communion only at Easter and were given only the consecrated host. For the early Swiss reformers, the Eucharist was a public rite of thanksgiving and remembrance in which individuals testified to their membership in the visible church. For others, the Lord's Supper not only reminded recipients of the rite's institution by Christ but also bestowed some spiritual benefit along with the physical reception of the bread and wine. What those benefits were, and how they were conveyed and received, would become a matter of contentious debate.

Martin Luther initiated discussion of the Eucharist and of the sacraments more generally with his 1520 treatise *On the Babylonian Captivity of the Church*. He rejected three points of medieval teaching and practice: withholding the chalice from the laity, making transubstantiation into an article of faith, and turning the Mass into a sacrifice offered to God rather than seeing it as Christ's testament offered to human beings. Proper preparation for communion consisted of awareness of one's sinfulness and trust in God's promise of forgiveness, not in making a complete sacramental confession or performing any kind of work.[1] In his 1523 revision of the Latin Mass, he condemned the Mass canon, whose prayers fostered the notion of sacrifice, and he recommended that Christ's words instituting the sacrament be

---

[1] WA 6: 502–526; LW 36: 19–57.

repeated out loud so that bystanders could hear this promise of forgiveness.[2] Other reformers quickly produced evangelical masses entirely in the vernacular. The language of the Mass, the lay chalice, the priest's power to transform the elements into Christ's body and blood, and especially the sacrifice of the Mass were issues on which all Protestants disagreed with the Roman church. Throughout the sixteenth century, conflict with Catholic authors on these issues formed the backdrop to the Protestant debate over the Lord's Supper, especially because Catholics used Protestant disagreement over the sacrament to argue that this proved that all of them were wrong.

In contrast to the debate with Catholics concerning the Mass, the intra-evangelical debate over the Lord's Supper evolved significantly. On one level, the Protestant Eucharistic controversy concerned the substance of Christ's body, understood in Aristotelian terms as that which made his body truly human. The reformers addressed several questions: Could that substantial or corporeal body be contained in the bread, and if so how – or was it even necessary to know how? Could Christ's substantial body be eaten physically in the sacrament, and if so was it received by all recipients or only by believers? When Christ said, "this is my body," was he speaking literally and so referring to the actual substance of his body, or was he speaking figuratively? Was Christ present in the elements in some way other than bodily, and if so, with what terms should that presence be described? The ambiguous use of both "Eucharist" and "sacrament" to refer to either the rite or the elements was also significant. Everyone could agree that Christ was somehow present in the rite, but those who argued for Christ's bodily presence in the bread regarded this agreement as subterfuge that drew attention away from the real question of the relationship between Christ's substantial body and the elements. The focus on Christ's substantial body also raised the issue of the nature of a truly human body and, more broadly, of the relationship between Christ's human and divine natures, and so Christology became a part of the debate as well.

On a deeper level, the debate raised questions about the nature of the sacraments: Who was the chief agent in the sacraments: God or human beings? Did a sacrament convey or confer anything to the recipient, and if so, what? What was the relationship between the external sacrament and the internal working of the Spirit? More specifically, could an external sacrament console consciences or increase faith? Was faith a necessary prerequisite for the beneficial reception of a sacrament, and did faith require

[2] WA 12: 205–220; LW 53: 22–30.

some level of cognition or assent? These questions obviously had implications for baptism as well.

Both sides developed communion liturgies that reflected their understanding of the sacrament. So that individuals could receive communion whenever they desired it, Luther retained communion as part of the main Sunday worship service in his 1526 German Mass. Those wanting to receive communion in Wittenberg were to be examined beforehand by the pastor to ensure that they understood they were receiving Christ's body and blood as a seal and promise of forgiveness that strengthened their faith. The Zurich liturgy introduced in the spring of 1525 emphasized the public and collective nature of communion, which was to be celebrated only four times a year. The communion services introduced in Strasbourg and Basel were influenced by the Zurich model, but in both cities communion was held monthly in each parish church. Calvin became familiar with the Strasbourg practice during his three-year stay in that city, and the communion service he introduced in Geneva in 1541 was influenced by the Strasbourg liturgy. Following the practice of Zurich and Bern, communion was celebrated only quarterly in Geneva, although Calvin would have preferred more frequent celebration of the Lord's Supper.[3]

Central to the development of rival understandings of the Lord's Supper, and of the sacraments more generally, were the confessions of faith that began to be written in 1529–1530. These codified an understanding of the sacrament worked out in previous debates and established a consensus among their signatories that shaped later discussions. They therefore served as important turning points in the public debate, which fell into four phases over the course of Calvin's lifetime.

PHASES OF THE EUCHARISTIC CONTROVERSY

The controversy began in late 1524, when Andreas Karlstadt published several vernacular pamphlets rejecting Christ's corporeal presence in the elements of bread and wine and attacking Luther's claim that the sacraments could assure troubled consciences of forgiveness. He argued that the sacrament instead was an occasion for individual recipients to remember Christ's suffering and death. Over the next several months, Huldrych Zwingli of Zurich and Johannes Oecolampadius of Basel both published Latin treatises rejecting Christ's corporeal presence and describing the sacrament as a

---

[3] Amy Nelson Burnett, "The Social History of Communion and the Reformation of the Eucharist," *Past and Present* 211 (2011): 77–119.

means of thanksgiving and remembrance. Against Anabaptist claims that the Lord's Supper should be celebrated only among committed believers and in private homes, Zwingli stressed that the rite was a public testimony of faith and should be celebrated together with all Christians in the city's churches. Oecolampadius drew from the writings of the church fathers to argue that the early church had not taught Christ's corporeal presence in the elements. In Strasbourg, Wolfgang Capito and Martin Bucer supported the Swiss position in their letters and publications, and in Silesia, Kaspar Schwenckfeld and Valentin Krautwald developed their own understanding of the Supper in treatises that circulated in manuscript. The Strasbourgers and Silesians differed from the Swiss in that they connected Christ's discourse on the spiritual eating of his flesh in John 6 with the institution of the Lord's Supper. As a consequence, they drew an explicit connection between spiritual and sacramental communion, but they too attacked the claim that Christ's body was corporeally present in the bread and wine.

In *Against the Heavenly Prophets*, his response to Karlstadt, Luther laid out his fundamental premise that God always worked through the external means of Word and sacraments. Even more important would be the printed debate waged in Latin between Johannes Brenz and Willibald Pirckheimer, who supported the Wittenberg position, and Johannes Oecolampadius. The Basel reformer allowed that the Spirit could use the external sacrament to convey Christ's benefits, but the Spirit was not bound to the sacrament, nor could Christ's human body, which had ascended into heaven, be present in the bread and wine of the Supper. Oecolampadius accused his opponents of teaching consubstantiation and impanation, two ways of conceptualizing the coexistence of the substances of body and bread that had been rejected by the medieval church. Zwingli went even further in polemical vernacular works against his Catholic opponents, arguing that it opposed the articles of the Creed to say Christ's body was in the sacrament. In his 1527 *Amica Exegesis* he introduced *alloiosis*, a figure of speech in which what was said of one thing was applied to another, to explain how Christ's statements about himself in the Gospel of John should be applied to either his divine or his human nature. Luther responded to his opponents in two vernacular treatises published in 1527 and 1528. In them he argued that "this is my body" could be understood as a synecdoche, a figure of speech that included both contents and container – in this case, body and bread. He also described how Christ's substantial body might be present in the bread and wine, and he suggested the term "sacramental union" for the connection between Christ's body and the elements. Ultimately, however, he rejected the use of reason and Aristotelian concepts to explain how Christ's body was present and received; what was necessary was simply to believe Christ's words, "this is my body."

By this time it was evident that there could be no agreement concerning whether Christ's substantial body was in the bread and wine. Political pressures on evangelicals in the Holy Roman Empire caused Landgraf Philipp of Hesse to arrange a meeting between the Wittenbergers and the Swiss and Strasbourg reformers in Marburg in October 1529. Despite three days of debate, neither side persuaded the other to abandon its position. The Landgraf pushed for a common statement of faith, however, and the Marburg Articles that resulted showed that the two sides could agree that as a common rule God used externals to convey his benefits. The Articles acknowledged, however, that on the fundamental question of Christ's bodily presence there was no agreement.

The Marburg Colloquy and the articles that resulted marked the first turning point in the debate, and they brought to light differences among Luther's opponents. Although Zwingli would reject the idea that the sacraments could convey or dispense grace, both Oecolampadius and the Strasbourgers could agree with the Wittenbergers as long as some freedom was left for the Spirit. This opened the way toward a common position that described how Christ and/or his benefits were conveyed through the elements of bread and wine.

Where the initial phase of the Eucharistic controversy was characterized by attempts to prove one's opponents were wrong concerning Christ's corporeal presence, the second phase was dedicated to finding points of agreement concerning what was received in the Supper, and by whom. This meant turning attention away from the location of Christ's body in heaven and focusing instead on the connection between spiritual and sacramental communion. It was complicated by Luther's insistence that communicants received Christ's body by mouth (*manducatio oralis*) and that all communicants, even the impious, received that body (*manducatio impii*). Political pressures on the south German cities remained an important factor, for they could not join the Schmalkaldic League, a defensive alliance against the Catholic emperor, unless they endorsed the Augsburg Confession.

Martin Bucer worked tirelessly through the first half of the 1530s to craft a formula concerning the Lord's Supper that would be acceptable to both sides. His counterpart in Wittenberg was Philipp Melanchthon rather than Luther, while the deaths of both Zwingli and Oecolampadius in the fall of 1531 meant that the chief spokesman for the Swiss churches was Heinrich Bullinger, Zwingli's successor in Zurich. Through correspondence, individual meetings, and small gatherings of theologians, terminology was hammered out that could be accepted by most of those involved. In March 1536, representatives of the Swiss churches endorsed the First Helvetic Confession (sometimes called the Second Basel Confession, after the city where the meeting was held) to be presented to Luther as a summary of their teachings. Two months later, delegates of the south German cities traveled to Wittenberg, where negotiations led to a statement acceptable to both sides concerning not only the Lord's Supper but also baptism and absolution.

The Wittenberg Concord of 1536 was not a mutual confession of faith, but rather a formulation of the sacramental theology of the south German churches that the Wittenbergers could accept as orthodox, even if it did not fully agree with their position. It emphasized positions held in common and depended on ambiguity and strategic silence to obscure disagreements. It stated that Christ's body and blood were not locally enclosed in the elements, and it rejected the reservation and display of the consecrated host. Through sacramental union, Christ's body was truly present and offered, and it was received even by the unworthy (*indigni*), a group that the south Germans – but not the Wittenbergers – distinguished from the impious (*impii*). The Concord said nothing about either the *manducatio oralis* or the location of Christ's body, thereby avoiding two issues on which the parties still disagreed.

Bucer spent the next two years attempting to persuade the south German and Swiss churches to accept the Wittenberg Concord. He was successful within the Holy Roman Empire, largely because endorsement enabled the cities to join the Schmalkaldic League, and in the Swiss Confederation he was able to win the support of Basel's church. But personal relations between Bucer and Bullinger broke down completely in the process, and at a meeting in May 1538 it became apparent that Zurich and the churches in its orbit would not accept the Wittenberg Concord. The Swiss rejection of the Wittenberg Concord ended the second phase of the controversy, and it divided the parties to the conflict not according to whether they believed that Christ's body was contained in the bread but rather according to whether they taught that in the sacrament Christ's true body was presented, offered, and received by both the worthy and the unworthy.

Jean Calvin had little knowledge of the first phase of the controversy and was only an observer in the second phase, but he became involved in the third phase, which lasted through the 1540s. The first half of that decade was a time of relative tranquility broken by a few public outbursts and significant underlying tensions as Strasbourg and Zurich vied for influence over the churches of what is now western Switzerland. As pastor of the French church in Strasbourg from 1538 to 1541, Calvin accepted the Variata, the version of the Augsburg Confession modified by Melanchthon to reflect the wording of the Wittenberg Concord. A Buceran faction had the upper hand in Bern, and with Calvin's return to Geneva in 1541, that city was also regarded as aligned with Strasbourg. After the emperor's victory over the Schmalkaldic League in 1547, however, Bucer was exiled to England, and the Buceran faction was expelled from Bern. Hoping to improve his relations with the pro-Zurich faction now dominant in Bern, Calvin began corresponding with Bullinger about the Lord's Supper. To reach agreement with Bullinger, Calvin abandoned Bucer's terminology and gave renewed prominence to Christology. The result was the Consensus Tigurinus of 1549, which moved the Genevan church away from Strasbourg and into alliance with Zurich. The Consensus Tigurinus was quickly endorsed by all the Swiss churches except Basel.

Publication of the Consensus Tigurinus in 1551 touched off the fourth phase of the Eucharistic controversy. The Hamburg pastor Joachim Westphal attacked the Consensus in two books published in 1552–1553. Calvin responded, and the public debate soon expanded to include others from both sides. Calvin's treatises from these years demonstrate that he was reading the contributions to the first phase of the Eucharistic controversy and incorporating their arguments into his own polemics against his opponents. In the heat of conflict, there was no attempt to distinguish between the two issues that had distinguished the first and second phases of the controversy. Rather than working out arguments to justify their own understanding of the Lord's Supper, participants now defended positions set forth in confessions of faith considered as authoritative. Where the Consensus Tigurinus served as a common confession for the Reformed, Lutherans were divided between those who drew on Luther's later writings and those more influenced by Melanchthon; the latter would be criticized as "crypto-Calvinists." Only with the 1577 Formula of Concord were most Lutherans able to agree on a common position concerning the Lord's Supper.

Calvin's understanding of the Lord's Supper evolved over time, as he first observed and then became involved in debates with the Lutherans. His rejection of Christ's corporeal presence placed him on the side of the Swiss and South German reformers, but his discussion of the sacraments in the first edition of the *Institutes of the Christian Religion* was strongly influenced by both early Wittenberg theology and Bucer's linkage of spiritual and sacramental communion. His alliance with Strasbourg through the second and third phase of the Eucharistic controversy is therefore not surprising. The collapse of the Strasbourg network after the Schmalkaldic War left

Geneva both theologically and politically isolated and demonstrated the perils of estrangement from Zurich. As one of the architects of the Consensus Tigurinus, Calvin would become a key participant in the public debate that confession provoked, and he would be fully associated with Zurich by the time of his death.

SUGGESTED FURTHER READINGS

Burnett, Amy Nelson. *Debating the Sacraments: Print and Authority in the Early Reformation.* New York: Oxford University Press, 2019.

Campi, Emidio, and Ruedi Reich, eds. *Consensus Tigurinus (1549): Die Einigung zwischen Heinrich Bullinger und Johannes Calvin über das Abendmahl. Werden – Wertung – Bedeutung.* Zurich: TVZ, 2009.

Davis, Thomas J. *The Clearest Promises of God: The Development of Calvin's Eucharistic Teaching.* New York: AMS Press, 1995.

Janse, Wim. "Calvin's Eucharistic Theology: Three Dogma-Historical Observations." In *Calvinus sacrarum literarum interpres: Papers of the International Congress on Calvin Research,* ed. Herman J. Selderhuis. Reformed Historical Theology 5. Göttingen: Vandenhoeck & Ruprecht, 2008, 37–69.

Jensen, Gordon A. *The Wittenberg Concord: Creating Space for Dialogue.* Lutheran Quarterly Books. Minneapolis, MN: Fortress Press, 2018.

Wandel, Lee Palmer, ed. *A Companion to the Eucharist in the Reformation.* Brill's Companions to the Christian Tradition 46. Leiden, The Netherlands: Brill, 2013.

29

Predestination in Early Modern Thought

Charles Raith II

If there is a theological locus that the popular mind associates with John Calvin, it is the doctrine of predestination, and in particular the notion of "double predestination." This association is not limited to the popular mind, to be sure; even scholars have attempted to make predestination the "center" of Calvin's theology. I do not here plan to tackle the issue of the place of predestination in Calvin's theological framework. My goal instead is to demonstrate the *lack of originality* of Calvin's teaching on predestination when placed against the backdrop of both medieval debates surrounding predestination and the theology of Calvin's fellow reformers.

Before diving into the argument, it must be noted that understanding Calvin on predestination requires understanding its *pastoral* and *polemical* context within the sixteenth century. Calvin drew on the doctrine of predestination as a way to undermine Pelagian tendencies found in the opponents' teaching on salvation and, in particular, the doctrine of merit.[1] He believed that the emphasis placed on merit put souls at risk while bolstering the problematical sacramental system of church. He was adamant regarding the practical dimensions of predestination, warning against "burying [predestination] in the secret council of God," which would make the doctrine "not only lacking in warmth but completely lifeless."[2] He addressed these problems not by producing a teaching *de novo* on predestination, rather he did so by siding with one position amongst many bequeathed to him from medieval scholastic debates on predestination – a position already taken by others

---

[1] Charles Raith II, "Calvin's Critique of Merit, and Why Aquinas (Mostly) Agrees," *Pro Ecclesia* 20 (2011): 154–155; Paul Helm, *Calvin at the Centre* (Oxford: Oxford University Press, 2009), 152.

[2] *Commentarius in Epistilorum Pauli ad Romanos*, T. H. L. Parker (ed.) (Leiden, The Netherlands: Brill, 1981), 187.27–29.

like Luther – while heavily polemicizing other approaches and radicalizing the implications of the position he chose. And like medieval scholastic theologians before him, he called upon Augustine's doctrine of predestination as an ally to address "Pelagian" teaching.

THE SCHOLASTIC HERITAGE ON PREDESTINATION

The doctrine of predestination had long been debated before the sixteenth century, particularly in those streams flowing from the reservoir of Augustine. It was a debate that would bequeath to early modern thought numerous options for approaching the topic. Debates surrounding the proper reception of Augustine's teaching on predestination were alive and well already in the ninth century thanks to Gottschalk, whose teaching drew considerable negative attention particularly as it related to reprobation. In sum, Gottschalk taught a form of "double predestination," that is, he applied the term *predestination* to *both* the elect receiving eternal life *and* the reprobate receiving eternal death. Gottschalk considered his teaching deeply Augustinian, and he cited Isidore of Seville, Gregory the Great and Fulgentius of Ruspe as holding a similar position. His opponents thought otherwise and developed alternative Augustinian theologies of predestination, whether from Amolo of Lyons, Hincmar of Reims, or Rabanus Maurus. Thus the Augustinian waters were already populated with options before the rise of scholasticism.

Scholastic engagement with Augustine's teaching on predestination became shaped in large part by Peter Lombard's *Sentences*. Yet this period witnessed a great deal of distinguishing, clarifying, nuancing, and precision that allowed unique approaches to the topic that went beyond the less clear positions found in Augustine. Although Calvin quoted Augustine on predestination and related issues, he was in fact approaching Augustine through the lens of these scholastic developments.

In the thirteenth century, predestination generally pertained to *God's eternal will* to grant human beings participation in glory. For this to occur, God acts externally to give grace for conversion from sin, sustain one in grace on the journey to eternal life, and grant eternal life to the one persevering in grace. Predestination in this view is thus an aspect of God; it reflects his eternal decision to bring people to glory. But not everyone is granted grace, and this leads to reprobation. Reprobation is simply God *not willing* to grant grace to certain individuals. Reprobation is not the same as punishment, rather, it is simply God's not giving of grace. Punishment is the result of sin, which has as its only causal basis the human being. To clarify in light of later developments, reprobation here is not understood as God's *willing* not to give grace, rather, it is simply God not willing the gift of grace. The only active willing of God is toward the predestined to grant them grace and bring them to glory. The notion of *particular* predestination, however, gives rise to the further question: Why are the ones who are predestined *predestined*? Why God predestined *particular* individuals and not others is understood broadly within the thirteenth century as being in the hidden will of God. That is, God's decision to grant grace to particular individuals is not based on any foreseen merits in the one given grace; nothing in the predestined could be considered a grounds or a cause for being predestined.[3]

Fourteenth-century theologians largely considered predestination as the *whole* of God's salvific work, that is, not just predestination as it relates to glory but predestination as encompassing all that God gives to bring one to glory, and the giving of glory. But two shifts mark the debates of the fourteenth century. First, the central issue for many fourteenth-century theologians pertained to the cause of predestination, with the main concern being to determine the extent of its gratuity and the roles that God and human beings play within predestination. In this discussion, analyzing the value of works done in the state of nature (i.e., works done prior to receiving justifying grace) became an important topic of interest, as well as the relation of these works to God's act of predestinating.[4] For God to predestine or reprobate without a cause seemed to run contrary to God's justice and goodness, but to root a cause in human activity seemed to impinge upon the gratuity of grace and predestination.

Most theologians agreed in continuity with the thirteenth century that no works done outside of grace could be considered *meritorious*. But disagreements arose over how to evaluate the works done outside of grace. Were all works done outside of grace tainted by sin and therefore sinful? Or could works be performed that were truly good (though not meritorious)? Giles of Rome, for example, equates truly good works with *meritorious* works, and thus because no meritorious works are done outside of grace, we must say that the works of ungraced human beings are at least venially sinful.[5] Thomas of Strassburg, however, differentiates between good and bad works

---

[3] This is not to say, however, that merit was not *part* of predestination. God's eternal decision as to *whom* to predestine does not include foreknowledge of a person's merit. But predestination as God's ordering of a person to glory does include merit. Meritorious works are part of the way God has ordered the path of grace leading to glory.

[4] Joseph L. Shannon, *Good Works and Predestination according to Thomas of Strassbourg, O.S.A.* (Baltimore, MD: The Watkins Printing Co., 1940), 23–24.

[5] Giles of Rome, *Commentarium in II Sententiarum* d. 40, q. 2, a.3 (Venice, 1581), 316.

and meritorious, demeritorious, and indifferent works. While all meritorious works are good works, not all good works are meritorious works; instead only those done in grace are meritorious works.[6] Thomas can therefore say both that ungraced human beings can produce no meritorious works *and* that ungraced human beings can produce truly good works, without needing to say they are in any way sinful. Instead, these works are simply indifferent to merit.[7] The position one holds necessarily impacts the presentation of the relation between ungraced and graced works, and this in turn becomes a factor when considering whether the works of the ungraced person play a role in God's predestinating activity.

Second, a major turn in theological reflection on predestination comes with Peter Aureol, for whom predestination is not so much an internal decision or ordering in God as it is the outward, external activities of God granting grace and glory. For Aureol, God's internal (and eternal) will is to save *all* people and not just particular people. This internal decision to save all people results in the external acts of predestination, that is, the granting of grace and glory. But if God wills all people to be saved, why are there some who are not predestined, that is, why do some participate in grace and glory and others do not (i.e., the reprobate)? The reason for Aureol is not due to God eternally electing some and not others; God elects all human beings. But his election of all human beings consists of a qualifier: God eternally elects all human beings *who do not put up an obstacle to grace*. These are the *kinds* of people that are the predestined. Not putting up an obstacle is not for Aureol a meritorious act of a person; it is simply a not willing. It is a not resisting rather than an active will not to resist (or as it will be later, an active will to prepare oneself). The reprobate, however, are those who *retain* an obstacle to grace. Thus we find that unlike Aquinas, Aureol includes the human response to grace within the reason for someone being predestined or reprobated. Again, God does not consider anything in the particular person predestined in his eternal decision to elect to salvation. God's eternal decision to elect to salvation entails the election of a *kind* of person, that is, the one who does not resist grace. Predestination (in distinction from election) is thus not about God's internal decision (as it is with Aquinas) but about the external acts of granting grace and glory. And the nonresistance of grace is

---

[6] Thomas of Strassbourg, *Commentaria super quator libros Sententiarum*, II, d. 40–41, q. 1, a. 2, fol. 197 r I (Strassbourg, 1490).

[7] Shannon, *Good Works and Predestination*, 26–30. Shannon notes that in Thomas of Strassbourg, there is a tendency "to favor man's natural powers, which is certainly not that which dominated in the later Augustinian school" (38).

not a positive meritorious act by which a person is predestined, but rather merely a passive nonresistance. One person actively resists (i.e., reprobation); another person only passively nonresists (i.e., predestination). Nevertheless, the "cause" now for both predestination and reprobation is the same, namely the human response to grace: "the cause of reprobation is the maintenance of an impediment foreseen from eternity; but the cause of predestination is the foreknowledge and foresight of the absence of any impediment with respect to he who is called predestined."[8] For Aureol, then, God predestines those not putting up an obstacle, while for Aquinas those God predestines will not put up an obstacle. Thomas of Strassbourg holds a similar position. For Thomas, God desires that all people be saved *contingent on their acceptance or rejection of grace*. Predestination and reprobation are contingent on a person's reaction to grace. A person who does not resist the attraction of grace makes good use of the will; a person who resists the attraction of grace makes bad use of the will. God's foreknowledge includes this acceptance and rejection and forms the reason for one's reprobation or predestination.[9]

While Aureol maintains that the predestined are those who simply do not resist grace, other theologians will go further and include a person's *active* preparation for grace as a cause for predestination. Not only is preparation a cause for predestination but also some will affirm that preparation is a *meritorious* cause for predestination, thus resulting in the view that a person can merit the gift of initial, justifying grace. William of Ockham, for example, asserts, "Good works in some way dispose someone to grace and, consequently, to an effect of predestination, although not sufficiently or strictly meritoriously."[10] Disagreements exist over whether Ockham held to the notion of predestination *post praevisa merita*. Either way, whether the preparation for grace is congruously meritorious, the controversial point is that God considers our work of preparation in his decision to grant grace.

---

[8] Aureol, *Borghese* 329, f. 439ra.

[9] I, d. 40, a. 2, fol. 110 r II. Thomas of Strassbourg runs explicitly contrary to Thomas Aquinas and Giles of Rome. For Strassbourg, if there was nothing in the person that played a role in being predestined or reprobated, and that all are equal with regard to both, and that God then makes a choice without any ratio for that choice on the part of human beings, God's justice would be impugned (I, d. 41, a. 1, a. 2, fol. 112 v II). Aquinas and Giles think otherwise because predestination is wholly gratuitous; see Aquinas, *ST* I, q. 23, a. 5, ad. 3; Giles of Rome, *Comm. ad Rom.* cap. 9, lect. 31.

[10] Ockham, *Ordinatio* IV in *Guilleli de Ockham Opera philosophica et theologica ad fidem condicum manuscriptorum edita*, Gideon Gal et al. (eds.) (St. Bonaventure, NY: Franciscan Institute, 1976–1985), 600.

This line of thinking did not go unchallenged. Perhaps one of the strongest opponents was Gregory of Rimini, who develops a theology of predestination very similar to that of Calvin (and Gottschalk).[11] Not only did Rimini retrieve the earlier consensus view that predestination is in God's eternal will and consists of his positive decision to grant grace and glory to particular individuals – and this without consideration of anything on the side of those particular individuals – Rimini further made reprobation *also* a positive determination of God's will. Reprobation is God's *will* not to will to have mercy on certain individuals: "predestination is understood as the eternal purpose of God by which He appointed some beforehand to whom to give grace. And thus, reprobation signifies the eternal purpose of God by which he preordained not to give grace to a person, but instead preordained eternal punishment."[12] For Rimini, predestination proper is still solely to salvation. But now reprobation is equally part of God's eternal, hidden *active* will, along with predestination.[13]

After Rimini, three main options for interpreting predestination and reprobation were in the air. One version, following Aquinas, held that predestination is God's eternal decision to grant grace and glory to particular individuals without importing any foresight of a person's response to grace as a causal basis for predestination, while reprobation is simply God's not willing grace and glory. Aureol's teaching, and modifications thereof, hold that God's eternal, electing decision is solely to save all human beings who do not put up an obstacle to grace, making the human response of (1) passive reception or (2) active rejection the deciding factor in predestination and

---

[11] Johnathan H. Rainbow calls Rimini, along with John Wyclif and John Hus, "latter day Gottschalks" (*The Will of God and the Cross: An Historical and Theological Study of John Calvin's Doctrine of Limited Redemption* [Allison Park, PA: Pickwick Publications, 1990], 46).

[12] Gregory of Rimini, *Lectura*, I, a. 1 (vol. 3, p. 322).

[13] It is important to keep in mind that for Rimini, reprobation is not punishment. Punishment corresponds to sin. Reprobation is merely the decision not to give grace. This is similar to Aquinas's position, although Rimini goes further by making God's not willing of grace an active, willing decision by God: "For to afflict or to punish is not to reprobate. Therefore, God neither reprobates someone so that He may punish, nor does He punish because He reprobated, but because the one whome He punishes has sinned or has been condemned by son, of which sin, moreover, divine reprobation is not the cause. For God does not reprobate someone by imparting wickedness, but by not imparting grace" (*Lectura* I, d. 40–41, a. 2 (vol. 3, p. 348). Giles of Rome has held a similar position. The reason people are damned is due to their sin, but the reason God reprobates some people is due to God's eternal will to do so: "before some good or bad is done, not from works but according to the divine election and proposition and vocation it is said that this one is elected and that one is reprobated" (*Commentaria Ep. ad Rom.* cap. 9, dubium 7).

reprobation. With Rimini's teaching, and modifications thereof, one finds that both predestination and reprobation are part of God's eternal, *active* will for human beings, neither of which takes into consideration foresight of a person's response to grace as a causal basis for determining predestination or reprobation.

THE SIXTEENTH CENTURY

The theologians of the sixteenth century, both Catholic and Protestant, developed their predestinarian theology by participating (even if at times without acknowledgment) in this medieval development. That is, the Reformers' doctrine of predestination did not fall from the sky, nor was it simply the result of biblical exegesis. Up until and within the Reformation era, the second position previously mentioned would elicit charges of "Pelagianism," while the third position (and the first, though to a lesser extent) would elicit charges of "determinism" and the eradication of free choice. It comes as no surprise, then, when Calvin began working out his theological alternative to what he judged to be rampant Pelagianistic teaching in his day – "The Schools consistently have gone from worse to worse, until at length, in their downward path, they have denigrated into a kind of Pelagianism"[14] – he would focus on the doctrine of predestination as fashioned in a manner similar to Rimini as a means of countering such theology.[15]

But Calvin was not alone nor even the first Reformer to draw on a particular strain of predestinarian reflection to counter problematic "Pelagian" elements of theology, and an argument can be made that Calvin's theology on this locus is little more than a restatement of the views of Martin Luther.[16] While we often think of Calvin's theology of predestination generating controversy, Luther's position, especially as found in his *De servo arbitrium* was such that he had to defend himself on more than one occasion

---

[14] *Inst.* 3.11.15.

[15] It is also worth noting that even Calvin's position on the controversial subtopic of "limited redemption" evidences his inheritance of a long tradition of reflection on this topic. Rainbow, *The Will of God and the Cross*, 8. Rainbow also shows Calvin's indebtedness to Bucer on this point (61–63).

[16] For Calvin's borrowing from Luther various "necessitarian" concepts surrounding the doctrines of providence and predestination, see Kiven S. K. Choy, "Calvin's Reception of Necessitarian Concepts," in Jordon J. Ballor et al. (eds.), *Church and School in Early Modern Protestantism* (Leiden, The Netherlands: Brill, 2013), 111–122.

against charges of necessitarianism, that is, that people's action are a product
of *force* or *compulsion*. Luther's attacks on human "free will" and his
emphasis on God's immutable, eternal, all-determining will left his opponents wondering whether there was anything left for human responsibility.
Luther affirmed as much but only using a number of distinctions – between
"free will" and "mutable will," "compulsion" and "immutability," and
"necessity of force" and "necessity of time," to name a few.[17] Worth noting
is how later Lutherans would disavow Luther's predestinarian teaching in *De
servo arbitrium* as Luther's "real" thinking on the issue by citing (as evidence
of a shift in Luther's thinking) Luther's own comments about *De servo
arbitrium* in his lectures on Genesis.[18] Tellingly, later Calvinists, however,
had a much more positive take on *De servo arbitrium* and employed it in the
service of their own predestinarian reflections – with some even citing it as
proof of the Calvinist position over the Lutheran.[19]

Kiven Choy highlights five "necessitarian" concepts surrounding the
doctrines of providence and predestination that Calvin borrowed from
Luther. The first is an active concept of divine omnipotence, such that
God is not to be conceived of as an abstract and/or "idle" deity or as the
"general principle of confused motion" but rather one that is "watchful,
effective, engaged in ceaseless activity," that is, one who "directs everything."[20] Second is an emphasis on the active and literal interpretation of
hardening and reprobation in scripture, such that when scripture says God
hardened Pharaoh's heart it is speaking "literally, as if he said, 'I will act so
that Pharaoh's heart maybe hardened.'"[21] Third is the use of the term *ordain*
to characterize reprobation, which Calvin also applies to the fall. The fourth
is a "nominalist or perhaps Scotist" emphasis on the divine will and its

---

[17] See John B. King Jr., *Predestination in Light of the Cross: A Critical Exposition of Luther's
Theology* (Vallecita, CA: Chalcedon, 2003), 25–36. King's entire project is to demonstrate that
"double predestination originated with Luther, not Calvin . . . Calvin followed Luther almost
to the letter in his view of double predestination" (vi). I will assume King means by
"originated" that Luther is the first *Reformer* to affirm it because "double predestination"
was affirmed before Luther.

[18] WA 43:457.33–463.17 (LW 5:42–50).

[19] Abraham Scultetus, *Vitalia, das ist ein christlich und freundlich Reyß-Gespräch* (Hanau:
Aubrius and Clement, 1618), 77–80. For more on the Lutheran-Calvinist reception of *De
servo arbitrium*, see Robert Kolb, *Bound Choice, Election, and Wittenberg Theological
Method: From Martin Luther to the Formula of Concord* (Grand Rapids, MI:
Eerdmans, 2005).

[20] Kolb, *Bound Choice, Election, and Wittenberg Theological Method,* 114.

[21] Ibid., 114.

inscrutability. The last is the qualification that God is not the proper cause of sinful activity due to the inherence fallenness of the will. Thus God's active providence is his use of "evil instruments" to accomplish his good purposes.[22] These points are highlighted in order, once again, to emphasize the unoriginality in Calvin's thought.

SUGGESTED FURTHER READING

Choy, Kiven S. K. "Calvin's Reception of Necessitarian Concepts." In *Church and School in Early Modern Protestantism*, ed. Jordon J. Ballor et al. Leiden, The Netherlands: Brill, 2013, 111–122.

Kolb, Robert. *Bound Choice, Election, and Wittenberg Theological Method: From Martin Luther to the Formula of Concord*. Grand Rapids, MI: Eerdmans, 2005.

Muller, Richard. *Christ and Decree: Christology and Predestination in Reformed Theology from Calvin to Perkins*. Durham, NC: Labyrinth, 1986 (repr. Grand Rapids, MI: Baker Academic, 2008).

Rainbow, Johnathan H. *The Will of God and the Cross: An Historical and Theological Study of John Calvin's Doctrine of Limited Redemption*. Allison Park, PA: Pickwick Publications, 1990.

Raith II, Charles. "Calvin's Critique of Merit, and Why Aquinas (Mostly) Agrees," *Pro Ecclesia* 20 (2011): 135–153.

---

[22] Ibid., 117.

The Challenge of Heresy

Servetus, Stancaro, and Castellio

Arnold Huijgen

INTRODUCTION

The challenge of heresy is inherent to any claim of orthodoxy by the Christian Church. The New Testament already states that there must be heresies so that those who are genuine believers may be recognized.[1] As deviation from the ecclesial norm of orthodoxy, heresy threatens the unity of the Church, and even the integrity of society at large, when Christianity is the official religion of the empire as it was from AD 380. Heresy was a revolution, an attack on the order of the world. While modern readers may be tempted to view heresy as some positive expression of individual creativity in matters of doctrine, perhaps an instance of freedom of speech, such ideas were alien to the early modern mind. The stereotype of the heretic was not a creative individual, but someone possessed by the devil, driven by pride, who hid his heresy under the cover of seeming piety. Of course, not all doctrinal errors, dissident beliefs, and practices, were heresies. Error became heresy by obstinate refusal to obey the Church, which had defined orthodox teaching and sought to correct errors. As Robert Grosseteste defined: "a heresy is an opinion chosen by human perception contrary to holy Scripture, publicly avowed and obstinately defended."[2]

The punishments for heretics were severe. Because heresy threatened the order of society, it was penalized under imperial law. The *Codex Iustinianus* (1.6.2) stipulated that Anabaptism (*rebaptizare*) was punishable by capital punishment, and § 106 of Charles V's *Constitutio Criminalis Carolina* condemned the denial of God, which surely included antitrinitarianism, as

[1] 1 Cor. 11:19, cf. Titus 3:10.
[2] Malcolm Lambert, *Medieval Heresy: Popular Movements from the Gregorian Reform to the Reformation*, 2nd ed. (Oxford: Blackwell, 1992), 5.

also worthy of capital punishment. A city that failed to comply with these laws and let heretics go, would place itself outside of the Christian world, and would become a target for several imperial sanctions. Such a city could face the same fate as Münster earlier, which was ruled by Anabaptists from February 1534 to June 1535. The theocratic reign, polygamy, abolishment of social classes, community property, in short the destruction of society, led to a shockwave across the European continent. When the bishop recaptured the city, the heretic insurgents were tortured and killed. The Münster scenario demonstrated not only that heresy went along with revolutionary political and societal ideas but also that acceptance of these ideas would render entire cities outlaws.

For Protestants, heresy was particularly problematic because they had deviated, and obstinately so, from the practices and teachings of the Roman Catholic Church. As a result, Protestants were often on the receiving end of accusations of heresy. Moreover, Protestants denied the ultimate authority of the Church and regarded only scripture as infallible, which made the question of who was heretical open for discussion. Under Protestant conditions, no one could sentence a final "anathema." Still, Protestants did accuse others of heresy. First and foremost, they saw the papal church entrenched in heresies, becoming the apocalyptic antichrist, against which they sought rebirth in the healthy doctrine of the Church Fathers and earlier scholastic theologians. This entailed differentiating mainstream Protestantism from radical elements that transgressed the boundaries of Catholic orthodoxy, such as Anabaptism and, above all, antitrinitarianism.

While there were a wealth of heresies in Calvin's context to choose from, the present chapter is limited to the famous case of Servetus, that of Stancaro, and Castellio's fierce critique of the persecution of heretics.

SERVETUS AND ANTITRINITARIANISM

Michael Servetus (1511–1553), a Spanish physician and *homo universalis*, was a heretic by any definition available at the time. He defied the most fundamental Christian doctrine of the Trinity, and presented heretical views on an impressive number of other doctrines. His theological system (at least in 1553) was a strange mix of heterodox beliefs that may be summed up as follows: (1) Creation and revelation: Servetus pictured reality as a hierarchy of ideas, with Christ above everything but directly under God. Revelation took place as emanation, resulting in a tendency toward pantheism. Servetus was accused of Valentinian gnosticism. (2) Trinity: Servetus regarded Christ and the Spirit as modes of revelation of the Father, not as persons in the true sense of the word. This ancient heresy of modalism, or Sabellianism, was curiously supplemented by the subordinatianist thought that the Father is the ultimate God above all creation, while the Son and the Spirit reveal the Father but also share in created reality. Thus, Servetus managed to combine two heresies that are usually considered opposites. (3) Christology: Servetus thought Christ was adored in the form of an angel in the Old Testament, and tended to deny Christ's true humanity. This was in line with Servetus's rejection of the councils of the early Church: Chalcedon in 451 had emphasized Christ's two natures. (4) Anabaptism: Servetus rejected infant baptism. (5) Pelagianism: Servetus denied original sin, and advocated pelagian optimism, combined with apocalyptic milleniarism. Servetus was "the complete heretic," and therefore "opposed by the total Christian community of his day and was found heretic by any and all standards."[3] In Geneva, Servetus was "merely" accused of Anabaptism, antitrinitarianism, and pantheism, and found guilty of the former two.

It is one thing to publish heretical ideas, but quite another to be executed as a heretic. Two works on the Trinity published by Servetus in 1531 and 1532 had already brought him in trouble. His views were condemned by Protestants and Roman Catholics alike, so Servetus went into hiding under the name Michael Villanovanus, after his birthplace Villanueva in Spain. While in Lyon, he exchanged letters with Calvin on the Trinity, until these became repetitious. In January 1553, Servetus's final book was published anonymously in Vienne: *Christianismi Restitutio* (*Restoration of Christianity*). The identity of the author was easily uncovered, however. Calvin used Servetus's publication to plead the case for five Calvinist pastors that were arrested in Lyon in 1552, posing the question to the French authorities and the Inquisition how five orthodox Protestants could be condemned as guilty of heresy, when a physician in Vienne (not far from Lyon) could publish such a heretical work.[4] Servetus was arrested and questioned by the Inquisition, but he managed to escape from prison. *In absentia*, Servetus was declared guilty of scandalous heresy, sedition, rebellion, and evasion of prison. Capital punishment was executed *in effigie*: a picture of Servetus was burned. Next, Servetus appeared in Geneva, where he was recognized by Calvin during an afternoon Sunday service. After several examinations by the civil authorities, a debate between Calvin and Servetus, and a consultation of the other Swiss

---

[3] Jerome Friedman, *Michael Servetus: A Case Study in Total Heresy* (Genève: Librairie Droz, 1978), 133, 136.

[4] See Frans Pieter van Stam, *The Servetus Case: An Appeal for a New Assessment*. Cahiers d'humanisme et renaissance 136 (Genève: Droz, 2017).

cities, Servetus was found guilty of antitrinitarianism and Anabaptism. During the trial, Servetus refused to be extradited to Vienne, but preferred to be tried in Geneva. Calvin's plea for the more humane decapitation was denied by the authorities and on October 27, 1553, Servetus was burned at the stake.

Although in popular imagery, the burning of Servetus in 1553 has often served as the ultimate example of Calvin's cruelty, Servetus would in fact have suffered the same fate elsewhere in Europe, the trial was a secular proceeding by a Genevan administration that was mostly hostile to Calvin at the time, and failure to punish Servetus would have caused Geneva enormous damage. Because antitrinitarianism was punishable by imperial law, Geneva would have put itself on the map as a second Münster if the verdict had been different from the verdict passed in Vienne. It was found necessary to oppress heresy to avoid an outburst of political sedition. Also, capital punishment was practiced in many similar cases during the sixteenth century and later, and Geneva, like many other similar cities, had only two major possibilities for penalty at its disposal: banishment and execution. In the case of Servetus and in the context of the sixteenth century, the Genevan council had no choice but to execute a total heretic.

Servetus was not the only antitrinitarian, which is important to contextualize his position and the Genevan verdict. Calvin had been accused of antitrinitarianism by Pierre Caroli because of his reluctance to use the traditional terminology, but he had successfully refuted these accusations in 1545. After the Servetus affair, antitrinitarian sentiments began fermenting in the Genevan Italian congregation, which was founded in 1542. The Swiss cities provided a refuge for Italians who had fled their home country in the face of the Inquisition. The jurist Matteo Gribaldi (1506–1564) expressed similar ideas to Servetus's in a meeting of the Italian church in 1554, and the physician Giorgio Biandrata (1516–1588) and five other members of the congregation did similarly in 1558, refusing to sign a confession of faith affirming the divinity of Christ and of the Holy Spirit. Afterward, he fled to Poland, where he eventually complied with the strict Unitarianism of Socinus. The philologist Valentino Gentile (±1520–1566) was imprisoned in Geneva in 1557 for antitrinitarianism and condemned to death, but he recanted. He then fled to join other antitrinitarians. He also went to Poland, which was counted as very tolerant at the time, where he contributed to the antitrinitarian confession of Pińczów (1563). When traveling back to Switzerland, he was arrested in Bern in 1566 and decapitated there because of his heresy.

So, as far as antitrinitarianism is concerned, it is clear that the entire Christian West considered it a heresy worthy of capital punishment, although the severity of their persecution varied locally and through time. At its core, it was a denial of Nicene orthodoxy, so antitrinitarian is a synonym for anti-Nicene, and went hand in hand with an orientation on the ante-Nicene Church Fathers. Groups of antitrinitarians and unitarians found a stronghold in Poland and Transylvania. People like Servetus, who could not or would not demonstrate their Nicene orthodoxy, and could not or would not flee to these countries, risked their lives.

STANCARO AND CHRIST'S MEDIATORIAL OFFICE

In pursuit of the line between heresy and orthodoxy, Francesco Stancaro (1501–1574) provides another interesting example. Though he was not an antitrinitarian, his doctrine was used by antitrinitarians. Born in Mantua, Italy, after his conversion to Protestantism, he went to Switzerland, where he started writing on theological matters. Wherever he came and whatever he wrote, dissension arose. Stancaro's signature doctrinal position was the idea that Christ is mediator only according to his human nature, not according to his divine nature. He developed this position in his resistance to the position of Andreas Osiander, who had attacked Melanchthon's forensic position on justification. While Melanchthon taught that sinners are justified by imput-ation of Christ's righteousness, Osiander emphasized justification as sharing in the essential righteousness of Christ through Christ's indwelling (*inhabi-tatio*) of the person. Justification, according to Osiander, is not being declared righteous (as Melanchthon taught), but being effectively made righteous because of the instilling of Christ's righteousness in humanity by Christ's divine nature. Staunch Lutherans like Joachim Mörlin criticized Osiander for jeopardizing the doctrine of justification. Stancaro, in his turn, advocated the opposite position from Osiander. While Osiander found Christ's mediatorial office primarily in his divinity, Stancaro stated that Christ was mediator only according to his humanity.

Stancaro was convinced of his own orthodoxy, and invoked particularly Peter Lombard's *Sentences* in support of his views. He thought he had reason to believe that Calvin and Peter Vermigli would support him because they had emphasized that Christ the mediator has suffered in his humanity, not according to his divinity. For Calvin, Christ's true humanity was necessary to bridge the rift between God and humans. Stancaro radicalized this idea by teaching that Christ was mediator only according to his humanity. Franceso Lismanini has rightly characterized Stancaro's teachings as *nudus homo pro nobis mediatore* (a mere man is our mediator). Stancaro's style radicalized too: in a public discussion in Berlin (1552), he accused his opponent Andreas

Musculus of Manichaeism and Eutychianism (mixing the two natures of Christ). He even engaged in publication wars with Melanchthon, whom he labeled "the Arius of the north," although Melanchthon was the most favorable toward the Reformed camp. In a letter to Calvin, Stancaro pressed him to choose between "arianism" and Stancaro's own position. Against Stancaro's expectations, Calvin and Vermigli did not support him. They stated that while Christ suffers according to his humanity, he is still mediator according to both natures. For as mediator, he not only suffers, but also reigns. In terms of the threefold office of Christ: he is not merely the suffering Priest but also the reigning King.

Stancaro was accused of nestorianism – that is, the separation of Christ's natures – at a synod in Pińczów (1559) by Jan Łaski and Francesco Lismanini. Stancaro appealed to Lombard, who describes the incarnation as a work of the Trinity. For Stancaro, Christ's humanity becomes the instrument by which the Trinity brings salvation to pass. Stancaro did not seem to notice that he was en route to denying Christ's divinity, and embracing adoptianism, arianism, and eventually antitrinitarianism. Stancaro's view of Christ as "mere man" played into the hands of the antitrinitarians. Meanwhile, Lutherans and Calvinists alike were united in the orthodox stance that Christ was mediator according to both natures because not only suffering belongs to the mediator but also his reign and intercession.

CASTELLIO ON TOLERANCE

In response to the execution of Servetus in Geneva, the former rector of the Genevan school, Sebastian Castellio (1515–1563), wrote two books: *De haereticis, an sint persequendi* (*On heretics: Whether They Should Be Persecuted*), published under a pseudonym in Basel, 1554, and *Contra libellum Calvini* (*Against Calvin's Book*, finished in 1554, but published only after Castellio's death, in 1612 in the Netherlands). Castellio denied that the power of the sword of civil government should interfere with the doctrine of the Church: "To kill a man is not to defend a doctrine, but to kill a man ... The defence of doctrine is not the affair of the magistrate but of the doctor."[5] So, Castellio advocated tolerance, which should not be misunderstood in the modern sense of skepticism. Castellio did not deny that heretics were in the wrong and in need of correction, he only stated that people should not be put to

---

[5] Sebastian Castellio, *Contra Libellum Calvini*, sig. E16r.

death for their religious convictions. Heretics must be corrected, not with fire or sword, but by patient persuasion.[6]

Castellio brought three arguments to the fore. First, the definition of *heresy*. Castellio thought the category of heresy was problematic because of doctrinal divisions: someone who was deemed orthodox in one city, was regarded as a heretic in the next. To stay alive, one needed to have as many religions as there are cities![7] Castellio made a distinction: besides the pious people, there are two other groups: heretics and *impii*, deniers of God and blasphemers. The heretics stand in between the pious and the deniers of God because they are misguided, although they are genuinely concerned with the renewal of faith. Importantly, for Castellio, heresy was about morals. Not only was the right moral life for Castellio more important than the right doctrine, it was also easier to judge whether a person lived in a morally sound way than whether he was orthodox in doctrine.

Second, heretics should not be put to death. Castellio's main arguments were (1) one can never be sure who is a heretic and who is not. Based analogously on the wheat and tares (Matt. 13:24–30), action should be postponed until Christ comes; (2) death meant the end of the possibility of conversion, which should be the chief end for the Church; and (3) to kill a man is against the Christian commandment to love one's neighbor. Castellio notes that Calvin before pleaded for religious toleration in cases in which their fellow believers were persecuted. He should do the same now.

Meanwhile, there was still the group of blasphemers. Remarkably, Castellio handed the small group of the actual blasphemers over to the civil magistrate, "not because of their religion, which they do not have, but because of their irreligion."[8] He seemed even to suggest that they could be sentenced to death, although he advocated that they be put in jail, so that they might improve their lives. That would be the true leniency of a Christian government.

Third, Castellio attacked Calvin. These two had had a history in Geneva, where Castellio had to leave because his view of the Song of Songs as merely a love song, and his views on predestination, although Calvin did not regard him as a heretic. In *Contra libellum Calvini*, Castellio makes Calvin personally responsible for every step of the Servetus trial, and pictures Calvin as having written his 1554 *Defence* with his hands covered in blood. Although

---

[6] Bruce Gordon, "To Kill a Heretic: Sebastian Castellio against John Calvin," in Geoff Kemp (ed.), *Censorship Moments: Reading Texts in the History of Censorship and Freedom of Expression* (London: Bloomsbury, 2014), 55–61.

[7] Castellio, *De haereticis*, 19.

[8] Castellio, *Contra libellum Calvini*, sig. K2r.

Calvin's role in the secular trial was only limited, Castellio was successful in smearing Calvin's image for centuries.

At the time Castellio's ideas were considered dangerous, hence his pseudonymous and posthumous publications. Castellio worked from the assumption that scripture was not always clear, and that doctrinal differences were not so serious a threat to the Church that temporal authorities would have to protect it. Castellio's works sparked such unrest in Basel that Castellio planned once more to emigrate to Poland, although he died in Basel before he could do so.

All in all, just as Calvin is not the tyrant Castellio pictures him to be, Castellio was not the unambiguous forerunner of the modern ideal of tolerance. He did, however, allow for more toleration of heretics than most of his contemporaries.

CONCLUSION

Heresy is a byproduct of any definition of orthodox Christianity. After the split of the Church in the West, the Protestants were left without a central authority to decide on orthodoxy, heterodoxy, and heresy. Moreover, the divisions among the Protestants aggravated the debate on heresy. Still, a consensus remained across confessional positions that the councils of the early Church marked the boundaries between orthodoxy and heresy: for all, Nicaea was the watershed between orthodoxy and heresy. This consensus was undergirded by the fact that denial of the Trinitarian dogma was forbidden by Emperor Charles's imperial law, while Anabaptism was deemed punishable by the Codex Iustinianus. In Calvin's context, Michael Servetus has the dubious honor to stand out as the complete heretic. By contrast, Francesco Stancaro provides an example of a theological concept that was rejected by almost all branches of Protestantism and that paved the way for antitrinitarianism and Unitarianism, but that nonetheless was not in itself anti-Nicaean. Castellio's plea for tolerance sounded unfit for sixteenth-century ears, although his defamation of Calvin was highly successful. Calvin would have to negotiate this changing world around the questions of heresy and toleration throughout his career.

SUGGESTED FURTHER READING

Friedman, Jerome. *Michael Servetus: A Case Study in Total Heresy*. Genève: Librairie Droz, 1978.
Gordon, Bruce. "To Kill a Heretic: Sebastian Castellio against John Calvin." In *Censorship Moments: Reading Texts in the History of Censorship and*

Freedom of Expression, ed. Geoff Kemp. London: Bloomsbury, 2014, 55–62.

Lambert, Malcolm. *Medieval Heresy: Popular Movements from the Gregorian Reform to the Reformation,* 2nd ed. Oxford: Blackwell, 1992.

McLelland. Joseph C. "The Italian Anti-Trinitarians." In *Bewegung und Beharrung: Aspekte des Reformierten Protestantismus, 1520–1650.* Festschrift für Emidio Campi. Studies in the History of Christian Traditions 144, ed. Christian Moser and Peter Opitz. Leiden, The Netherlands: Brill, 2007, 147–158.

Stam, Frans Pieter van. *The Servetus Case: An Appeal for a New Assessment.* Cahiers d'humanisme et renaissance 136. Genève: Droz, 2017.

Early Modern Christianity and Idolatry

Carlos M. N. Eire

Idolatry is a fighting word, feisty and judgmental, freighted with disapproval. After all, to call any sacred object an *idol* is to question its legitimacy.

The English word *idolatry* comes from the Greek *eidōlolatreia:* image or representation (*eidōlon*) + worship (*latreia*). The Greek term *eidōlon* can also signify a ghost or imaginary entity. In Christian usage, *idolatry* has always referred to falsehood, misdirected worship, and religion gone awry.

To delve into the issue of idolatry in the Reformation era – an issue of ultimate concern for Calvin – is to enter the eye of the storm, for the Protestant campaign against Catholic "idols" was not aimed simply against images, relics, and other venerated objects. What was ultimately at stake was the abolition of the complex system of rituals and symbols that encoded the beliefs of the Catholic Church and reified its sacredness, power, and legitimacy.

In 1509, when John Calvin was born, Western Christendom shared a common piety in which the material and spiritual realms were intricately interconnected. Heaven was never far from earth. Supernatural power, reified in the Catholic Church and its sacraments, could be accessed through countless material points of contact: sacred oil, holy water, consecrated hosts, rosaries, medals, images, shrines, and relics, to name but a few. Lighting a candle as one prayed before a statue of the Virgin Mary could intensify the efficacy of one's prayers. A pious glance at an image of St. Christopher in the morning could ensure protection from illness or accidents throughout the day. Burial in a Franciscan friar's habit could improve one's prospects in the afterlife. A pilgrimage to Santiago, in Galicia, where the body of the Apostle James had been deposited by angels, or to Walsingham, in Norfolk, where a vial of milk from the Virgin Mary was venerated, could make a lame man walk, or hasten a soul's release from purgatory. The map of Europe bristled with holy places and sacred spaces crammed with images and relics. Life pulsated with the expectation of the miraculous, and the constant allure of the sacred objects that facilitated them. In the minds of the faithful, and in much of the official teaching of the Catholic Church, physical encounters with the divine were not just possible but also routine. One could even eat the flesh of Christ in a consecrated wafer.

In the late Middle Ages, only a relatively small number of dissenters dared to denounce this intertwining of the natural and supernatural as "idolatry." Aside from the English Lollards and the Bohemian Hussites in the four-teenth and fifteenth centuries – who rejected the veneration of images and relics – the vast majority of Western Europeans embraced a piety that was intensely materialistic, and did so with apparent enthusiasm, as can be gauged by a measurable upswell in the creation of religious art and the building of chapels and shrines throughout the Catholic world, a phenom-enon that has led some historians to speak of "an immense appetite for the divine"[1] at the time of Calvin's birth, or of "an enormous unfolding of religion in daily life."[2]

John Calvin was a mere child when some Protestants began to wage war against idolatry in the early 1520s. At that time, as he put it, he was still trapped in a "profound abyss of mire" and "obstinately devoted to the superstitions of popery."[3] We can only guess at the details of Calvin's religious upbringing because he rarely wrote about it, but in one of his most popular treatises, The Inventory of Relics, he gave the world a glimpse of what he came to despise in the Catholic piety of his native Noyon.

> I remember what I saw them do to images in our parish when I was a small boy. On the eve of the feast of St. Stephen, they would adorn all the images with garlands and necklaces, those of the murderers who stoned him to death . . . in the same fashion as the martyr. When the poor women saw the murderers decked out in this way, they mistook them for Stephen's com-panions, and offered each of them his own candle. Even worse, they did the same with the devil who struggled against St. Michael.[4]

It was precisely this kind of observation of Catholics as the "other"– as deviants vastly different from himself – that allowed Calvin to formulate a theory of the origins of "false" religion and of the difference between such "idolatry" and the "true" religion he believed he was defending. To fully

---

[1] Lucien Febvre, "Une question mal posée: les origines de la Réforme française," *Au coeur religieux du XVI siècle* (Paris: Sevpen, 1957), 1–70.
[2] Johan Huizinga, *The Waning of the Middle Ages* (New York: Doubleday, 1954), 151.
[3] *Commentary on Psalms*, Preface, CO 31.22.
[4] *Inventory of Relics*, CO 6. 452.

understand how and why Calvin became one of the most formidable opponents of Catholic "idolatry," one must first become familiar with the historical
context of his struggle.

Protestant attempts to wipe out idolatry first surfaced in Wittenberg, in
late 1521, while Martin Luther was hiding at the Wartburg castle. The leader
of these assaults was Andreas Bodenstein von Karlstadt, Luther's senior
colleague. As Karlstadt saw it, if Christianity was to be reformed according
to biblical principles – *sola scriptura* – one could not ignore several key texts
that prohibited the veneration of physical objects.[5] Driven by a literal
interpretation of biblical condemnations of idolatry, Karlstadt instigated
some image breaking in Wittenberg. Luther did not agree with Karlstadt,
however, so he came out of hiding in early 1522 and drove his colleague out
of Wittenberg, along with all other iconoclasts (Gk. *eikon* = image + *klastes* =
breaker). Idolatry was no great concern for Luther. As he saw it, religious
images were "neither here nor there, neither evil nor good."[6] He also thought
that it was preferable to "tear images out of the heart through God's Word"
than to remove them from church walls.[7] Although he gradually developed
opposition to the veneration of images, and called for their removal "whenever they are worshiped in an idolatrous manner,"[8] Luther and his followers
would never focus on idolatry as much as Karlstadt or other Protestant
Reformers, especially Calvin.

Karlstadt would continue to oppose idolatry and to influence other early
Protestant Reformers, especially Anabaptists, but his impact would be
limited. The idolophobia inherited by Calvin would not come from him,
but rather from Ulrich Zwingli in Zurich. An admirer of the Dutch humanist
Desiderius Erasmus, who emphasized the supremacy of the Bible and the
superiority of a spiritual piety bereft of physical points of contact with the
divine, Zwingli had been preaching against the veneration of images and
relics since 1519, at least two years before Karlstadt's iconoclasm in Wittenberg. Zwingli's Bible-centered attack on idolatry intensified in 1522, and soon
led to the abolition of religious images and Catholic rituals, not just in
Zurich, but most of northern Switzerland over the next few years. Zwingli's
iconoclastic theology would become a central feature of the Reformed
Protestant tradition founded by him, and also of the young John Calvin
who was exposed to it in Paris.

---

[5] Such as Exodus 20:3–6 and Leviticus 19:4.
[6] *Invocavit Sermons*, LW 51.86.
[7] *Against the Heavenly Prophets*, LW 40.84.
[8] *Invocavit Sermons*, LW 51.86.

At the very heart of Zwingli's theology certain metaphysical assumptions derived from Neoplatonism – largely through Erasmus – gave shape to his idolophobia. The most essential of these was his belief in a sharp and unbridgeable dichotomy between the spiritual and material realms. As Zwingli saw it, matter was an obstacle to be overcome in one's spiritual life, and in religion as a whole because physicality always detracts from spirituality (*Quantum sensui tribueris, tantum spiritui detraxeris*). Moreover, Zwingli was convinced that matter, which was finite, could never convey what was truly spiritual or divine, which was infinite (*finitum non est capax infiniti*).[9]

Calvin would imbibe this theology as a student in Paris, through various individuals who were directly and indirectly influenced by Protestantism from Zwingli's Switzerland rather than from Luther's Wittenberg. Driven from France by persecution, Calvin would end up in Geneva in 1536, shortly after that city had just rid itself of all idols through an iconoclastic riot. What he would do with his idolophobic theology in that independent city state would shape Reformed Protestantism in innumerable ways, not just there, but throughout Western Europe, and even in North America.

Calvin's understanding of idolatry and his opposition to it can be best summarized by subdividing his idolophobia into four interrelated theological components, each of which have drastic and immediate social and political implications.

THE NATURE AND PURPOSE OF WORSHIP

Idolatry is such an important issue for Calvin that he tackles it at the very beginning of the final edition of his *Institutes*. According to him, the purpose of human existence is to know God and to glorify him through worship and obedience. This assumption is the foundation of his attack on idolatry, for, as he sees it, one cannot come to know God without yielding some worship to him.[10] This means that the very purpose of human existence and the destiny of the entire human race is inextricably tied to the need for correct worship, and, conversely, that incorrect worship – idolatry – is an absolute obstacle to the ultimate fulfillment of human existence. Or, as he also puts it, knowledge of "the right way to worship God" was "the whole substance of Christianity."[11]

---

[9] Huldrych Zwingli, *Zwinglis Sämtliche Werke* (Berlin: C. A. Schwetschke und Sohn 1905), 8: 194–195.

[10] *Institutes* I.1.1; I.5.9.

[11] *On the Necessity of Reforming the Church*, CO 6:459.

THE IMPERATIVE FOR SPIRITUAL WORSHIP

Calvin's primary concern in his struggle against Catholic idolatry is defending the glory of a God who is "entirely other" and "as different from flesh as fire is from water."[12] Reduced to a formula this concern became known as Calvin's chief maxim, *Soli Deo Gloria*, or "glory be to God alone."

As Calvin sees it, that glory is wholly spiritual, and the true foundation of correct worship was "to acknowledge God to be as He is,"[13] that is, as far superior to matter. This superiority of the spiritual dimension is at the center of Calvin's idolophobia, for he insists that God is always improperly worshiped in visible material symbols, and that "whatever holds down and confines the senses to the earth is contrary to the covenant of God; in which, inviting us to himself, he permits us to think of nothing but what is spiritual."[14] Calvin repeatedly maintains that God's glory is impugned through the improper mingling of spiritual and material in worship because God's honor is corrupted "by an impious falsehood" whenever any materiality or form is attached to him.[15] In sum, all considerations of God, even the simplest mention of His name, require a correct response: "As often as Scripture asserts that there is one God, it is not contending over the bare name, but also prescribing that nothing belonging to his divinity is to be transferred to another."[16]

THE EFFECT OF ORIGINAL SIN ON RELIGION

For Calvin, human corruption is the root of all idolatry. Although humans have an irresistible natural drive to search for the truth, which includes an inborn sense of the divine (*sensus divinitatis*) and natural bent for religious belief planted in them like a seed (*semen religionis*), that instinct is too warped by original sin to produce good results. In fact, this damage is so severe that instead of bringing humans closer to God, it severs them from Him, turning the *sensus divinitatis* and the *semen religionis* into the fountainhead of idolatry.

All have naturally something of religion born with them, but such is the blindness and stupidity, as well as the weakness of our minds, that our

---

[12] *Institutes* I.5.9; *Commentary on the Gospel of John*, CO 47:90.
[13] *Necessity*, CO 6:440.
[14] *Commentary on the Last Four Books of Moses*, CO 24:376.
[15] *Institutes* I.11.2.
[16] *Institutes* I.12.1.

apprehension of God is immediately depraved. Religion is thus the beginning of all superstitions, not in its own nature, but through the darkness
which has settled down upon the minds of men, and which prevents them
from distinguishing between idols and the true God.[17]

Calvin refines the theology of idolatry that he inherited from his
Reformed Protestant predecessors, including Zwingli, for he shifts the focus
from the ontological inferiority of matter – from the incapacity of the finite
to convey the infinite– to the effects of original sin in human beings. Idolatry
does not result from any insufficiency in matter, he argues, but rather from a
defect in human beings, who always "try to circumscribe God's infinite
essence, or to draw Him down from heaven and to place Him beneath the
elements of the earth."[18] This means, of course, that idolatry is naturally
inescapable for humans, "for each man's mind is like a labyrinth,"[19] and
"every one of us is, even from our mother's womb, a master craftsman of
idols."[20]

This uncontrollable idolatrous urge is what makes the abolition of idols
such a pressing necessity for Calvin. "So innate in us is superstition," he says,
"that the least occasion will infect us with contagion. Dry wood will not so
easily burn when coals are put under it, as idolatry will seize the minds of
men, when the opportunity present itself to them."[21] In other words, once
they are established, idols are irresistible.[22]

THE DANGERS OF IDOLATRY

This power inherent in all idols makes them very perilous, Calvin argues,
because their veneration always elicits divine punishments on earth, both
personal and communal – famine, pestilence, war, and innumerable dire
circumstances. The greater one's exposure to idols, the greater the risk,
Calvin warns, for idolatry does not just pollute the space in which it is
carried out but also the human beings who occupy that space. Consequently,
avoiding all contact with idolatry is necessary. "He alone keeps himself free,"
he said, "who does not even allow himself any faked imitation of idolaters,
but is abstinent to such an extent that he contracts no guilt or stain either by

---

[17] *Commentary on Psalm 97:7*, CO 32:44.
[18] *Commentary Books of Moses*, CO 24:392.
[19] *Institutes* I.5.12.
[20] *Commentary on Acts*, CO 48:562.
[21] *Commentary on 1 John*, CO 55.376.
[22] *On Fleeing the Rites of the Ungodly*, CO 5.253.

look, access, or nearness to idols."[23] The practical implications of such advice are immense, for the avoidance of Catholic piety could only lead to social segregation, constant friction, and the creation of two distinct communities wherever idolatry has not yet been vanquished.

Calvin's reference to "faked imitation of idolaters" offers a very clear glimpse of the social and political context of his idolophobia, for many of his faithful followers lived surrounded by idolatry, in locations where they were not just a minority, but where abstaining from Catholic rituals could result in persecution, even burning at the stake. For many Calvinists in France, especially, pretending to be a good Catholic was necessary for survival. Unlike the Swiss Reformed Protestants who had rid themselves of idolatry once and for all, Calvin's disciples in France and other states were still threatened by it. Idolatry, then, was not simply an abstract theological issue for them, but a matter of life and death.

One of Calvin's lifelong obsessions was the issue of dissembling Protestants who defended their behavior by arguing that physical contact with idolatry was harmless as long as one did not consent to it spiritually. Known as Nicodemites – a reference to the dissembling Nicodemus in the Gospel of John[24] – these dissemblers posed a great challenge to Calvin. They also imperiled the continued expansion of Reformed Protestantism, for their belief in the invulnerability of their inner spiritual life would have made the creation of a Reformed identity and of Reformed churches ultimately unnecessary or superfluous.

Between 1537 and 1562 Calvin published various treatises in which he condemned Nicodemism and all compromise with the "Babylonish pollution"[25] of Catholicism. His advice was not always embraced, as a friend in Paris let him know: "A number of people think your assertions are thoroughly wretched. They accuse you of being merciless and very severe to those who are afflicted and say that it is easy for you to preach and threaten over there [in Geneva], but that if you were here [in France] you would perhaps feel differently."[26]

Calvin's "merciless and severe" position on dissembling was solidly anchored in his theology of worship and his *soli Deo gloria* principle. The key issue is the meaning of worship and of the reverence due to God. All worship involves a transaction, Calvin insists, and that exchange contains an

---

[23] Ibid., 5.265.
[24] John 3:1–3.
[25] *On Fleeing*, CO 5.239.
[26] Letter from Antoine Fumée, CO 11.646.

objective transference of reverence and honor. In the case of correct spiritual worship, God receives the due honor and reverence; in idolatrous worship, however, He never receives it. Whether the worshiper consents to the transaction is irrelevant: to merely be physically present in idolatrous worship – even with disdain – is to offend God and to be polluted by the idolatrous setting. As Calvin puts it, "[T]here is a real kind of idolatry when one performs an external act that is contrary to the true service of God, even if it is done only for deception."[27] Or, as he pointedly asks: "[W]hat kind of religion can that be, which lies submerged under seeming idolatry?"[28]

Calvin's theological objection to dissembling had immense political repercussions, for it instantly turned all his followers into opponents of the Catholic status quo. But what were these recalcitrant Calvinists to do, really, when their rulers outlawed the "true service of God"? Calvin's advice left the faithful with only two difficult choices: exile or martyrdom. Naturally, Calvin saw exile as preferable, and so did thousands of his followers who fled to Reformed Protestant states. Staying put was dangerous and less preferable, but many more Calvinists chose to stay than to flee. The result was the creation of instability in France and other states where dissident Calvinists began to establish their own churches in defiance of the law. Gradually, from the 1540s through the 1560s, Calvinist minorities continued to grow in various states, despite harassment and persecution, and these minorities were aggressively and very visibly opposed to the religious status quo. Calvin's directives called on his followers to observe self-imposed segregation: "Consider it always forbidden to let anyone see you communicating in the sacrilege of the Mass, or uncovering your head before an image, or observing any kind of superstition ... through which the glory of God is obscured, his religion profaned, his truth corrupted."[29] That segregation would lead to the creation of vibrant dissident communities, especially in France, the Netherlands, England, and Scotland. And wherever Calvin's followers eventually assumed control, iconoclasm became a hallmark of their religious fervor.

Calvin refused to offer his followers a third option: resistance to idolatrous rulers. The closest he came to doing so was in the final edition of the *Institutes*, where he alluded to the possibility of resistance obliquely.[30] But some of his followers were less cautious, and even before his death in 1564,

---

[27] *Sermon against Idolatry*, CO 8.380.
[28] Letter to Martin Luther, CO 12.7.
[29] *On Fleeing*, CO 5.274.
[30] *Institutes* IV.20.31.

theories of violent resistance began to emerge and to be applied. In Scotland, for instance, John Knox – who had spent time as a refugee in Geneva – successfully resisted Queen Mary, dismantled the Catholic Church, and obliterated all its "idols." In addition, he argued that all true Christians were obligated to overthrow idolatrous rulers, regardless of their social or political status.[31] Eventually, Calvin's successor Theodore Bèze would counsel resistance too,[32] along with other Calvinist thinkers such as Pierre Viret and Philippe du Plessis-Mornay in France, and Christopher Goodman, John Ponet, and George Buchanan in England. Not surprisingly, one concept that runs through all these theories of resistance, linking them like some bright red thread, is that of idolatry, and more specifically, idolatry as interpreted by Calvin.

Resistance to idolatrous rulers could only lead to violence. France, home to a sizeable Calvinist minority, sank into civil war in 1562, and these Wars of Religion, as they came to be known, carried on until 1598 with unprecedented savagery and overabundant iconoclasm. War broke out in the Low Countries too, in 1566, after Calvinist iconoclasts ransacked hundreds of churches, ridding them of all traces of idolatry. Known as the Eighty-Years' War, that conflict would not be finally settled until 1648. In England, Calvinist opposition to the idolatrous "popery" of the Anglican Church would build momentum and culminate not just in a civil war and widespread iconoclasm but also in the beheading of King Charles I in 1649 and the establishment of a Puritan Commonwealth.

Calvinist idolophobia came to be regarded by Catholics as one of the defining hallmarks of Protestantism as a whole, and one of the most obvious proofs of its wrongfulness. In the early days of the Protestant Reformation, Catholic theologians such as Jerome Emser and John Eck defended the veneration of images and relics, but such texts were aimed at learned audiences rather than wide audiences.[33] The common folk who opposed Protestantism, for the most part, defended images intuitively and viscerally

---

[31] Knox, Letter to the Commonalty of Scotland, in *Selected Writings of John Knox: Public Epistles, Treatises and Expositions to the Year 1559* (Dallas, TX: Presbyterian Heritage Publications, 1558).

[32] Bèze, Théodore de, *Du droit des Magistrats sur leurs subjets : Traitté très-necessaire en ce temps, pour advertir de leur devoir, tant les magistrats que les subjets* (Genève: Jacob Stoerl, 1574).

[33] In 1522 Jerome Emser published "That One Should Not Remove Images of Saints from the Churches," responding directly to Karlstadt, and John Eck joined the attack with his "On Not Removing Images of Christ and the Saints." See *A Reformation Debate: Karlstadt, Emser, and Eck on Sacred Images*, trans. Bryan Mangrum and Giuseppe Scavizzi (Toronto: Centre for Reformation and Renaissance Studies, 1991).

rather than theologically, as essential to their piety and identity. The Council of Trent took up the issue of Protestant idolophobia at its 25th session in December 1563, a mere five months before Calvin's death, issuing a decree on the invocation of saints and the veneration of relics and sacred images, in which everything considered "idolatry" by Calvin was affirmed as good, proper, and necessary for everyone's well-being. Concerning relics, the council's decree had this to say:

> The holy bodies of holy martyrs, and of others now living with Christ ... are to be venerated by the faithful; through which bodies many benefits are bestowed by God on men; so that they who affirm that veneration and honour are not due to the relics of saints; or, that these, and other sacred monuments, are uselessly honored by the faithful; and that the places dedicated to the memories of the saints are in vain visited with the view of obtaining their aid; are wholly to be condemned, as the Church has already long since condemned, and now also condemns them.

Concerning images, Trent's condemnation of Calvinist idolophobia was equally clear and forceful:

> Images of Christ, of the Virgin Mother of God, and of the other saints, are to be had and retained particularly in temples, and due honour and veneration are to be given them; not that any divinity, or virtue, is believed to be in them, on account of which they are to be worshiped; or that anything is to be asked of them; or, that trust is to be reposed in images, as was of old done by the Gentiles who placed their hope in idols.

The sole admission of impropriety on image and relic veneration made by the Council of Trent – and its sole nod to Calvinist complaints – was a terse statement that said: "If any abuses have crept in amongst these holy and salutary observances, the holy Synod ardently desires that they be utterly abolished."[34] So, when all is said and done, after 1563, the materially focused piety regarded as "idolatrous" by Calvin and other Protestants was reinvigorated in Catholicism, not only because it was deemed theologically correct but also because it was acknowledged as an essential component of Catholic identity and a marker of difference vis-à-vis woefully perverse heretics. In the seventeenth century, especially, Baroque Catholic piety would emphasize with great exuberance everything despised by Calvinists.

The creation of two diametrically opposed kinds of Christian piety was the ultimate result of Calvinist idolophobia, and in an age when religion was

---

[34] *Canons and Decrees of the Council of Trent*, trans. H. J. Schroeder (London and St. Louis, MO: B. Herder, 1941), 215–216.

inseparable from every aspect of life, that bifurcation could only cause great turmoil and some measure of grief.

Tucked away precariously in Geneva, resolutely opposed to any compromise with false religion, Calvin waged war against idolatry forcefully until his dying day by writing against it, and by creating dissenting minorities and undermining the stability of various states that supported it. In the long run, his idolophobia, which was thoroughly theological, proved to be as thoroughly political, and its legacy as weighty and significant as all the hammers wielded in iconoclastic riots and as the axe that beheaded King Charles I.

SUGGESTED FURTHER READINGS

Benedict, Philip. *Christ's Churches Purely Reformed: A Social History of Calvinism.* New Haven, CT: Yale University Press, 2004.

Crew, Phyllis Mack. *Calvinist Preaching and Iconoclasm in the Netherlands, 1544–1569.* New York: Cambridge University Press, 1978.

Elwood, Christopher. *The Body Broken: The Calvinist Doctrine of the Eucharist and the Symbolization of Power.* Oxford: Oxford University Press, 1998.

Mochizuki, Mia. *The Netherlandish Image after Iconoclasm, 1566–1672 : Material Religion in the Dutch Golden Age.* Burlington, VT: Ashgate, 2008.

Zachman, Randall C. *Image and Word in the Theology of John Calvin.* Notre Dame, IN: University of Notre Dame, 2009.

Trinitarian Controversies

Rebecca Giselbrecht

Sixteenth-century Protestant reformers did not reinvent the Trinity; most preserved the medieval understanding of the doctrine of God, which the church agreed upon at the First Council of Nicaea in 325 and revised at the Council of Constantinople in 381. The remarkable continuity of the medieval consubstantial Trinity during the Reformation became increasingly relevant to framing standard Reformed theology as certain minds began to fancy antitrinitarianism. The consensus among the magisterial reformers was that sixteenth-century nonconformist "heretics" endangered traditional Christology and therefore the traditional Christian doctrine of God. At the inception of Protestant dogma, reforming theologians were forced to assess an old question of the utmost relevance to the church: If Christ is not human and divine – what is Christianity? Thus, putting the relation of God, the Son, and the Holy Spirit into words from a scriptural perspective occupied the reformers as it had the early church fathers. The early reformers who revisited church doctrine should have enjoyed a period of trial and error. However, in the broader Reformation context, the sixteenth-century characters, who pushed the orthodox envelope beyond tradition, had by the mid-sixteenth century compelled the reformers to exacting linguistic precision, which subsequently became a distinctive trait of Reformed theology.

NORMATIVE IDEALS OF THE TRINITY

Repetitive antitrinitarian attacks obliged the church to formulate and contextualize an orthodox doctrine of the Trinity. The third-century antitrinitarian Sabellian or Modalist heresy maintained the Father, the Son, and the Holy Spirit are different modes in which the one God reveals God self, a claim that disputes that three distinct persons unite in one eternal nature. In the fourth-century Arian Controversy, Arius (d. 336) rejected the sanctioned doctrine of the Trinity when he claimed the Son of God to be subordinate to God the Father. The church universal replied with the Nicene Creed, which preserved a concise and authoritative ecumenical doctrine of the Triune God – a source of contention throughout the Reformation and in ecumenical discourse to this day.

Each word of the Creed matters. *Homoousios*, for example, was prudently chosen; it means "of one substance with" and was essential to the doctrine of the Son. *Homoousios* underscores the sameness of the Father and the Son. Accepting this word was binding for the confession of faith required to belong to the universal church. Then, "the Son who *proceeds* from the Father" were words ascribed to name the correspondence between the Father and the Son. Thus, the word *filioque* (and from the Son), which was supposed to add precision and address heresy, became part of the Nicene-Constantinopolitan Creed of 381. A later addendum to the Nicene Creed in reply to another Arian heresy appeared first in sixth-century Spain: the Holy Spirit must proceed from the co-equal Father and Son. These are the sections of the Nicene Constantinopolitan Creed relevant to many of the sixteenth-century trinitarian controversies (changes from the Creed of 325 are in italic):

> We believe in one God ... And in one Lord Jesus Christ, ... begotten, not made, being of one substance with the Father; by whom all things were made; ... And in the Holy Ghost, *the Lord and Giver of life, who proceeds from the Father [and the Son], who with the Father and the Son together is worshiped and glorified.*

Despite a plethora of reformed catechisms and confessions of faith, the Nicene Creed continued to be the standard for normative trinitarian ideals for the Roman Church as well as the Magisterial Reformers throughout the sixteenth century. This commonly accepted basis lent a certain continuity to Western Christianity as such.

INTERPRETING SCRIPTURE

The humanist revolution that began in the fourteenth century revived the discourse around faith, and Johannes Gutenberg's printing press (1440) opened a public avenue for publishing the new ideas. The sixteenth-century religious reforms that followed caused contention within the church body, which was to be expected considering that an established universal religious system, its ideology, traditions, legal authority, and especially its source of authority were under review. Ergo, the reformers' writings and their responses to dissent were subject to scrutiny from without *and* within. The scriptural principle – *sola scriptura* – lent scripture the authority to interpret scripture; and scripture became the plumb line to resolve issues of polity and right doctrine including doctrinal controversies. *Ad fonte* (back to the source) lent verve to scholarship in *original* language texts. However, the Hebrew and Greek codices for translating the Bible were not all the same. Erasmus of Rotterdam (1466–1536), the sixteenth-century humanist scholar, was among the first to be entangled in the endless series of trinitarian controversies rekindled by the Reformation.

Erasmus observed that the *Johannine Comma* was not in 1 John 5:7–8 in the manuscripts that were available to him in Basel.[1] This type of *comma* is not a matter of punctuation but refers to a cluster of words in a scriptural text, in this case, inserted in the middle of the sentence.[2] Erasmus found traditional trinitarian words missing in the six Greek codices he had access to for translating. What had traditionally read: "For there are three that witness in heaven, the Father, the Word, and the Holy Spirit, and these three are one," he rendered what he found according to the scriptural principle: "And there are three that bear witness on the earth, the spirit and the water and the blood, and these three are one."[3] Edward Lee (1482–1544) and Diego Lopez de Ayala (1480–1560), among others, were outraged that Erasmus failed to include the indispensable explicit formulation of the doctrine of the Trinity in his *Novum Instrumentum*. After that, accused by his peers of Arianism, Erasmus went to great lengths in his 1519 edition, *Novum Testamentum*, to assure his colleagues and the church authorities that he was loyal to the trinitarian tradition. Still suffering unrelenting pressure in 1521, he then translated 1 John 5:7–8 from the Vulgate with the *comma* and provided annotations regarding the missing *comma*.

Calvin concurred with Erasmus's exclusion of the *comma* but included it nevertheless in both his 1551 French Bible translation and commentary on the Catholic Epistles; like Erasmus, he added a marginal comment noting the missing *comma* in earlier texts.

---

[1] For a lively history of the Johannine Comma, see David M. Whitford, "Yielding to the Prejudices of His Time: Erasmus and the Comma Johanneum," *Church History and Religious Culture* 95 (2015): 19–40.

[2] See Grantly McDonald, *Biblical Criticism in Early Modern Europe: Erasmus, the Johannine Comma and Trinitarian Debate* (Cambridge: Cambridge University Press, 2016), 71–86.

[3] Whitford, *Yielding to the Prejudices*, 24.

TRINITARIAN WORDS

Early reformers tended to sidestep creedal language for several good reasons. First, words beyond scripture that describe God are merely symbols and metaphors for an unspeakable God. Then, the understanding that scriptural authority trumps tradition had, in fact, unraveled the church universal beyond the comfort of many. Thus, the reforming theologians became acutely sensitive to words like *filioque*, which they knew had caused seemingly irreparable injury to the unity of the Eastern and Western churches after 1054. Although the second-generation codifying reformers had reason to avoid normative medieval trinitarian language, they were of one mind in support of traditional trinitarian principles.[4] Scriptural emphasis and reducing technical word usage were aspects of the early Reformation methodological choices, as were avoiding scholasticism and extrabiblical God talk. There was no doubt in anyone's mind that the traditionary term *Trinity* was not in the Bible. Moreover, the Reformation aspired to be a people's movement promoting the priesthood of all believers, which meant writing in the vernacular in accessible language and preaching in a way that was useful for the certainty of salvation for the many; whereby, philosophical language was considered counterproductive.

In 1521, Luther set the tone for reformed trinitarian discourse and heralded the trinitarian controversy to come when he wrote in *Against Latomus*: "What if my soul hates the word *homoousion*, and I do not wish to use it, I will not be a heretic" (LW 32:24).[5] Calvin felt the same, "I would that the words themselves were buried, provided that this faith were universally established: that Father and Son are one God, and yet neither is the Son the Father, nor the Spirit the Son, but that they are distinguished by a certain property" (Inst., 1.13.5). The two prophet's wishes did not materialize.

Sola scriptura was the focus of reformed teaching; albeit, by 1540 the second-generation magisterial reformers were forced by the many trinitarian controversies to reach for traditional dogmatic language.[6] Logical deduction and philosophy were merely second to scripture, yet the *loci* that they argued came from scripture within the centuries-old tradition. An entire list of reformers including Luther, Calvin, Bullinger, and Melanchthon willingly

---

[4] For a comprehensive overview of the Reformed trinitarian doctrine see Richard A. Muller, *Post-Reformation Reformed Dogmatics: The Rise and Development of Reformed Orthodoxy.* Vol. 4: *The Triunity of God* (Grand Rapids, MI: Baker Academic, 2003), 72–83.
[5] See Gary W. Jenkins, *Calvin's Tormentors: Understanding the Conflicts That Shaped the Reformer* (Grand Rapids, MI: Baker Academic, 2018), 17–18.
[6] Muller, *Post-Reformation Reformed Dogmatics*, 60.

adopted increasing universal terminology rather than experiment because the embittered antitrinitarian attacks and polemic were going beyond the orthodoxy of the creedal baselines set in tradition, which they had come to realize were nonnegotiable elements of the Christian faith. The words *ousia*, *hypostaseis*, one substance, person, and three *subsistences* in one substance began to pepper their works and epistles by the early 1540s. The second-generation Zurich reformer, Heinrich Bullinger (1504–1575), already proclaimed normative trinitarian doctrinal language in his sermons, the *Decades* – something that must have been mysterious to his congregation. Muller reports, "Bullinger did not hesitate to present the standard language of patristic and medieval orthodoxy – namely distinction of persons without the division of the essence and the coequality, consubstantiality, and coeternity of the persons."[7] Bullinger also referred to the *filioque* and traces of the Athanasian Creed and its trinitarian wording in his Second Helvetic Confession.[8]

The exegesis and hermeneutical rigor of the magisterial reformers eventually marched in lockstep with both the ontological and epistemological traditions of the medieval and early church. First, because the resistance and bitter opposition were divisive to the Protestant camps and, second, because the initial creative reformed thinking required orthodoxy to standardize the system of belief.

SIXTEENTH-CENTURY TRINITARIAN CONTROVERSIES

The medieval notions of either removing or punishing heretics were traditions of the church that sixteenth-century morality inherited. The legal mores of the past may explain why the freedom individuals took to think and act in the new social order, power structures, and the malleable contours of early modern religious authority were more than some were able to tolerate. Strictly speaking, heresy is a belief or opinion contrary to orthodox religious doctrine, and the Roman Church considered everyone who embraced the sixteenth-century Reformation heretical enemies of the church. The reforming church did not get much time to configure a strategy to consolidate orthodoxy or address extremes before different and radical conceptions engulfed the church.

The young Calvin's first brief encounter with heresy forebode how it would continue to plague his ministry. It was early in the Reformation

---

[7] Ibid., 82–83.
[8] Ibid., 82.

during the *Affaire des Placards* when anti-Catholic posters were nailed up around Blois, Rouen, Tours, Orléans, and Paris. King Francis I was highly displeased at the polemic against the Mass and in support of Zwingli's Eucharist that so-called heretics attached to the king's bedroom door. Calvin was in Paris and engaged in humanism at the time and felt compelled to quickly flee to Basel before he could be labeled a heretic or punished. Little did he know that the first "friend" Calvin knew as a refugee in Basel, Pierre Caroli, would later accuse him of being a heretic.[9]

Calvin's first public accusers were two pastors, Chapponeau and Courtois of Neuchâtel; these colleagues claimed Calvin did not afford the Trinity due respect because he failed to use *enough* trinitarian words in his first *Institutes* of 1536. Also in 1536, Pierre Caroli, now pastor to Lausanne, accused the Genevan pastors, Calvin, Guillaume Farel (1489–1565), and Pierre Viret (1511–1571) of antitrinitarianism. Caroli claimed that the confession of faith Calvin presented to the Council at Bern on November 10, 1536, was marked by Arian and Sabellian heresy.[10] Farel, Viret, and Calvin were found innocent, and Caroli fled Bern.

Later in August 1537, Calvin and Farel felt the need to confess their faith in a Triune God and the Nicene word *person* and make this clear in a published treatise: *Confessio de Trinitate propter Calumnias P. Caroli*, 1537 (CO 5:703–10). There were more rumblings when Calvin refused to sign the Athanasian Creed at the Synod of Lausanne in 1537. Calvin's reply to his provocateurs was to reword the introduction to his 1537 and 1538 catechism; following Erasmus's example, he did not add any trinitarian language to the catechism.

Calvin must have grown impatient with the accusations of heresy being hurled at him. In January 1546, Pierre Ameaux of Geneva accused him of false doctrine claiming Calvin denied any real distinction between the Persons in God even labeling the Genevan a Sabellian heretic. Calvin finally responded with an increased focus on Trinity and its visibility in his works and debates, as was the case with his reforming peers.[11] More difficult to navigate than assaults on reformed theology, however, were the antitrinitarian controversies brewing throughout Europe. The Italian, Polish, and Anabaptist heretics were particularly unsettling.

---

[9] Jenkins, *Calvin's Tormentors*, 20.
[10] See "Calvin" in Diarmaid MacCulloch, *All Things Made New: Writings on the Reformation* (Oxford: Allen Lane Penguin, 2016), 55–69.
[11] William E. Addis and Thomas Arnold, *A Catholic Dictionary* (New York: The Catholic Publication Society Co., 1887), 730.

Between 1548 and 1555, Farges Giorgio Blandrata, Valentius Gentile, and
Giorgio Paul Alciati, who were members of the Italian refugee congregation
in Geneva, were influenced by the writings of Servetus and Matteo Gribaldi.
Matteo Gibraldi contended that the Trinity is three people with God as the
supreme among these. The Genevan Council was concerned and asked
the entire Italian congregation to sign a confession of faith that included the
Trinity in 1558. Valentius Gentile insisted that the begetting of the Son and the
procession of the Spirit amount to a radical subordination of the second and
third persons, with the result that the Father alone is God: "The Father is a
unique essence ... the Father is the only true God; it is he who gives his
essence to the other persons of the Divinity."[12] The Italian heretics were put on
trial and exiled from Geneva. Calvin responded with *Impietas Valentini
Gentilis detecta* in 1559; Gentile was executed for his tritheism heresy in Bern
in 1566. Meanwhile the exiles of other heretics were brewing around the same
time in Zurich, but these were on another reformer's conscience.

The Radical Reformation was a seedbed for antitrinitarian theology as the
Anabaptist, Spiritistic, and free-thinking religious ideologies grew more
biblistic. These groups tended to disregard tradition and the ecumenical
councils. Petrus Gonesius (ca. 1530–1571), for example, authored the first
antitrinitarian confession in Poland arguing an almost Arian perspective. He
argued scripture teaches the oneness of God – and that God created his son;
the son was created but not from nothing. Gonesius and Fausto Socinus
(1539–1604) eventually provided the Polish group with unpublished manuscripts of Laelius Socinus (1525–1562), which, in turn, furthered the Radical
Italian Reformation. Bullinger gave Laelius Socinus refuge from Calvin in
Zurich. Socinus fared better than Bernardino Ochino (1487–1564), who was
banished from Zurich for his satirical writings on polygamy, divorce, and the
Trinity, which Bullinger considered heretical. Ochino died in Moravia exiled
from tolerant Poland. The Polish Unitarians propagated a hybrid religious
direction and, as Calvin saw it, heretical antitrinitarian theology. Antitrinitarians read scripture, but the various threads of their antitrinitarianism
embraced the logical fallacy of words – that the Trinity is not scriptural.

CONTINUED CONTROVERSY

Trinitarian controversy is inherent to the church because God and salvation
are beyond words. Calvin wrote, "What we think about him of ourselves is

[12] J. Gaberel, *Histoire de l'Église de Génève depuis le commencement de la Reformation jusqu'a
nos jours*, 3 vols. (Geneva: J. Cherbuliez, 1858–1862), II: 227.

but foolishness and all we can say about him is without savour" (Inst., I.13.2). Nicaea achieved an ecumenical agreement on how to talk about God, but theologians continued to challenge the consensus as their contexts changed throughout the Middle Ages. Trinitarian controversy finally divided the church universal into an Eastern and Western Christian church. The sixteenth-century Magisterial Reformers continued in the same trinitarian understanding as stated in the Nicene Creed but relied on the scriptural principle while trying not to ask random scholastic questions. One of the many ironies of Calvin's context was that he was already caught up in heresies and criticism before he got to Geneva; change left him little time to completely articulate his doctrine of God before he was confronted with heresies. Calvin stressed his trinitarian intentionality in the *Institutes* of 1536 (Inst., II.7; II.8). His trinitarian position did not change; on the contrary, it can be argued that the Trinity was the central *locus* for Calvin's thought.[13] Calvin was preoccupied with the same web of controversies that have always agitated the church. Yet, he upheld the orthodox position on the Trinity, "That is the true knowledge of God which we may have when we contemplate him in Christ the incarnate Word as in a mirror, for it is in and through his Spirit that God has revealed to us what he is like in himself" (Inst., 3.2.6,14).

SUGGESTED FURTHER READINGS

Butin, Philip Walker. *Revelation, Redemption, and Response: Calvin's Trinitarian Understanding of the Divine-Human Relationship.* Oxford: Oxford University Press, 1995.

Ellis, Brannon. *Calvin, Classical Trinitarianism, and the Aseity of the Son.* Oxford: Oxford University Press, 2012.

Gordon, Bruce. *Calvin.* New Haven, CT: Yale University Press, 2009.

Jenkins, Gary W. *Calvin's Tormentors: Understanding the Conflicts That Shaped the Reformer.* Grand Rapids, MI: Baker Academic, 2018.

McDonald, Grantly. *Biblical Criticism in Early Modern Europe: Erasmus, the Johannine Comma and Trinitarian Debate.* Cambridge: Cambridge University Press, 2016.

Muller, Richard A. *Post-Reformation Reformed Dogmatics: The Rise and Development of Reformed Orthodoxy.* Vol. 4: *The Triunity of God.* Grand Rapids, MI: Baker Academic, 2003.

---

[13] See Philip Walker Butin, *Revelation, Redemption, and Response: Calvin's Trinitarian Understanding of the Divine-Human Relationship* (Oxford: Oxford University Press, 1995).

Nijenhuis, Willem. "Calvin's Attitude towards the Symbols of the Early Church during the Conflict with Caroli." In *Ecclesia Reformata: Studies on the Reformation*. Leiden, The Netherlands: Brill, 1972.

Torrance, Thomas F. "Calvin's Doctrine of the Trinity," *Calvin Theological Journal* 25:2 (1990): 165–193.

Whitford, David M. "Yielding to the Prejudices of His Time: Erasmus and the Comma Johanneum," *Church History and Religious Culture* 95 (2015): 19–40.

33

❧

Nicodemism and Libertinism

Kenneth J. Woo

When Nicodemus approached Jesus under cover of night (John 3), he did so to keep from being seen with someone accused of taking liberties with Jewish tradition and morality. Both Nicodemus's strategy and the associations he sought to avoid took on new forms in early modern Europe. Nicodemism was the practice of hiding one's beliefs, usually to evade persecution. Libertinism included various forms of ethical indifference. Nicodemism and libertinism in the Reformation era are best understood in relation to the period's profound cultural changes. A proliferation of new religious confessions in early modern Europe put many believers at odds with their communities. The resulting fluidity of religious identity meant that what one practiced did not always correspond with what one believed. More urgently, landing on the wrong side of belief could have disastrous, even deadly, consequences. The stakes were high at a time when religious pluralism was widely viewed as impurity that put a society under threat of divine judgment. Borders dividing mainstream from deviant religion could change quickly, so that a person found herself having to either prove she belonged or hide that she did not. Widespread persecution forced migration and exile upon those who could no longer worship according to their beliefs. Yet not everyone had the luxury of leaving for friendlier environs. Traditions of martyrdom and accusations of crypto-religion emerged within Catholic, Protestant, and radically reformed communities alike.

Against the backdrop of such religious change, the threats of Nicodemism and libertinism come into focus amid fresh concerns to regulate social and religious boundaries by clearly distinguishing insiders from outsiders, believers from heretics, the social body from its diseases. Various forms of polemical literature populated society's margins with conceptions of "the other" – dangerous outsiders – that served as a foil for reinforcing a community's ideological purity vis-à-vis examples of corruption. That such threats could exist in the shared space of daily commerce and political structures, even religious worship, made them especially insidious. The "Nicodemite" and the "libertine" appeared as examples of "the other" in diverse contexts – pejorative terms applied freely to one's enemies, real or imagined. For these reasons and others, unveiling and illumining the shape and character of Nicodemism and libertinism is not a straightforward task. Both are known chiefly through the definitions of their critics. In some cases, they were conflated, with moral indifference said to promote religious dissimulation. More generally, historians must rely – often entirely – on biased accounts of offenses rarely conceded by the accused. In the case of Nicodemism, as the epithet suggests, the accused were intrinsically unknown. Yet the charges stuck. Despite their elusiveness to contemporaries and historians alike, Nicodemites and libertines exerted influence beyond their visibility to shape religious identity in early modern Europe.

NICODEMISM

Religious dissimulation was a problem that crossed confessional and geographical lines during the Reformation. While he was not the first to address this issue, Calvin helped name it. The term "Nicodemites" (*les Nicodémites*) first appears in the reformer's *Answer to the Nicodemites* (1544), where he attributes its coinage to evangelicals who appealed to the biblical Nicodemus to justify hiding among Catholics. For Protestant writers, the controversy centered on idolatry, specifically the Roman Eucharist at the heart of the Catholic Mass. They called on believers to reject such idolatrous rites in either of two ways: (1) refuse to participate, whatever the cost, with martyrdom a possible outcome; or (2) embrace exile by fleeing one's homeland to a place where one could worship God rightly. No other faithful options existed. Those who pressed this message included the Italian reformers Pier Paolo Vergerio and Peter Martyr Vermigli, the Frenchmen Guillaume Farel and John Calvin, and the Strasbourg reformer Wolfgang Musculus, who fled Augsburg for Bern after the 1548 Interim. Musculus's *Proscaerus* (1549) is a series of dialogues challenging what he and other reformers portrayed as a typical Nicodemite argument. The "Temporizer" conforms to changing times to avoid persecution, citing biblical examples such as Naaman the Syrian (2 Kings 5) and Nicodemus to argue that true faith can exist in one's heart regardless of one's external actions. Musculus's protagonist, "Eusebius," rejects this logic, insisting that genuine faith requires outward confession – a standard contention across evangelical anti-Nicodemite literature. Written in response to reports of Nicodemism at Augsburg, *Proscaerus* was translated into French and English (as the *Temporysour*) in 1555.

Sixteenth-century English audiences also encountered the wider European controversy over dissimulation in translations of Vermigli, Calvin, Heinrich Bullinger, and Pierre Viret. The wide reach of their anti-Nicodemite writings, adapted to new situations, attests to an international concern. Time and again, Protestants tempted to hide their true convictions were called to decide between serving God and human fear. These theologians argued that faithfulness required resistance or flight; pretending was never acceptable.

The prevalence of religious persecution in the experience of Reformed Protestants contributed to the urgency of addressing dissimulation. It was a necessity for believers seeking guidance for faithful practice in hostile environments. Yet the Reformed were neither alone nor united in their position on Nicodemism. Antoine Fumée, Calvin's friend in Paris, sided with those accusing the reformer of being too harsh toward Nicodemism from the safety of Geneva. Among Lutherans, Martin Luther's call for patience with reforming liturgical practices, as an expression of confidence in God's Word and love of one's neighbor, was influential (LW 51:69–100; WA 10.3:1–64). Yet, none other than Philip Melanchthon joined Reformed theologians who added their endorsements to a 1546 reprint of Calvin's writings against Nicodemism. Another Lutheran, Johann Wigand (d. 1587), wrote a book, *Neutrals and Mediators* (1552), echoing others' calls to constant, open confession of one's faith. Dutch spiritualists such as Dirck Coornhert (d. 1590) and David Joris (d. 1556) defended Nicodemism against its detractors, advocating for the priority of inward spirituality. For these writers, religious practices were certainly not worth dying over. Sects such as the Family of Love, founded by the mystic Hendrik Niclaes (d. 1570), gained notoriety for allegedly practicing Nicodemism, conforming indiscriminately to civil and ecclesial powers as a matter of principle and strategy for survival.

What began as a debate among reformers on the European Continent also surfaced in England. Anti-Nicodemite polemical works multiplied during the regimes of Mary I and Elizabeth I, the former witnessing a steady flow of such writings from underground and overseas presses. Marian exiles characterized Nicodemism in ways that evoked Continental Reformed critiques of closeted evangelicals, but also as a quintessentially Catholic defect. They accused leaders of the newly reimposed English Catholicism of biding time as Nicodemites under King Edward VI. Far fewer English Protestants, such as John Cheke (d. 1557), took a more moderate stance, calling for patient conformity in the face of idolatry. In Elizabethan England, Puritan authors used anti-Nicodemite rhetoric to attack moderates in the same church, while Catholic polemicists used it against "church papists" who conformed to English Protestantism.

This cross-confessional perspective on dissimulation reflects the broader horizons of Nicodemism, not only in early modern Europe but also in the late medieval period. Even before divergent Christian confessions arose in the German and Swiss reformations, persecution, forced conversions, and expulsions of thousands of Jews and Muslims from the Iberian Peninsula in the fifteenth-century contributed to the prevalence of crypto-religion among the *Converso* and *Morisco* communities, as well as to religious pluralism abroad. Indelible ethnic and cultural differences meant that even perfect confessional conformity fell short of the invisibility enjoyed by Christian Nicodemites, who were generally indistinguishable from their neighbors. Within Christianity, centuries-old strategies of dissembling religion to evade authorities, including the Inquisition, persisted among Lollards in England and Waldensians in the Alpine regions.

The possibility – even likelihood – of Nicodemism in any given setting framed by the realities and risks of religious pluralism in sixteenth-century Europe suggests that it was a reflexive response to fear of persecution. This underscores the difficulty of identifying any specific groups or individuals, much less any sort of coordinated organization between them. Nicodemites had many faces. Calvin's critique focused on the French context, wherein the reformer envisioned dissemblers throughout society – from clergy to commoners – all of whom shared a common defect: fear of human power and eagerness to avoid hardship (CO 6:597–602). Other groups had Nicodemite-like tendencies, including the "followers of Lucian," Epicureans, so-called Neutrals, and libertines. Each of these invited Calvin's scorn for espousing religion without commitment. Nicodemites were different: they were committed evangelicals who hid their faith out of fear, despite knowing that this displeased God. As a reaction to persecution, Nicodemism likely was pervasive, present in virtually every early modern European society to an extent we will never know. Even at the highest levels of government in Catholic France, for example, suspicions remained that large numbers of Protestant sympathizers, if not actual Nicodemites, sat among the magistrates in the Parlement of Paris – at least 20 percent of whom conveniently avoided a compulsory reaffirmation of Catholic faith in 1562.[1] Yet, despite the confident assertions of their adversaries, Nicodemites who succeeded in hiding left no trace.

Finally, two groups frequently associated with Nicodemism should be distinguished from the invisible phenomenon described in the preceding

---

[1] Mack P. Holt, *The French Wars of Religion*, 2nd ed. (Cambridge: Cambridge University Press, 2005), 41.

text. First, principled conformists held progressive beliefs alongside old practices without difficulty. These included French Catholics with evangelical sympathies who felt no tension in remaining firmly ensconced in the old church. The humanists that gathered at Meaux under Bishop Guillaume Briçonnet (d. 1534) provoked Calvin's anti-Nicodemite censure and perhaps influenced dissemblers. Yet there is no evidence that such reform-minded individuals, including Gérard Roussel and Jacques Lefèvre d'Étaples, hid convictions out of fear. Amid porous religious divisions in the early decades of reform in France, the Meaux Circle and evangelical groups flourished with support from the Queen of Navarre. Others, such as François Baudouin (d. 1573), openly sought rapprochement between Rome and the reformers. Calvin accused him of Nicodemite-like behavior for trying to harmonize incompatible religions. Rather than hide, such individuals disputed the reformers publicly, reversing the charge to paint doctrinaire inflexibility as the real idolatry. Second, there were those whose ideals deemphasized external forms of religion. These included Coornhert, whose defense of Nicodemism Calvin refuted in 1562 with a *Letter to a Certain Dutchman*. Other spiritualists espoused beliefs more properly categorized under varieties of libertinism. To these we now turn.

LIBERTINISM

Like Nicodemism, libertinism was a diverse category portrayed largely by its enemies. It, too, was nothing new. Antinomianism, as the rejection of moral norms, is arguably as ancient as humanity. In the Reformation era, libertinism did not fit neatly on either side of the divide between Catholics and Protestants that hardened in the 1530s. Some libertines remained within Catholicism, others aligned with emerging magisterial Protestant movements, while many espoused varieties of so-called Anabaptism and spiritualism associated with radical reform. Such confessional indifference is exemplified in the case of Anton Engelbrecht (d. 1558), the Strasbourg pastor denounced by Bucer as an "Epicurean" who pursued pleasure unscrupulously because Engelbrecht claimed that civil regulation of religion impeded faith. Engelbrecht eventually returned to the Catholic Church, though his views on the priority of personal, inward religion bore many similarities to those of spiritualists such as Sebastian Franck (d. 1543) and Caspar Schwenckfeld (d. 1561), both of whom also lived in Strasbourg for a time. Broadly speaking, spiritualism privileged the direct guidance of God's spirit over objective, external criteria, including scripture. Within the constellation of early modern spiritualists was a group known by detractors as "libertines," though they preferred to be called "spirituals." This loosely connected spiritual libertine movement with origins in the Low Countries provoked responses from both Catholics and Protestants, and should be distinguished from another kind of libertinism that arose largely as a response to political and personal conflicts in Calvin's Geneva.

Bearing similarities to the medieval Brethren of the Free Spirit and the followers of Eligius Pruystinck (d. 1544) who clashed with Luther, a new form of spiritual libertinism descended from the teaching of a certain Coppin, who was a preacher at Lille in the 1520s. Men such as Claude Perceval, Bertrand des Moulins, Quintin Thiery, and Antoine Pocquet spread libertine ideals across the Low Countries and into France. To the irritation of the Swiss reformers, the ecumenically minded Bucer welcomed these libertines in Strasbourg. While remaining in the Catholic Church and enjoying the support of Marguerite de Navarre, Thiery and Pocquet gained thousands of followers through their writings. Also known as "Quintinists," these "spirituals" embraced an extreme form of predestination rooted in pantheism. According to this teaching, a single divine spirit inhabits all things to bring about its purposes. There are striking similarities between ancient Gnostic views and the libertine insistence that spiritual regeneration is reintegration with the divine spirit – a return to innocence – such that the spirit directs a person's will immediately and infallibly. This, in turn, gives rise to a strict determinism: human actions follow divine prerogative in such a way that free will is but an illusion, an example of what libertines called *cuider* (imagination).

Cuider functions as a technical category applied broadly to human experience of reality. Christ's resurrection is not literal, but rather illustrates the pattern of regeneration experienced by all, in whom the "old man" dies and the perfected innocence of the spirit's making comes to reside. For the renewed, only the illusion of imperfection remains: *cuider* for those who are in fact already one with the spirit, and thus cannot wander from God's will. Traditional beliefs in the devil and demons, evil and sin, were for spiritual libertines nothing more than figments of the imagination. Such *cuider* should not trouble those whose steps are directed by God. Human responsibility vanishes when perceived distinctions between good and evil have no basis in reality. Guilt is an illusion. Immorality cannot apply to perfection. Spiritual libertinism rendered ethical questions irrelevant, the stuff of *cuider*. The regenerate can do no wrong.

Unsurprisingly, Protestants and Catholics alike condemned such beliefs. Reformers such as Farel, Viret, and Calvin attempted to expose and refute a movement they accused of spreading confusion across Europe. In early 1545,

Catholic authorities at Tournai executed Pierre Brully, pastor of the French congregation at Strasbourg, conflating his Protestant faith with elements of spiritual libertinism. Thus libertinism threatened evangelicals with both doctrinal corruption and guilt by association. While the earliest libertines were Christians, the relationship between libertinism and later spiritualist movements hostile to Christian belief is difficult to determine. This is due in part to the diversity within spiritualism, which included groups often having little else in common than a commitment to the priority of subjective experience. Indeed, simply to speak of distinctive groups runs the risk of overstating unity and coordination within and between sects and movements. In their writings against spiritual libertinism, Calvin, Farel, and Viret portray distinctive characteristics that were varied enough in their origins and influence to defy identifying adherents with precision. A further complication is the lack of libertine sources. We possess the writings of Thiery and Pocquet only in the works of their critics, such as Calvin's 1545 treatise *Against the Raving and Fantastical Sect of Libertines, Who Are Called "Spirituals"* (COR IV.1:43–171) and Farel's *Sword of the True Word* (1550), both of which contain lengthy quotations of the libertine sources they refute. Thus, historians must depend on secondhand testimonies to recreate the ideas and activities of individuals and communities about whom we know little more.

Another brand of libertinism captured Calvin's attention closer to home, asserting freedom for reasons more political than philosophical. The Frenchman equated these with a baser kind of intemperance and moral unrestraint. But the truth is less one-sided. With roots in the struggle for Genevan independence from Savoy that predate Calvin's arrival, this group of prominent citizens known as "patriots" or "the children of Geneva" (*les enfants de Genève*) came to be dismissed by Calvin as simply "libertines." Although instrumental in bringing Calvin back to Geneva after his brief exile (1538–1541), these libertines turned against the reformer and the city's predominantly French-immigrant clergy, who came to represent a new form of foreign oppression. Known also as Perrinists after their leader Ami Perrin, whose fondness for fine clothes and dancing offended clerical sensibilities, the Genevan libertines included other distinguished families, such as the Favres and Vandels. Understandably irked by practices such as the ministerial penchant for publicly rebuking prominent citizens from the pulpit or substituting biblical names for children at the moment of their baptism, libertines responded by challenging clergy and disrupting worship services. Philip Berthelier, for instance, resorted to conspicuous flatulence after Calvin objected to coughing during sermons. Campaigns against individuals provoked considerable backlash. Popular opinion was divided in a city undergoing dramatic shifts in demographics that disrupted balances in political power. Immigrants, many fleeing religious persecution, poured into Geneva from across Europe in the 1540s and 1550s, essentially doubling the city's population over the course of a decade. Such migration destabilized society across all strata, redrawing cultural and ideological boundaries between the mainstream and the margins, producing considerable social volatility.

Reaction to perceived overreach on the part of Geneva's pastors was swift and intense. In 1552, Genevans elected a number of Perrinists to significant positions, sending a clear message to the clergy that left Calvin convinced of his imminent dismissal. This would not happen. In 1555, a series of ill-conceived demonstrations shifted public favor toward the clergy, who seized the opportunity to consolidate power through formal proceedings against their adversaries. The subsequent banishing of Ami Perrin and other libertine leaders effectively ended their movement. While taking care to distinguish this nativist response to reform in Geneva from the spiritual libertinism previously described, one should nevertheless avoid constructing artificial barriers between libertinism as political activism and libertinism as philosophical commitment. The case of Jacques Gruet, for instance, blurs these divisions. The Genevan libertine, beheaded in 1547, was a cobelligerent of the Perrinists who simultaneously embraced anti-Christian views discovered only after his death.

CONCLUSION

So-called Nicodemites and libertines are two of the easier names to recognize among Calvin's numerous polemical opponents, as well as two of the most difficult groups to identify. Despite sharing certain traits, Nicodemism and libertinism were discrete phenomena the Frenchman attacked in print over nearly three decades, exhibiting little patience for those he accused of trifling with the things of God. While plenty of evidence exists for what Calvin thought about these problematic individuals, we possess few of their own words. As those who cloaked their beliefs beneath a convincing veneer of practices, successful Nicodemites were, by definition, undetected by their contemporaries, leaving to historians scant traces of their double lives. A similar source problem afflicts Calvin's libertines, whose flaws are known best through their accusers. Those charged with cowardly crypto-religion or moral turpitude – the core defects of Nicodemism and libertinism – would never claim such traits for themselves. Yet despite this potential for incongruity between reputation and reality, these groups occupied sizable space in the imaginations of others. In a time of great anxiety over religious identity, Nicodemites and libertines were useful categories to those looking to define their communities in contrast to common foes, a strategy that worked regardless of whether such enemies existed. As such, they constituted important elements of Calvin's context that help to unveil and illumine the contours of his thought, particularly as he invoked these groups to reinforce a vision of religious purity over against examples of unacceptable doctrine and practice.

SUGGESTED FURTHER READINGS

Eire, Carlos M. N. "Calvin and Nicodemism: A Reappraisal." *Sixteenth Century Journal* 10:1 (1979): 45–69.

Jenkins, Gary W. *Calvin's Tormentors*. Grand Rapids, MI: Baker Academic, 2018.

Martin, John Jeffries. "Marranos and Nicodemites in Sixteenth-Century Venice." *Journal of Medieval and Early Modern Studies* 41:3 (2011): 577–599.

Matheson, Peter. "Martyrdom or Mission? A Protestant Debate." *Archiv für Reformationsgeschichte* 80 (1989): 154–72.

Naphy, William G. *Calvin and the Consolidation of the Genevan Reformation*. Manchester: Manchester University Press, 1994.

van Veen, Mirjam. "Introduction." *Ioannis Calvini opera omnia: Dueno recognita et adnotatione critica instructa notisque illustrata*. Series IV: Scripta didactica et polemica, 9–41. Geneva: Droz, 2005.

Verhey, Allen, and Robert G. Wilkie, "Calvin's Treatise 'Against the Libertines.'" *Calvin Theological Journal* 15 (1980): 190–219.

Walsham, Alexandra. *Church Papists: Catholicism, Conformity, and Confessional Polemic in Early Modern England*. Suffolk: The Boydell Press, 1999.

Williams, George H. *The Radical Reformation*. 3rd ed. Kirksville, MO: Sixteenth Century Journal Publishers, 1992.

Zagorin, Perez. *Ways of Lying: Dissimulation, Persecution, and Conformity in Early Modern Europe*. Cambridge, MA: Harvard University Press, 1990.

PART V

∾

CALVIN'S INFLUENCES

34

ᖇ

Calvin and Luther

Christopher Boyd Brown

The historical question of the personal and theological relationship between Martin Luther and John Calvin has long been freighted with larger questions of Evangelical identity. Calvin, in his published and epistolary rhetoric, deliberately constructed the image of a positive but critical attitude toward Luther, which he used to establish his own place in the Reformation. Luther's own positive but qualified opinion of Calvin, however, came to be distorted by transmission by different parties in the theological disputes of the succeeding generation.[1]

The relationship between the two men – who were aware of each other, though they never directly corresponded or met in person – was heavily conditioned by the difference between their contexts. Calvin was 26 years younger than Luther; he was born and educated in France rather than in the Holy Roman Empire; and he was unable to read German and had access only to the minority of Luther's writings, which were written in Latin or had been translated into Latin or French. Though Luther was certainly known in France – not least through his 1521 condemnation by the Sorbonne – his work was much less accessible than it was in Germany.[2]

---

[1] For treatments of the relationship between Calvin and Luther, see B. A. Gerrish, "John Calvin on Luther," in Jaroslav Pelikan (ed.), *Interpreters of Luther: Essays in Honor of Wilhelm Pauk* (Philadelphia: Fortress, 1968), 67–96; Bruce Gordon, "Martin Luther and John Calvin," in Derek R. Nelson and Paul Hinlicky (eds.), *The Oxford Encyclopedia of Martin Luther* (Oxford: Oxford University Press, 2017). https://dx.doi.org/10.1093/acrefore/9780199340378 .013.313; Herman J. Selderhuis, "Luther and Calvin," in Alberto Melloni (ed.), *Martin Luther: A Christian between Reforms and Modernity (1517–2017)* (Berlin: De Gruyter, 2017), 401–416.

[2] See Olivier Millet, "Das Lutherbild in den französischen evangelischen und calvinischen Veröffentlichungen (1520–1560)," in Herman J. Selderhuis and J. Marius J. Lange van Ravenswaay (eds.), *Luther and Calvinism: Image and Reception of Martin Luther in the History and Theology of Calvinism* (Göttingen: V&R, 2017), 497–511. On the preponderance of Luther's publication in German over Latin from about 1519 onward, see Mark U. Edwards,

In Calvin's foundational work as an evangelical theologian – the 1536 first edition of the *Institutes* – he nonetheless made substantial use of Luther's *Small Catechism* (1529), *Babylonian Captivity of the Church* (1520), *Freedom of a Christian* (1520), and *Sacrament of the Body and Blood of Christ – Against the Fanatics* (1526).[3] Thus, for example, the first edition of the *Institutes* – unlike later ones – followed the sequence of Luther's catechism: Ten Commandments, Creed, prayer, and sacraments, followed by a section on Christian freedom. Luther was thus a major influence on basic structures of Calvin's evangelical theology, though not the only one – and notably, never explicitly named as a source in any edition of the *Institutes*. In 1556, Calvin recalled that his early reading of Luther (evidently the 1526 treatise on the sacrament) had turned him away from the ideas of Zwingli and Oecolampadius.[4] Though the context of that remark must be taken into account – Calvin was trying to establish his credentials as an heir of Luther in debate with a Lutheran – it does reflect the documentable early influence of Luther's theology on Calvin.

Calvin's appraisal of Luther's exegesis (much of which was published in Latin) was also one of nuanced appreciation. He appreciated Luther's "fruitful" doctrinal exposition but criticized his lack of sufficient attention to the history or details of language.[5] He encouraged Veit Dietrich to complete the publication of Luther's *Lectures on Genesis* even as other Lutherans found Calvin's criticisms of the commentary to be offensive.[6] Calvin's critical appreciation also seems to have been expressed by a series of French translations of some of Luther's exegetical works, which appeared in Geneva

---

Printing, Propaganda, and Martin Luther (Berkeley: University of California Press, 1994), 17–21.

[3] *Christianae religionis* Institutio (1536), OS 1: 11–283. See Alexandre Ganoczy, *The Young Calvin*, trans. David Foxgrover and Wade Provo (Philadelphia: Westminster, 1987), 137–145; Jean-François Gilmont, *John Calvin and the Printed Book*, trans. Karin Maag, Sixteenth Century Essays and Studies 72 (Kirksville, MO: Truman State University Press, 2005), 168–169; August Lang, "Die Quellen der *Institutio* von 1536," *Evangelische Theologie* 3 (1936): 100–112. For the Luther texts, see *Parvus Catechismus* (1529), WA 30/1: 283–345 (translated in Robert Kolb and Timothy J. Wengert, eds., *The Book of Concord* [Minneapolis, MN: Fortress, 2000], 345–367; *De captivitate Babylonica ecclesiae praeludium* (1520), WA 6: 497–573 (LW 36: 3–126); *Tractatus de libertate Christiana* (1520), WA 7: 42–73 (LW 31: 327–377); *Sermon von dem Sakrament des Leibes und Blutes Christi wider die Schwarmgeister* (1526), translated into Latin by Vincent Obsopoeus, *Martini Lutheri sermo elegantissimus, super sacramento corporis et sanguinis Christi* (1527), WA 9: 469, 479, 474–522 (German) (LW 36: 329–361).

[4] Calvin, *Secunda defensio piae et orthodoxae de sacramentis fidei*, CO 9: 51.

[5] Calvin to Viret, May 19, 1540, CO 11: 36.

[6] Calvin to Veit Dietrich, March 16, 1546, CO 12: 315–317 no. 781, col. 317; cf. Franciscus Burkhardt to Calvin, October 7, 1554, CO 15: 260; Selderhuis, "Luther and Calvin," 412.

between 1540 and 1558, in almost every case closely followed (or preceded) by Calvin's own treatment of the biblical book in question.[7]

In the 1530s, however, Calvin was at first less demonstrative about his debt to Luther. When Calvin emigrated to Switzerland and then to Strasbourg, Calvin entered circles of Evangelical theologians who were in closer connection with Luther. Amid the negotiations over Swiss acceptance of the 1536 Wittenberg Concord, Calvin was at first skeptical of Luther's role, criticizing his teaching on the Lord's Supper and his stubbornness and love for victory while acknowledging Luther's piety.[8] While in Strasbourg, Calvin attended the imperial religious colloquies of 1539–1541, making personal contact with Melanchthon and coming to Luther's attention for the first time in correspondence from the Wittenbergers who were also in attendance.[9]

In a letter to Bucer of October 14, 1539, Luther asks that his greetings be conveyed to Johann Sturm and John Calvin, "whose books I have read with singular pleasure."[10] Almost certainly, Luther had in mind Calvin's 1539 *Reply to Sadoleto*.[11] Calvin's reaction to Luther's greeting reveals both the importance and the challenges of the relationship between the two reformers to Calvin. In a November letter to Farel, Calvin reported with delight that Luther had approved of his book – which he took in particular as approval or at least toleration of his teaching on the Lord's Supper contained there. This was reinforced by an oral report sent by Melanchthon that, when certain people had tried to provoke Luther by pointing out how critical Calvin was of Luther and his followers in the passage,[12] Luther had responded with equanimity, saying, "I do hope that he will one day have a better opinion of us, but it is right for us to be somewhat tolerant of a gifted man."[13]

---

[7] See Millet, "Das Lutherbild in den französischen evangelischen und calvinischen Veröffentlichungen," 508–509.

[8] Calvin to Bucer, January 12, 1538, CO 10/2: 137–144

[9] See, e.g., Myconius to Luther, March 3, 1539, WA Br 8: 386–388.

[10] Luther to Bucer, October 14, 1539, WA Br 8: 568–569 (LW 50: 187–191).

[11] *Responsio ad Sadoleti epistolam*, CO 5: 365–416; OS 1: 457–489 (translated in John C. Olin, ed., *John Calvin and Jacopo Sadoleto: A Reformation Debate* [New York: Harper & Row, 1966; repr. Grand Rapids, MI: Baker, 1976], 49–94; LCC 22: 219–256). J. K. S. Reid, ed., *Calvin: Theological Treatises* (Philadelphia: Westminster Press, 1954), Library of Christian Classics Vol. 22, 219–256.

[12] Probably the passage discussing the Supper in the *Reply to Sadoleto* (CO 5: 399–400; Olin, *John Calvin and Jacopo Sadoleto*, 70–71; LCC 22: 237–238), but possibly the section from the 1539 *Institutes*, CO 1: 991–1038, especially 1003–1009. See Gerrish, "John Calvin on Luther," 73.

[13] Calvin to Farel, November 20, 1539 CO 10/2: 429–432, no. 197. Melanchthon's letter to Calvin is catalogued as MBW 2290, T8: 558–559.

Calvin declared himself "melted" [*fractus*] by Luther's generous spirit. Yet Calvin in his delight may have somewhat misconstrued what Luther meant by his response. Calvin's discussion of the Supper in the *Reply to Sadoleto* (and also in the 1539 *Institutes*) firmly rejects the "local" presence of Christ's body and blood. Yet, though Calvin elsewhere faults Luther for teaching this,[14] Luther explicitly rejected the idea of a local presence (like "straw filling a sack"), instead teaching that the body and blood were present "definitively" (present at a definite place as a whole without filling particular dimensions or displacing other bodies). Luther's discussion of this point, however, had appeared chiefly in German, in his 1528 *Confession Concerning Christ's Supper*, and was therefore not known to Calvin.[15] In Luther's eyes, then, Calvin was rejecting a position that Luther did not hold, and Luther's wish that Calvin might come to a "better opinion" of the Wittenbergers (*de nobis melius sensurum*) likely expresses the hope that Calvin would come to a "more accurate" appraisal of what Luther taught.[16]

Other reports of Luther's opinion recorded during his lifetime convey a similar mixture of approbation and critique of Calvin. In addition to Luther's 1539 letter to Bucer, there are two pieces of Luther's *Table Talk* that mention Calvin: one from 1540 and another that, though undated, must date from after summer 1545 because it mentions the April 1545 massacre of Waldensians in Provence at Corbières and Mérindol, ascribed to the instigation of Cardinal Sadoleto.[17] The 1540 *Table Talk* is provoked by a mention of Vadian's book against Schwenckfeld. Luther remarks that Vadian wants to refute others but stands in need of refutation himself. "In the same way," Luther continues, "Calvin dissimulates his opinion about the sacraments. They have gone astray and are unable to speak. For the expression of truth is simple. Do not read me much of their books!"[18] The later *Table Talk*

---

[14] See Calvin to Bucer, January 12, 1538, CO 10/2: 137–144, 138; *Petit Traicté de la Saincte Cene* (1541), CO 5: 429–460, cols. 459–460 (OS 1: 499–530, 528–529; LCC 22: 140–166, 164–165).

[15] Luther, *Vom Abendmahl Christi: Bekenntnis*, WA 26: 261–509, 326–341 (LW 37: 151–372, 214–230). Cf. Luther, *Kurzes Bekenntnis vom heiligen Sakrament* (1544), WA 54: 151–167, 153 (LW 38: 279–372, 301). The *Vom Abendmahl Christi* did appear in a Latin translation in Wittenberg in 1539, but Calvin seems to have been unaware of it: see WA 26: 255.

[16] Calvin first seems to engage with the category of definitive presence in his 1561 polemic against Heshusius, dismissing it as an irrational contradiction, without acknowledging that Luther had also taught this mode of presence: see *Dilucida explicatio sanae doctrinae de vera participatione carnis et sanguinis Christi* [*Clear Explanation of Sound Doctrine Concerning the True Partaking of the Flesh and Blood of Christ*], CO 9: 457–524, col. 474 (LCC 22: 257–324, 272).

[17] Luther, *Table Talk* 5303 (1540), WA TR 5: 51; *Table Talk* 6050 ([1545]), WA TR 5: 461.

[18] "Sic Caluinus de re sacramentaria occultat suam sententiam. Sie sein irr vnd konnens nicht reden. Quia veritatis oratio simplex est. Man leß mir ire bucher nicht vill!"

describes Calvin's efforts to persuade the Swiss to renounce their allegiance to the tyrant Sadoleto; Luther responds by describing Calvin as "a learned man, but strongly suspect for the error of the Sacramentarians."[19]

In light of these reports, and especially the late date of the latter, it is difficult to give historical credence to the posthumous narratives offered by the crypto-Calvinist Christoph Pezel and others that Luther had a late private change of heart about Calvin's theology of the Lord's Supper.[20] Instead, Luther's appraisal of Calvin is consistent both in its appreciation of Calvin's talents (which indeed sets him apart from the Zurich theologians for whom Luther had no such esteem) and in its criticism of Calvin's ambiguity or failure to grasp essential issues in discussing the Supper.[21] Luther appreciated Calvin's writings in defense of the Reformation – the *Reply to Sadoleto* and (according to a report from Francisco de Enzinas) the *Humble Exhortation to Charles V*.[22] Yet theologically, he regarded the Genevan reformer as a "Sacramentarian." One similar example of Luther's willingness to treasure the contributions of his contemporaries while noting their theological errors is his treatment of the hymnwriter Michael Weisse, of the Bohemian Brethren, whom Luther hailed as a "good poet" and whose

---

[19] "*vir doctus, sed valde suspectus de errore sacramentariorum.*"

[20] A collection of documents and anecdotes attempting to demonstrate Luther's goodwill toward Calvin's theology of the Supper was assembled by Christoph Pezel, *Außführliche, warhaffte und bestendige Erzehlung* (Neustadt a.d. Haardt: Wilhelm Harnischs Erben, 1600), 89–90, 137–139. Such accounts had begun circulating in Heidelberg in the 1550s (the so-called *Heidelberger Landlüge*) and were criticized by the Lutheran Joachim Mörlin, *Wider die Landlügen der Heidelbergischen Theologen* (Eisleben: Andreas Petri, 1555). According to the first account, Luther had said to Melanchthon just before departing for Eisleben in 1546 that he had gone "too far" in the controversy over the Supper and asked Melanchthon to make amends after his death. In the second account cited from Pezel, Luther is supposed to have read a copy of the Latin translation of Calvin's *Petit Traicté* and exclaimed, "This is a learned and pious man, to whom I could well have entrusted the whole matter from the beginning. ... If Zwingli and Oecolampadius had explained themselves this way at first, we would never have wound up in such far-reaching disagreement." This story may have arisen out of the ambiguity of which books of Calvin Luther had read at the time of his 1539 letter to Bucer. Cf. the discussion of these texts in Gerrish, "John Calvin on Luther," 94 n. 53.

[21] Cf. the description of Calvin's reception in Wittenberg circles by Luther's friend the Torgau schoolmaster Marcus Crodel (Crodel to Calvin, March 6, 1545, CO 12: 40 no. 619). Crodel is fulsome in his praise of Calvin and his writings, mentioning the *Reply to Sadoleto*, *Against Pighius*, and *Institutes* (though he mention's Luther's own opinion only with respect to the *Reply*). Crodel makes an exception, however, for Calvin's discussion of the Supper, "in which you seem all too much inclined to the opinion of Zwingli and Oecolampadius."

[22] Francisco Enzinas [Dryander] to Calvin, August 3, 1545, CO 12: 125–127. Cf. Calvin to Melanchthon, April 21, 1544, MBW 3531 T13: 186–188 (CO 11: 696–698, no. 544), where Calvin sends the work to Melanchthon asking for Luther's evaluation. For the *Supplex exhortatio ad Caesarem*, see CO 6: 453–534 (translated in excerpts in LCC 22: 183–216).

burial hymn Luther included in the Wittenberg hymnals even as he noted that Weisse had "become a bit of an Enthusiast concerning the Sacrament."[23]

If Luther's appreciation of Calvin was focused on his role as a defender of the Reformation against the papacy and empire, Calvin's own appreciation of Luther after 1539 was also focused on his public historical role, as he offered a public though qualified defense of Luther against both Roman Catholic and Evangelical critics. Calvin drafted a defense of the Wittenberg Concord, which he meant to publish with his 1540 *Commentary on Romans*, but he was dissuaded from publishing it by Melanchthon – perhaps because the Wittenberg theologian recognized Calvin's failure to grasp Luther's own position.[24] In his 1541 *Short Treatise on the Lord's Supper*, Calvin narrated the history of the Evangelical debate over the Lord's Supper, crediting Luther for condemning transubstantiation while noting that he had employed "similes which were a little harsh and rude" and did not clearly exclude a local presence. However, Zwingli and Oecolampadius, while rightly attacking the "execrable idolatry" of Christ's "carnal presence," had given the impression that they reduced the sacrament to "bare signs without any corresponding spiritual substance." Credit and blame were thus distributed between Wittenberg and Zurich in such a way as to position Calvin as pacific mediator.[25] In Calvin's 1543 *Humble Exhortation to Charles V*, Calvin identified Luther as the one whom (along with unnamed "others") God had raised up "to carry the torch before us to reveal the way of salvation"; it was Luther who had first exposed the "wicked opinions which had bewitched the whole world" concerning sin, grace, and Christ's righteousness. He had called attention to abuses with great modesty, for which he had been unjustly vilified by his opponents. It was Luther who had shown the path on which others now continued.[26] Calvin's praise of Luther was always such as to leave space for others – including himself – to improve upon him, and not only in matters such as the Lord's Supper where there was substantial difference between the two men. In defending the doctrine of the bondage of the human will against the Catholic controversialist Albert Pighius in 1543,

---

[23] Luther, *Preface to the Babst Hymnal* (1545), WA 34: 477 (LW 53: 333–334).

[24] Calvin drafted an acknowledgment of Luther's praise that he intended to include in the preface to his *Commentary on Romans*, but he was dissuaded from publishing it by Melanchthon: see CO 9: 841–846 (with a better text in Herminjard 6: 132–137); Calvin to Farel, January 10, 1540, Herminjard 6: 150–165, 165.

[25] Calvin, *Petit Traicté de la Saincte Cene* (1541), CO 5: 429–460, cols. 457–460 (OS 1 525–530: LCC 22: 140–166, 163–166).

[26] *Supplex exhortatio ad Caesarem*, CO 6: 453–534, cols. 459, 466, 473, 499, 524–525 (these passages are not included in the translation in LCC 22).

Calvin defended Luther and his theology while conceding that Luther had used hyperbole (though with justification, given the circumstances under which he was writing) and pointing out that Calvin, for his part, has sought to soften the form of expression of the doctrine to avoid giving offense.[27]

In private letters, too, Calvin defended and praised Luther even as he criticized his stubbornness and irascibility. Writing to Farel in 1540, Calvin noted how much greater a theologian Luther was than Zwingli and rebuked the claims of the Zurich theologians to preeminence. In 1543-1544, Luther caused a new uproar among the Swiss reformers with his 1543 letter to the Zurich printer Christoph Froschauer and 1544 publication of Luther's *Brief Confession*, in which he denounced the Zurich theologians as incorrigible Sacramentarian heretics.[28] Calvin, writing to Bullinger in the wake of Luther's renewed attack on the Swiss, faulted the "immoderate violence and obstinacy" of Luther's character and lamented the reopening of divisions in the Evangelical movement, though he blamed Nicholas von Amsdorf – "a man wholly insane and of no intelligence" – for spurring Luther on. Nevertheless, he admonished Bullinger to remember what a great man Luther was and what he had accomplished against the papal Antichrist. Calvin, for his part, declared that "even if [Luther] were to call me a devil, I would nonetheless give him the honor of acknowledging him to be an outstanding servant of God."[29] Calvin distanced himself from the conflict by pointing to his inability to read in German either Luther's recent treatises on the Supper or the writings of the Zurichers that had provoked him.[30] At the same time, in writing to Melanchthon, Calvin urged him to try to restrain Luther's vehemence and to help him deal more gently with learned men, "even if he has cause to criticize them."[31] Bullinger, at least, found Calvin's efforts to triangulate between Zurich and Wittenberg naïve; although Calvin claimed to be distancing himself from Bullinger and taking Bucer's side in favor of the Wittenberg Concord, Bullinger judged that Calvin was mostly in agreement with Zurich – and predicted that Luther would not approve of Calvin's position, unless he renounced what he had written previously.[32]

---

[27] *Defensio sanae et orthodoxae doctrinae de servitute et liberatione humani arbitrii adversus calumnias Alberti Pighii Campensis* (1543), CO 6: 225–404, cols. 249–251. Cf. Gerrish, "John Calvin on Luther," 79.

[28] Luther to Froschauer, August 31, 1543, WA Br 10: 384–387 no. 3908; *Kurzes Bekenntnis vom heiligen Sakrament* (1544), WA 54: 141–167 (LW 38: 279–319).

[29] Calvin to Bullinger, November 25, 1544, CO 11: 772–775, no. 586 (escol. 774f).

[30] Calvin to Farel, October 1544, CO 11: 754–755 no. 576. Cf. pastors of Zurich to Calvin, October 24, 1554, CO 15: 274, no. 2034.

[31] Calvin to Melanchthon, April 21, 1544, MBW T13: 186–188, no. 3531 (CO 11: 696–998, no. 544).

[32] Bullinger to Vadian, May 1544 (CO 11: 722–724 no. 555).

The one opportunity to put Luther and Calvin in direct epistolary conversation came in 1545, when Calvin included with one of his letters to Melanchthon a letter to Luther, dated January 21, 1545.[33] To Melanchthon, Calvin wrote that he feared Luther's irritability, and entrusted to Melanchthon's judgment the decision whether to deliver the letter to Luther.[34] In writing to Luther, Calvin greeted the elder reformer as "the most excellent pastor of the Christian church, my greatly esteemed father" and as "the most outstanding minister of Christ, a father whom I ought always to esteem." He described his efforts to persuade French "Nicodemites" to make an open confession of Evangelical faith and asked Luther to read and comment briefly on a letter that the Nicodemites had prepared in their defense[35] and two of his own treatises seeking to persuade them to abandon secrecy.[36] Calvin trusted that Luther's judgment would carry great weight with French evangelicals. He concluded with the poignant wish that an opportunity for direct conversation might, if postponed on earth, come to fruition in the kingdom of God.

In the end, however, Calvin's letter never reached Luther. Melanchthon wrote back to Calvin on April 17 reporting that he had decided to hold it back, saying that Luther had become suspicious and that he did not want his opinions on Nicodemites to be circulated.[37] Yet it may well be that it was Melanchthon who was reluctant to have Luther's views circulated; certainly Melanchthon's own opinion on the Nicodemites made greater allowance for human frailty and practical compromise than Calvin expected from Luther.[38] In any event, whether protecting Calvin's interests or his own, Melanchthon prevented the communication that Calvin had desired.

Calvin's selection of a topic – the importance of public confession of faith, rather than the doctrine of the Supper – was strategic for his own approach to Luther.[39] Yet, despite the failure of direct communication, it also marks an

---

[33] Calvin to Luther, January 21, 1545, WA Br 11: 26–29 (CO 12: 6–8).

[34] Calvin to Melanchthon, January 21, 1545, MBW 3803 T14: 123–127 (CO 12: 9–12 no. 606).

[35] Probably Capnius to Calvin, 1544, CO 11: 825–830 no. 600.

[36] Apparently (so WA Br 11: 28 n. 2) *De vitandis superstitionibus* und *Excusatio ad Pseudo-Nicodemitas* (see CO 6: xxxi and 537–588, 589–614). Though these treatises had been first published in French and did not appear in Latin until 1549, Calvin writes to Melanchthon that he has had them translated into Latin to send to Wittenberg (CO 12: 10; MBW T14: 124–125, no. 3803).

[37] Melanchthon to Calvin, April 17, 1545, MBW 3885 T14: 264–265 (cf. Melanchthon's draft, MBW 3884 T14: 263–264) (CO 12: 61–62 no. 632): "Multa enim suspiciose accepit, et non vult circumferri suas responsiones de talibus quaestionibus quales proposuisti."

[38] See Melanchthon to Calvin, April 17, 1544, MBW 3886 T14: 266–272 (CR 5: 734–739; CO 6: 621–624.)

[39] Cf. Gordon, "Martin Luther and John Calvin," 10.

important theological connection between the two reformers. As scholars have increasingly come to realize, an important part of Luther's political legacy to the next generation of Protestants was not the "quietism" often ascribed to him, but his encouragement, especially in his later years, of resistance against the persecutors of the Gospel.[40] Among the cycle of Genevan publications of Luther's works during Calvin's ministry was an excerpt from Luther's pungent *Against Hanswurst*.[41]

After Luther's death, Calvin continued to appeal to his legacy, to position himself not only in relation to other Swiss reformers but also in relation to Lutherans. In defending his theology of the Supper against Joachim Westphal and Tileman Hesushius, Calvin claimed to be upholding what Luther had regarded as central – God's activity in the Supper. Other questions, in Calvin's estimation, could be put to the side.[42]

Calvin's approval of Luther was sincere, yet it also served his own purposes of self-definition. And it was, as Calvin acknowledged, selective, relying on Calvin's own sometimes tendentious identification of what was central in Luther's concerns. To recast one of Calvin's efforts to describe the Eucharist, Luther was present in Calvin's theology *totum, sed non totus*. The pieces of Luther's theology are present in Calvin's teaching, but they are not held together as a whole in the way that Luther relates them. On some questions, Calvin wants to relate things that Luther held in high tension or even paradox: the distinction between Law and Gospel, for example.[43] In other matters, Calvin insisted on the necessity of maintaining the independence of things that Luther wanted to hold united: the humanity and divinity of Christ, but also the Spirit and the physical means of Word and sacraments.

Their differences of perspective are grounded perhaps in differences between Luther's Ockhamist training and Calvin's arguably Scotist background.[44] Calvin could argue, as realist theologians had since Anselm, that

---

[40] See, e.g., David Mark Whitford, *Tyranny and Resistance: The Magdeburg Confession and the Lutheran Tradition* (St. Louis, MO: Concordia, 2001); Christoph Strom, "Luthers Einfluss auf das calvinistische Verständnis von Obrigkeit und Recht," in Herman J. Selderhuis, and J. Marius J. Lange van Ravenswaay (eds.), *Luther and Calvinism: Image and Reception of Martin Luther in the History and Theology of Calvinism* (Göttingen: V&R, 2017), 79–100.

[41] Luther, *Antithese de la vraye et faulse eglise* ([Geneva : Jean Girard], 1545). The French text is excerpted from *Wider Hans Worst* (1541), WA 51: 476–531 (LW 41: 193–224).

[42] Calvin, *Defensio sanae et orthodoxae doctrinae de sacramentis* (1555), CO 9: 17–19 (OS 2: 270–272). Cf. n. 4.

[43] See Randall Zachman, *The Assurance of Faith: Conscience in the Theology of Martin Luther and John Calvin* (Minneapolis, MN: Fortress, 1993), 156–158.

[44] See Heiko Oberman, *Initia Calvini: The Matrix of Calvin's Reformation* (Amsterdam, The Netherlands: Koninklijke Nederlandse Akademie van Wetenschappen, 1991).

certain acts could be excluded from possibility because they were "unworthy" of God. In the Lord's Supper, Calvin defended God against the indignity of being "enclosed in corruptible elements."[45] The physical and corporeal, on the one hand, and the spiritual, on the other, were contraries. For Luther, God's omnipotence was demonstrated precisely in the possibility that God could choose to do things that seemed impossible to reason and its scale of values: not that Luther believed that the finite was capable of the infinite (*finitum capax infiniti*) but that divine omnipotence was capable of the finite. God could really hide *sub contrario*, and to encounter God there was the deep revelation of God's heart, not merely an accommodation to human weakness whose inevitable limitations had always to be lamented and kept in mind.

Steven Ozment provocatively claimed that Calvin brought Luther's Reformation full circle, "'re-Catholicizing' Protestant theology at its most sensitive point."[46] What was at stake was not so much soteriological dogma but epistemology: How can a person be assured that God is gracious toward him? Luther's consistent answer was that the individual should look to the proclaimed promise of the Gospel, baptism, absolution, and the Supper, which were the means to which God had bound Himself.[47] To look for the Spirit apart from the external Word and sacraments was fanaticism: "enthusiasm." Yet for Calvin, this answer was inadequate because preaching and the sacraments were promiscuous, "common also to the wicked."[48] External words or signs must be sharply distinguished from the Spirit who may be active along with them as a pipe is from the life-giving water that flows through it. Assurance, for Calvin, comes not from the external Word but from the internal testimony of the Spirit: "This inner call, then, is a pledge of salvation that cannot deceive us."[49] Thus, both Luther and Calvin insist that predestination must be understood from the Word. For Calvin, this means that the Bible describes God's predestination. But Luther also means that it is the proclaimed Word that carries out predestination by creating faith.[50] Where Luther insists on facing outward, Calvin finally turns inward.

---

[45] Calvin, *Petit Traicté de la Saincte Cene* (1541), CO 5: 429–460, col. 460: "ne pensant pas que le Seigneur Iesus soit abaissé iusque là, de estre enclos soubz quelques elemens corruptibles."

[46] Steven Ozment, *The Age of Reform* (New Haven, CT: Yale University Press, 1980), 374–380.

[47] See, e.g., the *Smalcald Articles* (1537/1538) 3.8.3–13, WA 50: 235–237 (Kolb and Wengert, eds., *The Book of Concord*, 322–323).

[48] Calvin, *Institutes* 3.24.8 (OS 4: 420).

[49] Calvin, *Institutes* 3.24.2 (OS 4: 412).

[50] Cf. Luther's reflection on the *De servo arbitrio* (WA 18: 600–787; LW 33) in *Lectures on Genesis* 26: 9 (WA 43: 458–463; LW 5: 42–50).

For Calvin, Luther was the man called by God to inaugurate the Reformation, whose central concerns he saw himself not only advancing but also refining. For Luther, Calvin was a learned and commendable ally in the cause of Reformation, one whom he was able to acknowledge without implying unqualified endorsement. The perception of possible agreement in the theology of the sacrament may have been grounded in Calvin's inability, largely because of differences in language, to grasp the distinction Luther made between Christ's local and definitive presence in the sacrament. The following generations were left with the task of reconciling or reaffirming the unresolved tensions between the witness of the two greatest theologians of the Reformation.

SUGGESTED FURTHER READINGS

Gerrish, B. A. "John Calvin on Luther." In *Interpreters of Luther: Essays in Honor of Wilhelm Pauk*, ed. Jaroslav Pelikan. Philadelphia: Fortress Press, 1968, 67–96.

Gordon, Bruce. "Martin Luther and John Calvin." In *The Oxford Encyclopedia of Martin Luther*, ed. Derek R. Nelson and Paul Hinlicky. Oxford: Oxford University Press, 2017, https://dx.doi.org/10.1093/acrefore/9780199340378.013.313.

Holder, R. Ward, ed. *Calvin and Luther: The Continuing Relationship*. Göttingen: Vandenhoeck & Ruprecht, 2013.

Meinhold, Peter. "Calvin und Luther," *Lutherische Monatschefte* 3:6 (1964): 264–269.

Selderhuis, Herman J. "Luther and Calvin." In *Martin Luther: A Christian between Reforms and Modernity (1517–2017)*, ed. Alberto Melloni. Berlin: De Gruyter, 2017, 1: 401–416.

35

Calvin and Melanchthon

Timothy J. Orr

Philip Melanchthon is undoubtedly one of the most significant figures to emerge from the Reformation. However, his legacy is frequently over-shadowed by Martin Luther and John Calvin – in large part because of his close relationship with both. Because of this, Melanchthon has infrequently been the focus of historical research, functioning much more frequently as a footnote to Luther or a sounding board for Calvin. Yet Melanchthon's work and writings shaped the religious landscape of Europe and he left an indelible influence on both Lutheranism and the Reformed tradition – particularly through his biblical scholarship and *Loci Communes*. The overlooking of Melanchthon is, to some extent, explained by the final years of his life, during which he was almost universally disdained for his perceived betrayal of Lutheran principles at the Leipzig Interim. Because of this, Melanchthon has frequently been disregarded or maligned in confessional histories of Lutheranism and the Reformed faith. In more recent years, however, the significance of Melanchthon's *Loci Communes*, his contributions to early modern biblical scholarship, his role in the political developments of the German Reformation, and his relationship with Calvin have come to be recognized as formative influences on the history of the early modern world.

EARLY LIFE AND INTRODUCTION TO THE REFORMATION

Philip Melanchthon was born on February 16, 1497, in Bretten with the name Philip Schwartzerdt. His father, who was armorer for the Count Palatine of the Rhine, passed away when Philip was only 11, leaving him in the care of his great-aunt and her brother, Johann Reuchlin, a famous humanist and Hebraist. Reuchlin convinced the young Philip to change his name from the German Schwartzerdt to the Greek Melanchthon in the style of humanists of the day. He also instilled in Melanchthon a love of ancient languages.

Melanchthon entered the University of Heidelberg at a very young age and proved to be a very capable scholar, continuing his studies in Tübingen to attain his master's degree. While teaching at the university, Melanchthon was first exposed to reforming ideas through his uncle and Desiderius Erasmus and came to believe that the purpose of the church was not adequately encapsulated by scholastic theology. Melanchthon came to have a reputation as an innovator and a dangerous thinker at Tübingen, frequently coming into conflict with other professors. However, thanks to the influence of his uncle, Melanchthon was offered a position, which he accepted, as a professor of Greek at the University of Wittenberg, where Martin Luther was already a member of the faculty.

Melanchthon and Luther very quickly became friends. Both saw themselves as members of an emerging humanist caste opposed to scholastic thought and worked together to propagate their ideas. Luther had published his *Ninety-Five Thesis* shortly before Melanchthon's arrival and, while the Luther Affair would grow to become an issue of international interest over the next few years, Melanchthon's support of Luther provided him with allies who were willing to support him on the grounds of their shared humanism – among them, Reuchlin. The two complemented each other well. Luther was outspoken and confident whereas Melanchthon would always be more reserved and far less comfortable with confrontation. The two shared very similar theologies, but not identical ones. However, even where they disagreed, Melanchthon and Luther never publicly corrected or reprimanded each other – which speaks volumes about Luther's respect and care for Melanchthon, as he was more than willing to publicly scold even close friends. Because of this friendship, Melanchthon occasionally withheld his opinions to appease the more confrontational Luther – even going so far as to break off relationships with both Erasmus and his great-uncle Reuchlin when the two sided against Luther. This strong sense of devotion would have lasting significance for the Reformed faith in Germany.

MELANCHTHON'S ACADEMIC CAREER

As the Luther Affair grew in significance, Melanchthon frequently supported his friend. He attended the Leipzig Disputation in 1919 and offered his comments on the proceedings. He collected Luther's sermons on Genesis and compiled them into a commentary that would be published in 1523. It was Melanchthon who proposed to Luther the idea of translating the New Testament into Greek while Luther wasted away in the Wartburg and it was Melanchthon, seeing the potential for Luther's translation, who encouraged him to

refine and develop the translation. Melanchthon was also a very talented translator and author. His works, while frequently overshadowed by Luther's, reflect a
greater mastery of both translation and organization. Although he was never the
most original thinker, because of his ability to understand and synthesize
complex ideas it was Melanchthon who would set the standard for biblical and
theological scholarship for much of the sixteenth century and beyond.

It can be argued that, by 1521, Melanchthon was a greater master of
Lutheran theology than Luther – an argument based on the publication of
Loci Communes. The year 1520 would prove to be a landmark for the Lutheran
Reformation. Luther published three of his most famous works over the
course of the year and then, in 1521, after the Diet of Worms, he vanished.
Luther was alive and in hiding in the Wartburg, but most people believed he
had been quietly killed by the emperor. This is when the *Loci Communes*
released, and it was in this environment of uncertainty and doubt that
Melanchthon's theological masterpiece flourished. The *Loci Communes*
quickly became a bestseller and, in Luther's absence, helped preserve the
Lutheran movement in Germany and then propel it to even greater notoriety.

The *Loci Communes* was the first systematic treatment of Protestant thought
and marked the emergence of a distinct Protestant ideology. The *Loci Communes* is marked by its embracing of a Lutheran anthropology, which down-
plays human capability and emphasizes the necessity of God's grace. This
marked a theological break between Melanchthon and other humanists, who
tended to emphasize humanity's capability. This is not to say that Melanchthon
ceased to be a humanist, but that from this point forward his humanism was
more methodological than it was constitutive in regard to his thinking. The *Loci
Commune* also marked a distinctively Protestant use of the Christian scriptures.
Borrowing yet more inspiration from Luther, Melanchthon framed almost
every point within the *Loci Communes* around scriptural evidence rather than
relying on the historical Christian tradition or even humanist philosophy. This
scriptural method of writing most likely later influenced the construction and
composition of Calvin's *Institutes of the Christian Religion*.

The *Loci Communes* had its roots in Melanchthon's teaching on the
writings of Paul, especially the Book of Romans. In 1519 Melanchthon had
published the *Theological Introduction to the Epistle of Paul and the Romans*.
His lectures on Romans are evidence of how quickly Luther's thought
influenced Melanchthon, and they develop, in Melanchthon's skilled prose,
Luther's ideas of Law and Gospel – emphasizing the condemnation of the
Law and the role of the Gospel in the pardoning of this condemnation.
Melanchthon's use of scripture throughout his career marked a new wave of
biblical scholarship that was defined by grammatical mastery and an

understanding of the original historical, geographical, and cultural context of the scriptures.

The *Loci Communes* is structured so that it clearly and, as simply as possible, explores the most significant concepts in Lutheran theology. Even its title, which translates to "common topics," indicates that this is not an obscure theological book, marking it from the outset as an explicitly anti-scholastic work. The book is organized into 10 topics beginning with "human will and virtue," and then discussing "sin," "law," "Gospel," "grace," "justification and faith," "the Old and New Testaments," "signs," "love," "magistrates," and "scandal," also referred to as adiaphora (issues that are not absolutely essential to the Christian faith but have some significance for its practice). Each of these chapters clearly discussed the most important aspects of these subjects for the Lutheran faith with frequent use of scripture as the sole necessary justification for Melanchthon's conclusions. Melanchthon does not pretend that the *Loci Communes* is an exhaustive exploration of these topics. Rather, it serves as a primer to draw readers, especially students or youths, into the material and to encourage them to consult the resources, especially the scriptures, that he has cited.

The 1521 edition of the *Loci Communes* was the most successful and significant of Melanchthon's academic works, but, much like with Calvin's *Institutes*, this was not the only edition. Melanchthon continued to work on the *Loci Communes* throughout his life and later editions were published in 1535, 1543, and 1559. In these later editions, Melanchthon expands both the number of topics and the depth of his discussion of them. The later editions also mark Melanchthon's developing theology as he slowly changed his views regarding human will and, significantly, the Eucharist. The *Loci Communes* soon came to have an international audience. One of the later editions was dedicated to Henry VIII in an attempt to sway him toward the Lutheran faith and, while the *Loci Communes* was initially written in Latin, it would be translated into German in 1536 and, with the help of John Calvin, into French shortly after Luther's death in 1546 with another edition published in 1551 – both of which were also prefaced by Calvin. The success of the *Loci Communes* propelled Melanchthon onto the national stage alongside Luther and made him a central player in the increasingly political conflict surrounding the Lutheran Reformation.

POLITICAL DEVELOPMENTS

While Melanchthon would consistently prove himself a uniquely talented scholar, his performance in the political arena was not always as impressive.

His generally irenic nature and desire to compromise whenever possible created a number of difficult circumstances for the Protestant movement. Almost immediately following the successful publication of his *Loci Communes*, the arrival of the Zwickau Prophets in Wittenberg challenged Melanchthon's amicable style of leadership. The Zwickau Prophets found a willing audience in Wittenberg in the form of Andreas Karlstadt, but their radical emphasis on the Holy Spirit as a source of authority over and above that of scripture did not sit well with most of the other reformers. However, Melanchthon was unwilling to challenge Karlstadt and was thus compelled to write to Luther, forcing him out of hiding at the Wartburg, to resolve the affair.

This highlights a significant aspect of Melanchthon's personality. He was not unwilling to oppose those opponents he thought were wrong in both writing and in action. He wrote strongly against the scholastics and the Roman Catholics and encouraged Luther to use overwhelming force against the revolting peasants in the 1524 Peasants' War. He even wrote approvingly to Calvin of his execution of Michael Servetus. However, Melanchthon struggled to challenge his friends, most notably Luther, and felt a great deal of guilt whenever he disappointed them. This sense of having disappointed those he cared for came to play a greater role in Melanchthon's life as he began to work more publicly for the advancement and unification of Protestantism.

After the Peasant's War, the attention of the Holy Roman Emperor, Charles V, turned toward the eastern conflict with the Ottoman Empire. To successfully wage war, Charles needed peace in Germany and thus called the disastrous Diet of Speyer in 1529 and then the Diet of Augsburg in 1530 to both discuss the war with the Ottomans and, if possible, resolve the religious dispute in Germany related to the Luther Affair. Because Luther was outlawed by the emperor, Melanchthon became the chief agent of the Lutheran cause to attend the Diets. The Diet of Speyer proved to be a legal setback for Protestants. So, when the Diet of Augsburg was called, Melanchthon saw this as an opportunity to unify the church in Germany and, to this end, he wrote the *Augsburg Confession*.

The *Augsburg Confession*, like the *Loci Communes*, would prove to be one of Melanchthon's most lasting legacies. In it, he laid out the fundamental aspects of Lutheran thought and critiqued those practices of Roman Catholicism that Lutheranism rejected or modified in a total of 28 articles. Melanchthon's purpose in writing the *Augsburg Confession* was to create a document that might reunify the German Church. Because of this, he struck an irenic tone and did not attack certain doctrines of the Roman Catholic

Church, most notably confession, as fervently as other reformers desired. Thus, while Luther publicly affirmed the theology of the *Augsburg Confession*, he privately felt that Melanchthon had conceded too much to their Catholic opponents and had not taken a firm enough stand at the Diet. However, despite Melanchthon's attempts to find common ground with Charles and the Catholic faction, the Diet of Augsburg failed to bring the two sides together and let to the creation of the Protestant Schmalkaldic League.

After the Diet of Augsburg, Melanchthon was drawn into several other public controversies, especially by Luther. Melanchthon's work with Luther on the approval of Philip of Hesse's bigamous marriage greatly affected his psychological well-being after the news of the marriage became public. Melanchthon was also forced to present the position of Protestantism yet again to Charles V at the signing of the Treaty of Frankfurt, which temporarily prevented further hostilities between Charles and the Schmalkaldic League. It was in Frankfurt that Melanchthon was introduced to John Calvin, who was representing the exiled churches in Strasbourg.

CONTESTED LOYALTIES

Calvin was, in 1539, in exile in Strasbourg after fleeing from Geneva. In Frankfurt, Calvin and Melanchthon first met and began to discuss the importance of unity in the church and how this could be applied to the Reformation. By all appearances, the two got along quite well and struck up a friendship that would last for the rest of Melanchthon's life. Over the course of their friendship, Calvin penned at least 14 letters to Melanchthon and Melanchthon wrote at least 8 in reply. The remainder of Melanchthon's life after the Frankfurt meeting can, in many ways, be considered a balancing act between the German and Swiss Reformations. Unfortunately for Melanchthon, this attempt to appease the increasingly volatile and contentious Protestant factions in Germany and still remain faithful to both his friends and his beliefs would lead to increasing criticism of his leadership and his theology.

The conflicts between Geneva and Wittenberg in which Melanchthon found himself embroiled were primarily centered on two issues – the Eucharist and human will insofar as it related to the salvation of humanity. Interestingly, Melanchthon's conflict with both German and Swiss reformers came about as his views on these subjects developed over time. His initial positions on both of these issues presented in the 1521 edition of his *Loci Communes* were in line with Luther as it regarded the physical presence of

Christ in the Eucharist and Calvin when it spoke of humanity's inability to play any role in the salvific process. Over time though, Melanchthon's positions evolved, and he came to hold a view of the Eucharist that was closer to Calvin's understanding than Luther's and a view of human anthropology and salvation that aligned more fully with synergists, such as the early Swiss reformer Huldrych Zwingli. This distanced him from Calvin and other German reformers who found the position too Catholic.

Throughout this development of Melanchthon's views, he managed to maintain his relationship with Luther and Calvin. Luther grew suspicious of Melanchthon's position on the Eucharist, but the two remained publicly united in their discussion with other reformers. This in turn led Calvin to write plaintively to Melanchthon, encouraging him to openly correct Luther's view of the Eucharist and publicly affirm Calvin's own formula, with which Melanchthon did more closely align. However, Melanchthon's admiration and friendship with Calvin could not compete with his devotion to Luther, and Melanchthon avoided responding to Calvin's letters.

After Luther's death in 1546, leadership of the German Reformation fell to Melanchthon. As before, Melanchthon proved less of a diplomat than he was a theologian. This was not because of his inability to compromise, but rather because of his desire to appease all sides. When war broke out between Charles V and the Protestant Schmalkaldic League, Melanchthon attempted to negotiate a peace through the Augsburg Interim. In this document, Melanchthon conceded almost every point of adiaphora to the Roman Catholics. This caused a great deal of anger among the other reformers, and Melanchthon responded by signing the Leipzig Interim, which conceded less but still quite a bit to the Catholic Germans. When the Leipzig Interim failed, Melanchthon was accused of betraying the true teachings of Luther for no gain. This led one of Melanchthon's former students, Matthias Flacias Illyricus, to break with Melanchthon and establish his own branch of the Lutheran church, called the Gnesio-Lutherans.

Flacias was not alone in his criticism of Melanchthon's behavior. Calvin in particular was also at a loss for why Melanchthon would so quickly surrender theological points to Catholicism, be they adiaphora or no. Despite his criticisms, Calvin still assisted in the French translation of Melanchthon's *Loci Communes,* and Melanchthon publicly supported Calvin's decision to execute Servetus. However, the damage was done. The remainder of Calvin and Melanchthon's relationship would largely consist of Calvin encouraging his older friend to speak out in favor of Calvin's positions on the Eucharist and predestination, but Melanchthon remained silent out of both theological disagreement and fear of further angering and distancing the Gnesio-Lutherans led by Flacias.

Calvin's last letter to Melanchthon in 1558 marked a shift in tone. It became clear that Melanchthon would not shift his position and was besieged on all sides by theological and political opponents, and Calvin's letter offered encouragement rather than reprimand. Melanchthon died on April 19, 1560. His passing was not much mourned by many in the Lutheran camp who saw him still as a weak-willed traitor. Interestingly though, even a year after his death, Calvin continued to speak glowingly of Melanchthon and publicly mourned his death, meaning that Melanchthon's passing may have been more mourned in Geneva than it was in Wittenberg.

SUGGESTED FURTHER READINGS

Dingel, Irene, Robert Kolb, Nicole Kuropka, and Timothy J. Wingert, eds. *Philip Melanchthon: Theologian in Classroom, Confession, and Controversy*. Gottingen: Vandenhoeck & Ruprecht, 2012.

Melanchthon, Philip. *Commonplaces: Loci Communes, 1521*, trans. Chris Preus. St. Louis, MO: Concordia Publishing House, 2014.

Pitkin, Barbara. "The Protestant Zeno: Calvin and the Development of Melanchthon's Anthropology." *The Journal of Religion* 84:3 (2004): 345–378.

Speelman, Herman A. *Melanchthon and Calvin on Confession and Communion: Early Modern Protestant Penitential and Eucharistic Piety*. Gottingen: Vandenhoeck & Ruprecht, 2016.

36

Calvin and the Swiss and South German Evangelicals

Peter Opitz

CALVIN IN THE NETWORK OF THE SWISS
AND SOUTH GERMAN REFORMATION

With his flight from Paris to Strassburg and arrival in Basel in January 1535, Calvin entered the sphere of the Swiss and South German Reformation.[1] Geographically, the Reformed towns of the Swiss Confederation lay within this area: Zurich, Bern (with its strong influence reaching west to Lausanne and Geneva), Biel, Basel, Schaffhausen, and St. Gallen, joined by a number of South German towns such as Mülhausen, Strassburg, and Constance. These towns all experienced the Reformation as an urban Reformation, introduced by elected town councilors.[2] The guilds often had significant influence. The town councilors believed themselves responsible for the construction of a Christian church in accord with the Word of God within the area covered by their political authority. Communications networks on various levels linked the towns with each other. Thus, variously constituted gatherings met regularly or as needed and, additionally, information was exchanged, the position of other towns on important questions was ascertained, and letters of recommendation for urban reformers or scholars were supplied. While the towns were conscious of their confessional bonds, each retained its full autonomy and went its own way when it came to the implementation and organization of the Reformation. The Zurich urban reformation served as a model, but as a source of inspiration not a type to be copied wholesale. Disputations often preceded the introduction of the Reformation in these towns, as had been the case in Zurich, with various Reformers from the

---

[1] This chapter was translated by Rona Johnston.
   Peter Opitz, *Leben und Werk Johannes Calvins* (Göttingen: Vandenhoeck & Ruprecht, 2009), 34–59.
[2] Bruce Gordon, *The Swiss Reformation* (Manchester: Manchester University Press, 2002).

Swiss and South German network participating.[3] The Reformers' role was to suggest how the reformation of the Christian community might be accomplished, but the political authorities rarely followed such suggestions without reservation, and discussion and conflict were the order of the day. However much they supported a reformation of Christendom, the political authorities were always concerned to retain decision-making rights, including in church affairs, in their own hands.

Theologically this area was strongly influenced by the Zwinglian reformation.[4] Between 1521 and 1529, the contribution made by Zwingli as adviser on theological and practical matters was significant, as his correspondence makes evident.[5] At the same time, we must be careful to avoid characterizing the Reformers of the Swiss and South German lands as the pupils of a single master. Many were highly educated, humanistic scholars equally well acquainted with the writings of Erasmus and other humanists as with the early texts of Luther and Zwingli. As independent thinkers they tested everything against their own reading of the Bible. In their efforts to purify Christianity of human tradition and idolatry and to be led only by the Word of God, however, they concurred more strongly with the theology of the humanist Zwingli than with that of Luther.[6] Additionally, Zwingli had been more insistent than Luther that the Reformation was located not in the teachings of a single person but in shared efforts to interpret Holy Scripture, a position that he both pronounced and practiced.

Calvin's work and thought as a Reformer were entirely located within this political and intellectual space and were deeply influenced by it. Conversely, Calvin gave this Swiss and South German Reformation a theological form that enabled it to transcend the boundaries of the area influenced by Zwingli and his contemporary comrades in arms, and ultimately to become an international "Calvinism."

All three places where Calvin lived and worked belonged, although in different ways, to the area of the Swiss and South German Reformation.

---

[3] Bernd Moeller and Thomas Kaufmann, *Zwinglis Disputationen: Studien zur Kirchengründung in den Städten der frühen Reformation*, 2nd ed. (Gottingen: Vandenhoeck & Ruprecht, 2011).

[4] Gottfried W. Locher, *Die Zwinglische Reformation im Rahmen der europäischen Kirchengeschichte* (Göttingen: Vandenhoeck & Ruprecht, 1979).

[5] *Huldreich Zwingli sämtliche Werke*, Emil Egli et al. (eds.) (Corpus Reformatorum 88–108, Berlin, Leipzig, and Zürich, 1905–2013) (henceforth: Z); for the correspondence see Vols. VII–XI.

[6] See Peter Opitz, "Calvin in the Context of the Swiss Reformation: Detecting the Traces," in H. J. Selderhuis and Arnold Huijgen (eds.), *Calvinus Pastor Ecclesiae: Papers of the Eleventh International Congress on Calvin Research* (Göttingen: Vandenhoeck & Ruprecht, 2016), 13–28.

Since 1501 Basel had been a full member of the Swiss Confederation and in 1529 the city had finally joined the Reformation. The principal figure of the Basel Reformation was Johannes Oecolampadius, who on December 10, 1522, shortly after his arrival in the city, had first made contact with Zwingli. A close theological working relationship and friendship had developed,[7] and the Basel Reformer not only supported Zwingli in 1528 at the Disputation of Bern but also accompanied him in 1529 to the Marburg Colloquy, where the Lord's Supper was discussed with Luther and Melanchthon. Following Oecolampadius's death in 1531, the leadership of the church in Basel was assumed by Osward Myconius, an old friend of Zwingli's. Myconius had taught at the Grossmünster in Zurich from 1516 to 1519 and again from 1524, and he had participated in Zwingli's call to Zurich.

During Calvin's stay in Basel in 1535/36, the city was the setting for two events that became significant for and documented the identity of the Swiss and South German Reformation. They also provide us with illustrative access to the network of relationships amongst Swiss and South German Reformers. The first event was the printing of a volume with the correspondence of Zurich Reformer Zwingli and Basel Reformer Oecolampadius.[8] In response to accusations from the Lutheran side that the Swiss and South German reformers were divided, a slew of leading reformers and representatives of towns from the Swiss and South German context contributed to the work. The volume begins with a life of Zwingli written by Myconius and a life of Oecolampadius written by Simon Grynäus, his subject's successor as professor in Basel. In a preface Martin Bucer, reformer in Strassburg, defended Zwingli's position on the Lord's Supper. Wolfgang Capito, Zurich Hebraists Konrad Pellikan and Theodor Bibliander, Guillaume Farel, and Johannes Zwick, reformer in Constance, also contributed. All in all, this volume containing the exchange between Zwingli and Oecolampadius was clear affirmation by all the contributors of their allegiance to the Swiss and South German Reformation. With its publication they lined themselves up openly against Luther, who thought the printing of texts by the Swiss reformers outrageous and sought to have it halted.

The second significant event in Basel in that year was the creation of the First Helvetic Confession, signed in the city in February 1536.[9] It documents

---

[7] See Z VII, 635; Z VIII, 345.

[8] *Ioannis Oecolampadii et Huldrichi Zvingli epostolarum libri quatuor* (Basel, 1536).

[9] "The First Helvetic Confession," in Philip Schaff, *The Creeds of Christendom*, Vol. 3: *The Creeds of the Evangelical Churches* (New York: Harper, 1877), 211–231, www.ccel.org/ccel/schaff/creeds3.iv.iv.html.

the unity of the Swiss and South German reformers and also their wrestling to produce a common position in light of their relationship with the Wittenberg Reformation. The signatories had gathered in Basel under the leadership of Oswald Myconius and Simon Grynäus and included representatives from Zurich (Heinrich Bullinger and Leo Jud), Bern (Kaspar Megander), St. Gallen, Schaffhausen, Biel, Mühlhausen, and Constance, joined finally by Martin Bucer and Wolfgang Capito.[10] Both the Strassburg Reformers had previously also been active in the Swiss Confederation. Together with Zwingli, from Zurich, and Oeclampadius, from Basel, they had participated in the 1528 disputation that preceded the introduction of the Reformation in Bern, and Capito had played a significant role at the Synod of Bern in 1532. Unfortunately, the surviving sources reveal little about Calvin's time in Basel. It is, however, inconceivable that he would not have encountered many of the scholars from this circle, a conclusion confirmed by Heinrich Bullinger, reformer in Zurich. Bullinger had succeeded Zwingli as head of the Zurich church, and during Calvin's time he was the most influential reformer in the Swiss Confederation. Calvin's role in Geneva was only possible because he had Bullinger's approval and support. Bullinger sent letters of recommendation for Calvin to Geneva, Bern, and Strassburg and threw his weight behind Calvin in all the Frenchman's various conflicts in Geneva. Calvin also met other reformers during his time in Basel, including Pierre Viret, who, like Farel, became a close friend.

Martin Bucer from Strassburg had also accompanied Zwingli in the fall of 1529 to the colloquy at Marburg, where he had represented the Zwinglian–South German position on the Lord's Supper. Bucer had sought out contact with Zwingli early on and, like Wolfgang Capito and other Strassburg reformers, felt himself close theologically to the Zurich reformer. Accordingly, Zwingli proved an influential voice when it came to constructing a Reformed church.[11] In 1530 a political union was even formed between Zürich, Strassburg, and Basel in defense of the Reformation. Geographical

---

[10]   James M. Kittelson, *Wolfgang Capito, from Humanist to Reformer* (Leiden, The Netherlands: E. J. Brill, 1975); *The Correspondence of Wolfgang Capito*, Erika Rummel (trans. and ed.), 3 vols. (Toronto: University of Toronto Press, 2005–2015).

[11]   See, e.g., Bucer to Zwingli: Z VII 454 (letter of May 23, 1521) and Capito to Zwingli: Z VIII, 299–305 (letter of February 6, 1525). Correspondence of the Strassburg reformers with Zwingli: Kaspar Hedio: 13 letters between 1519 and 1528; Martin Bucer: 24 letters between 1519 and 1528; Wolfgang Capito: 50 letters between 1520 and 1528. We know of 70 letters sent to Zwingli from Strassburg between 1521 and 1528; see www.irg.uzh.ch/static/zwingli-briefe/?n=Index.Personen.

distance and confessional developments in the empire meant, however, that
the alliance did not survive for long.

Geneva, too, the core site of Calvin's activities, should also be recognized
as located within the sphere of the Swiss and South German Reformation.
The city on the River Rhone was not politically a member of the Swiss
Confederation, but from 1536 it was under the protection and potent influence of Bern, militarily the strongest member of the Confederation and
theologically deeply influenced by Zurich since the introduction of the
Reformation in 1528. Geneva faced an uphill battle in any attempt to remain
politically and ecclesiastically independent of Bern. For one thing, all the
reformers and teachers active in Geneva were part of the Swiss and South
German communication network and participated in its theological
exchanges. Guillaume Farel, Geneva Reformer and close friend of Calvin's,
saw himself as missionary of Zwingli in western Switzerland and his
Sommaire is entirely in line with Zwingli's thought.[12] Much the same can
be said of Calvin's other friend and colleague Pierre Viret. Guillaume Farel,
Pierre Viret, Heinrich Bullinger, and Martin Bucer together make up the
most significant of Calvin's correspondents.

CALVIN'S COMMENTARY ON THE LETTER TO THE ROMANS (1540) IN THE CONTEXT OF THE BIBLICAL INTERPRETATION OF THE SWISS AND SOUTH GERMAN REFORMATION

For Calvin, interpretation of scripture *was* theology. In the pulpit he worked
through individual books of the Bible chapter by chapter, following the
tradition of preaching practiced in Zurich. In 1539/40 his first printed
commentary on a book of the Bible, on the Letter to the Romans, was
published in Strassburg. In the preface, dedicated to Simon Grynäus, Calvin
informed his readers about the context in which this project had been
undertaken.[13] The names he cited make evident that this work of biblical
interpretation was carried out within context and network of the Swiss and
South German reformation.[14] Such was certainly also the case for all his later
biblical commentaries.

---

[12] Guillaume Farel, *Sommaire et brève declaration* (1525), Arthur-L. Hofer (ed.) (Neuchâtel: Belle Rivière, 1980).

[13] CO 10b, 402–406; *Ioannis Calvini Commentarius in Epistolam Pauli ad Romanos*, T. H. L. Parker and D. C. Parker (eds.), Ioannis Calvini Opera Omnia [. . .] Series II: Opera Exegetica Veteris et Novi Testamenti, vol. XIII (Geneva: Droz, 1999), 7–12.

[14] See Kathy Ehrensperger and R. Ward Holder, eds., *Reformation Readings of Romans* (London: T&T Clark, 2008).

Simon Grynäus, dedicatee of Calvin's commentary on the Letter to the Romans, was a humanistic scholar from Wurttemberg who had joined the Reformation and recognized he was close to the Zwinglian reformation in his position on the Lord's Supper and other issues. Having first held a chair in Greek at Heidelberg, as a result of efforts by Oecolampadius from 1529 with some interruptions he taught Greek and theology at the university at Basel. During Calvin's stay in Basel, Grynäus was also lecturing on interpretation of scripture. Grynäus is in many ways typical of the Swiss and South German Reformation. He worked with Erasmus on the editing of ancient texts. He had a friendly relationship with Melanchthon, who like Grynäus had attended the Latin school at Pforzheim. He was closely woven into the correspondence network of the Swiss and South German Reformation and assisted in the construction of Reformed churches. Together with Myconius he composed the First Basel Confession (1534), and, as noted, he was also involved in the writing of the First Helvetic Confession (1536) and the editing of the correspondence between Zwingli and Oecolampadius. During his time in Basel, Calvin interacted with Grynäus, who was known for his detailed philological exegesis, an approach Calvin replicated. Calvin's observations on other commentaries on the Letter to the Romans bolster this depiction. He disapproved of what he identified as Melanchthon's concentration on only theological issues. Bucer was criticized for losing himself in the detail. Bullinger alone escaped censure and the Zurich reformer's commentaries on the letters of the New Testament were undoubtedly the most significant model for Calvin's own interpretation. Naturally, in the background was Erasmus's philological and rhetorical biblical interpretation, which the Swiss and South German Reformation had adopted. Calvin's later commentaries too, written in Geneva, are unthinkable without the exegetical tradition of the Swiss and South German Reformation, which had its roots in a humanistic turn to the languages of scripture and to a philological engagement with biblical texts that went back to even before the advent of Luther.[15]

With the establishment of the *Prophezei* in 1525, Zwingli created the first institution in which philologists worked together on interpretation of the Old Testament with recourse to the Hebrew text and the Septuagint, the earliest Greek translation of the Old Testament. The first complete translation of the Old Testament into German during the Reformation was a fruit

---

[15] See Peter Opitz, "The Exegetical and Hermeneutical Work of John Oecolampadius, Huldrych Zwingli and John Calvin," in Magne Saebø (ed.), *Hebrew Bible, Old Testament: The History of Its Interpretation, Vol. II, From the Renaissance to the Enlightenment, B Reformation* (Göttingen: Vandenhoeck & Ruprecht, 1996–2008), 106–159.

of the *Prophezei*. The Zurich *Lectorium*, established in 1532, grew out of this foundation, and Konrad Pellikan and Theodor Bibliander, leading scholars in Hebrew and Old Testament, could be secured as teachers. Zurich did not lead the way alone for long. In 1529, Hebraist Sebastian Münster was called to Basel. While the Strassburg Hohe Schule was not created until 1538, Strassburg reformers Capito and Bucer had long been among the leading Hebraists of the age. Capito had published a Hebrew grammar as early as 1518 and had subsequently dedicated himself to the interpretation of the Old Testament books of the Prophets. He published Oecolampadius's commentary on Ezekiel in Strassburg in 1532, along with a report by Grynäus on Oecolampadius's death. Martin Bucer provided commentaries on a whole run of biblical books. Anyone who has tackled Bucer's commentaries on the Psalms will readily appreciate Calvin's critical comment about their too great exhaustiveness, although Calvin, whose knowledge of Hebrew was certainly limited, was able to profit from Bucer's efforts.[16] The Geneva Academy, founded by Calvin in 1559, should be understood in light of these earlier examples from Reformed cities.

CALVIN'S ECCLESIASTICAL ORDINANCES FOR GENEVA (1542) IN THE CONTEXT OF THE ECCLESIOLOGY OF THE SWISS AND SOUTH GERMAN REFORMATION

Only a few months before Calvin's arrival in Geneva in the summer of 1536, the Genevans had finally expelled the bishop and resolved to adopt the Reformation. Calvin had been brought to Geneva, on the urging of Farel, to give the young Genevan church a form and an order. That would require a catechism that could be used to instruct the people in the Reformed faith and church ordinances that would regulate the communal life of the faithful according to the Word of God.[17] As in all other towns, these innovations were introduced on the orders of the Christian town council and under its oversight. With the abolition of the episcopal marriage court, Geneva also needed to create a new authority that would be responsible for and adjudicate on issues of marriage and Christian coexistence, while excommunication, a practice often abused by the Roman Church, had to be overhauled. Both issues were naturally bound in

---

[16] See Peter Opitz, "Calvin as Bible Translator: From the Model of the Hebrew Psalter," in Herman J. Selderhuis (ed.). *Calvinus sacrarum literarum interpres: Papers of the International Congress on Calvin Research (Emden 2006)*, (Göttingen: Vandenhoeck & Ruprecht, 2008), 9–26.

[17] Still important is Walther Köhler, *Zürcher Ehegericht und Genfer Konsistorium*, 2 vols. (Leipzig: Heinsius, 1932–1942).

with the Reformers' efforts to combat immorality and sinfulness and to foster a true Christian life in community. As is well known, Calvin fought for the creation of a consistory in Geneva, a body that was to guide the church and whose members were to be selected according to spiritual criteria. For years he would need to fight for the consistory's independence of the Council, with the consistory's claim to be able to exclude intransigent sinners temporarily from the Lord's Supper. Yet neither Calvin's understanding of excommunication nor the long-lasting debate in Geneva he prompted was entirely novel. The problem of implementing a church discipline in accord with the Word of God had accompanied the Swiss and South German Reformation from the beginning. Everywhere marriage courts were set up to deal with issues related to matrimony and morals, usually as a small body composed of representatives from the council and pastorate. Zurich led the way, in 1525, and was followed by other towns: Bern in 1528, Basel in 1529, and, finally, Strassburg in 1537. In 1525 and then again in 1529, the Strassburg Reformers Bucer, Capito, Hedio, and Zell had requested that the town council establish a marriage court on the Zurich model, and the composition and precise competencies of this body remained constantly debated.

The issue of excommunication proved particularly controversial. Although fundamentally accepted because it had been practiced in the early church and, according to the reformers, was scripturally justified, its implementation was controversial from the start. In Zurich, Zwingli had proposed exclusion from participation in the Lord's Supper be practiced, although the Council had not taken up his suggestion. Elsewhere in the Confederation it was also contentious. The decision about excommunication was finally left to each member of the Swiss Confederation individually. For Zwingli, it was essential that the local community be able to decide for itself, for the community formed the visible church. As the town councilors and representatives of the guilds were members of the local church, he did not insist on the creation of an additional independent consistory. Zurich and Berne forwent the practice of excommunication. There was no desire for new bishops who would control the conscience of the individual. Instead, as proposed by Bullinger, the communion liturgy contained the formulation that each person should examine himself or herself to ascertain whether he or she was worthy (see 1 Cor. 11:27–28).

The situation was different in Basel, where Oecolampadius strongly favored practicing excommunication.[18] Bucer and other Strasburg reformers

---

[18] Olaf Kuhr, "Calvin and Basel: The Significance of Oecolampadius and the Basel Discipline Ordinance for the Institution of Ecclesiastical Discipline in Geneva," *Scottish Bulletin of Evangelical Theology* (Spring 1998): 19–33, http://resources.thegospelcoalition.org/library/

adopted the same position.[19] In both towns, and in Strassburg in particular, considerable tensions between the political authorities and the reformers arose as a result.

It is therefore hardly surprising that these tensions were repeated some years later in Geneva.[20] That Calvin was eventually more successful in realizing his vision than his colleagues in other towns was connected to Geneva's inundation with Protestant refugees, who shifted the majority position within the city in his favor.

Calvin has often been identified as a pupil of Martin Bucer. Certainly, on issues that were particularly controversial in his own age (church discipline, predestination, interpretation of the Lord's Supper) he was somewhat closer to the Strassburg reformer than to Heinrich Bullinger. Yet a friendship still developed between the reformer in Zurich and the reformer in Geneva. When Bucer and Bullinger were struggling to agree on how they might respond to Luther's unwillingness to compromise on the Lord's Supper, Calvin sought to mediate, and the Consensus Tigurinus of 1549 could document unity within the Swiss and South Germany Reformation.[21] Geneva adopted the Second Helvetic Confession, composed by Bullinger, as its own confession. And in responding to the polemic of Lutheran Joachim Westphal, Calvin finally expressly aligned himself with Zwingli, writing that he and Zwingli had made progress in Christ's school, taking all thought captive that it might obey Christ (see 2 Cor. 10:5).[22] Their common harkening to the Word of God was for him far stronger than their differences on individual questions. Calvin fully fitted the mold of the Swiss and South German Reformation.

SUGGESTED FURTHER READING

Ganoczy, Alexandre. *The Young Calvin.* 1st American ed. Philadelphia: Westminster Press, 1987.

---

calvin-and-basel-the-significance-of-oecolampadius-and-the-basel-discipline-ordinance-for-the-institution-of-ecclesiastical-discipline-in-geneva.

[19] Amy Nelson Burnett, "Church Discipline and Moral Reformation in the Thought of Martin Bucer," *Sixteenth Century Journal* 22:3 (1991): 439–456.

[20] See F. P. van Stam, "Das Verhältnis zwischen Bullinger und Calvin während Calvins erstem Aufenthalt in Genf," in Peter Opitz (ed.), *Calvin im Kontext der Schweizer Reformation* (Zürich: Theologischer Verlag Zürich, 2003), 25–40.

[21] Emidio Campi und Ruedi Reich (eds.), *Consensus Tigurinus (1549): Die Einigung zwischen Heinrich Bullinger und Johannes Calvin über das Abendmahl/Werden – Wertung – Bedeutung* (Zürich: TVZ Theologischer Verlag Zürich, 2009).

[22] CO 9, 94; see Fritz Blanke, "Calvins Urteile über Zwingli," *Aus der Welt der Reformation* (Zürich and Stuttgart: Zwingli-Verlag, 1960), 18–47.

Gordon, Bruce. *The Swiss Reformation*. Manchester, UK: Manchester University Press, 2002.

Locher, Gottfried W. *Die Zwinglische Reformation im Rahmen der europäischen Kirchengeschichte*. Göttingen: Vandenhoeck & Ruprecht, 1979.

Opitz, Peter. *Leben und Werk Johannes Calvins*. Göttingen: Vandenhoeck & Ruprecht, 2009.

37

Calvin's Friends

Farel, Viret, and Beza

Michael W. Bruening

John Calvin did not create the French Reformed movement alone. At every step of the way, he was assisted by close friends and allies. Guillaume Farel preceded Calvin and established many of the key doctrines and practices that would come to define Calvinism. Pierre Viret was perhaps Calvin's closest friend and worked steadily to implement Calvin's vision of reform first in Lausanne and later in France, while also popularizing Calvinist theology in his many vernacular dialogues. And Theodore Beza emerged as an important theologian in his own right before taking over as Calvin's successor as head of the Geneva Company of Pastors, from which position he helped to guide the French Reformed churches during the Wars of Religion and to unify the Swiss Reformed churches behind a common theology.

Guillaume Farel (1489–1565) was a native of Gap in the French Dauphiné.[1] After studies at the University of Paris (1509–1517), Farel joined Jacques Lefèvre d'Étaples first at Saint-Germain (1517–1521) and later as part of the

---

[1] The standard biography of Farel is the Comité Farel, *Guillaume Farel: Biographie nouvelle* (Neuchâtel: Delachaux & Niestlé, 1930); see also Pierre Barthel et al., eds., *Actes du Colloque Guillaume Farel, Neuchâtel, 29 septembre–1ᵉʳ octobre 1980*, 2 vols. (Geneva: Revue de Théologie et de Philosophie, 1983); Elfriede Jacobs, *Die Sakramentslehre Wilhelm Farels* (Zurich: Theologischer Verlag, 1978); Jason Zuidema and Theodore Van Raalte, *Early French Reform: The Theology and Spirituality of Guillaume Farel* (Burlington, VT: Ashgate, 2011), which also contains English translations of some of his early works. An effort is underway to publish critical editions of all of Farel's published works; Guillaume Farel, *Oeuvres imprimées*, Reinhard Bodenmann et al. (eds.) (Geneva: Droz, 2009–). Farel's correspondence is found chiefly in Herminjard and the CO, but see also Dominique Quadroni, "Répertoire de la Correspondance de Guillaume Farel," in Barthel, *Actes de Colloque Guillaume Farel*, 2:3–104; also, several of his previously unedited letters are in Michael Bruening, ed., *Epistolae Petri Vireti: The Previously Unedited Letters and a Register of Pierre Viret's Correspondence* (Geneva: Droz, 2012).

reform circle of Meaux (1521–1523). After Bishop Guillaume Briçonnet revoked Farel's preaching privileges in 1523, Farel left France.

The next years of Farel's career were decisive not only for his own development but also for the entire history of Francophone Protestantism, for he joined with the Reformed ministers of Germany and Switzerland, whose influence would be lasting. From 1524 to 1526, Farel traveled among Basel, Zurich, Montbéliard, and Strasbourg. It was precisely at this point when the first Eucharistic controversy broke out between the Lutherans and the Reformed. Farel, having become friends during this period with Zwingli, Oecolampadius, and Bucer, firmly took their side in the controversy, leading French reform forever to follow Reformed rather than Lutheran theology and practice.

Farel firmly established this Reformed shift in two books that would shape the early Francophone Reformation: His *Summaire* (1529) became the earliest French manual of Reformed theology, and his *Maniere et Fasson* (1533) provided French Protestants with their first vernacular liturgy.[2] These were the theological and liturgical guides available to French-speaking evangelicals before Calvin's arrival in Geneva and continued to be used for several years after. Thus, their significance cannot be overstated, and their roots lay in Farel's experience of the theology and liturgy common in Basel, Strasbourg, and Zurich.

While Farel's years in these Reformed cities were theologically formative, the following decade, from 1526 to 1536, secured Farel's reputation as the most important early French Protestant missionary. Without Farel's missionary work, there may not have been a Protestant Geneva for Calvin to come to in 1536. During these years, Farel worked to establish Protestant churches in Bern's allied and subject territories. Resistance to Protestantism was strong among the local populations, and Farel was by no means successful everywhere. He did, however, win two major victories by helping to convert the important cities of Neuchâtel (1530) and Geneva (1535) to Protestantism.

The year 1536 marked a major turning point in Farel's career, not only because of Calvin's arrival in Geneva but also because of Bern's conquest of the Pays de Vaud, the Francophone region between Geneva and Bern that

---

[2] Guillaume Farel, *Le Sommaire de Guillaume Farel, réimprimé d'après l'édition de l'an 1534*, J.-G. Baum, ed. (Geneva: Jules-Guillaume Fick, 1867); idem, *La maniere et fasson qu'on tient en baillant le sainct baptesme* (Neuchâtel: Pierre de Vingle, 1533). English translations of both works are available in Zuidema and Van Raalte, *Early French Reform*, 117–179 (*Summaire*), 195–223 (*Maniere et fasson*).

includes the city of Lausanne. The Bernese conquest and subsequent Lausanne Disputation converted the entire region to Protestantism, thus effectively bringing to an end Farel's missionary period. Calvin's arrival was important as well for Farel. While several early French arrivals in Switzerland (e.g., Jean Lecomte, Thomas Malingre, and André Zébédée) continued to follow the Zwinglian theology that Farel had introduced to the region, Farel quickly lined up behind Calvin on the issues that divided the two wings of the Reformed movement, most notably the Eucharist, predestination, and ecclesiastical discipline and excommunication.

In 1538, when Calvin and Farel were exiled from Geneva, Farel took up the post he would occupy for the rest of his life as pastor in Neuchâtel (1538–1565). In this role, Farel sought to implement Calvin's vision of reform in the city, with varying degrees of success. He also remained Calvin's lifelong friend, correspondent, and advisor.[3]

In 1542, however, Pierre Viret (1509/10–1571) effectively replaced Farel as Calvin's best friend and most frequent correspondent.[4] Viret, long thought to have been born in 1511, seems, in fact, to have been born earlier, probably in 1509 or early 1510, thus making him approximately the same age as Calvin.[5] Viret was from Orbe, a common lordship governed jointly by Bern and Fribourg, and as such, one of Farel's early missionary stops. In 1531, Farel convinced Viret to join the evangelical ministry; like Farel, Viret was an active missionary in the Suisse romande until 1536. Viret and Farel dominated the discussion at the Lausanne Disputation that year, and Viret remained as the city's pastor afterward.

---

[3] Heiko Oberman argues, however, that Farel's marriage in 1558 to Marie Thorel, a 16- or 17-year-old French refugee, alienated Calvin from Farel because their correspondence shows a marked decline after this event. Oberman, "Calvin and Farel: The Dynamics of Legitimation in Early Calvinism," in idem, *John Calvin and the Reformation of the Refugees* (Geneva: Droz, 2009), 195–222.

[4] On Viret, the standard biography is Jean Barnaud, *Pierre Viret: Sa vie et son oeuvre (1511–1571)* (Saint-Amans: G. Carayol, 1911); see also Karine Crousaz and Daniela Solfaroli-Camillocci, eds., *Pierre Viret et la diffusion de la Réforme* (Lausanne: Antipodes, 2014). On his thought, see Robert Linder, *The Political Ideas of Pierre Viret* (Geneva: Droz, 1964); Georges Bavaud, *Le réformateur Pierre Viret, 1511–1571: Sa théologie* (Geneva: Labor et fides, 1986). Dominique Troilo has compiled a thorough bibliography of works by and about Viret: *L'Oeuvre de Pierre Viret: L'activité littéraire du Réformateur mise en lumière* (Lausanne: L'Age d'Homme, 2012). A still useful collection of excerpts from Viret's writings can be found in Charles Schnetzler et al., eds., *Pierre Viret d'après lui-même* (Lausanne: Georges Bridel, 1911). His correspondence is found chiefly in Herminjard and the CO, but see also Jean Barnaud, ed., *Quelques lettres inédites de Pierre Viret* (Saint-Amans: G. Carayol, 1911), and Bruening, *Epistolae Petri Vireti*, which also contains a complete register of his correspondence.

[5] Crousaz and Solfaroli-Camillocci, *Pierre Viret et la diffusion de la Réforme*, 7–9.

Viret was called temporarily to Geneva in early 1541 to help prepare the city for Calvin's return from exile. He remained in the city for nine months after Calvin's arrival, and this period appears to have been the turning point that bound the two so closely together. From 1542 on, Viret would be Calvin's most frequent correspondent. Upon his return to Lausanne, Viret would also become the leader of the Calvinist party in the Pays de Vaud. He frequently found himself at odds with the region's Zwinglian pastors and with the Bern City Council, as he argued for Calvinist interpretations of the Lord's Supper and predestination, as well as for the right of the consistory to excommunicate unrepentant sinners.[6]

Lausanne was a vitally important Reformed center during Viret's tenure there, for it contained French-speaking Europe's first Protestant institution of higher learning, the Lausanne Academy.[7] This was, indeed, the only school of its kind in Francophone lands until the Geneva Academy opened in 1559. The Lausanne Academy, therefore, produced the first cohorts of French-speaking pastors to be trained entirely by Protestant teachers. In addition, the Academy offered a thoroughly humanist education and attracted some of the most important Protestant intellectuals at the time; Mathurin Cordier, Theodore Beza, François Hotman, Conrad Gessner, Celio Secondo Curione, André Zébédée, Jean Ribit, and Eustache du Quesnoy all taught there during Viret's time in Lausanne. Viret and the academy's professors usually made common cause on the divisive issues of the day; consequently, the Lausanne Academy emerged as the strongest bastion of Calvinist thought outside Geneva during the Reformation.

The conflicts between the Bern City Council and the Calvinists in Lausanne peaked in 1558, when Viret and the professors insisted on greater authority for the church in administering discipline, including the right of excommunication. When the Bern City Council refused to go as far as Viret wanted, Viret delayed administering the Christmas Eucharist without permission from the Bernese, and they responded by banishing him in early 1559. Nearly all the Lausanne professors and many of the students followed him into exile. Most, like Viret, went to Geneva initially, and many, also like Viret, went from there into France. The Lausanne exile thus created probably the single-largest geographical shift of Francophone Protestant intellectuals between the 1534 Affair of the Placards and the 1572 St. Bartholomew's

---

[6] On these issues, see Michael Bruening, *Calvinism's First Battleground: Conflict and Reform in the Pays de Vaud, 1528–1559* (Dordrecht, The Netherlands: Springer, 2005).

[7] On the academy, see Karine Crousaz, *L'Académie de Lausanne entre Humanisme et Réforme (ca. 1537–1560)* (Leiden, The Netherlands: Brill, 2012).

Day Massacre. Lausanne's loss was Geneva's gain, and the Geneva Academy was able to open later that year at full strength, with a faculty and student body composed, in part, of exiles from Lausanne.

During his time in Lausanne, Viret also emerged as the most popular and prolific Calvinist author after Calvin. Viret aimed to make his friend's theology accessible to a wider audience by writing almost exclusively in the vernacular, frequently using dialogue, and employing humor and sharp polemic. His works appear to have circulated widely, in both Switzerland and France, and they made him one of the best known reformers in French-speaking Europe.

Thus, when Viret made it known that he wanted to move to France because of his poor health, requests came in from churches all over the kingdom asking for him to be sent to their town. In 1561, he left Geneva for France and spent the final decade of his life there. After a few months in Nîmes and Montpellier, he moved to Lyon (1562–1565), and finally to Béarn (1567–1571), which was under the jurisdiction of Jeanne d'Albret, the Protestant daughter of Marguerite de Navarre. While in France, Viret participated in several local and regional synods and presided at the 1563 National Synod of Lyon.

One of Viret's most important colleagues, first in Lausanne and later in Geneva, was Theodore Beza (1516–1605), or Théodore de Bèze.[8] Beza was a Frenchman, born in Vézelay, whose first love was literature but whose career brought him increasingly into the theological centers and quarrels of the Reformation. Early studies with Melchior Wolmar exposed him to evangelical teachings, but he did not fully embrace Protestantism until 1548. After leaving Paris for Geneva, Beza found employment at the Lausanne Academy

---

[8] A larger literature has emerged around Beza than around Farel and Viret. The standard biography of Beza is Paul-F. Geisendorf, *Théodore de Bèze* (Geneva: Labor et Fides, 1949), but see also Alain Dufour, *Théodore de Bèze, poète et théologien* (Geneva: Droz, 2006), and Backus, ed., *Théodore de Bèze (1519–1605): Actes du Colloque de Genève (septembre 2005)* (Geneva: Droz, 2007). For various aspects of Beza's theology, see, e.g., Jill Raitt, *The Eucharistic Theology of Theodore Beza: Development of the Reformed Doctrine* (Chambersburg, PA: American Academy of Religion, 1972); John S. Bray, *Theodore Beza's Doctrine of Predestination* (Nieuwkoop: De Graaf, 1975); Jeffrey Mallinson, *Faith, Reason, and Revelation in Theodore Beza, 1519–1605* (Oxford: Oxford University Press, 2003); Kirk Summers, *Morality after Calvin: Theodore Beza's Christian Censor and Reformed Ethics* (New York: Oxford University Press, 2017). For Beza's influential role in the French Reformation during the second half of the sixteenth century, see Scott Manetsch, *Theodore Beza and the Quest for Peace in France, 1562–1598* (Leiden, The Netherlands: Brill, 2000). The half-century-long project to publish all Beza's correspondence was completed in 2017, just before the death of its longtime editor, Alain Dufour; Beza, *Correspondance de Théodore de Bèze*, 43 vols., Hippolyte Aubert et al. (eds.) (Geneva: Droz, 1960–2017).

as professor of Greek (1549–1558). Known early on for his literary creations (e.g., his 1548 *Juvenilia* poetry and his 1550 tragedy *Abraham Sacrifiant*), Beza increasingly became involved in the theological quarrels of the 1550s, penning sharply worded polemics against Calvin's nemesis Sebastian Castellio, strongly supporting Calvin against Jerome Bolsec on predestination, and standing with Viret in his struggles with the Bernese for ecclesiastical discipline.[9] Unlike Viret, however, Beza was able to leave Lausanne voluntarily shortly before Bern's decision to banish Viret and his other colleagues.

In November 1558, Beza moved to Geneva, which would become home for the rest of his life. First, he took on the role as professor of Greek and rector of the newly opened Geneva Academy, and he was made a member of the Company of Pastors. Both roles would be enduring. Beza would remain an academy professor until 1599, and he would succeed Calvin as moderator of the Company of Pastors (1564–1580). The torch had been passed.

In addition to guiding the Geneva church, Beza became deeply involved in the affairs of the Reformed churches in France. Not long after his arrival in Geneva, Beza set off on a series of diplomatic trips into the kingdom, the most important of which was as delegate to the Colloquy of Poissy (1561). Although the colloquy failed to achieve its primary objective of closing the rift between the Catholic and Reformed churches in France, it solidified Beza's position as Calvin's heir apparent and as a leader of the Francophone Reformed churches. Over the next decades, Beza would intervene repeatedly in French church affairs, carrying on an extensive correspondence with pastors in the realm and presiding at the important National Synod of La Rochelle in 1571. In addition, in one of his most influential historical works, Beza edited the famous *Ecclesiastical History of the French Reformed Churches*.[10] Following the St. Bartholomew's Day Massacre, Beza penned

---

[9] Kirk Summers, *A View from the Palatine: The Iuvenilia of Théodore de Bèze, Text, Translation, and Commentary* (Tempe: Arizona Center for Medieval and Renaissance Studies, 2001); Theodore Beza, *Abraham Sacrifiant*, Keith Cameron, Kathleen Hall, and Francis Higman (eds.) (Geneva: Droz, 1967); idem, *De Haereticis a civili magistratu puniendis libellus, adversus Martini Belli farraginem et novorum Academicorum sectam* (Geneva: Robert Estienne, 1554) (this text against Castellio is more commonly known as the *Antibellius*); idem, "Summa totius Christianismi sive descriptio et distributio causarum salutis electorum, et exitii reprobrum, ex sacris literis collecta," in idem, *Volumen Tractionum Theologicarum*, 3 vols. (Geneva: Jean Crespin, 1570–1582), 1: 170–205 (this text from 1555 is better known as the *Tabula Praedestinationis*).

[10] Theodore Beza, *Histoire ecclésiastique des Églises Réformées au royaume de France*, 3 vols., G. Baum and E. Cunitz (eds.) (Paris: Fischbacher, 1883–1889).

The Right of Magistrates, an influential defense of the right to armed resistance against tyranny.[11]

Beza's leadership played an important role in the Swiss Confederation as well, helping to heal some of the wounds between Calvinists and Zwinglians that had opened during Calvin's and Viret's lifetimes. In particular, Beza led Geneva to support Heinrich Bullinger's Second Helvetic Confession (1565). And at the Colloquy of Montbéliard (1586) and Synod of Bern (1588), pastors from Bern, Zurich, and Basel rallied around Beza's theological interpretations of divisive issues such as the Eucharist and predestination.

In his *Icones*, Beza noted that "many call Calvin, Farel, and Viret ... the 'elite trio,' in such a way that the common proverb celebrates the wisdom of Calvin, the vehemence of Farel, and the eloquence of Viret."[12] It seems perfectly appropriate to add the *Icones*'s author here to turn the trio into a quartet, and one suspects the proverb would go on to celebrate the "diplomacy of Beza." Above all, one must understand that Calvin was not a solo act. The development of the Reformed movement, the propagation of Calvinism, and the long-term legacy of Calvin's Geneva all owed a great deal to his followers and friends, and to none more so than Farel, Viret, and Beza.

SUGGESTED FURTHER READINGS

Barnaud, Jean. *Pierre Viret: Sa vie et son oeuvre (1511–1571)*. Saint-Amans: G. Carayol, 1911.

Bray, John S. *Theodore Beza's Doctrine of Predestination*. Nieuwkoop: De Graaf, 1975.

Bruening, Michael. *Calvinism's First Battleground: Conflict and Reform in the Pays de Vaud, 1528–1559*. Dordrecht, The Netherlands: Springer, 2005.

Comité Farel. *Guillaume Farel: Biographie nouvelle*. Neuchâtel: Delauchaux & Niestlé, 1930.

Dufour, Alain. *Théodore de Bèze, poète et théologien*. Geneva: Droz, 2006.

Geisendorf, Paul-F. *Théodore de Bèze*. Geneva: Labor et Fides, 1949.

Mallinson, Jeffrey. *Faith, Reason, and Revelation in Theodore Beza, 1519–1605*. Oxford: Oxford University Press, 2003.

Manetsch, Scott. *Theodore Beza and the Quest for Peace in France, 1562–1598*. Leiden, The Netherlands: Brill, 2000.

---

[11] Theodore Beza, *Du droit des magistrats*, Robert Kingdon (ed.) (Geneva: Droz, 1970).

[12] "plusieurs appeloyent Calvin, Farel, et Viret ... le trepied d'eslite: en telle sorte que le commun proverbe celebroit le savoir de Calvin, la vehemence de Farel, et l'eloqence de Viret." Theodore Beza, *Les vrais portraits des hommes illustres* (Geneva: Slatkine, 1986), 127.

Linder, Robert. *The Political Ideas of Pierre Viret*. Geneva: Droz, 1964.

Oberman, Heiko. *John Calvin and the Reformation of the Refugees*, ed. Peter Dykema. Geneva: Droz, 2009.

Raitt, Jill. *The Eucharistic Theology of Theodore Beza: Development of the Reformed Doctrine*. Chambersburg, PA: American Academy of Religion, 1972.

Summers, Kirk. *Morality after Calvin: Theodore Beza's Christian Censor and Reformed Ethics*. New York: Oxford University Press, 2017.

Zuidema, Jason, and Theodore Van Raalte. *Early French Reform: The Theology and Spirituality of Guillaume Farel*. Burlington, VT: Ashgate, 2011.

38

Calvin's Critics

Bolsec and Castellio

Kirk Essary

Few figures from the Reformation era have remained as divisive as John Calvin. Whether because of Calvin's doctrine of predestination or his involvement in the execution of Michael Servetus in Geneva in 1553, his contemporary detractors found ample reason for dissension. Regarding the former, five-odd centuries have done little to ameliorate (and perhaps much to exacerbate) the *prima facie* severity of Calvin's specific brand of predestination, which maintains that God foreordained multitudes to eternal damnation before the creation of the world. Anyone who has been tasked with explaining the reformer's thoughts on this matter to undergraduates in a Christianity 101 course (or to an innocent bystander at the local watering hole) is keenly aware of its almost universal unattractiveness. This sentiment holds *a fortiori* for the execution of Servetus. Two key sixteenth-century figures, Jérôme-Hermès Bolsec and Sebastian Castellio, honed in on these two issues in a barrage of anti-Calvinist writings. In doing so, they painted the first broad strokes of what would prove to be an enduring image of Calvin as a dour and intransigent figure. Moreover, they forced Calvin and Geneva into a series of defensive responses that were formative in the process of confessionalization beginning in the 1550s, a crucial period for religious identity formation especially among Swiss Protestant churches.

JEROME BOLSEC

Not all Calvin's critics are created equal. Few, for example, vehemently criticized Calvin's doctrine of predestination while he was sitting there in the room; even fewer took the opportunity to pen a biography of Calvin that portrays the reformer as dying an unflattering – albeit divinely ordained – death by pubic crabs. Jérôme Bolsec did both. We know little about Bolsec's upbringing. He eventually became a Carmelite monk in Paris, and so was likely from the north of France. Sometime around 1545, Bolsec left (or was forced from) the Catholic Church, seemingly in the wake of a controversial sermon he had preached at St. Bartholomew's in Paris.[1] This led him to Protestant-friendly lands, in the first instance to Ferrara whose Duchess Renee was amenable to Huguenot refugees, where he likely took up the study of medicine for the first time.

By the time he landed near Geneva in 1550, he called himself a medical doctor, but he also retained interests in theology and would attend meetings in the city with the ministers in the Geneva *congrégation*. According to Theodore Beza, he spent much of his time in smaller towns on the outskirts of Geneva, although whether this was because the Genevans found him problematic (as Beza – no friend of Bolsec's – suggests) is difficult to assess. For a time he lived in Veigy (then technically in Bernese territory) and was close with Jacques de Bourgogne, Lord of Falais, for whom he served as a family physician.[2] From the beginning of his time there, Bolsec was an engaged participant in Reformed Protestantism.[3] However, his newfound theological orientation did not extend to Calvin's doctrine of predestination, which would result in a very public disagreement that would lead to his imprisonment and eventual banishment from Geneva.

The controversy began in full force when, on October 16, 1551, Bolsec attended the *congrégation* in Geneva and publicly denounced Calvin's specific understanding of predestination on the grounds that the eternal damnation of the reprobate was both unscriptural and entailed that God was the author of sin and evil.[4] Bruce Gordon sums up the matter nicely: "The accusation was neither new nor original, yet to state it openly in Geneva and in Calvin's presence was simultaneously audacious and idiotic."[5] According

---

[1] The best source for the Bolsec controversy, with the most extensive bibliography, is Philip Holtrop, *The Bolsec Controversy on Predestination from 1551 to 1555*, 2 vols. (Lewiston, NY: Edwin Mellen, 1993). See also Bruce Gordon, *Calvin* (New Haven, CT: Yale University Press, 2009), 205–215, for the controversy and the stress it put on the relationship between Geneva and other Swiss churches for years. For contemporary details on Bolsec's trial in Geneva, see Philip Hughes, ed. and trans., *The Register of the Company of Pastors of Geneva in the Time of Calvin* (Grand Rapids, MI: Eerdmans, 1966). On Bolsec's *Life of Calvin*, see especially Irena Backus, *Life Writing in Reformation Europe* (Burlington, VT: Ashgate, 2008), 125–186.

[2] Calvin had dedicated his 1546 *Commentary on First Corinthians* to de Falais, but was forced to retract the dedication in the reissued 1556 edition in part, no doubt, because of de Falais's public support of Bolsec during the controversy (a retraction that even makes it into Pierre Bayle's *Dictionnaire* in the entry on de Falais).

[3] For a brief overview of the years after Bolsec left Paris, see Holtrop, *The Bolsec Controversy*, 769–771.

[4] He had been reprimanded earlier by the *congrègation* for his views on predestination, on May 15, 1551, according to the *Register* (see op. cit. 132).

[5] Gordon, *Calvin*, 205.

to the Genevan *Register*, Bolsec denied that election and reprobation had been eternal decrees by God, and that "no other election or reprobation should be recognized than that which is seen in the believer or the unbeliever."[6] According to Beza, Calvin was not in the room when Bolsec started, but arrived before he finished and proceeded to give a lengthy refutation of Bolsec's arguments. That retort "satisfied" the assembly, according to the *Register*, but was obviously deemed insufficient as a punishment: Bolsec was arrested and his trial started *that day*. It would last for two-and-a-half months, during which time he remained imprisoned in Geneva. In brief, the charge was heresy (of the Pelagian stripe), although Philip Holtrop and other scholars have suggested that such charges were in fact a cover for the real worry on the part of the Genevan ministers: a possible insurrection fomented by Bolsec's "slanders" against Calvin's teaching.[7]

Indeed, Bolsec's challenge raised in the minds of some (including Geneva's ally in Zurich, Heinrich Bullinger's, it seems[8]) the problematic idea that Calvin might endorse the unpalatable notion of God as the author of sin. Apart from private concerns raised by Bullinger that Calvin's doctrine was perhaps problematic – which would lead to Calvin defending and clarifying his doctrine of predestination in print throughout the next decade – the Zurich church also suggested that Geneva had initially been too harsh on Bolsec, claiming that it was in everyone's interest if the issue was resolved peaceably. Rumors had circulated that Calvin and other ministers in Geneva wanted Bolsec executed as a heretic, but capitulated to Bernese pressure that he not be put to death. In any case, after a 10-week trial that involved discussions between Bolsec and the ministers on a range of doctrinal matters, the ex-Carmelite was banished from Geneva to the sound of a trumpet on December 24, 1551.

The affair did not end there, however. Bolsec merely retreated to nearby Bernese territory, settling there at the beginning of 1552, and continued to excite animus against Calvin among its denizens, denouncing the Genevan reformer as a heretic and the Antichrist. The execution of Michael Servetus for heresy in Geneva in 1553 did little to undercut Bolsec's accusations of Calvin as a tyrant, and Bolsec seems to have continued to publish anti-

---

[6] *Register*, 138. For the *Register*'s account of the whole trial, see ibid. 138–186.
[7] For full details of the trial, see Holtrop, *The Bolsec Controversy*, 414ff.
[8] For the Zurich letter, see the *Register*, 177–179; for the exchange between Bullinger and Calvin, see Cornelis Venema, "Bullinger's Correspondence on Calvin's Doctrine of Predestination, 1551–1553," *The Sixteenth Century Journal* 17:4 (1986): 435–450.

Calvinist tracts during this time, much to the chagrin of the Genevans.[9] While Bernese officials seem initially to have been sympathetic to Bolsec's objections to Calvin's doctrine of predestination and thus willing to put up with a gadfly, they could not in the end endure his protestations against the execution of Servetus, for they had endorsed the decision. Bolsec was thus finally banished from Berne, too, in the spring or early summer of 1555.[10]

The controversy over predestination and the banishment of Bolsec from Geneva undoubtedly (and understandably) left him raw. It is also the episode for which Bolsec is now most remembered in Calvin studies. However, it was his biography of Calvin, first published in Paris in 1577, that would have a lasting impact outside Reformed circles. It is a disparaging attack on all aspects of Calvin's life and thought. Irena Backus has referred to the *Vie de Calvin* as "a sort of upside-down saint's life."[11] It was published, in part, as an antidote to Beza's rather more right-side-up *Life of Calvin*, which contained many slanders against Bolsec, including a reference to his wife as a prostitute. Bolsec's biography's impetus, however, had a much longer incubation period: Chiara Lastraioli has shown that the contours of the *Vie de Calvin* had in fact been printed two decades earlier in the form of a 546-line poem.[12] In this pseudonymous lampoon, Calvin ("Jehan de Noyon") is depicted as both the Antichrist and a counterfeit pope.

Some of the more colorful details are lacking in the first draft, however. For example, the 1577 biography contains the charge that Calvin, while still a youth at Noyon, was arrested for sodomy and, as punishment, received a brand of the *fleur-de-lis*.[13] While no doubt a fabrication, the detail would be repeated often in anti-Calvinist circles well into the seventeenth century. The biography also expands upon Beza's earlier account of Calvin's death. According to Bolsec, it was rather more violent, consisting of "lice and vermin covering his body, and in particular a very stinky and deadly ulcer

---

[9] Holtrop, *The Bolsec Controversy*, 296–297.

[10] Ibid., 771–774.

[11] Backus, *Life Writing in Reformation Europe*, 162.

[12] Lastraioli, "D'un texte inconnu de Jérôme Bolsec contre Calvin," *Reformation and Renaissance Review* 10:2 (2008): 157–174. The text, of which there is only a single copy in the Bibliothèque Nationale de France, is *Le double des lettres envoyées à Passevent Parisien, par le Noble et excellent Pasquin Romain, contenant en vérité la vie de Jehan Calvin* (Paris: Pierre Gaultier, 1556).

[13] Backus points out that one Jean Cauvin, vicar of Noyon, was punished for his "dissolute lifestyle" in Paris, but not until 1553 when our Calvin had long been established in Geneva (*Life Writing in Reformation Europe*, 160 and n. 119). Bolsec presumably found this account in the records and used it, rather liberally, for his biography (but perhaps did not have access to it for the 1556 poem).

at the base of his genitals, where he was eaten miserably by worms."[14] To Bolsec, Calvin's death was akin to those of earlier persecutors of God's people, such as Antiochus Epiphanes and Herod the Great.[15] The *Vie de Calvin* was translated into Latin and into several vernaculars, proving to have a long life. The early English version was quickly suppressed, but as Peter Marshall has shown it did not stop English anti-Calvinists from referring to the reformer as "a sear-backt priest for sodomie."[16] As late as the 1640s, English Calvinists were still defending Calvin against this specific charge by his detractors. While Bolsec would eventually return to the Catholic Church and his biography would serve as the basis for much Catholic anti-Calvinist propaganda, the substance of his attacks on Calvin (both personal and theological) was developed during his time as a Reformed Protestant in Switzerland.

SEBASTIAN CASTELLIO

Like Bolsec, we know little about Sebastian Castellio's early years, but we can say that he was born in Savoy in 1515, and that he studied in Lyon from 1535 until 1540.[17] Unlike Bolsec, however, Castellio was once a close friend of Calvin. Castellio emigrated from France in 1540, perhaps after witnessing anti-Protestant persecution at Lyon. He went to Strasbourg where he met Calvin (who was exiled from Geneva at the time). Castellio followed Calvin back to Geneva and was instituted as the rector of the Collège de Rive in June 1541, but the arrangement would prove to be short-lived. Castellio aspired to be a preacher, but his ambitions were quashed because of doctrinal divergences from Calvin's teaching: he rejected Calvin's allegorization of both the Song of Songs and of Christ's descent into hell in the Nicene Creed. The failure to secure a pastoral position, followed by Castellio's public rebuke of the Genevan ministers for their lackluster efforts at caring for plague victims, ultimately led to the Savoyard's departure from Geneva in 1544.[18] He would eventually make his way to Basle, where he secured

---

[14] "[C]'est d'une mangeaison de poux et vermine partout son corps; et singulierèment, d'un ulcère très-puant et virulent au fondement et parties vergogneuses, où il était misérablement rongé de vers" (Bolsec, *Vie de Calvin* [Geneva: Principaux libraires, 1835], 83–84).

[15] Ibid., 84.

[16] Peter Marshall, "John Calvin and the English Catholics, c. 1565–1640," *The Historical Journal* 53:4 (2010): 857.

[17] For many biographical details, I follow Hans Guggisberg, *Sebastian Castellio, 1515–1563: Humanist and Defender of Religious Toleration in a Confessional Age,* Bruce Gordon (trans.) (London and New York: Routledge, 2003).

[18] See ibid., 36.

employment as a corrector in Johannes Oporinus's press before finally securing a position as professor of Greek at the University of Basle in 1553.

While Castellio is mostly remembered for his involvement in disputes over religious tolerance, and specifically his relationship to Calvin and Geneva, during this period the Savoyard humanist also worked on editions and translations of ancient Greek texts, especially while at Oporinus's press in Basle. These included not only on a bilingual Homer (where he emended the "infinite places of distorted Greek" while also "straightening out" the Latin[19]) but also editions of Herodotus, Thucydides, and Xenophon. As Marie-Christine Gomez-Géraud has pointed out, little scholarly work has been done on these other aspects of Castellio's career.[20] The polyglot Castellio also translated later religious works, for example Thomas à Kempis's classic *De imitatione Christi* (from Latin into French), and 30 dialogues by a fellow ex-Genevan Bernardino Ochino (from Italian into French). His most widely published sixteenth-century work was the *Dialogi sacri*, which he first published while living in Geneva, and whose purpose was the pedagogical instruction of youth in Latin through religious dialogues.

Servetus's execution in 1553 would lead Castellio to publishing *Concerning Heretics and Whether They Should Be Persecuted*, a thinly veiled rebuke of Calvin and Geneva. This work, along with the posthumously published *On the Art of Doubting*, established Castellio as "the first systematic theorist of toleration."[21] *Concerning Heretics*, a collection of writings by several authors in defense of religious toleration and freedom of conscience, was published in Basle in 1554 under the pseudonym Martin Bellius. It contained not only pieces penned by Castellio under additional pseudonyms but also excerpts from church fathers Augustine, Jerome, and Chrysostom, as well as sixteenth-century reformers Erasmus and Luther. Castellio has a knack for pointing out a variety of absurdities related to sectarianism in the religious atmosphere of the mid-sixteenth-century, and in this he followed Erasmus, his more famous predecessor at Basle. According to both, abstruse matters of high dogma ought not to result in dissension, much less persecution.[22]

---

[19] "Graeca infinitis locis depravata, emendavi. Latina vera ita correxi" (from Castellio's preface to the *Homeri opera Graecolatina* [Basle: Oporinus, 1561], fol. a2).

[20] "Qui parle encore de Sébastien Castellion?," *Australian Journal of French Studies* 52:3 (2015): 261–273.

[21] Hans Guggisberg, "The Defense of Religious Toleration and Religious Liberty in Early Modern Europe: Arguments, Pressures, and Some Consequences," *History of European Ideas* 4:1 (1983), 35–50, 38.

[22] In fact, the connection to Erasmus is more material, as Castellio was for a time living off of a stipend provided from Erasmus's estate, which was handled by Bonifacius Amerbach, with whom Castellio had become friends (see Gordon, *Calvin*, 229).

Shortly after, Castellio penned a direct attack on Calvin, the *Contra libellum Calvini*.[23] Though it was not printed until 1612, the text served as a point-by-point refutation of Calvin's published justification of Geneva's action in the Servetus affair, the *Defensio orthodoxae fidei* of 1554.[24] Composed in dialogue form, with Calvin's words cut and pasted directly from the *Defensio* and the interlocutor "Vaticanus" representing Castellio's rebuttal, it lays the blame for Servetus's execution squarely at Calvin's feet.

As Erika Rummel has pointed out, Castellio diverged crucially from Calvin over the question of the clarity of scripture on difficult doctrinal matters.[25] Castellio was sufficiently skeptical of the ease of biblical interpretation to argue that no one should be persecuted on the grounds of belief. The obscurity of some biblical passages simply do not lend themselves to certainty: "If they were not obscure, controversy would have ceased, for who is so demented that he would die for the denial of the obvious?"[26] Castellio was not merely posing rhetorical questions: he was a first-rate biblical scholar with expertise in both Hebrew and Greek. He first published his complete Latin translation of the Bible in 1551, a continuation of a project he had started with the *Moses Latinus* of 1546, which rendered the Pentateuch into classicizing Latin style. Castellio's efforts at biblical translation and commentary (he also published a fresh French translation in 1555), along with his keen interest in classical antiquity reveal his adeptness as a humanist exegete. It also led to some eccentricities, such as his willingness to interject passages from the ancient Roman-Jewish historian Josephus directly into his edition of the Bible (albeit in smaller type).

He also used the opportunity of biblical scholarship to continue his criticisms of Calvin and Geneva, and city officials in Basle were eventually forced to disallow his commentary on Romans 9 from appearing in the second edition of his Latin Bible in 1555 to ward off further strain with Geneva.[27] The *Annotations* on Romans 9 were thus not published until 1613, but they touch on many of the same themes as Bolsec's criticisms. Comprising 30 pages on election and predestination, Castellio emphasizes the idea that God does not will anyone to perish, but had created all with the hope

---

[23] For excerpts in English translation, see Sebastian Castellio, *Concerning Heretics*, Roland Bainton (trans.) (New York: Octagon Press, 1979), 265–287.

[24] For details, see Guggisberg, *Sebastian Castellio*, 105–110.

[25] Erika Rummel, *The Confessionalization of Humanism in Reformation Germany* (Oxford: Oxford University Press, 2002), 68.

[26] Castellio, *Concerning Heretics*, 218.

[27] Guggisberg, *Sebastian Castellio*, 110.

that they would be saved.[28] Adam sinned freely, not in accord with God's will, according to Castellio, for otherwise all is reduced to Stoic Fate.[29] Calvin is not mentioned by name, but again the target was clear, especially in the wake of the Bolsec controversy. Geneva did not stand idly by. In addition to the intervention to forestall the commentary's inclusion in the 1555 *Biblia*, Theodore Beza published a refutation of Castellio's version of the New Testament in 1563, complete with accusations of Pelagianism in the dedicatory letter (which was addressed to the church pastors of Basle).[30] It is a firm reminder that such disputes over dogma were not ancillary exercises, but were of utmost importance to Protestants attempting to define their confessional identities in this period.

While Bolsec's *Vie de Calvin* was popular in Catholic circles long after his death, Castellio's reputation flourished among humanist proponents of religious toleration – including preeminent figures of the Enlightenment such as John Locke and Voltaire, who considered him a forerunner to their own attempts at liberating consciences from the shackles of religious authoritarianism. Both Bolsec and Castellio were impressively consistent nonconformists in their religious views at a time when this was not politically prudent. They both criticized Calvin's doctrine of predestination and abhorred his involvement in the execution of Servetus, obstinately taking on the Genevan reformer at home and then abroad. In doing so, they were important actors in a defining moment for the Genevan church's development as it sought to carve out its peculiar niche during a crucial period of confessionalization. Calvinism (or at least one version of it) came into its own during these years, for better or worse, and Bolsec and Castellio played a still underappreciated role in its development.

SUGGESTED FURTHER READINGS

Backus, Irena. "Moses, Plato and Flavius Josephus. Castellio's Conceptions of Sacred and Profane in His Latin Versions of the Bible." In *Shaping the Bible in the Reformation: Books, Scholars, and Their Readers*, ed. Bruce Gordon and Matthew McLean. Leiden, The Netherlands: Brill, 2012, 133–166.

---

[28] *Annotationes Sebastiani Castellionis, in caput nonum ad Rom. Quibus materia Electionis et Praedestinationis amplius illustratur* (1613).

[29] Ibid., 29.

[30] *Responsio ad defensiones et reprehensiones Sebastiani Castellionis* (Geneva: Estienne, 1563). E.g., "Vellet enim omnes homines esse bonos, et salvos fieri" (fol. 6).

"The Issue of Reformation Scepticism Revisited: What Erasmus and Sebastian Castellio Did or Did Not Know." In *Renaissance Scepticisms*, ed. Gianenrico Paganini and José Neto. Dordrecht, The Netherlands: Springer Academic, 2009, 63–89.

Life Writing in Reformation Europe. Burlington, VT: Ashgate, 2008.

Bietenholz, Peter. *Encounters with a Radical Erasmus*. Toronto: University of Toronto Press, 2009.

Bruening, Michael. *Calvinism's First Battleground: Conflict and Reform in the Pays de Vaud, 1528–1559*. Dordrecht, The Netherlands: Springer Academic Press, 2005.

Castellio, Sebastian. *On Heretics*. Trans. Roland Bainton. New York: Octagon Press, 1979.

Guggisberg, Hans. *Sebastian Castellio, 1515–1563: Humanist and Defender of Religious Toleration in a Confessional Age*. Trans. Bruce Gordon. London and New York: Routledge, 2003.

Holtrop, Philip. *The Bolsec Controversy on Predestination from 1551 to 1555*, 2 vols. Lewiston, NY: Edwin Mellen, 1993.

Rummel, Erika. *The Confessionalization of Humanism in Reformation Germany*. Oxford: Oxford University Press, 2002.

Calvin's Lutheran Critics

Esther Chung-Kim

In the sixteenth century, the organizing effort of many Reformation leaders coalesced in a newly imagined pan-Protestant community. While differences emerged from early in the Reformation, the consistent effort to resolve disagreements attested to the desire to establish the Reformation throughout Europe. In 1540, John Calvin asserted that religious reforms for Germany could be applied to France, Spain, Italy, and elsewhere in the world, as Protestants sought "to restore those things that Christ handed down, the apostles commended, and the ancient and purer church observed," rather than to initiate something new.[1] But as the vision of a pan-Protestant church faded in the 1550s, a growing criticism of Calvin's views emerged among later Lutherans. In the aftermath of the Augsburg Interim in 1548, which resulted in a series of intra-Lutheran debates, and the widely publicized 1549 Zürich Consensus, the organizing efforts of German Reformers shifted toward preserving the genuine Lutheran legacy of the Reformation. Such confession building had major consequences for shaping the various forms of reformation and the aspiration to come up with a unifying vision "whether historical or supernatural or both, in compensation for the constant, ad hoc negotiation of relationships."[2] The disagreement over the management of the Wittenberg legacy led to the formation of multiple legacies within Protestantism.[3]

---

[1] Calvin, *Consilium pro Lutheranis quod Pontifex Romanus nuper Caesari dedit*, 1540; CO 5:489.
[2] Christopher Ocker, "Calvin in Germany," in Christopher Ocker et al. (eds.), *Politics and Reformations: Essays in Honor of Thomas A. Brady Jr*. Studies in Medieval and Reformation Traditions, Vol. 127 (Boston: Brill Academic, 2007), 317.
[3] Irene Dingel, "The Culture of Conflict in the Controversies Leading to the Formula of Concord (1548–1580)," in Robert Kolb (ed.), *Lutheran Ecclesiastical Culture, 1550–1675* (Leiden, The Netherlands: Brill, 2008), 15–64, here at 28.

STRASBOURG CONTEXT (1538–1541)

Calvin's years in Strasbourg allowed him to interact with reform leaders on the international scene of imperial politics.[4] With the support of Wolfgang Capito and Martin Bucer, Calvin met other German reformers, including Philip Melanchthon. During this period when political and religious leaders alike sought to support the possibility of a pan-Protestant alliance, Calvin as a young refugee pastor observed the deliberations of the Lutheran leaders in the Schmalkaldic League. German reformers who were navigating the politics of religion in the Holy Roman Empire saw Calvin as an ally but an outsider.[5] He advocated for the League's intervention, and the cooperation between Swiss and German Protestants.[6]

Deep in deliberations at the Colloquy at Worms, Strasbourg representatives, such as Capito, Bucer, Simon Grynaeus, and Jean Sturm responded to Geneva's request for Calvin's return by noting Calvin's contribution to the reform in Strasbourg and the negotiations in Worms. Their letter from Worms (November 13, 1540) recognized that Calvin was deeply involved in public affairs and ecclesiastical service for the French refugee church, as well as the expanding theological school. Because their current endeavor toward an imperial peace around evangelical reform was blossoming, Calvin had to remain because of his ministry to the French church in Strasbourg and his teaching of the scriptures in their school, where he instructed Germans, Italians, and the French to preach Christ.[7] In the midst of doctrinal negotiations with Catholic theologians and each other, Calvin and the Lutherans agreed on faith, justification, clerical marriage, the mass, and monastic vows. Concerning the Protestant stance on justification, Calvin praised Johannes Brenz's strong stance resisting compromise on this topic.[8] During 1540–1541 at the major imperial religious conferences of Hagenau, Worms, and Regensburg, Calvin subscribed to the *Confessio Augustana Variata* submitted by the Wittenberg group as a basis for a possible confession for all Protestants. Calvin also set out his Lord's Supper doctrine in the 1541 *Petit traité de la Sainte Cène* (Short

---

[4] Ocker, "Calvin in Germany," 315.
[5] Ibid., 323. While German princes sought to negotiate a transconfessional German coalition with the Schmalkaldic League and prince-bishops, Calvin identified the League's main goal in negotiation – a permanent peace that left confiscations of church properties intact.
[6] Ibid., 326–327.
[7] Calvin, Letter 253, *Argentoratenses et Basilienses Genevensibus*; CO 11:108.
[8] Ocker, "Calvin in Germany," 338.

Treatise on the Lord's Supper) in a manner that suggested his position was not overly remote from that of Wittenberg.[9]

CONTROVERSIES AND CONFESSIONS (1548–1577)

In the sixteenth century, the culture of controversy played a crucial role in redefining a variety of confessional documents and alternative interpretations of biblical teaching.[10] After Luther's death in 1546, the Protestant defeat at the Smalcald War in 1547, and the Augsburg Interim in 1548, Lutherans debated Luther's legacy as polemical writers dedicated themselves to "warn the public against their adversaries."[11] Lutheran polemics soon revealed Calvin as one of these adversaries.

In Calvin's 1550 Appendix to the *Tract on the True Method of Reforming the Church*, Calvin refuted an anonymous German printer, when he had learned that his earlier *Tract on the True and Genuine Reformation of the Church* was reprinted in Germany in a corrupted version including a critique.[12] While he conjectured that the printer wrote his censure in a drunken stupor, Calvin felt the need to address the topic because if he remained silent and allowed wrong ideas to persist, then "the children of God and the public good would be impaired."[13] The specific disagreements over the sanctification of infants and baptism by women prompted some Lutherans to anonymously challenge some of Calvin's points, eliciting Calvin's response and defense of his theological positions.

Building consensus in the absence of a papal or conciliar magisterium became an important activity among Lutheran and Reformed Christians alike.[14] Yet, after Luther's death, his followers focused on building consensus among their German factions. In the intra-Lutheran debates spurred by

---

[9] Irene Dingel, "Calvin in the Context of Lutheran Consolidation," *Reformation and Renaissance Review* 12.2–3 (2010): 155–187, here at 159.

[10] Dingel, "The Culture of Conflict," 15. Reformation disputes "were increasingly extended beyond the academic realm and making an impact in the public sphere, even emerging in the vernacular." Ibid., 16.

[11] Ibid., 18.

[12] Calvin, *Appendix Libelli Adversus Interim Adultero-Germanum, in qua Refutat Ioannes Calvinus Censuram Quandam Typographi Ignoti, de parvulorum sanctificatione, et muliebri baptism*, 1550; CO 7:675.

[13] Calvin, *Appendix Libelli Adversus Interim Adultero-Germanum*; CO 7:676.

[14] Timothy J. Wengert, "Philip Melanchthon and John Calvin against Andreas Osiander: Coming to Terms with Forensic Justification," in R. Ward Holder (ed.), *Calvin and Luther: The Continuing Relationship* (Göttingen: Vandenhoeck & Ruprecht, 2013), 63–87, here at 75.

reactions to the Interim, Philip Melanchthon and his followers sought to preserve Luther's doctrine of justification. This was understood as a forensic declaration of forgiveness so that one became righteous by the promise of God's mercy as opposed to Osiander's interpretation of justification, in which one became righteous by an indwelling of Christ's divinity.[15] While Calvin linked himself positively with Lutherans who rejected Osiander's view of justification, including Gnesio-Lutherans who dismissed Osiander's view, he was still deeply embattled with the same Gnesio-Lutherans on the Lord's Supper over the Lutheran view that Christ was substantially and corporeally present in the Lord's Supper.

The impact of the Interim in southern Germany led many pastors and their families into exile, which fueled resentment and fear of perverting Luther's teaching, accompanied by a zeal for preserving the reformation legacy.[16] At the colloquy of Worms in 1557, the delegation of Ernestine theologians, led by Viktorin Strigel but influenced by Matthias Flacius Illyricus, demanded a clear rejection of false teaching and false teachers within their own camp, preventing the formation of a united front of evangelical theologians.[17]

In the fraught area of confessional consolidation, sixteenth-century Lutherans shifted their perception of Calvin and his theology in response to two developments: (1) the Zurich Consensus (1549) along with the ensuing Lutheran-Reformed debates throughout the 1550s and (2) the experience of electoral Saxony's "crypto-Calvinism" in the 1570s.[18]

Earlier controversies over the Lord's Supper between Luther and Zwingli reemerged when the Zürich Consensus between Calvin and Heinrich Bullinger of the Zürich Church began circulating in northern Germany in the early 1550s. In 1552, Westphal, a pastor in Hamburg, called on Calvin to return to his original position on the Lord's Supper as delineated in Calvin's Short Treatise on the Lord's Supper in 1541. Westphal believed that sacraments should not be subsumed under faith but instead linked in such a way that they are distinct.[19] His critique was that Sacramentarians

---

[15] Ibid., 86.
[16] Dingel, "The Culture of Conflict," 29. Lutherans seeking to preserve evangelical congregations in times of crisis felt the need to "guard and protect Luther's reformation legacy and promote the Ernestine policy of drawing boundaries between them and their Albertine rivals, particularly in the wake of the painful losses of the post-Interim period." Ibid., 26.
[17] Ibid., 27.
[18] Dingel, "Calvin in the Context of Lutheran Consolidation," 156.
[19] Joachim Westphal, Collectanea sententiarum divi Aurelii Augustini Episcopi Hipponensis de Coena Domini (Collectanaea) (Ratisponae, January 1555), E6r.

collapsed the communion with Christ, forgiveness of sins, and salvation into the single act of faith in such a way that these benefits are taken out of the sacraments. For Westphal, faith depended on God's Word and the sacraments, because by the virtue of the action of the Holy Spirit, they produced, confirmed, and nurtured faith.[20]

For Westphal, the Word of Christ made the sacrament effective, not one's faith; for Augustine had said the word was added to the element to become the sacrament.[21] Hence Westphal, who saw common ground with the pre-1549 Calvin, felt that he had to disclose Calvin's duplicity by distinguishing between what Calvin said earlier and what he really meant, especially through the lens of the *Consensus*.[22] Westphal explained that when Calvin described the body of Christ as coming down by Christ's power, the ambiguous language confused the meaning of body as instead meaning vigor or power.[23] According to Westphal, eating the body of Christ in the Supper was for Calvin the same as to believe, accept, or commemorate the benefits of redemption, instead of receiving the body.[24] Interestingly, Westphal's argument reflected Calvin's earlier words against the Zwinglian limitation of the *communio Christi* to a partaking of Christ's blessings (and the equating of sacramental eating to faith) in Calvin's 1546 *Commentary on 1 Corinthians*.[25] According to Westphal, when Calvin said bodily presence, he meant the presence of the Holy Spirit and thus Calvin's deception was uncovered by his own words identifying himself within the Zwinglian camp.[26]

The strict Lutherans saw the Zürich Consensus as the full disclosure of a distant partner turned public adversary when Calvin collaborated with Bullinger, successor to Zwingli, who was Luther's opponent on the important and highly divisive doctrine of the Eucharist and its related doctrine of Christology. This sense of betrayal became obvious when Westphal

---

[20] Ibid., E6v.

[21] Westphal, *Adversus cuiusdam Sacramentarii falsam criminationem, iusta defensio* (*Iusta defensio*) (Francoforti, July 1555), G1v, 82.

[22] Wim Janse, "Joachim Westphal's Sacramentology," *Lutheran Quarterly* 22 (2008): 137–160, here at 142–143.

[23] Westphal, *Iusta defensio*, E5v, 58; *Apologia confessionis de Coena Domini, contra corruptelas et calumnias Ioannis Calvini* (*Apologia*) (Ursellis, 1558), 71–83.

[24] Westphal, *Iusta defensio*, E8r–F1r, 63–65.

[25] Janse, "Joachim Westphal's Sacramentology," 154, n. 87.

[26] Westphal, *Iusta defensio*, F1r–F2r, 65–7; E4v–E5r, 56–7. Thomas Davis argues that Calvin's agreement with Zurich in Consensus reveals the extent to which Calvin was willing to compromise but not a precise reflection of Calvin's own views. Thomas J. Davis, *This Is My Body: The Presence of Christ in Reformation Thought* (Grand Rapids, MI: Baker Academic, 2008), 131.

"assigned Calvin along with John à Lasco to the list of Sacramentarians, by citing a passage from the Zurich Consensus."[27] For the representatives of Wittenburg theology, the Consensus was a signal that Genevan theology had sided with Zwingli's successor in opposition to Luther's theology. Hence, Westphal offered a "rereading of Calvin and the *Petit traité*" to show the incompatibility of Genevan and Wittenberg doctrine.[28] In a marginal gloss soon after emphasizing the body and blood of Christ are really offered in the bread and wine, Westphal identified Calvin as in agreement with "*Panem esse figuram corporis Christi*," a telltale sign exposing Calvin as a Sacramentarian.[29]

With the Zurich Consensus triggering the Westphal-Calvin debates, many Lutherans were reinterpreting the earlier potential for partnership with the Genevan Reformer as a lost cause and even a growing threat. Many Lutherans saw Calvin's growing influence as rivaling Luther's legacy as leader of the Reformation, and they resisted this encroachment by criticizing Calvin's views. The accusation of crypto-Calvinism carried a sense of disloyalty to the Lutheran tradition, which led strict Lutherans to use the description of *crypto-Calvinist* as a derogatory label. Luther had spoken sparingly, but occasionally positively of Calvin.[30] But with the 1549 *Consensus Tigurinus*, a compromise agreement between Calvinists and Swiss Reformed, Lutheran opponents reacted to this agreement as "a damning piece of evidence that Calvin was a Zwinglian."[31] When Calvin sought Melanchthon's support in the persistent Eucharistic controversy, the Wittenberg professor declined.[32] Although Calvin saw himself as a mediator between different strands of the Reformation, the *Consensus* not only alienated the Lutherans but also caused problems with other Swiss cities, including Bern and Basel.[33] Consequently, in the 1550s the polemical exchange between Calvin and Westphal over the Lord's Supper set up Lutheranism and Calvinism as rival confessions. Despite the ongoing disagreement between Calvin and Westphal, attempts to find agreement continued when Theodore Beza and Jakob Andreae agreed to a compromise in

---

[27] Dingel, "Calvin in the Context of Lutheran Consolidation," 164.

[28] Ibid., 165–166.

[29] Westphal, *Farrago Confusanearum et Inter Se Dissidentium Opinionum de Coena Domini, ex Sacramentariorum libris congesta* (Magdeburg: Rodius, 1552), D2v.

[30] R. Ward Holder, "Calvin and Luther: The Relationship That Still Echoes," in R. Ward Holder (ed.), *Calvin and Luther: The Continuing Relationship* (Göttingen: Vandenhoeck & Ruprecht, 2013), 7–10, here at 7.

[31] Ibid., 7–8.

[32] Dingel, "Calvin in the Context of Lutheran Consolidation," 168.

[33] Charlotte Methuen, *Luther and Calvin: Religious Revolutionaries* (Oxford: Lion, 2011), 143.

the Göppingen confession of 1557. While this compromise failed and Calvin chided Beza for poor diplomacy, he also refused to join the public denunciation of the content of the Göppingen confession, clearly written for a Lutheran audience.[34] If Calvin desired to bridge the positions between Swiss theology and moderate Lutheranism, he would have to settle for a "neo-Philippist Lutheranism, adhering to the 1540 *Confessio Augustana Variata.*"[35]

Lutheran-Reformed debates were not isolated incidents, nor were they confined to the 1550s. Another Lutheran and former student of Melanchthon, Tilemann Heshusius (Hesshusen) challenged Calvin's use of the church fathers in the Eucharistic debates.[36] Concerning Christ's presence in the Lord's Supper, Hesshusen argued that Calvin's explanation was confused with contradictions, while Hesshusen's view clearly accepted the words of institution.[37] Bemoaning the misuse of the church fathers, Hesshusen claimed that Calvin obscured and diluted the proper wisdom of the ancient church by reviving the positions of Pelagius and Origen as the new Sabellians.[38]

In the 1570s, Wittenberg theologians tried to include some aspects of Calvinist teaching. When the Wittenberg Catechism published in 1571 showed Calvinist elements, likely drawing from a Philippist perspective, the Gnesio-Lutheran response decried this crypto-Calvinism or crypto-Philippism. In the desire to preserve the Lutheran legacy, a growing disenchantment with the Philippists, the Calvinists and similar religious commitments had political consequences. In April 1574, Elector of Saxony, August and his wife, Anna of Denmark, "became convinced that some of their most trusted councilors, along with several professors at the Wittenberg, had conspired secretly to change the public teaching of his lands. This feeling of betrayal aroused a harsh reaction, launching a campaign to cleanse the churches of 'Calvinist' tendencies."[39] Calvinism was no longer a distant threat, but rather a perilously close one. Such Lutheran rulers perceived Calvinist views as the "subversion of the guaranteed promise of salvation in

---

[34] Euan Cameron, "The Consensus Tigurinus and the Göppingen Eucharistic Confession: Continuing Instabilities in Geneva's Relationship with Zurich and the Lutheran World," *Reformation & Renaissance Review* 18:1 (2016): 72–84, here at 76.

[35] Cameron, "The Consensus Tigurinus and the Göppingen Eucharistic Confession," 83.

[36] Esther Chung-Kim, *Inventing Authority: The Use of the Church Fathers in Reformation Debates over the Eucharist* (Waco, TX: Baylor, 2011), esp. ch. 5.

[37] Tilemann Heshussen, *De Praesentia Corporis Christi in Coena Domini, contra Sacramentarios* (Jena, 1560), B4, 21.

[38] Ibid., L7, 172 and M4, 181.

[39] Dingel, "The Culture of Conflict," 60.

the sacrament, corporally and really experienced in the eating and drinking of bread and wine," and worried that doctrinal convergence with the Genevan Reformation could have ominous political consequences.[40] Lutheran politicians accepted Westphal's assessment of Calvinist views. Likewise, in articles 7 and 8 of the Formula of Concord (1577), the unifying efforts of Lutherans rejected the positions of Calvin and some of Melanchthon's students on the Lord's Supper.

In the post–Formula of Concord period, Lutheran-Reformed debates increasingly focused on their differences concerning Christ's two natures, emerging from disagreements over the Lord's Supper. For example, at the Colloquy of Montbéliard in 1586, Andreae and Beza stood as opponents in the debates over the Eucharist and Christology. To complicate matters, while Prince Elector, August, in his time sought to eradicate crypto-Calvinism with harsh measures, his son and successor, Christian I, initially showed a more welcoming approach to Calvinism. Christian's policy involved staff changes in schools and universities, abolishing exorcism, a feature of the Lutheran baptismal rite, and an edict dated September 28, 1588, banning criticism of Calvinists from the pulpit or inveighing against their doctrine.[41]

The vacillating between oppression and permission depending on region and ruler for Calvinist views in some ways promoted starker dividing lines and the need to publicize opposing views. In the Palatinate, Heidelberg Reformed theologian, David Pareus represented those who were sympathetic to and defended Calvinist views. When the Marburg Lutheran theologian, Aegidius Hunnius (1550–1603), appointed to Wittenberg in 1591, wrote a scathing analysis of Calvin's views in his 1593 *Calvinus iudaizans* (Calvin the Judaizer), Pareus set about vindicating Calvin with his retort: *Calvinus orthodoxus* (Calvin the Orthodox). Hunnius's view of Calvin, not necessarily representative of most Lutherans as its harsh tone clearly reflected his conflict with Pareus, still revealed an important aspect in the spectrum of Protestant identity formation.[42] In his extensive tract composed during his debate with Pareus, Hunnius retrospectively accused Calvin of devising a Judaizing theology, resulting in a faulty understanding of scripture. Hunnius was not simply "appealing to Christology in support of Lutheran real presence, instead, he brought up evidence of a non-scriptural, Christological

---

[40] Dingel, "Calvin in the Context of Lutheran Consolidation," 170.

[41] Ibid., 172–173.

[42] Ibid., 180. See also G. Sujin Pak, *The Judaizing Calvin* (New York: Oxford, 2010), esp. ch. 5.

teaching whose repercussions extended well beyond the area of the Lord's Supper."[43] Around this time, another Gnesio-Lutheran, Nikolaus Selnecker noted that Calvin was part of a triad, with Zwingli as his alleged theological precursor and Beza as his heir, in succession with Karlstadt, Oecolampadius, and Peter Martyr Vermigli, which meant that their exegesis and ensuing doctrinal propositions were in sharp contrast to the testimony of scripture and the Augsburg Confession.[44] The sense articulated earlier by Westphal of Calvin's duplicity in speaking of similar things as orthodox teachers but with a different mind carried over into the Lutheran-Reformed debates of the 1590s.[45]

However, this did not signal the end of criticism and conflict in German-speaking territories. When Polish reformer, John à Lasco tried to reconcile the Protestant churches in Poland, they could not agree on the issue of real or spiritual presence of Christ in the Eucharist.[46] In Danzig, the debate over the remaining elements left over after communion divided the Danzig clergy and the city. This debate showed that religious concerns articulated in Lutheran circles in German towns reverberated well beyond their borders to neighboring nations. German events were "doubtlessly known in such a city with close ties to other Hanseatic cities like Hamburg, where Westphal lived, and Bremen, where Albert Hardenburg had been removed from his office because of his Melanchthonian position."[47] The Danzig City Council took immediate action to maintain peace and stability of the church within the city, but also to prevent the Polish king and the Catholic bishops from gaining influence on the Danzig church again.[48] The struggle to define Protestant orthodoxy extended to the Polish-Prussian region, an area of cultural transition between Polish and German interests.[49]

In the context of intra-Lutheran debates and the political situation in the aftermath of the Interim, Lutherans desired to reach a consensus. Calvin hindered Lutheran unity by offering alternative interpretations that some Lutherans accepted. Therefore, Calvin's growing influence prompted

---

[43] Dingel, "Calvin in the Context of Lutheran Consolidation," 179.

[44] Ibid., 173–174.

[45] Westphal, *Iusta defensio*, E5r, 57. Westphal cites Irenaeus as teaching that that heretics imitate those who teach the Word correctly, when they speak in a similar manner as orthodox thinkers, but have a different mind.

[46] Henning P. Jürgens, "Intra Protestant Conflicts in 16th Century Poland and Prussia – The Case of Benedict Morgenstern," in R. Ward Holder (ed.) *Calvin and Luther: The Continuing Relationship* (Göttingen: Vandenhoeck & Ruprecht, 2013), 143–162, here at 150.

[47] Ibid., 150–151.

[48] Ibid., 151.

[49] Ibid., 144.

Lutherans to define themselves against him and Heinrich Bullinger, his partner in the *Consensus*, whose influence was also expanding. When earlier efforts toward cooperation changed to competition over religious authority, Calvin was on the other side. From the Lutheran perspective, Calvin was now competing for the position of leadership that Luther once held as the recognized leader of the Reformation. While many lesser-known reformers engaged in the work of religious reform in various contexts,[50] Lutherans wanted to maintain Luther's legacy with limited variance – deviation would only confirm the Catholic accusation that Protestant disunity demonstrated their confusion and departure from orthodoxy.

SUGGESTED FURTHER READINGS

Cameron, Euan. "The Consensus Tigurinus and the Göppingen Eucharistic Confession: continuing instabilities in Geneva's relationship with Zurich and the Lutheran world," *Reformation & Renaissance Review* 18:1, 72–84.

Chung-Kim, Esther. *Inventing Authority: The Use of the Church Fathers in Reformation Debates over the Eucharist* (Waco: Baylor, 2011).

Dingel, Irene. "Calvin in the Context of Lutheran Consolidation," *Reformation and Renaissance Review* 12.2-3 (2010): 155–187.

Holder, R. Ward. "Calvin and Luther: The Relationship that Still Echoes," in *Calvin and Luther: The Continuing Relationship*, ed. R. Ward Holder (Göttingen: Vandenhoeck & Ruprecht, 2013), 7–10.

Methuen, Charlotte. *Luther and Calvin: Religious Revolutionaries* (Oxford: Lion, 2011).

Pak, G. Sujin. *The Judaizing Calvin: Sixteenth-Century Debates over the Messianic Psalms* (New York: Oxford, 2010).

Steinmetz, David. *Reformers in the Wings: From Geiler von Kaysersberg to Theodore Beza* (New York: Oxford, 2001).

---

[50] David Steinmetz, *Reformers in the Wings* (New York: Oxford, 2001).

40

❧

Calvin's Catholic Critics

Ralph Keen

Was Calvin another Luther? Certainly in the early decades of the Reformation it was a common perception among Catholics that the evangelicals were united in their opposition to Roman tradition and hierarchy, and that subtle differentiations were of little consequence when seeking to curtail a movement that challenged the authority of the Catholic Church. Thus it is not rare to find "Lutheran" used as the generic term for evangelicals, a term intended to contrast not with "Catholic" but "Christian." (The term reciprocates the pejorative "Papist" and the reverence for the pope it implies.) Given the ease with which Catholic opponents grouped all evangelicals together with little concern for points of difference among them, Calvin was indeed seen as another Luther and, like his counterpart in Wittenberg, a dangerous enemy of the church.

The overwhelming impression from Catholic polemical writings before 1700 is that Calvin's primordial disobedience was his assertion of authority to interpret scripture independently of the Roman tradition. In such impertinence Calvin was indeed another Luther, or Zwingli, or any of a dozen other biblical humanists seeking the meaning of scriptural revelation behind the accumulated tradition. It was evidently less important to attend to the nuances of every position Calvin advanced to refute it. In the following discussion we will offer some samples from the Catholic tradition in which Calvin and his unwieldy heir, Calvinism, are the targets of polemical rhetoric.

The argument of continuity of tradition, a unifying theme in much Counter-Reformation writing, became in anti-Calvinian polemics an argument that Calvin misinterpreted the tradition and hence deviated from it. The Reformers' claim of conformity with early tradition was joined to an assertion that the Catholic Church had deviated from it in later centuries and that they, the Reformers, were restoring Christian teaching and practice to their original forms. The defense of Patristic tradition in Romanist writings of the sixteenth and seventeenth centuries was a component of the narrative of continuity through which Catholic authors sought to refute evangelical claims that the Roman church had broken from the tradition.

EARLY REACTIONS

The 1539 pamphlet exchange between Calvin and Cardinal Jacobo Sadoleto (1477–1547), in which Sadoleto exhorted the Genevan people to return from the apostasy of following Calvin, contained a Catholic argument for the continuity of the Catholic tradition that would run as a thread through the polemical literature. Sadoleto's point was that the Genevans were choosing an authority different from the order that has been transmitted over time and were thus imperiling their salvation. Because of their political organization, the Genevans bore responsibility and – unlike the monarchical form in the German territories – had a duty to avoid becoming an apostate state.

Johannes Cochlaeus (1479–1552), one of the earliest and most vociferous opponents of the Reformation, turned his attention to Calvin toward the end of his life. He wrote a 1549 *Response* concerning the Interim, the decree by which certain liturgical and devotional elements of the Catholic Church were declared admissible in evangelical churches as "indifferent" things: that is to say, practices that were soteriologically immaterial. As he had done in his polemics against the Lutherans, Cochlaeus held Calvin responsible for the disruption of the social order and the "most harsh and bloody civil wars among the Swiss people."[1] Cochlaeus attacked Calvin as a "very prideful hater" (*Calumniator superbissimus*) in rejecting the compromise proposal of the emperor (sig. A6). It was not Calvin's attack on the substance of the Interim (which would have restored practices he considered idolatrous) that drew Cochlaeus's reproach, but the disobedience to the political order that generated the Interim. A similar concern for the preservation of the old order marked Cochlaeus's 1548 Confutation of Calvin's attack on the Council of Trent.[2] For Cochlaeus and his contemporaries, evangelical reform began in disobedience to the Church and ended in sedition.

Calvin's intellect and persuasive ability made him particularly threatening to the old order. The jurist and humanist François Baudouin (1520–1573), a

---

[1] *De Interim Brevis Responsio Ioan. Cochlaei, Ad Prolixvm Conuitiorum & Calumniarum librum Ioannis Caluini* (Mainz: Franz Behem, 1549), sig. A3^v.

[2] Cochlaeus, *Johannis Calvini in Acta Synodi Tridentinae Censura et eiusdem brevis confutatio. Circa duas praecipue calumnias* (Mainz: Franz Behem, 1548).

reconvert from Calvinism to Catholicism, composed in 1562 a *Response* to Calvin (part of an extended acrimonious exchange) in which he defended himself against attacks on his character and reputation. Describing himself as uncultivated and vulnerable in comparison with Calvin's eloquence and fame, Baudouin painted Calvin as an aggressive opponent of all who disagreed with him. "But God will I hope disrupt your cruel and insidious plans, and what you attack me with will fall upon your head and increase your infamy."[3] As with Cochlaeus, Baudouin's critique of Calvin included a detailed defense of the social and ecclesiastical order in which harmony was the product of rulers ensuring conformity to the teachings of the church as articulated in councils and by popes. Baudouin's *Response* marks the end of his efforts to reconcile evangelical and Catholic camps (he had been at the Colloquy of Poissy the year before), and he returned the next year to the Catholic Church.

Among specific doctrines, the Reformed doctrine of the Eucharist aroused substantial reaction. For example, René Benoit (1521–1608) attacked Calvin's position on the Lord's Supper in a treatise accompanied by an appeal to Catherine de Medici in which he reminds her that "the word of our God and eternal savior teaches us that the prelates must be the light, and through good works and the preaching of the pure word of God, which they are bound to know and preach."[4] Advising Calvin to remain submissive to the Catholic Church (sig. B1), Benoit appealed to "the sacred scriptures, the holy councils and doctors," to affirm that "the true, natural and substantial body of Jesus Christ, which was attached to the Cross, is truly (albeit miraculously) contained in the sacred Host" (sig. B3). There had never been, Benoit adds, a person more maliciously opposed to the truth of the Gospel than Calvin (sig. B3–3^v). In Benoit's view, Calvin plainly displayed his intention to remove Christ from the sacrament and reduce it to a mere sign (sig. B5^v). If that is the case, Benoit asks, what was the difference between the Old Law and the New? (sig. C4). Benoit derided Calvin as an instrument of Satan for depriving Christians of the means of grace (sig. F4).

Michael Baius (1513–1589) also defended the sacramental means of grace in several treatises on the merit of good works and the sacraments in general. In the latter, Baius accused Calvin of being "crafty in speaking, impudent in lying, sly in explaining, and so bloated with arrogant presumption in

---

[3] François Baudouin, *Responsio altera ad Ioan. Calvinum* (Paris: Guillaume Morel, 1562), sig. C7.

[4] René Benoit, *Une brieve et succincte refutation de la coene de Iean Calvin* (Antwerp: Philippe Tronasius, 1566), sig. A4.

resisting the truth of the Holy Scriptures and every tradition, of councils as much as of the ancient writers, that he seems to be moved not by a human spirit but a diabolical one."[5] Baius took pains to demonstrate that the seven sacraments, being among the good works that defined the life of faith, were (along with faith) the means of being accepted by God (sig. G6). Calvin preached that the sacraments are "not for sanctification but for teaching and the practice of faith" (sig. H4).

For Richard Smyth (1500–1563), royal chaplain under Mary Tudor and later (and briefly) chancellor of the Recusant college at Douai, Calvin and other Reformed theologians were reintroducing Pelagianism by asserting that baptism did not justify. "What is this impudence of yours?," Smyth asks Calvin, "what ignorance? Paul also says that we are regenerated and reborn in baptism, and that God saves us through it [Titus 3:5], and Peter testifies that baptism saves us [1 Pet. 3:25]."[6] For Smyth, Calvin's position on baptism removed the need for contrition and penance, as well as the other sacraments that the Catholic Church considered the means to salvation. If the sacraments were dispensable, it followed that all else that flowed from the authority of the church – the social order – was likewise vulnerable.

BELLARMINE AND THE JESUIT REACTION

The dominant narrative of the Counter-Reformation foregrounds the Society of Jesus, both for its chartered purpose and the range and depth of its principals. In both scope and influence, the most substantial critique of Calvin during the seventeenth century was that of Robert Bellarmine (1542–1621), author of the *Controversies of the Christian Faith*. Bellarmine's organizing concept in this work was the similarity of the movements of his own time to heresies of the early church, which meant that Patristic condemnations could be applied to the work of the various Reformers. Likewise, pointing to ways in which the Reformers allegedly misread the Fathers served to expose their ignorance of the tradition and thus their inability to represent the tradition.

In his treatment of the sacraments, Bellarmine offered a critique of Calvin's position as articulated in the 1547 *Antidote to the Council of Trent*

---

[5] Michael Baius, *De meritis operum libri duo, eiusdem de prima hominis iustitia et virtutis impiorum libri duo. Eiusdem de sacramentis in genere contra Calvinum liber unus* (Louvain: Johann Bogard, 1565), sigs. G4ᵛ-5.

[6] Richard Smyth, *De infantium baptismo, contra Ioannem Caluinum, ac de operibus supererogationis, & merito mortis Christi, aduersus eundem Caluinum, & eius discipulos* (Louvain: Johann Bogard, 1562), sig. A7ᵛ.

and other works. Directly calling several of Calvin's propositions lies (*mendacia*), Bellarmine attacked Calvin's claims at *Institutes* IV.14.14 and 14.17 that the Scholastics hold that the sacraments confer grace without faith being present and that the cause of justification and the power of the Holy Spirit were contained in the elements.[7] The elements, he stated, were instrumental causes only, and they did not act as vessels containing the power to make righteous. Bellarmine's argument that the sacraments were not efficacious *ex opere operato* continued a Catholic critique of the evangelical position already a century old: Luther had held that the Catholic Church located the power of the sacraments in the work.

Bellarmine offered a trenchant critique of Calvin's definition of a sacrament.[8] Claiming that Calvin's definition was a conflation of the views of Luther and Zwingli (each of which, in Bellarmine's view, he attacked), Bellarmine challenged the view at *Institutes* III.2 that faith cannot be lost. "From this it follows," stated Bellarmine, "that true faith, without which the sacraments have no benefit, belongs to the predestined and can in no way belong to those who are not."[9]

When not exposing the errors of the Reformers, Bellarmine sought to expose their ignorance. Regarding the work of the sacraments *ex opere operato*, for example, Bellarmine claimed he could not tell whether Calvin's view reflected his malice or his ignorance. Likewise, among the "lies" of Calvin's that Bellarmine attacked is the claim at *Institutes* IV.19.12 that the Church Fathers recognized only two sacraments. Bellarmine cited in response both Cyprian and Augustine on confirmation, affirming that for the latter the sacrament of chrism was as much a sacrament as baptism.

Regarding councils and the church, the defining of which occupied Reformers since before the start of the Council of Trent, Bellarmine singled out Calvin's claim at *Institutes* IV.9.1–2 that coming together in Christ's name was nothing other than coming together with his authority. "For what Calvin says, that assembling in the name of Christ is to congregate in such a way that Christ alone presides, and has no equal but only subjects, is neither known in scripture nor well enough known for recognizing legitimate councils."[10] Bellarmine continued by attacking Calvin's view as ambiguous and obscure because such vague conditions for a council meant that there

---

[7] Robert Bellarmine, *De controversiis Christianae fidei*, section "De sacramentis in genere," I.4, in *Opera omnia*, Vol. 3, ed. Xisto Riario Sforza (Naples: Josephus Giuliano, 1858), 21.

[8] Ibid., I.16 (*Opera*, 3: 43–46).

[9] Ibid., 3: 44.

[10] Bellarmine, *De controversiis*, "De conciliis," I.10, in *Opera*, Vol. 2 (Naples: Josephus Giuliano, 1857), 23–24.

would be no way to tell true councils from false (24). Elsewhere in the same work Bellarmine attacked, with scriptural verses like 2 Kings 8 (as well as the New Testament and the Fathers) Calvin's view that a council did not represent the whole church (41).

At the heart of the division between the Roman and Reformed churches was the definition of the church. On this question Bellarmine found five heretical statements in Calvin's conception of the church, from the idea that it was the congregation of the predestined to supposed affinities with Pelagians, Novatians, and Donatists (74). Bellarmine accused Calvin of deviating from Melanchthon and Brenz, for example, who saw the church as a mixture of good and bad persons, not recognizing that for the Reformers, the visible church and the eschatological invisible church were separate concepts. In Bellarmine's view, the idea of two churches was not found in scripture or Augustine, although he acknowledged that some Catholics had this idea (88). The true church was the visible church, he states, and was recognized as such throughout scripture and "wherever the word Church is found," while Calvin offered only Numbers 20:4 (which Bellarmine claims he misuses). Calvin's understanding of the invisible church as the true one allowed him to affirm that the church cannot err; Bellarmine asserted by contrast that the church that cannot err was "the universe of the faithful as much as the universe of bishops" (265–266).

In 1650 the Jesuit Jean Adam (1608–1684) sought to deploy Augustine against Calvin, arguing that Calvin "unjustly usurped" the Church Father's writings on grace, freedom, and predestination.[11] The authority of the church, said Adam, was indubitable, and only those properly charged with preaching could stand on that authority (sig. B1). Adam invoked Vincent of Lerins on tradition as a deposit of which the church was a custodian rather than an author, adding that the defenders of the tradition must also be the enemies of all innovations and that the Church Fathers were not only explicators of the faith but harsh opponents of all heretics (sig. B1^v–2). The Calvinists, according to Adam, misused scripture by questioning the accuracy of various early versions and revising their own translations (sig. B6–6^v), and claimed adherence to scripture while reading it according to "vostre seule imagination" (sig. C2); moreover, they refused to see that scripture has provided the basis for condemning all earlier heresies (sig. C2^v). Was it not strange, Adam asked the Calvinists, that they taught that Holy Scripture

---

[11] Jean Adam, *Calvin defait par soy-mesme et par les armes de S. Avgvstin qv'il avoit inivstement vsvrpées sur les matieres de la grace, de la liberté, & de la predestination* (Paris: Gaspar Metvras, 1650).

was as clear as the rays of the sun to all souls that have the faith, while they disputed among themselves about the canon and meaning of scripture (sig. C5^v)?

The shape of the *Institutes* was an invitation for the Paris Jesuit Pierre Coton (1564–1626) to compose his own *Institution Catholique* (1610 with later editions) in four books, as an "antidote" to Calvin's four-part work.[12] Coton shared the common view that Calvin misused the Church Fathers, and his work added copious quotations from them often in extended side-notes and blocks set apart from the body of the text, so that the reader had access to the texts that Calvin allegedly misused. (These excerpts were in the original languages, something of an anomaly in a vernacular work.)

JANSENISM

Whereas the Jesuit approach to Calvinism as found in Bellarmine's work was grounded in demonstrating that Protestant assumptions about the sole authority of scripture cannot sustain claims of continuity with tradition, the Jesuits' most vehement adversaries within the Catholic Church drew attention to the Calvinists' reading of the tradition. Jansensim was a movement begun after the death of Cornelius Jansen (1585–1638) and the publication of his *Augustinus*. As the title indicates, Jansenius was intent on correcting what he saw as an erroneous appropriation of the Augustinian legacy.

In seeking to reconcile human freedom with the working of grace, for example, Jansenius accused Calvin of erroneously denying that humans can sin: for if freedom is removed, so is culpability for sin.[13] Describing his effort to defend freedom while preserving the working of grace, Jansenius defined freedom as "indifferent," immaterial to one's salvation: "in defending indifferent freedom we refute Calvin without diminishing the error of Pelagius" (sig. Y2^v). The shadow side of recovering the Augustinian legacy was identification of those against whom Augustine wrote; and the Calvinists (despite their own protestations to the contrary and the common evangelical claim that the Romanists attributed too much to human nature) were the Pelagians.

---

[12] Pierre Coton, *Institution catholique, où est déclarée et confirmée la vérité de la foy, contre les hérésies et superstitions de ce temps. Divisé en quatre livres qui servent d'antidote aux quatre de l'Institution de Jean Calvin*, 2nd ed. (Paris: C. Chappelet, 1612).

[13] Cornelis Jansenius, *Augustinus, seu doctrina Sancti Augustini de humanae naturae sanitate, aegritudine, medicina adversus Pelagianos et Massilienses* (Paris: Michel Soly, 1641), sig. Ee3^v.

The Calvinists, Jansenius insists, were enemies of the authority of the church and warriors against the Fathers (sig. B5); and the testimony of the tradition was sufficient refutation. Invoking what he saw as the uninterrupted tradition that included Albert, Thomas, and Bonaventure as well as Alexander of Hales and Durand of St. Pourçain, Jansenius asserted that these stood against the "corrupt weapons" that Calvin employed: "Truth, not falsehood, must destroy errors" (sig. Bb4). While Jansenius admitted that Calvin was in accord with Augustine, in other points he claimed that Calvin attributed to Augustine the opposite of what Augustine stated (sig. Ii4). The general impression of Calvin that Jansenius wished to convey was that of a theologian occasionally, even accidentally, in accord with the tradition, but whose intentional distancing from it rendered him a heretic.

The Jansenist Antoine Arnauld (1612–1694) sought to demonstrate that Calvinism convicted itself of heresy in advancing impious dogma, focusing among other things on Reformed denial of certainty of righteousness and predestination. In *Le Calvinisme convaincu de nouveau de dogmes impies* (1682) he attempted to expose the contradictions that undermine both the Calvinists' claim to internal coherence and their assertion of conformity with the Fathers. All Catholics, Arnauld stated, have detested these claims since the days of Calvin and Beza.[14] Arnauld attacked the Calvinists (and, it should be noted, did not single out Calvin) for an inversion of morality ("renversement de la morale"), a charge he had leveled against them a decade before.[15] In Arnauld's view, the Calvinists' position on the certitude of salvation was manifestly contrary to scripture, giving Christians occasion to yield to the sins that tempt them, and running directly against Jesus's instructions to his disciples.[16]

Toward the end of the century, Antoine Blache (1635–1714) sought to instruct reconverts to the Catholic Church from that of the "pretended Reformed" ("Pretendus Reformez") who had brought schism and heresy.[17] With elevated polemical rhetoric Blache started by exposing the "contradictions and absurdities" in Calvin's doctrine of the "pretend church," asserting

---

[14] Antoine Arnauld, *Le Calvinisme convaincu de nouveau de dogmes impies* (Cologne: Pierre Binsfelt, 1682), sig. A8ᵛ.

[15] Antoine Arnauld, *Le renversement de la morale de Jesus-Christ par les erreurs des Calvinistes touchant la justification* (Paris: Guillaume Desprez, 1672).

[16] Arnauld, *Le Calvinisme convaincu*, sigs. N11ᵛ–12.

[17] Antoine Blache, *Refutation de l'heresie de Calvin, par la seule doctrine de Mrs de la R. P. R. pour affermir sans dispute les nouveaux convertis dans la foy de l'Eglise catholique. Avec des extraits de plusieurs lettres de Saint Augustin, où il paroist que la conduite du Roy, à l'égard des Calvinistes de France, est conforme à la doctrine de ce Pere* (Paris: Antoine Lambin, 1687), sigs. i2ᵛ–3.

that the religion of Calvin taught nothing true (sig. A1–2). The church that Christ saw as a unity was, says Blache, the enemy of schism and heresy, which only trouble and divide believers; thus "every person of good sense recognizes the need to grant to the Church the power to condemn" heresies (sig. D1). The Calvinists, according to Blache, were moved by their particular spirit against the body of the Church; and they did not have the church but rather deprived themselves of the power that Christ gave to the visible body of his church (sig. D3ᵛ).

The consistent theme in the Catholic rhetoric against Calvin was schism. Calvin's presumption in defining the church and in setting the rules by which it was to live was nothing less than schism according to Catholics who saw Rome rather than Geneva as the site of ecclesiastical authority. Geneva was an apostate church, led by heretical leaders among whom Calvin was the eponymous *primus inter pares*. In claiming conformity to the Patristic tradition and usurping the designation "Catholic" while deviating from the trajectory culminating in the Roman Catholic Church of his time, Calvin had set himself up in a form of opposition to the Catholic Church that gave defenders of the latter little choice but to condemn him as a false teacher.

SUGGESTED FURTHER READINGS

Keen, Ralph. "The Critique of Calvin in Jansenius's *Augustinus*." In *Crossing Traditions: Essays on the Reformation and Intellectual History in Honour of Irena Backus*, ed. Maria-Cristina Pitassi and Daniela Solfaroli Camillocci. Leiden, The Netherlands: Brill, 2018, 405–415.

Zachman, Randall C., ed. *John Calvin and Roman Catholicism: Critique and Engagement, Then and Now*. Grand Rapids, MI: Baker, 2008.

41

❧

Calvin and the Anabaptists

Mirjam van Veen

The unhappy encounter between Anabaptists and Reformed in Wismar in 1553 is a striking example of how confusing the sixteenth-century religious landscape was. In the early 1550s a group of Anabaptists under the leadership of Menno Simons managed to live peacefully in the small German Hanseatic town Wismar. They met informally in the private homes of members of their community. Apparently Wismar's authorities turned a blind eye toward this group of Anabaptists. This mode of peaceful coexistence between a predominantly Lutheran population and a minority of Anabaptist refugees came to an end when a group of Dutch Reformed refugees arrived in the city. Unlike the Anabaptists, these Reformed refugees were unwilling to compromise. They endeavored to establish their own ecclesiastical organization and claimed their own church building to worship God in a pure Reformed manner.

These Reformed refugees belonged to the wave of Protestants who had left England after Mary's ascension to the throne in 1553. The group was self-confident. According to Marten Micron, one of their leaders, the world had never seen a church as pure as theirs. The boy-king Edward VI had granted them extensive privileges, partly because he hoped that this refugee church would serve as a bulwark against Anabaptist influences in England. After Mary's ascension to the throne, the group tried to reestablish their church in a new land. They first went to Denmark, but the Danish court insisted on their accommodation to the Lutheran settings. After this, the Dutch continued their journey to find a safe haven, including in Wismar that December.

As soon as their vessel entered Wismar's harbor the Reformed found themselves in trouble. By that time it was winter and – as the story goes – ice prevented them from reaching land. The Anabaptists helped the Reformed, but the Reformed leadership took this help as an attempt to convert members of their flock to Anabaptism. A debate between Anabaptists and Reformed ensued, but as usual this debate went nowhere. The Reformed blamed the Anabaptists for adhering to an erroneous doctrine; the Anabaptists blamed the Reformed for adhering to a halfhearted Reformation and for not taking sanctification seriously enough. The debate did, however, draw the attention of Wismar's authorities. They decided to expel both groups of refugees. The Reformed happily published their account of the disputation with the Anabaptists, making the Reformed victory known to the world. The Anabaptists blamed the Reformed for not being true pilgrims of the Lord and for putting Anabaptists' lives at risk. After all, the actions of the Reformed had provoked the authorities to take measures not only against the Reformed but also against the Anabaptists.[1]

In a sense the Reformed refugees in this case represented the more radical wing of the Reformation. Whereas the Anabaptists were able to cope with life in a Lutheran city, the Reformed provoked Lutheran anger, which quickly led to their expulsion from the city. Wismar's events are only one reason to modify the normal historiography. After George Williams's groundbreaking study on the Radical Reformation, scholars have continued to describe the Anabaptists as the more radical wing of the Reformation. According to this framework, Lutherans and Reformed had been ready to take the Constantinian framework for granted and didn't feel the need to question the decisions on for example the Trinity and the humanity of Christ of the early church. The Anabaptists, however, made a plea for a return to what they portrayed as the apostolic church, thus doing away with the decisions of the early church. This distinction between the radical and the magisterial Reformation makes sense and is helpful to understand the different roles Anabaptism, Lutheranism, and Reformed Protestantism played within early modern societies. It is also a useful framework to understand the numerous debates on the humanity of Christ or on the Trinity.[2] In that sense, their plea for a return to the Apostolic Church was more radical than the Lutheran and Reformed plea to do so.[3]

The distinction between radical and magisterial reformation, however, blurs the complexities of the relationship between Anabaptists and Reformed. Part of the explanation of the numerous clashes between

---

[1] M. van Veen, "Ware pelgrims. Dopers-gereformeerd ongemak in Wismar (1553)," *Doopsgezinde Bijdragen* 43 (2017): 53–62.

[2] See J. H. Wessels, *De leerstellige strijd tusschen Nederlandsche Gereformeerden en Doopsgezinden in de zestiende eeuw* (Assen: Van Gorcum & Comp, 1945).

[3] G. H. Williams, *The Radical Reformation*, 3rd ed. (Kirksville, MO: Sixteenth Century Journal Publishers, 1992).

Anabaptists and Reformed is that they simply resembled each other too closely. During the first half of the sixteenth century the Reformed struggled to draw boundaries between their own movement and the Anabaptists. In the first part of my contribution I will elaborate on this process of differentiation, taking baptism as an example. In the second part I will show how, depending on the positions within societies, old divergent views could also merge. I will focus on the Servetus case as an example of how the two movements were also deeply influenced by each other's views.

Anabaptists and Reformed that found their offspring in Zurich had their roots in common. Ulrich Zwingli, Konrad Grebel, and Felix Mantz shared an ardent desire to bring the church back to its apostolic beginnings. During the process of Reformation, however, it turned out that these allies differed on what this meant. The Anabaptist conviction that infant baptism belonged to the human inventions that polluted the church had far-reaching consequences. The decision to baptize adults after a confession of the faith implied that one only became a church member after making a deliberate choice to do so. The place of such a voluntary church within a society was different from a church that encompassed the whole population. This debate on infant or adult baptism marked a break with the Middle Ages, during which the unity between the civic and ecclesiastical society had been uncontested. In the Anabaptist vision members of one and the same civic society ceased to belong necessarily to one and the same church. The Anabaptist voluntary church necessitated a rethinking of the link between the civic and the ecclesiastical society and ultimately of the link between church and state. If the ecclesiastical community differed from the civic community why then should the state rule the two communities?[4]

Whereas Anabaptists were clear on their ideas regarding baptism, Reformed struggled to define their position. Guillaume Farel presents us with a striking example of the Reformed difficulties to reach clarity. While other leading Reformed ministers were engaged in a polemical battle against the Anabaptists, describing their movement as a serious threat to the Reformation, Farel insisted that brotherly love would suffice to convince the Anabaptists that the Reformed were right and the Anabaptist wrong. His description of baptism was ambiguous, to say the least, because he linked it with a confession of faith. Such a confession of faith, of course, presupposed

---

[4] On the clash in Zürich between Reformed and Anabaptists see especially: A. Strübind, *Eifriger als Zwingli. Die frühe Taüferbewegung in der Schweiz* (Berlin: Duncker & Humblot, 2003).

adult baptism.[5] Farel's view was not exceptional within the Reformed world. Johannes Oecolampadius seems to have taken an in between position as well. The Anabaptist leader Balthasar Hubmaier was at least sure that Johannes Oecolampadius agreed with his view on baptism.[6] Hubmaier had good reasons for his assumption. In his correspondence with Hubmaier, Oecolampadius pointed at the doctrine of the covenant to explain why it was allowed to baptize children. At the same time, he assured Hubmaier that he approved of his baptismal practice and that he hoped it would please everybody.[7] In the mid-1530s, the Reformed apparently reached clarity on adult baptism. However, the Lutheran accusation that the Reformed presented a sort of "Anabaptism-light" was not entirely without ground. The Reformed refusal to accept emergency baptism, for instance, questioned the necessity of the baptismal ceremony. If children could reach eternal bliss without baptism, was it even necessary to be baptized?

The Reformed choice to continue infant baptism had a decisive impact on the kind of church they promoted. John Calvin's church in Geneva in fact replaced the medieval Catholic Church. Hence the unity between the civic and the ecclesiastical community remained intact and church-state relationships remained to a large extent unaltered. The Anabaptist choice for adult baptism implied a different ecclesiastical model with different church-state relationships. At first sight, the two movements reached well-defined position in the late 1530s. By that time it became clear that Anabaptists and Reformed went different directions. Disputes on economic questions like slavery, usury, and the tithe showed that the Reformed were far more inclined to accommodate themselves to the given structures of society than the Anabaptists. In 1531, Heinrich Bullinger wrote his extensive rebuttal of the Anabaptist view, which became a sort of standard work against the Anabaptists, not only among the Reformed but also among Catholics.[8]

[5] G. Farel, *Sommaire et brève déclaration* [1529], A. L. Hofer (ed.) (Neuchâtel: Édition "Belle Rivière, 1980), 110. In his 1534 edition Farel left this statement unaltered. G. Farel, *Sommaire, 1534*, J. G. Baum (ed.) (Genève: Editions Belle Rivière 1867), 34.

[6] E. Staehelin, ed., *Briefe und Akten zum Leben Oekolampads* (New York and London: Johnson, 1971 (reprint), Bd 2, no. 582, 192. Cf. J. Yoder, *Täufertum und Reformation in der Schweiz. I. Die Gespräche zwischen Täufern und Reformatoren 1523–1538* (Karlsruhe: Mennonitischer Geschichtsverein, 1962), 60.

[7] Oecolampadius answered to Hubmaier in two successive letters. Oecolampadius to Hubmaier [Basel 18. January 1525] (Staehelin, ed., *Briefe und Akten*, Bd 1, ep. 239, 344–345); Oecolampadius to Hubmaier [Basel, toward the end of January 1525] (Staehelin, ed., *Briefe und Akten*, Bd 1, ep. 243, 355–356).

[8] H. Bullinger, *Von demm unverschampten fräfel, ergezlichem verwyrren, undd unwarhafftem leeren, der selbsgesandten Widertöufferen, vier gespräch Bücher, zů verwarnenn den einfalten* (1531). On the interconfessional use of Bullinger's writing see, for example, P. J. A. Nissen, *De*

The Anabaptists pinpointed their position in the Schleitheim Confession demarcating their positions on baptism, the ban, the Lord's Supper, separation, shepherds in the church, the sword, and the oath against the Reformed. Calvin's reply against the Schleitheim Confession, published in 1544, was very much a summary of the main points under debate between Reformed and Anabaptists. In his polemical treatise, Calvin focused on baptism, church-state relationships, and the human nature of Christ.[9] The subsequent polemic between Reformed and Anabaptists reads like a repetition of former arguments. A characteristic of the polemic is the Reformed search for differences: Reformed authors criticized the Anabaptists praying in silence, Anabaptist women uncovering their head while being baptized and Anabaptist measures against mixed marriages (which they opposed as well).

Reformed had to stress these differences because these distinctions were not overly apparent. On many occasions, it seemed as if Anabaptism was simply a more consistent variant of the Reformed movement. The Reformed made a plea for a return to scripture, but the Anabaptist were ready to question all doctrines that couldn't univocally traced back to a biblical foundation. The Reformed made a plea for the sanctification of daily life, but Anabaptist holiness surpassed the Reformed ability to pursue a reformation of manners. The Anabaptist ability to be more consistent than the Reformed was a consequence of their minority position. The Reformed endeavor to replace the medieval church necessitated compromise. A church without spot or winkle was simply incompatible with the attempt to encompass the entire society.[10]

How closely intertwined the Anabaptist-Reformed polemic was with their position in the society became obvious in the debate on the Servetus affair. During this debate, the Anabaptist and the Reformed positions changed in two respects: the Anabaptists became more critical of Servetus's thought and started to show comprehension for Reformed attempts to check his

---

katholieke polemiek tegen de Dopers: reacties van katholieke theologen op de Doperse beweging in de Nederlanden (1530–1650) (1991).

[9] On Calvin and the Anabaptists see W. Balke, Calvijn en de Doperse Radikalen (Amsterdam, The Netherlands: Ton Bolland, 1973). In my introduction to Calvin's treatise against the Anabaptists I analyze the circumstances that induced Calvin to take up his pen, as well as the link between Calvin's treatise and the Schleitheim articles. J. Calvin, Brieve Instruction pour armer tous bons fideles contre les erreurs de la secte commune des anabaptistes (Genève: Jean Girard, 1544 [CO 7.45–142]).

[10] See also: M. van Veen, "Religieus Schermvechten. Dopers-Gereformeerde Disputaties in de Zestiende Eeuw," in V. Soen and P. Knevel (eds.), Religie, hervorming en controverse in de zestiende-eeuwse Nederlanden (Herzogenrath: Shaker Publisher, 2013), 88.

influence; the Reformed, however, distanced themselves from Calvin's actions against Servetus and started to show comprehension for Servetus's critique of old ecclesiastical doctrines.

During the famous heresy trial against Miguel Servetus (1553), the Anabaptist and the Reformed ideas on the role of the state clashed. According to Calvin, secular authorities had to purge societies from erroneous doctrines. The state was responsible for the well-being of its inhabitants; the well-being of the souls was certainly part of this responsibility. Although it was the Genevan state that put Servetus to death, Calvin certainly supported the death penalty against Servetus and readily cooperated with it. Calvin's explanation of Deuteronomy shows that the Servetus's case was perfectly in line with Calvin's thought on the exclusion of heretics from society. His eagerness to provide authorities of Vienne with information against Servetus also testifies to Calvin's determination to silence Servetus.[11]

The Radical Reformation didn't have any positive expectations from the state. Based on a sharp distinction between the carnal and the spiritual world, they denoted secular authorities as carnal and incapable of judging spiritual matters. But there was more. These dissenters simply had many negative experiences with secular authorities. David Joris certainly shared this dualistic worldview, but he was also upset by the measures taken against him. He testified that he wanted to live peacefully and in accordance with his conscience. He simply found the persecutions against him unjust.[12] The Servetus trial provoked an outcry of frustration and anger from dissenters, who criticized Calvin's use of carnal weapons in matters of faith and warned that a Genevan tyranny had replaced the papal tyranny. In his treatise on the killing of heretics, Castellio suggested that Calvin had in fact changed his opinion. As long as he had been persecuted he had claimed the freedom of faith, but as soon as he had come to power he denied others the freedom he had claimed for himself.[13]

This debate between Anabaptism and Reformed Protestantism was indeed closely connected with the positions the two movements occupied within the

---

[11] On the Servetus-case see: F. P. van Stam, *The Servetus Case: An Appeal for a New Assessment* (Geneva: Droz, 2017). J. Calvin, *Sermons sur le Deuteronomie* (CO27, 246). G. Baum, E. Cunitz, and E. Reuss ed., *Ioannis Calvini Opera quae Supersunt Omnia* (Brunswick and Berlin, Germany: 1863–1900).

[12] M. van Veen, "David Joris' Memoryaell," *Doopsgezinde Bijdragen* 33 (2007): 31–40; M. van Veen, "'Contaminated with David Joris's blasphemies': David Joris's Contribution to Castellio's De haereticis an sint persequendi," *Bibliothèque d'Humanisme et Renaissance* 69 (2007): 313–326.

[13] On this outcry of indignation see especially: U. Plath, *Calvin und Basel in den Jahren 1552–1556* (Zürich: Theologischer Verlag Zürich, 1974).

society. Reformed that faced persecutions had a different perspective than
their brothers and sisters that acquired an uncontested majority position,
although persecutions stirred Reformed thought in different directions. In
the case of Wismar, for example, the Lutheran polemic made it all the more
important for the Reformed to present themselves as the embodiment of
peace and order.[14] They used a similar strategy as Calvin had done in his 1536
Institutes and emphasized the differences between the Reformed and Anabaptists. On other occasions the persecutions created a bond between the
two movements. Mathilde Monge showed how Reformed in the German
Rhineland were even willing to help persecuted Anabaptists.[15]

In the Dutch Republic the Reformed hesitated about whether the state was
indeed called to purge societies of heresies. Ministers in the province of
Friesland called on magistrates to check Anabaptist influence and translated
Theodore Beza's treatise on the persecution of heretics. According to them,
heretics should indeed be killed.[16] Other Reformed ministers took a position
that came close to the Anabaptist position. Emden's minister Bernhard
Buwo, for example, disagreed with the Anabaptist view on baptism, but
argued that Anabaptist ideas should be countered by words and arguments,
not by the use of fire and sword.[17] Many Reformed declined to defend
Calvin's support of Servetus's execution. The polemic between Dirck Volckertsz Coornhert and Reformed ministers presents us with a striking
example. Coornhert challenged his opponents to defend Calvin's actions
against Servetus, but they refused to do so, arguing that this was not the
subject of their debate.[18] Reformed writers describing the Servetus affair

---

[14] O. P. Grell, "Exile and Tolerance," in O. P. Grell and B. Scribner (eds.) *Tolerance and
Intolerance in the European Reformation* (Cambridge: Cambridge University Press, 1996),
164–181.

[15] M. Monge, *Des communautés mouvantes. Les "societés des frères chrétiens" en Rhénanie du
Nord Juliers, Berg*, Cologne vers 1530–1694 (Geneva: Droz, 2015), 212–213.

[16] *Een schoon tractaet des Godtgheleerden Theodori Bezae van de Straffe welcke de wereltlijcke
overicheydt over de ketters behoort te oeffenen/ teghen Martini Belli tsamenraepsel/ ende der
secte der nieuwe Academisten. Overgheset inde Nederduytsche sprake door de Dienaers des
G. Woorts binnen Sneeck. Met een voorrede/ vervatende mede int corte een verhael van tgene
sick tusschen de Magistraet met de Dienaers des woorts der Stede voorschreven, ende de
Wederdoopers aldaer heeft toeghedraghen* (Franeker: Gillis van den Rade, 1601).

[17] [B. Buwo], *Een frundtlicke thosamensprekinge van twe personen, van de Döpe der yungen
unmundigen kynderen* (Emden: Gellius Ctematius 1556), a8r/v. Adriaan van Haemstede held
a comparable position. A. J. Jelsma, *Adriaan van Haemstede en zijn martelaarsboek*
('s-Gravenhage: Boekencentrum, 1970), 123.

[18] M. Roobol, *Disputation by Decree: The Public Disputations between Reformed Ministers and
Dirck Volckertsz Coornhert as Instruments of Religious Policy during the Dutch Revolt
(1577–1583)* (Leiden, The Netherlands: Brill, 2010), 24–25.

started to inform their readers on what had happened without ever approving of Calvin's position on the matter.

After the seventeenth century, Reformed Protestants often treated the Servetus affair as a regrettable accident that had little in common with the Reformed movement per se. They reasoned that Calvin had been unable to quit the Catholic settings within one generation. Being born and raised within the medieval system, he had been unable to distance himself entirely from the papal inquisition. Servetus had had good reason to ask questions about the Trinity and the humanity of Christ. After all, Reformed Protestantism was based on scripture and on reason. This made the debate about these church doctrines seemingly inevitable. Anabaptists, however, started to assure their readers that they had nothing in common with Servetus's erroneous nonsense. They regretted the death penalty against Servetus, but were also ready to state that he had gone too far. Once again, the frontiers between Anabaptism and Reformed Protestantism became porous and vague, with the Anabaptists assuring their readers that they did accept the doctrines of the patristic church and with the Reformed assuring their readers that they were always open to a reasonable debate, even on the Trinity.[19]

Hence the relationship between Anabaptists and Reformed continued to be a striking example of how confused the early modern religious landscape often was. Historians have recently started to emphasize "religious ambiguity" instead of confessionalization as a concept to understand the religious landscape of early modern Europe. The relationship between Reformed and Anabaptists highlights these ambiguities. Believers crossed confessional boundaries and the two movements mutually influenced each other. This approach is, I think, highly useful to understand the often complex relationship between Anabaptists and Reformed as well as their often changing positions.

SUGGESTED FURTHER READINGS

Balke, W. *Calvijn en de Doperse Radikalen.* Amsterdam: Ton Bolland, 1973.
Heal, B., and A. Kremers. *Radicalism and Dissent in the World of Protestant Reform.* Göttingen: Vandenhoeck & Ruprecht, 2017.

[19] M. van Veen, "Dutch Anabaptist and Reformed Historiographers on Servetus' Death: Or How the Radical Reformation Turned Mainstream and How the Mainstream Reformation Turned Radical," in B. Heal and A. Kremers (eds.), *Radicalism and Dissent in the World of Protestant Reform* (Göttingen: Vandenhoeck & Ruprecht, 2017), 162–172.

Plath, U. *Calvin und Basel in den Jahren 1552–1556*. Zürich: Theologischer
    Verlag Zürich, 1974.
Strübind, A. *Eifriger als Zwingli. Die frühe Taüferbewegung in der Schweiz*.
    Berlin: Duncker & Humblot, 2003.
Williams, G. H. *The Radical Reformation*. 3rd ed. Kirksville, MO: Sixteenth
    Century Journal Publishers, 1992.

PART VI

∽

CALVIN'S RECEPTION

Our Context

International Calvinism

Mack P. Holt

It is well known that the Reformed Church spread farther and faster than any of the other Protestant reformations, expanding to various Swiss cities, France, the Netherlands, the British Isles, much of the Holy Roman Empire, Hungary, and Poland-Lithuania during Calvin's own lifetime or shortly after his death in 1564. And in the seventeenth century it flourished even farther afield, expanding permanently to North America and southern Africa. Moreover, much of this growth and expansion was directly tied to a larger narrative of persecution, emigration, and refuge. But to refer to this phenomenal growth as the creation of international Calvinism conceals as much as it reveals. For one thing, we might better speak of international Calvinisms in the plural, as it was hardly the same church that was exported across much of western and central Europe and then the globe. As other chapters in this volume explain very explicitly, the Reformed religion had to adapt and restyle itself virtually everywhere it went to survive in very different political, economic, and sociocultural climates. For another, international Calvinism had no Calvinist international, either institutionally or structurally, to foster and maintain close and permanent relations among the various Reformed churches. This was hardly surprising given Calvin's own inclination that each church should be self-governing. So, what, then, can we mean by the term *international Calvinism*?

In one sense, then, international Calvinism was an "imagined community," not in terms of a nationalist identity suggested by Benedict Anderson, but as a transnational and spiritual identity. One key to understanding Reformed churches wherever they existed was the notion of a special covenant with God. This had less to do with any understanding of the doctrine of predestination – never as central to Calvin's own ideas as many nineteenth-century Reformed theologians have led us to believe – than with a sincere belief that the Reformed were God's chosen people with a destiny to fulfill in this world, akin to their spiritual forebears, the Hebrews of the Old Testament. As Calvin often reminded his own parishioners, they were the new Israelites, and that Old Testament history was also their own history. It is clear that for French Huguenots struggling for survival in Catholic France and for Dutch Calvinists under Spanish suppression, they used this self-image of the successors to the Children of Israel both to justify their struggles as well as to boost their identity as God's chosen people.[1] Nevertheless, there was more to international Calvinism than simply an imagined sense of common identity. In fact, it appears that many Reformed communities were also bound together in the sixteenth and seventeenth centuries in several distinct and explicit ways: intellectually, commercially and financially, as well as militarily. The remainder of this chapter will attempt to contextualize these three spheres in which Reformed communities not only sought to construct a common Reformed identity but also to build more permanent and lasting connections for Calvinists across Europe and indeed around the globe.

The intellectual bonds linking Reformed communities everywhere in Europe clearly began with the Reformed seminaries and academies where most of their pastors trained for the ministry. The Genevan Academy founded by Calvin in June 1559 was hardly the first of these, as Reformed academies founded in Zurich, Strasbourg, Bern, and Lausanne served as models for the new academy in Geneva. They also contributed to its faculty, as Calvin hired the young professor of Greek from Lausanne, Theodore Beza, to be the Genevan Academy's first rector. Moreover, in other cities attracted to the Reformation such as Basel, Ghent, and Heidelberg, older Catholic universities had been transformed into Reformed academies of higher learning. And in due course, brand new institutions such as Leiden University, founded in 1575 after that city's ultimate victory over the Spanish army after a lengthy siege, provided yet more outlets for the training of Reformed ministers. Moreover, by the early seventeenth century, Leiden University had managed to surpass the academy in Geneva and other Swiss cities in terms of faculty, students, and curriculum. Just as the political

---

[1] See Charles H. Parker, "French Calvinists as the Children of Israel: An Old Testament Self-Consciousness in Jean Crespin's *Histoire des Martyrs* before the Wars of Religion," *Sixteenth Century Journal* 24 (1993): 227–248; G. Groenhuis, "Calvinism and National Consciousness: The Dutch Republic as the New Israel," in *Church and State since the Reformation*, Vol. 7 of *Britain and the Netherlands*, A. C. Duke and C. A. Tamse (eds.) (The Hague: Nijhoff, 1981), 119–133; and Ole Peter Grell, "The Creation of a Calvinist Identity in the Reformation Period," in Per Ingesman (ed.), *Religion as an Agent of Change: Crusades, Reformation, Pietism* (Leiden, The Netherlands: Brill, 2016), 149–165.

leadership of international Calvinism shifted from Geneva to Amsterdam after the death of Beza in 1605, the intellectual leadership of the movement shifted from Geneva to Leiden. What all the Reformed academies and universities shared in common was a curriculum dominated by the intense study of Latin, Greek, and Hebrew, as well as theology, law, and history, though a Providential history to be sure. Not every student at these academies was training for the ministry, as many became lawyers, merchants, bankers, and teachers. The curriculum was littered with the Latin and Greek classics – Homer, Aristotle, Cicero, Ovid, Polybius, Livy, Xenophon, and Vergil, for example – as one would expect from Calvin's and Beza's own humanist training. And despite the theological differences that emerged after Calvin's death in 1564 – such as whether Christ died for the sins of all or just for the sins of the elect, whether God decided who would be saved and who would be damned before or after the Fall, or especially the Arminian controversy over predestination – these institutions of higher learning nevertheless provided a common body of thought and way of understanding the world for the Reformed. Calvin strongly believed that to have a Christian community, a strong foundation of Christian teaching and learning was an absolute necessity.[2]

In addition to a solid foundation of educational institutions, another strength of international Calvinism was a network of printers. Just as Luther's Reformation in Wittenburg turned that city from a publishing backwater into an international printing powerhouse, Calvin did the same in Geneva and Lyon, while Reformed cities such as Emden, Zurich, and Basel also became major print centers. In addition, the Wechel family established Frankfurt as a major outlet for Reformed printing by the end of the sixteenth century. In the Netherlands, first Antwerp, then Amsterdam and Delft, served the reformed community there. This network of printers provided Reformed churches all over Europe not only with vernacular Bibles, psalters, and texts for the students at Reformed academies and universities, but they also kept them up to date with news in myriad printed forms from the civil wars in France to the Dutch revolt.[3] Thus, even though there was no umbrella institution administering to the needs of Reformed

---

[2] Gillian Lewis, "The Geneva Academy," in Andrew Pettegree, Alastair Duke, and Gillian Lewis (eds.), *Calvinism in Europe, 1540–1620* (Cambridge: Cambridge University Press, 1994), 35–63; and Karin Maag, *Seminary or University? The Genevan Academy and Reformed Higher Education, 1560–1620* (Aldershot: Scolar Press, 1995).

[3] See Andrew Pettegree, *The French Book and the European Book World* (Leiden, The Netherlands: Brill, 2007); and R. J. W. Evans, "The Wechel Presses: Humanism and Calvinism in Central Europe, 1572–1627," *Past and Present,* suppl. 2 (1975): 1–74.

churches across Europe, there were intellectual ties that in many ways united them, founded upon a solid network of academies of higher learning and a vibrant community of printers sympathetic to the cause.

A second link that tied most of the Reformed communities together was a vast economic network of trade and commerce. Born from a legacy of persecution, emigration, and refuge, a network of wealthy merchants extended across much of western Europe: from Lucca at the southern extreme, to Scotland at the northern extreme, and as far east as Poland and as far west as Ireland. Many of these merchants had connections to Geneva, as some even studied at the Geneva Academy. Thus, by the end of the sixteenth century a widespread Reformed diaspora emerged, which not only provided a much needed communication link across Europe, but also produced a vast charitable relief operation for persecuted Calvinists, as became strikingly visible during the Thirty Years' War. How this commercial network of Calvinist merchants, aided and abetted by ministers and elders throughout, functioned as an astringent to bind these far-flung Reformed congregations together is best seen by examining some specific case studies.

Four wealthy merchant families – the Calandrini, Burlemachi, Diodati, and Turettini families – all fled their native Lucca in Tuscany in the 1560s because of the persecution they experienced due to their Reformed faith.[4] Over three generations and the course of 50–60 years, the experiences of repeated persecution, exodus, and exile came to reinforce not only their identities as persecuted Calvinists founded on election and providence but it also integrated them into other Reformed communities through intermarriage and extensive financial and commercial support. Following their migration through France, the Netherlands, the German Empire, Switzerland, and England demonstrates how an extensive Calvinist diaspora not only came into being but also how this diaspora survived. Their family histories and memoirs were, at the same time, providential and biblical histories, and they were written down and shared with other Reformed communities everywhere they went. Thus, their stories were both read and retold by generations of Calvinists who never knew these Italian immigrants, and they served to reinforce their own identities as members of the elect.

To take just one example, Giuliano Calandrini settled originally in Lyon after fleeing Lucca. Later on, two of his three sons, Giovanni and Cesare, along with their extensive families of 11 and 13 children, respectively,

---

[4] This entire section is based on Ole Peter Grell, *Brethren in Christ: A Calvinist Network in Reformation Europe* (Cambridge: Cambridge University Press, 2011).

eventually moved to major European cities such as Frankfurt, Stade, Antwerp, Nuremberg, Amsterdam, and London. They and their children managed to create and join commercial and financial enterprises with other Reformed refugee merchants, at the same time establishing links through marriage with prominent Reformed Dutch, Walloon, and English merchant families. Moreover, they fully participated in the Reformed "stranger" churches wherever they went, not just as members, but also as deacons and elders. This shared network of Calvinist exiles, cemented by their shared commercial and financial ventures, made it possible to aid other godly members of the elect who were less fortunate than they in escaping persecution. And one particular way in which the financial resources of successful Reformed families such as these came to benefit the entire Calvinist diaspora was in raising money for those most heavily persecuted, such as the Calvinists in the German Palatinate in the early seventeenth century.

The defeat of the army of Elector Palatine Frederick V's army at the White Mountain just outside Prague in 1620 at the start of the Thirty Years' War, followed by the subsequent occupation of the Upper and Lower Palatinate by Habsburg troops, resulted in large numbers of refugee Calvinist ministers, artisans, schoolmasters, and their families, who were expelled from their homeland. Many of them fled to Nuremberg where they were taken in and supported by the local Reformed community. From Nuremberg, Cesare Calandrini's son, Jeremiah, took charge of collecting aid and monies for them from both Amsterdam and Paris. His brother Benedict, who lived in London, supervised the collection of aid from England and Ireland. But the support led by the Calandrini brothers was just the tip of the iceberg, as money flowed in from Reformed communities all over Europe, and especially from England, Scotland, and Ireland where about 40 percent of the total was raised. The sustenance provided by Calvinists all over Europe to their "brethren in Christ" from the Palatinate in 1622 was just one of numerous episodes of Reformed charity collected for the exiled and persecuted members of the elect. They constructed a welfare safety net whenever it was needed, which happened often in the sixteenth and seventeenth centuries.

One other commercial tie uniting Calvinists all over Europe was the way in which they used certain consumer goods as both symbols of their Reformed identity and history as well as objects of utilitarian function. Tin-glazed earthenware cups, plates, bowls, pots, tankards, and jugs, otherwise known as delftware, were originally brought to the Netherlands from Italy and Spain before 1500. The manufacture of this majolica pottery soon took root in Haarlem, Amsterdam, Rotterdam, and above all Delft, which after 1620 became the commercial center for such pottery. It was decorated and painted by hand, usually with either biblical or political images. The most common images were scenes from the Old Testament, with the most prominent of all being Abraham's sacrifice of Isaac and the temptation of Adam and Eve. The most common image from the New Testament was that of the prodigal son. All these images resonate with the providential history that Calvinists everywhere carried with them, and these pieces of decorated pottery turned up all over the Netherlands, Germany, Switzerland, and above all, in England. There they also carried explicit political messages, whether a modest message such as "God save Elizabeth our Queene," to more explicit support for William and Mary, underpinning the legitimacy of a Calvinist king who had a very contested claim to the English throne. Above all, as Alexandra Walsham has shown, objects such as these pieces of delftware were "badges of belonging to the imagined community of the godly."[5]

In addition to intellectual and commercial links uniting Calvinists across western Europe, there was also a surprising military link. Moreover, this link was based on much more than the familiar foreign policy decisions made by monarchs like Queen Elizabeth to support the Dutch rebels in their fight against Philip II of Spain, or the Count-Duke of the Palatinate's support for Bohemian rebels against the Habsburgs. Those actions were based just as much on significant geopolitical motives as on religion. Nevertheless, despite the conclusions of nearly all present-day military historians that professional soldiers were motivated primarily by socioeconomic motives or perhaps a desire for honor, there is ample evidence that many of the officers who fought in these conflicts were enjoined to participate in them by a deep commitment to their Reformed faith.[6] For example, from 1562 to 1642 – that is, from the start of the French Wars of Religion to the start of the English Civil War – an average of about three thousand Englishmen per year served in foreign armies in the Netherlands and in France fighting for Calvinism. Given the premium placed on self-reflection by Calvin, many of the officer corps were not only literate but also they kept diaries and memoirs and often wrote historical accounts of their military action. What stands out in all these writings, according to David Trim, are the explicit references to Reformed

---

[5] This entire paragraph is based on Alexandra Walsham, "Domesticating the Reformation: Material Culture, Memory, and Confessional Identity in Early Modern England," *Renaissance Quarterly* 69 (Summer 2016): 566–616, quote on 580.

[6] This entire section is based on the splendid article by David Trim, "Calvinist Internationalism and the English Officer Corps, 1562–1642," *History Compass* 4:6 (2006): 1024–1048.

theology, history, and memory. For instance, they tended to show that these officers considered the collective Reformed church as Israel, based on a Calvinist understanding of the Bible. Moreover, they considered that their mission and duty was to support this church, not as an international church, but as a transnational community of the godly. One particularly good example was Geoffrey Gates's *The Defence of Militarie Profession* published in London in 1579. Gates was a sometime lawyer in Lincoln's Inn from a devout family in Essex, but he was also a professional soldier who fought in France during the French Wars of Religion. He compared the Calvinists fighting in the Netherlands against Spanish Catholics, and the Huguenots fighting in France against French Catholics, as the godly fighting against the enemies of Israel. He described the army of William, Prince of Orange as "the very Army of the Lord God of Hostes." Gates clearly believed, as did many other officers who wrote such accounts, that they were God's soldiers fighting God's own wars of religion, and that they had to fight for the Reformed cause everywhere in Europe, not just in their own homeland. Thus, in the sixteenth century officers like Gates clearly prefigured the more explicit Calvinist divines who addressed this topic in treatises, pamphlets, and sermons during the Civil War in seventeenth-century England.

What I have tried to suggest is that there may not have been any Calvinist international in any institutional sense in early modern Europe, but Reformed churches all over Europe clearly shared important links and forged networks among themselves to survive and even flourish. These communities did not consider themselves as part of an international church, but more a transnational *ecclesia* that did not recognize national boundaries. Without these networks of support and collective identity and memory, it is doubtful that the Reformed church could have grown and spread so widely within a century of Calvin's death.

SUGGESTED FURTHER READINGS

Benedict, Philip. *Christ's Churches Purely Reformed: A Social History of Calvinism*. New Haven, CT: Yale University Press, 2002.

Gordon, Bruce, ed. *Protestant History and Identity in Sixteenth-Century Europe: The Later Reformation*. Aldershot: Ashgate, 1996.

Grell, Ole Peter. *Brethren in Christ: A Calvinist Network in Reformation Europe*. Cambridge: Cambridge University Press, 2011.

Hirzel, Ernst, and Martin Salmann, eds. *John Calvin's Impact on Church and Society, 1509–2009*. Grand Rapids, MI: William B. Eerdmans, 2009.

Murdock, Graeme. *Beyond Calvin: The Intellectual, Political, and Cultural World of Europe's Reformed Churches, c. 1540–1620*. London and New York: Palgrave Macmillan, 2004.

Oberman, Heiko A. "*Europa Afflicta*: The Reformation of the Refugees." *Archiv für Reformationsgeschichte* 83 (1992): 91–111.

Pettegree, Andrew. *Emden and the Dutch Revolt*. Oxford: Oxford University Press, 1992.

Foreign Protestant Communities in Sixteenth-Century London. Oxford: Oxford University Press, 1986.

Pettegree, Andrew, Alastair Duke, and Gillian Lewis, eds. *Calvinism in Europe, 1540–1620*. Cambridge: Cambridge University Press, 1994.

Prestwich, Menna, ed. *International Calvinism, 1541–1715*. Oxford: Oxford University Press, 1985.

Trim, David. "Calvinist Internationalism and the English Officer Corps, 1562–1642." *History Compass* 4:6 (2006): 1024–1048.

43

∾

Calvin Legends

Hagiology and Demonology

Jennifer Powell McNutt

In 1695, Andrea Pozzo was commissioned to oversee the erection of a Baroque altar at the church of the Gesù in Rome in celebration of Ignatius Loyola. French sculptor, Pierre Le Gros the younger, contributed a striking marble tableau to the project entitled, "Religion Overthrowing Heresy and Hatred."[1] With notable skill, Le Gros depicted religion as a young woman hurling firebolts at hatred and heresy represented by an old man, and the viewer is left with little question as to the identity of those levied with the grievous charge of heresy. As religion attacks heresy with a righteous anger, the figure of heresy topples backward, stepping upon a book with Martin Luther's name written on the spine; meanwhile, the putto in the forefront of the tableau earnestly tears the writings of Ulrich Zwingli and John Calvin. The boldness of the tableau's message and its unshakeable confidence in the Roman Catholic cause is fitting to its time; polarization between Protestants and Catholics due to post-Reformation warfare and confessionalization on the eve of the Enlightenment is surely no better illustrated.[2] Calvin's inclusion in the tableau alongside first-wave reformers, Luther and Zwingli, is something of a backhanded compliment, which speaks to his enduring

---

[1] John Barber, *The Road from Eden: Studies in Christianity and Culture* (Palo Alto, CA: Academica Press, 2008), 295.

[2] Protestants were vulnerable at this juncture in European history due to the political maneuvers of Louis XIV, King of France and worked actively toward theological alliance: Jennifer Powell McNutt, *Calvin Meets Voltaire: The Clergy of Geneva in the Age of Enlightenment* (Burlington: VT: Ashgate, 2014), 47–52; Martin Klauber, "The Drive Toward Protestant Union in Early Eighteenth-Century Geneva: J.-A. Turrettini on the 'Fundamental Articles' of the Faith," *Church History* 61:3 (September 1992): 334–349; Richard Whatmore, *Against War and Empire: Geneva, Britain, and France in the Eighteenth Century* (New Haven, CT: Yale University Press, 2012).

perceived significance within the history of the church, acknowledged even by opponents. The tableau also illustrates how Reformation leaders, particularly, and Protestant communities, broadly, were charged in an enduring way with a litany of misdeeds including heresy as well as treason, licentiousness, and sedition. Early modern slander favored these accusations, and they functioned in an interconnected way as the unsavory inheritance of key Reformation leaders and communities including Calvin and Geneva. Indeed, it was due to these very accusations that Calvin first entered the Reformation fray as advocate on behalf of the struggling, emerging Reformed community in France.

ENTERING THE LIMELIGHT

In 1536, Calvin became a vocal proponent of the Reformation cause with the first edition of his *Institutes of the Christian Religion* prefaced by a dedication to King Francis I. In the aftermath of the Placard Affair (October 18, 1534), which rattled the king right out of his bedchamber into launching a royal campaign of persecution against Protestants, Calvin's volume stressed the bleak conditions faced by France's evangelical constituents for their faith: shackled, beaten, publicly humiliated, tortured, impoverished, cursed, and forced into exile.[3] Calvin writes,

> The poor little church has either been wasted with cruel slaughter or banished into exile, or so overwhelmed by threats and fears that it dare not even open its mouth.... Meanwhile no one comes forward to defend the church against such furies.[4]

Driven by the dire nature of the situation, Calvin as trained lawyer and self-made theologian emerged in the public eye as defender of the Protestant cause against what he regarded as rampant rumor and misinformation circulating: "I know with what horrible reports they have filled your ears and mind, to render our cause as hateful as possible to you."[5] Diligently, Calvin addressed each accusation levied against the community: religious heresy, sedition, political treason, theological innovation, ecclesiastical schism, and moral licentiousness. Turning slander on its head, he compared the treatment of Protestants with the treatment of the Apostles.[6] By

---

[3] John Calvin, *Institutes of the Christian Religion*, John McNeill (ed.), Ford Lewis Battles (trans.), Vol. 1 (Philadelphia: Westminster Press, 1960), 14.

[4] Ibid., 11.

[5] Ibid., 9–10.

[6] Ibid., 29.

presenting the theological views of the *Institutes* as the true articulation of the Huguenot cause and the core of the Gospel message, Calvin wrote expressly for the purpose of contesting the demonizing of the Protestant movement.[7] In the end, this determination to gain a hearing for the Protestant cause led to both the elevation and distortion of his reputation. The public face of the Huguenot cause in the context of persecution rendered Calvin vulnerable to personal attack as well.[8]

TARGET OF ATTACK

As events unfolded, the vitriol directed at the movement began leveling attacks against Calvin that he was not keen to brush off. Bruce Gordon's work notes how Calvin spent a considerable amount of time and energy responding to personal accusations: "He was ferociously defensive of his reputation and few things could rouse his ire more rapidly than the suggestion that his name was in bad odour or that he was being traduced by an opponent. Perceived slights and insults cut deeply and were frequently recounted in letters to intimates."[9] Calvin's heightened concern for preserving his reputation was also a consequence of the way in which his personal reputation became closely linked with the success of the Reformation in France. If he was maligned, so was the cause.

These dynamics were complicated by the fact that, as successor to Luther and Zwingli, Calvin found it necessary to distinguish his convictions from Catholicism as well as other versions of Protestantism throughout Reformation Europe. As Karin Maag writes, "[T]o clear the ground for his understanding of Reformed Protestantism to take root, Calvin had to fight a polemical battle on multiple fronts at the same time."[10] According to Calvin, this felt at times like he was "under pressure from all sides at the same moment" as he also maintained a tremendous work load.[11] The challenges he

---

[7] Calvin's treatise to Emperor Charles V, "On the Necessity of Reforming the Church," addresses slander against Protestantism: *John Calvin: Tracts and Letters*, Henry Beveridge (ed. and trans.), Vol. 1 (Carlisle, PA: The Banner of Truth Trust, 2009), 124.

[8] Karin Maag, "Hero or Villain? Interpretations of John Calvin and His Legacy," *Calvin Theological Journal* 41 (2006): 229.

[9] Bruce Gordon, *Calvin* (New Haven, CT: Yale University Press, 2009), 145.

[10] Maag, "Hero or Villain?," 228.

[11] See Calvin's dedication to Philip Melanchthon: *The Bondage and Liberation of the Will*, A. N. S. Lane (ed.), G. I. Davies (trans.) (Grand Rapids, MI: Baker Books, 1996), 4–5; Max Engammare, "Calvin the Workaholic," in Irena Backus and Philip Benedict (eds.), *Calvin and His Influence, 1509–2009* (New York, NY: Oxford University Press, 2011), 67–83. The polemical side of Calvin has frequently overshadowed the pastoral dimensions of his identity

faced were certainly multifaceted, particularly because the demonizing of his reputation was not merely the work of Roman Catholic opponents but estranged and antagonistic members of the Protestant community as well.

As Calvin assumed advocacy of the Protestant cause, embraced the task of pastoral leadership, dramatically expanded his publications, and rose in prominence among the reformers, scrutiny over his reputation led to his becoming a target of attack.

THE DEMONIZING OF CALVIN

Although the demonizing of Calvin often echoed accusations broadly raised against the Protestant cause, defamation was also exceptionally directed at him. Examples from the apologetics of his supporters indicate that Calvin was susceptible to accusations of forming a "new popedom" similarly guilty of hording wealth and indulging luxurious living as a spin on his success in shaping Geneva's church and Reformed churches beyond.[12] Calvin's new theocracy in Geneva was power hungry and revealed its true colors of tyranny with the execution of the antitrinitarian Michael Servetus.[13] Meanwhile, his contested involvement in the Conspiracy of Amboise raised questions about his role in advancing treason and insurrection in France.[14] According to one story, Calvin was no better than a charlatan for paying a man to feign death so that he could carry out the "miracle" of raising him from the dead.[15] Meanwhile, the falsified claim that Calvin's dispassionate severity led him to execute his own stepson and stepdaughter for acts of fornication and adultery, respectively, continues to circulate today.[16]

Yet, Calvin was nothing if not a supreme heretic for those at odds with him, a perception with a long publishing life.[17] During his time, his theology was described as a "new" Gospel,[18] and his hometown of Noyon was

---

and work well into twentieth-century historiography. More recently, Randall Zachman, Elsie McKee, and Scott Manetsch have emphasized the pastoral dimensions of Calvin's work, identity, and legacy in their scholarship.

[12] Theodore Beza, "Life of John Calvin," in Henry Beveridge (ed. and trans.), *John Calvin: Tracts and Letters*, Vol. 1 (Carlisle, PA: The Banner of Truth Trust, 2009), xcix.

[13] Ibid., c.

[14] Ibid., lxxvii–i.

[15] Ibid., c.

[16] Maag traces the emergence and continuation of this claim: "Hero or Villain?," 234.

[17] In 1891, correspondence between T. H. Hinchman and James Bell was published in the book, *John Calvin: His Errors, Ignorance, Misconceptions, and Absurdities and the Errors of Presbyterianism, Disclosed and Exposed*.

[18] Willem van der Lindt, *Recueil d'aucunes mensonges de Calvin, Melanthon, Bucere et autres nouveaux* (Paris, 1561).

applauded for refusing to embrace his influence.[19] Soon after his death, the Roman Catholic Augustinian Claude de Sainctes accused Calvin of atheism due to his views on the doctrine of God and the Eucharist.[20] In the end, Calvin was harangued for advancing antitrinitarian theology on multiple occasions[21] and lambasted for mistreating antitrinitarians in the case of Michael Servetus.[22] The latter claim would prove the most enduring due in part to Voltaire's popular writings in the eighteenth century identifying Calvin with an "atrocious soul" for his treatment of Servetus.[23]

But the label of heretic was not merely the result of Catholic polemical writings. In the Protestant world, Calvin launched his ministry in Geneva under suspicion of unorthodoxy due to his colleague, Pierre Caroli, who became an early antagonist and troubled him many years afterward. Though Caroli began as a member of the reform-minded Circle at Meaux and was later named chief preacher at Lausanne, he spent much of his adult life struggling to navigate between Protestant and Catholic loyalties. His ambivalence is evident in the many times that he changed religious affiliation over the course of his ministry and by how he managed the theology and praxis surrounding prayers for the dead. Calvin regarded Caroli as a self-seeking leader, who left Protestant teachings vulnerable to accusations of hypocrisy and perceptions of internal discord.[24] In turn, Caroli accused Calvin, Guillame Farel, and Pierre Viret of the antitrinitarian heresies of Arianism and Sabellianism.[25] Caroli was found at fault at the Disputation of Lausanne (1536) and by the delegation at Berne; nonetheless, rumors circulated in Protestant circles that Geneva's clergy guided by Calvin advanced unorthodox views on the doctrine of God.[26] The fact that Calvin was expelled subsequently from Geneva on an unrelated matter exacerbated the perception for some that Calvin was guilty of heresy.[27] In the end, the damage that Caroli inflicted on Calvin's reputation was minor

[19] Antoine de Mouchy, *De veritate Christi* (Paris, 1570). Archdeacon at Noyon, Jacques Le Vasseur encouraged this trend of distancing the city from Calvin's heretical reputation in the seventeenth century.

[20] Sainctes, *Declaration d'aucuns atheismes de la doctrine de Calvin et Beze* (Paris, 1568).

[21] Italian Catholic priest Franciscus Stancarus of Mantua charged Protestants including Calvin with Arianism for describing Christ as Mediator.

[22] See Sebastian Castellio's *On Heretics*: Martin Bellius [pseud.], *De haereticis* (Basel, 1554).

[23] McNutt, *Calvin Meets Voltaire*, ch. 4.

[24] *John Calvin: Tracts and Letters*, Jules Bonnet (ed.), David Constable (trans.), new ed., Vol. 4 (Carlisle, PA: The Banner of Truth Trust, 2009), 49. Upon arriving in Basel, Caroli accused Farel of attempting to murder him in Geneva: Gordon, *Calvin*, 50.

[25] Calvin pointed to his catechism in defense: *Tracts*, 4: 54.

[26] Numerous letters recount these matters: ibid., 47–58, 150–157.

[27] Beza, "Life of John Calvin," xcix.

compared to the defamation he suffered in perpetuity by fellow Protestant refugee, Jérôme Bolsec.

In 1577, more than 10 years after Calvin's passing, Bolsec released an anti-biography of Calvin that proved devastating to his reputation.[28] The bad blood between them had begun years before. In 1551, Bolsec entered into public confrontation with Calvin over the doctrine of predestination. Stung by his subsequent banishment from Geneva and the Protestant Synod of Lyon's condemnation in 1563, Bolsec was driven back into the arms of the Catholic Church and keen to counter Theodore Beza's portrayal of Calvin's character and life written soon after Calvin's death. Bolsec was intent upon destroying the elevated remembrance of the Protestant reformers,[29] and his antipathy for Calvin was overt as he also subverted a genre of biography used classically and exclusively for praise.[30] Bolsec's Calvin embodied immorality, cruelty, sedition, and tyranny to the core. He described Calvin as the son of a blasphemous father and the father of a homosexual son, branded with an iron for his immorality (a lenient punitive measure at the time). Bolsec's Calvin was little more than a sexual deviant, who was convicted of sodomy in his hometown of Noyon and died of crab lice due to rampant promiscuity. Calvin's dishonor was complete when Bolsec elevated a rumor of a death-bed renunciation of all his writings. Although Bolsec admitted to basing his stories on gossip, he gained a wide readership as numerous editions were published throughout the century and beyond. Calvin would never know the character assassination that Bolsec penned, but the depiction would trouble his legacy for generations.[31]

In particular, Bolsec's work created space and opportunity for Catholic opponents to question the soundness of Calvin's character and teaching.[32] Reference to Calvin became a staple in Catholic histories about heresy.[33] For example, Florimond de Raemond linked the antitrinitarian teaching of Pierre Statorius of the Polish Brethren with Calvin's impact.[34] Jacques

---

[28] Bolsec's *Histoire de la vie moeurs, actes, doctrine, constance et mort de Jean Calvin jadis minister de Genève* (Paris: G. Mallot, 1577; Lyon: Jean Patrasson, 1577).

[29] Irena Backus, *Life Writing in Reformation Europe: Lives of Reformers by Friends, Disciples, and Foes*. St. Andrews Studies in Reformation History (Burlington, VT: Ashgate, 2013), 154.

[30] Ibid., 155.

[31] Backus argues that this type of anti-biography was motivated by prospects for reconverting French Protestants: ibid., 162.

[32] Beza, "Life of John Calvin," lxxvi.

[33] Including Gabriel Dupréau, Wilhelmus Lindanus, Florimond de Raemon, and Laurentius Surius.

[34] Raemond, *L'Histoire de la naissance, progrez et décadence de l'hérésie de ce siècle divisee en huit livres* (Paris: Chez Veuve Guillaume de la Nove, MDCX). See Book 4: 455.

Desmay used the records at Noyon to depict Calvin from his youth as seeking innovation and practicing clerical immorality only to return to Catholicism on his deathbed.[35] In 1651, Cardinal Richelieu published on the errors of Protestantism in three volumes.[36] Heresy went hand in hand with debauchery, and Calvin was again prominently accused of sexual degeneracy and tyranny, which revived Bolsec's narrative of Calvin's conviction of sodomy and subsequent branding. Such demonizations of Calvin would not go unanswered. Alternate narratives were also advanced among Calvin's contemporaries, and after his death as his work grew in significance for the Protestant cause.

THE HAGIOLOGY OF CALVIN

Calvin was not without his allies and advocates from the start of his ministry. As he made his mark on the movement, he began to receive notable acclaim from Protestant brethren identifying him as an indispensable leader with a brilliant grasp of theology. By 1539, Calvin received word of Luther's favor,[37] confirmed by Philip Melanchthon.[38] Yet, few knew Calvin better than his faithful colleague in ministry, friend, and successor, Theodore Beza, and no one nurtured, protected, and advocated for the good remembrance of Calvin more than he. Consequently, just months after Calvin's death,[39] Beza published Calvin's commentary on Joshua posthumously along with *L'histoire de la vie et mort de Calvin*.[40] Nicolas Colladon, a French refugee and lawyer, expanded this version into a second edition with an apologetic edge. In 1575, a new version was published by Beza along with Calvin's correspondence,[41] and the task continued a century later with Antoine Teissier's French translation.

---

[35] Desmay, *Remarques considérables sur la vie et mœurs de Jean Calvin, hérésiarque* (1621).

[36] *Traitté qui contient la méthode la plus facile et la plus assurée pour conuertir ceux qui se sont séparés de l'Église* (1651).

[37] *Tracts*, 4: 167; LW 50 (Philadelphia: Fortress Press, 1975), 190–191.

[38] Beza reports Melanchthon called Calvin, "The Theologian": Beza, "Life of John Calvin," xxxvi.

[39] *Commentaires de M. Iehan Calvin, sur le livre de Josué. Avec une preface de Theodore de Besze, contenant en brief l'histoire de la vie et mort d'iceluy* (Geneva: François Perrin, 1564).

[40] See D. Ménager, "Théodore de Bèze, biographe de Calvin," *Bibliothèque d'Humanisme et Renaissance* 45:2 (1983): 231–255.

[41] J.-R. Armogathe, "Les vies de Calvin aux xvie et xviie siècles," in P. Joutard (ed.) *Historiographie de la Réforme* (Neuchâtel: Delachaux & Niestlé, 1977), 45–59.

Beza's Calvin cut a sympathetic swath and increasingly so as the editions developed.[42] Like a devoted son to a father, Beza described Calvin as a brilliant, hard-working leader, who was gifted in theology, leadership, and organization according to all who encountered him.[43] By shaping the story of Calvin's life around the relentless challenge of incessant antagonists and external opponents, Calvin emerges as faithful in his calling to proclaim the Gospel while working tirelessly to advance orthodoxy.[44] To Beza, Calvin modeled a "Christian Hercules," subduing the monsters of heresy "by that mightiest of all clubs, the Word of God."[45] Beza frequently complimented Calvin for his moderation and patience in responding to controversy, and when Calvin was particularly severe toward others, Beza tended to give warrant for the response.[46] Though naturally grave in temperament, for Beza, "there was no man who was more pleasant."[47] In the midst of his struggles with Catholics, Anabaptists, and Libertines,[48] Beza's Calvin was weighed down by sorrow for the persecution of his brethren,[49] and he grieved and advocated for those facing persecution.[50] As refugees streamed into the city, Beza's Calvin advanced pastoral care.[51] As the city grappled with plague, he put his life on the line by volunteering to care for the sick.[52] Even as his health rapidly deteriorated,[53] Calvin gave every ounce of himself to the cause to the point of being carried to meetings of the congregation. Ultimately, Beza's narrative treated Satan as the primary opponent working against Calvin's ministry to thwart his faithful work at every turn,[54] which Beza interpreted as a sign of Calvin's faithfulness.[55] In the end, Calvin's reputation spread far and wide with Christians flocking to Geneva from all over Christendom seeking to establish Italian, English, and Spanish

---

[42] Beza's first edition was not apologetically motivated: Backus, *Life Writing in Reformation Europe*, xxii. Moreover, Beza notes the complexity of celebrating Calvin's contributions without presenting him as a Protestant saint: "Life of John Calvin," xx.

[43] Beza, "Life of John Calvin," xxxviii–xxxix, xliii.

[44] Ibid., xlii.

[45] Ibid., xcix. Beza's comments are reminiscent of Luther's depiction as "Hercules Germanicus" by Hans Holbein (1520).

[46] Ibid., xlviii–xlix.

[47] Ibid., xcviii.

[48] Ibid., xlv.

[49] Ibid., lxxxi.

[50] Ibid., lxxi–lxxiii; lxxix.

[51] Ibid., xli.

[52] Ibid., xlii.

[53] Ibid., lxxxii.

[54] Ibid., xliii.

[55] Ibid., xlvi.

churches, perhaps the greatest sign of God's blessing on Calvin's ministry according to Beza.[56]

Advancing a noble memory of Calvin's life and contribution was not lost with the passing generations. Charles Drelincourt's *Défense de Calvin* (Geneva, 1667) was written expressly to combat Cardinal Richelieu's disparaging depiction of Calvin as no better than a common criminal. Drelincourt's apology was dedicated to the pastors and professors of Geneva with profuse appreciation for Calvin's theological writings as inspired by the Holy Spirit and for his moral fiber, as one who lived "one of the most beautiful and most holy lives which has ever been on the earth."[57] In the eighteenth century, the memory of John Calvin required defense again by the direct descendants of his pastoral legacy, this time against French philosophes Voltaire, and they would not neglect their stewardship of his memory.[58] In the early twentieth century, Geneva would prove its devotion again for the 400th anniversary of Calvin's birth when the International Monument to the Reformation was erected. There Calvin stands larger than life at 5 m tall and prominently leading the way. The man who requested and received burial in an unmarked grave was deemed too significant to be forgotten by his posterity.

HUMANIZING CALVIN

Assessing the Calvinography of the past can leave one with a disjointed picture that does not always fit neatly into a Protestant/Catholic divide.[59] Though Calvin's hagiography has been deemed decidedly limited, this does not suitably appreciate the way in which Calvin's name grew to become inextricably linked, even interchangeable, with Geneva's reputation.[60] For example, in September 1552, Calvin cautions the Church of London against the tendency to turn him into an "idol" and Geneva into a "Jerusalem."[61] One will not soon forget Scottish Reformer John Knox's famous words identifying Geneva with "the most perfect school of Christ that ever was in the earth since the days of the Apostles. In other places, I confess Christ to be

[56] Ibid., xxxix.

[57] Drelincourt, *La défense de Calvin contre l'outrage fait à sa mémoire dans un livre qui à pour titre, traité qui contient la méthode la plus facile et la plus assurée pour convertir ceux qui se sont séparés de l'église, par le cardinal de Richelieu* (Genève: Pour Jean Ant et Samuel De Tournes, 1667), 3.

[58] McNutt, *Calvin Meets Voltaire*, ch. 4.

[59] Term used by Backus for descriptions of Calvin by others.

[60] See McNutt, *Calvin Meets Voltaire*, ch. 1.

[61] Referenced in Alain Dufour's "Le Mythe de Geneve au Temps de Calvin," *Revue Suisse D'Histoire*, Vol. 9 (Zurich, 1959), 508.

truly preached; but manners and religion to be so sincerely reformed, I have not yet seen in any other place."[62] Gratitude for Geneva was a compliment owed to Calvin just as villainizing Geneva for its heresy, debauchery, and sedition ultimately fell at his feet. As Calvin rose in prominence, the trend of identifying Geneva as the "Rome of Protestantism" or the new Jerusalem gained momentum well into the Enlightenment era.[63] Persisting polarized views have been identified as the "myth of Geneva"[64] while recognizing the symbiotic relationship it shares with Calvin's name and reputation. In response to oscillating attitudes, scholarship trends over the last century have largely tended to demote the singular impact that Calvin had on the Reformed tradition[65] as well as to humanize his biography for a more measured appreciation of his contribution to Christian history and theology.[66]

SUGGESTED FURTHER READINGS

Backus, Irena. *Life Writing in Reformation Europe: Lives of Reformers by Friends, Disciples and Foes.* St. Andrews Studies in Reformation History. Burlington, VT: Ashgate, 2013.

Dompnier, Bernard. *Le venin de l'hérésie. Image du protestantisme et combat catholique au XVIIe siècle.* Paris: Le centurion, 1985.

Jenkins, Gary W. *Calvin's Tormentors: Understanding the Conflicts That Shaped the Reformer.* Grand Rapids, MI: Baker Academic, 2018.

McNutt, Jennifer Powell. *Calvin Meets Voltaire: The Clergy of Geneva in the Age of Enlightenment.* Burlington, VT: Ashgate, 2014.

Zachman, Randall, ed. *John Calvin and Roman Catholicism: Critique and Engagement Then and Now.* Grand Rapids, MI: Baker Academic, 2008.

---

[62] "John Knox to Mrs. Locke, 9 December 1556," in David Laing (ed.), *The Works of John Knox*, Vol. 4 (New York: AMS Press, 1966), 240.

[63] Geneva continued to be described as another "Jerusalem" and "Rome": see McNutt, *Calvin Meets Voltaire*, ch. 1.

[64] Dufour, "Le Mythe de Geneve au Temps de Calvin," 489–518.

[65] See Richard Muller's work.

[66] Richard Stauffer, *The Humanness of John Calvin*, George Schriver (trans.) (Birmingham, AL: Abingdon Press, 1971).

44

Calvin and Calvinism in Early Modern England, Scotland, and Ireland

Crawford Gribben

In the England, Scotland, Ireland and their colonies, throughout the sixteenth and seventeenth centuries, no intellectual system may have exercised greater structural or imaginative significance than the theology of John Calvin. In this context, the influence of Calvin's ideas far outweighed the circulation of his published works, and the tradition of translating his publications into English, especially in the second half of the sixteenth century, continued as his ideas were received, adapted and disseminated in the distinctive and sometimes tumultuous religious environments of the Tudor and Stuart territories. These ideas took impressive hold. By the middle of the seventeenth century, Calvinist ideas had moved from the margins to the centre of the religious, cultural and political life of the three kingdoms, feeding into the outbreak of civil war and facilitating the revolution that in turn created the short-lived Cromwellian republic. Simultaneously, Calvinism began to variegate, as the Reformed theologies that circulated within and occasionally between the English, Scottish and Irish churches took on distinctive flavours, in reaction to which, and with the goal of uniting these divided Reformed churches, Calvinist theologians created some of the most important of the early modern confessions of faith. One of the longest of these, the Westminster Confession of Faith (1647), was intended to achieve, but never achieved, the doctrinal unity of the three established churches, though it remains a constitutional benchmark of Presbyterian denominations around the world. Despite some extraordinary achievements, Calvinist theology was in decline by the end of the seventeenth century, being defended by a shrinking number of clergy and adherents of established and dissenting churches, haunted by its association with political instability and

constitutional chaos, and challenged by the presuppositions of the early
Enlightenment and the emergence of trans-Atlantic evangelicalism as a
variety of popular Protestantism better adapted to the religious circumstances of the early eighteenth century.

THE MARIAN EXILES

The Protestant Reformation of the English church had begun under
Henry VIII and continued, with much greater doctrinal clarity and precision,
under Edward VI, before being partially reversed under Mary I and settled,
with various degrees of commitment, under Elizabeth I, James VI/I and
Charles I. This reformation was facilitated by networks and personal relationships that were established in the 1550s, when many of those who would
become the leaders of these reforms met in exile. The efforts made by Mary
to re-establish the Catholic faith had led to the most sustained period of
religious persecution in English history, with the notorious 'fires of Smith-
field' consuming almost 300 Protestant martyrs between 1555 and 1558,
including 1 archbishop and 4 bishops as well as almost 60 women and
children. Escaping for their lives, a further eight hundred Protestant refugees
migrated to the intellectual centres of the Calvinist Reformation, where, in
locations such as Frankfurt am Main, Basel and Geneva, they collaborated
with theologians of other nationalities to create the defining texts of the
theological system that by the later sixteenth century would become the
doctrinal consensus of the established churches of England, Scotland and
Ireland, and a source, as well as a foil, for the churches of their colonies.

The communities of exiles, while disagreeing on certain aspects of the
form of a truly Reformed church, created a shared literary culture, the key
achievements of which would exercise extraordinary influence in popu-
larising the principal themes of Calvin's theology. Developing the arguments of John Bale's study of *The Image of Both Churches* (1547), exile
writers rooted their anti-Marian polemic and their theological and
confessional-historical constructions in an apocalyptic register. John Olde
translated Rudolf Gualter's *Antichrist* (1556), and published his own *Short
Description of Antichrist* (1557) in the same year that Bartholomew
Traheron's lectures on Revelation and Robert Pownall's *Admonition to
the towne of Callys* invoked the apocalyptic themes to warn of impending
judgement upon the English church. John Knox's *First Blast of the
Trumpet against the Monstrous Regiment of Women* (1558) challenged
the propriety of female monarchical rule, aiming to subvert Mary but
appearing in time to do the same for Elizabeth, her Protestant successor

who translated the opening passage of the *Institutes*.[1] In 1557, William Whittingham prepared what became the first English New Testament to include verse divisions, a text that presaged the first full Geneva Bible (1560), the fruit of his scholarly collaboration with Miles Coverdale and Christopher Goodman, which included hundreds of thousands of words of theological and exegetical annotations in defence of Reformed theology. The Geneva Bible, in its various editions, became the central text of Calvinist Reformation in England, where 140 printings of its most popular edition appeared between 1560 and 1644, and where, between 1575 and 1618, at least one new edition of the text appeared annually. The Geneva Bible had similar influence in Scotland, where in the form of its 1599 edition, it retained a monopoly on Bible publication until 1610. It was never printed in Ireland, where the market for Reformed print was small, undeveloped and always depended upon imports, or in the new world. Providing popular readers with maps, illustrations, introductions and explanatory annotations, and sporting the innovation of verse divisions, Geneva Bibles were 'used and pored over by three generations of English Protestants before the Civil War',[2] and likely did more than anything else to popularise the principal ideas of the Genevan reformer among those most critical of the established churches and their hesitant reformations. Its achievements were supported by the work of John Foxe. The historical themes he explored in his drama *Christus Triumphans* (1556) were developed in his *Acts and Monuments* (1563), a massive narrative that in its millions of words traced the history of the true church through centuries of persecution. The 'Book of Martyrs', as the *Acts and Monuments* was also known, appeared in multiple editions of various lengths, and was circulating in around 10,000 copies by the end of the seventeenth century, with its arguments echoing throughout the genre of historical-confessional polemic that it helped to inspire. Even in the 1680s, the 'Book of Martyrs' could be 'esteemed (as the learned confess) the next of all human penn'd Books to the sacred Bible'.[3] The print culture that was developed by exiles from Mary's England established the themes and

[1]   Janel Mueller and Joshua Scodel, eds., *Elizabeth I: Translations, 1544–1589* (Chicago: University of Chicago Press, 2009), 203–287; Andrew Pettegree, 'The Reception of Calvinism in Britain', in Wilhelm H. Neuser and Brian G. Armstrong (eds.), *Calvinus sincerioris religionis vindex* (Kirksville, MO: Truman State University Press, 1997), 267–289.
[2]   Christopher Hill, *Antichrist in Seventeenth-Century England* (London: Oxford University Press, 1971), 3–4.
[3]   John Foxe, *Acts and Monuments* (London: 1684), i. [a]^r.

tropes that would define Calvinism across the three nations until the end of the seventeenth century.

CALVINISM AND THE CULTURES OF EARLY MODERN PRINT

In the later sixteenth century, the programme for Protestant Reformation moved from a Lutheran to a Calvinist agenda, and from an English to a British and Irish agenda, partly as a consequence of the print culture of the Marian refugees and partly as a consequence of the translation into English of Calvin's works and of the wide circulation of his ideas in catechisms, confessions of faith, sermons and other publications. Calvin's reputation was established in print, and illustrated how translators, editors and publishers thought that he might be most effectively introduced to English-language reading publics whose interest in his work the Marian refugees had primed. The translation and publication of Calvin's work predated Mary's accession, and notably increased in the aftermath of her death. But Calvin's reputation had to be promoted. A number of his publications appeared in translation in 1548: *A faythful and moost Godlye treatyse concernynge the most sacret sacrament of the blessed body and bloude of oure sauioure Christe* was described as having been 'co[m]piled by Iohn Caluyne, a man of no lesse lernyng and literature, then Godlye studye, and example of liuyng', while *The mynde of the godly and excellent lerned man M. Ihon Caluyne, what a faithfull man, whiche is instructe in the Worde of God, ought to do, dwellinge amongest the papistes* set out its commendation of the author in its title, and *Of the life or conuersation of a Christen man* (1549) was advertised as work by 'maister Iohn Caluyne, a man of ryghte excellente learnynge and of no lesse godly conuersation'. As English readers grew in their regard for his character and achievements, London printers serviced their demand by publishing an edition of his homilies (1553), as well as editions of his catechism, in both French (1552) and English (1556). *The forme of prayers and ministration of the sacraments, &c. vsed in the Englishe Congregation at Geneua* (1556) may have described Calvin as a 'famous' 'godly learned man', but this world of illicit print was not propitious for the making of a Protestant reputation.

The publication of Calvin's works suddenly ramped up after the death of Mary and the accession of Elizabeth in 1558. Printers rushed to supply multiple editions of his sermons, catechisms and books of church order. In the later sixteenth century, Calvin's reputation rested supremely upon the achievement of his *Institutes of the Christian Religion*, which was widely circulated. Thomas Norton's translation of the final Latin text of the *Institutes* (1559) was published in London in 1561, 1562, 1574, 1582, 1587,

1599, 1611 and 1634. Abridged versions of the *Institutes* were prepared by Edmond Bunnie (1580) and William Lawne (1585, 1586, 1587), while aphorisms lifted from the text were published in Latin in 1595 and in English in 1596, offering the general reader access to an expensive and technically demanding volume that, its publishers claimed, enjoyed unique 'acceptation and general approbation'.[4] An enterprising London publisher marketed a Spanish translation of the *Institutes* in 1597, with uncertain results. Other editions of the text were likely aimed at different kinds of reader: London printers published Latin editions of the *Institutes* in 1576, 1579, 1583 and 1584, with another appearing from the Oxford University printer in 1655. But the appearance of this Oxford edition was late and rare, suggesting that a great deal of demand for the *Institutes* was being met by its circulation in second-hand copies, and that the appetites of English-language readers had changed from the preoccupations of the late sixteenth century. Throughout the period, Calvin's works continued to circulate on the second-hand market, through lending libraries, and were likely imported into Scotland and Ireland, even as English publishers were selling fewer editions of his work. In the mid-sixteenth century, Calvin's works had appeared suddenly in the marketplace of English print, and their disappearance from publishers' lists at the beginning of the seventeenth century was just as rapid. But this was a sign of the success, not the failure, of Calvin's ideas. And there was, ultimately, no significance in the fact that his works were never published in Scotland or Ireland, nor the *Institutes* in the new world, for it was in the very different contexts of the Scottish and Irish national churches, and the churches of the New England colonies, that Calvin's ideas were put on their firmest institutional foundation.

THE ECLIPSE OF CALVINISM

As the market for Calvin's published works declined, his ideas were widely and variously disseminated in the expanding print culture of early modern England, as well as in the much smaller print cultures of Scotland and Ireland, even as they were adapted to the distinct circumstances of each of these nations and developed to create the distinctive cultures of transnational and trans-Atlantic Puritanism. This process of local adoption threw up some ironies: the Scots Confession (1560), which provided the doctrinal

---

[4] 'To the reader', *Aphorismes of Christian religion: or, a verie compendious abridgement of M. I. Calvins Institutions set forth in short sentences methodically by M. I. Piscator: and now Englished according to the authors third and last edition*, by H. Holland (1596), n.p.

standard for the Calvinist Reformation of the Church of Scotland for almost
one century, contained no reference to justification by faith, but generated
fewer complaints than did the 39 Articles of the Church of England (1563),
which provided a more balanced summary of Reformed doctrine while
attracting criticism from the emerging Puritan party, whose key commitments were reflected in the Irish Articles (1615), the double-predestinarian,
apocalyptically anti-Catholic and consequently short-lived doctrinal platform of the Church of Ireland. Nevertheless, by the end of the sixteenth
century, and despite these local peculiarities, Calvinist ideas were supporting
the doctrinal consensus of the three established churches, despite their
having different systems of church government, and motivating the concerns of some of their critics, even as James VI/I, the Scottish king who had
recently also acceded to the English crown, dispatched a delegation to the
Synod of Dort with the purpose of finding a middle way in the dispute
within the Dutch church that threatened to undermine the distinctive claims
of the Calvinist Reformation across Europe. James could represent his
Calvinism as a system of political and religious moderation because this
theology, represented in the confessions of faith of his three established
churches, was also taught in catechisms, defended in university disputations,
preached in sermons and elaborated upon by philosophical and creative
writers from Francis Bacon to William Shakespeare to John Donne. Within
this consensus, Calvin was not regarded as the fountainhead of true theology, nor as being uniquely or distinctively associated with the system of
doctrine that has come to bear his name. His name, where it was cited at all,
was most often listed as part of a sequence of Reformed theologians, and his
ideas were celebrated not because they were his but because they were
thought to be biblical. Consequently, Calvin's ideas could be sustained,
adapted, challenged or transfigured even as his contribution to the shaping
of Reformed theology went unacknowledged.

    The eclipse of Calvin within Calvinism occurred as this theological system
took on local colour. Whatever their differences, the Protestant theological
cultures of England, Scotland and Ireland rallied around a number of ideas
by which they were distinguished from the Continental Reformed churches.
The British and Irish churches took advantage of the fact that trans-national
Calvinism lacked a central confessional text – unlike the Lutheran churches,
which had rallied around the Augsburg Confession (1530) – to develop an
emphasis upon the Sabbath that was distinctive within international Protestantism, as well as a famously self-reflexive spirituality. This approach,
which was simultaneously legalistic and pietistic, was codified in the major
seventeenth-century confessions of faith. But these theological statements

were never as effective as their framers had hoped. Neither could they stifle theological creativity. The Westminster Confession was adapted by Congregationalists in 1658, and this redaction was in turn modified by Baptists in 1677. This confessional tradition appropriated some new ideas into the Reformed mainstream, including the covenant of redemption, an agreement between the members of the Trinity before creation to achieve the salvation of the elect, and the active imputation of the righteousness of Christ in justification. These ideas became commonplaces in high Calvinist circles by the end of the seventeenth century, but they were always contested by others who also claimed the identity of Reformed. Debates about justification in the 1670s crossed divisions between the established and dissenting churches in Britain and Ireland, and reached across the Atlantic. Participants on both sides of this debate believed that the gospel was at stake, and appealed for support to central texts in the Calvinist tradition.

But, for all the raising of stakes, the dispute was about the boundaries of Reformed theology, and about who had the right to set them. As competition between denominations diffused religious authority, individuals looked increasingly to their own resources to establish religious truth. The emergence of evangelicalism in the 1730s was both a cause and consequence of the erosion of Calvinism, and undermined the aspiration of individuals across British and Irish Protestant spectrum to see their churches finally settle upon a shared orthodoxy. As born-again Protestants came increasingly to emphasise subjective piety over objective statements of faith, they abandoned or modified the sources to which earlier generations within the same Calvinist tradition had made their appeal, so that Calvinism lost is doctrinal centre. Calvin's theology had provided British and Irish Protestants with so many strategies for spirituality, systems of government for the church and competing doctrines of church-state relations that hopes for the healing of divisions among early modern Christians were perpetually frustrated.

CONTESTED LEGACIES

After the Restoration (1660), Calvinism was eclipsed within the British and Irish churches. In terms of popular religion, Calvinism was most secure in New England, where it had permeated the new society that the early colonists had created. Scotland remained a puritan nation, with solid ecclesiastical institutions that would be settled on Presbyterian models after the Glorious Revolution (1689–1690). Calvinism was increasingly contested within the Church of England, and was more popular within dissent, even as a number of key dissenting communities moved into Arminianism and

Unitarianism. Among those who returned to Calvin during this period was Lucy Hutchinson, whose translation from the *Institutes* was part of her turn towards serious religion in the aftermath of her husband's death.[5] In southern and western Ireland, where the number of Protestants remained small, Calvinist theology was socially irrelevant, while in the north of the island, where Presbyterians retained strong links with Scotland, it was infused with unstable political overtones and presented a serious threat to stable government. In the late sixteenth and early seventeenth centuries, Calvin's ideas had infused religious, political and imaginative cultures. In the mid-seventeenth-century, they had driven a revolution and underwritten a government that, for the first time, effectively controlled the three Stuart nations. But, by the end of the seventeenth century, popular culture and religious politics had moved on, and Calvin's ideas were being regarded as useful for little more than religion. Even in the new world, the revivals of the 1730s were evidence not of the success of Calvinist thought, but of its failure, and of the impossibility of its being renewed. No system of thought had done more to shape the imagination and experience of individuals and institutions in early modern England, Scotland, Ireland and their colonies. But, by the end of the seventeenth century, as an intellectual system exercising any significant degree of structural and imaginative significance, the theology of John Calvin had had its day.

SUGGESTED FURTHER READINGS

Dawson, Jane. *John Knox*. New Haven, CT: Yale University Press, 2016.
Gribben, Crawford. *John Owen and English Puritanism: Experiences of Defeat*. Oxford: Oxford University Press, 2016.
Hart, D. G. *Calvinism: A History*. New Haven, CT: Yale University Press, 2013.
Tyacke, Nicholas. *Anti-Calvinists: The Rise of English Arminianism c. 1590–1640*. Oxford: Clarendon Press, 1990.
Wallace, Dewey D. *Shapers of English Calvinism, 1660–1714: Variety, Persistence, and Transformation*. Oxford: Oxford University Press, 2011.

---

[5] Elizabeth Clarke, David Norbrook and Jane Stevenson, eds., *The Works of Lucy Hutchinson* (Oxford: Oxford University Press, 2018), 2: 59–76.

Calvinism in the Early Modern Netherlands and the Dutch Atlantic World

Christine Kooi

Writing on the religious culture of the early modern Dutch Republic, the eminent historian Johan Huizinga once observed, "The foreigner who wishes to understand our history begins with the assumption that the Republic was indisputably a Calvinist state and a Calvinist land." To this Huizinga, a Groninger with Mennonite antecedents, wryly rejoined, "We Dutch know better."[1] Indeed, although in the popular imagination Calvinism and the Netherlands are virtually synonymous, the actual history of this relationship is, of course, far more complicated. In the Netherlandish context John Calvin, or rather the religious movement his ideas helped to inspire, had to compete with a wide variety of other equally zealous and committed groups intent on religious reform. Although Calvinism would "win" the Reformation in the Netherlands by becoming the only publicly sanctioned religion of the independent Dutch state, it would also have to coexist with a wide variety of religious movements and sects throughout its history. The Dutch Republic was not Calvinist, but Calvinist and pluralist.

The roots of this lay in the inchoate and eclectic reformation(s) that swept through the Low Countries during the sixteenth century. The call for church reform had already sounded long and loud in the homeland of Erasmus well before Luther. Luther's writings and ideas first showed up in the Habsburg Netherlands in 1518, and in the course of the 1520s enough evangelical activity cropped up in the region's teeming cities to alarm the Habsburg central government into creating inquisitorial institutions to combat heresy in the region. By the 1530s, some of these dissidents took a distinctly millenarian turn, culminating in the notorious episodes of Anabaptist

---

[1] J. Huizinga, *Nederland's beschaving in de 17e eeuw* (Groningen: Wolters-Noordhoff, 1984), 62.

rebellion in Münster and Amsterdam. This radicalization further exacerbated the Habsburg crackdown, and by mid-century hundreds of Netherlanders were being prosecuted for heresy.

In this chaotic milieu emerged the first signs of a Reformed movement of religious protest. Around mid-century, Reformed proselytizers appeared in the French-speaking south, in such towns as Tournai and Valenciennes. They had come up through the porous border with the kingdom of France, where a robust Reformed network had already formed, inspired by missionaries from Geneva. The international Reformed movement now extended its reach into the Netherlands. From the southern cities, Reformed preachers made their way northward into the bigger, richer towns of Flanders and Brabant, especially the great commercial metropolis of Antwerp. As a world emporium, Antwerp traded not just in goods but also ideas, and by the 1560s the city was home to a thriving Reformed community.[2] From Antwerp, evangelical missionaries proselytized in the rest of the region. Thus, although Calvinism would become associated with the northern Netherlands, it really got its start in the southern heartlands (roughly present-day Belgium). It was during this formative decade, the 1560s, that preacher Guido de Bres wrote up the movement's first normative statement of belief, the Belgic Confession.

All this dissident activity caused the Habsburg government, now headed by Philip II, the King of Spain, to redouble its judicial efforts to stamp out heresy. This in turn sparked further discontent among the town governments and nobles responsible for local government in the region. The heavy-handedness of the inquisitorial process, which arrested citizens, incarcerated them, and tried them outside normal local jurisdictions, coupled with unhappiness about other Habsburg centralizing policies that tried to collect power at local expense, prompted the emergence of a political opposition movement by 1565. Led by some of the nobility, this bloc successfully pressured the Brussels government to ease some of the repressive measures against religious dissenters.

The result was the "Wonderyear" of 1566. By that spring, evangelicals were organizing open-air meetings complete with sermons and psalm singing. Within a short time, some local magistracies were allowing Reformed communities to appropriate buildings to use openly as churches and gathering places. For the first time, at least in some localities, Netherlandish Reformed Christians were able to worship freely. For some extremists, however, this was not enough. Among the most radical Reformed there was a deep antipathy to Catholic worship, which to them was an

---

[2] Guido Marnef, *Antwerp in the Age of Reformation: Underground Protestantism in a Commercial Metropolis, 1550–1577* (Baltimore, MD: Johns Hopkins University Press, 1996), 61–87.

unacceptable form of idolatry. In August 1566, a mob of evangelicals, stirred up by passionate preaching, invaded a Catholic chapel in a village in western Flanders, destroying images, breaking windows, and generally decimating the church fabric. Word spread, and before long more churches were being attacked. Over the next two months this iconoclastic fury spread in a northeasterly direction, engulfing most of the major Netherlandish towns from Flanders to Groningen. In some cases local magistracies stood by helplessly, in others they hid church ornaments before they could be destroyed, and in still others they aided the iconoclasts in an effort to keep the mobs orderly. No matter how it played out, it was to contemporaries a deeply shocking event.

The iconoclastic fury also convinced Philip II that a still harder policy was needed against heresy. He installed a new military regime under the control of the Duke of Alba, who ruled the Low Countries with a heavy hand. Alba set up a special court, the Council of Troubles, which specifically targeted rebels and heretics. Thousands of people were rounded up and tried for heresy and treason. Many charged with Reformed heresy were executed, and still more fled into exile, principally to safe havens in England and the Holy Roman Empire.

Exile proved to be a formative experience for Netherlandish Calvinism. It was the most committed Calvinists, preachers and layfolk alike, who during their exile in places like London, Frankfurt, Emden, and Wesel, began to plot their return and, more importantly, imagine what their re-formed church would be like when they were once again home. In exile refugees found themselves free to organize their worship according to what they saw as biblical norms. A group of Reformed leaders met in the north German town of Emden in 1571 and there crafted a Reformed church order that they hoped to implement in the time of return. This order envisioned a hierarchical, conciliar polity, comprising local consistories, regional classes, and provincial and national synods. These bodies would enforce both doctrine and morals and would make sure that the Gospel was correctly preached.

Much to the surprise of many, the day of return came. The Reformed opposition's political allies, led by the armies of Prince William of Orange, took control of the provinces of Holland and Zeeland in the spring of 1572. In the wake of these armies came exiles, political and religious. Reformed militants successfully established nascent congregations in the towns of these occupied provinces, and they held their first provincial synod in Holland in the summer of 1572. Church organization based on the model proposed in Emden was soon established. By 1573 they had successfully lobbied for the suppression of Catholic worship in these regions. Despite the political leadership's attempts to broker some kind of religious peace among the confessions, the Calvinists effectively blocked public worship by any church but their own.

Thus, in the independent provinces of Holland and Zeeland, which eventually formed the core of what became by the late 1580s the United Netherlands or Dutch Republic, a new state created out of the Netherlandish wars, the Calvinists triumphed. Thanks to their support of the political revolt against Philip II, they secured for their confession the privileged status of "public church." That is, the Reformed church was only one with the right to worship publicly. It secured control over nearly all ecclesiastical buildings once belonging to the disestablished Catholic Church, its preachers were paid out of publicly administered funds, it provided the chaplains for the Republic's armed forces, and it provided the new state with its official religious identity.

A monopoly on the public worship of God did not, however, mean a monopoly on popular allegiance. Indeed, until about the middle of the seventeenth century, Calvinists made up a plurality rather than a majority of the young state's population. There were two principal reasons for this. Firstly, the urban oligarchs who controlled the Republic insisted on the principle of freedom of conscience as expressed in the 1579 Union of Utrecht, the closest thing the Republic had to a founding document. Consequently, the regents required no one to join the public church. Secondly, the Reformed church agreed with this stipulation, insisting that joining the communion of saints was a voluntary act. Church authorities set up high standards for membership – submission to ecclesiastical discipline and public profession of faith – requirements that many of the Republic's inhabitants balked at. These two factors conspired to keep the Reformed church, despite its privileged status, a minority among the inhabitants, with membership perhaps as little as 10 percent of the adult population at the end of the sixteenth century.

What about the rest? Although many Dutch eschewed membership in the public church, a substantial portion of them attended Reformed worship without partaking in the sacraments. These "sympathizers" (liefhebbers) probably made up a large part of the congregation on any given Sunday in any given church, but their numbers are virtually impossible to obtain. The very imprecise numbers that historians have been able to reconstruct suggest that up till the middle of the seventeenth century, members of the Reformed church membership made up anywhere from 15 to 30 percent of most civic congregations, at least in the province of Holland. In very rough terms, the provinces of Friesland, Groningen, Drenthe, and Zeeland were overwhelmingly Protestant (principally Reformed and Mennonite), while Holland, Utrecht, Gelderland, and Overijssel had more mixed populations, with Catholics making up close to half the population.[3] This religious variegation across provinces would remain fairly consistent throughout the Republic's history.

Aside from the *liefhebbers*, the rest of the Republic's confessional complexion included principally Catholics, Mennonites, Lutherans, Jews, and various smaller Christian sects. Their numbers are also hard to come by, but Joke Spaans's pathbreaking 1989 study of the city of Haarlem's religious culture in the period 1577–1620 is quite suggestive: it revealed a civic population in 1620 that was roughly 20 percent Reformed, 14 percent Mennonite, 12.5 percent Catholic, and 1 percent Lutheran. The rest of the city's population, more than half, does not appear to have formally aligned with any confession at all, though many of them were likely *liefhebbers*.[4] Dutch Calvinism was thus surrounded by multiconfessionalism.

During its first 50 years as the public church, the Reformed church did not pay much attention to the religious pluralism outside its walls and wrestled primarily with internal controversies. It was preoccupied with figuring out its own identity, for despite all the meticulous work done by Reformed worthies, both in exile and upon their return, there was still no complete consensus about the precise nature of the new church's autonomy, doctrine, and organization. Reformed Christianity in the early Dutch Republic was not a Calvinist monolith. Controversies erupted in several cities in Holland and Utrecht about the relationship between the public church and civic authorities, and a few preachers questioned church teachings about discipline. In the specific cases of the cities of Leiden and Utrecht, these conflicts became quite bitter. Urban magistrates, who expected to superintend the public church, bristled at its demands for independence and autonomy. A minority of dissident preachers, such as Caspar Coolhaes in Leiden and Herbert Duifhuis in Utrecht, advocated for less rigid, more supple understandings of church discipline, membership, and doctrine. These controversies roiled the Reformed church in the 1570s and 1580s and then resurfaced a generation later in the 1610s, when the public church faced its worst crisis: the Arminian controversy. Jacobus Arminius (1560–1609), a theologian at the University of Leiden, proposed a reinterpretation of the doctrine of

---

[3] Willem Frijhoff and Marijke Spies, *1650: Hard-Won Unity: Dutch Culture in a European Perspective* (Assen, The Netherlands: Van Gorcum, 2004), 352.

[4] Joke Spaans, *Haarlem na de Reformatie: Stedelijke cultuur en kerkelijk leven, 1577–1620* (The Hague: Hollandsche Historische Reeks, 1989), 104.

predestination that allowed for more human agency in the process of salvation; his colleague Franciscus Gomarus (1563–1641) vociferously opposed this opinion as heretical, insisting that God alone was the author of salvation. What started as an academic dispute soon inflamed the whole Reformed church in controversy in the 1610s. The vast majority of preachers and congregations affirmed Gomarus's position, which they held as closer to the ideas of Calvin and Béza. But a minority of preachers and congregations, principally in Holland, favored Arminius's interpretation.

The Arminian controversy within the Dutch Reformed church mirrored a larger political debate that gripped the whole Dutch Republic: how and whether to continue to prosecute the war against Habsburg Spain. Since 1609 a 12-year truce with Spain was in effect, and the Republic's political elites soon divided into prowar and propeace factions. The Arminian minority within the public church supported the peace party, comprising mostly Holland urban oligarchs who preferred commerce to conflict; the Holland regents effectively became the Arminians' political patrons. Meanwhile the Gomarist majority within the Reformed church, staunch sectarians who saw hated Catholic Spain, supported the war party. Eventually the war faction, led by the Stadholder Maurice of Nassau, staged a coup in 1618 that unseated the peace party in Holland. The Gomarists took the opportunity created by this political moment to call the National Synod of Dordrecht, a seven-month gathering of Reformed worthies from across the Republic (as well as a number of international observers). The Synod expelled the Arminians from the public church and, for the first time, established what its doctrinal orthodoxy was, particularly on the question of soteriology. From now on, the Gomarist position on salvation, insisting that there was no human role in the process, would be the official doctrine of the church, with no dissenters tolerated.

With its own internal disputes settled by 1619, the Reformed church began to pay more attention to the tolerated confessions, especially the Catholics. The Reformed directed a considerable amount of theological and rhetorical ire at the Catholic Church, seeing it very much as a sectarian enemy, the very church the Calvinists believed they had reformed. The Republic's toleration of Catholics, as uneven and inconsistent as it was, was to them a grave threat to the spiritual health of the commonwealth. The public church frequently lobbied local and provincial governments to do something about "popish impudence" through the 1600s, with little success. It also complained, to a lesser degree, about Mennonites, Arminians, Lutherans, and any number of sectaries who found safe harbor in the Republic. But, although local authorities made occasional attempts to constrain religious minorities, the "winners" of the Netherlandish Reformation had to live alongside its "losers."

This would also prove true as the Dutch Republic exported its culture to its colonial possessions in southern Africa and the Americas[5]. The Reformed church, in the person of ministers and visitors of the sick, traveled with the East and West India Companies as the Republic established colonies in the Americas and Africa among populations of highly mixed ethnicity and religion, and thus pluralism defined Dutch Calvinism's experience abroad as well as at home.

Between the 1620s and 1660s, Reformed congregations and consistories were set up in Dutch colonies in New Netherland, the West Indies, Brazil, and the Cape; all of them fell under the supervision of the classis of Amsterdam and the directors of the Companies, who jointly appointed ministers. They worshiped and exercised church discipline in the manner prescribed by the Synod of Dordrecht. The colonial church was entirely subordinated to the Companies, which wielded governmental as well as commercial authority in the colonies. The church was intended to serve the company personnel and settlers who worked in these regions and not so much, at least in the seventeenth century, as a missionary church to indigenous peoples. What proselytizing the colonial Reformed church did was primarily directed against rival Christian groups, such as Catholics in Brazil and Protestant dissenters in New Netherland. Serving the church in a colonial capacity was considered a hardship by most clergy, with its meager pay and congregations of rough-and-ready colonials. Indeed the size of congregations in the American and African possessions was exceedingly small. Congregations in the Cape Colony, for example, numbered anywhere from 50 to 100 members even by 1700.[6] In New Netherland, congregations appeared to have ranged from 100 to 500 members in the seventeenth century.[7] Culturally, the Dutch Reformed church exercised perhaps its greatest influence in the Cape Colony, where it would contribute substantially to a sense of group identity among European (white) settlers.

How much moral suasion the Dutch Reformed church was able to exercise in the early modern era, in the colonies or at home, is open for

[5] Yudha Thianto examines Dutch Calvinism in Asia in Chapter 46.

[6] G. J. Schutte, "De Gereformeerde kerk onder de Verenigde Oostindische Compagnie," in *Het Calvinistisch Nederland: Mythe en werkelijkheid* (Hilversum, The Netherlands: Verloren, 2000), 67.

[7] Jaap Jacobs, *New Netherland: A Dutch Colony in Seventeenth-Century America* (Leiden, The Netherlands: Brill, 2005), 292–295.

debate. The church could exercise discipline, but only on its own members. The church was officially sanctioned and publicly privileged, of course, but political authorities kept a sharp eye on it, and it had to coexist in a relatively free society with a host of non-Reformed Christianities. Dutch Calvinism, in its Netherlandish context, was characterized by a strong biblicism, a commitment to discipline in belief and behavior, a marked anti-Catholic bias, and a preference for ecclesiastical autonomy. These qualities did not make it a universal or inclusive church and, as Johan Huizinga noted more than a half-century ago, they did not make the Dutch Republic, including its colonial satellites, a Calvinist nation.

SUGGESTED FURTHER READINGS

Deursen. A. Th. van. *Bavianen en slijkgeuzen: Kerk en kerkvolk ten tijde van Maurits en Oldenbarnevelt.* Franeker: Van Wijnen, 1998.

Duke, Alastair. *Reformation and Revolt in the Low Countries.* London: Hambledon Press, 1990.

Gerstner, Jonathan N. "A Christian Monopoly: The Reformed Church and Colonial Society under Dutch Rule." In *Christianity in South Africa: A Political, Social and Cultural History*, ed. Richard Elphick and Rodney Davenport. Berkeley: University of California Press, 1997, 16–30.

Jacobs, Jaap. *New Netherland: A Dutch Colony in Seventeenth-Century America.* Leiden, The Netherlands: Brill, 2005, esp. ch. 5.

Kooi, Christine. *Liberty and Religion: Church and State in Leiden's Reformation, 1572–1620.* Leiden, The Netherlands: Brill, 2000.

Nijenhuis, Willem. "Variants within Dutch Calvinism in the Sixteenth Century." In *Ecclesia Reformata: Studies on the Reformation.* Leiden, The Netherlands: Brill, 1972, 2: 163–182.

Pettegree, Andrew. *Emden and the Dutch Revolt: Exile and the Development of Reformed Protestantism.* Oxford: Clarendon Press, 1992.

Schutte, G. J. *Het Calvinistisch Nederland: Mythe en werkelijkheid.* Hilversum, The Netherlands: Verloren, 2000.

Spohnholz, Jesse. "Confessional Coexistence in the Early Modern Low Countries." In *A Companion to Multiconfessionalism in the Early Modern World*, ed. Thomas Max Safley. Leiden, The Netherlands: Brill, 2011, 47–73.

Woltjer, J. J., and M. E. H. N. Mout. "Settlements: The Netherlands." In *Handbook of European History 1400–1600*, ed. Thomas A. Brady et al. Leiden, The Netherlands: Brill, 1995, 385–415.

46

❦

Calvin in Asia

Yudha Thianto

Calvin's theology and ecclesiastical practices reached the shores of Asia by way of the Dutch and their efforts to monopolize spice trading in the South and Southeast Asia regions starting from the late sixteenth through the seventeenth centuries. Following the Union of Utrecht of January 1579,[1] the two northern provinces of the Netherlands, Holland and Zeeland, acknowledged only one branch of Protestantism, namely Calvinism, as the accepted form of religion. While the other five provinces declared that people were free to choose their own form of religion, in practice, the Reformed church became the privileged church in the Dutch Republic. When the Dutch under the leadership of Cornelis de Houtman arrived in Banten (or Bantam) in the northwest corner of Java in 1596 to begin their exploration of monopoly of spice trading, they paved the way for Calvinism to be introduced to the majority of the Southeast Asian regions.

To prevent competitions amongst their own people, the Dutch formed the Dutch East India Company, or the *Vereenigde Oostindische Compagnie* (VOC) in 1602.[2] The company, the first one among its kind to ever be established, proved to be effective. Under the leadership of the *Heeren XVII*, or the "17 Gentlemen," the VOC received authority from the Dutch government to act as an independent entity that could print its own money, do trading with local princes and regents, take plunder of defeated enemy ships, and wage wars when necessary. The VOC was successful in planting its power in the East Indian archipelago. At first the company built its

---

[1] For text of the Union of Utrecht see Herbert H. Rowen, *The Low Countries in Early Modern Times: A Documentary History* (New York: Harper & Row, 1972), 69–74.

[2] G. L. Balk, F. Van Dijk, and D. J. Kortlang, eds., *The Archives of the Dutch East India Company (VOC) and the Local Institutions in Batavia (Jakarta)* (Leiden, The Netherlands: Brill, 2007).

headquarters on the island of Ambon, in the Moluccas islands where spices grew the best. After the Dutch defeated Jacatra (now Jakarta) on the northern coast of West Java in 1619, the Dutch renamed the city Batavia and moved the VOC headquarters there. Batavia would soon become the most important port and the center of VOC's operation. From the East Indian archipelago the VOC spread its trading power to Malabar on the southwest coast of India, Ceylon (now Sri Lanka), as well as Formosa (now Taiwan), and farther north to Deshima and Hirado in Japan.

Dutch ministers sailed to the East Indies together with the merchants and VOC workers. These ministers soon started Reformed worship services at the port cities where the VOC offices were built. The primary tasks of the ministers and the comforters of the sick (*ziekentroosters*) were to take care of the spiritual well-beings of the Netherlanders. However, very soon they also reached out to the indigenous people to bring them into the Calvinistic faith. The ministers conducted Reformed worship services in the fort cities in some parts of the East Indies.

The Portuguese had been present in the region long before the Dutch set their feet on the East Indies. In 1512, Antonio Abreu led a small fleet of Portuguese ships to navigate the Strait of Bangka, a narrow strip separating the island of Sumatra from the island of Bangka, through the Java Sea, to the Moluccas in their search of spices.[3] Prior to their arrival in the islands of the East Indies the Portuguese had traded with the people of Goa in South India and Malacca. As a result of the contacts between the Portuguese and the indigenous people of the region, Portuguese became widely used and would later became one of the *lingua franca* of the people, together with Malay, which had already been a widely used language in the region.

The Jesuit missionaries spread Roman Catholicism in Asia beginning from the middle of the sixteenth century. Francis Xavier was in Goa, India, for some time, before he embarked on his missionary journey in Southeast Asia with a final destination of Japan. He landed in the Moluccas in January 1546 and stayed there until May 1547. Particularly, he worked on the islands of Ambon, Ternate, and Halmahera.[4] Before Xavier arrived in the Moluccas many other Jesuit missionaries had come to the archipelago and baptized indigenous people into the Roman Catholic faith. Dissatisfied with the behavior of the Portuguese in the archipelago who did not display good examples of how to live as Christians to the new converts, Xavier strove to

---

[3] Ian Burnet, *East Indies* (Halmahera, New South Wales: Rosenberg, 2019), 34–35.
[4] Susan Schröter, ed., *Christianity in Indonesia: Perspectives on Power* (Berlin: Lit Verlag, 2010), 36.

educate the people. He provided the people with a catechetical instruction as well as a guide of how to live religiously, and gave instructions to the Jesuit missionaries regarding how to teach Catholic hymns to the indigenous people in their mother tongue.

The Dutch faced a challenging competition with the Jesuits in their effort to spread Calvinism in this part of Asia. The Jesuit missionaries had established some footholds in bringing Christianity to the region. Thus, in bringing Calvinism to the East Indies, the Dutch had to compete with Roman Catholicism. Carrying the theological beliefs of Calvin in the previous century, the Dutch were convinced that only their version of Christianity was the true religion and thus the only way to heaven. They believed that Roman Catholicism was marred by superstition and therefore not a true teaching of Christianity. The rivalries between the Dutch and the Iberians on matters pertaining to the monopoly of spice trading were soon followed by competition in establishing the Reformed church in the archipelago. The VOC's success in driving away the Iberians from the most parts of the East Indies paved the way for Calvinism to gain ground in the area. When the majority of the Portuguese were driven away from the archipelago, the indigenous people who embraced Roman Catholicism needed to receive spiritual care. The Dutch ministers and other church workers employed by the VOC, namely the visitors of the sick and the schoolmasters, enfolded these ex-Catholics into the Reformed church.

In the early seventeenth century, several Reformed ministers came from the Netherlands to the East Indies. Among the early ministers who came to the archipelago were Caspar Wiltens and Sebastian Danckaerts.[5] Danckaerts arrived in Java in 1616, was the minister in Bantam (or Banten) in 1616–1617, and then a preacher in Ambon between 1618 and 1622. He went back to the Netherlands in 1623, but then returned to Batavia and preached there from 1624 until his death in 1634. Wiltens preached on the islands of Batjan and Makian starting in 1612, and served on the islands in the Moluccas, including Ambon, until his death in 1619. Together the two ministers published a Dutch-Malay dictionary that was instrumental in building communication between the Dutch and the Malay-speaking people. Danckaerts translated the Heidelberg Catechism into Malay in 1623 and this translation

---

[5] For list of the Dutch ministers in the Moluccas and the rest of the East Indies, as well as records of churches and schools in the archipelago at time of the VOC, see Hendrik Niemeijer and Th. Van den End, *Bronnen betreffende Kerk and School in de gouvernementen Ambon, Ternate en Banda ten tijde van de Verenigde Oost-Indische Compagnie (VOC) 1605-1791*, 6 vols. (The Hague: Huygens ING, 2015).

strengthened the presence of Calvinism in Asia.[6] As the Heidelberg Catechism was fundamental in teaching the basics of Reformed Christianity in the Calvinistic regions in Europe, the catechism also became one significant instrument to teach the Christians in Asia the rudiments of Christian belief. A few other catechetical materials were also published in Malay by the VOC. Schoolteachers and visitors of the sick often took the work of itinerant catechism teachers who traveled from village to village, and even house to house to catechize young children.

The first Reformed church service was held in Batavia in 1620.[7] To govern the Reformed churches in the East Indies, the Dutch published the church order of Batavia, or the *Batavia Kerkenordening*, in 1624.[8] For the most part, this church order followed the church order of the Dutch Reformed church accepted by the Synod of Dordt in 1618–1619, with certain articles added to be applied to the churches in the East Indies. When the church order underwent revision in 1643, there were notable additions that reflected the church's efforts to be more contextually sensitive. The addition also included specific instructions to the churches beyond the East Indian archipelago, most notably the churches in Malabar, India.[9] The church order noted that for the Christians in the Malabar region, Portuguese was still commonly used, and therefore the scripture reading would be taken from the Bible in Portuguese. While many parts of the East Indies used Malay as their lingua franca, Portuguese remained in several regions. Several catechisms were published in Portuguese for the benefit of the Portuguese-speaking reformed believers. One notable catechism was a translation of Philip Van Marnix's catechism entitled *Compendioso Exame dos Principaes Puntos de Religiano Christiano*, translated by Abraham Rogerius and published in 1688.[10]

The Dutch Reformed church had a strict regulation in which only ordained ministers had the authority to preach their own sermons. Given

---

[6] Sebastian Danckaerts, *Catechismus attau Adjaran derri agamma Christaon. Bersalin derri bahassa Hollanda dalam bahassa Maleya derri pada Sebastian Danckaerts* (The Hague: n. p., 1623).

[7] Baron Van Hoevell, *Tijdschrift voor Nederlandsch Indië, Vol. 2* (Zaltbommel: Joh. Noman and Son, 1887), 2.

[8] "Kerkorde voor de kerken in Oost-Indië (1624)," in Hendrik Niemeijer and Th. Van den End (eds.), *Bronnen betrefende Kerk en School in de gouvernementen Ambon, Ternate end Banda ten tijde van de Verenigde Oost-Indische Compagnie (VOC), 1605-1791, Vol. 4,* (The Hague: Huygens ING, 2015), 98–110.

[9] "Kerkorde voor de gemeente te Batavia, 7 december 1643," in Niemeijer and Van den End, eds., *Bronnen betrefende Kerk en School, Vol. 4,* 124.

[10] Philip Van Marnix, *Compendioso Exame dos Principaes Puntos de Religiano Christiano* (Amsterdam, The Netherlands: Paulus Mattheyszon, 1688).

the lack of sufficient ordained ministers to serve in the churches scattered throughout the regions, the church mobilized schoolmasters and visitors of the sick to lead worship services, while prohibiting these people to preach their own sermons. They were only allowed to read sermons written and published by ordained ministers. The wealth of printed sermons by these ordained ministers revealed the way Calvin's theology gained its foothold in Asia. Sebastian Danckaerts, Caspar Wiltens, and later Franchois Caron had their collection of sermons published and circulated long after they died.[11] Caron was born in Japan and, after receiving his theological education from Utrecht and Leiden, he went to Batavia in 1660, and later preached in Ambon between 1661 and 1674. He returned to the Netherlands in 1679 and died there in 1706.[12]

In keeping with the pattern of teaching that Calvin and other Reformers established less than a century earlier, Caron's sermons centered on the elaboration and explication of the Ten Commandments, the Lord's Prayer, and the Apostles' Creed. Caron published 40 sermons, consisting of 12 sermons on the Apostles' Creed, 10 sermons on the Ten Commandments, 7 sermons on the Lord's Prayer, and 11 sermons for Easter, Pentecost, Christmas, and special days.[13] These sermons are demonstrations of the application of Calvin's theology in the context of the church in the East Indies.

Reformed churches in Asia had consistories in important parts of the regions under the jurisdiction of the VOC. Archives of consistory records from several parts of the regions bear witness to the similarity of practice between these Asian churches and that of Calvin's Geneva. There are consistory records found from the Dutch Reformed churches in Formosa (Taiwan), Ceylon (Sri Lanka), and Batavia. Given the fact that the churches in Asia faced issues that could be quite different from those of Reformed churches in Europe, these consistory records show much wider scope of problems that ministers in these Asian places had to deal with, compared with the consistory records of the church in Geneva. In addition to issues regarding morality and daily Christian conducts, the records of the Tayouan (Taiwan) consistory also reveal problems that had to do with the tasks of visitors of the sick, school-masters, and the day-to-day administration of the church.[14]

---

[11] Yudha Thianto, *The Way to Heaven: Catechisms and Sermons in the Establishment of the Dutch Reformed Church in the East Indies* (Eugene, OR: Wipf & Stock, 2014).

[12] Niemeijer and Van den End, eds., *Bronnen betrefende Kerk en School, Vol. 4,* 49.

[13] Franchois Caron, *Voorbeeldt des openbaren Godstdiensts* (Amsterdam, The Netherlands: Paulus Matthyszon, 1693).

[14] Kerckboeck van Formosa 1643–1649, in *Resoluties van de kerkenraad van Taiwan (Formosa), 1643 October 5–1649 Juni,* Hoge Regering 4451, Arsip Nasional Republik Indonesia, Jakarta.

The consistory records of the Wolvendaal Church, Colombo, Sri Lanka, bore close resemblance to those of the Genevan church in the time of Calvin.[15] Even two hundred years after Calvin's time, the Reformed ministers in Colombo still had to deal with issues pertaining to the way the Reformed church may or may not interact with their Roman Catholic neighbors, adultery and divorce, and domestic violence. In addition, the church in Colombo also wrestled with the issue of slavery, freed slaves, and the baptisms of children of slaves. In general, the ministers tended to allow baptisms of the children of slaves, provided the parents were already baptized in the Reformed church. Difficulty arose when the parents were not officially married. In such cases, the church decided to withhold baptisms of the children until the parents show good Christian conduct, which, among other recognizable manifestations, included being lawfully married.

Singing the metrical psalms was an important part of the worshiping communities in the Calvinist churches in Asia under the power of the VOC. The 1643 Church Order of Batavia carefully set the order of worship in churches, with the emphasis on the prayers, sermon, and the singing of the psalms.[16] The church order emphasized the need of the indigenous people to sing the psalms in their native tongues. In singing these psalms at churches, the churches were instructed to employ the so-called English way, namely by way of the use of a cantor who led the congregation to sing one line at a time. Taking a similar approach taken by the Genevan church, the church order emphasized that little children must be taught to sing the psalms as well. The church order provided specific instructions to schoolmasters to teach their students to sing at school, and also to the visitors of the sick to lead hospital patients in singing at least one psalm per day. Similar instruction was also given to the visitors of the sick who worked in the orphanages.

As early as 1629, the VOC published translations of some metrical psalms and hymns into Malay to be used at churches, schools, and orphanages. These psalms and ecclesiastical songs were published together with the earliest Malay translation of the Gospel of Mathew by Albertus Ruyl.[17] It is

---

[15] Klaus Koshorke, ed., Summaries of the Minutes of the Consistory of the Dutch Reformed Church in Colombo Held at the Wolvendaal Church, Colombo, 1735–1797 (May 16, 2008), www.aecg.evtheol.lmu.de/cms/fileadmin/DRC/DRC_Volume4A-2.pdf (accessed March 26, 2019).

[16] Church Order of Batavia 1643, articles 42, 86, and also the appendix of the church order articles 3–4.

[17] Albert Ruyl, Het Nieuwe Testament: dat is het Nieuwe Verbondt onses Heeren Jesu Christi: In Neder-duytsch ende Malays na der Grieckscher waerheyt Overgeset (Enckhuysen: Jacobsz Palensteyn, 1629).

clear through this publication that the Dutch wanted to bring the custom of Reformed worship style into the East Indies. In 1542, the Genevan church published its first psalter.[18] As early as 1541 Calvin insisted that the church in Geneva must know how to sing hymns – which, for Calvin were mostly the Psalms – as people's expression of prayer and praise to God. The 1541 Ecclesiastical Ordinances of the city of Geneva also specified that to help adults learn the Psalms, little children should be taught how to sing so that they could help their parents to learn the doctrines of the church through singing the Psalms.[19] It is very obvious that the Dutch Reformed church adopted the custom of the Reformed church in Geneva. As the Dutch came to the Indies, they also brought this custom and introduced psalm singing to the new Christians in the archipelago. In addition to the metrical Psalms, the Reformed church in Geneva under the direction of Calvin also versified the Lord's Prayer, the Apostles' Creed, and the Ten Commandments and included them as the so-called ecclesiastical songs. The church in Geneva also added the Song of Mary, the Song of Zechariah, and the Song of Simeon into the collection of the hymns or the so-called ecclesiastical songs. The Reformed church in the Netherlands adopted the practice of the Genevan church in its worship practice. The three pillars of the Christian faith, namely the Apostles' Creed, the Ten Commandments, and the Lord's Prayer became the standard teaching for the church. As it was evident through the circulated sermons of the Dutch ministers in the East Indies, these three pillars were also deemed significant for the people in the Indies to understand and internalize. Therefore, sermons based on these three basic standards of Christianity became very fundamental in the establishment of the Reformed church in Asia. The Dutch's dedication to Calvinism became a very strong motivation to transplant its theology and ecclesial practices in Asia, including the tradition of singing the metrical Psalms and ecclesiastical songs. This effort, however, was wrapped in the larger context of colonialization. And thus, we can also see that the work to bring Reformed Protestantism to the people was also politically and commercially motivated.

The acceptance and growth of Calvinism in the East Indies is observable through the increase of the number of Dutch ministers sent to the archipelago, as well as the gradual rise of indigenous unordained church workers and

---

[18] For the earliest publication of the metrical psalms in the city of Geneva see [John Calvin], *La Forme des prieres et chantz ecclesiastiqes, auec la maniere d'administrer les Sacremens, & consacrer le Mariage: selon la coustume de l'Eglise Ancienne* (n.p., 1542).

[19] John Calvin, "Ecclesiastical Ordinances 1541," in Philip E. Hughes, *The Register of the Company of Pastors of Geneva in the Time of Calvin* (Grand Rapids, MI: Eerdmans, 1966), 45.

schoolteachers over time. In the first decade of the seventeenth century, the Reformed church in the Netherlands sent only two ordained ministers, but in the subsequent decades of the seventeenth century, the churches in the East Indies received a total of 163 ministers from the Netherlands. The number grew even larger in the eighteenth century, resulting in a total of 650 ministers sent to the archipelago over two centuries. Reformed churches grew the fastest in the fort cities where the VOC had its headquarters and on the islands where spices grew the best. Batavia saw a steady growth of the number of Reformed Protestants, requiring the port city to get an increase of ministers to be sent there, starting with 2 in in 1625, going to a total of 10 ministers at the beginning of the eighteenth century, and in 1750 alone Batavia received 12 ministers. In the Moluccas, including the Banda islands, there were 5 ordained ministers in 1625, moving up to 23 by 1700. By the middle of the eighteenth century the Dutch Reformed church started to allow indigenous people to be appointed unordained church workers under the VOC, mostly as schoolteachers and catechism teachers. In 1753 there were 58 school indigenous teachers and 82 catechism teachers throughout the archipelago.[20] These numbers provide us with a look at how Reformed Protestantism grew in the East Indies over time. The steady increase in the number of the ministers sent into various parts of the East Indies was proportional to the growth and acceptance of Calvinism in the VOC regions across Southeast Asia.

Calvinism in the form of Presbyterianism reached the Korean Peninsula toward the end of the nineteenth century. First encounters between the Koreans and Presbyterianism was traceable to the conversion of Seo Sang-Ryun (1848–1926) who met Scottish Presbyterian missionaries John Ross and John McIntyre spreading the gospel in Northeast China. Accepting Christianity around 1880, Seo soon established the first Presbyterian church in Solnae, within the Korean territory.[21] In 1885, Horace Underwood, a Protestant missionary from a Dutch Reformed background, came to Korea. He started to translate the New Testament into Korean around the turn of the century. Another Presbyterian missionary, S. A. Moffett, started the Pyeong Yang Seminary in 1901. His son Samuel H. Moffett was educated at Princeton Seminary and inspired a stream of Korean Christian leaders to

---

[20] F. A. Van Lieburg, "Het personeel van de Indische kerk: een kwantitatieve benadering," in G. J. Schutte (ed.), *Het Indisch Sion: De Gereformeerde kerk onder de Verenigde Oost-Indische Compagnie* (Hilversum, The Netherlands: Verloren, 2002), 83–84.

[21] In-Sub Ahn, "John Calvin's Reception in North-East Asia," *Chongshin Theological Journal* 16:1 (2011): 159.

receive theological education at his alma mater. One of the earliest Koreans to be educated at Princeton was Park Hyong Nong. Among Korean Christians, Park's name is almost identical with conservative Calvinism. At the end of World War II, the division of Korea into the Republic of Korea in the South and the Democratic People's Republic of Korea in the North affected the growth of Calvinism in the peninsula. In South Korea however, Presbyterianism remains the dominant branch of Christianity.

SUGGESTED FURTHER READINGS

Balk, G. L., F. Van Dijk, and D. J. Kortlang, eds. *The Archives of the Dutch East India Company (VOC) and the Local Institutions in Batavia (Jakarta).* (Leiden: Brill, 2007).

Burnet, Ian. *East Indies.* New South Wales: Rosenberg, 2019.

Schutte, G. J. ed. *Het Indisch Sion: De Gereformeerde kerk onder de Verenigde Oost-Indische Compagnie.* Hilversum: Verloren, 2002.

Thianto, Yudha. *The Way to Heaven: Catechisms and Sermons in the Establishment of the Dutch Reformed Church in the East Indies.* Eugene, OR: Wipf & Stock, 2014.

47

Calvin's Theological Legacy from the Seventeenth through the Nineteenth Centuries

Keith D. Stanglin

Calvin's legacy from the seventeenth through the nineteenth centuries is not monolithic. His is a multifarious legacy, perhaps fitting for a towering figure whose life and writings exhibit such a breadth of interest and talent. The complexity also reflects the fact that, beginning with his contemporaries and continuing through the subsequent centuries, supporters and opponents alike have had their way with Calvin, and they have done so in a variety of times and places. This brief essay can only scratch the surface and address some of the highlights of Calvin's reception during these three centuries, with a few opinions cited along the way.

The reception of Calvin is bound up with the fact that his name became nearly interchangeable with the Reformed tradition. In other words, the reception of Calvin is inextricably linked to the reception of so-called Calvinism. Although Calvin was a central figure in the sixteenth-century Reformed movement, he was not the sole figure. He was one among many Reformed theologians who, before the last third of the sixteenth century, were as influential – and, in some cases, more dominant – including Ulrich Zwingli, Johannes Oecolampadius, Martin Bucer, Wolfgang Musculus, Heinrich Bullinger, and Peter Martyr Vermigli. When and how did Calvin's name begin to stand for non-Lutheran Reformed theology? In other words, why did the Reformed tradition become synonymous with Calvin and not with any of these other figures?

In short, though there were many factors, it was the quantity, quality, and accessibility of Calvin's writings that secured his immediate legacy. At the top of the list is the *Institutes*, which enjoyed ever-increasing fame. Through the centuries, the *Institutes* went from being one prominent work of Reformed theology to first among equals to simply preeminent, evident especially in its many translations, reprintings, and citations.[1] Next to the *Institutes*, Calvin's commentaries, covering nearly every book of the Bible, were just as influential and important in securing his place above other Reformed theologians.[2] As it was during his lifetime, so it remained: Calvin always had his detractors and defenders, and his works gave both sides plenty of grist for the mill.

It should go without saying that the term *Calvinist* began as a neologism invented by Calvin's opponents. Perhaps the earliest use of this term was during the Eucharistic controversy between Calvin and the Lutherans. Throughout his 1560 treatise on the Lord's Supper, the Lutheran Tilemann Heshusen refers to the Zwinglians (*Zwinglianer*), Calvinists (*Calvinisten*), Papists (*Papisten*), and Lutherans (*Lutherischen Christen*), reflecting the confessionalization that was taking place.[3] Heshusen knew of Oecolampadius, Heinrich Bullinger, Vermigli, Joannes a Lasco, and other Reformed theologians,[4] but he only had categories named for Zwingli and Calvin. Thus, the first prevalent use of "Calvinist" is in the context of the debate about Christ's Eucharistic presence and is distinguished from Zwinglian. In his written response to Heshusen, Calvin repeats "Calvinists" four times without specifically denouncing it.[5] The context makes clear, though, that he is simply repeating Heshusen's expression and does not intend to endorse the term.

It was through controversies within the broad Reformed camp that Calvin and Calvinist came to stand principally not for Eucharistic teaching but for the doctrine of absolute predestination. Cambridge was a case in point. In 1595, William Barrett preached a sermon in opposition to unconditional

[1] See Bruce Gordon, *John Calvin's* Institutes of the Christian Religion: *A Biography*. Lives of Great Religious Books (Princeton, NJ: Princeton University Press, 2016), 60–67. Gordon's book is a very good survey of the subsequent, varied legacy of Calvin and his most famous book from the sixteenth century to the present day.

[2] Richard A. Muller, "Demoting Calvin: The Issue of Calvin and the Reformed Tradition," in Amy Nelson Burnett (ed.), *John Calvin, Myth and Reality: Images and Impact of Geneva's Reformer* (Eugene, OR: Cascade Books, 2011), 8–9, 11–13.

[3] Tilemann Heshusen, *Bekandtnuß vom heyligen Nachtmal des Herrn Jesu Christi* (Nuremberg: Johann vom Berg and Ulrich Newber, 1560), A7r–A8v, et passim.

[4] Ibid., B7r.

[5] John Calvin, *Clear Explanation of Sound Doctrine concerning the True Partaking of the Flesh and Blood of Christ in the Holy Supper, in order to Dissipate the Mists of Tileman Heshusius*, in *Tracts Containing Treatises on the Sacraments, Catechism of the Church of Geneva, Forms of Prayer, and Confessions of Faith*, Vol. 2, Henry Beveridge (trans.) (Edinburgh: Calvin Translation Society, 1849), 502, 510, 526, and 563. Cf. Richard A. Muller, *Calvin and the Reformed Tradition: On the Work of Christ and the Order of Salvation* (Grand Rapids, MI: Baker Academic, 2012), 54 n. 5.

predestination. He cited such Reformed theologians as Vermigli, Theodore Beza, Girolamo Zanchi, and Franciscus Junius, "calling them by the odious names of Calvinists and other slanderous words, branding them with the harshest mark of reproach."[6] Like Heshusen, Barret is satisfied to lump other respected figures under the category of Calvinist. The difference is that being a Calvinist is not now about Eucharistic presence but about a specific type of predestinarianism. Later, in 1598, William Perkins of Cambridge noted that his doctrine of predestination is pejoratively called "the Calvinists doctrine."[7]

Although absolute predestination is properly Augustinian and, among sixteenth-century Protestants, was already advocated by Luther, Zwingli, and others, the association of absolute predestination with Calvin was reinforced during the Arminian debates within the Dutch Reformed Church. During the late 1590s, in his written correspondence with Junius, Jacob Arminius distinguished three opinions on predestination that can be found in Reformed churches. The first opinion he attributes to Calvin and Beza, the second to Thomas Aquinas, and the third to Augustine. Junius acknowledges that many other opinions could be gathered, but he does not dispute the categories, and he agrees that these are the opinions "of easily the chief men (*virorum facile principum*)."[8]

With Arminius's Dutch Reformed sympathizers, known as the Remonstrants, Calvin's position as the primary representative of absolute predestination and of everything contra-Remonstrant strengthened, particularly in the intense controversies leading up to and following the Synod of Dordt (1618–1619), when polemic was heightened on both sides. Reinier Telle and his kinsman, the Remonstrant minister Henricus Slatius, are typical examples. Telle translated Sebastian Castellio's *Contra libellum Calvini* into Dutch in 1613. Among Slatius's Dutch pamphlets were *The Tyrannies, Abuses*

---

[6] William Barrett, "Recantatio Mri. Barret," in William Prynne, *Anti-Arminianisme: Or the Church of Englands Old Antithesis to New Arminianisme* ([London:] Imprinted [by Elizabeth Allde for Michael Sparke],1630), 58–59, 68–69; John Strype, *The Life and Acts of John Whitgift, D.D.*, 3 vols. (1718; reprint, Oxford: Clarendon Press, 1822), 3: 318–319; Thomas Fuller, *The History of the University of Cambridge since the Conquest*, appended to *The Church-History of Britain, from the Birth of Jesus Christ, until the Year M.DC.XLVIII* (London: for John Williams, 1655), 151.

[7] William Perkins, *A Treatise of the Manner and Order of Predestination*, in *The Workes of . . . Mr. William Perkins*, Vol. 2 (London: John Legatt, 1631), 605.

[8] Jacob Arminius and Franciscus Junius, *Jacobi Arminii amica cum Francisco Junio de praedestinatione per litteras habita collatio*, in *Opera theologica* (Leiden, The Netherlands: Govert Basson, 1629), 459–461; *The Works of James Arminius*, 3 vols., James Nichols and William Nichols (trans.), London edition (1825–1875; reprint, Grand Rapids, MI: Baker, 1986), 3: 18–20.

and Lies of John Calvin (1616) and John Calvin: Cruel, Bitter, Deceitful (1619).[9] In general, the pamphlet material coming from the Remonstrant perspective disparaged the "Calvinists," which had become a term synonymous with Contra-Remonstrants.[10] Calvinists were lampooned for worshiping the "new God of Geneva" and falling at the feet of the "Calf," a clear reference to Calvin.[11] Johannes Uytenbogaert contended that the Contra-Remonstrants have tried to take the name Reformed when, in reality, they are rightly Calvinists and sectarians.[12] In later Remonstrant theology and historiography, "Calvinian" and "Calvinist" became standard ciphers for the Contra-Remonstrant theology of Dordt.[13]

The elevation of Calvin to Contra-Remonstrant sainthood is reflected memorably in the Remonstrant political broadsheet from 1618 popularly known as Op de Waeg-schael (On the Balance), which depicts, on one scale pan, Arminius's works and, on the other, two books – Calvin's Institutes and a book labeled simply "Beza." In the picture, those books outweigh Arminius's works only because Prince Maurits lays his sword alongside the Institutes.[14] Two points are relevant here. First, the Contra-Remonstrant side, influenced as it was by a number of Reformed theologians besides Calvin, is represented simply by Calvin's Institutes in the foreground, with Beza, visually and metaphorically, slipping into the background. Second, the print implicitly links Calvin with coercion by the sword, a reputation that

---

[9] Freya Sierhuis, The Literature of the Arminian Controversy: Religion, Politics, and the Stage in the Dutch Republic (Oxford: Oxford University Press, 2015), 87–88.

[10] E.g., see [Reinier Telle,] Retortie ofte Weder-steeck, Ghegheven met de smadelijcke Sift by eenighe bittere Calvinisten, ende Calumniateurs in Figuren af-ghebeeldet... (1619); [Henricus Slatius,] Amsterdamsche Nouvellos, dat is/ Nieuwe Tydinghen/ Van 'tghene datter onlancx is ghepasseert in Bohemen/ Hongarien/... (1620).

[11] Sierhuis, Literature of the Arminian Controversy, 148–149, 164–165.

[12] [Johannes Uytenbogaert,] Redenen, Waerom men in goede Conscientie metten Nederlandtschen Contra-Remonstranten/ die haer den name van Ghereformeerde toe-eyghenen... (Freiburg, [1619]).

[13] E.g., see Simon Episcopius, Apologia pro confessione sive declaratione sententiae eorum, qui in Foederato Belgio vocantur Remonstrantes, super praecipuis articulis religionis Christianae (1630), 45v–46r; Geeraert Brandt, The History of the Reformation and Other Ecclesiastical Transactions in and about the Low-Countries, 4 vols. (London: T. Wood for Timothy Childe, 1720–1723). See especially throughout volume 4.

[14] See W. P. C. Knuttel, Catalogus van de pamfletten-verzameling berustende in de Koninklijke Bibliotheek, no. 2770 (The Hague: Algemeene Landsdrukkerij, 1889), I/1: 532. For background and further details on this broadsheet, see Jeremy Dupertuis Bangs, "Beyond Luther, beyond Calvin, beyond Arminius: The Pilgrims and the Remonstrants in Leiden, 1609–1620," in Keith D. Stanglin, Mark G. Bilby, and Mark H. Mann (eds.), Reconsidering Arminius: Beyond the Reformed and Wesleyan Divide (Nashville, TN: Abingdon/Kingwood Books, 2014), 61–64; Sierhuis, Literature of the Arminian Controversy, 151–152.

goes back to the Michael Servetus affair and would haunt Calvin's legacy through the centuries.

In addition to the Lutheran and Reformed branches, Roman Catholics also came to identify Calvin with unconditional predestination and related doctrines. This link was particularly clear in the *de auxiliis* controversy between the Dominican Bañezians and the Jesuits, during which there was no shortage of name calling. Some Jesuit texts attributed the Dominican opinion to that of Calvin and at the same time denied that the Jesuits teach (semi-)Pelagianism. In 1607, the papal decision to suspend judgment was made: "Deservedly [the pope] frees the Bañezians from the charge of Calvinism and the Jesuits from Pelagianism. The debate is not over dogma, but over the explanation of dogma; neither party is to be condemned."[15] The exclusive association of Calvin with these controversial doctrines is further evident in a Dutch Catholic broadsheet from 1611. Calvin and the "Calvinist sect" are charged, among other things, with making God the author of sin, denying human free will, and claiming that human good works are nothing more than sin. It provides a typology and description of four Calvinist divisions and observes that the disunity among the Calvinists is a sign of a false church.[16]

In sum, already by the early seventeenth century, "Calvinist" became a slur employed by Lutherans, Roman Catholics, and even among some Reformed to describe their opponents. It was used first by the Lutherans to specify Calvin's doctrine of Christ's Eucharistic presence. More frequently, however, Calvin and Calvinist came to stand for the theological perspectives related to unconditional predestination. Although these doctrines had not been the exclusive property of Calvin, and they came to characterize the Reformed tradition at large, nevertheless they became nearly synonymous with the legacy of Calvin, thanks almost entirely to Calvin's posthumous opponents.

As Calvin increasingly was seen by opponents as the chief figure of Reformed theology, some Reformed theologians devoted increasing energy to defending Calvin. For instance, the Anglican John Yates, in 1616, defended Calvin against Arminius and Robert Cardinal Bellarmine.[17] Moyse Amyraut was perhaps the most prominent mid-seventeenth-century theologian who

---

[15] Geerardus Schneemann, ed., *Controversiarum de divinae gratiae liberique arbitrii Concordia initia et progressus* (Freiburg: Herder, 1881), 292. Cf. ibid., 290–291, 295–296.

[16] [Richard Verstegen,] *Oorspronck ende teghenwoordighen staet van de Calvinische secte, alsoo die nu verscheyden is in vier principale deelen* (Antwerp: Robert Bruneau, 1611); Knuttel, *Catalogus van de pamfletten*, no. 1925, I/1: 372.

[17] Gordon, *Calvin's* Institutes, 61–62.

fancied himself a follower of Calvin, though, in his attempt to enlist Calvin for his own hypothetical universalism, his contemporaries generally thought that he misrepresented Calvin.[18] By the latter part of the seventeenth century, Reformed figures slowly began to accept the label of Calvinist no longer as an insult but as a proper designation, yet with varying degrees of comfort. Dewey Wallace affirms that John Edwards, for example, was "self-consciously Calvinist, repeatedly and proudly using the label as a designation for his viewpoint," and he also showed interest in Calvin.[19] Stephen Hampton, however, is less confident about the eagerness of Edwards and of other seventeenth-century English Reformed theologians to identify themselves as Calvinist, seeing rather more reluctance.[20] At any rate, by the eighteenth century, Reformed apologists were more gladly self-designating as Calvinists with little or no hesitation. This eager acceptance of the Calvin legacy is seen in the predestination controversies during the English evangelical revivals, when Augustus Toplady voiced his support for "doctrinal Calvinism."[21] The promotion of Calvin as the primary spokesman for the Reformed faith necessarily led to the demotion of other prominent Reformed thinkers in the tradition.

This so-called Calvinism dominated the North American colonies during the Great Awakening, but, during the Second Great Awakening in the new American republic, Calvinism, along with Calvin's reputation, experienced a steady decline. Yet the familiar, dual reception of Calvin – either adored or abhorred – continued into the nineteenth century. I would suggest that, under each of these two types of reception, there were both theological and sociopolitical reasons for supporting or denouncing Calvin and the range of thought that his name signified, resulting in four distinct (though occasionally overlapping) portraits.[22]

---

[18] Muller, *Calvin and the Reformed Tradition*, 55.

[19] Dewey D. Wallace, *Shapers of English Calvinism, 1660–1714: Variety, Persistence, and Transformation*. Oxford Studies in Historical Theology (Oxford and New York: Oxford University Press, 2011), 9–13, 205. Cf. Muller, *Calvin and the Reformed Tradition*, 55.

[20] Stephen Hampton, *Anti-Arminians: The Anglican Reformed Tradition from Charles II to George I*. Oxford Theological Monographs (Oxford: Oxford University Press, 2008), 5–7.

[21] Augustus Toplady, *Historic Proof of the Doctrinal Calvinism of the Church of England*, 2 vols. (London: for George Keith, 1774).

[22] Three of these legacies (all but my first category) are discussed in R. Bryan Bademan, "'The Republican Reformer': John Calvin and the American Calvinists, 1830–1910," in Johan de Niet, Herman Paul, and Bart Wallet (eds.), *Sober, Strict, and Scriptural: Collective Memories of John Calvin, 1800–2000*. Brill's Series in Church History 38 (Leiden, The Netherlands, and Boston: Brill, 2009), 267–291. For another overview of Calvin's legacy and the reasons behind it, see Karin Y. Maag, "Hero or Villain? Interpretations of John Calvin and His Legacy," *Calvin Theological Journal* 41:2 (2006): 222–237.

First, Calvin remained the poster child for absolute predestination, which
was seen as Calvinism's central dogma, and so Calvin's theological reputation continued to suffer at the hands of opponents of this doctrine. In a
nation forged by a revolution whose watchword was freedom, Calvin's
denial of human free choice in salvation did not play to most crowds.
Instead, Methodist, Restorationist, and other adaptations of Arminian or
anti-Calvinist soteriology dominated the Second Great Awakening.[23] Along
with its content, the method of Calvin's theology also came under scrutiny.
Some critics censured Calvin for his illogical appeal to mystery while others
cited him for his excessive theological speculation, neither of which was
welcome in a context that valued the intellectually simple and concrete over
the complex and abstract.[24] For many, then, Calvin was not to be trusted
theologically.

Second, in the mind of his critics Calvin was still the intolerant tyrant who
engaged in *ad hominem* attacks against his opponents and who, to his
everlasting shame, burned Servetus.[25] The treatment of Servetus was controversial in Calvin's own day, but it was particularly unhelpful in a post-
Enlightenment culture that took religious toleration for granted. Therefore,
not only was Calvin regarded as theologically unsound but he was also no
model of Christian virtue. These two features of Calvin were anticipated by
the eighteenth-century historian, J. L. von Mosheim, who derided both his
character and his "gloomy" doctrines.[26]

Third, for those who identified as Reformed or Calvinist, Calvin continued to be, as Bryan Bademan puts it, "a hero of Christian understanding
and piety."[27] By the nineteenth century, Calvin's position as the theological
touchstone for the Reformed tradition was secure. This fact does not imply
uniformity of interpretation. Among those who called themselves Calvinists

---

[23] E.g., see "A Sampling of Anticlerical and Anti-Calvinist Christian Verse," in Nathan
O. Hatch, *The Democratization of American Christianity* (New Haven, CT: Yale University
Press, 1989), 227–243.

[24] E.g., see the polemical comments of the Methodist J. A. Waterman in "Converting Power,"
Millennial Harbinger 1st series, 4 (1833): 491–492; and of the Restorationist Alexander
Campbell in "Letter to William Jones," *Millennial Harbinger* 1st series, 5 (1834): 586–587;
"Calvinism and Arminianism," *Millennial Harbinger* 3rd series, 3 (1846): 326.

[25] E.g., Waterman, "Converting Power," 491–492. For recent treatments of the Servetus affair,
see Bruce Gordon, *Calvin* (New Haven, CT: Yale University Press, 2009), 217–232; and Jeff
Fisher, "Housing a Heretic: Johannes Oecolampadius (1482–1531) and the 'Pre-History' of the
Servetus Affair," *Reformation and Renaissance Review* 20:1 (2018): 35–50.

[26] Johann Lorenz von Mosheim, *Institutes of Ecclesiastical History Ancient and Modern*. 3 vols.
in 1, James Murdock (trans.) (New York: Robert Carter & Brothers, [1871]), 3: 159–171,
191–195.

[27] Bademan, "Republican Reformer," 274.

and sought to reclaim the spirit and form of Calvin's theology, there could be deep disagreement over that common heritage and its application to the new American context.[28] The common feature, however, was in their primary appeal to Calvin for support.

Fourth, in the post-Enlightenment context, Calvin was increasingly admired for his contribution as a champion of human freedom and political republicanism. Given Calvin's reputation as the "Zeus of Lake Geneva,"[29] this aspect of Calvin's legacy seems to be the most counterintuitive. The strong version of this affirmation may be traced back to the writings of George Bancroft in the 1830s. It was Calvinist Presbyterians and Congregationalists, not Anglicans, who generally supported the American Revolution. As episcopal polity is analogous to political monarchy, both of which suppress the freedom of the people, so Presbyterian polity is analogous to a republic, both of which balance individual liberties with submission to proper authorities. As the genius behind the Presbyterian system, Calvin was seen as a pioneer of freedom – even, as it came to be expressed in the modern period, religious freedom.[30] To be sure, before Bancroft, it was common to attribute the freedoms enjoyed in the United States ultimately to the Protestant Reformers, including Calvin. In 1835, the American Restoration Movement leader Alexander Campbell, who was no particular fan of Calvin's theology, claimed, "We Americans owe our national privileges and our civil liberties to the protestant reformers."[31]

These portraits of Calvin are based in historical truth but are also shaped and appropriated according to the needs of those who appealed to him. Already by the early seventeenth century, Calvin was rarely, if ever, associated primarily with his significant contributions to covenant theology, Eucharistic presence, general revelation, the offices of Christ, or other teachings. He was pulled into the ongoing controversies on grace and predestination and made to take sides on civil and religious freedom. In the mid-nineteenth century, Anglophones would see the first major

---

[28] E.g., the debates among Calvinists Charles Hodge, John Nevin, and Edwards Amasa Park are discussed in Douglas A. Sweeney, "'Falling Away from the General Faith of the Reformation?' The Contest over Calvinism in Nineteenth-Century America," in Thomas J. Davis (ed.), *John Calvin's American Legacy* (Oxford: Oxford University Press, 2010), 111–146.

[29] As one of Calvin's former students called him, according to Gordon, *Calvin's* Institutes, 49.

[30] On this point, see Bademan, "Republican Reformer"; and D. G. Hart, "Implausible: Calvinism and American Politics," in Davis, ed., *John Calvin's American Legacy*, 65–88.

[31] Alexander Campbell, *Christianity Restored* (1835; reprint, Rosemead, CA: Old Paths Book Club, 1959), 3.

biographies and critical studies of Calvin,[32] which, along with the work of the Calvin Translation Society, would help to nuance the received picture of the Geneva Reformer. These various legacies, discernible in nineteenth-century North America, would set the stage for more widespread and even global use of Calvin in the twentieth century.

SUGGESTED FURTHER READINGS

Bademan, R. Bryan. "'The Republican Reformer': John Calvin and the American Calvinists, 1830–1910." In *Sober, Strict, and Scriptural: Collective Memories of John Calvin, 1800–2000*, ed. Johan de Niet, Herman Paul, and Bart Wallet. Brill's Series in Church History 38. Leiden, The Netherlands, and Boston: Brill, 2009, 267–291.

Davis, Thomas J., ed. *John Calvin's American Legacy*. Oxford: Oxford University Press, 2010.

Gordon, Bruce. *Calvin*. New Haven, CT: Yale University Press, 2009.

John Calvin's Institutes of the Christian Religion: A Biography. Lives of Great Religious Books. Princeton, NJ: Princeton University Press, 2016.

Maag, Karin Y. "Hero or Villain? Interpretations of John Calvin and His Legacy." *Calvin Theological Journal* 41:2 (2006): 222–237.

Muller, Richard A. "Demoting Calvin: The Issue of Calvin and the Reformed Tradition." In *John Calvin, Myth and Reality: Images and Impact of Geneva's Reformer*, ed. Amy Nelson Burnett. Eugene, OR: Cascade Books, 2011, 3–17.

Calvin and the Reformed Tradition: On the Work of Christ and the Order of Salvation. Grand Rapids, MI: Baker Academic, 2012.

Sierhuis, Freya. *The Literature of the Arminian Controversy: Religion, Politics, and the Stage in the Dutch Republic*. Oxford: Oxford University Press, 2015.

---

[32] Bademan, "Republican Reformer," 272–273.

48

The Reception of John Calvin in the Twentieth and Twenty-First Centuries

Bruce Gordon

Through the twentieth century and into the twenty-first John Calvin has remained the subject of considerable theological and cultural debate as scholars and church leaders have struggled to distil the essence of his thought and to recognize its possible applications for the modern world. From liberal Protestants to Karl Barth, Baptists to the new Calvinists, a broad spectrum of interpreters, adherents, and critics have been attracted to the writings of the French reformer. Further, with the massive expansion of churches in the Global South and majority world Calvin's works have found new audiences in varied ecclesiastical contexts, from Korea and China to Africa. Translations proliferate while virtually all the reformer's works are now readily available online.

It will hardly surprise that schools of Calvin interpretation in the West during the twentieth century have rarely proved easy to demarcate. Distinctions such as liberal or conservative are of little assistance for understanding the central role played by the reformer in the development of Reformed thought. Indeed, we should proceed with a number of caveats, beginning with the recognition that the Frenchman's work was never read in isolation; it was always located within a particular context. Next, as was ever the case, the invoking of the name John Calvin or of his theology is something quite separate from serious engagement with his writing. Like other great works of Christian theology, the *Institutes of the Christian Religion* remains a book far more often referenced than read. For many students and laypeople, their sole encounter with this literary masterpiece is through a decontextualized reading of Calvin's treatment of predestination in the third book. Consequently, it is not straightforward to track the reformer's influence in the labyrinthine world of twentieth-century theological debates, education, and church life. We should remain justly suspicious of all claims to have recovered the "authentic Calvin" from the Reformation and to have identified how he is to be applied to the contemporary world. Nevertheless, this chapter will attend briefly to some of the principle movers and readers to demonstrate the diversity of influential interpretations of the Genevan reformer.

Let us open with the transatlantic relationship of several of the most engaged readers of John Calvin from the late nineteenth and early twentieth centuries: the Dutchmen Abraham Kuyper (1837–1920), Herman Bavinck (1854–1921), and their friend and colleague who brought their ideas to America, Benjamin B, Warfield (1851–1921). Kuyper's story belongs largely to developments in the Dutch church during the nineteenth century, when as a pastor in the Dutch church he advocated for Calvin's *Institutes* as a model for theological and ecclesiastical reform. Kuyper, a journalist and later politician, saw in Calvin and his successors a faith that could embrace the diversity of the modern societies emerging in the nineteenth century. His views on Calvinist theology and its relationship to politics, science, and culture were set out in his Stone Lectures, delivered at Princeton University in 1898.

In many respects, Herman Bavinck, although lesser known, was the more formative figure for what became known as neo-Calvinism, a movement that continues to have a strong following. Like Kuyper, Bavinck traveled in the United States and cultivated numerous friendships among leading theologians. His many writings included an influential essay, "Calvin and Common Grace," that appeared in the *Princeton Theological Review* in 1909. Like his theological mentor Kuyper, Bavinck, too, had a high view of Calvin's *Institutes*, which he regarded as the Frenchman's "clear, deep and harmonious insight into Christian truth [such] as to render any subsequent modification unnecessary."[1]

The man who had invited Kuyper and Bavinck to America in 1901 and 1908 was the redoubtable Benjamin B. Warfield, who remained professor of theology at Princeton until 1921. Without doubt, Warfield was the most influential interpreter of Calvin in the United States during the opening decades of the twentieth century. He wrote extensively on Calvin, declaring him to be model for the church and a figure who had been much maligned by subsequent generations. Warfield's interpretation of Calvin had emerged out of the bitter division between Princeton and Mercersburg in the nineteenth century over the legacy of Reformation Reformed theology, and Warfield remained a distinctive and commanding voice. He saw Calvin as

---

[1] Benjamin B. Warfield, Émile Doumergue, and William Park Armstrong, *Four Studies by Émile Doumergue, August Lang, Herman Bavinck, and Benjamin B. Warfield* (New York: Fleming H. Revell, 1909), 117.

an original thinker and praised, in particular, the Frenchman's Christology as found in book two of the *Institutes*.

Above all, in Europe the nineteenth century had witnessed the creation of a John Calvin more palatable to liberal Protestantism. Averting their eyes from such doctrines as predestination, many Reformed writers chose to identify in the Genevan reformer a man of progress and vision, a prophet to the modern world. Perhaps the most enduring symbol of this reinterpretation was the Reformation monument inaugurated in Geneva in 1909, which emphasized Calvin's prominence among the company of sixteenth-century men. Liberals in particular had to come to terms with the major blot on Calvin's reputation, the execution of Michael Servetus in 1553. For supporters and critics alike, some form of atonement was necessary, including the erection of a memorial to Servetus in 1903.

The most influential French interpreter of Calvin in this period was the pastor Émile Doumergue (1844–1937), whose seven-volume *John Calvin: The Man and His Times* (1899–1927) remains essential reading a century later. Doumergue's Calvin was the quintessential Frenchman, the most original and prophetic Reformation figure, and a herald of modern progressive thought. The biography was a literary achievement of the highest order, a monumental work of erudition and style.

Following the devastation of World War I the landscape of Calvin studies in Europe and America changed radically. Among Reformed theologians, the titan to emerge was the Swiss Karl Barth (1886–1966), whose engagement with Calvin dated to his early years as a pastor. In what became a much quoted passage, Barth wrote in 1922, "Calvin is a waterfall, a primitive force, something demonic, coming down from the Himalayas, absolutely Chinese, wonderful, mythological. I lack the organs, the suction cups, to take in this phenomenon, not to mention presenting it rightly.... I could cheerfully sit down and spend the rest of my life with Calvin."[2] In many respects, Calvin never did leave Barth's side, and Barth offered seminars on the Frenchman right up to the end of his teaching. Also in 1922 he held his seminal lectures on Calvin. Yet the relationship between the sixteenth-century reformer and the giant of twentieth-century theology was fraught, marked by difficulties, disagreements, and controversial interpretations. Barth departed from Calvin on the reformer's doctrine of God and its ensuing teaching on predestination. Famously, or infamously, Barth offered a stunning rebuke to his erstwhile friend and colleague

---

[2] Eberhard Busch, *Karl Barth: His Life from Letters and Autobiographical Texts*, John Bowden (trans.) (London: SCM Press, 1976), 138.

Emile Brunner on the subject of natural theology, revealing the profoundly different ways that the two men read Calvin.

Another major figure of post–World War I Calvin scholarship was the Dutchman Hermann Bauke (1886–1928), who took on a question repeatedly posed in the nineteenth and early twentieth centuries – and still controversial today: What constitutes the central doctrine of Calvin's *Institutes*? Bauke's *Die Probleme der Theologie Calvins* appeared in 1922. Rejecting the idea that such a foundational doctrine was to be found, Bauke turned to the character of Calvin's theology as a distinctive expression of the reformer's thought. The characteristic theological form of Calvin consisted for Bauke in three closely related aspects: a formal-dialectial rationalism, a complex of opposites, and a formal biblicism.[3]

The influence of Barth was enormous, particularly among those who came to be known as the "neo-Orthodox," a term that Barth rejected. This controversial concept centered on the idea of restoring an older, more authentic Reformation tradition of theology against the tenets of Protestant liberalism. The movement took shape in the 1930s in Europe and across the Atlantic and played a crucial role in the revival of interest in Calvin studies. One of the most significant figures was Wilhelm Niesel (1903–1988), who owed a great deal to both Barth and other neo-Orthodox theologians. Niesel's great work was his *Theology of Calvin*, published in 1938 and translated into English in 1956. Like Bauke, Niesel looked to the relationship of form and content in Calvin's writing, finding the *Institutes* to be less a book of doctrinal statements, and more a text shaped by its central message of God's self-revelation in Christ.[4] Niesel's position was later challenged by Princeton Theological Seminary's Edward Dowey (1918–2003), who argued that the central doctrine of Calvin's work was humanity's knowledge of God as creator and redeemer, which is the core of the *Institutes*. Dowey's major work, published in 1952 and entitled *Knowledge of God in Calvin's Theology*, argued that Calvin's *Institutes* was fundamentally determined by the twofold knowledge of God that opens the first book. *Knowledge of God*, without doubt one of the most significant studies of Calvin in America in the postwar period, continues to be debated and was reprinted as recently as the 1990s.

Also of the post–World War I generation was Wilhelm Pauck (1901–1981), a German immigrant and later professor of theology at Chicago. Pauck likewise was a critic of liberalism for what he saw as its misunderstanding

---

[3] Cornelius P. Venema, *Accepted and Renewed in Christ: The "Twofold Graces of God" and the Interpretation of Calvin's Theology* (Göttingen: Vandenhoeck & Ruprecht, 2015), 16.
[4] Ibid., 19.

of Calvin, but he was by no means an uncritical reader of the reformer. Pauck saw Calvin not only as a major theological figure, but as a man of the church. As a result, the revival of interest in Calvin would not in his view be sufficient for the restoration of orthodox Reformed Christianity as espoused by Barth and Brunner.[5]

A particularly charged issue to emerge from neo-Calvinism was the question of whether a distinction between Calvin and his successors could be posited, the so-called "Calvin against the Calvinists" debate. The most significant critic of this discontinuity has been Richard Muller, who has argued that the claim has several serious flaws. He does not accept that Calvin defined the Reformed tradition, which embraced a much broader cast of characters and confessions. While recognizing that there was considerable development in that tradition away from Calvin, he has rejected as superficial the dichotomy between a pure Calvin tradition and the corruptions of his successors.

Other landmarks of Calvin scholarship appeared in America following World War II, including John McNeill's *The History and Character of Calvinism*, in which its author saw Calvin's message for the present age as the recovery of the sovereign and redeeming God. Among educators of Reformed clergy, the works of the neo-Orthodox theologians dominated in the period from the 1950s to the 1970s, with the contributions of Emil Brunner and Karl Barth enjoying particular attention. As Stephen Crocco has observed, "Barth's interpretation of Calvin – his effort to take Calvin where Calvin could not get himself, but where Barth thought the logic of his theology pointed – made a lasting impact on American theology."[6] The Barthian Calvin in America became more dependent on the Holy Spirit than deductive forms of theological argument.

The 1960s brought a major development in the study of Calvin in the English-speaking world with the new translation of the *Institutes of the Christian Religion* by Ford Lewis Battles, and edited by John T. McNeill. Battles worked not alone, but with a small group of scholars, including Princeton Theological Seminary's Dowey, who prepared much of the scholarly apparatus for books one and two. The edition, which continues to be the standard English translation, was provided with subheadings taken from the German edition of Otto Weber.

---

[5] Stephen D. Crocco, "Which Calvinism? John Calvin and the Development of Twentieth-Century American Theology," in Thomas J. Davis (ed.), *John Calvin's American Legacy* (Oxford: Oxford University Press, 2010), 179.

[6] Ibid., 183.

Alongside the English *Institutes*, one of the most influential works on Calvin's theology was also translated and printed by a major trade press in the United States. François Wendel's *Calvin: The Origin and Development of his Thought* appeared with Harper & Row in 1963. The book, which has remained a standard read for both students of Calvin and a broader audience, traced Calvin's life along with the evolution of his thought from the perspective of a liberal Protestant author. Wendel wrote of the *Institutes*, "[T]he 1559 edition stands out among its predecessors by its greater coherence. Never did the author succeed so well in mastering the enormous material that he had to organize."[7]

The 1960s and the rise of social histories of the Reformation saw Calvin increasingly portrayed both in Geneva and as a major player in the wider European Reformation. The leader in this field of scholarship was Robert Kingdon, whose students have continued his legacy of archival research, including the editing of the Genevan Consistory records. At the same time, one of the most influential works on Calvin, a book that combines theology and history, was Alexandér Ganoczy's *Young Calvin* (English translation 1966). Ganoczy's book was one of the first influential works on Calvin by a Catholic scholar.

Through the 1970s, 1980s, and 1990s scholarship on Calvin continued to flourish within the academy, although one searches in vain for consensus on the major theological questions such as his central theological arguments, the character of his doctrine of predestination, and whether he held to limited atonement. The field is too densely populated for an adequate account of the new lines of Calvin research that range across the theological spectrum, but certain names stand out for their pioneering work, including David Steinmetz, Brian Gerrish, Paul Helm, Richard Muller, Susan Schreiner, Olivier Millet, and Randall Zachman. The rise of feminist theology also brought new perspectives to Calvin research, beginning with the work of Jane Dempsey Douglass and her 1985 study *Woman, Freedom and Calvin*.

Particularly in the United States, Calvin's status as a reformer received a major boost in 2009 with the 500th anniversary of his birth. A plethora of conferences and commemorations were accompanied by an avalanche of new scholarship looking at all aspects of his life, work, and influence. The moment was propitious as Calvin was enjoying a revival amongst the wider public through the preaching and writing of such prominent figures as John Piper, Tim Keller, and Carl Trueman. The extraordinary success of the

---

[7] Cited in Bruce Gordon, *John Calvin's Institutes of the Christian Religion* (Princeton, NJ: Princeton University Press, 2016), 163.

novels of Marilynne Robinson, notably *Gilead*, has done a great deal to put Calvin and Calvinism at the center of literary and cultural discussions.

Away from Europe and North America, the reception of Calvin has found new life in the rapid growth of Reformed churches in Africa, Asia, and South America. While Presbyterianism had long been vibrant in Korea, following the work of American missionaries, and the Dutch Reformed Church was established in South Africa, new readerships and students also emerged in the late twentieth century in Indonesia, China, and Brazil. Translations of the *Institutes* into Chinese and Portuguese have appeared in recent years, bearing witness to the diverse circumstances in which the sixteenth-century Frenchman continues to be read and consulted, and also regarded as an authority.

One of the major stories of Calvinism in the twentieth century took place in South Africa, where the Dutch Reformed Church was long associated with apartheid. As John W. de Gruchy remarked in 2009 at the International Calvin Congress held in Geneva, "[B]y the 1960s, Calvinism was widely understood, whether on the part of black South Africans, white English-speaking liberal Protestants, or Catholics both Anglican and Roman, as the creed that legitimized Apartheid."[8] And he added, "For the vast majority in South Africa, Calvinism meant bad religion, and Calvin in his own right is little known except as someone who, it is assumed, taught a perverse racist understanding of Christianity."[9]

By the 1970s, leading black theologians were beginning to offer interpretations of Calvin's theology that rejected the unholy alliance with apartheid. Figures such as Dougles S. Bax, Beyers Naudé, and Lebakeng Ramotschabi Lekula were drawing on Calvin and other Reformed writers to offer penetrating critiques of the established theology of the Dutch Reformed Church. Much of the discussion concerned the use of the writings of Abraham Kuyper to defend the separation of blacks and whites.

The emergence of black theology in the United States through the work of James Cone and others had a tremendous impact on African writers. Amongst the most prominent was Allan Boesak, a Reformed pastor who had read Calvin and Barth closely during his studies in the Netherlands. Boesak turned Calvin against the supporters of apartheid. In a 1981 address to the Alliance of Black Reformed Christians, Boesak said, "For Reformed

---

[8] Ibid., 167.
[9] John de Gruchy, "Calvin(ism) and Apartheid in South Africa in the Twentieth Century: The Making and Unmaking of Racial Ideology," in Irena Backus and Philp Benedict (eds.), *Calvin and His Influence, 1509–2009* (Oxford: Oxford University Press, 2011), 310.

Christians, government is not 'naturally' an enemy. We believe with Calvin that governments are instituted by God for the just and legitimate administration of the world.... In terms of any modern concept of democracy, as well as in terms of Calvin's understanding of legitimacy, the South African government is neither just nor legitimate."[10]

In 2010 a new translation of Calvin's *Institutes* appeared in Mandarin, the latest development in the remarkable spread of the reformer's work in China during the post–World War II period. In the 1950s, the first Chinese translation of the *Institutes* appeared in Hong Kong, and by the 1990s Calvin's works were widely available to Christians in Taiwan, Singapore, and Hong Kong, while in mainland China writing on Calvin began to be published from the 1980s. The reception of the French reformer in China was mediated through, among other writers, Max Weber, with Calvin taken as a prophet of progress, modernization, and openness to the West.

With the rise of the Chinese house churches in the 1990s there was a newfound enthusiasm for John Calvin, whose work was seen as "forward looking, rational, intellectually serious and favourable to making money."[11] In a 2009 lecture in Basel, Chinese theologian Aiming Wang drew attention to how "Calvin arouses the attention of Chinese intellectuals and elites in the current period of transition to its modernization."[12] The research of Andrew Chow has shown that urban, intellectual, and increasingly affluent Chinese Christians are drawn to Calvin on account of his clear and emphatic teaching on the institutional church.[13]

Attention to the broader audiences for Calvin's work leads us to the growth of Reformed churches such as the Presbyterian Church of Brazil, which has more than a million members and the Protestant Church in Western Indonesia, which is only slightly smaller. More anecdotal in its implications is the decision by George Sabra, president of the Near East School of Theology in Beirut, to translate Calvin's *Institutes* into Arabic for the first time for both Christian and Muslim readers.

John Calvin remains a deeply controversial figure, regarded by many as the symbol for the worst of Christian intolerance. Yet, throughout the twentieth century and still now in the twenty-first century, his work

---

[10] Quoted in Gordon, *John Calvin's Institutes*, 177–178.

[11] Andrew Brown, "Chinese Calvinism Flourishes', *Guardian*, May 27, 2009.

[12] Aiming Wang, "The Importance of John Calvin for the Protestant Church in China," in C. Stückelberger and R. Bernhardt (eds.), *Calvin Global: How Faith Influences Societies* (Geneva: Globethics.net, 2009), 179–194.

[13] Andrew Chow, "Calvinist Public Theology in China Today," *International Journal of Public Theology* 8 (2014): 158–175.

continues to be read and be cited in theological and ecclesiastical debates. Consensus on his life and thought remains elusive, but without doubt he remains the most controversial reformer of the sixteenth century.

SUGGESTED FURTHER READINGS

Backus, Irena, and Philip Benedict, eds. *Calvin and His Influence, 1509–2009*. Oxford: Oxford University Press, 2011.

Barth, Karl. *The Theology of John Calvin*, trans. Geoffrey W. Bromiley. Grand Rapids, MI: Eerdmans, 1995.

Bratt, James D. *Abraham Kuyper: Modern Calvinist, Christian Democrat*. Grand Rapids, MI: Eerdmans, 2013.

Davis, Thomas J. *John Calvin's American Legacy*. Oxford: Oxford University Press, 2010.

Gordon, Bruce. *John Calvin's Institutes of the Christian Religion*. Princeton, NJ: Princeton University Press, 2016.

McNutt, Jennifer Powell. *Calvin Meets Voltaire: The Clergy of Geneva and the Age of Enlightenment 1685–1798*. Burlington, VT: Ashgate, 2013.

Conclusion

Calvin and Calvinism: A Variety of Portraits

R. Ward Holder

William Bouwsma, the celebrated intellectual historian, published his *John Calvin: A Sixteenth Century Portrait*, in 1987.[1] That probing analysis did not seek so much to write a complete biography of John Calvin as to understand him and the modern world that, in Bouwsma's estimation, had ignored Calvin.[2] As an intellectual historian, Bouwsma turned to the evidence from Calvin's own writings, and found him to be suspended between the labyrinth and the abyss.[3] Bouwsma believed that getting to the intellectual character of Calvin would provide a better portrait, and grant the modern world a view of a figure who had left an indelible mark on the mind of the modern Christian world. The depth and breadth of response within the small group of professional Calvin scholars to Bouwsma's book suggested that, at the very least, he had touched a nerve – and that nerve was not within Calvin, but within those who could broadly be called Calvinists.

This volume has now come to a close, and I wish to make a parallel claim, one that I would argue has been inspired by Bouwsma's thought. While Bouwsma saw a complex Calvin who moved back and forth between his struggles with being lost in the labyrinth and falling into the abyss, the present volume seeks to broaden that canvas, showing a variety of portraits that are responses to a variety of impulses. Calvin moved in a complex world that many saw as disintegrating. He lived through wars, bouts of plague, and religious struggles so violent that people believed that it was better to kill their religious opponents instead of tolerating them. He dwelt in an

---

[1] William Bouwsma, *John Calvin: A Sixteenth Century Portrait* (Oxford: Oxford University Press, 1987).
[2] Ibid., 1.
[3] Ibid., esp. Parts II and IV.

intellectual world that was attempting to recast some of its most closely held beliefs while living the religious lives governed by those beliefs – metaphorically rebuilding the boat in which they were sailing. He moved in a world of relationships – exchanging warm greetings with friends, trading barbs with colleagues, and throwing damnation at those he felt were dangerous. In other words, Calvin was constantly moving not merely between the Scylla and Charybdis of the labyrinth and the abyss but also through a rich, satisfying, and sometimes terrifying mix of impulses both social and intellectual.

As the final section of the volume made clear, Calvin was not the only one subject to contexts. Our own readings of Calvin come through our understanding of the mediated traditions in which we stand. Calvinism spread out of Geneva in the second half of the sixteenth century, probably much to the detriment of the reading of Calvin. But when we take seriously the contexts in which Calvin lived and thought, as well as our own, we place ourselves in the best position to understand him not as a caricature, but as the early modern man who lived in a rich and complex world, a world without which his thought is rendered almost meaningless. Should we truly wish to understand Calvin, we must grasp the many contexts that influenced him, as well as those that set our own contexts. This is true whether our interest is historical, theological, or intellectual. When we do that, Calvin becomes less the theologian, or the preacher, or the biblical exegete, and far more a complex man living in a complex time – a time that still affects our own.

Bibliography

PRIMARY SOURCES

Adam, Jean. *Calvin defait par soy-mesme et par les armes de S. Avgvstin qv'il avoit inivstement vsvrpées sur les matieres de la grace, de la liberté, & de la predestination.* Paris: Gaspar Meturas, 1650.

Archives d'Etat de Genève, Registres du Consistoire, vols. 1–21.

Arminius, Jacob, and Franciscus Junius. *Jacobi Arminii amica cum Francisco Junio de praedestinatione per litteras habita collatio.* In *Opera theologica.* Leiden, The Netherlands: Govert Basson, 1629. ET, *The Works of James Arminius.* 3 vols., trans. James Nichols and William Nichols. London edition, 1825–1875 (repr., Grand Rapids, MI: Baker, 1986).

Arnauld, Antoine. *Le renversement de la morale de Jesus-Christ par les erreurs des Calvinistes touchant la justification.* Paris: Guillaume Desprez, 1672.

Le Calvinisme convaincu de nouveau de dogmes impies. Cologne: Pierre Binsfelt, 1682.

Baius, Michael. *De meritis operum libri duo, eiusdem de prima hominis iustitia et virtutis impiorum libri duo. Eiusdem de sacramentis in genere contra Calvinum liber unus.* Louvain: Johann Bogard, 1565.

Barrett, William. "Recantatio Mri. Barret." In William Prynne, *Anti-Arminianisme: Or the Church of England's Old Antithesis to New Arminianisme.* [London:] Imprinted [by Elizabeth Allde for Michael Sparke], 1630.

Baudouin, François. *Responsio altera ad Ioan. Calvinum.* Paris: Guillaume Morel, 1562.

Bellarmine, Robert. De controversiis Christianae fidei, I.4. In *Opera omnia,* Vol. 3, ed. Justin Louis Pierre Fèvre. Naples: Josephus Giuliano, 1857.

Benoit, René. *Une brieve et succincte refutation de la coene de Iean Calvin.* Antwerp: Philippe Tronasius, 1566.

Beza, Th. *Een schoon tractaet des Godtgheleerden Theodori Bezae van de Straffe welcke de wereltlijcke overicheydt over de ketters behoort te oeffenen/*

teghen Martini Belli tsamenraepsel/ende der secte der nieuwe Academisten. Overgheset inde Nederduytsche sprake door de Dienaers des G. Woorts binnen Sneeck. Met een voorrede/vervatende mede int corte een verhael van tgene sick tusschen de Magistraet met de Dienaers des woorts der Stede voorschreven, ende de Wederdoopers aldaer heeft toeghedraghen. Franeker: Gillis van den Rade, 1601.

Beza, Theodore. *Responsio ad defensiones et reprehensiones Sebastiani Castellionis.* Geneva: Estienne, 1563.

Bèze, Théodore de. *De Haereticis a civili magistratu puniendis libellus, adversus Martini Belli farraginem et novorum Academicorum sectam.* Geneva: Robert Estienne, 1554.

Volumen Tractionum Theologicarum. 3 vols. Geneva: Jean Crespin, 1570–1582.

Histoire ecclésiastique des Églises Réformées au royaume de France. 3 vols., ed. G. Baum and E. Cunitz. Paris: Fischbacher, 1883–1889.

Correspondance de Théodore de Bèze. Travaux d'Humanisme et Renaissance. 43 vols., ed. Hippolyte Aubert et al. Geneva: Droz, 1960–2017.

Abraham Sacrifiant. Textes littéraires français 135, ed. Keith Cameron, Kathleen Hall, and Francis Higman. Geneva: Droz, 1967.

Du droit des magistrats. Les Classiques de la pensée politique, ed. Robert Kingdon. Geneva: Droz, 1970.

Les vrais portraits des hommes illustres. Geneva: Slatkine, 1986.

Biblia Latina cum Glossa Ordinaria, Facsimile Reprint of the Editio Princeps Adolph Rusch of Strassburg 1480/81, introduction by Karlfried Froehlich and Margaret T. Gibson. Brepols: Turnhout, 1992.

Blache, Antoine. *Refutation de l'heresie de Calvin, par la seule doctrine de Mrs de la R. P. R. pour affermir sans dispute les nouveaux convertis dans la foy de l'Eglise catholique. Avec des extraits de plusieurs lettres de Saint Augustin, où il paroist que la conduite du Roy, à l'égard des Calvinistes de France, est conforme à la doctrine de ce Pere.* Paris: Antoine Lambin, 1687.

Bolsec. *Vies de Jean Calvin et de Théodore de Bèze.* Geneva: Principaux libraires, 1835.

Brandt, Geeraert. *The History of the Reformation and Other Ecclesiastical Transactions in and about the Low-Countries.* 4 vols. London: T. Wood for Timothy Childe, 1720–1723.

Bullinger, H. *Von demm unverschampten fräfel, ergezlichem verwyrren, undd unwarhafftem leeren, der selbsgesandten Widertöufferen, vier gespräch Bücher, zů verwarnenn den einfalten* (1531).

[Buwo, B.] *Een frundtlicke thosamensprekinge van twe personen, van de Döpe der yungen unmundigen kynderen.* Emden: Gellius Ctematius, 1556.

Cajetan, Tommaso de Vio. *Commentarii illustres planeque insignes in quinque mosaicos libros.* Paris: Guilielmus de Boffozel, 1539.

Calvin, John. *Sermons sur le Deuteronomie* (CO27).

Letter 253, *Argentoratenses et Basilienses Genevensibus*; CO 11:106–113.

Consilium pro Lutheranis quod Pontifex Romanus nuper Caesari dedit, 1540; CO 5:487–508.

Brieve Instruction pour armer tous bons fideles contre les erreurs de la secte commune des anabaptistes. Genève: Jean Girard, 1544 (COR IV/2).

Appendix Libelli Adversus Interim Adultero-Germanum, in qua Refutat Ioannes Calvinus Censuram Quandam Typographi Ignoti, de parvulorum sanctificatione, et muliebri baptism, 1550; CO 7:675–686.

Clear Explanation of Sound Doctrine concerning the True Partaking of the Flesh and Blood of Christ in the Holy Supper, in order to Dissipate the Mists of Tileman Heshusius. In *Tracts Containing Treatises on the Sacraments, Catechism of the Church of Geneva, Forms of Prayer, and Confessions of Faith*, vol. 2, trans. Henry Beveridge. Edinburgh: Calvin Translation Society, 1849, 495–572.

Calvin's Tracts: Tracts Relating to the Reformation, Vol. 3, ed. Henry Beveridge. Edinburg: Calvin Translation Society, 1851.

Treatise on Relics, ed. Anthony Uyl. Edinburgh: Johnson and Hunter, 1854.

Ioannis Calvini Opera quae supersunt omnia, ed. Baum et al., 59 tomes. Brunswick, Germany: C. A. Schwetschke et Filium, 1863–1900.

Commentarius in Epistilorum Pauli ad Romanos, ed. T. H. L. Parker. Leiden, The Netherlands: Brill, 1981.

Treatises against the Anabaptists and against the Libertines, ed. and trans. Benjamin W. Farley. Grand Rapids, MI: Baker Books, 1982.

Sermons on 2 Samuel: Chapters 1–13, trans. Douglas F. Kelly. Edinburgh: Banner of Truth Trust, 1992.

Campbell, Alexander. "Letter to William Jones." *Millennial Harbinger* 1st series, 5 (1834): 584–590.

"Calvinism and Arminianism." *Millennial Harbinger* 3rd series, 3 (1846): 325–329.

Christianity Restored. Rosemead, CA: Old Paths Book Club, 1959 (reprint of 1835).

Caron, Franchois. *Voorbeeldt des openbaren Godstdiensts.* Amsterdam, The Netherlands: Paulus Matthyszon, 1693.

Castellio, Sebastian. *De haereticis an sint persequendi et omnino quomodo sit cum eis agendum, Luteri et Brentii, aliorumque multorum tum veterum tum recentiorum sententiae* (S. van der Woude, facsimile-uitgave). Genève: Droz, 1954.

De haereticis, an sint persequendi (On heretics: Whether they should be persecuted) (1554).

Contra libellum Calvini (Against Calvin's Book) (1612).

Annotationes Sebastiani Castellionis, in caput nonum ad Rom. Quibus materia Electionis et Praedestinationis amplius illustrator. Gouda, 1613.

On Heretics, trans. Roland Bainton. New York: Octagon Press, 1979.

Cochlaeus. *Johannis Calvini in Acta Synodi Tridentinae Censura et eiusdem brevis confutation. Circa duas praecipue calumnias.* Mainz: Franz Behem, 1548.

De Interim Brevis Responsio Ioan. Cochlaei, Ad Prolixvm Conuitiorum & Calumniarum librum Ioannis Caluini. Mainz: Franz Behem, 1549.

Colloque de Poissy 2011: au coeur de la laïcité, dialogue et tolérance, actes des 10 et 11 septembre 2011. Paris: Mare & Martin, 2012.

Consilium ... de Emendanda ecclesia. Rome: n.p., 1538. English translation in John Olin, ed., The Catholic Reformation: From Cardinal Ximines to the Council of Trent. New York: Fordham University Press, 1990, 65–79.

Coton, Pierre. *Institution catholique, où est déclarée et confirmée la vérité de la foy, contre les hérésies et superstitions de ce temps. Divisé en quatre livres qui servent d'antidote aux quatre de l'Institution de Jean Calvin,* 2nd ed. Paris: C. Chappelet, 1612.

Danckaerts, Sebastian. *Catechismus attau Adjaran derri agamma Christaon. Bersalin derri bahassa Hollanda dalam bahassa Maleya derri pada Sebastian Danckaerts.* The Hague: n.p., 1623.

Episcopius, Simon. *Apologia pro confessione sive declaratione sententiae eorum, qui in Foederato Belgio vocantur Remonstrantes, super praecipuis articulis religionis Christianae* (1630).

Farel, Guillaume. *La Maniere et fasson qu'on tient en baillant le sainct baptesme en la saincte congregation de dieu: et en espousant ceulx qui viennent au sainct mariage, et à la saincte Cene de nostre seigneur, ès lieux lesquelz dieu de sa grace a visité, faisant que selon sa saincte parolle ce qu'il a deffendu en son eglise soit rejecté, et ce qu'il a commandé soit tenu. Aussi la maniere comment la predication commence, moyenne et finit, avec les prieres et exhorations qu'on facit à tous et pour tous, et de la visitation des malades.* Neuchâtel: Pierre de Vingle, 1533.

Le Sommaire de Guillaume Farel, réimprimé d'après l'édition de l'an 1534, ed. J.-G. Baum. Geneva: Jules-Guillaume Fick, 1867.

Sommaire et brève déclaration [1529], ed. A. L. Hofer. Neuchâtel: Editions Belle-Rivière, 1980.

Oeuvres imprimées, ed. Reinhard Bodenmann et al. Travaux d'Humanisme et Renaissance. Geneva: Droz, 2009–.

Fuller, Thomas. *The History of the University of Cambridge since the Conquest.* Appended to *The Church-History of Britain, from the Birth of Jesus Christ, until the Year M.DC.XLVIII.* London: for John Williams, 1655.

Ganzer, Klaus, and Karl-Heinz zur Mühlen, gen. eds. *Akten der deutschen Reichsreligionsgespräche im 16. Jahrhundert.* Göttingen: Vandenhoeck & Ruprecht, 2000–2007.

1. Bd. *Das Hagenauer Religionsgespräch (1540),* ed. Wolfgang Matz et al. (2 vols.)

2. Bd. *Das Wormser Religionsgespräch (1540/41)*, ed. Heinz Volker Mantey, Norbert Jäger, and Christoph Stoll (2 vols.)

3. Bd. *Das Regensburger Religionsgespräch (1541)*, ed. Norbert Jäger, Saskia Schultheis, and Christoph Stoll.

Giles of Rome. *Commentarium in II Sententiarum*. Venice, 1581.

Hendrik Niemeijer, and Th. Van den End. *Bronnen betreffende Kerk and School in de gouvernementen Ambon, Ternate en Banda ten tijde van de Verenigde Oost-Indische Compagnie (VOC) 1605–1791*. 6 vols. The Hague: Huygens ING, 2015.

Herminjard, A.-L. *Correspondance des réformateurs dans les pays de langue française*. 9 vols. Geneva: H. Georg, 1866–1897.

Heshusen, Tilemann. *Bekandtnuß vom heyligen Nachtmal des Herrn Jesu Christi*. Nuremberg: Johann vom Berg and Ulrich Newber, 1560.

De Praesentia Corporis Christi in Coena Domini, contra Sacramentarios. Jena: Drucker, 1560.

Hoevell, Baron Van. *Tijdschrift voor Nederlandsch Indië, Vol. 2*. Zaltbommel: Joh. Noman and Son, 1887.

Hughes, Philip E. *The Register of the Company of Pastors of Geneva in the Time of Calvin*. Grand Rapids, MI: Eerdmans, 1966.

Jansenius, Cornelis. *Augustinus, seu doctrina Sancti Augustini de humanae naturae sanitate, aegritudine, medicina adversus Pelagianos et Massilienses*. Paris: Michel Soly, 1641.

Jussie, Jean de. *A Short Chronicle: A Poor Clare's Account of the Reformation in Geneva*, ed. and trans. Carrie F. Klaus. Chicago: University of Chicago Press, 2006.

Knuttel, W. P. C. *Catalogus van de pamfletten-verzameling berustende in de Koninklijke Bibliotheek*, vol. I/1. The Hague: Algemeene Landsdrukkerij, 1889.

Koschorke, Klaus, ed. *Summaries of the Minutes of the Consistory of the Dutch Reformed Church in Colombo Held at the Wolvendaal Church, Colombo, 1735–1797*.

Luther, Martin. "Wider das papsttum vom teufel gestiftet." In *D. Martin Luthers Werke (Weimarer Ausgabe)*. Weimar: Harmann Böhlau, 1883–2009, 136:54, 206–99. English tradition in Jaroslav Pelikan et al., eds., *Luther's Works*. Philadelphia: Fortress Press and St. Louis: Concordia Publishing, 1956–2002, 55:41, 263–376.

The Schmalkald Articles, trans. William Russell. Minneapolis, MN: Fortress Press, 1995.

Mallinson, Jeffrey, ed. *Lutheranism vs. Calvinism: The Classic Debate at the Colloquy of Montbéliard 1586, Jakob Andreae and Theodore Beza*, trans. Clinton Armstrong. Saint Louis, MO: Concordia Publishing House, 2017.

Marnix, Philip Van. *Compendioso Exame dos Principaes Puntos de Religiano Christiano*. Amsterdam, The Netherlands: Paulus Mattheyszon, 1688.

Melanchthon, Philip, and Sachiko Kusukawa. *Philip Melanchthon: Orations on Philosophy and Education*. Cambridge: Cambridge University Press, 1999.

Melanchthon, Philip. *Commonplaces: Loci Communes, 1521,* trans. Chris Preus. St. Louis, MO: Concordia Publishing House, 2014.

Perkins, William. *A Treatise of the Manner and Order of Predestination. In The Workes of . . . Mr. William Perkins, volume 2, 603–41.* London: John Legatt, 1631.

Registers of the Consistory of Geneva in the Time of Calvin, Vol. 1, ed. Thomas A. Lambert and Isabella M. Watt, trans. M. Wallace McDonald. Grand Rapids, MI: Eerdmans, 2000.

Registres du Consistoire de Genève au temps de Calvin (1542–1557). 11 vols., ed. Isabella M. Watt et al. Geneva: Droz, 1996–2017.

Ruyl, Albert. *Het Nieuwe Testament: dat is het Nieuwe Verbondt onses Heeren Jesu Christi: In Neder-duytsch ende Malays na der Grieckscher waerheyt Overgeset.* Enckhuysen: Jacobsz Palensteyn, 1629.

Schroeder, H. J., ed. *The Canons and Decrees of the Council of Trent.* St. Louis, MO: Herder, 1941.

Scultetus, Abraham. *Vitalia, das ist ein christlich und freundlich Reyß-Gespräch.* Hanau: Aubrius and Clement, 1618.

Servetus, Michael. *Christianismi Restitutio (Restoration of Christianity)* (1553).

[Slatius, Henricus.] *Amsterdamsche Nouvellos, dat is/ Nieuwe Tydinghen/ Van'tghene datter onlancx is ghepasseert in Bohemen/ Hongarien/. . .* (1620).

Smyth, Richard. *De infantium baptismo, contra Ioannem Caluinum, ac de operibus supererogationis, & merito mortis Christi, aduersus eundem Caluinum, & eius discipulos.* Louvain: Johann Bogard, 1562, sig. A7^v

Strype, John. *The Life and Acts of John Whitgift, D.D.* 3 vols. Oxford: Clarendon Press, 1822 (reprint of 1718),

[Telle, Reinier.] *Retortie ofte Weder-steeck, Ghegheven met de smadelijcke Sift by eenighe bittere Calvinisten, ende Calumniateurs in Figuren af-ghebeeldet. . .* (1619).

Thomas of Strassbourg. *Commentaria super quator libros Sententiarum.* Strassbourg, 1490.

Toplady, Augustus. *Historic Proof of the Doctrinal Calvinism of the Church of England.* 2 vols. London: for George Keith, 1774.

[Uytenbogaert, Johannes.] *Redenen, Waerom men in goede Conscientie metten Nederlandtschen Contra-Remonstranten/ die haer den name van Ghere-formeerde toe-eyghenen. . .* Freiburg, [1619].

van Formosa, Kerckboek. 1643–1649, in *Resoluties van de kerkenraad van Taiwan (Formosa), 1643 October 5–1649 Juni,* Hoge Regering 4451, Arsip Nasional Republik Indonesia, Jakarta.

[Verstegen, Richard.] *Oorspronck ende teghenwoordighen staet van de Calvinische secte, alsoo die nu verscheyden is in vier principale deelen.* Antwerp: Robert Bruneau, 1611.

Viret, Pierre. *Quelques lettres inédites de Pierre Viret,* ed. Jean Barnaud. Saint-Amans: G. Carayol, 1911.

Epistolae Petri Vireti: The Previously Unedited Letters and a Register of Pierre Viret's Correspondence, ed. Michael Bruening. Travaux d'Humanisme et Renaissance 494. Geneva: Droz, 2012.

Westphal, Joachim. *Farrago Confusanearum et Inter Se Dissidentium Opinionum de Coena Domini, ex Sacramentariorum libris congesta*. Magdeburg: Rodius, 1552.

Collectanea sententiarum divi Aurelii Augustini Episcopi Hipponensis de Coena Domini (Collectanaea). Ratisponae, January 1555.

Adversus cuiusdam Sacramentarii falsam criminationem, iusta defensio (Iusta defensio). Francoforti, July 1555.

Apologia confessionis de Coena Domini, contra corruptelas et calumnias Ioannis Calvini (Apologia). Ursellis, 1558, 71–83.

William of Ockham. *Ordinatio IV*, in *Guilleli de Ockham Opera philosophica et theologica ad fidem condicum manuscriptorum edita*, ed. Gideon Gal et al. St. Bonaventure, NY: Franciscan Institute, 1976–1985.

SECONDARY SOURCES

Abray, Lorna Jane. *The People's Reformation: Magistrates, Clergy, and Commons in Strasbourg, 1500–1598*. Ithaca, NY: Cornell University Press, 1985.

Addis, William E., and Thomas Arnold. *A Catholic Dictionary*. New York: The Catholic Publication Society Co., 1887.

Ahn, In-Sub. "John Calvin's Reception in North-East Asia." *Chongshin Theological Journal* 16:1 (2011): 151–175.

Amalou, Thierry. "Holy War or Sedition? The Prophetism of Parisian Preachers and Catholic Militancy, 1558–1588." *French Historical Studies* 38:4 (October 2015): 611–631.

Arand, Charles, et al. *The Lutheran Confessions: History and Theology of the Book of Concord*. Minneapolis, MN: Fortress Press, 2012, 177–183.

Babel, Antoine. *Histoire économique de Genève*. Geneva: Jullien, 1963.

Backus, Irena. "Moses, Plato and Flavius Josephus: Castellio's Conceptions of Sacred and Profane in His Latin Versions of the Bible." In *Shaping the Bible in the Reformation: Books, Scholars, and Their Readers*, ed. Bruce Gordon and Matthew McLean. Leiden, The Netherlands: Brill, 2001, 143–166.

Backus, Irena. *Historical Method and Confessional Identity in the Era of the Reformation*. Leiden, The Netherlands: Brill, 2003.

Life Writing in Reformation Europe. Surrey: Ashgate, 2008.

"The Issue of Reformation Scepticism Revisited: What Erasmus and Sebastian Castellio Did or Did Not Know." In *Renaissance Scepticisms*, ed. Gianenrico Paganini and José Neto. New York: Springer Academic, 2009, 63–89.

ed. *Théodore de Bèze (1519–1605): Actes du Colloque de Genève (septembre 2005)*. Travaux d'Humanisme et Renaissance 424. Geneva: Droz, 2007.

Bademan, R. Bryan. "'The Republican Reformer': John Calvin and the American Calvinists, 1830–1910." In *Sober, Strict, and Scriptural: Collective Memories of John Calvin, 1800–2000*. Brill's Series in Church History 38, ed. Johan de Niet, Herman Paul, and Bart Wallet. Leiden, The Netherlands, and Boston: Brill, 2009, 267–291.

Balk, G. L., F. Van Dijk, and D. J. Kortlang, eds. *The Archives of the Dutch East India Company (VOC) and the Local Institutions in Batavia (Jakarta)*. Leiden, The Netherlands: Brill, 2007.

Balke, Willem. *Calvin and the Anabaptist Radicals*, trans. Willem Heynen. Grand Rapids, MI: Eerdmans, 1981.

Bangs, Jeremy Dupertuis. "Beyond Luther, beyond Calvin, beyond Arminius: The Pilgrims and the Remonstrants in Leiden, 1609–1620." In *Reconsidering Arminius: Beyond the Reformed and Wesleyan Divide*, ed. Keith D. Stanglin, Mark G. Bilby, and Mark H. Mann. Nashville, TN: Abingdon/ Kingwood Books, 2014, 39–69.

Barnaud, Jean. *Pierre Viret: Sa vie et son oeuvre (1511–1571)*. Saint-Amans: G. Carayol, 1911.

Barnes, Andrew E. *The Social Dimension of Piety: Associative Life and Devotional Changes in the Penitent Confraternities of Marseilles (1499–1792)*. New York: Paulist Press, 1994.

Baron, Salo W. "John Calvin and the Jews." In *Harry Austryn Wolfson Jubilee*, Vol. 1. Jerusalem: American Academy for Jewish Research, 1965, 141–163.

Barth, Karl. *The Theology of John Calvin*, trans. Geoffrey W. Bromiley. Grand Rapids, MI: Eerdmans, 1995.

Barthel, Pierre, et al., eds. *Actes du Colloque Guillaume Farel, Neuchâtel, 29 septembre–1er octobre 1980*. 2 vols. Cahiers de la Revue de Théologie et de Philosophie 9. Geneva: Revue de Théologie et de Philosophie, 1983. Cited chapter: Dominique Quadroni, "Répertoire de la Correspondance de Guillaume Farel." 2:3–104.

Battles, F. L. *Interpreting John Calvin*. Grand Rapids, MI: Baker Books, 1996.

Baumgartner, Frederic J. *Henry II: King of France, 1547–1559*. Durham, NC: Duke University Press, 1988.

Bavaud, Georges. *Le réformateur Pierre Viret, 1511–1571: Sa théologie. Histoire et société 10*. Geneva: Labor et fides, 1986.

Bedouelle, Guy. *The Reform of Catholicism, 1480–1620*, trans. James K. Farge. Toronto: Pontifical Institute of Medieval Studies, 2008.

Bell, David A. "Unmasking a King: The Political Uses of Popular Literature under the French Catholic League, 1588–89." *The Sixteenth Century Journal* 20 (1989): 371–386.

Bell, Dean Phillip, and Stephen G. Burnett, eds. *Jews, Judaism, and the Reformation in Sixteenth-Century Germany.* Leiden, The Netherlands: Brill, 2006.

Benedict, Philip. "The Saint Bartholomew's Day Massacres in the Provinces." *Historical Journal* 21:2 (1978): 205–225.

——— *Rouen during the Wars of Religion.* Cambridge: Cambridge University Press, 1981.

——— *Christ's Churches Purely Reformed: A Social History of Calvinism.* New Haven, CT, and London: Yale University Press, 2002.

——— *Graphic History: The "Wars, Massacres, and Troubles" of Tortorel and Perrissin.* Geneva: Droz, 2007.

Benedict, Philip, and Nicolas Forneron, eds. *L'organisation et l'action des églises réformées de France (1557–1563): Synodes provinciaux et autres documents.* Geneva: Droz, 2012.

Benedict, Philip, Guido Marnef, and Henk van Nierop, eds. *Reformation, Revolt, and Civil War in France and the Netherlands, 1555–1585.* Amsterdam, The Netherlands: Royal Netherlands Academy of Arts and Sciences, 1999.

Benedict, Philip, Silvana Seidel Menchi, and Alain Tallon, eds. *La Réforme en France et en Italie: Contacts, comparaisons et contrastes.* Collection de l'École française de Rome, 384. Rome: École française de Rome, 2007.

Bernstein, Hilary J. *Between Crown and Community: Politics and Civic Culture in Sixteenth-Century Poitiers.* Ithaca, NY: Cornell University Press, 2004.

Berthoud, Gabrielle, ed. *Aspects de la propagande religieuse.* Geneva: Droz, 1957.

Bétant, E.-A. *Notice sur le Collège de Rive.* Geneva: Fick, 1866

Bietenholz, Peter. *Encounters with a Radical Erasmus.* Toronto: University of Toronto Press, 2009.

Birnstiel, Eckart. *La Diaspora des Huguenots: Les réfugiés protestants de France et leur dispersion dans le monde (XVIe–XVIIIe siècles).* Paris: Honoré Champion, 2001.

Binz, Louis. *Vie Religieuse et Reforme Ecclesiastique Dans le Diocese De Geneve, Pendant le Grand Schisme et la Crise Conciliaire, 1378–1450.* Geneva: Alex Jullien, Libraire, 1973.

——— *A Brief History of Geneva,* trans. by Jean Gunn. Geneva: Chancellerie d'Etat, 1985.

Bizer, Ernst. *Studien zur Geschichte des Abendmahlsstreits im 16. Jahrhundert,* 2nd ed. Darmstadt: Wissenschaftliche Buchgesellschaft, 1962.

Blair, Ann. *Too Much to Know: Managing Scholarly Information before the Modern Age.* New Haven, CT, and London: Yale University Press, 2011.

Blaisdell, Charmarie. "Calvin's Letters to Women: The Courting of Ladies in High Places." *Sixteenth Century Journal* 13: 3 (Autumn 1982): 67–84.

Bohatec, J. *Budé und Calvin. Studien zur Gedankenwelt des französischen Humanismus,* Graz: Böhlaus, 1950.

Bouvier, Nicole, et al. *Geneva, Zurich, Basel: History, Culture, and National Identity.* Princeton, NJ: Princeton University Press, 2014.

Bonney, Richard. *The European Dynastic States 1494–1660.* Reprint edition. Short Oxford History of the Modern World. Oxford: Oxford University Press, 1991.

Borgeaud, Charles. *Histoire de l'université de Genève: l'académie de Calvin.* Geneva: Georg & Co., 1900.

Bouwsma, William J. *John Calvin: A Sixteenth-Century Portrait.* Oxford: Oxford University Press, 1988.

Brady, Thomas A., Jr. *Ruling Class, Regime, and Reformation at Strasbourg, 1520–1555.* Leiden, The Netherlands: Brill, 1978.

The Politics of the Reformation in Germany: Jacob Sturm (1489–1553) of Strasbourg. Atlantic Highlands, NJ: Humanities Press, 1997.

Brandt, Geeraert. *The History of the Reformation and Other Ecclesiastical Transactions in and about the Low-Countries.* 4 vols. London: T. Wood for Timothy Childe, 1720–1723.

Bray, John S. *Theodore Beza's Doctrine of Predestination.* Bibliotheca humanistica and reformatorica 12. Nieuwkoop: De Graaf, 1975.

Breuer, Mordechai. "The Jewish Middle Ages." In *German-Jewish History in Modern Times,* ed. Michael A. Meyer. New York: Columbia University Press, 1990, 1:7–77.

Bratt, James D. *Abraham Kuyper: Modern Calvinist, Christian Democrat.* Grand Rapids, MI: Eerdmans, 2013.

Breen, Q. *John Calvin: A Study in French Humanism,* Hamden, CO: Archon Books, 1968.

Broomhall, Susan. *Women and Religion in Sixteenth-Century France.* New York: Palgrave Macmillan, 2006.

Bruening, Michael W. *Calvinism's First Battleground: Conflict and Reform in the Pays de Vaud, 1528–1559.* Dordrecht, The Netherlands: Spring, 2005.

Burnett, Amy Nelson. *The Yoke of Christ: Martin Bucer and Christian Discipline.* Kirksville, MO: Sixteenth Century Publishers, 1994.

"The Myth of the Swiss Lutherans: Martin Bucer and the Eucharistic Controversy in Bern." *Zwingliana 32* (2005): 45–70.

"The Social History of Communion and the Reformation of the Eucharist." *Past and Present* 211 (2011): 77–119.

"From Concord to Confession: The Wittenberg Concord and the Consensus Tigurinus in Historical Perspective." *Reformation and Renaissance Review* 18 (2016): 47–58.

Debating the Sacraments: Print and Authority in the Early Reformation. New York: Oxford University Press, 2019.

Burnett, Amy Nelson, and Emidio Campio, eds. *A Companion to the Swiss Reformation.* Leiden, The Netherlands: Brill, 2016.

Burnet, Ian. *East Indies.* Kenthurst, New South Wales: Rosenberg, 2019.

Burns, J. H., and Mark Goldie, eds. *The Cambridge History of Political Thought, 1450–1700*. Cambridge: Cambridge University Press, 1991.

Butin, Philip Walker. *Revelation, Redemption, and Response: Calvin's Trinitarian Understanding of the Divine-Human Relationship*. Oxford: Oxford University Press, 1995.

Bynum, Carolyn W. *Holy Feast and Holy Famine: the Religious Significance of Food to Medieval Women*. Berkeley and Los Angeles: University of California Press, 1987.

Calvin et l'humanisme. Actes du symposium d'Amiens et Lille III, edited by B. Boudou and A.-P. Pouey-Mounou. Genève: Droz, 2012.

Cameron, Euan. *The Reformation of the Heretics: The Waldenses of the Alps, 1480–1580*. Oxford: Clarendon Press, 1984.

The European Reformation. Oxford: Clarendon Press, 1991.

"The Consensus Tigurinus and the Göppingen Eucharistic Confession: Continuing Instabilities in Geneva's Relationship with Zurich and the Lutheran World." *Reformation and Renaissance Review* 18:1 (2016): 72–84.

Campbell, Alexander. "Letter to William Jones." *Millennial Harbinger* 1st series, 5 (1834): 584–590.

"Calvinism and Arminianism." *Millennial Harbinger* 3rd series, 3 (1846): 325–329.

Christianity Restored. Rosemead, CA: Old Paths Book Club, 1959 (reprint of 1835).

Campi, Emidio, and Ruedi Reich, eds. *Consensus Tigurinus (1549): Die Einigung zwischen Heinrich Bullinger und Johannes Calvin über das Abendmahl. Werden – Wertung – Bedeutung*. Zurich: TVZ, 2009.

Carpi, Olivia. *Les Guerres de religion: Un conflit franco-français 1559–1598*. Paris: Ellipses Marketing, 2012.

Carroll, Stuart. *Noble Power during the French Wars of Religion: The Guise Affinity and the Catholic Cause in Normandy*. Cambridge: Cambridge University Press, 1998.

Carruthers, Mary. *The Book of Memory; A Study of Memory in Medieval Culture*. Cambridge: Cambridge University Press, 1990.

Chambers, B. T. *Bibliography of French Bibles. Fifteenth- and Sixteenth-Century French- Language Editions of the Scriptures*. Geneva: Droz, 1983.

Choy, Kiven S. K. "Calvin's Reception of Necessitarian Concepts." In *Church and School in Early Modern Protestantism*, ed. Jordon J. Ballor et al. Leiden, The Netherlands: Brill, 2013, 111–122.

Christin, Olivier. *Une Révolution symbolique: L'iconoclasme huguenot et la reconstruction catholique*. Paris: Les Editions de Minuit, 1991.

Chung-Kim, Esther. *Inventing Authority: The Use of the Church Fathers in Reformation Debates over the Eucharist*. Waco, TX: Baylor, 2011.

Comité Farel. *Guillaume Farel: Biographie nouvelle écrite d'après les documents originaux par un groupe d'historiens, professeurs et pasteurs de Suisse, de France et d'Italie*. Neuchâtel: Delauchaux & Niestlé, 1930.

Conner, Philip. *Huguenot Heartland: Montauban and Southern French Calvinism during the Wars of Religion*. Aldershot: Ashgate, 2002.

Coster, Will. *Baptism and Spiritual Kinship in Early Modern England*. Brookfield, VT: Ashgate, 2002.

Cottret, Bernard. *Terre d'exil: L'Angleterre et ses réfugiés français et wallons, de la Réforme à la Révocation de l'édit de Nantes*. Paris: Aubier, 1985.

Jean Calvin: A Biography. Grand Rapids, MI: Eerdmans, 2009.

Crawford, Katherine B. "Love, Sodomy, and Scandal: Controlling the Sexual Reputation of Henry III." *Journal of the History of Sexuality* 12:4 (October 2003): 513–542.

Crew, Phyllis Mack. *Calvinist Preaching and Iconoclasm in the Netherlands, 1544–1569*. New York: Cambridge University Press, 1978.

Crousaz, Karine. *L'Académie de Lausanne entre Humanisme et Réforme (ca. 1537–1560)*. Education and Society in the Middle Ages and Renaissance 41. Leiden, The Netherlands: Brill, 2012.

Crouzet, Denis. *Les guerriers de Dieu: La violence au temps des troubles de religion vers 1525–vers 1610*. 2 vols. Seyssel: Champ Vallon, 1990.

Curley, Edwin. "Castellio's Erasmian Liberalism." *Philosophical Topics* 31:1 (2003): 47–73.

Daussy, Hugues. Le parti huguenot: Chronique d'une désillusion *(1557–1572)*. Geneva: Droz, 2014.

Davis, Natalie Z. "City Women and Religious Change." In *Society and Culture in Early Modern France*. Stanford, CA: Stanford University Press, 1975, 65–96.

Society and Culture in Early Modern France: Eight Essays. Stanford, CA: Stanford University Press, 1975.

Davis, Thomas J. *The Clearest Promises of God: The Development of Calvin's Eucharistic Teaching*. New York: AMS Press, 1995.

This Is My Body: The Presence of Christ in Reformation Thought. Grand Rapids, MI: Baker Academic, 2008.

Davis, Thomas J., ed. *John Calvin's American Legacy*. Oxford: Oxford University Press, 2010.

De Boer, Erik. *The Genevan School of the Prophets*. Geneva: Droz, 2012.

de Greef, Wulfert. *The Writings of John Calvin: An Introductory Guide*. Grand Rapids, MI: Baker Books, 1993.

De Gruchy, John W. *John Calvin: Christian Humanist and Evangelical Reformer*. Eugene, OR: Cascade, 2013.

Dentière, Marie. *Epistle to Marguerite de Navarre: And, Preface to a Sermon by John Calvin*, ed. and trans. Mary B. McKinley. Chicago: University of Chicago Press, 2004.

Detmers, Achim. *Reformation und Judentum: Israel-Lehren und Einstellungen zum Judentum von Luther bis zum frühen Calvin.* Stuttgart: Kohlhammer, 2001.

Deursen. A. Th. van. *Bavianen en slijkgeuzen: Kerk en kerkvolk ten tijde van Mauritsen Oldenbarnevelt.* Franeker: Van Wijnen, 1998.

Diefendorf, Barbara B. *Beneath the Cross: Catholics and Huguenots in Sixteenth-Century Paris.* Oxford: Oxford University Press, 1991.

The Saint Bartholomew's Day Massacre: A Brief History with Documents. Boston: Bedford/St. Martin's Press, 2009.

Dingel, Irene. "The Culture of Conflict in the Controversies Leading to the Formula of Concord (1548–1580)." In *Brill's Companion to the Christian Tradition: Lutheran Ecclesiastical Culture, 1550–1675,* ed. Robert Kolb. Leiden, The Netherlands: Brill: 2008, 15–64.

"Calvin in the Context of Lutheran Consolidation." *Reformation and Renaissance Review* 12:2–3 (2010): 155–187.

Dingel, Irene, Robert Kolb, Nicole Kuropka, and Timothy J. Wingert, eds. *Philip Melanchthon: Theologian in Classroom, Confession, and Controversy.* Gottingen: Vandenhoeck & Ruprecht, 2012.

Dowey, Edward A., Jr. *The Knowledge of God in Calvin's Theology,* 3rd ed. Grand Rapids, MI: Eerdmans, 1994.

Droz, Eugénie. *Chemins de l'hérésie. textes et documents.* 4 vols. Geneva: Slatkine, 1970–1976.

Dufour, Alain. *Théodore de Bèze, poète et théologien.* Cahiers d'Humanisme et Renaissance 78. Geneva: Droz, 2006.

Duke, Alastair. *Reformation and Revolt in the Low Countries.* London: Hambledon Press, 1990.

Dyrness, William A. *Reformed Theology and Visual Culture: The Protestant Imagination from Calvin to Edwards.* Cambridge: Cambridge University Press, 2004.

Edwards, Mark U. *Printing, Propaganda, and Martin Luther.* Berkeley: University of California Press, 1994, 17–21.

Eire, Carlos M. N. "Calvin and Nicodemism: A Reappraisal." *Sixteenth Century Journal* 10:1 (1979): 45–69.

War against the Idols. Cambridge: Cambridge University Press, 1986.

Reformations: The Early Modern World. New Haven, CT: Yale University Press, 2016.

Ellis, Brannon. *Calvin, Classical Trinitarianism, and the Aseity of the Son.* Oxford: Oxford University Press, 2012.

Elwood, Christopher. *The Body Broken: The Calvinist Doctrine of the Eucharist and the Symbolization of Power.* Oxford: Oxford University Press, 1998.

Engammare, Max. *On Time, Punctuality, and Discipline in Early Modern Calvinism,* trans. Karin Maag. New York and Cambridge: Cambridge University Press, 2010.

Eurich, Amanda. "Women in the Huguenot Community." In *A Companion to the Huguenots*, ed. Raymond A. Mentzer and Bertrand Van Ruymbeke. Leiden, The Netherlands: Brill, 2016, 118–149.

Evans, R. J. W. "The Wechel Presses: Humanism and Calvinism in Central Europe, 1572–1627." *Past and Present*, suppl. 2 (1975): 1–74.

Fabisch, P. *Dokumente zur Causa Lutheri: 1517–1521.* Münster: Aschendorff, 1988.

Farge, James K. *Orthodoxy and Reform in Early Reformation France: The Faculty of Theology of Paris, 1500–1543.* Leiden, The Netherlands: Brill, 1985.

"Early Censorship in Paris: A New Look at the Roles of the Parlement of Paris and of King Francis I." *Renaissance and Reformation* 25:2 (1989): 173–183.

"Noel Beda and the Defense of the Tradition." In *Biblical Humanism and Scholasticism in the Age of Erasmus*, ed. Erika Rummel. Leiden, The Netherlands: Brill, 2008, 143–164.

Fehleison, Jill. *Boundaries of Faith: Catholics and Protestants in the Diocese of Geneva.* Kirksville, MO: Truman State University Press, 2010.

Fenlon, Dermon. *Heresy and Obedience in Tridentine Italy: Cardinal Pole and the Counter Reformation.* London: Cambridge University Press, 1973.

Finley-Croswhite, Annette. *Henri IV and the Towns: The Pursuit of Legitimacy in French Urban Society, 1589–1610.* Cambridge: Cambridge University Press, 1999.

Fisher, J. D. C. *Christian Initiation in the Medieval West: A Study in the Disintegration of the Primitive Rite of Initiation.* Chicago: Hillenbrand Books, 2004 (reprint of 1965 original).

Fisher, Jeff. "Housing a Heretic: Johannes Oecolampadius (1482–1531) and the 'Pre-History' of the Servetus Affair." *Reformation and Renaissance Review* 20:1 (2018): 35–50.

Foster, Herbert Darling. "Geneva Before Calvin (1387–1526) The Antecedents of a Puritan State." *The American Historical Review* 8:2 (January 1903): 217–240.

Foucault, Michel. *Essential Works of Foucault 1954–1984.* Vol. 1: Ethics: Subjectivity and Truth, ed. Paul Rabinow and trans. Robert Hurley. London: Penguin, 2000.

Franklin, Julian, ed. and trans. *Constitutionalism and Resistance in the Sixteenth Century: Three Treatises by Hotman, Béza and Mornay.* New York: Pegasus, 1969.

Friedman, Jerome. *Michael Servetus: A Case Study in Total Heresy.* Genève: Librairie Droz, 1978.

Frijhoff, Willem, and Marijke Spies. *1650: Hard-Won Unity. Dutch Culture in a European Perspective.* Assen: Van Gorcum, 2004.

Froehlich, Karlfried. "Always to Keep the Literal Sense in Holy Scripture Means to Kill One's Soul: The State of Biblical Hermeneutics at the

Beginning of the Fifteenth Century." In *Literary Uses of Typology from the Late Middle Ages to the Present*, ed. Earl Miner. Princeton, NJ: Princeton University Press, 1977, 20–48.

Gaberel, J. *Histoire de l'Église de Génève depuis le commencement de la Reformation jusqu'a nos jours*. 3 vols. Geneva, 1858–1862.

Galpern, A. Neal. *The Religions of the People in Sixteenth-Century Champagne*. Cambridge, MA: Harvard University Press, 1976.

Gamble, Richard. "Calvin's Controversies." In *The Cambridge Companion to Jean Calvin*, ed. Donald McKim. Cambridge: Cambridge University Press, 2004, 188–206.

    ed. *The Organizational Structure of Calvin's Theology*. New York: Garland, 1992.

Ganoczy, Alexandre. *The Young Calvin*, trans. David Foxgrover and Wade Provo. Philadelphia: Westminster, 1987.

Garside, Charles. *Zwingli and the Arts*. New Haven, CT: Yale University Press, 1966

Garrisson, Janine. *Royauté, renaissance et réforme*. Paris: Le Seuil, 1991.

Gauna, Max. *Upwellings: First Expressions of Unbelief in the Printed Literature of the French Renaissance*. London: Associated University Presses, 1992.

Geisendorf, Paul-F. *Théodore de Bèze*. Geneva: Labor et Fides, 1949.

Gerrish, B. A. "John Calvin on Luther." In *Interpreters of Luther: Essays in Honor of Wilhelm Pauck*, ed. Jaroslav Pelikan. Philadelphia: Fortress Press, 1968, 67–96.

Gerstner, Jonathan N. "A Christian Monopoly: The Reformed Church and Colonial Society under Dutch Rule." In *Christianity in South Africa: A Political, Social and Cultural History*, eds. Richard Elphick and Rodney Davenport. Berkeley: University of California Press, 1997, 16–30.

Gilmont, Jean-François. *The Reformation and the Book*. Aldershot: Ashgate, 1996.

    Le livre réformé au XVIe siècle. Paris: Bibliothèque nationale de France, 2005.

    John Calvin and the Printed Book. Kirskville, MO: Truman State University Press, 2005.

Gomez-Géraud, Marie-Christine. "Qui parle encore de Sébastien Castellion?" *Australian Journal of French Studies* 52:3 (2015): 261–273.

Gordon, Bruce. *The Swiss Reformation*. Manchester: Manchester University Press, 2002.

    Calvin. New Haven, CT: Yale University Press, 2009.

    "To Kill a Heretic: Sebastian Castellio against John Calvin." In *Censorship Moments: Reading Texts in the History of Censorship and Freedom of Expression*, ed. Geoff Kemp. London: Bloomsbury, 2014, 55–61.

    John Calvin's *Institutes of the Christian Religion: A Biography*. Lives of Great Religious Books. Princeton, NJ: Princeton University Press, 2016.

"Martin Luther and John Calvin." In *Oxford Encyclopedia of Religion*.

ed. *Protestant History and Identity in Sixteenth-Century Europe: The Later Reformation*. Aldershot: Ashgate, 1996.

Gordon, Bruce, and Matthew McLean, eds. *Shaping the Bible in the Reformation: Books, Scholars and Their Readers in the Sixteenth Century*. Boston and Leiden, The Netherlands: Brill, 2012.

Gowing, Laura. *Domestic Dangers: Women, Words, and Sex in Early Modern London*. Oxford: Oxford University Press, 1998.

Graham, Michael F. *The Uses of Reform: "Godly Discipline" and Popular Behavior in Scotland and Beyond, 1560–1610*. Leiden, The Netherlands: Brill, 1996.

Greengrass, Mark. *The French Reformation*. Oxford: Wiley-Blackwell, 1991.

France in the Age of Henry IV: The Struggle for Stability, 2nd ed. New York: Longman, 1995.

The European Reformation, c. 1500–1618. London: Longman, 1998.

Grell, Ole Peter. "Exile and Tolerance." In *Tolerance and Intolerance in the European Reformation*, ed. O. P. Grell and B. Scribner. Cambridge: Cambridge University Press, 1996, 164–181.

Brethren in Christ: A Calvinist Network in Reformation Europe. Cambridge: Cambridge University Press, 2011.

"The Creation of a Calvinist Identity in the Reformation Period." In *Religion as an Agent of Change: Crusades, Reformation, Pietism*, ed. Per Ingesman. Leiden, The Netherlands: Brill, 2016, 149–165.

Grendler, Paul F. "The Universities of the Renaissance and Reformation." *Renaissance Quarterly* 57:1 (Spring 2004): 1–42.

Grislis, Egil. "Calvin's Doctrine of Baptism." *Church History* 31:1 (1962): 46–65.

"Martin Luther and Menno Simons on Infant Baptism." *Journal of Mennonite Studies* 12 (1994): 7–25.

Groenhuis, G. "Calvinism and National Consciousness: The Dutch Republic as the New Israel." In A. C. Duke and C. A. Tamse, eds. *Church and State Since the Reformation*, Vol. 7 of *Britain and the Netherlands*. The Hague: Nijhoff, 1981, 119–133.

Grosse, Christian. *L'excommunication de Philibert Berthelier: Histoire d'un conflit d'identité aux premiers temps de la Réforme genevoise (1547–1555)*. Geneva: Société d'Histoire et d'Archéologie de Genève, 1995.

Les rituels de la cène: Le culte eucharistique réformé à Genève (XVIe–XVIIe siècles). Geneva: Droz, 2008.

"Aux origines des pratiques consistoriales de pacification des conflits: Le 'Conseil de paix,' (1527–1529)." In *Les registres du Conseil de la République de Genève sous l'Ancien Régime: Nouvelles approches, nouvelles perspectives*, ed. Sandra Coram-Mekkey. Geneva: Archives d'Etat de Genève and Fondation de l'Encyclopédie de Genève, 2009, 29–63.

Guggisberg, Hans. "The Defense of Religious Toleration and Religious Liberty in Early Modern Europe: Arguments, Pressures, and Some Consequences." *History of European Ideas* 4:1 (1983): 35–50.

Sebastian Castellio, 1515–1563: Humanist and Defender of Religious Toleration in a Confessional Age, trans. Bruce Gordon. New York: Routledge, 2003.

Gwynn, Robin. *Huguenot Heritage: The History and Contribution of the Huguenots in Britain*. Brighton: Academic Press, 2001.

Hampton, Stephen. *Anti-Arminians: The Anglican Reformed Tradition from Charles II to George I*. Oxford Theological Monographs. Oxford: Oxford University Press, 2008.

Hancock, Ralph C. *Calvin and the Foundations of Modern Politics*. Ithaca, NY: Cornell University Press, 1989.

Hanley, Sarah. "The French Constitution Revised: Representative Assemblies and Resistance Right in Sixteenth-Century France." In *Society and Institutions in Early Modern France*, ed. Mack P. Holt. Athens, GA: University of Georgia Press, 1991, 36–50.

Hanlon, Gregory. *Confession and Community in Seventeenth-Century France: Catholic and Protestant Co-existence in Aquitaine*. Philadelphia: University of Pennsylvania Press, 1993.

Hart, D. G. "Implausible: Calvinism and American Politics." In *John Calvin's American Legacy*, ed. Thomas J. Davis. Oxford: Oxford University Press, 2008, 65–88.

Hatch, Nathan O. *The Democratization of American Christianity*. New Haven, CT: Yale University Press, 1989.

Hein, Lorenz. *Italienische Protestanten und ihr Einfluss auf die Reformation in Polen während der beiden Jahrzehnte vor dem Sandomirer Konsens (1570)*. Leiden, The Netherlands: E. J. Brill, 1974.

Helm, Paul. *Calvin at the Centre*. Oxford: Oxford University Press, 2009.

Hendrix, Scott H. *Martin Luther: Visionary Reformer*. New Haven, CT: Yale University Press, 2015.

Henisch, Bridget Ann. *Fast and Feast: Food in Medieval Society*. University Park: Pennsylvania State University Press, 1976.

Higman, Francis. *The Style of John Calvin in his French Polemical Treatises*. Oxford: Oxford University Press, 1967.

Jean Calvin: Three French Treatises. London: Athlone Press, 1970.

Censorship and the Sorbonne: A Bibliographical Study of Books in French Censured by the Faculty of Theology of the University of Paris, 1520–1551. Geneva: Droz, 1979.

"The Question of Nicodemism." In *Calvinus ecclesiae Genevensis Custos: die Referate des Congrès International des Recherches Calviniennes vom 6-9 September 1982 in Genf*, ed. Wilhelm H. Neuser. Frankfurt: Peter Lang, 1984, 165–170.

"Calvin's Works in Translation." In *Calvinism in Europe, 1540–1620*, ed. Andrew Pettegree, Alastair Duke, and Gillian Lewis. Cambridge: Cambridge University Press, 1994, 82–99.

Piety and the People: Religious Printing in French, 1511–1551. Aldershot: Ashgate, 1996.

Lire et découvrir : la circulation des idées au temps de la Réforme. Geneva: Droz, 1998.

Hill, Kat. *Baptism, Brotherhood, and Belief in Reformation Germany: Anabaptism and Lutheranism, 1525–1585*. Oxford: Oxford University Press, 2015.

Hillerbrand, Hans, ed. *The Oxford Encyclopedia of the Reformation*, 4 vols. New York: Oxford University Press, 1996. For dated but still helpful overviews, which have informed this article, see the following entries: Vinzenz Pfnür, "Colloquies," Vol. 3, 375–383; Alois Schmid, "Hagenau, Colloquy of," Vol. 2, 208; Alois Schmid, "Marburg, Colloquy of," Vol. 3, 2–4; Robert Kolb, "Maulbronn, Colloquy of," Vol. 3, 34–35; Jill Raitt, "Montebéliard, Colloquy of," Vol. 3, 84–85; Donald Nugent, "Poissy, Colloquy of," Vol. 3, 281–282.

Hirzel, Ernst, and Martin Salmann, eds., *John Calvin's Impact on Church and Society, 1509–2009*. Grand Rapids, MI: Eerdmans, 2009.

Histoire du Collège de France. I. La création 1530–1560, ed. A. Tuilier. Paris: Fayard, 2006.

Holder, R. Ward. *Crisis and Renewal: The Era of the Reformations*. Louisville, KY: Westminster John Knox, 2009.

"Calvin and Luther: The Relationship that Still Echoes." In *Calvin and Luther: The Continuing Relationship*, ed. R. Ward Holder. Göttingen: Vandenhoeck & Ruprecht, 2013, 7–10.

Holt, Mack P. *The Duke of Anjou and the Politique Struggle during the Wars of Religion*. Cambridge: Cambridge University Press, 1986.

"Putting Religion Back into the Wars of Religion." *French Historical Studies* 18 (1993): 524–551.

The French Wars of Religion, 1562–1629, 2nd ed. Cambridge: Cambridge University Press, 2005.

ed. *Renaissance and Reformation France: 1500–1648*. Oxford: Oxford University Press, 2002.

Holtrop, Philip. *The Bolsec Controversy on Predestination from 1551 to 1555*. 2 vols. Lewiston, NY: Edwin Mellen, 1993.

Höpfl, Harro. *The Christian Polity of John Calvin*. Cambridge: Cambridge University Press, 1992.

"The Ideal of *Aristocratia Politia Vicina* in the Calvinist Political Tradition." In *Calvin and His Influence, 1509–2009*, ed. Irena Backus and Philip Benedict. Oxford: Oxford University Press, 2011, 46–66.

Hotman, François. *Francogallia*, ed. and trans. Ralph E. Giesey and J. H. M. Salmon. Cambridge: Cambridge University Press, 1973.

Huizinga, Johan. *Nederland's beschaving in de 17e eeuw.* Groningen: Wolters-Noordhoff, 1984.

Huppert, George. *Public Schools in Renaissance France.* Urbana: University of Illinois Press, 1984.

Israel, Jonathan I. *European Jewry in the Age of Mercantilism 1550–1750*, 3rd. ed. London: Littman, 1998.

Jacobs, Elfriede. *Die Sakramentslehre Wilhelm Farels.* Zürcher Beiträge zur Reformationsgeschichte 10. Zurich: Theologischer Verlag, 1978.

Jacobs, Jaap. *New Netherland: A Dutch Colony in Seventeenth-Century America.* Leiden, The Netherlnds: Brill, 2005.

Janse, Wim. "Calvin's Eucharistic Theology: Three Dogma-Historical Observations." In *Calvinus sacrarum literarum interpres: Papers of the International Congress on Calvin Research*, ed. Herman J. Selderhuis. Reformed Historical Theology 5. Göttingen: Vandenhoeck & Ruprecht, 2008, 37–69.

"Joachim Westphal's Sacramentology." *Lutheran Quarterly* 22 (2008): 137–160.

"The Sacraments." In *The Calvin Handbook*, ed. Herman J. Selderhuis. Grand Rapids, MI: Eerdmans, 2009, 344–355.

Jedin, Hubert. *A History of the Council of Trent*, trans. Ernest Graf. 3 vols. St. Louis, MO: Herder, 1957–1961.

Jenkins, Gary W. *Calvin's Tormentors.* Grand Rapids, MI: Baker Academic, 2018.

Jensen, De Lamar. *Confrontation at Worms: Martin Luther and the Diet of Worms.* Provo, UT: Brigham Young University Press, 1973.

Jensen, Gordon A. *The Wittenberg Concord: Creating Space for Dialogue.* Lutheran Quarterly Books. Minneapolis, MN: Fortress Press, 2018.

Jouanna, Arlette. *La France du XVIe siècle, 1483–1598*, 3rd ed. Paris: Presses Universitaires de France, 2016.

Jürgens, Henning P. "Intra Protestant Conflicts in 16th Century Poland and Prussia – The Case of Benedict Morgenstern." In *Calvin and Luther: The Continuing Relationship*, ed. R. Ward Holder. Göttingen: Vandenhoeck & Ruprecht, 2013, 143–162.

Karant-Nunn, Susan. "Continuity and Change: Some of the Effects of the Reformation on the Women of Zwickau." *Sixteenth Century Journal* 13:2 (1984): 17–42.

The Reformation of Ritual: An Interpretation of Early Modern Germany. London: Routledge, 1997.

"'Suffer the Little Children to Come unto Me, and Forbid Them Not': The Social Location of Baptism in Early Modern Germany." In *Continuity and Change: The Harvest of Late Medieval and Reformation History*, ed. Robert J. Bast and Andrew C. Gow. Leiden, The Netherlands: Brill, 2000, 359–378.

Kaufmann, Thomas. "'Our Lord God's Chancery' in Magdeburg and Its Fight against the Interim." *Church History* 73 (2004): 566–582.

Luther's Jews. Oxford: Oxford University Press, 2017.

Kelley, Donald R. *The Beginning of Ideology: Consciousness and Society in the French Reformation*. Cambridge: Cambridge University Press, 1981.

Kelly, Joan. "Did Women Have a Renaissance?" In *Women, History, and Theory: The Essays of Joan Kelly*. Chicago: University of Chicago Press, 1984, 19–50.

King, John B., Jr. *Predestination in Light of the Cross: A Critical Exposition of Luther's Theology*. Vallecita, CA: Chalcedon, 2003.

Kingdon, Robert M. *Adultery and Divorce in Calvin's Geneva*. Cambridge, MA: Harvard University Press, 1995.

Geneva and the Coming of the Wars of Religion in France, 1555–1563. Reprint edition with a foreword by Mack. P. Holt and a postface by Robert M. Kingdon. Geneva: Droz, 2007 [1956].

Kingdon, Robert M. (with Thomas A. Lambert). *Reforming Geneva: Discipline, Faith, and Anger*. Geneva: Droz, 2012.

Klaus, Carrie F. "Architecture and Sexual Identity: Jeanne de Jussie's Narrative of the Reformation in Geneva." *Feminist Studies* 29:2 (Summer 2003): 278–297.

Knecht, R. J. *Renaissance Warrior and Patron: The Reign of Francis I*. Cambridge and New York: Cambridge University Press, 1996.

Catherine de Medici. New York: Longman, 1998.

The Rise and Fall of Renaissance France: 1483–1610, 2nd ed. Oxford: Wiley-Blackwell, 2002.

Hero or Tyrant? Henry III, King of France, 1574–1589. Aldershot: Ashgate, 2014.

Köhler, Walther. *Zwingli und Luther: Ihre Streit über das Abendmahl nach seinen politischen und religiösen Beziehungen*. 2 vols. Quellen und Forschungen zur Reformationsgeschichte 6–7. Gütersloh: Bertelsmann, 1924–1953 (repr. Gütersloh, 2017).

Kolb, Robert. *Bound Choice, Election, and Wittenberg Theological Method: From Martin Luther to the Formula of Concord*. Grand Rapids, MI: Eerdmans, 2005.

Konnert, Mark W. *Civic Agendas and Religious Passion: Châlons-sur-Marne during the French Wars of Religion, 1560–1594*. Kirksville, MO: Truman State University Press, 1997.

Kooi, Christine. *Liberty and Religion: Church and State in Leiden's Reformation, 1572–1620*. Leiden, The Netherlands: Brill, 2000.

Krans, Jan. *Beyond What Is Written: Erasmus and Beza as Conjectural Critics of the New Testament*. Boston and Leiden, The Netherlands: Brill, 2006.

Kretscher, Georg, "The Imperial Diet of Regensburg and the 1541 Variata of the Augsburg Confession." In *Piety, Politics, and Ethics: Reformation*

Studies in Honor of George W. Forrell, ed. Carter Lindberg. Kirksville, MO: Sixteenth Century Journal Publications, 1984, 85–102.

La Buissière, Groupe de. *Pratiques de la confession des pères du désert à Vatican II. Quinze études d'histoire.* Paris: Editions du Cerf, 1983.

Lambert, Malcolm. *Medieval Heresy: Popular Movements from the Gregorian Reform to the Reformation*, 2nd ed. Oxford: Blackwell, 1992.

Lane, A. N. S., "Calvin and Article 5 of the Regensburg Colloquy." In *Calvinus Praeceptor Ecclesiae: Papers of the International Congress on Calvin Research, Princeton, August 20–24, 2002*, ed. Herman J. Selderuis. Geneva: Librairie Droz, 2004, 233–263.

"A Tale of Two Imperial Cities: Justification at Regensburg (1541) and Trent (1546–1547)." In *Justification in Perspective: Historical Developments and Contemporary Challenges*, ed. Bruce McCormack. Grand Rapids, MI, and Edinburgh: Baker Academic/Rutherford House, 2006, 119–145.

Lang, August. "Die Quellen der *Institutio* von 1536." *Evangelische Theologie* 3 (1936):100–112.

Lastraioli, Chiara. "D'un texte inconnu de Jérôme Bolsee contre Calvin." *Renaissance and Reformation Review* 10:2 (2008): 157–174.

Lehner, Ulrich L., Richard A. Muller, and A. G. Roeber, eds. *The Oxford Handbook of Early Modern Theology, 1600–1800.* New York and Oxford: Oxford University Press, 2016.

Leppin, Volker. *Martin Luther: A Medieval Life.* Grand Rapids, MI: Baker, 2017.

Lescaze, Bernard, *Sauver l'âme, nourrir le corps.* Geneva: Hospice Général, 1985.

Lestringant, Frank. *Le Huguenot et le sauvage: L'Amérique et la controverse coloniale, en France, au temps des guerres de religion (1555–1589)*, 3rd ed. Geneva: Droz, 2004.

Lexutt, Athina. *Rechtfertigung im Gesprach. Das Rechtfertigungsverstandnis in den Religionsgesprachen von Hagenau, Worms und Regensburg, 1540/41.* Gottingen: Vandenhoeck & Ruprecht, 1996.

Lienhard, Marc. "Strasbourg in Calvin's Time." In *John Calvin: The Strasbourg Years (1538–1541)*, ed. Matthieu Arnold. Eugene, OR: Wipf and Stock, 2018, 1–22.

Lindberg, Carter. *The European Reformations*, 2nd ed. Hoboken, NJ: Wiley Blackwell, 2009

Linder, Robert. *The Political Ideas of Pierre Viret.* Travaux d'Humanisme et Renaissance 64. Geneva: Droz, 1964.

Lottin, Alain, et al. *Les Affrontements religieux en Europe (1500–1650).* Paris: PU Paris-Sorbonne, 2009.

Love, Ronald S. *Blood and Religion: the Conscience of Henri IV.* Montréal: McGill-Queen's University Press, 2001.

Lualdi, Katharine J. "A Body of Beliefs and Believers: Sacramental Confession and Parish Worship in Reformation France." In *Penitence in the Age of Reformations*, ed. Katherine J. Lualdi, and Anne T. Thayer. Aldershot: Ashgate, 2000, 134–151.

Lugioyo, Brian. *Martin Bucer's Doctrine of Justification: Reformation Theology and Early Modern Irenicism.* Oxford and New York: Oxford University Press, 2010.

Luria, Keith P. *Sacred Boundaries: Religious Coexistence and Conflict in Early Modern France.* Washington, DC: The Catholic University of America Press, 2005.

Luther, Martin, and Kurt Aland. *Martin Luther's 95 Theses: With the Pertinent Documents from the History of the Reformation.* Saint Louis, MO: Concordia Publishing House, 2004.

Lynch, Joseph H. *Godparents and Kinship in Early Medieval Europe.* Princeton, NJ: Princeton University Press, 1986.

Maag, Karin. *Seminary or University? The Genevan Academy and Reformed Higher Education, 1560–1620.* Aldershot: Scolar Press, 1995.

Melanchthon in Europe: His Work and Influence Beyond Wittenberg. Grand Rapids, MI: Paternoster, 1999.

"Hero or Villain? Interpretations of John Calvin and His Legacy." *Calvin Theological Journal* 41:2 (2006): 222–237.

"Schools and Education." In *A Companion to the Swiss Reformation*, ed. Amy Burnett and Emidio Campi. Leiden, The Netherlands: Brill, 2016, 520–541.

MacCulloch, Diarmaid. *All Things Made New: Writings on the Reformation.* Westminister: Allen Lane Penguin, 2016.

Mackensen, Heinz. "The Debate between Eck and Melanchthon on Original Sin at the Colloquy of Worms." *Lutheran Quarterly* 11 (1959): 42–56.

"Contarini's Theological Role at Ratibson in 1541." *Archiv für Reformationsgeschichte* 51 (1960): 36–57.

Mallinson, Jeffrey. *Faith, Reason, and Revelation in Theodore Beza, 1519–1605.* Oxford Theological Monographs. Oxford: Oxford University Press, 2003.

Manetsch, Scott M. *Theodore Beza and the Quest for Peace in France, 1562–1598.* Studies in Medieval and Reformation Thought 79. Leiden, The Netherlands: Brill, 2000.

Calvin's Company of Pastors: Pastoral Care and the Emerging Reformed Church, 1536–1609. Oxford: Oxford University Press, 2013.

Margolf, Diane C. "Adjudicating Memory: Law and Religious Difference in Early Seventeenth-Century France." *Sixteenth Century Journal* 27:2 (Summer 1996): 399–418.

Marshall, Peter. "John Calvin and the English Catholics, c. 1565–1640." *The Historical Journal* 53:4 (2010): 857.

Martin, John Jeffries. "Marranos and Nicodemites in Sixteenth-Century Venice." *Journal of Medieval and Early Modern Studies* 41.3 (2011): 577–599.

Martin, Paul-E. *Trois Cas de Pluralisme Confessionnel aux xvie et xviie siècles, Genève, Savoie, France.* Geneva: A. Jullien, 1961.

Matheson, Peter. *Cardinal Contarini at Regensburg.* Oxford: Clarendon Press, 1972 (repr. Eugene, OR: Wipf and Stock Publishers, 2014).

"Martyrdom or Mission? A Protestant Debate." *Archiv für Reformationsgeschichte* 80 (1989): 154–172.

The Rhetoric of the Reformation. Edinburgh: T&T Clark, 1998.

McDonald, Grantly. *Biblical Criticism in Early Modern Europe: Erasmus, the Johannine Comma and Trinitarian Debate.* Cambridge: Cambridge University Press, 2016.

McLelland, Joseph C. "The Italian Anti-Trinitarians." In *Bewegung und Beharrung: Aspekte des Reformierten Protestantismus, 1520–1650.* Festschrift für Emidio Campi, ed. Christian Moser and Peter Opitz. Studies in the History of Christian Traditions 144. Leiden, The Netherlands: Brill, 2007, 147–158.

McKee, Elsie. *The Pastoral Ministry and Worship in Calvin's Geneva.* Travaux d'humanisme et Renaissance 556. Geneva: Droz, 2016.

McKee, Elsie Anne. *Katharina Schütz Zell: The Life and Thought of a Sixteenth-Century Reformer.* Leiden, The Netherlands: Brill, 1999.

McNally, Robert E. "The Council of Trent and the German Protestants." *Theological Studies* 25 (1964): 1–22.

McNutt, Jennifer Powell. *Calvin Meets Voltaire: The Clergy of Geneva and the Age of Enlightenment 1685–1798.* Burlington, VT: Ashgate, 2013.

Meinhold, Peter. "Calvin und Luther." *Lutherische Monatshefte* 3:6 (1964): 264–269.

Mentzer, Raymond A. *Heresy Proceedings in Languedoc, 1500–1560.* Transactions of the American Philosophical Society 74:5. Philadelphia: American Philosophical Society, 1984.

"Ecclesiastical Discipline and Communal Reorganisation among the Protestants of Southern France." *European History Quarterly* 21 (1991): 163–183.

Blood and Belief: Family Survival and Confessional Identity among the Provincial Huguenot Nobility. West Lafayette, IN: Purdue University Press, 1994.

ed. *Sin and the Calvinists: Morals Control and the Consistory in the Reformed Tradition.* Kirksville, MO: Sixteenth Century Publishers, 1994.

"The Persistence of 'Superstition and Idolatry' among Rural French Calvinists." *Church History* 65 (1996): 220–233.

Mentzer, Raymond A., and Andrew Spicer, eds. *Society and Culture in the Huguenot World, 1559–1685.* Cambridge: Cambridge University Press, 2002.

Methuen, Charlotte. *Luther and Calvin: Religious Revolutionaries*. Oxford: Lion, 2011, 143.

Millet, Olivier. *Calvin et la dynamique de la parole, étude de rhétorique réformée*. Paris: Champion, 1992.

Minnis, A. J., and A. B. Scott, *Medieval Literary Theory and Criticism, c. 1100–c. 1375: The Commentary-Tradition*. New York and Oxford: Oxford University Press, 1988.

Mochizuki, Mia. *The Netherlandish Image after Iconoclasm, 1566–1672: Material Religion in the Dutch Golden Age*. Burlington, VT: Ashgate, 2008.

Monge, M. *Des communautés mouvantes. Les "sociétés des frères chrétiens" en Rhénanie du Nord Juliers, Berg, Cologne vers 1530–1694*. Geneva: Droz, 2015.

Monheit, Michael L. "Young Calvin: Textual Interpretation and Roman Law." *Bibliothèque d'Humanisme et Renaissance* 59:2 (1997): 263–282.

Monter, E. William. *Calvin's Geneva*. London: Wiley, 1967.

"Historical Demography and Religious History in Sixteenth-Century Geneva." *The Journal of Interdisciplinary History* 9:3 (Winter 1979): 399–427.

"Women in Calvinist Geneva." *Signs* 6:2 (Winter 1980): 189–209.

Judging the French Reformation: Heresy Trials by Sixteenth-Century Parlements. Cambridge, MA: Harvard University Press, 1999.

Mosheim, Johann Lorenz von. *Institutes of Ecclesiastical History Ancient and Modern*. 3 vols. in 1; trans. James Murdock. New York: Robert Carter & Brothers, [1871].

Mouw, Richard J. "Baptism and the Salvific Status of Children: An Examination of Some Intra-Reformed Debates." *Calvin Theological Journal* 41:2 (2006): 238–254.

Mühling, Andreas. *Heinrich Bullingers europäische Kirchenpolitik*. Bern and New York: Peter Lang, 2001.

Muller, Richard. *Christ and Decree: Christology and Predestination in Reformed Theology from Calvin to Perkins*. Durham, NC: Labyrinth, 1986 (repr. Grand Rapids, MI: Baker Academic, 2008).

The Unaccommodated Calvin: Studies in the Foundation of a Theological Tradition. Oxford: Oxford University Press, 2000.

Post-Reformation Reformed Dogmatics: The Rise and Development of Reformed Orthodoxy, Vol. 4: The Triunity of God. Grand Rapids, MI: Baker Academic, 2003.

"Demoting Calvin: The Issue of Calvin and the Reformed Tradition." In *John Calvin, Myth and Reality: Images and Impact of Geneva's Reformer*, ed. Amy Nelson Burnett. Eugene, OR: Cascade Books, 2011, 3–17.

Calvin and the Reformed Tradition: On the Work of Christ and the Order of Salvation. Grand Rapids, MI: Baker Academic, 2012.

Mullett, Michael. *John Calvin*. New York: Routledge, 2011.

Murdock, Graeme. *Beyond Calvin: The Intellectual, Political, and Cultural World of Europe's Reformed Churches, c. 1540-1620.* London and New York: Palgrave Macmillan, 2004.

Murdock, Graeme, Andrew Spicer, and Penny Roberts, eds. *Ritual and Violence: Natalie Zemon Davis and Early Modern France.* Past and Present Supplement 7. Oxford: Oxford University Press, 2012.

Naphy, William G. *Calvin and the Consolidation of the Genevan Reformation.* New York and Manchester: St. Martin's Press and Manchester University Press, 1994.

"The Reformation and Evolution of Geneva's Schools." In *Reformations Old and New,* ed. B. Kümin. Aldershot: Scolar, 1997, 185-202.

"Genevan National Security and Defence Spending." *War in History* 5:4 (1998): 379-399.

"Genevan Diplomacy and Foreign Policy, c. 1535-1560." In *En Marge de la Confédération,* ed. W. Kaiser, C. Sieber-Lehmann, and C. Windler. Basel: Schwabe, 2001, 189-219.

"Calvin's Church in Geneva: Constructed or Gathered? Local or Foreign? French or Swiss?" In *Calvin and His Influence, 1509-2009,* ed. Irena Backus and Philip Benedict. Oxford: Oxford University Press, 2011, 102-118.

"Calvin's Consistory: Secular Court?" In *L'Intime du Droit à la Renaissance,* ed. M. Engammare, A. Vauautgaerden, and F. Bierlaire. Geneva: Librairie Droz, 2014, 397-408

"Consistories." In *Judging Faith, Punishing Sin,* ed. C. Parker and G. Starr-Lebeau. Cambridge: Cambridge University Press, 2017, 104-116.

"From Prince-Bishopric to City-State." In *Layered Landscapes,* ed. E Nelson and J. Wright. Oxford: Routledge, 2017, 134-149.

Nauert, Charles G. "Humanism as Method: Roots of Conflict with the Scholastics." *The Sixteenth Century Journal* 29:2 (Summer 1998): 427-438.

Humanism and the Culture of Renaissance Europe, 2nd ed. Cambridge: Cambridge University Press, 2006, 17-18.

Neusser, W. H. "Calvin and Luther: Their Personal and Theological Relationship." *Hervormde Teologiese Studies* 38 (1982): 89-103.

Neusser, Wilhelm. "Calvin's Beitrag zu den Religionsgesprächen von Hagenau, Worms und Regensburg (1540/41)." In *Studien zur Geschichte and Theologie der Reformation. Festschrift für Ernst Bizer,* ed. Luise Abramowski and J. F. Gerhard Goeters. Neukirchen-Vluyn: Neukirchener Verlag, 1969, 213-237.

"Calvin's Attitude towards the Symbols of the Early Church during the Conflict with Caroli." In *Ecclesia Reformata: Studies on the Reformation.* Leiden, The Netherlands: Brill, 1972, 73-96.

Ecclesia Reformata: Studies on the Reformation, Vol. 2. Leiden, The Netherlands: Brill, 1972, 163-182.

"Variants within Dutch Calvinism in the Sixteenth Century." In *Ecclesia Reformata: Studies on the Reformation*. Leiden, The Netherlands: Brill, 1972, 48–61.

"The Limits of Civil Disobedience in Calvin's Last-Known Sermons: Development of His Ideas on the Right of Civil Resistance." In *Ecclesia Reformata: Studies on the Reformation*, Vol. 2. Leiden, The Netherlands: Brill, 1994, 73–97.

Neusser, Wilhelm, and Brian Armstrong, eds. *Calvinus Sincerioris Religionis Vindix: Calvin as Protector of the Purer Religion*, Vol. 36. Kirksville, MO: Sixteenth Century Essays and Studies, 1997.

Nissen, P. J. A. *De katholieke polemiek tegen de Dopers: reacties van katholieke theologen op de Doperse beweging in de Nederlanden (1530–1650)* (1991).

Nugent, Donald. *Ecumenism in the Age of Reformation: The Colloquy of Poissy*. Cambridge, MA: Harvard University Press, 1974.

Oberman, Heiko A. "Die Nicodemiten: Ausharren Statt Flucht." In *Die Wirkung Der Reformation: Probleme und Perspectiven*. Stuttgart: Franz Steiner Verlag Wiesbaden GMBH, 1987, 32–46.

Initia Calvini: The Matrix of Calvin's Reformation. Amsterdam, The Netherlands: Koninklijke Nederlandse Akademie van Wetenschappen, 1991.

"*Europa Afflicta*: The Reformation of the Refugees." *Archiv für Reformationsgeschichte* 83 (1992): 91–111.

"Calvin and Farel: The Dynamics of Legitimation in Early Calvinism." In *John Calvin and the Reformation of the Refugees*, ed. Peter Dykema. Travaux d'Humanisme et Renaissance 464. Geneva: Droz, 2009, 195–222.

Ocker, Christopher. "Calvin in Germany." In *Politics and Reformations: Essays in Honor of Thomas A. Brady Jr.*, ed. Christopher Ocker et al. Studies in Medieval and Reformation Traditions, Vol. 127. Boston: Brill Academic, 2007, 313–341.

Old, Hughes Oliphant. *The Shaping of the Reformed Baptismal Rite in the Sixteenth Century*. Grand Rapids, MI: William B. Eerdmans, 1992.

Olin, John C., ed. *John Calvin and Jacopo Sadoleto: A Reformation Debate*. New York: Harper & Row, 1966 (repr. Grand Rapids, MI: Baker, 1976).

Olson, Jeannine. *Calvin and Social Welfare*. Selinsgrove, PA: Susquehanna University, 1989.

O'Malley, John. *Trent and All That*. Cambridge, MA: Harvard University Press, 2002.

Ortmann, Volkmar. *Reformation und Einheit der Kirche : Martin Bucers Einigungsbemühungen bei den Religionsgesprächen in Leipzig, Hagenau, Worms und Regensburg 1539–1541*. Mainz am Rhein: Philipp von Zabern, 2001.

Ozment, Steven. *The Age of Reform*. New Haven, CT: Yale University Press, 1980.

The Reformation in the Cities: The Appeal of Protestantism to Sixteenth-Century Germany and Switzerland. New Haven, CT: Yale University Press, 1980.

Pak, G. Sujin. *The Judaizing Calvin: Sixteenth-Century Debates over the Messianic Psalms*. New York: Oxford, 2010.

Parker, Charles H. "French Calvinists as the Children of Israel: An Old Testament Self-Consciousness in Jean Crespin's *Histoire des Martyrs* before the Wars of Religion." *Sixteenth Century Journal* 24 (1993): 227–248.

Parker, Charles H., and Gretchen Starr-LeBeau, eds. *Judging Faith, Punishing Sin: Inquisitions and Consistories in the Early Modern World*. Cambridge: Cambridge University Press, 2017.

Parker, T. H. L. *John Calvin: A Biography*. Philadelphia: Westminster, 1975.

Calvin's New Testament Commentaries. Louisville, KY: Westminster/John Knox, 1993 (original 1971).

Calvin's Old Testament Commentaries. Louisville, KY: Westminster/John Knox, 1993 (original 1986).

Parrow, Kathleen. *From Defense to Resistance: Justification of Violence during the French Wars of Religion*. Transactions of the American Philosophical Society 83:6. Philadelphia: American Philosophical Society, 1993.

Pellerin, Daniel. "Calvin: Militant or Man of Peace?" *The Review of Politics* 65:1 (Winter 2003): 35–59.

Perrenoud, Alfred. *La population de Genève XVIe–XIXe siècles*. Geneva: Jullien, 1979.

Peter, Rodolphe, and Jean-François Gilmont, Bibliotheca Calviniana. *Les oeuvres de Jean Calvin publiées au XVIe siècle*, 3 vols. Geneva: Droz, 1991–2000.

Petrini, Sylvie Moret. "Ces Lausonnois qui 'pappistent': Ce que nous apprennent les registres consistoriaux lausannois (1538–1540)." *Revue historique vaudoise* 119 (2011): 139–151.

Pettegree, Andrew. *Foreign Protestant Communities in Sixteenth-Century London*. Oxford: Oxford University Press, 1986.

Emden and the Dutch Revolt. Oxford: Oxford University Press, 1992.

"Nicodemism and the English Reformation." In *Marian Protestantism: Six Studies*. Aldershot: Scolar Press, 1996, 86–117.

"The Reception of Calvinism in Britain." In *Calvinus Sincerioris Religionis Vindex. Calvin as Protector of the Purer Religion*, ed. Wilhelm Neuser and Brian Armstrong. Kirksville, MO: Sixteenth Century Essays and Studies, 1997, 267–289.

The French Book and the European Book World. Leiden, The Netherlands: Brill, 2007.

The Book in the Renaissance. New Haven, CT, and London: Yale University Press, 2010.

Brand Luther: 1517, Printing, and the Making of the Reformation. New York: Penguin Press, 2015.

Pettegree, Andrew, and Arthur der Weduwen. *The Bookshop of the World: Making and Trading Books in the Dutch Golden Age.* London: Yale University Press, 2019.

Pettegree, Andrew, Alastair Duke, and Gillian Lewis, eds. *Calvinism in Europe, 1540–1620.* Cambridge: Cambridge University Press, 1994.

Pitkin, Barbara. "The Protestant Zeno: Calvin and the Development of Melanchthon's Anthropology." *The Journal of Religion* 84:3 (2004): 345–378.

Plath, U. *Calvin und Basel in den Jahren 1552–1556.* Zürich: Theologischer Verlag Zürich, 1974.

Potter, David. *A History of France, 1460–1560: The Emergence of a Nation State.* New York: St. Martin's Press, 1995.

"Kingship in the Wars of Religion: The Reputation of Henri III of France." *European History Quarterly* 25 (1995): 485–528.

Potter, Mary. "Gender Equality and Gender Hierarchy in Calvin's Theology." *Signs* 11:4 (Summer 1986): 725–739.

Prestwich, Menna, ed. *International Calvinism, 1541–1715.* Oxford: Oxford University Press, 1985.

Price, David H. "Maximilian I and Toleration of Judaism." *Archiv für Reformationsgeschichte* 105 (2014): 7–29.

Rabe, Horst. "Zur Entstehung des Augsburger Interims 1547/48." *Archiv für Reformationsgeschichte* 2003: 6–104.

Racaut, Luc. *Hatred in Print: Catholic Propaganda and Protestant Identity during the French Wars of Religion.* Aldershot: Ashgate, 2002.

Rainbow, Johnathan H. *The Will of God and the Cross: An Historical and Theological Study of John Calvin's Doctrine of Limited Redemption.* Allison Park, PA: Pickwick Publications, 1990.

Raith II, Charles. "Calvin's Critique of Merit, and Why Aquinas (Mostly) Agrees." *Pro Ecclesia* 20 (2011): 135–153.

Raitt, Jill. *The Eucharistic Theology of Theodore Beza: Development of the Reformed Doctrine.* AAR Studies in Religion 4. Chambersburg, PA: American Academy of Religion, 1972.

The Colloquy of Montebéliard: Religion and Politics in the Sixteenth Century. New York: Oxford University Press, 1993.

Rashdall, Hastings. "The Origines of the University of Paris." *The English Historical Review,* 1:4 (October 1886): 639–676.

The Universities of Europe in the Middle Ages, Vol. 1. Oxford: Clarendon Press, 1895.

Reid, Jonathan A. *King's Sister – Queen of Dissent: Marguerite of Navarre (1492–1549) and Her Evangelical Network. 2 vols. Studies in Medieval and Reformation Traditions, 139.* Leiden, The Netherlands: Brill, 2009.

Rein, Nathan Baruch. "Faith and Empire: Conflicting Visions of Religion in a Late Reformation Controversy – The Augsburg Interim and Its Opponents, 1548–50." *Journal of the American Academy of Religion* 71 (2003): 45–74.

Reinburg, Virginia. "Liturgy and the Laity in Late Medieval and Reformation France." *Sixteenth Century Journal* 23 (1992): 526–547.

Riggs, John. *Baptism in the Reformed Tradition: A Historical and Practical Theology.* Louisville, KY: Westminster John Knox, 2002.

Roberts, Penny. *A City in Conflict: Troyes during the French Wars of Religion.* Manchester: Manchester University Press, 1996.

"Royal Authority and Justice during the French Religious Wars." *Past and Present* 184 (August 2004): 3–32.

Robert, Michèle. *"Que dorénavant chacun fuie paillardise, oisiveté, gourmandize. . ." Réforme et contrôle des mœurs. La justice consistoriale dans le Pays de Neuchâtel (1547–1848).* Neuchâtel: Alphil-Presses universitaires suisses, 2016.

Robbins, Kevin C. *City on the Ocean Sea, La Rochelle, 1530–1650: Urban Society, Religion and Politics on the French Atlantic Frontier.* Leiden, The Netherlands: Brill, 1997.

Roelker, Nancy L. *Queen of Navarre: Jeanne d'Albret, 1528–1572.* Cambridge, MA: Harvard University Press, 1968.

"The Role of Noblewomen in the French Reformation." *Archiv für Reformationsgeschichte/Archive for Reformation History* 63 (1972): 168–195.

One King, One Faith: The Parlement of Paris and the Religious Reformations of the Sixteenth Century. Berkeley: University of California Press, 1996.

Roney, John B., and Klauber, Martin I., eds., *The Identity of Geneva.* London: Greenwood, 1998.

Roobol, M. *Disputation by Decree: The Public Disputations between Reformed Ministers and Dirck Volckertsz Coornhert as Instruments of Religious Policy during the Dutch Revolt (1577–1583).* Leiden, The Netherlands: Brill, 2010.

Roper, Lyndal. *The Holy Household: Women and Morals in Reformation Augsburg.* Oxford: Oxford University Press, 1989.

Martin Luther: Renegade and Prophet. New York: Random House, 2017.

Rowen, Herbert H. *The Low Countries in Early Modern Times: A Documentary History.* New York: Harper & Row, 1972.

Ruderman, David B. *Early Modern Jewry.* Princeton, NJ: Princeton University Press, 2010.

Rummel, Erika. *The Humanist-Scholastic Debate in the Renaissance and Reformation.* Cambridge, MA: Harvard University Press, 1995.

The Confessionalization of Humanism in Reformation Germany. Oxford: Oxford University Press, 2002.

Sæbø, Magne, ed. *Hebrew Bible/Old Testament,* Vol. 2: *From the Renaissance to the Enlightenment.* Göttingen: Vandenhoeck & Ruprecht, 2008.

Salmon, J. H. M. *Renaissance and Revolt: Essays in the Intellectual and Social History of Early Modern France.* Cambridge: Cambridge University Press, 1987.

Sandberg, Brian. "'Generous Amazons Came to the Breach': Besieged Women, Agency and Subjectivity during the French Wars of Religion." *Gender and History* 16:3 (November 2004): 654–688.

Schaff, Philip. *The Creeds of Christendom*, Vol. 3: *The Creeds of the Evangelical Churches*. New York: Harper, 1877. www.ccel.org/ccel/schaff/creeds3.iv.iv.html.

History of the Christian Church, Vol. 8: *Modern Christianity. The Swiss Reformation*, 3rd ed. revised. New York: Charles Scribner's Sons, 1892.

Schilling, Heinz. *Civic Calvinism in Northwestern Germany and the Netherlands, Sixteenth to the Nineteenth Centuries*. Kirksville, MO: Sixteenth Century Publishers, 1991.

Schmidt, Heinrich Richard. "Morals Courts in Rural Berne during the Early Modern Period." In *The Reformation in Eastern and Central Europe*, ed. Karin Maag. Aldershot, and Brookfield, VT: Scolar Press/Ashgate, 1997, 155–181.

Schneemann, Geerardus, ed. *Controversiarum de divinae gratiae liberique arbitrii Concordia initia et progressus* Freiburg: Herder, 1881.

Schnetzler, Charles, et al., eds. *Pierre Viret d'après lui-même*. Lausanne: Georges Bridel, 1911.

Schreiner, Stefan. "Jüdische Reaktionen auf die Reformation." *Judaica* 39 (1983): 150–168.

Schröter, Susan, ed. *Christianity in Indonesia: Perspectives on Power*. Berlin: Lit Verlag, 2010.

Schulz Hequet, Suzanne. *The 1541 Colloquy at Regensburg: In Pursuit of Church Unity*. Saarbrücken, Germany: VDM Verlag Dr. Müller, 2009.

Schutte, G. J. *Het Calvinistisch Nederland: Mythe en werkelijkheid*. Hilversum: Verloren, 2000.

ed. *Het Indisch Sion: De Gereformeerde kerk onder de Verenigde Oost-Indische Compagnie*. Hilversum: Verloren, 2002.

Schwendemann, Wilhelm. *Reformation und Humanismus: Philipp Melanchthon und Johannes Calvin*. Frankfurt: Peter Lang, 2013.

Scott, Tom. *The Swiss and Their Neighbors, 1460–1560: Between Accommodation and Aggression*. Oxford: Oxford University Press, 2017.

Selderhuis, Herman J. *John Calvin: A Pilgrim's Life*, trans. Albert Gootjes. Downers Grove, IL: IVP Academic, 2009.

ed. *The Calvin Handbook*. Grand Rapids, MI: Eerdmans, 2009.

Selderhuis, Herman J., J. Marius, and J. Lange van Ravenswaay, eds. "Calvin and Wittenberg." In *The Calvin Handbook*, ed. Herman J. Selderhuis. Grand Rapids, MI: Eerdmans, 2009, 57–63.

Selderhuis, Herman J., J. Marius, and J. Lange van Ravenswaay, "Luther and Calvin." In *Martin Luther: A Christian between Reforms and Modernity (1517–2017)*, ed. Alberto Melloni. Berlin: De Gruyter, 2017, 401–416.

Luther and Calvinism: Image and Reception of Martin Luther in the History and Theology of Calvinism. Göttingen: Vandenhoeck & Ruprecht, 2017.

Shannon, Joseph L. *Good Works and Predestination according to Thomas of Strassbourg, O.S.A.* Baltimore, MD: The Watkins Printing Co., 1940.

Shepardson, Nikki. "The Rhetoric of Martyrdom and the Anti-Nicodemite Discourses in France, 1550–1570." *Renaissance and Reformation/Renaissance et Réforme*, n.s. 27:3 (Summer 2003): 37–61.

Sierhuis, Freya. *The Literature of the Arminian Controversy: Religion, Politics, and the Stage in the Dutch Republic.* Oxford: Oxford University Press, 2015.

Smalley, Beryl. *The Study of the Bible in the Middle Ages.* Notre Dame, IN: University of Notre Dame Press, 1964.

Smith, William Bradford. "Lutheran Resistance to the Imperial Interim in Hesse and Kulmbach." *Lutheran Quarterly* 19 (2005): 249–275.

Spaans, Joke. *Haarlem na de Reformatie: Stedelijke cultuur en kerkelijk leven, 1577–1620.* The Hague: Hollandsche Historische Reeks, 1989.

Speelman, Herman A. *Melanchthon and Calvin on Confession and Communion: Early Modern Protestant Penitential and Eucharistic Piety.* Gottingen: Vandenhoeck & Ruprecht, 2016.

Spierling, Karen. *Infant Baptism in Reformation Geneva: The Shaping of a Community, 1536–1564.* Aldershot: Ashgate, 2005 (repr. Louisville, KY: Westminster John Knox, 2009).

Spierling, Karen E., Erik A. de Boer, and R. Ward Holder, eds. *Emancipating Calvin: Culture and Confessional Identity in Francophone Reformed Communities. Essays in Honor of Raymond A. Mentzer, Jr.* Leiden, The Netherlands: Brill, 2018.

Spitz, Lewis. *The Religious Renaissance of the German Humanists.* Cambridge, MA: Harvard University Press, 1963, 275.

"Humanism and the Reformation." In *Transition and Revolution: Problems and Issues in European Renaissance and Reformation History*, ed. Robert Kingdon Minneapolis, MN: Burgess, 1974.

Spohnholz, Jesse. "Confessional Coexistence in the Early Modern Low Countries." In *A Companion to Multiconfessionalism in the Early Modern World*, ed. Thomas Max Safley. Leiden, The Netherlands: Brill, 2011, 47–73.

Sproxton, Judy. *Violence and Religion: Attitudes Toward Militancy in the French Civil Wars and the English Revolution.* London: Routledge, 1995.

Staedtke, Joachim. *Heinrich Bullinger Bibliographie. Beschreibendes Verzeichnis der gedruckten Werke von Heinrich Bullinger.* Zürich: Theologischer Verlag, 1972.

Staehelin, E. *Briefe und Akten zum Leben Oekolampads.* Leipzig: M. Heinsius Nachfolger, 1934, Bd 2.

Stam, Frans Pieter van. *The Servetus Case: An Appeal for a New Assessment.* Cahiers d'humanisme et renaissance 136. Genève: Droz, 2017.

Starkey, Lindsay J. *Presenting Christian Doctrine : Philip Melanchthon's Method for Reading Scripture in His 1521 Loci Communes* (2008).

Steinmetz, David. *Calvin in Context.* New York: Oxford University Press, 1995.

Reformers in the Wings: From Geiler von Kaysersberg to Theodore Beza. New York: Oxford, 2001.

Stephens, Peter. "Bullinger's Defence of Infant Baptism in Debate with the Anabaptists." *Reformation and Renaissance Review* 4:2 (2002): 168–189.

Stjerna, Kirsi. *Women and the Reformation.* Malden, MA: Blackwell Publishing, 2009.

Strübind, A. *Eifriger als Zwingli. Die frühe Taüferbewegung in der Schweiz.* Berlin: Duncker & Humblot 2003.

Sutherland, Nicola M. *The Massacre of St. Bartholomew and the European Conflict, 1559–1572.* London: Macmillan, 1973.

The Huguenot Struggle for Recognition. New Haven, CT: Yale University Press, 1980.

Summers, Kirk. A View from the Palatine: The *Iuvenilia* of Théodore de Bèze, Text, Translation, and Commentary. Medieval and Renaissance Texts and Studies 237. Tempe: Arizona Center for Medieval and Renaissance Studies, 2001.

Morality after Calvin: Theodore Beza's Christian Censor and Reformed Ethics. Oxford Studies in Historical Theology. New York: Oxford University Press, 2017.

Swanson, Robert. *Religion and Devotion in Europe, c. 1215–c. 1515.* Cambridge: Cambridge University Press, 1995.

Sweeney, Douglas A. "'Falling Away from the General Faith of the Reformation'? The Contest over Calvinism in Nineteenth-Century America." In *John Calvin's American Legacy*, ed. Thomas J. Davis. Oxford: Oxford University Press, 2010, 111–146.

Suerbaum, Almut, George Southcombe, and Benjamn Thompson, eds. *Polemic: Language as Violence in Medieval and Early Modern Discourse.* London and New York: Routledge, 2016.

Szabari, Antònia. *Less Rightly Said: Scandals and Readers in Sixteenth-Century France.* Redwood, CA: Stanford University Press, 2009.

Tallon, Alain. *La France et le Concile de Trente, 1518–1563.* Bibliothèque des Écoles françaises d'Athènes et de Rome 295. Rome: École française de Rome; Paris: Diffusion de Boccard, 1997.

Tavard, George. "Calvin and the Nicodemites." In *Calvin and Roman Catholicism*, ed. Randall Zachman. Grand Rapids, MI: Baker Academic, 2007, 59–78.

Taylor, Larissa. *Soldiers of Christ: Preaching in Late Medieval and Reformation France.* Oxford: Oxford University Press, 1992.

Terpstra, Nicholas. *Religious Refugees in the Early Modern World: An Alternative History of the Reformation.* Cambridge: University of Cambridge Press, 2015.

Thévenaz, Louis-J. *Histoire du Collège de Genève*. Geneva: Département de l'instruction publique, 1896 (Geneva: Slatkine reprints, 2009).

Thianto, Yudha. *The Way to Heaven: Catechisms and Sermons in the Establishment of the Dutch Reformed Church in the East Indies*. Eugene, OR: Wipf & Stock, 2014.

Tingle, Elizabeth C. *Authority and Society in Nantes during the French Wars of Religion, 1559–1598*. Manchester: Manchester University Press, 2006.

Todd, Margo. *The Culture of Protestantism in Early Modern Scotland*. New Haven, CT: Yale University Press, 2002.

Torrance, Thomas F. "Calvin's Doctrine of the Trinity." *Calvin Theological Journal* 25:2 (1990): 165–193.

Trigg, Jonathan D. *Baptism in the Theology of Martin Luther*. Leiden, The Netherlands: Brill, 2001.

Trim, David. "Calvinist Internationalism and the English Officer Corps, 1562–1642." *History Compass* 4:6 (2006): 1024–1048.

Troilo, Dominique. *L'Oeuvre de Pierre Viret: L'activité littéraire du Réformateur mise en lumière*. Lausanne: L'Age d'Homme, 2012.

Tulchin, Allan A. *That Men Would Praise the Lord: The Triumph of Protestantism in Nîmes, 1530–1570*. Oxford: Oxford University Press, 2010.

"Church and State in the French Reformation." *Journal of Modern History* 86:4 (December 2014): 826–861.

Tylenda, Joseph N. "The Calvin-Westphal Exchange: The Genesis of Calvin's Treatises against Westphal." *Calvin Theological Journal* 9 (1974): 182–209.

Universal Short-Title Catalogue. www.ustc.ac.uk/.

Van der Linden, David. *Experiencing Exile: Huguenot Refugees in the Dutch Republic, 1680–1700*. Farnham: Ashgate, 2015.

Van't Spijker, Willem. *Calvin: A Brief Guide to His Life and Thought*, trans. Lyle D. Bierma. Louisville, KY: Westminster John Knox, 2009.

van Veen, Mirjam. "Introduction." In *Ioannis Calvini opera omnia: Dueno recognita et adnotatione critica instructa notisque illustrata*. Series IV: Scripta didactica et polemica. Droz: Geneva, 2005, 9–41.

"'Contaminated with David Joris's Blasphemies': David Joris's Contribution to Castellio's De haereticis an sint persequendi." *Bibliothèque d'Humanisme et Renaissance* 69 (2007): 313–326.

"David Joris' Memoryaell." *Doopsgezinde Bijdragen* 33 (2007): 31–40.

"Religieus Schermvechten. Dopers-Gereformeerde Disputaties in de Zestiende Eeuw." In *Religie, hervorming en controverse in de zestiende-eeuwse Nederlanden*, ed. V. Soen and P. Knevel. Herzogenrath: Shaker Publisher, 2013.

Die Freiheit des Denkens: Sebastian Castellio, Wegbereiter der Toleranz, 1515–1563. Eine Biographie. Essen: Alcorde, 2015.

"Dutch Anabaptist and Reformed Historiographers on Servetus' Death: or How the Radical Reformation Turned Mainstream and How the

Mainstream Reformation Turned Radical." In Radicalism and Dissent in the World of Protestant Reform, ed. B. Heal and A. Kremers. Göttingen: Vandenhoeck & Ruprecht, 2017, 162–172.

"Ware pelgrims. Dopers-gereformeerd ongemak in Wismar (1553)." *Doopsgezinde Bijdragen* 43 (2017): 53–62.

"Johan Jakob Wettstein's (1693–1754) Use of Sebastian Castellio (1515–1563)." In Sebastian Castellio (1515–1563) – Dissidenz und Toleranz. Beiträge zu einer internationalen Tagung auf dem Monte Verità in Ascona 2015, ed. B. Mahlmann-Bauer. Göttingen: Vandenhoeck & Ruprecht, 2018, 575–588.

Venema, Cornelis. "Bullinger's Correspondence on Calvin's Doctrine of Predestination, 1551–1553." *The Sixteenth Century Journal* 17:4 (1986): 435–450.

Verhey, Allen, and Robert G. Wilkie. "Calvin's Treatise 'Against the Libertines.'" *Calvin Theological Journal* 15 (1980): 190–219.

Vester, Matthew, ed. *Sabaudian Studies: Political Culture, Dynasty, and Territory 1400–1700.* Kirksville, MO: Truman State University Press, 2013.

Vischer, Manfred, *Bibliographie der Zürcher Druckschriften des 15. und 16. Jahrhunderts.* Baden-Baden: Koerner, 1991.

Vogel, Lothar. *Das zweite Regensburger Religionsgespräch von 1546. Politik und Theologie zwischen Konsensdruck und Selbstbehauptung.* Gütersloh: Gütersloher Verlagshaus, 2009.

Wabuda, Susan. "Equivocation and Recantation during the English Reformation: The 'Subtle Shadows' of Dr. Edward Crome." *Journal of Ecclesiastical History* 44 (1993): 224–242.

Wallace, Dewey D. *Shapers of English Calvinism, 1660–1714: Variety, Persistence, and Transformation.* Oxford Studies in Historical Theology. Oxford and New York: Oxford University Press, 2011.

Walsham, Alexandra. *Church Papists: Catholicism, Conformity, and Confessional Polemic in Early Modern England.* Suffolk: The Boydell Press, 1999.

"Domesticating the Reformation: Material Culture, Memory, and Confessional Identity in Early Modern England." *Renaissance Quarterly* 69 (Summer 2014): 566–616.

Walzer, Michael. *The Revolution of the Saints: A Study in the Origins of Radical Politics.* Cambridge, MA: Harvard University Press, 1965.

Wandel, Lee Palmer, ed. *A Companion to the Eucharist in the Reformation.* Brill's Companions to the Christian Tradition 46. Leiden, The Netherlands: Brill, 2013.

Waterman, J. A. "Converting Power." *Millennial Harbinger* 1st series, 4 (1833): 487–492.

Watt, Jeffrey R. "The Reception of the Reformation in Valangin, Switzerland, 1547–1588." *Sixteenth Century Journal* 20 (1989): 89–104.

The Making of Modern Marriage: Matrimonial Control and the Rise of Sentiment in Neuchâtel, 1550–1800. Ithaca, NY: Cornell University Press, 1992.

"Women and the Consistory in Calvin's Geneva." *Sixteenth Century Journal* 24:2 (1993): 429–439.

"Calvinism, Childhood, and Education: The Evidence from the Genevan Consistory." *The Sixteenth Century Journal*, 33:2 (Summer 2002): 439–456.

"Childhood and Youth in the Genevan Consistory Minutes." In *Calvinus Praeceptor Ecclesiae: Papers of the International Congress on Calvin Research*, ed. Herman Selderhuis. Geneva: Droz, 2004, 41–62.

Watt, Jeffrey R., and Isabella M. Watt, eds. *Registres du Consistoire de Genève au Temps de Calvin*, Vol. 10, 14 February 1555–6 February 1556. Geneva: Librairie Droz, 2016.

Weldler-Steinberg, Augusta. *Geschichte der Juden in der Schweiz vom 16. Jahrhundert bis nach der Emancipation.* 2 vols. Zürich: Schweizerischer Israelitischer Gemeindebund, 1966–1979.

Wendel, François. *Calvin: Origins and Developments of His Religious Thought*, trans. Philip Mairet. Grand Rapids, MI: Baker Books, 1997 (original 1950).

Wengert, Timothy J. "Philip Melanchthon and John Calvin against Andreas Osiander: Coming to Terms with Forensic Justification." In *Calvin and Luther: The Continuing Relationship*, ed. R. Ward Holder. Göttingen: Vandenhoeck & Ruprecht, 2013, 63–87.

"Philip Melanchthon: Speaking for the Reformation." *The Expository Times* 126:7 (2015): 313–325

Wessels, J. H. *De leerstellige strijd tusschen Nederlandsche Gereformeerden en Doopsgezinden in de zestiende eeuw.* Assen: Van Gorcum & Company, 1945.

Whitford, David M. *Tyranny and Resistance: The Magdeburg Confession and the Lutheran Tradition.* St. Louis, MO: Concordia Publishing House, 2001.

"Yielding to the Prejudices of His Time: Erasmus and the Comma Johanneum." *Church History and Religious Culture* 95 (2015): 19–40.

Wiesner, Merry. "Beyond Women and the Family: Toward a Gender Analysis of the Reformation." *Sixteenth Century Journal* 18:3 (1987): 311–321.

"Protestant Movements." In *The Ashgate Research Companion to Women and Gender in Early Modern Europe*, ed. Allyson M. Poska, Jane Couchman, and Katherine A. McIver. Burlington, VT: Ashgate, 2013, 129–148.

Williams, George H. *The Radical Reformation*, 3rd ed. Kirksville, MO: Sixteenth Century Journal Publishers, 1992.

Wolfe, Michael. *The Conversion of Henri IV: Politics, Power, and Religious Belief in Early Modern France.* Cambridge, MA: Harvard University Press, 1993.

"The Strange Afterlife of Henri III: Dynastic Distortions in Early Bourbon France." *Renaissance Studies* 10:4 (December 1996): 474–489.

Woltjer, J. J., and M. E. H. N. Mout, "Settlements: The Netherlands." In *Handbook of European History 1400–1600*, eds. Thomas A. Brady et al. Leiden, The Netherlands: Brill, 1995, 385–416.

Wood, James B. *The King's Army: Warfare, Soldiers, and Society during the Wars of Religion in France, 1562–1572.* Cambridge: Cambridge University Press, 1996.

Wright, David F. "Why Was Calvin So Severe a Critic of Nicodemism?" In *Calvinus Evangelii Propugnator: Calvin, Champion of the Gospel: Papers Presented at the International Congress on Calvin Research, Seoul, 1998,* ed. David F. Wright, A. N. Lane, and Jon Balserak. Grand Rapids, MI: Calvin Studies Society, 2006, 66–90.

Yoder, J. H. *Täufertum und Reformation im Gespäch: dogmengeschichtliche Untersuchung der frühen Gesprächen zwischen schweizerischen Täufern und Reformatoren.* Zürich: EVZ Verlag 1968.

Zachman, Randall. *John Calvin as Teacher, Pastor, and Theologian: The Shape of His Writings and Thought.* Grand Rapids, MI: Baker Academic, 2006. *Image and Word in the Theology of John Calvin.* Notre Dame, IN: University of Notre Dame, 2007.

Zagorin, Perez. *Ways of Lying: Dissimulation, Persecution, and Conformity in Early Modern Europe.* Cambridge, MI: Harvard University Press, 1990.

Zell, Katharina Schütz. *Church Mother: The Writings of a Protestant Reformer in Sixteenth-Century Germany,* trans. Elsie McKee. Chicago: University of Chicago Press, 2006.

Ziegler, Donald J. *Great Debates of the Reformation.* New York: Random House, 1969.

Zuidema, Jason, and Theodore Van Raalte. *Early French Reform: The Theology and Spirituality of Guillaume Farel.* St. Andrews Studies in Reformation History. Burlington, VT: Ashgate, 2011.

Index